M000087293

Latina Issues
Fragments of Historia(ella) (Herstory)

Edited with an introduction by

Antoinette Sedillo López
University of New Mexico
School of Law

GARLAND PUBLISHING, INC.
A MEMBER OF THE TAYLOR & FRANCIS GROUP
New York & London
1999

Contents

Introduction

Colonization

Indian women
were given
or gave themselves
(rape)
reproduced
(birth)
cared for children; and,
when they could,
worked to produce
wealth
for Spaniards under rules
(colonization)
dictated by Spaniards (men).

Spaniards
satisfied their needs;
they accumulated
wealth
and passed it on
to their white children (men).

Spaniards left their mark
on the faces, bodies,
names
of the children
(colonization)
and on the backs and bodies
of the women
whose earth brown faces
will never disappear.

—Antoinette Sedillo López

A history of Latino peoples would be incomplete without a history of Latinas. Their
stories are just beginning to be researched and told. There are more stories about Latinas
in the development of Latino peoples than the often-told stories of La Malinche, the
interpreter and betrayer of Indian people, of La Llorana, the mythical woman who

weeps for her children, and the Virgin of Guadalupe, the Indian apparition of the Mother of Christ. This collection explores the fragments of history available about Latinas in the United States and highlights their emerging voices.

Not quite comfortable with the white women's movement and white feminists, Latinas bring women-centered challenges to Latino movements and politics. When public policy focuses on women and minorities, women of color tend to be rendered invisible since policy makers usually concentrate on white women and minority men. This volume attempts to make Latina history visible and Latina voices heard. It focuses solely on women — not to marginalize Latina stories but to showcase them. Each of these articles illustrates Latina perspectives on colonization, gender, race, and class.

Latina History

Adelaida R. Del Castillo's essay challenges many of the myths about Malentzin-Tenepal, also known as La Malinche, the native woman who served as Cortes' interpreter. Although largely vilified as a traitor to her race, Del Castillo looks at the woman in historical context and describes political and social conditions at the time to explain the logic of the choices Malentzin-Tenepal made. She examines all the historical aspects of Malentzin-Tenepal's involvement in the conquest of the native people of Mexico and finds that Malentzin-Tenepal embodies decisive action that syncretized two worlds, causing a new one to emerge — our own. Thus, she was not a mythical figure but a dynamic force in the making of history.

Historian Deena J. González discusses the lives of widowed women in Santa Fe immediately after the territory became American following the Mexican-American War. She describes the dislocation of native Spanish-speaking residents. She looks at census records and court documents to capture a snapshot of the living conditions of widowed women. She finds that they were targets of con games by the Americans, the state, and the church, and had to struggle to survive the changing economic and social order imposed by the American conquest.

Vicki Ruíz addresses an important methodological question in the quest for Latina history — the use of missionary records. She examines missionary records in El Paso to expose the attempts to Americanize and recruit Mexican-American women. She explores the way women select and create cultural norms and discusses the fluidity of cultural interaction.

Mario García wrote a case study of Mexican women in El Paso that looked at household compositions, working conditions, and problems. He finds that they labored in the home, selling piecework, taking in laundry, and working as domestics. They served as the guardians of Mexican cultural traditions, which ironically maintained women in a position subordinate to the husband in the family. He describes their gradual move toward outside employment because of financial need. He points out their poor wage differentials and depicts their attempts to organize to overcome poor treatment in the workplace.

Lourdes Miranda King writes of issues facing Puertorriqueñas in the United States. She refutes stereotypes of Puerto Rican women and outlines employment, child care, and educational issues they face in the United States. In Puerto Rico, the role of women is being redefined with industrialization. She calls for the women's rights movement to respect Puerto Rican women's cultural values and to address basic issues of human rights for both men and women.

Denise Segura pursues an analysis of Chicanas in the labor market. She points out that the Chicana experience is usually subsumed under the "larger" questions of race or class. Feminists also approach the study of women of color as secondary to the gender questions. Segura attempts to join the race, class, and gender frameworks. Analyzing demographic and statistical analysis of census records for Chicanas and white women, she uses current theoretical models of education and employment theory to demonstrate that Chicanas suffer from triple oppression of race, gender, and class.

Mary Romero studied the work experience of Chicana private housekeepers. She conducted interviews with twenty-five Chicanas living in a western city to gather detailed information about their working experience. She finds that unlike white women in domestic service, minority women often find themselves trapped in an occupational ghetto.

Yolanda Prieto looks at the factors affecting high rates of employment among Cuban women in New Jersey. She finds that despite traditional cultural norms discouraging work outside the home (indeed some Cubans fled Cuba because of its "destruction of the family" in requiring women to work outside the home), many Cuban women engage in paid employment. The major reason Cuban women gave for working outside the home was to help the family financially. Thus, the women viewed working outside the home as an extension of their family obligation. Specifically, Cuban families were aspiring to a middle-class lifestyle similar to what they had in Cuba.

Carlos G. Velez-I wrote an ethnography of ten Mexican-American women who were sterilized without their consent and of their attempts to seek legal redress. He analyzes the cultural and psychological effects of the loss of the ability to bear children. He provides an anthropological view of the effects of sterilization on these women and describes their social disengagement from their community, their cultural disruption, and their depression. He concludes with a description of the trial in which these women sought damages for the forced sterilization — and lost. The judge found for the doctors, despite the fact that the doctors could not independently recall any one of the cases but asserted that their usual custom and practice was to perform a sterilization with a woman's consent. Velez-I concludes that the judge used the women's linguistic and cultural difference against them to justify the doctor's actions.

Emerging Latina Voices

The second part of this reader highlights some of the writings of Latina feminists. They write from a perspective that is woman-centered yet conscious of race and class issues. In encompassing the complexities of race, gender, and class, they make important contributions to women's studies as well as to Latino studies.

Virginia Martinez provides an overview of legal issues affecting Latinas and the failure of the women's movement and the Chicano movement to address Chicana issues. She describes the Chicana rights project and the possibilities of legislation and

University of Texas, 1986.

Cotera, Martha. *Diosa y Hembra: The History and Heritage of Chicanas in the U.S.* Austin, Texas: Information Systems Development, 1976.

———. *Profile on the Mexican American Woman.* Austin, Texas: For sale by National Educational Laboratory Publishers, 1976.

Darabi, Katherine, and Vilma Ortiz. "Childbearing among Young Latino Women in the United States." 77 *American Journal of Public Health* 25 (1987).

Espinosa, Leslie, and Angela P. Harris. "Embracing the Tar-Baby-LatCrit Theory and the Sticky Mess of Race." 85 *California Law Review* 1585 (1997).

Facio, Elisia. *Understanding Older Chicanas, Sociological and Policy Perspectives* (Thousand Oaks, Ca.: Sage , 1996).

Garcia, Karen. "Gender and Ethnicity in the Emerging Identity of Puerto Rican Women." 3 *Latino Studies Journal* 3 (1992).

Gonzales, Deena J. "Chicana Ideneity Matters." In *Culture and Difference: Critical Perspectives on the Bicultural Experience in the United States,* edited by Antonia Darder (Westport, Conn.: Bergin and Garvey, 1995).

Gonzalez, Rosalinda M. "Chicanas and Mexican Immigrant Families, 1920–1940." *Decades of Discontent: The Women's Movement, 1920–1940,* 2nd ed. (Boston: Northwestern University Press, 1987).

Hernandez-Truyol, Berta Esperanza. "Borders (En)gendered: Normativities, Latinas, and a Latcrit Paradigm." 72 *New York University Law Review* 882 (1997).

———. "Building Bridges — Latinas and Latinos at the Crossroads: Realities, Rhetoric and Replacement." 25 *Columbia Human Rights Law Review* 369 (1994).

———. "Sex, Culture and Rights: A Re/conceptualization of Violence for the Twenty-First Century." 60 *Albany Law Review* 607 (1997).

Herrera-Sobek, and Helena Maria Viramontes. *Chicana Creativity and Criticism: New Frontiers in American Literature* (Albuquerque, New Mexico: University of New Mexico Press, 1996).

Holmquaist, Kirsten L. "Cultural Defense or False Stereotypes? What Happens When Latina Defendants Collide with the Federal Sentencing Guidelines." 12 *Berkeley Women's Law Journal* 45 (1997).

Hurtado, Aida. "Relating to Privilege: Seduction and Rejection in the Subordination of White Women and Women of Color." 14 *Signs: Journal of Women in Culture and Society* 833 (1989).

Iglesias, Elizabeth M. "Rape, Race and Representation: The Power of Discourse, Discourses of Power, and the Reconstruction of Heterosexuality." 49 *Vanderbilt Law Review* 869 (1996).

Kohpahl, Gabriele. *Voices of Guatemalan Women in Los Angeles: Understanding their Immigration* (New York, London: Garland Publishing, 1998).

Lopez, Antoinette Sedillo. "A Comparative Analysis of Women's Issues: Toward a Contextualized Methodology." 10 *Hastings Women's Law Journal* 101 (1999).

———. "Evolution." XIX *La Herencia* 22 (Fall 1998).

———. "Family Secrets." V *Circles: Buffalo Women's Journal of Law and Social Policy* 68 (1997).

———. "Grandma's Hands." *La Herencia* (Fall 1999) (forthcoming).

———. "On Privilege." 2 *American University Journal of Gender and the Law* 217 (1994).

———. "Testimony." 6 *American University Journal of Gender and the Law* (1998).

Montoya, Margaret E. "*Máscaras, Trenzas y Greñas:* Un/masking the Self While Un/braiding Latina Stories and Legal Discourse." 15 *Chicano/Latino Law Review* 1 (1994).

Mora, Magdalena, and Adelaida Del Castillo, eds. *Mexican Women in the United States: Struggles Past and Present.* Los Angeles: Chicano Studies Research Center Publications, University of California, 1980.

Moraga, Cherrie, and Gloria Anzaldua, eds. *This Bridge Called My Back: Writings of Radical Women of Color.* New York: Kitchen Table, Women of Color Press, 1983.

Mūniz, Vicky. *Resisting Gentrification and Displacement: Voices of Puerto Rican Women of the Barrio* (New Yorkm London: Garland Publishing, 1998).

Ontiveros, Maria L. "Fictionalizing Harrassment: Disclosing the Truth." 93 *Michigan Law Review* 1373 (1995).

Ortiz, Silvia, and Jesus Manuel Casas. "Birth Control and Low Income Mexican-American Women: The Impact of Three Values." 12 *Hispanic Journal of Behavioral Sciences* 83 (1990).

Pardo, Mary. *Mexican American Women Activists: Identity and Resistance in Two Los Angeles Communities* (Philadelphia, Penn.: Temple University Press, 1998).

Pesquera, Beatriz, and Denise Segura. "With Quill and Torch: A Chicana Perspective on the American Women's Movement and Feminist Theroies." In *Chicanas/Chicanos at the Crossroads: Social, Economic, and Political Change,* David Maciel and Isidro Ortiz, eds. (Tucson: University of Arizona Press, 1996).

Platt, Kamala. "Chicana Strategies for Success and Survival: Cultural Poetics of Environmental Justice from the Mothers of East Los Angeles." 18.2 *Frontiers* 48 (1997).

Prieto, Yolanda. "Continuity or Change? Two Generations of Cuban American Women." 113 *New Jersey History* 47 (1995).

Rivera, Jenny. "Domestic Violence Against Latinas by Latino Males: An Analysis of Race, National Origin, and Gender Differences." 14 *Boston College Third World Law Journal* 231 (1994).

Rodriguez, Clara. "On the Declining Interest in Race." 3 and 4 *Women Studies Quarterly* (1988).

Romero, Mary. "Twice Protected? Assessing the Impact of Affirmative Action on Mexican-American Women." 5 *Ethnicity and Women* 135 (1986).

Ruiz, Vicki. *From Out of the Shadows: Mexican Women in Twentieth Century America* (New York: Oxford University, 1998).

Russel y Rodriguez, Monica. "Confronting Anthropology's Silencing Praxis: Speaking Of/From a Chicana Consciousness." 4:1 *Qualitative Inquiry* 15 (1998).

Sanchez, Rosaura. "Reconstructing Chicana Gender Identity." 9:2 *American Literary History* 350 (1997).

Spencer, Laura Gutierrez. "Mirrors and Masks: Female Subjectivity in Chicana Poetry." 15:2 *Frontiers* 69 (1994).

Trujillo, Carla. *Living Chicana Theory* (Berkeley, Calif.: Third Woman Press, 1998).

Ybarra, Lea. "When Wives Work: The Impact on the Chicano Family." 44 *Journal of Marriage and the Family* (1982).

Latina Issues

Malintzin Tenépal:
A Preliminary Look
into a New Perspective

ADELAIDA R. DEL CASTILLO

INTRODUCTION

History, literature and popular belief normally introduce us to the story and image of Doña Marina, La Malinche,[1] in either of three ways: (1) the woman is oftentimes presented very simply and insignificantly as just another part of the necessary back-drop to Cortés' triumphant conquest or, as is more commonly done, (2) her portrayal assumes synonymity with destruction when she is singled out as the sole cause of the fall of the "patria" and becomes the scapegoat for all Mexican perdition thereafter while, on the other hand, (3) romanticists find themselves almost instinctively driven to depicting Doña Marina as the misguided and exploited victim of the tragic love affair which is said to have taken place between herself and Hernán Cortés.

  The above approaches for depiction of Doña Marina do no justice to the image of this Mexican woman in that the following historical aspects are not taken into full consideration:

1. Quetzalcoatl—the prophet and his religion;
2. Aztec religion—in particular, the works of Tlacaelel;
3. The political milieu of the Aztec empire at the time of the conquest;
4. The situation of the Indian peoples under Aztec rule;

Adelaida R. Del Castillo majored in Social Linguistics at the University of California, Los Angeles and is a staff writer for the *Sin Fronteras* newspaper.
© 1974 Adelaida R. Del Castillo. Reprinted by permission. First published in *Encuentro Femenil*.

he take care of the earth and himself and, as such, he could never condone human sacrifice: flowers, fruits, and poems would suffice for him. However, much to his dismay, man continued to destroy life and eventually forced Quetzalcoatl to leave his world; he had betrayed Quetzalcoatl's goodwill. Thus, man merited his own punishment when Quetzalcoatl chose to destroy him once and for all just as the flood of God destroyed Noah's generation. It was man who persisted in being negative. On the other hand, the blood cult of Huitzilopochtli selfishly drained human life. Huitzilopochtli demanded the hearts of men, he did not bestow them upon men. He was the warrior, not the peacemaker.

One need only compare some of the prerequisites for the selection of an Aztec priest with the actual deeds that such a priest would have to perform to realize that some kind of deterioration had already taken place, that two diametrically opposed philosophies were now existing side by side. For example, on the one hand, Aztec doctrine specifically stipulated that any criteria for the selection of high priests would have to entail that those chosen for this order should be virtuous, passive, considerate, humble, loving, timorous of God, and compassionate. On the other hand, we know for a fact that priests behaved quite the contrary to what was expected of them according to those traditional doctrines (most likely, those doctrines which remain unaltered by Tlacaelel). Laws made it mandatory that EVERYONE witness Huitzilopochtli's priests perform the brutal sacrifices of not just hundreds, but actually thousands of men, women, and children. The extent to which these priests indulged themselves in human sacrifice can only be understood as maniacal. The extent to which genocide, the mutilization of victims, and anthropophagy became commonplace was all indicative of a moral degeneracy. Contrary to what we've been told, it must have terrified one to think that perhaps some day one would have to be sacrificed accordingly; in fact, because there was always panic, fainting, and crying among victims, priests were forced to drag these victims up the pyramids by the hair and sometimes even drug them. If one was to believe in the philosophy of Quetzalcoatl, as the Aztecs presumably did, how then could one maintain a belief in the perpetual genocide which the worship of Huitzilopochtli entailed? What virtue was there to a sacrificial orgy of bloodthirsty madmen?

It wasn't really surprising, then, that Malintzin Tenépal should prefer to worship the image of Quetzalcoatl as opposed to that of Huitzilopochtli. As a Mayan slave, Malintzin began to understand the trials of the common indio, especially of those

7

indios burdened by Aztec dominance, if not the threat of it. She saw with her own eyes, and must have experienced as well, all the injustices that the indios suffered under the military state of Huitzilopochtli. Perhaps Malintzin was given some sense of deliverance when she recognized that the Spaniards resembled Quetzalcoatl in more ways than was to be expected for a mere coincidence.

THE ARRIVAL

It was the Aztec priests themselves who had recorded the expected date of Quetzalcoatl's return. Quetzalcoatl had prophesied: "On the day One Reed [April 21st] and the year One Reed [1519] I shall return. I will come from the east like the Morning Star." On a Thursday afternoon of April 21st, 1519, Hernán Cortés and his Spanish expedition landed on the island of San Juan de Ulúa. No sooner had they done so when, out of nowhere, Mexica (Aztec) ambassadors sent by the great Motecuhzoma himself welcomed the white strangers by presenting them with the Treasure of Quetzalcoatl.[6] The Mexicas had now acknowledged Quetzalcoatl's return. Ironically, Christianity (the Spanish faith), as stated in Revelations 22:16, proclaimed: "I, Jesus, have sent mine angel to testify unto you these things in the churches. I am the root and the offspring of David and the bright and Morning Star." The Morning Star had indeed returned and his coming had been heralded among the Indian world by the revival of old superstitions and the observation of omens in the sky, in the water and on earth.

Just before his arrival at San Juan de Ulúa, Cortés had fought a tenacious battle with the indios of Tabasco who, in the end, finally surrendered to him. Soon after, several Tabascan indios approached the Spanish camp and presented Cortés with many gifts of gold and women, one of whom was Malintzin Tenépal herself.

Malintzin not only made communication between the two worlds possible, she made it meaningful as well. The indios recognized that this woman was also Indian and that she was in a position to help them through her direct influence on and contact with the Conquistador himself. In fact, the extent to which the indios recognized the dual leadership of both Cortés and Malintzin can be better understood when we learn that the indios referred to both as "Malinche."

8

When the indios realized through their own defeat that Cortés was indeed a powerful force, they came to seek his help, but spoke with Doña Marina directly. They complained to them of the cruelties they were subjected to under Aztec dominance. They described how the Mexicas pillaged their settlements and raped their daughters in front of them. They told them of how the Aztecs took victims en masse for their bloody sacrifices and of how they were expected to pay tribute in heavy taxes. Many Indian peoples could no longer endure these injustices so that occurrences of rebellious outbreaks were not unusual. But, because the Aztec empire was more of a loose confederation (perhaps not even that) of Indian nations[7] ruled more for fiscal than for political purposes, the conquered peoples were able to retain much of their own political and cultural autonomy as nations. Unlike the Romans, the Aztecs made no attempt to "Aztecize" or integrate those conquered into the empire. They were simply used as a resource for exploitation. Aztec political thought had no conception of anything beyond the city. Similar to the Greek "polis," the Aztecs saw the "altepetl" (city) as the fundamental autonomous unit.

In effect, when Doña Marina is accused of being "una traidora a la patria," one wrongly assumes that there was a "patria" (similar to the patrias of today). The fact is, there were many Indian nations within the Aztec Empire and these nations were always attempting, through one rebellion or another, to regain their former independence.

It was not unusual for Indian nations to resist Aztec dominance by refusing to pay them tribute and by sometimes even resorting to killing the calpixqui[8] and whatever men accompanied him. For instance, when the province of Cuetlaxlan on the Gulf of México, rebelled, the Cuetlaxtecs forced the Mexican tax-collectors into a house and quickly set fire to it.

It is willful to forget that the concept of Mexican nationalism (la patria) was introduced only long after the conquest of México and *not* before. Nationalism might have been easier to implement after the conquest since, by this time, many Indian nations had already encountered the viability of allying themselves and working together as one political force.

Again, we cannot accuse Doña Marina of having betrayed the Indian peoples as a whole for it was they who had decided it would be to their advantage to help free themselves from the yoke of Aztec dominance. In effect, the whole nature of the Aztec Empire decreed its own self-destruction in that it was the subjected peoples of the Empire who eventually joined together to make its downfall a reality.

THE NEXUS

On Sunday of March 20, 1519, Malintzin Tenépal was baptized in the Tabascan lands of Cuetla. Her baptism was her emergence into another world for only as Christians could there be any interaction between her and the white strangers who came to destroy in the name of God. Bartolomé de Olmedo, the priest among them, had christened her "Doña Marina." Already she had been among these men five days and she had seen their wounds fester and bleed—indeed they were capable of bleeding. She learned that they reeked of filth, that they quarreled among themselves, and that they hungered for gold and young women like herself. Surely these were not gods!

Before being baptized, Doña Marina was first catechized and converted into the Catholic faith by Gerónimo de Aquilar, Cortés' Mayan interpreter.[9] It must not have been difficult for one threatened and horrified by the cruelties of Huitzilopochtli to reach out for the tenderness of the Virgin Mother Mary lovingly holding her child; Mary who seemed so unlike the mother Cimatl. Many were surprised at how Doña Marina had so readily grasped the Christian faith. Fray Christobal de Alameda writes of her: "Esta india de hermosura nada vulgar, era dotada de una viveza de espiritu; y assi [sic] pudo en breve imponerse en las verdades de nuestra Religión, Sus Sagrados Mysteriós y en la lengua castellana: sirviendo de interprete fidelíssima: no solo para facilitar la conquista: sino tambien, el Cathequismo de aquellas gentes." And Doña Marina herself tells us through the words of Bernal Díaz del Castillo: "que se encontraba más feliz que antes, pues había sido instruída en la fe cristiana y abjurado la sangrienta religión de los aztecas. . . ."

Although Doña Marina must have soon realized that the white strangers were not gods of themselves, she must have recognized that these very same crude and brutal men were the carriers (not necessarily the preachers) of a unifying force which promised peace to all. The fact that there were too many similarities between these men and Quetzalcoatl's faith and image suggested more than a mere coincidence. For example, some of the similarities between Doña Marina's indigenous faith and Catholicism include the following: both made use of a priestly hierarchy and both believed in baptism by immersion, in communion with the holy body, in

10

confession (to Tezcatlipoca, for example), and both celebrated in the memory of the dead, believed in a hell, the limbo of children, and in a paradise (Tlalocan). Besides there being a great similarity between the Aztec godless Cihuacoatl (snake-woman) and Eve, both faiths practiced fasting and abstinence, both espoused the presentation of new-born children in the temple, the gift of the first fruits to the gods, and both believed in the destruction of the world by evil spirits. Both Jesus and Quetzalcoatl were conceived through a virgin-birth, both were white, light-haired, and bearded and wore robes of which Quetzalcoatl's was embroidered with red and black crosses.

It was more than a coincidence that these Christians should also arrive from the east, the direction from which Quetzalcoatl had predicted he would arrive, on exactly the same date which he had also set for his return. Cortés must have also given the impression that he was "heaven sent" when he introduced himself to the Indian peoples as having come "de parte del primer señor (King Carlos V of Spain) que había en el mundo." It's quite possible, then, that these men might have represented manifestations of Quetzalcoatl's will to Doña Marina as indeed they had to the rest of the Indian world including Motecuhzoma himself. Doña Marina's faith in Quetzalcoatl was reified in her Christianity.

From the very onset of her participation in the conquest of México, Marina not only translated per se as did Gerónimo de Aquilar, but on her own initiative, beckoned by her precocious intelligence, she resourcefully mitigated possible violence between indio and Spaniard through her own persuasion. She alone (she made Gerónimo de Aquilar dispensable when she learned Spanish) could determine and give validity to the negotiations and treaties which went on between the Spanish aggressors and her indio world. Within thirty days, Doña Marina developed from a mere slave gift to a strategic asset.

It's quite possible that if Doña Marina soon realized that the Christians were not gods in themselves, she might have also recognized the fact that these conquistadores had come to interfere in her indigenous totality to the extent of upsetting it forever; indeed, they had come endowed with the power to destroy her entire culture.[10] Why then did Marina choose to protect and guide these men? Again, it's quite possible that her faith in the Word of God, those prophecies of Quetzalcoatl which predicted his coming along with the formation of a new world, motivated her particular actions in the conquest of México (i.e., the destruction of her own existing indio reality).

11

welcome. The Emperor Motecuhzoma had sent word to the Cholulans to befriend the white men. However, Motecuhzoma later
changed his mind (ever since the appearance of the white men,
the Emperor had been beseiged by indecisiveness and great
anxieties as to the nature of these strangers) and plotted to have
them ambushed by both Cholulan and Aztec military forces,
dividing whatever prisoners were left to be later used as sacrificial
victims. Fortunately for the Spaniards, Doña Marina's pleasing
character won the favor of an old Cholulan cacica who beckoned
Marina to leave the white men for fear that she might suffer the
imminent disaster intended for them. Marina pretended to go
along with the old woman's plans only to get more information
concerning the ambush; later she excused herself from the old
lady's presence on the pretext of going to pack some clothes, but
instead rushed to Cortés to inform him of the plot. Cortés was
outraged! Although Cortés had ulterior motives himself, he could
not understand why he had been welcomed in friendship only to
be destroyed in cold-blooded treachery! He felt that his Christian
ethics of trust and fidelity had been violated. In retaliation, he
counter-plotted just as evil an ambush as was intended for him.

In the end, Cortés and his Indian allies managed to
massacre more than 60,000 indios in just a matter of hours. The
audacity and intensity of such a massacre was heard of throughout
the land. Motecuhzoma was bewildered. In spite of everything,
the Christians had emerged victorious once again.

Doña Marina must have been as bewildered as the great
Emperor himself; never before had she witnessed such merciless
cruelty on behalf of the leader of the Christians. In informing him
of the Cholulan plot, she sought to save his life, for he was in
danger. Most likely, she assumed that Cortés would have reacted
against the Cholulans in very much the same way that he reacted
against the Tlaxcalan spies—he overlooked their betrayal and sued
for peace. Cortés was always willing to make peace with the
Indian peoples simply because it was to his advantage to do so.
How, then, was Marina to have known that Cortés would react
like a madman and commit the darkest massacre in all the history
of México?

Cortés' actions demonstrated to the indio world that he
was not to be deceived in any way, and perhaps his actions were
also intended as a warning to the great Motecuhzoma—he who
had initiated the plot.

Cortés was now preparing to march on to the center of
the Empire itself—México-Tenochtitlán. Motecuhzoma had done

everything within his power to prevent the Spaniards from advancing further. His oracles had warned him that the white strangers brought his empire's doom. Before Cortés left the deathridden city of Cholula, he made peace with them and made both the Cholulans and Tlaxcalans resolve the turmoil that had made them enemies for so long. The Spaniards and their Indian allies then proceeded to march on to Tenochtitlán.

On November 8, 1519, the Spanish expedition reached the city of México-Tenochtitlán, and for the first time Motecuhzoma and Hernán Cortés met each other. The great Motecuhzoma, whom no one dared to look directly in the face, humbly welcomed the Spaniards to his city. Cortés, however, was not content with Motecuhzoma's humble generosity—instead he wanted to arrest him and hold him as a hostage in case things turned to the worst within the city (as they had in Cholula).

On the day of the arrest, Cortés was accompanied by some of his best men and, of course, Doña Marina, without whom he never went anywhere. He requested an audience with the Emperor which was immediately granted. Cortés was the first to begin conversation on what had recently occurred in Cholula, but Motecuhzoma denied that he had had anything to do with the plot. Cortés then requested the great Emperor to "transfer" his living quarters to Cortés' place of residence as proof of his innocence (the arrest had commenced). After this the conversation went as follows:

Motecuhzoma: "When was it ever heard that a great prince, like myself, voluntarily left his own palace to become a prisoner in the hands of strangers!"

Cortés assures him that he would not go as a prisoner.

Motecuhzoma: "If I should consent to such a degradation my subjects never would!"

The discussion continued very much along the same lines, but Cortés was patient. Finally Motecuhzoma offered the persistent Spaniards one of his daughters or sons to be taken in his stead. But the Spaniards were not amenable. They refused.

Many hours had gone by and still no agreement had been reached between the two men. At this moment, the impatient Velásquez de León shouted: "Why do we waste words on this barbarian? We have gone too far to recede now. Let us seize him, and, if he resists, plunge our swords into his body!" Alarmed by his aggressive manner, Motecuhzoma turned to Doña Marina and

15

asked her what it was that Velásquez had just said. Marina, realizing that his life was in danger, did her best to try and persuade Motecuhzoma to accompany the insistent Spaniards. She explained: "Señor, yo como vasalla vuestra deseo vuestra felicidad, y como confidente de estos hombres se sus secretos y conozco su resolución. Si os avenis a lo que os propone, os trataran con el honor y distinción que se debe a vuestra real persona: si persistis en vuestra resistencia corre peligro vuestra vida." (Clavijero.) Motecuhzoma conceded.

But Motecuhzoma was right, the Mexicas could never accept the fact that their king had been taken prisoner by the imposing strangers. In spite of the Emperor's protests, the Aztec populace attacked Cortés' residence and, had it not been for his daring escape from the city on the night of "la noche triste," the indios would definitely have destroyed the entire Spanish expedition along with its allies. Cortés lost most of his forces during his desperate flight from México that night (noche triste), but fortunately for him and the allied forces, Doña Marina was alive, both indios and Spaniards had given up their lives to secure hers.

The broken Cortés returned to the land of his Tlaxcalan allies to recuperate (in every sense of the word!). The Tlaxcalans welcomed him faithfully in friendship and made him at home in their province, but already Cortés, as shattered as he was, was making plans for his return to the great city. The Tlaxcalans reinforced his Spanish forces and helped him build his ships. When all was ready, Doña Marina talked to the armed forces and encouraged them in their divine struggle: "Que se alegrasen y esforzasen mucho, pues veían que nuestro Señor nos encaminaba para haber victoria a nuestros enemigos." This time not even the powers of the formidable Huitzilopochtli could save the Indian peoples; even the name of their new king, Cuauhtemoc, "the falling eagle," presaged a downfall.

Everyone in high spirits, the march to México-Tenochtitlán resumed once again. None realized that there would be no true victors, but only the emergence of a new people inherently born with the tenacity of both the indio who fought heroically against fate and the Spaniard who, in spite of his greatest defeat, was determined to conquer.

In the midst of the horror of destroyed bodies, of disease and wounds and the stench of decaying corpses of both men and animals, Marina shed her own blood with that of the men. In the midst of all this death, she made love to a decaying Cortés, thus giving birth to a new people.

It was Quetzalcoatl, the Feathered Serpent, who came down to earth from the heavens to create life from the bones of the dead to bring forth a new people. Now, it was these people whom Cortés had come to destroy. Their Indian world would end in the year Ce Acatl, "one reed" (1519 A.D.)—the Feathered Serpent had predicted it; but a new world, a new people, would spring forth from the old as had happened before. The life cycle continued. Doña Marina gave birth to the mestizo child, Martín Cortés Tenépal—la raza cósmica.

THE OUTCOME

Because history is notorious for depicting the female as being one of the main causes for man's failures, it's extremely important that we understand the ethics with which historians, most of whom have been men in the past, distribute blame and justice. Apparently, what seems to be involved here is an unconscious acceptance of morals which blindly depict the male force as one which generally strives to do good in spite of the ever-present influence of the opposite sex. Woman is perceived as being one whose innately negative nature only serves to stagnate man, if not corrupt him entirely. So just as Eve was chosen long ago by misogynistic men to represent the embodiment of "the root of all evil" for western man, Mexico's first and most exceptional heroine, Doña Marina "la Malinche" now embodies female negativity (traición) for our Mexican culture. Yet, why is Doña Marina demeaned and obscured in history?

I believe that her negative portrayal in history and, thereby, in popular belief, can be attributed to two things: (1) misinterpretation of her role in the conquest of Mexico and (2) an unconscious, if not intentional misogynistic attitude toward women in general, especially toward self-assertive women, on the part of western society as a whole.

Popular Mexican heroines such as la Adelita, Juna Gallo, y la Valentina are admired not because they acted according to their own convictions, but because their behavior is interpreted as being imitative of masculine behavior, they took on a masculine attitude and became "machas." History, or should I say documentors of history, can tolerate and even condone this type of behavior from females because it's still within a masculine norm.

Doña Marina, on the other hand, is not a "macha." But, just the same, her submission is to her own convictions. Her

actions in the conquest of México are the reification of those
convictions. She and her faith in God are her own motivation to
action. Although she does not imitate the crude behavior of her
male companions, her courage is insurmountable. Yet few writers
find her admirable.

In *Tiempo Mexicano*, for example, Carlos Fuentes helps
to condemn this woman when he states that La Malinche "genera
la traición y la corrupción en la mujer," which is comparable to
saying that we as mexicanas not only have to contend with Eve's
great sin, but with Malinche's as well, we, unfortunately, receive
a double dose of corruption! Such a statement is confusing primarily because it really doesn't seem to make any sense, and yet
it's so damaging. If, for example, Malinche is understood to
represent a positive character, as she is by some people, the above
statement makes little sense in that goodness (positivity) is not
conducive to corruption. If, on the other hand, we do understand
Malinche to be representative of evil, are we to honestly believe
that she actually generates evil to the rest of the female sex? I
think not. To be sure, Carlos Fuentes is being metaphorical, but
even so, his statement is revealing of a condescending, if not
contemptuous attitude toward women. Fuentes implies that if
women are rotten creatures, it's not, their fault; we're not even
acknowledged as creatures responsible for our own actions. Blame
Malinche. She generates the evil! In the end, only a woman could
be responsible for others' faults. Carlos Fuentes' rationale is not
atypical of the kind of misogynistic reasoning which portrays
women as being "innately" evil and, thereby, justifiably in need
of male domination.

Not only is Marina depicted as the destructive traitoress,
she is also known as "la mala mujer," the lustful whore whose only
motivation is her own selfishness. Margaret Shedd, who perhaps
doesn't realize the crass liberties she's taken, gives us to understand
in her novel, *Malinche and Cortés,* that Marina is so phallically
fixated that if it weren't for Cortés' own overpowering size,
Marina would certainly have settled for his horse! It's discouraging
to read how Shedd finds it so easy to depict Doña Marina, a Mexican historical figure if nothing else, as a rampant nymphomaniac!
What gives her, what gives anybody, the right to accuse Doña
Marina of such behavior? On what do they base their accusations?
If, in fact, Doña Marina did love Hernán Cortés, as every author
who's written about her has either implied or openly stated, there
could be nothing promiscuous about her relationship with him.

Isn't promiscuity a state of non-love, i.e., a lack of being loved? Unfortunately, words like *whore*, which Shedd uses frequently to describe Marina, are as loosely used and exploited as are those at whom they are directed. As such, popular belief depicts the mexicana/chicana as having an affinity for being a loose, treacherous female.

Because I see Marina as primordial to any conceptualization of "mexicanidad" based on "el mestizaje" that she initiates, it behooves me to understand her: she is the beginning of the mestizo nation, she is the mother of its birth, she initiates it with the birth of her mestizo children. Even her baptism is significant. She is, in fact, the first Indian to be christianized (catechized and baptized to Catholicism) in her native land, that land which metamorphizes into our mundo mestizo—again she is the starting point! Thus any denigrations made against her indirectly defame the character of the mexicana/chicana female. If there is shame for her, there is shame for us; we suffer the effects of these implications.

It was only after I had familiarized myself with the history of the conquest of México and the story of Doña Marina that it became evident to me that statements such as "la Malinche fue nada más que una traidora a la patria" were at most anachronistic, if not flatly untrue. I came to realize that the young Doña Marina was not "solamente la intérprete y amante de Cortés" as is popularly believed.

It was only after some consideration into religion that it became evident to me that Doña Marina's role in the conquest was just as profound as she was difficult to understand. A careful look at what is known about her and her times seems to indicate the immense probability that Doña Marina's participation in the conquest of México was a manifestation of her faith in a godly force— the prophecies of Quetzalcoatl. It is because of this faith that she sees the destruction of the Aztec empire, the conquest of México, and as such, the termination of her indigenous world as inevitable.

It is to this faith that she submits entirely. Never once did Marina's determination waiver, and never did she complain about insufferable conditions as did her male companions. Bernal Díaz del Castillo makes it a point in his chronicles to write of Marina's unflinching courage throughout her participation in the conquest: "Digamos como doña Marina, con ser mujer de tierra, que esfuerzo varonil tenía, que con oir cada día que nos habían de matar y comer nuestras carnes, y habernos visto cercados en

19

las batallas pasadas, y que ahora todos estamo heridos, y dolien-
tes, jamás vimos flaqueza en ella, sino muy mayor esfuerzo de
mujer."[11]

To say that Doña Marina endured these hardships because of her love for Cortés, as authors have written, is to be
naïve. Love of the opposite sex is in no way to be compared with
love (belief) of a godly force. It was this latter force which provided her with the physical and spiritual stamina with which to
encounter the hardships and atrocities of the conquest. Religious
belief necessarily entails a comprehensive philosophy which puts
the world and us in proper perspective in relation to the intangible
supernatural force. This gives order and meaning to everything
around, and supplies dictum for proper behavior within that
order. As such, even the absurd—the nonsensical—serves a purpose, and can be meaningful.

Kierkegaard tells us that when one succumbs to complete
faith in God, there can be no doubt whatsoever in His Word no
matter what it may entail.[12] With God all things are possible, opposites may occasionally exist side by side; a life giving force, a
peacemaker such as Quetzalcoatl may demand and bring about
the destruction and death of an entire world, such as he had
predicted he would do. His prophecies eventually became manifest, and the indios of that past world were indeed expecting the
reification of such prophecies.

A true believer never doubts the Word of God. For
example, when God asked Abraham to kill his beloved son, Abraham did not question God as to his motives for such a request.
Abraham responded faithfully by what Kierkegaard calls "the
virtue of the absurd"; for it is absurd that God should ask Abraham, who had always been good and faithful to Him, to perform
such a deed.

But because Abraham IS faithful, he is at one with God;
and although he may not totally understand, he resigns himself
to the absurdity of the situation. Because God has willed it there
is virtue in it. All things are possible with God, even the absurd.
By "virtue of the absurd," Doña Marina helps to bring the destruction of her own world and of her own self, that it all made little
sense is besides the point. The Lifegiver had decreed death.

Having chosen to act on behalf of her religious faith, like
most religious activists, Doña Marina's reward was martyrdom.
Marina was to die by the age of approximately twenty-two,
spending most of her youth on the road alongside Hernán Cortés,

after which he married her off to the Spaniard ingrate, Don Juan Jaramillo. Her children were tortured and robbed of their rightful inheritance. Don Martín Cortés Tenépal, natural son of Hernán Cortés and Doña Marina, was accused of treason and tortured by the Spaniards to obtain a confession, after which he was executed. María Jaramillo, legitimate daughter of Don Juan Jaramillo and Doña Marina, was robbed of her inheritance of land and money by her own father soon after Doña Marina's death (most likely caused by smallpox). After all Doña Matina had endured to bring forth a new world, few recognized or acknowledged her merits and contributions to it. No one, not Cortés,[13] not the Catholic Church, nor her own husband, not even history itself, nor the mestizo nation she gives birth to realize the great injustice they have done her by obscuring her in defamation.

EPILOGUE

In *The Labyrinth of Solitude*, Octavio Paz tells that when a mexicano "repudiates La Malinche—the Mexican Eve—[he] breaks his ties with the past, renounces his origins, and lives in isolation and solitude." Here we see that Paz clearly acknowledges the existence of a nexus between ourselves and La Malinche as mexicanos, but he also sees her as being representative of "the cruel incarnation of the feminine condition," this being the belief that there exists an innate feminine vulnerability which transforms women into "chingadas." Clearly this has very belittling overtones and destructive implications concerning the feminine character.

Nevertheless, Octavio Paz, being the sensitive and intelligent man that he is, has convincingly managed to come up with a "reasonable" explanation of the female's doom to become the "chingada" he believes we as women must eventually become. Evidently, it all goes back to fundamentals, man's main interest in woman—her body. In so many words, Paz gives us to understand that a woman's nature (the physical condition of her body) is by its very essence always being "violated."

After considering an exposition of the word "chingar," Paz concludes that it is an aggressive masculine verb which connotes "an emergence from oneself to penetrate another by force" and, thus, consummating a violation. This penetration can take many forms: it can be sexual, physical, or even mental; but because it can only be achieved by force, the nature of the action

21

is one of being closed to the vulnerability of being retaliated against or used. The one who receives this closed, aggressive action must be passive and open, the penetration (violation) thereby being made possible. Thus, if the verb connotes aggressive masculinity, its object is passive femininity. Hence, if the "chingon" is the male penetrator, then the "chingada" is the "violated female" for she supposedly receives the action. But as far as Octavio Paz is concerned, even if a woman willingly partakes in the act of lovemaking, the fact that she is "penetrated" constitutes a violation. He puts it this way: "In effect, every woman—even when she gives herself willingly (in Octavio's eyes, woman is more of a "donor" than a participant)—is torn open by the man, is the "Chingada." Our "feminine condition," according to him, dooms us by nature to being "open" and "violated" by "penetration" (I suppose virgin-mother-saints are the only females exempt from such a fate).

Because Octavio Paz sees the conquest of México as a violation in itself, he must necessarily see Doña Marina as the violated mother for she is mistress to the leader of the conquest. We as mestizos are then "the offspring of violation," we are all "hijos de la chingada." In effect, Octavio Paz reaffirms the belief that if La Malinche is to be demeaned and denigrated naturally her children will have to be considered accordingly.

Unfortunately, for all of us, man has always been the dictating force in determining what our female nature is really all about regardless of whether or not his impressions are true. His only criterion being that his definition of us be relevant to him and "his world." This, in fact, is what the poet Octavio Paz is doing when he associates the pure act of making love with a woman as a direct violation of that woman irrespective of her motivations!

Octavio's statements also imply to me that to lose one's virginity (to be "torn open") is by nature a violation. But just exactly by whose nature is it a violation? It is certainly not by woman's nature to abstain from the act of loving. Virginity (mental, physical, or whatever it may mean to us) is more an obsession created by and for the use of men than an actual feminine state of being. Probably, what comes most naturally between a man and a woman is copulation. Taking into consideration that one of our primary biological functions is to reproduce the species, there is nothing unnatural or negative in the act of sexual intercourse. There is no inherent "violation" involved in such an act; indeed, Paz is being the poet.

In spite of this oversight, Octavio Paz chooses to use terms such as "torn open," "penetrate" and "violate" as well as the dialectic of the "closed" and the "open."

I perceive the situation differently. Terms like "penetrate" are already loaded with unbalanced energies which help to slant the presentation. Such a word implies that it only takes the participation of one force (the active) to fulfill the act although actually two entities are involved, whereas terms like "copulation" or "sexual intercourse," as medical as they may sound, leave one the alternative of envisioning two equally active participants, both giving and receiving. I could have, for example, chosen to describe Octavio's "violation" as actually being that of the male, in the sense that a woman can be understood to "engulf" the man, actually consuming him entirely in the act of loving; making him the overwhelmed! However, such an interpretation would have been just as capricious as Octavio's. Nevertheless, I should like to point out that just as it is necessary and natural for us to eat through our mouths, it is necessary and natural and essential to the survival of the species for man and woman to partake of sexual intercourse. We can't say that a woman is violated just because she participates in copulation, any more than we can say that we violate the mouth every time we eat, although there is a definite "penetration" involved. Associations such as those given by Octavio Paz can only be attributed to an "ego-testicle" worldview.

Actually, for Paz to have written that woman is violated even when she has willingly consented to the act of love is to imply that woman is not capable of reciprocating, which is to imply sexual impotence. For example, Octavio wrotes: "The Chingada [La Malinche] is even more passive. Her passivity is abject: she does not resist violence, but is an inert heap of bones, blood and dust." As sexually inferior, woman can only be passive while he is active: we can only receive, we cannot give. The act is presented as being one between unequals. However, the very act of love tells us differently. When two people make love, they are one with each other, each giving and receiving, they are equally participating. There is no such thing as a violation between lovers, between equals; on the contrary, there is only complementing of one another.

It is unusual to associate love with violence. Our biological function of procreation denies that an offence has taken place, and the very act of love prevents it. Of course, I don't deny the fact that many women are actually violated or that some may

Indians	*Spaniards*
1. shields of leather & wood	1. body armor of steel
2. headpieces made of leather or cloth	2. helmets of steel
3. bow and arrow with obsidian heads	3. crossbow (greater distance) and steel-tipped arrow
4. darts and stones	4. muskets & canon (great distance)
5. lances	5. 20' lances of wood with iron or copper heads
6. wooden clubs with sharp obsidian chips protruding	6. steel sword
7. canoe	7. boat & ship
8. the need to use a greater amount of ammunition to wound or slay a well protected Spaniard	8. easier to wound or slay the unprotected indio with their powerful weapons
9. nothing comparable to the horse	9. the horse
10. superstition	10. advanced tactics of war & military strategems
11. everything to lose	11. nothing to lose but their lives

The Indios did have the advantage of possessing greater numbers, but eventually more and more Indian nations allied themselves to the Spanish forces.

11. Bernal Díaz del Castillo's Spanish is a bit archaic, but still comprehensible to the modern speaker of Spanish. His direct translations for Indian words are exactly that, and in no way representative of the Indian language. He, for example, interprets the great Motecuhzoma's name as being "Montezuma" and goes even further when it comes to Huitzilopochtli's name, which he interprets as "Huichilobos" and, in turn, ends up as "Witchywolves" when Spain's distinguished historian, Salvador de Madariaga, translates it into English.

12. Kierkegaard, Sören, *Fear and Trembling / Sickness unto Death*, trans. Walter Lowie (New York: Princeton University Press, 1954).

13. In his famous letters of correspondence to King Carlos V, Cortés shrewdly refers to Doña Marina as just "an Indian woman" (Second Letter), then again as "the female interpreter" (Second Letter), then for the third and last time he mentions her by name in his Fifth Letter as "the interpreter . . . , who is Marina." By doing so, he minimizes her significance in the conquest making it seem as if he were solely responsible for the success of the conquest.

BIBLIOGRAPHY

Braden, Charles S. *Religious Aspects of the Conquest of Mexico.* North Carolina, 1930.

———— . *The Broken Spears,* ed. Miguel León-Portilla. Boston, 1969.

Cantu, Caesar C. *Cortés and the Fall of the Aztec Empire.* California, 1966.

Conquistador Anonimo. *Relación de algunas cosas de Nueva España.* México, 1938.

Cortes, Hernando. *Cartas y Relaciones al Emperado Carlos V.* Escritas 1519–26. Translated and edited with notes and comments by Francis A. MacNutt, 2 vols., under the title *Letters of Hernando Cortés to Charles V.* New York, 1908.

26

CRONICA DE LA CONQUISTA. *Relación de Andrés de Tapia.* Mexico, 1939.
DIAZ DEL CASTILLO, BERNAL. *The Conquest of New Spain,* trans. and ed. by J. M. Cohen. Baltimore, 1963.
——— . *Historia verdadera de la conquista de la Nueva España.* España, 1942.
FUENTES, CARLOS. *Tiempo mexicano.* México, 1971.
GOMEZ DE OROZCO, FEDERICO. *Doña Marina.* México, 1942.
GONZALO RUIZ, FELIPE. *Doña Marina (La india que amó a Cortés).* España, 1944.
HERNANDO, LIC. CARLOS. *Mujeres célebres de México.* Ed. Lozano, San Antonio, Texas, U.S.A.
IXTLIXOCHITL DE ALBA, FERNANDO. *Relación de la venida de los españoles y principio de la ley evangélica.* México, D.F.
KIERKEGAARD, SOREN. *Fear and Trembling / Sickness unto Death,* trans. by Walter Lowie. New York, 1954.
KRUGER, HILDA. *Malinche o el adios a los mitos.* México, 1944.
LEANDER, BIRGITTA. *Herencia Cultural del Mundo Nahuatl.* México, 1972.
LEON-PORTILLA, MIGUEL. *Los antiguos mexicanos a través de sus crónicas y cantares.* México, D.F.
——— . *Nezahualcoyotl, Poesia y Pensamiento.* México, 1972.
LONG, HANIEL. *Malinche (Doña Marina).* Santa Fe, New Mexico, 1939.
MADARIAGA, SALVADOR DE. *Hernán Cortés, Conqueror of Mexico.* New York, 1969.
McHENRY, PATRICK J. *A Short History of Mexico.* New York, 1962.
PAZ, OCTAVIO. *The Labyrinth of Solitude, Life and Thought in Mexico,* trans. by Lysander Kemp. New York, 1961.
PRESCOTT, W.H. *The History of the Conquest of Mexico,* 3 vols. Philadelphia, 1874.
RAMOS-OLIVEIRA, ANTONIO. *Hernán Cortés y Sus Parientes Los Juarez.* México, 1972.
RODRIGUEZ, DR. GUSTAVO. *Doña Marina.* México, 1935.
ROGERS, KATHARINE M. *The Troublesome Helpmate, A History of Misogyny in Literature.* Seattle, 1966.
ROMEROVARGAS YTURBIDE, LIC. IGNACIO. *Organización política de los pueblos de Anáhuac.* México, 1957.
SEJOURNE, LAURETTE. *Pensamiento y Religión en el México Antiguo.* México, 1957.
SHEARER, TONY. *Lord of the Dawn, Quetzalcoatl.* California, 1971.
SHEDD, MARGARET. *Malinche and Cortés.* Garden City: Doubleday & Company, Inc., 1971.
SOMONTE, MARIANO G. *Doña Marina, "La Malinche."* México, 1969.
SOUSTELLE, JACQUES. *Daily Life of the Aztecs,* trans. by Patrick O'Brian. California, 1961.
TIBON, GUTIERRE. *Diccionario Etimologico compensado de nombres propios de personas.* México, D.F.
TORQUEMADA, FRAY JUAN. *Los veintiun libros rituales monarchia Indiana.* España, 1723.
VAILLANT, GEORGE C. *Aztecs of Mexico.* Penguin Books, 1941.
VASCONCELOS, JOSE. *Breve Historia de México.* México, 1944.

3

The Widowed Women of Santa Fe: Assessments on the Lives of an Unmarried Population, 1850-80

DEENA J. GONZÁLEZ

This essay examines the lives of Spanish-Mexican widows living in Santa Fe, New Mexico, between 1850 and 1880. The terms *widow* and *widowhood* can be misleading, however, and require qualification. For some groups of southwestern women a more apt description would be "unmarried," a category that included not only widows but also the far larger community of women who were divorced, separated, or deserted. Placing Santa Fe's widows under the broader category of unmarried women reflects accurately their lives and makes possible the use of material from the censuses that did not enumerate widows separately.

Determining the exact number of widows in Santa Fe is more difficult than for most groups of white westering women. Although the censuses portrayed many women heading households and some elderly unmarried women living within several types of family groups, the number of widows remains undetermined because only the 1880 census specified marital status. Comparisons with earlier Mexican enumerations provide few clues. And the 1845 census for Santa Fe is lost entirely. Still, the task of counting the presence of widows in the population at large or deciphering the patterns of their lives is not impossible. It simply requires applying — and this can be generalized to include all Latin American women — more imaginative criteria to the evidence. Residential habits, income distribution, occupations, and stages in the life cycle thus can embellish the portrait of unmarried women when statistics or other factors cannot.

Unmarried women merit special consideration for another reason: Latin

American societies and communities consistently exhibited higher percentages of unmarried females than those of the United States. Studies on
Peru and parts of the Mexican frontier have found that perhaps 7 to 10
percent of the adult population in certain areas could be classified as widows.
Moreover, if Latin American societies and communities traditionally included a large number of unmarried women, widowhood would carry
different connotations and would be regarded differently. The censuses and
some wills provide evidence that this was the case. They also indicate that
Spanish-Mexican Santa Fe, like many parts of Latin America, continued its
precapitalist economic practices, so that in their families widows as well as
other members contributed to the household economy. The censuses, in
particular, portray women at work — sewing, laundering, and providing other
services for the Euro-American men who poured into town after 1848 when
the war with Mexico ended and the United States annexed New Mexico.

Yet another problem confronts any study of Spanish-Mexican women but
is used here as a theme for examining their lives. Most white women
moving into the southwestern United States after the war participated in
the systematic effort to control or acquire property and settle in former
Mexican territory. On the other side of that effort stood Native and Spanish-
Mexican women, who experienced firsthand the white westering impact.
For them, the signing of the Treaty of Guadalupe-Hidalgo, between the
United States and Mexico, marked a turning point. Beginning in 1848 even
the Spanish-Mexican widow — seemingly protected because she lived among
her family and because her community contained so many others in her
situation — experienced the effects of conquest.

In this essay I inquire into a woman's widowhood but place it within
the postwar period's surrounding turmoil and accompanying economic displacement. I focus on specific characteristics of a widowed population as
well as on impinging socioeconomic forces and argue that a widow's life
was shaped by the interplay of a changing society and an economy imposed
on her by wealthy newcomers, and not solely by her widowhood.

When the United States-Mexican War ended in 1848, all women in Santa
Fe faced generally dismal economic circumstances. Only two years earlier,
they had heard General Stephen Watts Kearny proclaim peace and promise
prosperity. His army, Kearny declared, had come "as friends, to better your
condition."[1] When people first watched the soldiers occupy the area peace-
fully, perhaps they anticipated better times. Since 1820 they had witnessed
traders trek to Santa Fe, introduce manufactured items, and alter the town's

protection against such spiraling costs. Even worse, shortages frequently developed. The same amount of crops and number of livestock continued to support the expanding population.[20] The scarcity of commodities led Sister Blandina Segale of the Sisters of Charity to report in the late 1870s that many poor women came into the plaza on Sundays, begging for food while trying to exchange precious possessions like Indian blankets.[21]

Spanish-Mexican women could do little against rising inflation. They had previously supplemented their incomes by raising hens for the eggs but never in sufficient quantity to compete with farmers from the outlying areas in the marketing of chickens. Now women began raising the animals. Local men bought sheep and pastured them on plots outside the urban area. The flocks proved to be a nuisance, in both instances. Sheep devoured good grasses and left the hillsides bare; chickens were noisy and difficult to keep penned. Regardless, the locals could not compete with the newcomers who invested in the more lucrative commodities of cattle and hogs. Such changes had a rippling effect that extended all the way to diet: beef and pork replaced chicken and mutton as delicacies. Cattle and hogs, which the immigrant class purchased as rapidly as possible and leased out to pasture, became unofficial currency worth more than some luxury items. The value of chickens and sheep fell correspondingly.[22]

Postwar Santa Fe was a town turned upside down. Ethnically, it had changed substantially with the arrival of U.S. soldiers and citizens. But the 1870s witnessed unprecedented migration—over 1,300 new men entered Santa Fe (table 3). Their cash flowed in and around the territorial capital lining the pockets of retailers and politicians. Investors used their money to construct new mercantile establishments, a hotel, homes, a hospital, and an orphanage. Yet the economy of the 1870s continued to fluctuate, and its instability affected Spanish-Mexican families. The burgeoning population once more induced food shortages and lowered buying power. The male migrants upset ethnic and sex balances as never before. Men with money in the 1870s increasingly forced locals into menial work. Women in particular struggled under the pressing challenge of changing markets, a new demography, and different occupations. In a matter of decades dual jobs marked their lot.[23]

Social and economic inequalities were most glaring for unmarried women. As used here, the term "unmarried" signifies all adult women who, when enumerated by the census, were living without men. Perhaps 10 percent of adult females had lived or would live with men but were never "legally married." As many as 20 percent outlived their male partners. Placing such

Table 3. Santa Fe's Changing Demography, 1850-80

	1850	1860	1870	1880
Total Population	4,320	4,555	4,847	6,767
Female	2,166 (50%)	2,247 (49%)	2,488 (52%)	2,662 (38%)
Male	2,154 (50%)	2,308 (51%)	2,359 (49%)	4,105 (62%)
Ethnic Background				
Spanish-surnamed females	2,126 (49%)	2,160 (47%)	2,438 (50%)	2,532 (37%)
Spanish-surnamed males	1,915 (44%)	1,995 (44%)	1,803 (37%)	2,178 (32%)
Non–Spanish-surnamed females	40	87	50	130
Non–Spanish-surnamed males	(7%) 239	(9%) 313	(13%) 556	(31%) 1,927
Female-Headed Households				
Total Households	930	879	1,216	1,461
Unmarried, Spanish-surnamed female heads of households	201 (22%)	253 (29%)	322 (26%)	183 (13%)[a]

SOURCES: U.S. Census Bureau, Original Schedules of the Seventh, Eighth, Ninth, and Tenth Censuses of Population, for Santa Fe (microfilm, NMSRC).
[a] Only those enumerated as widows make up this number.

women in the broadest possible category reflects accurately their common status — women without men.

Among all groups, women over 15 without husbands remained at the bottom of the hierarchy, in income and jobs. From 1850 to 1880, such women made up at least 10 percent of the adult population. Not just work or marital status determined their low position. The majority headed their own households; at least 5 percent lived with women who appeared to be their widowed mothers.[24]

These and other figures were slightly inflated by the number of women whose husbands were away at the mines or, after 1870, laboring for the railroad farther south. The percentage of women "abandoned" will never be known. Additionally, the number legally married and subsequently separated went unrecorded. Nevertheless, other key features of these women's lives coupled with their large number in the population (table 3) suggest that they were the group most adversely affected by the changes in their community.

Despite the renewed growth of the town, single mothers prospered least of all. More headed households in these decades, and their average family size grew by almost one child. Once able to count on relatives or neighbors, such women now found their traditional supporters similarly constrained. The census graphically marked the pattern. On pages enumerating the Spanish-Mexican populace, the euphemistic phrase "at home" rarely described women's work. Rather, the most common occupations were laundress and seamstress, undertaken by mothers and daughters of all ages.[25] Whereas the 1850 census had been peppered with such skilled and semi-skilled trades as "midwife," "confectioner," and "farmer," the next two enumerations (1860, 1870) rarely listed vocations that veered from domestic and cleaning services. The wages paid (table 1) suggest that women did not take these jobs in unprecedented numbers for the extra money but from necessity.

The percentages of single women heading households (table 3) and their deteriorating net worths offer additional insights into women's plight. About 90 percent of all such women had children with their own surname. Across the three decades, their average households grew by one child and an additional adult, almost always a relative, but on occasion, a boarder. These women were not marrying their children's fathers. A randomly selected set of fifty single female heads of household with children of the same surname in 1860 showed not a single male as head of these households a decade later, while the women headed a slightly larger family. Of the fifty, eight listed adopted children in the household.

In 50 percent of the families, children over the age of 15 also worked, thereby aiding the household economy. Mothers heading households with working children appeared slightly better off than either single women listed within a household or women who apparently had no children. But the same random sample yielded the pattern of larger numbers of women per household working as laundresses, seamstresses, and domestics. Few revealed net worths extending beyond $100. Hence, a husbandless or unmarried condition alone did not bind them as a group. Equally pernicious was the growing family and dual, low-paying jobs.

Among these women, age helped determine rank or position. Women between 30 and 80 were most likely to be listed as heads of household. Those between ages 15 and 30 tended to live with their parents, often with sisters or other relatives. The link between age and residence lends credence to the possibility that some who appear to have been unmarried were women whose husbands were away and who had temporarily moved in with relatives. But tracing another group of fifteen mothers in their thirties between the 1860 and 1870 censuses revealed no such pattern and found them still listed without adult men of a different surname. The selection highlighted, however simplistically, the remoteness of temporary separation. It attested to an equally strong possibility that the majority of adult women who appeared to be unmarried lived permanently without male partners and might have been widows.

Within this group of women, widowhood became a distinguishing characteristic. Widowhood also affected how women survived the growing disparities of their time. Unfortunately, because the census did not list familial relationships, age, income, residential arrangement, and ethnicity must also be correlated to marital status to determine how widows and other husbandless women survived inflation and intrusion.[26]

Demographically, Spanish-Mexican Santa Fe had indeed begun to change, but a few patterns remained the same and suggest reasons for the hardy endurance of women without male partners. Few Spanish-Mexican women ever lived alone. Across the four censuses in this period, fewer than twenty resided by themselves. All lived with what appear to have been sons, daughters, or other relatives. A majority of women over 40 headed their households, but some (approximately 30 percent) were counted within a household headed by another woman or an adult man of her surname. Commonly, the husbandless mother, the widow, and other unmarried women lived either with their daughters and sons-in-law, next door to them, or with a married son. Another general pattern, typical of at least half the unmarried women, was that of a single woman heading a household but living in it with an unmarried son, usually in his twenties. Roughly another 10 percent of such mothers made up that group.[27]

Residentially, it could be argued, Santa Fe remained a town of old habits. Women's living arrangments portrayed a community still clustering around neighborhoods, the barrios, with related persons forming the nucleus in most homes. Juxtaposing residence habits, customs, and marital condition depicts a population consistently relying on each other in years of unprecedented growth and change. Women's net worth must thus be evaluated against the specific characteristics of their households. A woman in these decades heading a family sustained it. In a majority of cases she lived without a male partner; in all cases, she labored. Living among relatives, taking several jobs, or remaining unmarried as well as age combined in diverse patterns to insure the household's and the community's survival.

The unmarried Spanish-Mexican woman remained an integral part of her society. She lived and worked with relatives, sons or daughters, married or unmarried. Frequently, she adopted children or cared for children other than her own. These circumstances identify the extent of her incorporation and leadership in family and community life. The widow followed the same pattern. No one thought to place a member of society in a hospital, asylum, or poorhouse; before 1880 Santa Fe had few such institutions.[28]

More important, however, Spanish-Mexican culture either revered its aged or respected their productivity. In one census, about 40 percent of unmarried women over the age of 50 worked as laundresses and seamstresses.[29] Their specific tasks sustained a community under siege. Utilitarian worth undoubtedly joined with cultural mores to secure the position of the elderly and the unmarried. In that regard, the widow of 50 years and older helped households weather the upheaval.

To understand these women of the postwar era only as hard workers or mere survivors or simply to look at their ages when widowed or unmarried is misleading. Santa Fe's women did not pass easily between stages of their lives. Specific profiling — the single mother' heading a family, the widow living with her family, the young mother working as a seamstress living with a sister who worked as a laundress — points out how varied, yet universally constrained, each subgroup was.

Marital status obviously influenced survival but also affected the ability to stave off the impact of colonization. Similarly, parenting and grandparenting continued in spite of circumscribing economic and political tumult. Yet a key difference separated these women from the westering woman or Euro-American women generally: Santa Fe's women existed primarily inside the unending, all-embracing pressure of conquest. And it affected every stage of their lives.

Work, disparate property and income distributions, and marital status suggest initially a deepening schism between unmarried women and affluent immigrating men. With so many unmarried women living on the verge of poverty, especially single mothers, widows might have proved most susceptible to the influx of strangers and their cash. In fact, although widows were generally at the bottom of the social and economic ladder in other parts of the Far West, such was not entirely the case in Santa Fe insofar as women's finances can be measured and their status assessed.[30] Widows indeed emerged at the low end of the economy, but, in comparison to all women without male partners, appeared to be slightly more prosperous. And society did not always hold them in low esteem.

These assessments are based on several sources. Few Spanish-Mexican women left written letters or diaries, but they wrote a significant number of wills and testaments. Women comprised about one-third of the authors of 220 wills listed in probate court journals after 1850 and before 1880.[31] Of additional wills located in private family papers, widows wrote about thirty. Furthermore, wills provide exactly the insights missing for other unmarried women. While these wills shed light on the circumstances of all women, that a significant portion were drawn up by widows skews the resulting portrait of unmarried women. But the most prosperous of the unmarried group as a whole, widows looked destitute in comparison with the riches that male immigrants had accumulated and willed.

In addition to will making, another distinguishing feature of widows sets them apart: they had maintained or had held a legally sanctioned relationship with a man, sanctioned by the courts and by the church. Their better financial position might have derived as well from their husbands. But Spanish-Mexican women traditionally held and owned property in their maiden names. They could dispose of it without a husband's signature, and the wills reflected the tendency to retain and pass on inherited property. María de la Sur Ortiz bequeathed her land and another house farther south in San Isidro. She had inherited the property from her father. In 1860 María Josefa Martínez did the same and passed on land, livestock, and furniture to her children and grandchildren.[32] Marriage might have sustained the property for these women or made it unnecessary to sell it, but the land originally belonged to a parent or a wife's family. It was entrusted but not surrendered in marriage.

Many women maintained farms and property apart from their husbands. They rarely drew additional income from it, nor did ownership of farmland indicate general prosperity. New Mexicans had developed a regard for land and concept of ownership that differed markedly from that of the immigrants, even in 1850.[33] Accumulation was relatively unknown because most people inherited land and few bought up acres. One of the most common expressions in wills and testaments is "I leave a plot I bought from _____." Many Santa Fe residents, female and male, continued to own small pastures, but not acreage, outside of town. They used them for grazing or willed them in perpetuity, passing the land to sons and daughters. In some cases the land had been part of an old, divided grant; in others it had been acquired by trade. In *hijuela,* the giving of a share of property, some had received acreage or pasturage. The land did not necessarily carry a peso or dollar value, but it was useful in the exchange market of families or friends.[34]

Moreover, the Productions of Agriculture schedules following each census

indicated how little acreage Spanish-Mexicans owned. Few were listed as
farmowners in the county. [35] The worth they assigned the land stayed well
below its true value on the open market until 1870, when the entry of the
railroad was being discussed.

María Josefa Martínez owned twenty acres outside of town; the census
found her residing in Santa Fe with her children and claiming a net worth
of $50. Her house and furniture alone would have been worth that. Ob-
viously, she did not include her farmland.[36] Unlike inhabitants of other
parts of northern New Mexico, Santa Fe's people did manage to hold on to
these inherited shares, at least for a time. Land prices, by census indication,
had not yet skyrocketed, and much of the pasturage remained in Spanish-
Mexican hands. With that in mind, widows who owned land or pastures
could hardly be distinguished financially from those who did not.

In another regard, however, a prosperous widow stood alone. She became
the woman most subject to the avarice of the greedy politician or the
enterprising merchant, something of a pawn in their hands. The widow
Chaves, her first name not given, symbolized the extent to which a widow
with property might be victimized.[37] By no means poor, the widow Chaves
was preyed upon because she had some means and because the immigrant
men with whom she dealt carried to Santa Fe prejudices about women's
intelligence or wherewithal.[38]

As Territorial Secretary William G. Ritch reported it, the widow Chaves
wanted to write her will. In bad health, unable to read or write English,
and finding her own attorney absent, the widow asked a law clerk, Edwin
Dunn, to draw up the document. Only later, when her son examined the
will, did she learn that the stranger had written in donations to the church
and the poor. To her horror, she told a friend of Ritch's, it appeared that
the law clerk and the priest who was to have received the money had
colluded to dupe her.[39]

Several aspects of the tale are important. Each has something to say about
the position of Spanish-Mexican widows in Santa Fe after the war and about
how outsiders had begun to control women's lives. First, the story was
relayed to Ritch by a friend. As a third-hand account, it casts aspersions as
much on Ritch as on the conspiring clerk and suspicious priest. Ritch
subtitled the document, "How a lawyer and a priest undertook to fix the
will of a widow lady in the interest of Truchard [the priest]."[40] That
description alone hints at Ritch's anti-Catholicism and his guiding assumption that the U.S. government could relieve Spanish-Mexicans of the ubiq-

uitous Catholic oppression operating in the form of powerful priests. It was a belief uniformly shared by territorial officials.

Ritch twisted his friend's recollections to end on the same note: the widow accused the priest publicly, and in response he began excommunication procedures and would rescind them only if she sought his forgiveness. Of course, she did not ask for it. Smugly, Ritch wound the narrative to its suggestive finale. As a Catholic, Chaves continued to profess her beliefs, fully expecting to be buried in a Catholic rite, but "she had not the supreme confidence in the priesthood that she once had. Nor would she yield to them in matters which appertained to her business and were entirely foreign to the Church."[41] Even women, Ritch seemed to say, were ready for reform. If the wealthier could be converted, perhaps the rest would follow. In any case, the widow Chaves made him hopeful about the Spanish-Mexican willingness to accept change and to embrace it.

Ritch's concerns emerge clearly from his report of the episode. His account also offers insightful commentary into the lives of women in a decade of rising immigration and significant upheaval. Even Ritch could not ignore what motivated the widow Chaves. She was wealthy and thus atypical, a descendant of an affluent family, the Armijos, he said. On a strictly financial level, she reflected the concerns of the wealthiest members of the community. She had married well; her husband, a merchant, Ritch believed, had left a large inheritance to his daughters, giving them each $17,000. One of the daughters was an invalid and incapacitated to the point of being confined to an institution. The daughter intended to leave her brother her share of the estate, but a New Mexico law of that period prevented invalids from bequeathing any one sibling more than one-third of their inheritance. Presumably, this complicated legal situation motivated the widow Chaves to seek assistance from the conniving law clerk.[42]

Despite her wealth, or because of it, Chaves was vulnerable. But her son had uncovered the problem in the will drafted by Dunn and pointed out the way in which women, even wealthier ones, coped with the matters at hand. When institutions like the court or church failed, others stepped in and took over. In this instance, family became the basis upon which to resolve the controversy. Evidently not regarding it as a "private" matter, Chaves had shown the will to her son. After all, it concerned him. Or perhaps Chaves sensed that something was amiss. In any case, her reliance on the son attested to, and identified, the primacy of family. Further, Chaves asked her neighbor, "the widow of Juan Delgado and mother of Juan," to witness her burning the disputed will.[43] Son and neighbor thus rectified the impropriety and helped ease Chaves's situation.

Ritch's efforts to the contrary, the helpers demonstrated the continuing social and cultural tendencies that undermined most attempts at Americanization. At a minimum, the repeated failures of the territorial government and the church illustrated how unpredictable the institutions or their leaders could be. In the final analysis, Chaves had been forced to rely on family and friends, her own kind. They sustained her while new lawyers and a French priest served only to confuse and anger her. The widow Chaves might have been Ritch's champion, but he and his cronies were not hers.

The widow Chaves's experience was repeated throughout the postwar decades, but especially in the 1870s, when the bulk of eastern men arrived and their railroad began approaching Santa Fe. Probate records in that period showed women filing wills as never before (table 4). One book in the court records has been lost, but the remaining materials indicate that the number of women writing their final testaments after 1877 and depositing them before a local magistrate, with two witnesses present, rose dramatically.[44] The rising number owed something to the influx of new people and the havoc they created.

Not all of the women writing wills did so to counter the presence of strangers. Some had even married the newcomers.[45] Some testaments had been framed by widows of mixed marriages.[46] But mixed marriages were complicated by the prevailing social disruptions of the time. In the 1870s, more than ever, such relationships had become primarily a matter of class.

An 1880 sample of non–New Mexico born males married to New Mex-

Table 4. Female Wills and Testaments in Santa Fe County

Wills	Number	Percentage of Composers with Spanish Surnames
Listed in the Index	75	95
Book B, 1856-62	6	99
Book C, 1859-70	6	99
Book D, 1869-77	3	98
Book E, 1877-97	36	95
Missing	24	90

SOURCES: Santa Fe County Records, Wills and Testaments, Index, Books B, C, D, and E, 1856-97, NMSRC, Santa Fe.

ican females bearing Spanish first names implicated economic background
in the likelihood of intermarriage. It showed that the majority of such men
were craftsmen, semiskilled tradesmen, and, often, of Irish ancestry. An
1870 selection yielded similar results and revealed the male partners of
mixed marriages worth less than those who remained unmarried or who
brought their wives to Santa Fe.[47] Religion also played a role in the selection
of marriage partners and, along with class, encouraged intermarriage between
Euro-American Catholics and Spanish-Mexican women.

By the 1870s intermarriage had become a custom with important ramifications for a community experiencing a Euro-American onslaught. It
offered Spanish-Mexican women — women with few choices and limited
means — a degree of stability. For men without women, entering a new and
decidedly different community, marriage afforded opportunities for financial
success. Most transplanted easterners left their relatives behind, but the
women they married in Santa Fe were privy to an entire network of extended
family contacts. A tailor or blacksmith thus had his job virtually secured
by his wife's family and friends. Equally important for the woman, the
eastern or European-born husband stepped into *her* world. Her contact with
people of his race or culture required little of her except by association with
him. Even then, she had family or neighbors who spoke her language and
who could assist if she found herself lost or confused. Despite imbalances
in culture, class, and sense of place, people continued to marry across racial
and cultural lines. It remained an important option available to the enterprising woman.[48]

But it was not the only option. The unmarried women who wrote wills
pointed to another solution. The majority did not marry the immigrants;
women displayed minimal interest in easing men's transition to life in a
new society. Instead, they sought stability in their own worlds; they sought
to impose order on a world increasingly changed by easterners and their
ways. For more and more of these women, the act of writing a will offered
a measure of control over their circumstances. Spanish-Mexican women
had followed the custom for generations; worldly possessions, however
meager, required proper care.[49] The custom took on added significance in
the postwar period. Its assumption of stability contrasted sharply with an
enveloping sense of disorder; further, it promised children a continuity, a
certainty, that their parents lacked.[50]

If more wills attested to a need for order during the turmoil, then their
actual composition conveyed another message. Their language, expressed
purposes, and stated desires portrayed timeless concerns. "Prometo deberle

a nadien nada" — "I am beholden to none" — told the community that the person was leaving the world in good shape. All debts, no matter how small, were recorded with the saying, "I order the following things paid," or, "I ask that the following be collected." Some women listed the debts payable immediately; few exceeded the small amounts of one or five dollars. These women sought to clarify personal and public affairs, to join the two arenas and, by doing so, to preserve harmony in the community.

Within the wills, the arrangement and order of key phrases signaled the extent of women's subordination. "Fui casada y belada" — "I was married to, and watched over by" — usually followed the standard and lengthy proclamations to church and saints.[51] Sometimes a prayer was included, indicating the testator's deep faith as well as her position in the world. God and saints, marriage and husband, and finally children regulated life for women. Next to religious commitment, marriage connoted the second significant phase in a woman's life, and motherhood the third. How the community accounted for the large and growing numbers of unmarried women, given these lifeways, remains a mystery. But one possibility is that a woman who fulfilled even two of the more significant roles was well regarded. As the census recorded, many women who remained unmarried or who had been widowed were also mothers. The majority clustered in their old neighborhoods, and almost every fifth household contained an unmarried woman over the age of 30.[52]

These wills, so often written by unmarried women, starkly expose a community's ideals and mores out of alignment with the realities of many women's lives. "I was watched over by" became a moot point in the wills of at least one-third of these women because they were widowed — some had been widowed longer than they had been married.[53] It might have been more accurate, as with the widow Chaves's friend and neighbor who was widowed, but also a mother, to have brought forward motherhood, after religious commitment, as the next crucial phase in a woman's life. Wills and other documents show that a widowed mother valued both a past marriage and her parenting. In fact, in the neighbor's case, whether widowed or married, the complex middle ground the majority of Spanish-Mexican women occupied was exposed. The short but telling description calling the widow Delgado the wife of Juan and mother of a son by the same name made explicit her dependency, reliance, or regard for her husband and son. Depicting them as widows or as mothers, however, does not define such women's economic circumstances more broadly, especially because they were restricted more than ever by immigrating men with money.

45

Calling a woman a widow, like terming her wife or mother, conveyed a certain status in Spanish-Mexican Santa Fe. It often did not overlook her reliance on men or children, but told the community that she was a full-fledged member of the society. Not sequestered, rarely living alone, and often heading a family, the widow had to be so included. Yet as a woman without a male partner, she felt increasing pressure from several sides. At home she had fallen victim to the outsider's better economic position. She had few places to turn for support or assistance: even the church, once a traditional sanctuary, was full of new influences and customs.

Yet, as the court documents indicate, the unmarried women and widows writing wills were coping and ordering their lives around people first, institutions second. Some intimately connected to the new church adapted to the changing scene. Sister Dolores Chávez y Gutiérrez, was widowed, entered a convent, and ministered to the poor; for her, the convent was a refuge as well as a life of service.[54]

In the tumultuous decade of the 1870s, will making reflected another alternative to disorder. Women continued to file wills with priests and judges. Perhaps they trusted both; perhaps they should have trusted neither. The widow Chaves had been duped by both church and state. The attorney was as much at fault as the priest, even if the tale exaggerated the influence of one over the other. Yet by 1870 territorial officials had succeeded in passing legislation designed to undermine the power of the church. Bishop Lamy was forced to protect the interests of the church but sometimes that meant helping merchants. He had sold church property to make way for a store. He excommunicated many priests, and this, more than his economic policies, irked Spanish-Mexicans. Factions developed between Lamy's supporters and those upset about his developing collusion with merchants, attorneys, and politicians. Everyone could see that Lamy's immediate goal was to free the church from supposed corruption but that his long-term interest was to advance its economic standing and, if necessary, to try his hand at local and territorial politics.

The melding of both types of institutions, religious and political, predicted other disastrous consequences for the unmarried women, impoverished or not. Bishop Lamy and Territorial Secretrary Ritch occupied different arenas, but they took on the same role — to Americanize. In other parts of the frontier land had changed hands as never before; by some estimates 80 percent of the original Spanish land grants had fallen into newcomers' hands.[55] Lamy himself owned 2,000 acres outside of town. In the resulting confluence, where church, politics, and the economy joined forces, Spanish-

Mexican women recognized a shift that had to be accommodated. The rate at which they filed wills exemplified that recognition.

The world had changed, and women turned to a new court system to make sense of it. Word of mouth, now an unreliable system, did not suffice for dispensing possessions and leaving a mark in life. The witnesses brought into the courtroom were almost always other women, relatives or friends, and reliable. Altogether, a minimum of five people knew what a will contained. If the judges were suspect, at least the community knew a person's final wishes. Never much of a secret, the written document now conveyed a strong public message to residents and newcomers alike; it was an act of faith, but it had its practical side as well.

Among widows, and all women, drawing up a will had become an act demonstrating more than mere orthodoxy or practical commitment. Irrespective of religious meaning or other symbolism, the document laid a life to rest, giving a dying woman (the majority said they were gravely ill) a sense of order and perhaps revivifying her. This final act also bridged life in the present with the hereafter.

The dispersal of worldly possessions, in the Catholic mind, must have connected temporal and spiritual worlds.[56] One was known and measurable — or could be regulated — the other, imagined and unquantifiable. Underneath Catholicism's hierarchy, and over the underlying economic disruptions of the period, wills unveiled a continuing commitment to life's arrangements: religious expressions and devotion remained at the forefront of a dying widow's thoughts, her relationship to her husband, sanctified by church and community, and her relation to a succeeding generation. Not just heirs, but children, marked her existence. Even her final act reflected a spirit and continuity that sustained her.

In the topsy-turvy decades following the war, poverty, death, and general precariousness prevailed. The censuses recorded high death rates among men, which also contributed to the numbers of unmarried women. The conflicts with Natives continued to dominate village life and affected even as large a settlement as Santa Fe.[57] But that alone did not account for the record number of deaths. The newspapers described smallpox and influenza epidemics. Enumerators included at the end of the census other diseases. "The diseases most prevalent have been pleuresy, pneumonia, and fever especially among the poorer class of people."[58] They also noted accidental deaths. "Pablo Lovato, a servant, was killed working a deep acequia [water-ditch] when he was buried by the caving in of one side."[59]

Accidents and illness accounted for some deaths, but when correlated to church burial records, a discrepancy appears. More women than men were buried during this period (table 5). If many unmarried women were being widowed, one would expect to find more adult men than women dying and their burials recorded. Men's burials in almost every year lend some credibility to the point that many unmarried women in the censuses before 1880 were temporarily separated. Or husbands who labored in other towns and died might have been buried in cemeteries away from Santa Fe, and the local parish therefore would not have counted them.

The widows who died were consistently older than the men who died. The 1860 death schedules recorded five such women, all over 40. Only one died of injury, the others of diseases. A 94-year-old developed bladder problems. An 80-year-old did not survive a ten-day illness. Scarlet fever claimed the life of Guadalupe Ortiz, who was 60. María Ortiz, her sister, was 70 and lingered for six months until dropsy killed her.[60]

These women had experienced great changes in their lifetimes. They died before the harshest transformations of the 1870s took hold. Yet in spite of the intrusion that circumscribed their lives, they led a full and rich existence. That should not obscure, however, the number who were impoverished and those who were mothers; of the latter, a larger group per decade headed households. The money entering Santa Fe did little to help them.

Unmarried women had become a fact of life in postwar Santa Fe. They had always been present in Spanish-Mexican communities, but never had their numbers soared as they did after the war. Not all of their troubles could be attributed solely to the military presence or to the politicians who

Table 5. Burial Record: Random Sample for the County of Santa Fe, Archdiocese of Santa Fe

	1852	1860	1870	1878
Wives	10 (22%)	3 (16%)	12 (13%)	34 (27%)
Husbands	9 (20%)	1 (5%)	10 (11%)	19 (15%)
Daughters	8 (37%)	3 (32%)	15 (35%)	21 (37%)
Sons	9	3	16	26
Total buried	46	19	89	127
Total uncategorized	1 (2%)	2 (11%)	11 (12%)	11 (9%)
All others[a]	9 (20%)	7 (37%)	25 (28%)	16 (13%)

SOURCES: Archives of the Archdiocese of Santa Fe (microfilm reel 88, NMSRC, Santa Fe).
[a] Infants, for example, are included in this figure.

attempted to bind Santa Fe to the Union. But the circumstances of this period encouraged dependence among unmarried women already exceedingly vulnerable either to politicians or to merchants.

On the other side of the political and economic spectrum were the numerous attorneys and federal appointees arriving in Santa Fe. Although federal appointments were not permanent, the individual wealth of each officer marked the steady march toward higher incomes and richer people. The surveyor general of the 1850s, William Pelham, stated a net worth of $26,500. By 1870 Pelham had been replaced by Thomas Spencer, who claimed an estate of $60,000.[61] Each of the highest government positions and most skilled trades saw escalating improvement — for men.

Meanwhile, unmarried women's finances declined. Their buying power fell, the percentage of those living without a male partner rose, their families grew, and they witnessed a declining net worth during decades of unprecedented transformation. Emphasizing their marital status and ignoring the context in which it occurred would be misleading. They did not live apart or immune from the general dislocations of the period. In that regard, even the widow was not alone. She stood in a very long line of women experiencing conquest in the most fundamental way, as it affected their economy and families.

In Spanish-Mexican communities throughout the Southwest, the role and position of widows and other unmarried women have long been understood but never discussed. Their position may raise many disquieting questions. In this case, however, widows and all unmarried women shed light on the entire frontier. Dislocation and disparity had become facts of life, and yet women subsisted. Barter and exchange practices continued to serve them well, and many probably survived because the old skills had not eroded entirely. Gardening continued in Santa Fe's barrios, and the products were given and traded to relatives and neighbors alike.[62] Extended family networks provided the security needed to raise children, and no matter how difficult reliance on relatives could become, such new institutions as hospitals or orphanages did not yet replace such dependence.

Life for the unmarried woman, the widow included, also exhibited a certain fluidity. Some married, or remarried, the new men in their midst. Others made wills to provide for a future generation. In that manner they might have been like other southwesterners. But they remained Spanish-Mexican women speaking Spanish and not English, practicing Catholicism and not Protestantism, residing in neighborhoods several centuries old, with roots stretching far back. Their story differed fundamentally from the stories of women to whom they might be compared, including Mormon women, city women, or westering women.[63]

To be sure, Santa Fe widows and others who were unmarried shared a language and religion with other Spanish-Mexican women of the Southwest, with Catholic women, and perhaps with the majority of working widows. But I have not been concerned with similarities for two reasons. First, not much information on other unmarried groups exists as yet; and the unifying impulse in such scholarship detracts seriously from the ability to consider these women on their own terms, from the inside out. Second and equally important, further research about the general cultural regard in which widows were held in nineteenth-century Spanish-Mexican communities needs to be done. I have suggested the methods of their survival in this essay, but I have not lost the focus on their financial situation and the general political imbalances pervading their lives. As women of the Spanish-Mexican frontier, they survived the worst decades of turmoil.

At the end of the 1870s, when the railroad tracks had nearly reached Santa Fe, unmarried women stood at another critical juncture. Families and the community were changing; no longer did many groups reside on the periphery, isolated from the government or its institutions. Rather, Spanish-Mexicans were at the center of continuing colonization, their ways irrevocably altered. As immigrants became residents, the unmarried women faced difficult choices. They had persevered, but as the iron horse pushed toward their community, even more pernicious forms of intrusion threatened. They had little choice but to accommodate.

NOTES

1. Ralph Emerson Twitchell, *The Story of the Conquest of Santa Fe: New Mexico and the Building of Old Fort Marcy, A.D. 1846* (Santa Fe: Historical Society of New Mexico, 1921), 30.

2. For evidence of the impact of the Santa Fe trade of the 1820s on residents, see Max Moorhead, *New Mexico's Royal Road: Trade and Travel on the Chihuahua Trail* (Norman: University of Oklahoma Press, 1958); on the nature of conquest in these earlier decades, see David J. Weber, ed., *Foreigners in Their Native Land: Historical Roots of the Mexican-Americans* (Albuquerque: University of New Mexico Press, 1973).

3. On the fort, see L. Bradford Prince, *Old Fort Marcy, Santa Fe, New Mexico: Historical Sketch and Panoramic View of Santa Fe and Its Vicinity* (Santa Fe: New Mexico Historical Publications, 1892). On the army, see Gunther Barth, *Instant Cities: Urbanization and the Rise of San Francisco and Denver* (New

York: Oxford University Press, 1975), 65-67. On wages, see John Taylor Hughes, *Doniphan's Expedition: An Account of the Conquest of New Mexico* (Cincinnati: J. A. & U. P. James, 1848), 52.

4. Dyer War Journal, Oct. 1847, Alexander B. Dyer Papers, Museum of New Mexico, Santa Fe.

5. Alvin Sunseri, *Seeds of Discord: New Mexico in the Aftermath of the American Conquest, 1846-1861* (Chicago: Nelson-Hall, 1979).

6. Howard Roberts Lamar, *The Far Southwest, 1846-1912: A Territorial History* (paper ed., New York: W. W. Norton, 1970), 66-67.

7. Ibid., 83.

8. For an example of the disparities, see U.S. Census Bureau, Original Schedule of the Eighth Census of Population, for Santa Fe, New Mexico (microfilm, New Mexico State Records Center, Santa Fe), 22, 26, 28, 31, hereafter cited as NMSRC.

9. U.S. Census Bureau, Original Schedule of the Seventh Census of Population, for Santa Fe, New Mexico (microfilm, Coronado Collection, University of New Mexico, Albuquerque), 1. See Eighth Census, for Santa Fe, 39.

10. Quoted in James Josiah Webb, Memoirs, July 1844, Museum of New Mexico.

11. Ibid., 44.

12. On the politicians, see Lamar, *Far Southwest,* ch. 4. On the merchants, see Barth, *Instant Cities,* 72, 73.

13. David Meriwether to Building Commissioners, Sept. 1853, William G. Ritch Collection, Box 11, Henry E. Huntington Library, San Marino, Calif.

14. See, for example, Jean Baptiste Lamy to Archbishop Purcell, Sept. 2, 1851, Archives of the Archdiocese of Santa Fe, Loose Diocesan Documents, number 14, 1-3. On the masons, see Sister Blandina Segale, *At the End of the Santa Fe Trail* (reprint ed., Milwaukee: Bruce Publishing, 1948), 81.

15. Lamy to Purcell, Sept. 2, 1851, 2.

16. On the rising costs, see Segale, *End of the Santa Fe Trail,* 105-6; for comparisons, see Sunseri, *Seeds of Discord,* 21-22.

17. Lamar, *Far Southwest,* 103.

18. U.S. Census Bureau, Original Schedules of the Eighth and Ninth Censuses of Population, for Santa Fe, New Mexico (microfilm, NMSRC).

19. On eggs, see Segale, *End of the Santa Fe Trail;* on mules, see Sunseri, *Seeds of Discord,* 30-31.

20. Productions of Agriculture Schedules," in U.S. Census Bureau, Original Schedules of the Seventh and Eighth Censuses of Population, for Santa Fe County (microfilm, NMSRC), 1-7, 1-8.

21. Segale, *End of the Santa Fe Trail,* 104.

22. Sunseri, *Seeds of Discord,* 28, 31.

23. For examples, see U.S. Census Bureau, Original Schedule of the Ninth Census of Population, for Santa Fe (microfilm NMSRC).

24. U.S. Census Bureau, Original Schedules of the Seventh, Eighth, Ninth, and Tenth Censuses of Population, for Santa Fe (microfilm, NMSRC).

25. For examples, see the Seventh Census, 1, 32, 50; Eighth Census, 16, 17, 29; Ninth Census, 12, 23, 25; Tenth Census, 9, 15, 29.

26. For widows in other parts of the Far West, see Joyce D. Goodfriend, "The Struggle for Survival: Widows in Denver, 1880-1912," and Maureen Ursenbach Beecher, Carol Cornwall Madsen, and Lavina Fielding Anderson, "Widowhood among the Mormons: The Personal Accounts," herein.

27. U.S. Census Bureau, Original Schedules of the Seventh, Eighth, Ninth, and Tenth Censuses of Population, for Santa Fe (microfilm, NMSRC).

28. Lamar, *Far Southwest*, 91; on St. Vincent's Hospital, see U.S. Census Bureau, Original Schedule of the Tenth Census of Population, for Santa Fe (microfilm, NMSRC), 17; and the Santa Fe *New Mexican*, Oct. 13, 1865; on the orphanage, see Thomas Richter, ed., "Sister Catherine Mallon's Journal (Part One)," *New Mexico Historical Review* 52 (1977):135-55.

29. U.S. Census Bureau, Original Schedule of the Eighth Census of Population, for Santa Fe (microfilm, NMSRC).

30. On Denver, see Goodfriend, "Struggle for Survival"; on Texas, see Arnoldo de Leon, *The Tejano Community, 1836-1900* (Albuquerque: University of New Mexico Press, 1982), 107, 109, 110, 189; on Los Angeles, see Barbara Laslett, "Household Structure on an American Frontier: Los Angeles, California, in 1850," *American Journal of Sociology* 81 (1975):109-28, and Richard Griswold del Castillo, *The Los Angeles Barrio, 1850-1890: A Social History* (Berkeley: University of California Press, 1979).

31. Santa Fe County Records, Wills and Testaments, 1856-97, Index, Books B, C, D, E (Manuscript Division, NMSRC).

32. Will of Maria de la Sur Ortiz, Apr. 1860, will of María Josefa Martínez, Aug. 1860, Santa Fe County Records, Book B, 1856-62.

33. For a distinction on attitudes and concepts toward land, see Roxanne Dunbar Ortiz, *Roots of Resistance: Land Tenure in New Mexico, 1680-1980* (Los Angeles: Chicano Studies Research Center Publications and the American Indian Center, 1980). For a different assessment, see Victor Westphall, *Mercedes Reales: Hispanic Land Grants of the Upper Rio Grande Region* (Albuquerque: University of New Mexico Press, 1983).

34. On hijuela, see Westphall, *Mercedes Reales*, 225. For examples on the loss of land and hijuelas, see the requests to collect debts for land sold in the will of Dolores Montoya, May 21, 1881, and will of María Josefa Montoya, Aug. 9, 1883, Santa Fe County Records, Wills and Testaments, Book E, 1877-97.

35. "Productions of Agriculture," in U.S. Census Bureau, Original Schedules of the Eighth and Ninth Census of Population, for Santa Fe County (microfilm, NMSRC), 1-8, 1-7.

36. U.S. Census Bureau, Original Schedule of the Ninth Census of Population, for Santa Fe (microfilm, Huntington Library), 22.

37. Official Reports of the Territorial Secretary, Summer 1876, William G. Ritch Collection, RI 1731.

38. See Deena J. González, "The Spanish-Mexican Women of Santa Fe: Patterns of Their Resistance and Accommodation, 1820-1880" (Ph.D. diss., University of California, Berkeley, 1985).

39. On the widow Chaves and who she might have been, see U.S. Census Bureau, Original Schedule of the Eighth Census of Population, for Santa Fe (microfilm, NMSRC), 5; in the same census, "Productions of Agriculture," 1; will of Teresa Chávez, Jan. 1, 1871, Santa Fe County Records, Wills and Testaments, 1856-97, Book D.

40. Official Report, Ritch Collection, RI 1731, 1. For further information on Truchard, see Lamar, Far Southwest, 174; Santa Fe New Mexican, July 20, 1877; will of María Nieves Chávez, Dec. 1870, Santa Fe County Records, Wills and Testaments, 1856-97, Book D.

41. Official Report, Ritch Collection, RI 1731.

42. Ibid., RI 1731; on the law, see L. Bradford Prince, comp., General Laws of New Mexico from the "Kearny Code of 1846" to 1880 (Albany: Torch Press, 1880), 52.

43. She may have been the widow Trinidad Delgado; see U.S. Census Bureau, Original Schedule of the Tenth Census of Population, for Santa Fe (microfilm, NMSRC), 27.

44. See Santa Fe County Records, Wills and Testaments, 1856-97, Book E.

45. On intermarriages in an earlier period and a different assessment, see Darlis Miller, "Cross-cultural Marriages in the Southwest: The New Mexico Experience, 1846-1900," New Mexico Historical Review 57 (1982):334.

46. See, for example, Santa Fe County Records, Legitimacy and Adoption Records, 1870-82 (Manuscript Division, NMSRC), 5-6.

47. U.S. Census Bureau, Original Schedules of the Ninth and Tenth Censuses of Population, for Santa Fe (microfilm, NMSRC).

48. For an estimate on the number of white men marrying Spanish-Mexican women, see Miller, "Cross-cultural Marriages," 334.

49. For samples of wills in the first half of the nineteenth century, see will of Rafaela Baca, Apr. 26, 1804, will of María Micaela Baca, Apr. 22, 1830, will of Bárbara Baca, Dec. 30, 1838, Twitchell Collection (Manuscript Division, NMSRC).

50. For assistance with these ideas, I thank Helena M. Wall, Pomona College. See her use of court records in her study of British North America, "Private Lives: The Transformation of Family and Community in Early America" (Ph.D. diss., Harvard University, 1983).

51. See, for example, will of Desidéria Otero, Dec. 22, 1870, Santa Fe County Records, Wills and Testaments, 1856-97, Book D; will of Francisca Quirón, Apr.

30, 1857, Santa Fe County Records, Wills and Testaments, 1865-97, Book B; will of Rafaela Baca, Apr. 26, 1804, Twitchell Collection, Wills and Estates, 1.

52. U.S. Census Bureau, Original Schedules of the Seventh, Eighth, and Ninth Census of Population, for Santa Fe (microfilm, NMSRC).

53. For examples, see will of María Miquela Lucero, Feb. 4, 1858, Mariano Chávez Family Papers (Manuscript Division, NMSRC), 1; will of Maria Josefa Martínez, May 23, 1860, Santa Fe County Records, Wills and Testaments, 1856-97, Book B. The two women can be found in the Tenth Census, 31, 62.

54. Segale, End of the Santa Fe Trail, 117-22. For a discussion of the convent as a refuge in Latin America, see Asuncion Lavrin, "Values and Meaning of Monastic Life for Nuns in Colonial Mexico," Catholic Historical Review 58 (1972):367-87.

55. Ortiz, Roots of Resistance, 93. For an analysis that blames Manuel Armijo for selling land to Euro-Americans, see Westphall, Mercedes Reales, 147-49; on Lamy, see Lamar, Far Southwest, 102-3.

56. For statements reflecting the connection, see the prayers in the will of María Teresa García, Nov. 24, 1879; will of Dolores Montoya, May 12, 1881, Santa Fe County Records, Wills and Testaments, 1856-97, Book E.

57. Lamar, Far Southwest, 133; on the general social disquietude and specific incidents of violence, see the Santa Fe New Mexican, Jan. 20, 1865, Jan. 12, 1867, Jan. 14, 1868, Aug. 30, 1870.

58. "Death Schedules," in U.S. Census Bureau, Original Schedule of the Eighth Census of Population, for Santa Fe (microfilm, NMSRC), 1. On a smallpox epidemic, see the Santa Fe New Mexican, July 20, 1877.

59. U.S. Census Bureau, Original Schedule of the Eighth Census of Population, for Santa Fe (microfilm, NMSRC), 4.

60. "Death Schedules," in U.S. Census Bureau, Original Schedule of the Eighth Census of Population, for Santa Fe County (microfilm, NMSRC), 2-3.

61. On Pelham, see U.S. Census Bureau, Original Schedule of the Eighth Census of Population, for Santa Fe (microfilm, NMSRC), 21; on Spencer, see the Ninth Census, 49.

62. For an observation of the gardens, see the letters of Sarah Wetter, Sept. 14, 1869, to her mother, Henry Wetter Papers, Museum of New Mexico. On the importance of produce, see the will of María Josefa Martínez, May 23, 1860, Santa Fe County Records, Wills and Testaments, 1856-97, Book B; on fruit exchange, see the Santa Fe New Mexican Review, Sept. 3, 4, 1883.

63. On the small number of English-speaking women in postwar Santa Fe, see table 1; for a general description, see Miller, "Cross-cultural Marriages," 339.

Vicki Ruíz

Dead Ends or Gold Mines?: Using Missionary Records in Mexican-American Women's History

Peggy Pascoe and Valerie Matsumoto clearly delineated the theoretical issues we face as feminist historians.[1] Expanding on their essays, I would like to discuss what is often ill perceived as the flip side of theory — that is, methodology. How do we use institutional records (for example, missionary reports, pamphlets, and newsletters) to illuminate the experiences and attitudes of women of color? How do we sift through the bias, the self-congratulation, and the hyperbole to gain insight into women's lives? What can these records tell us of women's agencies?

I am intrigued (actually, obsessed is a better verb) with questions involving decisionmaking, specifically with regard to acculturation. What have Mexican women chosen to accept or reject? How have the economic, social, and political environments influenced the acceptance or rejection of cultural messages that emanate from the Mexican community, from U.S. popular culture, from Americanization programs, and from a dynamic coalescence of differing and at times oppositional cultural forms? What were women's real choices? And, to borrow from Jürgen Habermas, how did they move "within the horizon of their lifeworld"?[2] Obviously, no set of institutional records can provide substantive answers, but by exploring these documents in the framework of these larger questions, we place Mexican women at the center of our study, not as victims of poverty and superstition (as they were so often depicted by missionaries) but as women who made choices for themselves and for their families.

Frontiers, vol. XII, no. 1, © Frontiers Editorial Collective.

33

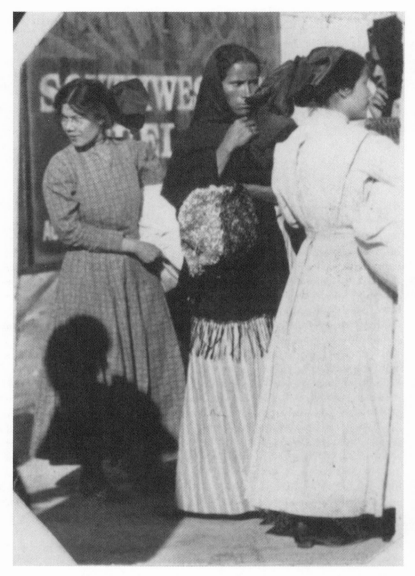

Fig. 1. Las solas: Mexican women arriving in El Paso, 1911. (Courtesy of Rio Grande Historical Collections, University Archives, New Mexico State University, Las Cruces, New Mexico.)

34

Pushed by the economic and political chaos generated by the Mexican Revolution and lured by jobs in U.S. agribusiness and industry, over one million Mexicanos migrated northward between 1910 and 1930. When one thinks of Mexican immigration, one typically visualizes a single male or family group. However, as depicted in figure 1, women also traveled as *solas* ("single women"). Mexicanos settled into the existing barrios and forged new communities in the Southwest and Midwest.[3] El Paso, Texas, was their Ellis Island, and many decided to stay in this bustling border city. In 1900, the Mexican community of El Paso numbered only 8,748 residents, but by 1930, its population swelled to 68,476. Over the course of the twentieth century, Mexicans have comprised over one-half of El Paso's total population.[4] Inheriting a legacy of colonialism wrought by Manifest Destiny, Mexicans, regardless of nativity, have been segmented into low-paying, low-status jobs. Perceived as cheap labor by Anglo businessmen, they have provided the human resources necessary for the city's industrial and commercial growth. Education and economic advancement proved illusory as segregation in housing, employment, and schools served as constant reminders of their second-class citizenship. To cite an example of stratification, from 1930 to 1960, only 1.8 percent of El Paso's Mexican work force held high white-collar occupations.[5]

Segundo Barrio or South El Paso has served as the center of Mexican community life. Today, as in the past, wooden tenements and crumbling adobe structures house thousands of Mexicanos and Mexican Americans alike. For several decades, the only consistent source of social services in Segundo Barrio was the Rose Gregory Houchen Settlement House and its adjacent health clinic and hospital. The records of Houchen Settlement form the core of this study.

Founded in 1912 on the corner of Tays and Fifth in the heart of the barrio, this Methodist settlement had two initial goals: (1) to provide a Christian rooming house for single Mexicana wage earners and (2) to open a kindergarten for area children. By 1918, Houchen offered a full schedule of Americanization programs — citizenship, cooking, carpentry, English instruction, Bible study, and Boy Scouts. The first Houchen staff included three female Methodist missionaries and one "student helper," Ofilia Chávez.[6] Living in the barrio made these women sensitive to the need for low-cost, accessible health care. Infant mortality in Segundo Barrio was alarmingly high. Historian Mario García related the following example: "Of 121 deaths during July [1914], 52 were children under 5 years of age."[7]

In 1920, the Methodist Home Missionary Society responded (at last) to Houchen appeals by assigning Effie Stoltz, a registered nurse, to

35

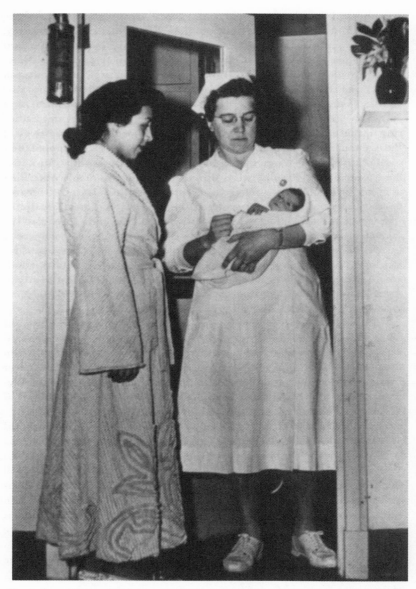

Fig. 2. From 1937 to 1976, over 12,000 babies were born at Newark hospital. Although mother and child are unidentified, the nurse is Dorothea Muñoz. (Courtesy of Houchen Community Center.)

36

the settlement. Stoltz's work began in Houchen's bathroom, where she operated a first-aid station. More importantly, she persuaded a local physician to visit the residence on a regular basis, and he, in turn, enlisted the services of his colleagues. Within seven months of Stoltz's arrival, a small adobe flat was converted into the Freeman Clinic. Run by volunteers, this clinic provided prenatal exams, well-baby care, and pediatric services; in 1930, it opened a six-bed maternity ward. Seven years later, it would be demolished to make way for the construction of a more modern clinic and a new twenty-two-bed maternity facility — the Newark Methodist Maternity Hospital. Health care at Newark was a bargain. Prenatal classes, pregnancy exams, and infant immunizations were free. Patients paid for medicines at cost, and during the 1940s, $30 covered the hospital bill (see figure 2). Staff members would boast that for less than $50, payable in installments, neighborhood women could give birth at "one of the best-equipped maternity hospitals in the city."[8]

Houchen Settlement did not linger in the shadows of its adjacent hospital; from 1920 to 1960, it coordinated an array of Americanization activities. These included age- and gender-graded Bible studies, music lessons, Camp Fire Girls, scouting, working girls' clubs, hygiene, cooking, and citizenship classes. Staff members also opened a day nursery to complement the kindergarten program.

In terms of numbers, how successful was Houchen? The records to which I had access gave little indication of the extent of the settlement's client base. Fragmentary evidence for the period 1930 to 1950 suggests that perhaps as many as 15,000 to 20,000 people per year (or approximately one-fourth to one-third of El Paso's Mexican population) utilized its medical and/or educational services. Indeed, one Methodist cited in the 1930s pamphlet boasted that the settlement "reaches nearly 15,000 people."[9]

As a functioning Progressive-era settlement, Houchen had amazing longevity from 1912 to 1962. Several Methodist missionaries came to Segundo Barrio as young women and stayed until their retirement. Arriving in 1930, Millie Rickford would live at the settlement for thirty-one years. Two years after her departure, the Rose Gregory Houchen Settlement House (named after a Michigan schoolteacher) would receive a new name, Houchen Community Center. As a community center, it would become more of a secular agency staffed by social workers and, at times, Chicano activists.[10] In 1991, the buildings that cover a city block in South El Paso still furnish day-care and recreational activities. Along with Bible study, there are classes in ballet folklorico, karate, English, and aerobics. Citing climbing insurance

37

costs (among other reasons), the Methodist church closed the hospital and clinic in December 1986 over the protests of local supporters and community members.[11]

From 1912 until the 1950s, Houchen workers placed Americanization and proselytization at the center of their efforts. Embracing the imagery and ideology of the melting pot, Methodist missionary Dorothy Little explained: "Houchen settlement stands as a sentinel of friendship . . . between the people of America and the people of Mexico. We assimilate the best of their culture, their art, their ideals and they in turn gladly accept the best America has to offer as they . . . become one with us. For right here within our four walls is begun much of the "Melting" process of our 'Melting Pot.' "[12]

To "become one with us" no doubt included a conversion to Methodism. It is important to remember that these missionaries were, indeed, missionaries, and they perceived themselves as harbingers of salvation. In "Our Work at Houchen," it was expressed this way: "Our Church is called El Buen Pastor . . . and that is what our church really is to the people — it is a Good Shepherd guiding our folks out of darkness and Catholocism [sic] into the good Christian life." Along similar lines, one Methodist pamphlet printed during the 1930s equated Catholicism (as practiced by Mexicans) with paganism and superstition. The settlement's programs were couched in terms of "Christian Americanization," and these programs began early.[13]

Like the Franciscan missionaries who trod the same ground three centuries before, the women of Houchen sought to win the hearts and minds of children. Although preschool and kindergarten students spoke Spanish and sang Mexican songs, they also learned English, U.S. history, biblical verses — even etiquette à la Emily Post[14] (see figure 3). The settlement also offered a number of afterschool activities for older children. These included "Little Homemakers," scouting, teen clubs, piano lessons, dance, Bible classes, and story hour. For many years, the most elaborate playground in South El Paso could be found within the outer courtyard of the settlement (see figure 4). A life-long resident of Segundo Barrio, Elsa Chávez remarked that her mother let her play there on the condition that she not accept any "cookies or Kool-Aid," the refreshments provided by Houchen staff. Other people remembered making similar bargains with their mothers. They could play on the swings and slide, but they could not go indoors.[15] How big of a step was it to venture from the playground to story hour?

Settlement proselytizing did not escape the notice of barrio priests. Clearly troubled by Houchen, a few predicted dire consequences for those who participated in any Protestant-tinged activities. One priest

38

Fig. 3. The task of "Christian Americanization" began early. Here, kindergarten students are taught to say grace during snack time. (Courtesy of Houchen Community Center.)

Fig. 4. For many years, the big attraction for neighborhood children was the settlement's elaborate playground. (Courtesy of Houchen Community Center.)

39

Fig. 5. As part of a prenatal class, a Houchen nurse demonstrates the "proper" way to bathe an infant. (Courtesy of Houchen Comunity Center.)

went so far as to tell neighborhood children that it was a sin even to play on the playground equipment. Others, however, took a more realistic stance and did not chastise their parishioners for utilizing Methodist child-care and medical services. Perhaps as a response to both the Great Depression and suspected Protestant inroads, several area Catholic churches began distributing food baskets and establishing soup kitchens.[16]

Children were not the only people targeted by Houchen. Women, particularly expectant mothers, received special attention. Like the proponents of Americanization programs in California, settlement workers believed that women held a special guardianship over their families' welfare. As head nurse Millie Rickford explained, " 'If we can teach her [the mother-to-be] the modern methods of cooking and preparing foods and simple hygiene habits for herself and her family, we have gained a stride' "[17] (see figure 5).

Houchen's "Christian Americanization" programs were not unique. Between 1910 and 1930, religious and state-organized Americanization projects aimed at the Mexican population proliferated throughout the Southwest. These efforts varied in scale from settlement houses to night classes, and the curriculum generally revolved around cooking, hygiene,

40

Fig. 6. This dance recital captures the Eurocentric orientation advocated by Houchen residents. Settlement workers believed that their students could "melt" within the "melting pot." (Courtesy of Houchen Community Center.)

English, and civics. Music seemed a universal tool of instruction. One rural Arizona schoolteacher excitedly informed readers of the *Arizona Teacher and Home Journal* that, for the "cause of Americanization," her district had purchased a Victrola and several records, including two Spanish melodies, the " 'Star Spangled Banner,' 'The Red, White, and Blue,' 'Silent Night,' [and] 'Old Kentucky Home.' "[18] Houchen, of course, offered a variety of musical activities, beginning with the kindergarten rhythm band of 1927. During the 1940s and 1950s, missionaries offered flute, guitar, ballet, and tap lessons. For 50¢ per week, a youngster could take dance or music classes and perform in settlement recitals[19] (see figure 6). The last figure is not atypical; there apparently were several instances when youngsters were clothed in European peasant styles. For instance, Alice Ruiz, Priscilla Molina, Edna Parra, Mira Gomez, and Aida Rivera, representing Houchen in a local Girl Scout festival held at the Shrine temple, modeled costumes from Sweden, England, France, Scotland, and Lithuania.[20] Some immigrant traditions were valorized more than others. Celebrating Mexican heritage did not figure into the Euro-American orientation pushed by Houchen residents.

41

Settlement workers held out unrealistic notions of the American dream, romantic constructions of American life. It is as if they endeavored to create a white, middle-class environment for Mexican youngsters, complete with tutus and toe shoes. Cooking classes also became avenues for developing particular tastes. As Minerva Franco recalled, "I'll never forget the look on my mother's face when I first cooked 'Eggs Benedict' which I learned to prepare at Houchen."[21] The following passage taken from a report dated February 1942 outlines, in part, the perceived accomplishments of the settlement: "Sanitary conditions have been improving — more children go to school — more parents are becoming citizens, more are leaving Catholicism — more are entering business and public life — and more and more they are taking on the customs and standards of the Anglo people."[22]

There are numerous passages and photographs in the Houchen collection that provide fodder for sarcasm among contemporary scholars. As a Chicana historian, I am of two minds. I respect the settlement workers for their health and child-care services, but I cringe at their ethnocentrism and their romantic idealization of "American" life. Yet, before judging the maternal missionaries too harshly, it is important to keep in mind the social services they rendered over an extended period of time, as well as the environment in which they lived. For example, Houchen probably launched the first bilingual kindergarten program in El Paso, a program that eased the children's transition into an English-only first grade. Nor did Houchen residents denigrate the use of Spanish, and many became fluent Spanish-speakers themselves. The hospital and clinic, moreover, were important community institutions for over half a century.[23]

Furthermore, settlement workers could not always count on the encouragement or patronage of Anglo El Paso. In a virulently nativist tract, a local physician, C. S. Babbitt, condemned missionaries like the women of Houchen for working among Mexican and African Americans. In fact, Babbitt argued that religious workers were "seemingly conspiring with Satan to destroy the handiwork of God" because their energies were "wasted on beings . . . who are not in reality the objects of Christ's sacrifice."[24] Perhaps more damaging than this extremist view was the apparent lack of financial support on the part of area Methodist churches. The records I examined revealed little in terms of local donations. The former Michigan schoolteacher whom the settlement was named after bequeathed $1,000 for the establishment of an El Paso settlement. The Women's Home Missionary Society of the Newark, New Jersey Conference proved instrumental in raising funds for the construction of both the Freeman Clinic and the Newark Methodist Maternity

42

Hospital. When the clinic first opened its doors in June 1921, all of the medical equipment — everything from sterilizers to baby scales — were gifts from Methodist groups across the nation. The Houchen Day Nursery, however, received consistent financial support from the El Paso Community Chest and, later, the United Way. In 1975, Houchen's board of directors conducted the first communitywide fund-raising drive. Volunteers sought to raise $375,000 to renovate existing structures and to build a modern day-care center. But the Houchen fund-raising slogan — "When people pay their own way, it's your affair . . . not welfare" — makes painfully clear the conservative attitudes toward social welfare harbored by affluent El Pasoans.[25]

The women of Houchen appeared undaunted by the lack of local support. For over fifty years, these missionaries coordinated a multifaceted Americanization campaign among the residents of Segundo Barrio. But how did Mexican women perceive the settlement? What services did they utilize? And to what extent did they internalize the romantic notions of "Christian Americanization"?

Examining Mexican women's agency through institutional records is difficult; it involves getting beneath the text. Furthermore, one must take into account the selectivity of voices. In drafting settlement reports and publications, missionaries chose those voices that would publicize their "victories" among the Spanish-speaking. As a result, quotations abound that heap praise upon praise on Houchen and its staff. For example, in 1939, Soledad Burciaga emphatically declared, "There is not a person, no matter to which denomination they belong, who hasn't a kind word and a heart full of gratitude towards the Settlement House."[26] Obviously, these documents have their limits. Oral interviews and informal discussions with people who grew up in Segundo Barrio give a more balanced, less effusive perspective. Most viewed Houchen as a Protestant-run health-care and afterschool activities center, rather than as the "light-house" [sic] in South El Paso.[27]

In 1949, the term *Friendship Square* was coined as a description for the settlement house, hospital, day nursery, and church. Missionaries hoped that children born at Newark would participate in preschool and afternoon programs and that eventually they and their families would join the church, El Buen Pastor. And a few did follow this pattern. One of the ministers assigned to El Buen Pastor, Fernando García, had himself been a Houchen kindergarten graduate. Emulating the settlement staff, some young women enrolled in Methodist missionary colleges or served as lay volunteers. Elizabeth Soto, for example, had attended Houchen programs throughout her childhood and adolescence. Upon graduation from Bowie High School, she entered Asbury

43

College to train as a missionary and then returned to El Paso as a Houchen resident. After several years of service, she left settlement work to become the wife of a Mexican Methodist minister. The more common goal among Houchen teens was to graduate from high school and perhaps attend Texas Western, the local college. The first child born at Newark Hospital, Margaret Holguin, took part in settlement activities as a child and later became a registered nurse. According to her *comadre*, Lucy Lucero, Holguin's decision to pursue nursing was "perhaps due to the influence" of head nurse Millie Rickford. Lucero noted, "The only contact I had had with Anglos was with Anglo teachers. Then I met Miss Rickford and I felt, 'Hey, she's human. She's great.' " At a time when many (though certainly not all) elementary schoolteachers cared little about their Mexican students, Houchen residents offered warmth and encouragement.[28] Based on the selectivity of available data, one cannot make wholesale generalizations about Friendship Square's role in fostering mobility or even aspirations for mobility among the youth of Segundo Barrio. Yet, it is clear that the women of Houchen strove to build self-esteem and encouraged young people to pursue higher education.

Missionaries also envisioned a Protestant enclave in South El Paso, but, to their frustration, very few people responded. The settlement church, El Buen Pastor, had a peak membership of 150 families. The church itself had an intermittent history. Shortly after its founding in 1897, El Buen Pastor disappeared; it was officially rededicated as part of Houchen in 1932. However, the construction of an actual church on settlement grounds did not begin until 1945. In 1968, the small rock chapel would be converted into a recreation room and thrift shop as the members of El Buen Pastor and El Mesias (another Mexican-American church) were merged together to form the congregation of the Emmanuel United Methodist Church in downtown El Paso. In 1991, a modern gymnasium occupies the ground where the chapel once stood.[29]

Based on the selective case histories of converts, I suggest that many of those who joined El Buen Pastor were already Protestant. The Dominguez family offers an example. In the words of settlement worker Ruth Kern: "Reyna and Gabriel Dominguez are Latin Americans, even though both were born in the United States. Some members of the family do not even speak English. Reyna was born . . . in a Catholic home, but at the age of eleven years, she began attending The Methodist Church. Gabriel was born in Arizona. His mother was a Catholic, but she became a Protestant when . . . Gabriel was five years old."[30]

The youth programs at Houchen brought Reyna and Gabriel together. After their marriage, the couple had six children, all born at

44

Newark Hospital. The Dominguez family represented Friendship Square's typical success story. Many of the converts were children, and many had already embraced a Protestant faith. In the records I examined, I found only one instance of the conversion of a Catholic adult and one instance of the conversion of an entire Catholic family.[31] It seems that those most receptive to Houchen's religious messages were already predisposed to that direction.

The failure of proselytization cannot be examined solely within the confines of Friendship Square. It is not as if these Methodist women were good social workers but incompetent missionaries. Houchen staff member Clara Sarmiento wrote of the difficulty in building trust among the adults of Segundo Barrio: "Though it is easy for children to open up their hearts to us we do not find it so with the parents." She continued, "It is hard especially because we are Protestant, and most of the people we serve . . . come from Catholic heritage."[32] I would argue that the Mexican community played an instrumental role in thwarting conversion. In a land where the barrio could serve as a refuge from prejudice and discrimination, the threat of social isolation could certainly inhibit many residents from turning Protestant. During an oral interview, a woman who participated in Houchen activities for over fifty years, Estella Ibarra, described growing up Protestant in South El Paso: "We went through a lot of prejudice . . . sometimes my friends' mothers wouldn't let them play with us. . . . When the priest would go through the neighborhood, all the children would run to say hello and kiss his hand. My brothers and I would just stand by and look. The priest would usually come . . . and tell us how we were living in sin. Also, there were times when my brother and I were stoned by other students . . . and called bad names."[33]

When contacted by a Houchen resident, Mrs. Espinosa admitted to being a closet Protestant. As she explained, "I am afraid of the Catholic sisters and [I] don't want my neighbors to know that I am not Catholic-minded." The fear of ostracism, though recorded by Houchen staff, did not figure into their understanding of Mexicano resistance to conversion. Instead, they blamed time and culture. As Dorothy Little succinctly related, "We can not eradicate in a few years what has been built up during ages."[34]

Although a Protestant enclave never materialized, settlement women remained steadfast in their goals of conversion and Americanization, goals that did not change until the mid- to late fifties. Historians Sarah Deutsch and George Sanchez have noted that sporadic, poorly financed Americanization programs made little headway in Mexican communities. Ruth Crocker also described the Protestant settlements in

45

Gary, Indiana, as having only a "superficial and temporary" influence.[35] Yet, even long-term sustained efforts, as in the case of Houchen, had limited appeal. This inability to mold consciousness or identity demonstrates not only the strength of community sanctions but, more significantly, the resiliency of Mexican culture and the astuteness of Mexicanos. Mexican women derived substantive services from Friendship Square in the form of health care and education; however, they refused to embrace the romantic idealizations of American life. Wage-earning mothers who placed their children in the day nursery no doubt encountered an Anglo world quite different from the one depicted by Methodist missionaries, and, thus, they were skeptical of the settlement's cultural ideations (see figure 7). Clara Sarmiento knew from experience that it was much easier to reach the children than their parents.[36]

How did children respond to the ideological undercurrents of Houchen programs? Did Mexican women feel empowered by their interaction with the settlement, or were Methodist missionaries invidious underminers of Mexican identity? In getting beneath the text, the following remarks of Minerva Franco, which appeared in a 1975 issue of *Newark-Houchen News*, raise a series of provocative questions. "Houchen provided . . . opportunities for learning and experiencing. . . . At Houchen I was shown that I had worth and that I was an individual."[37] What did she mean by that statement? Did the settlement house heighten her self-esteem? Did she feel that she was not an individual within the context of her family and neighborhood? Some young women imbibed Americanization so heavily that they rejected their identity. In *No Separate Refuge*, Sarah Deutsch picked up on this theme as she quoted missionary Polita Padilla, "I am Mexican, born and brought up in New Mexico, but much of my life was spent in the Allison School where we had a different training so that the Mexican way of living now seems strange to me." Others, like Estella Ibarra and Rose Escheverría Mulligan, saw little incompatibility between Mexican traditions and Protestantism. Growing up in Los Angeles, Mulligan remembered her religion as reaffirming Mexican values. In her words, "I was beginning to think that the Baptist Church was a little too Mexican. Too much restriction."[38]

Houchen documents reveal glimpses into the formation of identity, consciousness, and values. The Friendship Square calendar of 1949 explicitly stated that the medical care provided at Houchen "is a tool to develop sound minds in sound bodies; for thus it is easier to find peace with God and man. We want to help people develop a sense of values in life." In an era of bleaching creams, the privileging of color — with

Fig. 7. A wage-earning mother on her way to work escorts her children to the Houchen Day Nursery. (Courtesy of Houchen Community Center.)

47

white as the pinnacle — was an early lesson. Relating the excitement of kindergarten graduation, day nursery head Beatrice Fernandez included in her report a question asked by Margarita, one of the young graduates. "We are all wearing white, white dress, slip, socks and Miss Fernandez, is it alright if our hair is black?"[39] Houchen activities were synonymous with Americanization. A member of the settlement Brownie troop encouraged her friends "to become 'an American or a Girl Scout' at Houchen." Scouting certainly served as a vehicle for Americanization. The all-Mexican Girl and Boy Scout troops of Alpine, Texas, enjoyed visiting El Paso and Ciudad Juárez in the company of Houchen scouts. In a thank-you note, the Alpine Girl Scouts wrote, "Now we can all say we have been to a foreign country."[40]

It is important to remember that Houchen provided a bilingual environment, not a bicultural one. Spanish was the means to communicate the message of Methodism and Christian Americanization. Whether dressing up children as Pilgrims or European peasants, missionaries stressed "American" citizenship and values; yet, outside of conversion, definitions of those values or of "our American way" remained elusive. Indeed, some of the settlement lessons were not incongruous with Mexican mores. In December 1952, an Anglo settlement worker recorded in her journal the success of a Girl Scout dinner: "The girls learned a lot from it too. They were taught how to set the table, and how to serve the men. They learned also that they had to share, to cooperate, and to wait their turn."[41] The most striking theme is that of individualism. Missionaries emphasized the importance of individual decisionmaking and individual accomplishment. In recounting her own conversion, Clara Sarmiento explained to a young client, "I chose my own religion because it was my own personal experience and . . . I was glad my religion was not chosen for me."[42]

The Latina missionaries of Houchen served as cultural brokers as they diligently strove to integrate themselves into the community. Until 1950, the Houchen staff usually included one Latina. During the 1950s, the number of Latina (predominately Mexican-American) settlement workers rose to six. Mary Lou López, María Rico, Elizabeth Soto, Febe Bonilla, Clara Sarmiento, María Payan, and Beatrice Fernandez had participated in Methodist outreach activities as children (Soto at Houchen) and had decided to follow in the footsteps of their teachers. In addition, these women had the assistance of five full-time Mexican lay persons.[43] It is no coincidence that the decade of greatest change in Houchen policies occurred at a time when Latinas held a growing number of staff positions. Friendship Square's greater sensitivity to neighborhood

48

needs arose, in part, out of the influence exerted by Mexican clients in shaping the attitudes and actions of Mexican missionaries.

I will further suggest that although Mexican women utilized Houchen's social services, they did not, by and large, adopt its tenets of "Christian Americanization." Children who attended settlement programs enjoyed the activities, but Friendship Square did not always leave a lasting imprint. "My Mom had an open mind, so I participated in a lot of clubs. But I didn't become Protestant," remarked Lucy Lucero. "I had fun and I learned a lot, too." Because of the warm, supportive environment, Houchen settlement is remembered with fondness. However, one cannot equate pleasant memories with the acceptance of the settlement's cultural ideations.[44]

Settlement records bear out the Mexican women's selective use of Houchen's resources. The most complete set of figures I viewed was for the year 1944. During this period, 7,614 people visited the clinic and hospital. The settlement afternoon programs had an average monthly enrollment of 362, and 40 children attended kindergarten. Taken together, approximately 8,000 residents of Segundo Barrio utilized Friendship Square's medical and educational offerings. In contrast, the congregation of El Buen Pastor in 1944 included 160 people.[45] Although representing only a single year, these figures indicate the importance of Houchen's medical facilities and of Mexican women's selective utilization of resources.

Implemented by a growing Latina staff, client-initiated changes in Houchen policies brought a realistic recognition of the settlement as a social service agency, rather than as a religious mission. During the 1950s, brochures describing the day nursery emphasized that, although children said grace at meals and sang Christian songs, they would not receive "in any way indoctrination" regarding Methodism. In fact, at the parents' request, Newark nurses summoned Catholic priests to the hospital to baptize premature infants. Client desire became the justification for allowing the presence of Catholic clergy, a policy that would have been unthinkable in the not-too-distant past.[46] Finally, in the new Houchen constitution of 1959, all mention of conversion was dropped. Instead, it conveyed a more ecumenical, nondenominational spirit. For instance, the goal of Houchen Settlement was henceforth "to establish a Christian democratic framework for — individual development, family solidarity, and neighborhood welfare."[47]

Settlement activities also became more closely linked with the Mexican community. During the 1950s, Houchen was the home of two chapters — one for teenagers and one for adults — of the League of

49

United Latin American Citizens (LULAC), the most visible and politically powerful civil rights organization in Texas.[48] Carpentry classes — once the preserve of males — opened their doors to young women, although on a gender-segregated basis. Houchen workers, moreover, made veiled references to the "very dangerous business" of Juárez abortion clinics; however, it appears unclear whether or not the residents themselves offered any contraceptive counseling. But during the early 1960s, the settlement, in cooperation with Planned Parenthood, opened a birth control clinic for "married women." Indeed, a Houchen contraception success story was featured on the front page of a spring newsletter: "Mrs. G.————, after having her thirteenth and fourteenth children (twins), enrolled in our birth control clinic; now for one and one half years she has been a happy and non-pregnant mother."[49]

Certainly, Houchen had changed with the times. What factors accounted for the new directions in settlement work? The evidence on the baptism of premature babies seems fairly clear in terms of client pressure, but to what extent did other policies change as the result of Mexican women's input? The residents of Segundo Barrio may have felt more comfortable expressing their ideas, and Latina settlement workers may have exhibited a greater willingness to listen. Though it is a matter of pure speculation at this point, a working coalition of Mexican women that spanned the missionary-client boundary may have accounted for Houchen's more ecumenical tone and greater community involvement. In reviewing Houchen's history, I would argue that Mexican clients, not the missionaries, set the boundaries for interaction. For most women, Houchen was not a beacon of salvation but a medical and social service center run by Methodists. They consciously decided what resources they would utilize and consciously ignored or sidestepped the settlement's ideological premises. Like women of color in academia, they sought to take advantage of the system without buying into it.

Houchen provides a case study of what I term *cultural coalescence*. Immigrants and their children pick, borrow, retain, and create distinctive cultural forms. There is not a single hermetic Mexican or Mexican-American culture but rather permeable *cultures* rooted in generation, gender, region, class, and personal experience. Chicano scholars have divided Mexican experiences into three generational categories: Mexicano (first generation), Mexican-American (second generation), and Chicano (third and beyond).[50] But this general typology tends to obscure the ways in which people navigate across cultural boundaries, as well as their conscious decisionmaking in the production of culture. However, bear in mind that people of color have not had unlimited

50

choice. Racism, sexism, imperialism, persecution, and social, political, and economic segmentation have all constrained the individual's aspiration, expectations, and decisionmaking. As an example, young women coming of age during the 1920s may have wanted to be like the flappers they saw on the silver screen or read about in magazines, but few would do more than adopt prevailing fashions. Strict parental supervision, including chaperonage, and the reality of poverty and prejudice served to blunt their ability to emulate the icons of a new consumer society. Young women encountered both the lure of Hollywood and the threat of deportation and walked between the familiarity of tradition and the excitement of experimentation.[51]

The ideations of Americanization were a mixed lot. Religious and secular Americanization programs, the elementary schools, movies, magazines, and radio bombarded the Mexican community with a myriad of models, most of which were idealized, stylized, unrealistic, and unattainable. Even the Spanish-language press promoted acculturation, especially in the realm of consumer culture. Aimed at women, advertisements promised status and affection if the proper bleaching cream, hair coloring, and cosmetics were purchased. "Siga las Estrellas" [Follow the Stars] beckoned one Max Factor advertisement.[52]

By looking through the lens of cultural coalescence, we can begin to discern the ways in which people select and create cultural forms. The fluidity of cultures offers exciting possibilities for research and discussion. Institutional records, like those of Houchen, are neither dead ends nor gold mines but points of departure. Creating the public space of the settlement, Methodist missionaries sought to alter the "lifeworld" of Mexican immigrants to reflect their own idealized versions of life in the United States. Settlement workers can be viewed as the narrators of lived experience. And Houchen records reflect the cognitive construction of missionary aspirations and expectations. In other words, the documents revealed more about the women who wrote them than those they served. At another level, one could interpret the cultural ideations of Americanization as indications of an attempt at what Jürgen Habermas has termed "inner colonization."[53] Yet, the failure of such projects illustrates the ways in which Mexican women appropriated desired resources, both material (infant immunizations) and psychological (self-esteem), while, in the main, rejecting the ideological messages behind them. The shift in Houchen policies during the 1950s meant more than a recognition of community needs; it represented a claiming of public space by Mexican women clients. Cultural coalescence encompasses both accommodation and resistance, and Mexican women acted,

---

51

FRONTIERS

not reacted, to the settlement impulse. When standing at the cultural crossroads, Mexican women blended their options and created their own paths.

NOTES

1. I thank Valerie Matsumoto for her unflagging encouragement and insightful comments. I gratefully acknowledge Tom Houghteling, Houchen Community Center executive director, and members of the Houchen board for their permission to use settlement materials. This essay was completed with the support of a University of California, Davis, Humanities Institute Fellowship.

2. Steven Seidman, ed., *Jürgen Habermas on Society and Politics: A Reader* (Boston: Beacon Press, 1989), p. 171.

3. Mario T. García, *Desert Immigrants: The Mexicans of El Paso, 1880–1920* (New Haven: Yale University Press, 1981), pp. 144–145. On a national level, Mexicans formed the "third largest 'racial' group" by 1930, outnumbered only by Anglos and African-Americans, according to T. Wilson Longmore and Homer L. Hitt, "A Demographic Analysis of First and Second Generation Mexican Population of the United States: 1930," *Southwestern Social Science Quarterly*, 24 (September 1943): 140.

4. Oscar J. Martínez, *The Chicanos of El Paso: An Assessment of Progress* (El Paso: Texas Western Press, 1980), pp. 17, 6.

5. Martínez, *Chicanos*, pp. 29–33, 10. Mario García meticulously documents the economic and social stratification of Mexicans in El Paso; see García, *Desert Immigrants*. In 1960, the proportion of Mexican workers with high white-collar jobs jumped to 3.4 percent, according to Martínez, *Chicanos*, p. 10.

6. "South El Paso's Oasis of Care," *paso del norte*, 1 (September 1982): 42–43; Thelma Hammond, "Friendship Square," (Houchen report, 1969), part of an uncataloged collection of documents housed at Houchen Community Center, El Paso, Texas, and hereafter referred to as [HF] (for Houchen Files); "Growing With the Century" (Houchen report, 1947) [HF].

7. García, *Desert Immigrants*, p. 145; Effie Stoltz, "Freeman Clinic: A Resume of Four Years Work" (Houchen pamphlet, 1924) [HF]. It should be noted that Houchen Settlement sprang from the work of Methodist missionary Mary Tripp, who arrived in South El Paso in 1893. However, it was not until 1912 that an actual settlement was established, according to "South El Paso's Oasis of Care," p. 42.

8. Stoltz, "Freeman Clinic"; Hammond, "Friendship Square"; M. Dorothy Woodruff and Dorothy Little, "Friendship Square" (Houchen pamphlet, March 1949) [HF]; "Friendship Square" (Houchen report, circa 1940s) [HF]; "Health Center" (Houchen newsletter, 1943) [HF]; "Christian Health Service" (Houchen report, 1941) [HF]; *El Paso Times*, October 20, 1945.

9. "Settlement Worker's Report" (Houchen report, 1927) [HF]; letter from Dorothy Little to E. Mae Young, dated May 10, 1945 [HF]; letter from Bessie Brinson to Treva Ely, dated September 14, 1958 [HF]; Hammond, "Friendship Square"; Elmer T. Clark and Dorothy McConnell, "The Methodist Church and Latin Americans in the United States" (Board of Home Missions pamphlet, circa 1930s) [HF]. My very rough estimate is based on the documents and records to which I had access. I was not permitted to examine any materials then housed at Newark Hospital. The most complete statistics on utilization of services are for the year 1944 and are given in the letter from Little to Young. Because of the deportation and repatriation drives

52

74

of the 1930s in which one-third of the Mexican population in the United States was either deported or repatriated, the number of Mexicans in El Paso dropped from 68,476 in 1930 to 55,000 in 1940; by 1960, it had risen to 63,796, according to Martínez, *Chicanos*, p. 6.

10. *El Paso Herald Post*, March 7, 1961; *El Paso Herald Post*, March 12, 1961; "Community Centers" (Women's Division of Christian Service pamphlet, May 1963); "Funding Proposal for Youth Outreach and Referral Report Project" (April 30, 1974), from the private files of Kenton J. Clymer, Ph.D.; *El Paso Herald Post*, January 3, 1983; *El Paso Times*, August 8, 1983.

11. Letter from Tom Houghteling, executive director, Houchen Community Center, to the author, dated December 24, 1990; Tom Houghteling, interview with the author, January 9, 1991.

12. Dorothy Little, "Rose Gregory Houchen Settlement" (Houchen report, February 1942) [HF].

13. Ibid.; "Our Work at Houchen" (Houchen report, circa 1940s) [HF]; Woodruff and Little, "Friendship Square"; Jennie C. Gilbert, "Settlements Under the Women's Home Missionary Society," (pamphlet, circa 1920s) [HF]; Clark and McConnell, "The Methodist Church."

14. Anita Hernandez, "The Kindergarten" (Houchen report, circa 1940s) [HF]; "A Right Glad New Year" (Houchen newsletter, circa 1940s) [HF]; Little, "Rose Gregory Houchen Settlement"; "Our Work at Houchen"; Woodruff and Little, "Friendship Square." For more information on the Franciscans, see Ramón Gutiérrez, *When Padre Jesus Came, the Corn Mothers Went Away: Marriage, Sexuality, and Power in New Mexico, 1500–1846* (Stanford, Calif.: Stanford University Press, 1991).

15. "Settlement Worker's Report"; letter from Little to Young; letter from Brinson to Ely; Friendship Square calendar for 1949 [HF]; Lucy Lucero, interview with the author, October 8, 1983; Elsa Chávez, interview with the author, April 19, 1983; discussion following presentation on "Settlement Houses in El Paso," given by the author at the El Paso Conference on History and the Social Sciences, August 24, 1983, El Paso, Texas. (Tape of presentation and discussion is on file at the Institute of Oral History, University of Texas, El Paso.) Elsa Chávez is a pseudonym used at the person's request.

16. Discussion following "Settlement Houses in El Paso" presentation. The Catholic church never established a competing settlement house. However, during the 1920s in Gary, Indiana, the Catholic diocese opened up the Gary-Alerding Settlement with the primary goal of Americanizing Mexican immigrants. The bishop took such action to counteract suspected inroads made by two local Protestant settlement houses. See Ruth Hutchinson Crocker, "Gary Mexicans and 'Christian Americanization': A Study in Cultural Conflict," in *Forging Community: The Latino Experience in Northwest Indiana, 1919–1975*, eds. James B. Lane and Edward J. Escobar (Chicago: Cattails Press, 1987), pp. 115–134.

17. "Christian Health Service"; "The Freeman Clinic and the Newark Conference Maternity Hospital" (Houchen report, 1940) [HF]; *El Paso Times*, August 2, 1961; *El Paso Herald Post*, May 12, 1961. For more information on Americanization programs in California, see George J. Sanchez, " 'Go After the Women': Americanization and the Mexican Immigrant Woman, 1915–1929," in *Unequal Sisters: A Multicultural Reader in U.S. Women's History*, eds. Ellen Carol DuBois and Vicki L. Ruíz (New York: Routledge, 1990), pp. 250–263. The documents reveal a striking absence of adult Mexican male clients. The Mexican men who do appear are either Methodist ministers or lay volunteers.

18. Sanchez, " 'Go After the Women,' " pp. 250–283; Sarah Deutsch, *No Separate Refuge: Culture, Class, and Gender on the Anglo-Hispanic Frontier in the American*

53

Southwest, 1880–1940 (New York: Oxford University Press, 1987); "Americanization Notes," *Arizona Teacher and Home Journal*, 11 (January 1923): 26. The Methodist and Presbyterian settlements in Gary, Indiana, also couched their programs in terms of "Christian Americanization," according to Hutchinson Crocker, "Gary Mexicans," pp. 118–120.

19. "Settlement Worker's Report"; Friendship Square calendar for 1949; letter from Brinson to Ely; Chávez interview.

20. News clipping from the *El Paso Times* (circa 1950s) [HF].

21. Sanchez, " 'Go After the Women,' " p. 260; *Newark-Houchen News*, September 1975. I agree with George Sanchez that Americanization programs created an overly rosy picture of U.S. life. In his words: "Rather than providing Mexican immigrant women with an attainable picture of assimilation, Americanization programs could only offer these immigrants idealized versions of American life" (Sanchez, " 'Go After the Women,' " p. 260).

22. Little, "Rose Gregory Houchen Settlement."

23. "Settlement Worker's Report"; Hernandez, "The Kindergarten"; "A Right Glad New Year"; Little, "Rose Gregory Houchen Settlement"; "Our Work at Houchen"; Woodruff and Little, "Friendship Square"; "South El Paso's Oasis of Care"; *El Paso Herald Post*, March 7, 1961; *El Paso Herald Post*, March 12, 1961; *El Paso Herald Post*, May 12, 1961.

24. C. S. Babbitt, *The Remedy for the Decadence of the Latin Race* (El Paso, Tex.: El Paso Printing Company), p. 55 (presented to the Pioneers Association of El Paso, Texas, July 11, 1909, by Mrs. Babbitt, widow of the author; pamphlet courtesy of Jack Redman).

25. "Account Book for Rose Gregory Houchen Settlement (1903–1913)" [HF]; Hammond, "Friendship Square"; "Growing With the Century"; *El Paso Times*, September 5, 1975; Stoltz, "Freeman Clinic"; Woodruff and Little, "Friendship Square"; *El Paso Times*, October 3, 1947; "Four Institutions. One Goal. The Christian Community" (Houchen pamphlet, circa early 1950s) [HF]; Houghteling interview; "A City Block of Service" (script of Houchen slide presentation, 1976) [HF]; *El Paso Times*, January 19, 1977; speech given by Kenton J. Clymer, Ph.D., June 1975 (Clymer Files); *El Paso Times*, May 23, 1975; *Newark-Houchen News*, September 1975. It should be noted that in 1904 local Methodist congregations did contribute much of the money needed to purchase the property upon which the settlement was built. Local civic groups occasionally donated money or equipment and threw Christmas parties for Houchen children, according to "Account Book"; *El Paso Herald Post*, December 14, 1951; *El Paso Times*, December 16, 1951.

26. Vernon McCombs, "Victories in the Latin American Mission" (Board of Home Missions pamphlet, 1935) [HF]; "Brillante Historia de la Iglesia 'El Buen Pastor' El Paso" (Young Adult Fellowship newsletter, December 1946) [HF]; Soledad Burciaga, "Yesterday in 1923" (Houchen report, 1939) [HF].

27. This study is based on a limited number of oral interviews (five to be exact), but they represent a range of interaction with the settlement, from playing on the playground to serving as the minister for El Buen Pastor. It is also informed by a public discussion of my work on Houchen held during an El Paso teachers' conference in 1983. Most of the educators who attended the talk had participated, to some extent, in Houchen activities and were eager to share their recollections (cf. note 13). I am also indebted to students in my Mexican-American history classes when I taught at the University of Texas, El Paso, especially the reentry women, for their insight and knowledge.

28. Woodruff and Little, "Friendship Square"; Hammond, "Friendship Square"; "Greetings for 1946" (Houchen Christmas newsletter, 1946) [HF]; Little, "Rose

54

Gregory Houchen Settlement"; Soledad Burciaga, "Today in 1939" (Houchen report, 1939) [HF]; "Our Work at Houchen"; "Christian Social Service" (Houchen report, circa 1940s) [HF]; Fernando García, interview with the author, September 21, 1983; *El Paso Times*, June 14, 1951; Lucero interview; Vicki L. Ruíz, "Oral History and La Mujer: The Rosa Guerrero Story," in *Women on the U.S.–Mexico Border: Responses to Change* (Boston: Allen and Unwin, 1987), pp. 226–227; *Newark-Houchen News*, September 1975.

29. Spanish-American Methodist News Bulletin, April 1946 [HF]; Hammond, "Friend-ship Square"; McCombs, "Victories"; "El Metodismo en la Ciudad de El Paso," *Christian Herald*, July 1945 [HF]; "Brillante Historia"; "The Door: An Informal Pamphlet on the Work of the Methodist Church Among the Spanish-speaking of El Paso, Texas" (Methodist pamphlet, 1940) [HF]; "A City Block of Service"; García interview; Houghteling interview. From 1932 to 1939, services for El Buen Pastor were held in a church located two blocks from the settlement.

30. A. Ruth Kern, "There Is No Segregation Here" (Methodist Youth Fund Bulletin, January–March 1953), p. 12 [HF].

31. Ibid.; "The Torres Family" (Houchen report, circa 1940s) [HF]; Estella Ibarra, interview with Jesusita Ponce, November 11, 1982; Hazel Bulifant, "One Woman's Story" (Houchen report, 1950) [HF]; "Our Work at Houchen."

32. Clara Sarmiento, "Lupe" (Houchen report, circa 1950s) [HF].

33. Ibarra interview.

34. Bulifant, "One Woman's Story"; letter from Little to Young.

35. Deutsch, No Separate Refuge, pp. 64–66, 85–86; Sanchez, " 'Go After the Women,' " pp. 259–261; Hutchinson Crocker, "Gary Mexicans," p. 121.

36. Sarmiento, "Lupe." In her study, Ruth Hutchinson Crocker also notes the propensity of Protestant missionaries to focus their energies on children and the selective uses of services by Mexican clients. As she explained, "Inevitably, many immigrants came to the settlement, took what they wanted of its services, and remained untouched by its message" (Hutchinson Crocker, "Gary Mexicans," p. 122).

37. *Newark-Houchen News*, September 1975.

38. Deutsch, *No Separate Refuge*, pp. 78–79; Ibarra interview; interview with Rose Escheverria Mulligan, vol. 27 of *Rosie the Riveter Revisited: Women and the World War II Work Experience*, ed. Sherna Berger Gluck (Long Beach, Calif.: CSULB Foundation, 1983), p. 24.

39. Friendship Square calendar for 1949; Beatrice Fernandez, "Day Nursery" (Houchen report, circa late 1950s) [HF].

40. "Friendship Square" (Houchen pamphlet, circa 1950s) [HF]; letter to Houchen Girl Scouts from Troop 4, Latin American Community Center, Alpine, Texas, May 18, 1951 [HF].

41. "A Right Glad New Year"; News clipping from the *El Paso Times* (circa 1950s); "Our Work at Houchen"; Little, "Rose Gregory Houchen Settlement"; Anglo settlement worker's journal, entry for December 1952 [HF].

42. *Newark-Houchen News*, September 1975; Sarmiento, "Lupe."

43. Datebook for 1926, settlement worker's private journal, entry for Friday, September 9, 1929 [HF]; "Brillante Historia"; "Report and Directory of Association of Church Social Workers, 1940" [HF]; "May I Come In?" (Houchen brochure, circa 1950s) [HF]; "Friendship Square" (Houchen pamphlet, 1958) [HF]; Mary Lou López, "Kindergarten Report" (Houchen report, circa 1950s) [HF]; Sarmiento, "Lupe"; "Freeman Clinic and Newark Hospital" (Houchen pamphlet, 1954) [HF]; *El Paso Times*, June 14, 1951; "Houchen Day Nursery" (Houchen pamphlet, circa

55

1950s) [HF]; *El Paso Times*, September 12, 1952. Methodist missionaries seem to have experienced some mobility within the settlement hierarchy. In 1912, Ofilia Chávez served as a "student helper"; forty years later, Beatrice Fernandez would direct the preschool.

44. Chávez interview; Martha González, interview with the author, October 8, 1983; Lucero interview; *Newark-Houchen News*, September 1974.

45. Letter from Little to Young; "The Door"; Woodruff and Little, "Friendship Square."

46. "Houchen Day Nursery"; "Life in a Glass House" (Houchen report, circa 1950s) [HF].

47. Program for first annual meeting, Houchen Settlement and Day Nursery, Freeman Clinic and Newark Conference Maternity Hospital (January 8, 1960) [HF]. It should be noted that thirty years later, there seems to be a shift back to original settlement ideas. Today, in 1991, Houchen Community has regularly scheduled Bible studies, according to letter from Houghteling to the author.

48. Program for Houchen production of "Cinderella" [HF]; letter from Brinson to Ely. For more information on LULAC, see Mario T. García, *Mexican Americans: Leadership, Ideology, and Identity, 1930–1960* (New Haven: Yale University Press, 1989).

49. Bulifant, "One Woman's Story"; "News From Friendship Square" (spring newsletter, circa early 1960s) [HF].

50. As an example of this typology, see García, *Mexican Americans*, pp. 13–22, 295–302. Richard Griswold del Castillo touches on the dynamic nature of Mexican culture in *La Familia: Chicano Families in the Urban Southwest, 1848 to the Present* (Notre Dame, Ind.: University of Notre Dame Press, 1984).

51. A more developed elaboration of these themes may be found in my essay, " 'Star Struck': Acculturation, Adolescence, and the Mexican American Woman, 1920–1940," in *Building With Our Hands: New Directions in Chicana Scholarship*, eds. Adela de la Torre and Beatríz Pesquera (Berkeley: University of California Press, forthcoming).

52. Ibid.; *La Opinion*, June 5, 1927; *La Opinion*, January 8, 1938.

53. My understanding and application of the ideas of Jürgen Habermas have been informed by the following works: Jürgen Habermas, *Moral Consciousness and Communicative Action*, trans. Christian Lenhardt and Sherry Weber Nicholsen, intro. Thomas McCarthy (Cambridge, Mass.: MIT Press, 1990); Steven Seidman, ed., *Jürgen Habermas on Society and Politics*; Nancy Fraser, *Unruly Practices: Power, Discourse, and Gender in Contemporary Social Theory* (Minneapolis: University of Minnesota Press, 1989); and Seyla Benhabib and Drucilla Cornell, "Introduction: Beyond the Politics of Gender," in *Feminism As Critique*, eds. Seyla Benhabib and Drucilla Cornell (Minneapolis: University of Minnesota Press, 1987).

56

The Chicana in American History: The Mexican Women of El Paso, 1880–1920—A Case Study

Mario T. García

The author is a member of the history and Chicano studies departments in the University of California, Santa Barbara.

ALTHOUGH MEXICAN WOMEN have made significant contributions to the growth of a Chicano working class in the United States, their history has received little attention. Interpretive and historiographical pieces have been written, but no in-depth scholarship on the subject has emerged.[1] One factor that may explain this shortcoming is the absence of female Mexican

The author wishes to thank Ramón Eduardo Ruiz, W. Elliot Brownlee, Mary Brownlee, and Ileana Rodríguez for their helpful comments on this paper.

[1]General and interpretive works based on secondary sources include Martha P. Cotera, *Diosa y Hembra: The History and Heritage of Chicanas in the U.S.* (Austin, 1976); María Linda Apodaca, "The Chicana Woman: An Historical Materialist Perspective," *Latin American Perspectives*, IV (Winter and Spring 1977), 70–89; and Flor Saiz, *La Chicana* (N.p., 1973). For contemporary history based on recent census data, see Laura E. Arroyo, "Industrial and Occupational Distribution of Chicana Workers," *Aztlán*, IV (1973), 343–382; and Rosaura Sánchez, "The Chicana Labor Force," in Rosaura Sánchez and Rosa Martínez Cruz, *Essays on La Mujer* (Los Angeles, 1977), 3–15. On historiography, see Judith Sweeney, "Chicana History: A Review of the Literature," in Sánchez and Martínez Cruz, *La Mujer*, 99–123; and Rosalinda M. González, "A Review of the Literature on Mexican American Women Workers in the U.S. Southwest, 1900–75" (Unpublished paper available in the Chicano Studies Library, University of California, Berkeley). Also, consult the following bibliographies which have sections on history: Roberto Cabello-Argandoña, Juan Gómez-Quiñones, and Patricia Herrera Durán, eds., *The Chicana: A Comprehensive Study* (Los Angeles, 1975); and Cristina Portillo, Graciela Rios, and Martha Rodríguez, eds., *Bibliography of Writings on La Mujer* (Berkeley, 1976). For interpretive articles on contemporary

Pacific Historical Review

© 1980, by the Pacific Coast Branch, American Historical Association

American historians. Moreover, Chicano history, like most history, while showing slow but healthy development recently, only now has begun to focus on the role of Mexican American women.[2] A "Chicana" writer finds it "disheartening" to discover scant mention of women in the latest publications on Chicano history.[3] Yet "her history" is an integral part of the Mexican saga in the Southwest. As one scholar has observed, Chicano history without the Chicana would be "false" and "truncated."[4] This study attempts to help correct the omission of women in Chicano history and suggests some of the major research areas that might be explored, using the case study of Mexican women in El Paso, Texas, between 1880 and 1920.[5]

Women of Mexican descent appear early in the story of the Southwest. On the whole, most were wives and mothers, and their story has yet to be told. Wives accompanied their husbands on the long and perilous trek to the United States during the late nineteenth and early twentieth centuries. The family, of course, represented the most important institution transferred across the border by Mexican immigrants. The Dillingham Commission report of 1911 on the state of foreign immigration to the United States, authorized by the United States Senate, noted that a high percentage of Mexican laborers in western

Chicanas, the following sample can be consulted: Noemi Lorenzana, "La Chicana: Transcending the Old and Carrying Out a New Life and Self-Image," De Colores, II (1975), 6–14; Jennie V. Chávez, "An Opinion: Women of the Mexican-American Movement," Mademoiselle, LXXXII (April 1972), 150–152; and Adal Riddel, "Chicanas and El Movimiento," Aztlán, (1974), 155–165. For a more recent and general treatment, see Alfredo Mirandé and Evangelina Enríquez, La Chicana: The Mexican-American Woman (Chicago, 1979).
[2]For a discussion of recent publications in Chicano history, see Juan Gómez Quinoñes and Luis Arroyo, "On the State of Chicano History: Observations on Its Development, Interpretation, and Theory, 1970–1974," Western Historical Quarterly 1976), 155–185.
[3]Noemi Lorenzana, "Hijas de Aztlán," De Colores, I (Summer 1974), 43.
[4]Sweeney, "Chicana History," 99–100.
[5]Besides being the most important point of entry for Mexican immigrants, El Paso also served as a major urban employer of Mexican workers. Mexican men, for example, readily found jobs at the smelter, the railroad yards, in construction, clerical work, and in a variety of other low-skilled occupations. A special El Paso census conducted in 1916 recorded that out of a total population of 61,482, Mexicans represented 32,724 or 54.8 percent of the city's inhabitants. Except for San Antonio, El Paso by 1920 contained the largest urban concentration of Mexicans in the U.S., and the border city was the only southwestern metropolis possessing more Mexicans than Anglo Americans. For more on El Paso and its Mexican population, see Mario T. García, "Obreros: The Mexican Workers of El Paso, 1900–1920" (Ph.D. dissertation, University of California, San Diego, 1975); and Oscar J. Martínez, Border Boom Town: Ciudad Juárez since 1848 (Austin, 1978).

industries had brought their wives from nearby Mexico. According to the commission, some 58.2 percent of Mexican railroad workers in the survey reported that their wives were with them in the United States. This figure was much higher than that for other immigrant railroad workers in the West who had arrived from more distant lands, such as southern Europe and Asia, and the commission suggested, although without evidence, that "the conditions under which section hands live are less uninviting to the Mexican women than to the women of any other race."[6] One railroad line, the Santa Fe, by 1910 was encouraging the migration of Mexican families in order to stabilize working conditions. As a Santa Fe engineer put it, hiring married men resulted in better and more productive workers.[7] Investigators for the Dillingham Commission also discovered a similar condition in urban-related work. Sixty percent of Mexicans employed as construction workers by street railways, for example, admitted they had their wives with them.[8]

In Mexico at the turn of the century, the urban working class and rural family appear to have constituted a strong social and economic institution. Ernesto Galarza, in his autobiographical *Barrio Boy*, recalls that his family in rural Nayarit included not only his mother (who divorced Galarza's father prior to his birth), but also his aunt, three uncles, and two cousins. In the Galarza household, the men went to labor in the fields during the day while the women and children remained and performed the housework and cooking.[9]

Leaving Mexico and entering the United States, the Mexican family seems to have remained strong and retained its native character rather than being weakened by the immigration process. The majority of Mexican immigrant families, as revealed in a sample taken from a 1900 El Paso census, were either nuclear or extended (see Table 1). Over half of the immigrant household units were nuclear families living by themselves or in an augmented relationship with nonrelated household resi-

---

[6]"Immigrants in Industries, Part 25: Japanese and Other Immigrant Races in the Pacific Coast and Rocky Mountain States," 61 Cong., 2 sess., *S. Doc. 633* (1911), Vol. III, Part I, pp. 11–12 (cited hereafter as *Dillingham Commission*).

[7]Judith Fincher Laird, "Argentine, Kansas: The Evolution of a Mexican-American Community: 1905–1940" (Ph.D. dissertation, University of Kansas, 1975), 121.

[8]*Dillingham Commission*, Part 25, Vol. III, Parts I and II, pp. 39 and 86.

[9]Ernesto Galarza, *Barrio Boy* (Notre Dame, 1971), 3–71.

TABLE 1
HOUSEHOLD COMPOSITION, EL PASO, 1900
(PERCENTAGES ROUNDED OFF)

	Mexican National	Mexican American	Non-Spanish Surname
Nuclear family households			
Husband, wife and children	38% (58)	45% (11)	29% (65)
Husband, wife, no children	7% (10)	4% (1)	10% (23)
Broken families			
Husband and children	3% (4)	0 (0)	3% (7)
Wife and children	19% (30)	0 (0)	9% (21)
Single-person households	7% (12)	4% (1)	20% (42)
Extended-family households[a]	13% (20)	16% (4)	5% (13)
Augmented-family households[b]	11% (17)	30% (7)	19% (40)
Extended-augmented family households[c]	0 (1)	0 (0)	2% (6)
Total Number (393)	(152)	(24)	(217)

[a] Nuclear family living with one or more relatives.
[b] Nuclear family living with nonfamily members, such as lodgers, in the same household.
[c] Nuclear family living with both relatives and nonfamily members
SOURCE: U.S. *Manuscript Census, 1900.*

dents, such as boarders. In addition, 13 percent were extended families. More Mexican immigrant families lived in nuclear households than did non-Spanish surname families. Perhaps reflecting greater personal mobility, a larger percentage of non-Spanish surnamed individuals resided in single-person households than did Mexican immigrants. On the other hand, more broken homes could be found among the Mexican immigrant population, especially those involving a mother and her children; however, it is possible that in some cases husbands were not recorded due to jobs outside the city. Still considerably more Mexican Americans than Mexican immigrants lived in nuclear families. Many Mexican Americans also apparently took in boarders.[10] Since the 1910 and 1920 manuscript cenuses are not

[10]U.S. manuscript census, 1900, El Paso County, Vols. 35 and 36. There are 3,123 family units included in the 1900 census for the city of El Paso. To acquire a representative sample, every eighth unit was recorded commencing with the second unit of the First Ward (the census encompassed El Paso's four wards). The total number of units in the sample amounted to 393. For sample methodology, see Peter R. Knights, *The Plain People of Boston, 1830–1860: A Study of City Growth* (New York, 1971), 3–10. I wish to thank Carl V. Harris of the Department of History, University of California, Santa Barbara, for his assistance in determining the sample. In a study of the Mexican

yet available to scholars, no comparisons can be made, but it is possible that over this twenty-year period a pattern of chain migration set in and extended-family households grew among Mexican immigrants as other relatives arrived, especially those from the northern Mexican states.

Although some Mexican women in El Paso and throughout the urban Southwest contributed to household incomes by taking in wash or lodgers, no disintegration took place in the traditional pattern of men being the chief wage-earners and women doing household work. The sample taken from the El Paso census of 1900 shows that no mothers and few daughters, most of the latter being too young, in an immigrant family headed by the father worked outside the home.[11] As wife and mother the Mexican housewife was primarily responsible for caring for the Mexican male worker and her family. Under a division of labor which relegated nearly all of them to house-work, Mexican women, like most women, had to maintain the male work force as well as reproduce it. Within the family, Mexican males not only found relief from their job alienation, but nourishment for another day's hard work. Consequently, the family, and the women's role in it, performed a significant economic task.[12]

Too poor to afford their own domestics, Mexican women in the border city performed their housework under depressed living conditions. "Chihuahuita," the largest Mexican settlement in El Paso and adjacent to the Rio Grande River border, contained the city's worst and most congested housing. While no legal restrictions prohibited Mexicans from living in the better homes found in American neighborhoods, lack of occuptional

community in Los Angeles between 1850 and 1890, Richard Griswold del Castillo also found that most Mexican immigrants lived in nuclear families. Griswold del Castillo, "La Familia Chicana: Social Change in the Chicano Family of Los Angeles, 1850−1890," *Journal of Ethnic Studies*, III (Spring 1975), 41−58.

[11]*Manuscript Census, 1900.* In a sample of 152 immigrant households, of those with a working father not one unit contained a mother working outside the home and only seven units had working daughters.

[12]For interpretive works on the role of women as housewives and mothers, see Shiela Rowbotham, *Woman's Consciousness, Man's World* (Middlesex, England, 1973); Rowbotham, *Hidden from History: Rediscovering Women in History from the 17th Century to the Present* (New York, 1976); Alva Buxenbaum, "The Status of Women Workers," *Political Affairs*, LII (Nov. 1973), pp. 31−42; and Wally Secombe, "The Housewife and Her Labour under Capitalism," *New Left Review*, LXXXII (Jan.−Feb. 1974), 3−24.

mobility, in addition to race and cultural prejudice, kept Mexicans segregated in *barrios* (slums). Mexicans adjusted to these conditions, however, because of acquaintance with poverty, plus the mistaken belief they would soon return to Mexico with ample savings.

Unfortunately, the adjustment of Mexicans left them open to exploitation and neglect by landlords and city officials. Due to their small wages, Mexican workers had to live in *jacales*—adobe homes—with dirt floors. Reporter Lewis Gilbert of Missouri noted in a visit to El Paso in 1900 that the huts, home to the Mexicans, had from one to three rooms. In sharp contrast to their adobe houses, the Missourian observed, Americans built their structures of bricks. For heating and cooking, the Mexicans gathered firewood from timber that flowed down the Rio Grande. Some resorted to stealing coal from nearby railroad cars. Tragically, the burning of these fuels often led to fires which destroyed the jacales. Furthermore, little sanitation existed in the Mexican barrios. Since they did not own property, except for their huts, Mexicans found it difficult to acquire municipal services paid by local property taxes. American property owners in Chihuahuita, who rented land to Mexicans, delayed improvements by claiming they could not afford increased taxes. Unlike the American sections, for example, the Mexican districts contained few sidewalks or paved streets. In 1897 the Spanish language newspaper, *El Monitor*, complained about poor street conditions in the Mexican area where rubble and latrines could be found. Already crowded, the addition of new immigrants and refugees, especially during the Mexican Revolution of 1910, only increased the high population density of Chihuahuita. Jacales at times housed two or three families. Although tenements had replaced some of the huts by 1916, the new buildings quickly became congested and unsanitary due to the Mexican's poverty, continued immigration, and neglect by landlords.[13]

Under these conditions, Mexican housewives did the hard manual labor which allowed immigrant families to live on husband's and sometimes childrens' limited earnings. Mexican

---

[13]*El Paso Times*, Jan 9, 1900, p. 6; *El Monitor*, Oct. 31, 1893, p. 3. Also, see chapter 5, "Chihuahuita: The Making of a Barrio," in García, "Obreros," 212–260.

women had to haul water for washing and cooking from the river or public water pipes. To feed their families, they had to spend time marketing, often in Cuidad Juárez across the border, as well as long, hot hours cooking meals and coping with the burden of desert sand both inside and outside their homes. Besides the problem of raising children, unsanitary living conditions forced Mexican mothers to deal with disease and illness in their families. Diphtheria, tuberculosis, typhus, and influenza were never too far away. Some diseases could be directly traced to inferior city services. Charity official, Mrs. E. Kohlberg, complained in 1909 that much of the increase in tuberculosis among the Mexican population could be blamed on the sanitation department which swept the streets of Chihuahuita without first sprinkling them with water, "thus scattering dust in every direction and releasing millions of germs." As a result, Mexican mothers had to devote much energy caring for sick children, many of whom died. The *El Paso Times* commented later in 1909 that out of thirty-six deaths during the previous week, twenty involved children less than three years of age. Almost all were Mexicans. "Death seems to be a frequent and common visitor in the homes of the Mexican element," the newspaper remarked. Lack of sewers, water, paved sidewalks, and streets plus overcrowded homes made housework one of the most arduous jobs in the Mexican settlement.[14]

The Mexican housewife, although oppressed under a sexual division of labor, helped sustain the family's male workers and indirectly El Paso's economy which grew and prospered from the labor of Mexicans. Without the woman's housework, Mexican men could not have adjusted so easily to an American urban environment. "If we are to understand the lives of the working class," one scholar stresses, "we must look at the lives of the women as well as those of the men, in the household as well as in the workplaces."[15]

---

[14]García, "Obreros," 238–244; *Times*, Nov. 24, 1909, pp. 1–2, and May 13, 1910, p. 4.

[15]Susan J. Kleinberg, "Technology and Women's Work: The Lives of Working Class Women in Pittsburg, 1870–1900," *Labor History*, XVII (1976), 58. Interpreting the modern role of housewives as a result of industrial capitalism, Ann Oakly writes that "the work of women has received very little serious sociological or historical attention. Their unpaid work in the home has scarcely been studied at all." Ann Oakly, *Women's Work: The Housewife, Past and Present* (New York, 1976), 3–78.

322   PACIFIC HISTORICAL REVIEW

Besides their roles as housewives, Mexican women guarded
Mexican cultural traditions within the family. Not only did the
family represent the most fundamental institution brought by
Mexican immigrants, but it proved to be the most resistant
barrier to American assimilation.[16] Due to a lack of economic
options, much Mexican popular culture in El Paso and throughout the Southwest centered on family activities. It is difficult
with the scarcity of documentation on Mexican families to
present an accurate picture of family life in El Paso, but
anthropologist Manuel Gamio noted certain customs being
practiced during the 1920s by Mexican immigrant families in El
Paso as well as other Mexican settlements throughout the
United States. Gamio observed that while Mexican immigrants
accepted American material goods, they also retained earlier
customs. These included folklore, songs and ballads, birthday
celebrations, saints' days, baptisms, weddings, and funerals in
the traditional style. Because of poverty, a lack of physicians in
the barrios, and adherence to traditional customs, Mexicans
continued to use medicinal herbs. Immigrant women interviewed by Gamio acknowledged that for the most part they
cooked "Mexican style."[17] Mexican folk customs both inside and
outside the family also included a variety of oral traditions.
These involved *cuentos* (Mexican tales), children's stories, leg-
ends, ghost and goblin stories, such as "La Llorona" (The
Weeper) and *dichos*—sayings and proverbs. Perhaps the most
popular form of oral literature were the songs and ballads called
corridos which were based on the Spanish romance and which
the Mexicans sang in Spanish with their families and fellow-

[16]Ernesto Galarza, "Mexicans in the Southwest: A Culture in Process," in Edward H.
Spicer and Raymond H. Thompson, eds., *Plural Society in the Southwest* (New York, 1972),
276–277.

[17]Manuel Gamio, *Mexican Immigration to the United States* (New York, 1971; originally
published Chicago, 1930), 76–83, and Gamio, *The Life Story of the Mexican Immigrant* (New
York, 1971; originally published Chicago, 1931), 82–83, 161–166. The existence of
such folk traditions emphasizes what Emilio Willems discovered in his study of the
German Rhineland town of Negle: the persistence of earlier preindustrial cultural
practices within a modernized society or what sociologist Herbert J. Gans refers to as an
"urban village." See Emilio Willems, "Peasantry and City: Cultural Persistence and
Change in Historical Perspective—A European Case," *American Anthropologist*, LXXII
(1970), 528–543; and Herbert J. Gans, *The Urban Villages* (New York, 1962). Also, see
Herbert G. Gutman, *Work, Culture and Society in Industrializing America* (New York, 1976),
3–78.

workers. Singing in the family involved songs sung by mothers
to their children or while doing housework. According to one
folklorist, singing formed part of the evening's entertainment
along with prose narratives, riddles, and games. All family
members participated in these evening performances and the
singing ranged from *corridos* to children's songs.[18] In addition,
Mexican women instilled in their children faith in Mexican
Catholic beliefs and practices. Although Mexican culture in El
Paso and along the border changed over the years as Americanization modified various customs and values, Mexican housewives must nevertheless be credited with helping to keep alive
native culture, thus making it easier for Mexican immigrants to
adjust and work in the United States.[19]

While housework formed the most important work activity
for Mexican women, some in El Paso also found jobs outside the
home. El Paso, for example, had one of the earliest concentrations of Mexican female wage workers in the United States.
Mexican women, as other women, worked either to augment
the earnings of male family members or due to the loss of the
male breadwinner. As one scholar correctly observes, "work was
not a choice but a necessity."[20] A sample of 393 El Paso
households taken from the 1900 manuscript census reveals that
almost a fifth (17.11 percent) of Mexican households contained
a working woman. American women also had to enter the labor

---

[18] Américo Paredes, *A Texas-Mexican Cancionero: Folksongs of the Lower Border* (Urbana,
1976), xvii, xix—xxii; and Gamio, *Life Story*, 218.

[19] While Mexican women aided in the retention of cultural traditions within the family,
it should also be pointed out that such traditions maintained the woman in a subordinate
position within the family. For sociological, anthropological, and psychological views on
the Mexican family in the United States, see Maxine Baca Zinn, "Chicanas: Power and
Control in the Domestic Sphere," *De Colores*, II, no. 4 (1975), 19—31; Zinn, "Political
Familism: Toward Sex Role Equality in Chicano Families," *Aztlán*, VI (1976), 13—26;
Miguel Montiel, "The Social Science Myth of the Mexican American Family," *El Grito*, III
(1970), 56—63; Miguel Montiel, "The Chicano Family: A Review of Research," *Social
Work*, XVIII (March 1973), 22—31; Robert Staples, "The Mexican-American Family: Its
Modification over Time and Space," *Phylon*, XXXVII (1971), 179—192; Nathan Murillo,
"The Mexican American Family," in Carrol A. Hernández, *et al.*, eds., *Chicanos: Social and
Psychological Perspectives* (St. Louis, 1976), 15—25; Peter Uhlenberg, "Marital Instability
among Mexican Americans: Following the Patterns of Blacks?" *Social Problems*, XX
(Summer 1972), 49—56; Betty Garcia-Bahne, "La Chicana and the Chicano Family," in
Sánchez and Martínez Cruz, *La Mujer*, 30—47; and Leo Grebler, *et al.*, eds., *The Mexican-
American People* (New York, 1970), 350—377.

[20] Apodaca, "The Chicana Woman," 71.

force and the census sample indicates that 11.21 percent of American households had a female worker. Mexican women who worked, according to the census, were either unmarried daughters, mothers with no husbands, or single women. Of the 31 Spanish surnamed households in the sample with a working female, 17 had daughters or other young relatives with jobs while the remaining 14 contained working mothers with no husbands or single women. On the other hand, married Mexican women, both foreign and native born, within a nuclear or extended family, did not work. The sample revealed no instance of a woman with an employed husband having a job.[21] Age and fertility help explain this condition. In the 1900 sample, 41.08 percent of married Mexican immigrant women were between fifteen and thirty years of age, a period when women generally give birth. Moreover, 38.44 percent of married Mexican immigrant women were between thirty and forty, a period when most women had children at home. Indeed, 77.44 percent of all married Mexican immigrant women in El Paso had children twelve years of age or under or children listed as attending school; of these 39.93 percent had children five years of age and under.[22]

If age and fertility worked against Mexican women finding jobs outside the home, so too did Mexican cultural traditions. Mexican men resented women, especially wives, working or wanting to work for wages. Most males believed their work a man's duty and that woman's consisted of raising children and keeping house.[23] As one working class newspaper in Mexico during the age of Porfirio Díaz emphasized: "To be a wife is to be a woman preferably selected amongst many other women, for her honesty, for her religiousness, for her amiability, . . . for

---

[21] *Manuscript Census, 1900.*

[22] *Ibid.* Virginia Yans-McLaughlin in her study of Italian immigrant families in Buffalo also discovered a preponderance of married immigrant women of child-bearing age who did not work outside the home. See Yans-McLaughlin, *Family and Community: Italian Immigrants in Buffalo, 1880–1930* (Ithaca, 1977), 180–217. Most married women of child-bearing age in the United States in the early twentieth century did not work. Valerie Kincade Oppenheimer, *The Female Labor Force in the United States* (Berkeley, 1970), 1–63.

[23] For attitudes of Mexican men toward wage-working women, see Paul S. Taylor, "Mexican Labor in Los Angeles Industry" (unpublished manuscript, Paul S. Taylor Collection, Bancroft Library, University of California, Berkeley), part 2; and Gamio, *Life Story,* 46.

her industriousness, [and] for her docility. . . ."[24] Despite such attitudes, the Mexican family in the United States did not remain static. Over the years more Mexican women, especially daughters, became wage-workers to augment the family income. Also, as the economy expanded, especially during the "Roaring Twenties," El Paso and southwestern industries and services began to recruit more Mexican women workers. Mexican men may have more easily accepted their daughters working outside the home than their wives, but the cultural challenge and adjustment that resulted from wage-working women within the traditional male-dominated Mexican family represents a little understood and important topic for future research.[25]

The increase in Mexican female wage-workers in El Paso by 1920 can be seen in census figures for that year. The census reported that 3,474 foreign-born females, almost all Mexicans, ten years of age and older were engaged in a gainful occupation. Foreign-born female wage-workers represented half of all females ten years and over who held jobs in El Paso. Most female workers in El Paso (3,112 females or 45 percent of all employed women) did "women's work." The two largest occupations were servants (1,718) and laundresses (710)—jobs familiar to women in Mexico—where the majority of Mexican working women could be found. Due to deficiencies in skills and schooling, as well as prejudice against them, few Mexican women, unlike their American counterparts, were in such skilled professional occupations as teaching, nursing, or office work.[26] Table 2

---

[24] As quoted in Margaret Towner, "Monopoly Capitalism and Women's Work during the Porfiriato," *Latin American Perspectives*, IV (Winter–Spring 1977), 93. Like Mexican men, most males in the United States did not look with favor on women, especially married ones with children, working outside the home. Oppenheimer, *Female Labor Force*, 40–42.

[25] McLaughlin points out in her study of Italian immigrant families in Buffalo that acculturation, including women working outside the home, did not necessarily lead to a breakdown of traditional male authority in the family. See McLaughlin, "Patterns of Work and Family Organization: Buffalo's Italians," in Michael Gordon, ed., *The American Family in Social Historical Perspective* (New York, 1973), 140. A recent study suggests that increased numbers of married Mexican women are now working. See Rosemary Santana Cooney, "Changing Labor Force Participation of Mexican American Wives: A Comparison with Anglos and Blacks," *Social Science Quarterly*, LVI (1975), 252–261.

[26] U.S. Bureau of the Census, *Fourteenth Census of the United States, 1920: Population* (Washington, D.C., 1923), IV, 263; U.S. manuscript census, 1900; and Carlos B. Gill, "Mascota: A Mexican World Left Behind" (Ph.D. dissertation, University of California, Los Angeles, 1975), 127.

TABLE 2
NUMBER AND PERCENTAGE OF SPANISH-SURNAMED
DOMESTICS AND LAUNDRESSES, 1889, 1910, AND 1920

Year	Number	Percent of Total Workers (Mexican and American)
	DOMESTICS	
1889	61	49.73
1910	447	65.37
1920	1528	76.18
	LAUNDRESSES	
1889	40	34.90
1910	220	64.48
1920	516	92.17

SOURCE: El Paso city directories for 1889, 1910, and 1920. The 1890 city directory was not used because no copies for that year could be found. The discrepancy between the 1920 census figures and those of the city directory is probably the result of a more limited survey by the compilers of the city directory.

shows the number and percentage of Spanish-surnamed women listed as domestics and laundresses in the city directories of 1889, 1910, and 1920.

Victor S. Clark, a Bureau of Labor inspector, noted in 1908 that Mexican "immigrant women have so little conception of domestic arrangements in the United States that the task of training them would be too heavy for American housewives."[27] Yet domestic work proved to be the most readily available source of jobs for Mexican women. Clark correctly recognized that women from preindustrial cultures might have difficulty adjusting to the new electrical devices of middle-class American homes, although he failed to understand that the employment of Mexican maids saved southwestern housewives from having to buy the new appliances. Mexican domestics did their work by hand. Elizabeth Rae Tyson, who grew up in El Paso, remembered the extensive use of Mexican maids by American families. "Owing to the large Mexican majority," she recalled,

. . . almost every Anglo-American family had at least one, sometimes two or three servants: a maid and laundress, and perhaps a nursemaid

---

[27]Victor S. Clark, "Mexican Labor in the United States," *U.S. Bureau of Labor Bulletin No. 78* (Washington, D.C., 1908), reprinted in Carlos E. Cortés, *et al.*, eds., *Mexican Labor in the United States* (New York, 1974), 496.

or yardmen. The maid came in after breakfast and cleaned up the breakfast dishes, and very likely last night's supper dishes as well; did the routine cleaning, washing and ironing, and after the family dinner in the middle of the day, washed dishes again, and then went home to perform similar service in her own home.[28]

Mexican women, besides working as servants, found other employment opportunities. Many worked as washerwomen, either in American homes or in their own as well as in the various laundries of El Paso. In laundries, they learned such other skills as the use of sewing machines and received from $4 to $6 a week. In 1917 the El Paso Laundry, the largest in the city, employed 134 Spanish-surnamed workers out of a total of 166 employees, and Mexican women, mostly doing collar and flatwork, composed what appears to have been over half of the Mexican employees. That same year the Elite Laundry had 76 Spanish-surnamed female workers out of a total of 128 employees. Another of the larger laundries, the Acme, employed 75 Spanish-surnamed females out of 121 employees in 1917. The same pattern prevailed in the smaller laundries. For example, the Post Laundry had 33 Spanish-surnamed women in their work force of 49. While many of these laundresses lived in El Paso, some came from Cuidad Juárez. The daughter-in-law of Frank Fletcher, who owned the Acme Laundry, remembers that when she arrived in 1926, a laundry truck picked up the Mexican women at the border, took them to work, and returned

---

[28]As quoted in Mary Wilson Barton, "Methodism at Work among the Spanish-Speaking People of El Paso, Texas" (M.A. thesis, University of Texas, El Paso, 1950), 15. Some Mexican women also worked as maids in office buildings. See Pay Roll, Mills Building, Sept. 1, 1911, in H. Stevens Collection, No. 761, University of Texas, El Paso, library. The continued employment of Mexican domestics after 1920 in El Paso suggests that the use of new household technology by middle-class Americans did not lead to a total displacement of Mexicans as domestics. It appears that Mexican women, many of them commuter workers from Ciudad Juárez, learned the use of the new technology and at the same time continued to receive low wages. The 1970 census for El Paso lists 1,394 women as private household workers out of a total Spanish-language or Spanish-surname working population of 54,789 (U.S. Bureau of the Census, *Census of Population, 1970—Character of the Population*, Part 45: *Texas* [Washington, D.C., 1973], Sect. 1, p. 714). The persistence of Mexican women as domestics in El Paso and along the border goes counter to the national trend of the new household technology replacing domestics. See Ruth Schwartz Cowan, "The 'Industrial Revolution' in the Home: Household Technology and Social Change in the 20th Century," *Technology and Culture*, XVII (1976), 1–23.

them in the evening to the international bridge. The use of nonresident Mexican women limited already low wages.[29]

In addition to service jobs, some Mexican women labored as production workers, especially in El Paso's early garment factories. In 1902 Bergman's factory, which turned out shirts and overalls, reported that it had three American women and a large number of Mexican females. Yet, according to a newspaper account, Bergman concluded that he could get more and better work out of his Americans and consequently paid them $10 to $14 a week while the Mexicans received no more than $9 a week. Several years later, in 1919, the El Paso Overall Company advertised in a Spanish-language newspaper that it needed Mexican women for sewing and for general work. Mexican women likewise worked in the Kohlberg cigar factory. Although the exact nature of their work cannot be determined, 22 Mexican women out of 113 employees labored in the plant in 1917. Some women also found jobs as clerks and sales personnel in the downtown stores. An *El Paso Times* ad in 1905 read: "Wanted - 5 experienced American and Spanish salesladies." The Mexican newspaper, *El Día*, in 1919 praised Panchita Salas for her "work and charm" at the El Globo Department Store run by the Schwartz family. That same year, the White House Department Store, one of El Paso's largest, publicized in *La Patria* that it needed young women clerks in all its departments. Still other Mexicans worked as cooks or dishwashers in restaurants. In more unfortunate cases, Mexican women sold food on the streets of Chihuahuita.[30]

Finally, as in other societies, some women inhabited the saloons and gambling halls of the red-light district. The *Lone Star*, an early El Paso newspaper, in 1885 expressed shock over a twelve-year-old Mexican girl's activities. "It is rumored," the newspaper sermonized, "that she is a prostitute and most any hour of the day she can be seen in the streets with different men." When the city government enforced an ordinance in

[29]*La Patria*, Sept. 12, 1919, p. 4; *Labor Advocate*, Oct. 31, 1919, p. 4; *El Paso Herald*, June 23–24, 1917, p. 7; July 28–29, 1917, p. 16; May 26–27, 1917, p. 15; Dec. 15–16, 1917, p. 4; and telephone interview with Mrs. Frank Fletcher, Jr., El Paso, Aug. 15, 1975.
[30]*Times*, Sept. 26, 1902, p. 8; *La Patria*, Oct. 30, 1919, p. 4; *Herald*, June 9–11, 1917, p. 15; *Times*, Dec. 19, 1905, p. 7; *El Día*, Feb. 18, 1919, p. 3; *La Patria*, Oct. 30, 1919, p. 4; *Times*, Dec. 8, 1903, p. 7; and *Herald*, Aug. 1, 1916, p. 14.

1903 to move the district further from the center of El Paso, the *Times* reported that many of the prostitutes "propose to go across the river, among the number being the Mexicans, which include the dance hall girls." Two years later when Lou Vidal attempted to open his dance hall, police raided the establishment and arrested his employees, which included dance hall girls María González, Josefa González, Lola Beltran, and Senida García.[31]

Not only did employers hire Mexican women for jobs characterized as "women's work," but they paid them the lowest wages in the city. Although it appears that poor wages for Mexican women can be partly explained by their work inexperience and initial low productivity, employers nevertheless used such arguments to maintain wage differentials between Mexicans and Americans and to insure profits for themselves. As a result, persistent low wages for all Mexicans, men and women, whether for economic or racial reasons, or both, served to support job and educational discrimination against Mexicans in El Paso, which kept them in a state of restricted economic mobility and near poverty.[32]

Specific attention to the wages of Mexican women in El Paso occurred as the result of hearings held in the border city in November 1919 by the Texas Industrial Welfare Commission. During three days of testimony by employers as well as female employees, the commission discovered that Mexican workers in the laundries and factories of the city received less pay than American women in other industries. The Mexicans also obtained less than the salaries of laundry and factory workers in other Texas cities who performed similar work but did not face Mexican competition. According to the commission, these differences made it more difficult to set a minimum wage throughout the state. The reason for the problem, the commission stated, could be found in the Mexican's lower standard of living,

---

[31] *Lone Star*, Aug. 22, 1885, p. 3; *Times*, Feb. 4, 1903, p. 2; Feb. 3, 1905, p. 3. For information on El Paso's redlight district, see C. L. Sonnichsen, *Pass of the North* (El Paso, 1968), 277–304. In 1910, the city government abolished the red-light district.

[32] On occupational and educational differences between Mexicans and Americans in El Paso, see Mario T. García, "Racial Dualism in the El Paso Labor Market, 1880–1920," *Aztlán*, VI (1975), 197–218. For a recent theoretical treatment of race and class, see Mario Barrera, *Race and Class in the Southwest: A Theory of Racial Inequality* (Notre Dame, Ind., 1979).

330 PACIFIC HISTORICAL REVIEW

"and that is a condition which, it seems, cannot be remedied."
The members of the commission concluded, although without
evidence, that "the Mexican workers find it possible to 'live
comfortably' on a wage that Anglo workers would regard as
'starvation wages.' "[33]

Despite the commission's conclusions, Mexican women who
appeared before it refuted those who claimed that Mexicans did
not need higher wages because they had a lower standard of
living. One group of laundry workers who had gone on strike
for higher wages testified that the laundries had paid them $4 to
$5 a week. Manuela Hernández, who had worked for several
years at the Acme Laundry, told the commission in Spanish that
she received $11 a week. While her wages made her the highest
paid Mexican woman in the plant, American women averaged
$4 to $6 more, although it is not clear if the Americans
performed the same work. "I find it difficult to live on my
wages," Hernández commented, "which I turn in to the family
budget." She estimated that it would take $16 a week for her
family to live "comfortably." María Valles testified that she
worked at the Elite Laundry and received $4.50 a week. She
lived with her family and supported a nine-year-old daughter.
"I have to support her and myself," she stated, "but I have to
make great sacrifices, some days going without food, for lack of
means." She believed she could live well on $15 a week. Mexican
women employed in the El Paso Overall Company also testified
before the commission about their need for higher wages. The
El Paso Herald described one of these workers, Daniela Morena,
as "a woman along in years," who stated that she made $7 to $8 a
week and supported her mother and two children. She believed
that she required at least $15 a week, "but if alone might get
along with $8 or $9 a week, as she 'dressed very humbly.' "
Other garment workers gave similar testimonies. The Mexican
women's arguments, unfortunately, had little impact. Low wages
for Mexicans, both men and women, continued to characterize
the El Paso economy.[34]

---

[33]*Times*, Nov. 20, 1919, p. 5.
[34]*Ibid.*, and *Herald*, Nov. 20, 1919, p. 10. For a more thorough discussion of the Texas
Industrial Welfare Commission's hearing in El Paso, see García, "Racial Dualism,"
201–206.

In addition to their roles as housewives and wage workers, a third major activity of Mexican women in the United States was their participation in labor unions and labor strife. Though relatively few women were active in unions or labor protests, Mexican women nonetheless were involved in some of the largest and most important labor strikes in the Southwest.[35] In El Paso, the laundry strike of 1919 is illustrative of the numerous class conflicts of the post-World War I years in the United States.[36] Unlike domestics who worked alone, the Mexican laundresses labored in close physical proximity in the same plant. Consequently, a sense of community developed in the laundries that helped promote the organization of workers who demanded higher wages and union recognition. In October 1919 some of the Mexican women, together with state and local American Federation of Labor organizers, established the Laundry Workers' Union. The union then began to organize workers, almost all Mexican women, in the Acme Laundry of El Paso. When this plant refused to accept the union and fired two of the organizers, Isabel and Manuela Hernández, the rest of the almost two hundred workers went on strike demanding that the employers rehire their co-workers. "We asked for the reinstatement of the two girls . . . ," Acme employee Francisca Sáenz told a meeting of the Mexican strikers. "Isabel Hernandez," she explained, "is a marker, sorter and inspector getting $11 a week with four years experience and Manuela is getting the same wages as marker and sorter and started in six years ago." F. B. Fletcher, the president and manager of Acme, denied any knowledge of a union and claimed he had dismissed the two workers for other reasons. According to Fletcher, one of the women had been fired because "she had made talk about the laundry that was not to his liking. . . ." As for the other,

---

[35]The two most significant strikes involving Mexican women are the San Antonio Pecan strike in 1938 and the more recent Farah strike in El Paso in the early 1970s. Seedon C. Menefee and Orin C. Cassmore, *The Pecan Shellers of San Antonio: The Problem of Underpaid and Unemployed Mexican Labor* (Washington, D.C., 1940); Harold A. Shapiro, "The Workers of San Antonio, Texas, 1900–1940" (Ph.D. dissertation, University of Texas, Austin, 1952); and The San Francisco Bay Area Farah Strike Support Committee, *Chicano Strike at Farah* (San Francisco, 1974).

[36]On the numerous incidents of class strife in the United States in 1919, such as the steel strike and the Seattle general strike, see Jeremy Brecher, *Strike* (Greenwich, Conn., 1972), 133–180.

Fletcher alleged that she had been working at another laundry while insisting she had been sick and claiming pay from the Acme.[37]

When three other laundries attempted to do the work of Acme, the Mexican women at those plants joined the strike. Owners of two more laundries at first agreed to recognize the union, but then changed their minds. The women at these places also struck. In a few days somewhere between 300 and 575 workers, including some men, had gone on strike against all of El Paso's laundries. At a meeting of the Central Labor Union where representatives of the A. F. of L. addressed the laundry workers, the Mexican women unanimously agreed to stand by the union. "Truly this was a sight that would do the heart of any one good to see these girls and women," the *Labor Advocate*, the A. F. of L. organ in El Paso, reported. "[S]ome of them hardly in their teens and some of them bent with age, standing up and solemnly promising that no matter what may come or what may happen, they would stand together for the mutual good of their fellow workers."[38]

Besides the workers' own solidarity, the A. F. of L.'s support proved important in maintaining the strike. The Central Labor Union not only endorsed the action, but various locals raised funds for the women strikers. The *Herald* reported shortly after the work stoppage that the machinists of both the El Paso & Southwestern Railroad and the Galveston, Houston & San Antonio Railroad had gathered $400 for the laundry union in addition to $100 donated by the carpenter's local. Other unions which contributed included those representing plumbers, iron-workers, bricklayers, electrical workers, sheetmetal workers, freight handlers, musicians, plasterers, painters, and taxi drivers. The Central Labor Union also organized a committee headed by William J. Moran, the *Advocate*'s editor, to negotiate a settlement with the laundries. The A. F. of L.'s willingness to organize and assist the Mexicans, however, did not represent a departure from Samuel Gompers' policy of excluding alien

[37] *Advocate*, Oct. 24, 1919, p. 1 and Oct. 31, 1919, p. 1; *Herald*, Oct. 27, 1919, p. 4; and *Times*, Oct. 28, 1919, p. 3.
[38] *Advocate*, Oct. 24, 1919, p. 1 and Oct. 31, 1919, p. 1; *Herald*, Oct. 30, 1919, p. 4; *Times*, Oct. 31, 1919, p. 8; and *La Patria*, Oct. 31, 1919, p. 8.

workers. "The strike of the Laundry Workers in our area is somewhat unique," the *Advocate* editorialized, "for often we have taken it for granted that these workers were practically all Mexicans, hence we gave but little concern, but this is not the case. True it is, that they are nearly all of Mexican origin but they are by no means all of Mexican citizenship. The large majority are residents of El Paso and citizens of the nation, but nevertheless, let us look at the facts that are fundamentally the cause of this strike." Besides the nonrecognition of the union by the laundries and the dismissal of the women organizers, the strike concerned the low wages paid to the workers. These ranged from $4 to $6 a week. In comparison, laundry workers in Fort Worth, Dallas, Galveston, Houston, and San Antonio averaged $14 a week. "[T]here is no question," the *Advocate* stated, "but that the treatment of the laundry workers of El Paso has been disgraceful and disgrace rests upon the laundry owners."[39]

The laundry workers obtained further assistance from various Mexican social organizations in El Paso, composed of both Mexican Americans and Mexican nationals. *La Patria*, the city's major Spanish-language newspaper, expressed its support of the Mexican women and called upon other Mexican groups to do likewise. Although it did not usually favor strikes, believing them to be counterproductive as well as the work of radicals and agitators, *La Patria* believed the laundry workers' struggle was a just one: "[I]f our congenial women compatriots deserve praise," *La Patria* emphasized, "so too does the Central Labor Union and other American unions who have provided unselfish assistance as well as moral support." A delegation of twelve women and four men from the laundry union also received the endorsement of the influential mutual society, the Círculo de Amigos, which had been organized by Mexican American city employees. In a letter to all Mexican societies, Círculo officials expressed their support of the strikers "who are giving an example of character, strength and racial solidarity." Believing it important not to abandon the women in their hour of need, the Círculo called on

---

[39]*Herald*, Oct. 30, 1919, p. 4; *Advocate*, Oct. 27, 1919, p. 4; *Times*, Oct. 28, 1919, p. 1; *Herald*, Oct. 27, 1919, p. 4; *Times*, Oct. 28, 1919, p. 1; *Advocate*, Oct. 24, 1919, p. 1 and Oct. 31, 1919, p. 1.

all other Mexican organizations and the Mexican community to attend an informational meeting on how best to "help our sisters." To raise funds for the workers, the Círculo sponsored a dance.[40]

Hearing of the laundry strike, some Mexican workers outside El Paso voiced their support. José L. Payen of Local No. 84 of the International Union of Mine, Mill, and Smelter Workers of Metcalf, Arizona, stressed at an El Paso strike rally the need for unionization and justice for workers. Payen, however, put forth a class ideology which went beyond the more limited union consciousness of the Mexican women and the Central Labor Union:

Comrades in arms, we, who through our labor turn our sweat into gold, should be united, especially in these times when it appears the world is going to encounter a terrible catastrophe. We should be united to demonstrate to the capitalists that our religion is our Union and our weapon is the strike and our sights a brilliant future created through the honorable medium of our labor, and if anyone dares to destroy our sacred ideals, then they will pay the price, and we will be satisfied that we have done our sacred duty.[41]

Despite organized labor's support and that of the Mexican societies, the laundry workers faced considerable opposition. El Paso newspapers, with the exception of the *Labor Advocate* and *La Patria*, carried reports favorable to the laundry owners. A *Herald* reporter, after a visit to the Acme Laundry, noted that the entire plant appeared to be clean and well-ventilated. Besides sanitary toilets and cooking facilities, the *Herald* writer informed his readers that he had found "a Victrola in the upstairs main room where Mr. Fletcher says the girls have dances each noon." Interviewed by the *Herald*, Fletcher denied that the average wage given laundry workers amounted to $5.50 a week. Acme, according to Fletcher, paid an average of $9 a week for a nine-hour day and a fifty-four-hour week. Fletcher, however, neglected to tell the reporter what he would testify before the Texas Welfare Commission less than a month later: that the $9 average resulted from paying Mexican workers an

---

[40] *La Patria*, Nov. 1, 1919, pp. 3–4; Nov. 3, 1919, p. 2; and Nov. 11, 1919, p. 3.
[41] *Ibid.*, Nov. 11, 1919, p. 2.

average of $6 per week and American workers $16.55 a week. Although the *Herald* believed that workers, especially foreigners, needed to be awarded "fair pay for a fair day's work," it also agreed with New Mexico Governor O. A. Larrazolo, who warned that "reckless agitators [from] within were foes more dangerous to the United States than any foes without."[42] The *Herald* did not specifically link the Mexican women with radicalism, but the newspaper's concern with class agitation could not help but influence public opinion against the Mexicans.

To emphasize growing class conflict not only in the United States but also along the U.S.-Mexican border, both the *Herald* and the *Times* carried reports during the strike that literature printed by the Industrial Workers of the World had been seized by El Paso border officials. Some of the literature, claimed the newspapers, had been printed in Spanish and had been distributed to Mexican workers in the United States. The newspapers observed that the "Wobblie" pamphlets advocated nationalization of all industries and land in Mexico, free love, and the overthrow of existing governments. While no evidence exists of I.W.W. influence in the laundry strike nor among El Paso workers, the *Herald* nevertheless warned citizens:

That the I.W.W. has advance guard going about the country blazing the trail for the main body and the city of El Paso has already been so blazed is the interpretation placed by some to the presence on the wall of a men's rest room in El Paso of the following lines of mystery:

W
J T N G E T N G No. 2
I WW
TEX[43]

While hurt by unfavorable newspaper publicity, the laundry workers' main problem concerned the owners' ability to hire strikebreakers as well as retain some of their employees. F. Ravel, proprietor of the Excelsior Laundry, refused to sign a union contract because his operation had not been seriously hampered by the strike. "Some of my Mexicans quit," he told a

---

[42]*Herald*, Oct. 31, 1919, p. 3; Nov. 20, 1919, p. 10; and Oct. 30, 1919, p. 6.
[43]*Ibid.*, Nov. 17, 1919, p. 1; and *Times*, Nov. 18, 1919, p. 13.

reporter, "and I put Americans in their places. In a few weeks every workman in my shop will be American." Ravel contended that American labor proved to be more productive and efficient than Mexican. Besides hiring unemployed Americans, the laundries also found it easy to hire numerous Mexican workers both in El Paso and Cuidad Juárez. The *Advocate* pointed out that even though 486 women and men had gone on strike, hundreds of other Mexicans were asking for work in the laundries. How many of these were citizens and how many were not is impossible to determine. Frustrated, the strikers verbally attacked their replacements by calling them "scabs" and labor leaders demanded that the city government stop the laundries from employing other workers. The city attorney, however, ruled that no municipal ordinance prohibited employers from hiring whom they pleased.[44] Unfortunately for organized labor and the Mexican women, the A.F. of L.'s own refusal to organize or support Mexican alien workers only added to the availability of Mexican strikebreakers.

To compound their problems, the laundry workers failed to maintain the laundry drivers' support, despite an initial endorsement by the Laundry Drivers' Union. "As the first blow in a fight against Bolshevism," the *Herald* noted, "the American Legion endorsed Friday the action of the ten drivers for the Acme Laundry who withdrew from their union and stood by their employers." Unlike the laundry workers, all of the truck drivers were Anglo-Americans. The Mexican women received an additional setback when an ad appeared in the *Herald* signed by thirty-four workers, including twenty-seven Mexicans, who had remained on the job at the El Paso Laundry. Addressed "To the Public," the notice stated that the undersigned "old employees" of the laundry "have at all times been treated in a most considerate manner, and our welfare has never been neglected; . . . we are not in sympathy with the laundry workers' unfair strike and positively will not support it."[45]

El Paso's laundry strike continued until the end of 1919, but it had been lost almost from the start. The existence of a large

---

[44]*Advocate*, Dec. 19, 1919, p. 1; *La Patria*, Nov. 1, 1919, pp. 1 and 4; and *Herald*, Oct. 31, 1919, p. 5.
[45]*Times*, Oct. 31, 1919, p. 8; *Herald*, Oct. 31, 1919, p. 3; and Nov. 4, 1919, p. 8.

pool of surplus Mexican labor both in El Paso and across the border proved to be the decisive factor. Although no doubt irritated by the strike, and by the fear of class disturbances in the city, laundry owners simply hired other workers, both Mexican and American. Hampered by El Paso's large number of Mexican aliens, plus its refusal to organize or support them, the A.F. of L. assisted as best as possible the laundry workers, but could not overcome organized labor's liabilities along the border. As for the Mexican women who went on strike, it appears most never regained their jobs. Their struggle, however, represents one of the earliest displays of union consciousness and ethnic solidarity among Mexican female workers in the United States. The fact that many of the women apparently were Mexican Americans rather than Mexican nationals must also be seen as a major factor in the laundry workers' ability to organize. More permanent, knowledgeable, and secure in their rights as American citizens, unionization of Mexican American workers symbolized a process of acculturation to an industrial and urban culture.[46] Hence, the laundry strike of 1919 stands as an example of Mexican women workers in the United States actively resisting class exploitation and in the process forging their own history.

This case study of Mexican women in El Paso between 1880 and 1920 has attempted to demonstrate some of the major research themes on women that might be pursued in Chicano history. The general topics of Mexican women as housewives, as wage workers, and as participants in unionization and labor strife constitute the most important activities that have affected Mexican women in the United States. An investigation of them by historians of the Chicano experience will contribute not only to an understanding of the history of Mexican American women, but to the history of all Mexicans north of the border. The history of Chicanos, especially Chicano workers, is only half complete without an appreciation of the contributions Mexican women have made. As one Mexican American woman has concluded: "History is filled with the activities of the Chicana."[47]

---

[46] For a treatment of industrialization's impact on early women factory workers, see E. P. Thompson, *The Making of the English Working Class* (New York, 1963), 413–417.

[47] Apodaca, "The Chicana Woman," 88.

Puertorriquenas In The United States

THE IMPACT OF DOUBLE DISCRIMINATION

By Lourdes Miranda King

The Puerto Rican woman is too often pictured as a passive female, bending first to the will of her father, then of her husband—an obscure figure shuffling to the needs of her children and the men in her family.

This image has become an excuse to justify excluding her from full participation in the life of the United States. It reinforces the Anglo American stereotype of the Latin woman as childlike, pampered, and irresponsible.

The view supports the notion that Puerto Rican women deserve their subordinate status. After all, are not many of them employed in service occupations and as unskilled labor? That must mean they are suited only for demeaning work and is proof enough that they belong in that category. If one adds the prevalent assumption that Puerto Rican women are all alike, the stereotype is complete.

In many ways, the image of the Puerto Rican woman is similar to that of Puerto Rican men. That

Lourdes Miranda King is a former professor of Spanish literature, and a founder of the National Conference of Puerto Rican Women.

© Lourdes Miranda King 1974

20

103

image is embellished by the perception of Latin men as indolent skirtchasers, in addition to being irresponsible and undependable. They, too, are at the bottom of the occupational ladder—which serves, in turn, to justify their exclusion and discrimination.

The adoption of the terms *macho* and *machismo* from Spanish to describe the supreme male chauvinist reflects the Latin male stereotype. Is it a coincidence that earlier the English borrowed *Don Juan,* the stereotype of the great lover?

Surely, other cultures have created words and literary figures to portray the traits of lovers, "banty-roosters," and authoritative males. If such spontaneous labels faithfully reflect life, as has been pointed out, then the selection of words from one culture for the popular language of another must reflect deep-rooted value judgments and cultural assumptions.

Official statistics show the disastrous results brought about by false assumptions. The overall situation of Puerto Ricans in the United States attests to the low esteem in which they are held. By any standards, Puerto Ricans are a severely deprived ethnic group.

A Profile

In 1972, Puerto Ricans had lower median incomes ($6,210 for a family of four), higher unemployment rates (9.6 percent in New York), and lower educational attainment (8 median years of schooling) than any other group in the United States, including blacks. Puerto Rican men are concentrated in the lower paying occupations, such as operatives, laborers, and service workers. Of all Puerto Rican families, 27.9 percent have incomes below $5,000; 12 percent have incomes below $2,000.

As did others before them, Puerto Ricans came to the mainland United States in search of work and improved economic opportunities. They arrived by plane in massive numbers during the late 1940s, mostly as unskilled workers entering a specialized economy.

Unlike previous immigrants, however, Puerto Ricans are American citizens. They all retained a nostalgic hope of returning to Puerto Rico—a new type of non-European immigrant.

On arrival, Puerto Ricans encountered numerous problems—their scanty knowledge of English, differences in customs, experience in a racially mixed society which ill prepared them for confronting racial inequities. All these factors conspired to sour the "American dream."

Today, even such fundamental facts as our numbers within the population are unclear. The 1.4 million count of the 1970 Census understates the true total, especially in New York. There, 200,000 Puerto Ricans remained uncounted, according to the Center for Social Research of the City University of New York.

Although approximately 60 percent of the Puerto Rican population in the United States is concentrated in New York City, that is not the only place where Puerto Ricans live. Substantial numbers are dispersed throughout the country—in New Jersey, Pennsylvania, Connecticut, Florida, Massachusetts, Illinois, Ohio, Indiana, Wisconsin, and as far west as California and Hawaii.

It is within this context that one must view the status of the Puerto Rican woman in the United States. Her situation is intertwined with that of the Puerto Rican male in American society. Both question their sense of worth, both feel the impact of discrimination as members of a minority. As a young woman told me, "Our men don't have equal rights or equal pay. We are all fighting for the same thing; both male and female are oppressed."

How Puerto Rican men are treated when they try to enter the so-called "mainstream of society" greatly influences Puerto Rican women. If, as has been the case, the Puerto Rican man is defeated or does not fare well, the woman bears the brunt of this treatment.

The Puerto Rican Woman

The Puerto Rican woman becomes a part of the cycle of failure. She drops out of school at an early age or enters the labor force at the lowest level, in the hope that her earnings will help lift her family out of poverty. Or her family unit may disintegrate through separation or divorce, leaving her the sole provider and head of household.

The Puerto Rican woman in the United States fits the historical pattern of the immigrant woman who worked alongside her man, sharing the burden of work and responsibilities. Unlike any other woman who has preceded her, however, she is a member of a group in continuous flux, moving between the United States and Puerto Rico for varying lengths of time throughout her life.

Studies have shown that women predominate among the return

22

migrants to Puerto Rico. Some are single young women who have lost their jobs; others are older women whose children have left home. A still larger group is composed of women who have returned after a marital break-up.

It is not unusual to find women working in the United States whose children are cared for by grandmothers or other relatives in Puerto Rico, or to find wives and children living in Puerto Rico while their husbands find work in the mainland, or to find working wives in Puerto Rico "pioneering the resettlement" of husband and children—different patterns, yet with the same divisive effect on families. The woman is thrust into the role of sole supporter, creating the new immigrant woman and incidentally destroying the myth of the passive female.

As has been the case in other minority groups, the woman frequently has had more access to the larger Anglo-American society than has the Puerto Rican man. I have often heard, "When we came to the United States, my mother was able to get a job first while my father was still looking."

For many reasons, Puerto Rican women found employment more readily. Sexist attitudes permitted hiring a woman for a lower wage than a Puerto Rican man. Either they were seen as less of a threat in the white male hierarchy, or the available opportunities were so-called "women's jobs"—that is, unskilled.

In many communities with a concentration of Puerto Ricans, the pattern of employment was reversed and women had a lower unemployment rate. As late as 1969, according to the study, *Poverty Area Profiles: The New York*

Puerto Rican: "Whereas normally the jobless rate for women is higher than for men, among Puerto Rican workers the pattern was reversed. Adult men 25-54 had a rate of nearly 8 percent, compared with less than 4 percent for women in this age group."

The Census Bureau attempted to explain this difference:

Puerto Rican men in their prime, no matter what their employment status, are as firmly attached to the labor force as men in their prime generally, while Puerto Rican women tend more readily than women generally to withdraw from the labor force upon being laid off, or to re-enter it only when recalled or when accepting a new job. The short average duration of unemployment among these women in part reflects these unusual patterns of labor force entry and exit, and makes for low jobless rates.

Later data and trends belie this simplistic and confusing explanation. The low rate of unemployment is more likely caused by "dropping out" of a labor force which does not offer useful work —considering women's supreme difficulties in finding a job and their childbearing and child rearing functions. The harm was done, however, and a generation of Puerto Ricans were led to believe that Puerto Rican women were better off than their men.

The Myth of Success

In spite of a current 10 percent unemployment rate for Puerto Rican women in New York (the highest unemployment of any group in that city) and the decrease during the past decade in

the level of Puerto Rican female participation in the job market from 38 to 28 percent (which runs against the national trend), the myth of female success was firmly entrenched among the Puerto Rican communities on the mainland. The belief prevailed that any attempt at upgrading the status of Puerto Rican women would of necessity take jobs away from the men, downgrading the Puerto Rican man and the Puerto Rican family.

As one woman told me, "We have so many bread and butter issues and such few human resources that we have to establish priorities and my main interest is toward Puerto Rican issues, regardless of sex." She added, however, "as long as the women's movement is fighting for those things which we as a minority group are fighting for—such as equal rights, the end to poverty, and expansion of child care centers —we are with them."

The aversion toward focusing on the status of the Puerto Rican woman has been detrimental to both males and females. It blatantly ignores the economic facts. The Women's Bureau of the U.S. Department of Labor has found that: "There were 19.2 million married women (husband present) in the labor force in March 1972; the number of unemployed men was 3.1 million. If all the married women stayed home and unemployed men were placed in their jobs, there would be 16.1 million unfilled jobs."

History has shown that gains in income by the productivity of a new group do not come at the expense of existing groups.

Many of the Puerto Rican community leaders who have swal-

23

lowed the myth of female success are women. They have been made to feel guilty about their leadership role in relation to Puerto Rican men, even though more than half of the Puerto Rican population is composed of women. I was horrified—and mortified—when a prominent Puerto Rican woman leader was telling me about her tribulations in locating a young male to serve as president of a Puerto Rican youth leadership group.

"The most promising candidate, and the one most likely to be elected, was a young woman," she said. "I quickly had to come up with a boy to back for president ... There are just too many women leaders in the Puerto Rican community already." Although clearly not the most qualified, the boy was elected president.

The Puerto Rican woman in the United States then is caught between two forces. On the one hand, she is entrapped within the bleak economic and political powerlessness affecting the Puerto Rican population in general. On the other hand, she suffers from the socialization of sex roles which causes her to have guilt feelings about the fulfillment of her potential and its expression in a society which looks down its aquiline Anglo nose at her and her people. Above it all, the statistics verify that her situation is worse than even she might be willing to admit.

Some Comparisons

The Puerto Rican woman in the mainland United States feels the impact of double discrimination as a woman and as a Puerto Rican —often as a woman, a black, and a Puerto Rican. The Puerto Rican man has a median income of

$5,613 a year; the Puerto Rican woman earns $2,784 a year. Of all Puerto Rican males, 12 percent have incomes below $2,000, compared to 34 percent of all Puerto Rican women. The men complete 9.3 years of school, while women finish 8.8 years.

Unemployment among Puerto Rican women is a whopping 17.8 percent—the highest rate among any Spanish origin group, and almost three times higher than the national average. The Puerto Rican male unemployment rate, although high, is 8.8 percent.

The Puerto Rican woman is often prevented from working by the number of small children in the family who need her care and attention, for the Puerto Rican population in the mainland United States is extremely young. The median age is 18 years. Of all Puerto Rican families, 76 percent have children under 18, and of all Puerto Ricans living in this country, 28.7 percent are under 10 years old.

This situation is further aggravated by the greater family responsibilities and income needs of larger families. Over half of these families have more than five members in the family.

Lack of child care facilities specifically geared to the language and cultural needs of the Puerto Rican child (bilingual child care centers, since Spanish is the language spoken in 73 percent of Puerto Rican homes) often force the mother either to stay at home, or to ship her children off to a willing relative in Puerto Rico.

If she does brave that obstacle, she starts her day earlier than the average worker in order to dress and feed her children before taking them to be cared for in someone's

home. In any case, knowing that her children are being raised by another person often a thousand miles away under less than adequate conditions, or that they are roaming the streets alone after school, becomes a source of further worry and stress.

For 105,000 Puerto Rican families in the United States, female employment and earnings are vital. Those families (29 percent of the total number of Puerto Rican families) are headed by Puerto Rican women. Yet official figures show that only 12.7 percent of those Puerto Rican women were able to work full-time all year, compared to 80.3 percent of white and 73.5 percent of black female heads of households who worked at full-time jobs. Only 23.6 percent of such Puerto Rican women worked part of the year.

We all know that a part-time job is not enough to support a family above the poverty level. Should it astound us, then, to find that a shocking 65 percent of the Puerto Rican families headed by women were living in poverty in 1971? This is much higher than the 27 percent of all white female-headed families and 54 percent of all black female-headed families living at the poverty level.

Among the migrants returning to Puerto Rico, more than one-fifth were women heads of households. Jose Hernandez, in *Return Migration to Puerto Rico*, found that 42.8 percent of the female heads of household were married women whose spouses were absent. He concludes: "It is clear that this category contained many survivors of family breakage at the 'launching stage' . . . ."

When she is able to work, the Puerto Rican woman faces serious disadvantages. She lacks sufficient education and training to command a decent salary, thus compounding her housing, health, and overall problems further. Lack of full command of English is yet another obstacle.

And always present are the subtle pressures of finding her values as a Puerto Rican threatened and misunderstood. Since her livelihood depends on it, she has to prove herself constantly—among men and women—in the larger society, straining to conform.

I am always saddened when I see Puerto Rican women with hair dyed flaming red or yellow. Is it not the ideal of beauty to be a long-limbed, slim-hipped blonde? As the Anglo woman chases a male-determined standard of beauty, the Puerto Rican woman pursues that same standard established by cultures other than her own. She can't stretch herself, but she can always color her hair.

Women in Puerto Rico

Any discussion of the Puerto Ricans in the United States would be incomplete if it did not cover their place of origin, the island of Puerto Rico.

The situation in Puerto Rico helps to debunk further the stereotype of a passive Puerto Rican woman. The woman in Puerto Rico, despite the discrimination which persists against the woman employed outside the home, has played an unusually important role, especially in public and academic life. Even before gaining the right to vote in 1932, she has been active and outspoken—from the courageous Indian Cacica Yuisa in 1514, to Mariana Bracetti (Brazo de Oro), who embroidered the standard of the Grito de Lares

proclaiming the 24-hour Puerto Rican republic in 1868, on down throughout Puerto Rican history.

A complete list would be too long, but some must be included: Lola Rodríguez de Tio, patriot, poet, and revolutionary author of Puerto Rico's anthem, La Borinqueña; Ana Roque de Duprey, journalist, ardent feminist, and founder of the first feminist organization in the island; Trinidad Padilla de Sanz (La Hija del Caribe), writer, and Isabel Andreu de Aguilar, professor, suffragette, and author of the first memorandum addressed to the Puerto Rican Legislature demanding women's right to vote.

Others are María Cadilla de Martínez, educator, painter, and historian; María Martínez de Péres Almirioty, elected to the Puerto Rican Senate in 1936; and —also in the political arena— Felisa Rincón de Gautier, for 23 years mayor of San Juan and president in 1954 of the Inter-American Congress of Municipalities.

However impressive these women are, it would be less than fair to cite them as the only examples of the strength, dignity, and sense of justice which have characterized the Puerto Rican woman throughout our history. Nameless, yet very much in my mind, are the thousands of women who in their daily struggle have been the main source of strength and the stabilizing force within Puerto Rican culture. It is because of my strong faith in the Puerto Rican woman that I see her as the vehicle by which men and women will reach equality and fulfillment.

New Trends

As the economy of Puerto Rico becomes more industrialized, a new

social base is being created—the urban working class. With the emergence of this class, the role of the woman is being redefined. Increasingly, the authority of the father and the husband is being questioned. The dogma of male authority and the culturally defined role of the wife as subordinate to the husband is giving way to the emancipation of the Puerto Rican woman, especially as she becomes more economically independent of man.

Between 1962 and 1971, for instance, the rate of women's participation in the labor force rose from 22 to 27.1 percent. This trend is comparable to that in the mainland United States. In 1970, Puerto Rico had 253,000 working women—30.1 percent of the total labor force. That same year on the mainland 34 percent of the labor force was composed of women.

To understand the roles of women in Puerto Rican society, we should keep in mind the uncertainties which the political situation in the island has created for both its men and women. For over 400 years Puerto Rico has suffered the rigors of colonization. This is a reality which many Puerto Ricans still have to face in order to understand the complex relationships which have influenced our character, and to a great extent, determined our conduct. The migration experience and the patterns it molded, as well as the economic situation which propelled that migration, are cases in point.

The Pill

A devastating example of particular importance to women is the vast testing of experimental drugs carried out in Puerto Rico by American drug firms. Only now

26

are the facts beginning to emerge concerning a 1957 experimental study of the birth control pill on 338 Puerto Rican women. In this field study, five Puerto Rican research subjects died; they were not attended by physicians, nor autopsied.

As Dr. Edmond Kassouf stated before the Subcommittee on Monopoly of the Senate Select Committee on Small Business, "Five such deaths in a research series of 350 is high. All five deaths are, in fact, reasonable suspects for a pill link." The Food and Drug Administration had no record of the deaths. The drug company did not report them and declared the drug safe, restricting death risk data to the continental United States.

The Puerto Rican study was the basis for approval of the new drug application for the birth control pill. A hoax was perpetrated on thousands of unsuspecting women, not to mention the Puerto Rican women of the initial research studies. Aware of this situation, certain segments of the population in Puerto Rico have become suspicious of any official attempts at population control, fearful of "genocide" of the Puerto Rican population.

On the other hand, studies have shown that Puerto Ricans do not adhere to the anti-birth control beliefs and practices which characterize many Latin countries. For years female sterilization, or "la peración," has been the most known, available, and widely used method of limiting the size of a family. Sterilization is part of the overall health program of the Puerto Rican government and is encouraged by physicians throughout the island. As is the case elsewhere, the woman thus bears the responsibility for family control.

The subject of abortion has received great attention recently. Before many States in the mainland United States had legalized abortion, Puerto Rico was a mecca to well-off American women, who flocked to have surgical abortions performed in private clinics. Wealthy Puerto Rican women also underwent abortions at will. However, their poorer sisters died by the hundreds and continue to do so, as a result of self-induced abortions. Some employ the crudest of instruments; others impair their health and that of their unborn child by drinking concoctions or taking any number of pills. The power of the purse still determines what should be an individual decision.

The Women's Movement

The Puerto Rican woman, both in Puerto Rico and in the United States, must examine the issues surrounding the women's movement. Today, the participation of Puerto Rican women in the women's movement in the United States has been limited to a small core of middle class professional women and, to a lesser degree, working class women who have always had to struggle for survival. Others active in the movement have been completely "assimilated" into the American middle class structure, sometimes rejecting that which is unique about our culture. However, a small group of Puerto Rican women with clearly defined priorities have chosen to work through the women's movement as part and parcel of the advancement of all Puerto Ricans.

Unfortunately, the women's rights movement has barely started to reach the ordinary middle class woman who, through the "success" of some man, has vicariously achieved "success" as defined by our society, and has built her life around her family, her house, and the incessant acquisition of material goods—never realizing that she is but a man away from poverty.

For all Puerto Rican women, the movement must concentrate on education concerning the issues involved and the true distinction between the women's rights movement and the negative image of "women's liberation" created by the media. Although we have been mistakenly led to believe that radical feminists advocate doing so, Puerto Rican women are not going to divorce themselves from their cultural heritage or be alienated from their men.

The Puerto Rican woman's views on the qualities of womanhood, her strong family ties, and her respect for the family as an institution will accept a movement which asserts, but not one which divides. If the movement appeals to the basic issue of human rights for both men and women, to the values inherent in the freedom of men and women from sexism in their relationships, to the fact that a woman with freedom of choice also frees the man to decide what he wants to do with his life—if it appeals to the real issues involved and not the image—then Puerto Rican women will support it.

It has been basic misunderstanding of the movement as anti-male, anti-family, and somehow sexually promiscuous which has made it difficult for more Puerto Rican women—as well as Anglo American women, I might add—to embrace the cause of feminism.

27

LABOR MARKET STRATIFICATION: THE CHICANA EXPERIENCE*

By Denise Segura

Analyzing the experience of Chicanas,[1] or women of Mexican descent in the United States, is a difficult and often cumbersome task. Although the fastest-growing population group in the country is of Mexican origin, the scarcity of critical social science literature on Chicanas seems to belittle this fact. Within sociological analyses, the Chicana experience is rarely of central concern and usually is subsumed under the "larger" race or class question. Similarly, feminist scholarly work approaches the study of Chicanas and other women of color as secondary to the universal condition of gender oppression.

This paper seeks to join a feminist analysis of gender to labor sociology within the context of the distinct labor market experiences of Chicanas in the United States. A central tenet of this paper is that Chicanas suffer from the "triple oppression" of race, gender and class that is unique to them as women of color. The manner in which this triple oppression manifests itself varies according to the specific social arena. But whether it is within the family, the school, or the labor market, the interplay between the stratification axes of race, class and gender must be analyzed.

The first part of this paper will focus on the labor market to illustrate one outcome of the tripartite stratification of Chicanas. Focusing on the past decade (1970-1980), I shall undertake a four way comparison between white males and females and Mexican (and Spanish origin) men and women. The jobs Chicanas have held will be examined and compared to those of white women in order to isolate possible racial stratification mechanisms. At the same time, the occupations in which Chicanas have been employed will be compared to those of men to view stratification by gender in the labor market. To locate the dynamic of class, I shall examine such variables as family and personal income, education and occupations. It will be demonstrated that these socio-economic variables interact negatively for Chicanas, resulting in their lower class position relative to the white

*Special thanks to Tomás Almaguer, Lupe Friaz, Karla Hackstaff, Arlie Hochschild, Don Mar and Jennifer Pierce for their helpful comments on earlier drafts of this paper.

population.

In an attempt to account for the occupational segregation of Chicanas, the second half of this paper will examine the process of stratification itself within the tradition of labor market segmentation theory. The failure of this approach, as well as others, to adequately address the dynamic of race and gender will be critically evaluated. Finally, I will discuss future directions for research on Chicana labor in our society.

Chicanas: A Demographic Profile

An essential first step in an analysis of Chicana labor is the compilation of a demographic profile of the population.[2] Armed with this knowledge, an examination of various explanations for the persistent poverty and low occupational status of Chicanas in this country can be attempted.

In 1980, 14.06 million persons of Spanish origin were counted by the U.S. Census Bureau.[3] In California, 3.6 million Hispanic residents were identified, or 19.2 percent of the total state population.[4]

The past decade has witnessed significant growth in the labor force participation of all women, including Chicanas (Appendix A). In 1970, 39.4 percent of all Chicanas over the age of sixteen, worked for wages in California as compared to 41.7 percent of all white women.[5] White males and Chicanos had labor force participation rates of 78.0 and 79.0 percent, respectively.[6]

In 1980, these figures climbed significantly, with California Chicana labor force participation rising to 51.3 percent—a percentage slightly smaller than the 51.7 percent of white women.[7] It should be noted that the 1970 and 1980 census figures are not strictly comparable due to different enumerating procedures and more extensive self-identification categorizations in 1980. Nevertheless, the figures can provide us with indications of labor market trends for both populations.[8]

The above information is an important first step in becoming acquainted with Chicana activity in the paid work force. It would seem that the differences between Chicanas and white females working in California have lessened in a 10-year period to a relatively insignificant four-tenths of one percent.

The narrow employment gap between Chicanas and white women in California is probably due to the fact that the large number of labor intensive businesses (especially agriculture, electronics, and apparel factories) located in California require a greater supply of semi- and unskilled labor than in other states. This regional variation is important to consider in terms of labor demand and Chicana employment (Briggs, Fogel and Schmidt, 1977; Kane, 1973; Fogel,

1968; Cornelius, 1982). It could be hypothesized that the greater employment of Chicanas is related to the strength of the California economy. The implication of this hypothesis is that the scope and range of Chicana employment is not so much the reflection of individual choice, but rather is strongly related to regional demand.

Income and Occupations

Our next task is to examine the income and occupational profiles of Chicanas in comparison to Chicanos, white women and white men. This four way comparison is necessary to demonstrate the importance of the interplay between the structural variables of race, gender and class. In addition, this type of comparison will reveal certain implications for the feminist movement and the Chicano movement as both women and Chicanos struggle for social and economic parity with white males.

Table 1. Median Family Income in
Current Dollars for Selected Years in the U.S.

	1969	1974	1979
White			
All Families	$9,794	$13,408	$20,502
Married Couples	10,241	14,183	21,824
Single Female Head	5,500	7,405	11,452
Spanish Origin			
All Families	$7,348	$9,540	$14,569
Married Couples	n.a.	10,803	16,839
Single Female Head	3,654	4,854	6,639

Source: U.S. Bureau of the Census, *Current Population Reports*, Series P-20, No. 363, "Population Profile of the United States: 1980," Washington, D.C.: USGPO, 1981.

It is readily apparent that the family income of Spanish-origin families, 60 percent of whom are Chicano, is significantly smaller than that of the majority population (see Table 1). In addition, 25.7 percent of all Chicano families lived below the official poverty level in 1980, compared to 10.2 percent of white families. The smaller income of Chicano families has important consequences for education and future labor market options as we shall examine later.

Diversity within the Chicano population is not reflected in the occupational profile of this group. Nationally, Chicanas are concentrated in the low-paying clerical, operative and service occupations (Appendix B). This same pattern is true in California (see Table 2A). Of primary concern is the fact that little movement appears to have occurred within the last decade with respect to the types of jobs Chicanas have held.

During the 1970's, Chicana labor force participation was consistently high in the service sector in California. At the same time, Chicanas registered a small 3.8 percent decline in blue collar employment with a correspondingly small rise in white collar jobs. Although Chicana employment in the operative levels declined by one-third, they continued to be over-represented in these low-paying, largely seasonal and unstable job categories.[9] Chicano males are also concentrated in these jobs. Neither white males nor females are frequently employed within the operative category.

The vulnerability of women working as operatives is well-described by Cristina Ramirez, an ILGWU (International Ladies Garment Workers Union) organizer:

> When I went to work, the guy that used to give the work out, he
> used to tell me that if I was good to him he would give me the
> best work. Like if I'd go out with him and stuff like that.[10]

Chicanas and other operative workers are subject to work assignments and dismissal based on subjective criteria that make this type of work rank among the least desirable occupations in the labor force.

In light of the marginal pay and working conditions of many operative jobs, it is significant that there are 66 percent more Chicanos in this occupational category than either white males or females. Recent literature suggests that this type of employment is becoming less acceptable to native-born Chicanos (Maram, 1980; Baca and Bryan, 1980). Thus, employers have come to rely increasingly on Mexican immigrant labor to meet their need for cheap, seasonal labor (Cornelius et al., 1982; Sassen-Koob, 1980).

An examination of the occupational distribution of white women reveals that nationally 66 percent are concentrated within white collar employment (Appendix B). In California 75 percent of all white women holding paying jobs are concentrated in the white collar sector (see Table 2A). The gain in white collar employment has been much more modest for Chicanas (four percent). Particularly notable is the 50 percent increase in participation of both white women and Chicanas at the executive and managerial levels. In terms of percentages, white women are twice as likely as Chicanas to be employed in this relatively high paying occupational category. This suggests that the racial barriers among women have not been broken down by time and affirmative action. This social tendency becomes even more apparent when we find that Chicano males have shown even less progress in gaining access to managerial white collar occupations than Chicanas.

Table 2a. Occupational Employment Patterns for
White Women and Chicanas for 1970 and 1980 in California

| | 1970 | | 1980 | |
	White	Chicana	White	Chicana
Total, 16 years and over	2,519,594	259,255	3,369,325	763,471
White Collar Workers	70.2%	42.5%	76.0%	46.6%
Executive, Administrative and Managerial	4.9	2.0	10.7	4.8
Professional	}17.1	}6.4	15.0	6.0
Technicians			3.0	1.8
Sales	8.5	5.0	13.3	8.2
Clerical	39.6	29.1	34.0	26.2
Blue Collar Workers	11.9%	32.8%	8.0%	29.0%
Craft Workers	1.7	2.2	2.4	5.0
Operatives (including Transport)	10.9	29.2	4.0	19.0
Laborers	--*	1.4	1.4	4.7
Service Workers	17.1%	20.6%	15.2%	20.0%
Private Household	2.4	4.3	--*	3.3
Protective Services	--*	--*	--*	--*
Non-private Occupations	14.6	16.3	14.0	16.5
Farm and All Other Occupations	--*	4.0%	2.8%	4.4%

* Less than .01% reported working in this occupation.

Note: All figures have been converted to percentages and may not equal 100 percent due to rounding.

Source: 1970 data for white women: Composed from U.S. Bureau of the Census, *General Social and Economic Characteristics, Part 6: California,* Table 54, p.397 (April, 1973). 1970 data for Chicanas: U.S. Bureau of the Census, 1970, Census of Population, *Subject Reports,* "Persons of Spanish Origin," PC(2)-1C (June, 1973). 1980 data: Composed from 1980 Census/EEP Special File, "Summarized Occupational Categories by Race, Hispanic Origin and Sex: California."

Table 2b. Occupational Employment Patterns for White Men and Chicanos for 1970 and 1980 in California

	1970 White	1970 Chicano	1980 White	1980 Chicano
Total, 16 years and over	4,234,065	491,905	4,536,827	1,177,574
White Collar Workers	47.1%	20.9%	52.6%	22.2%
Executive, Administrative and Managerial	12.8	4.3	15.8	5.4
Professional	}18.2	}6.5	14.7	4.1
Technicians			3.8	1.6
Sales	8.3	3.4	11.6	4.8
Clerical and kindred	7.8	6.7	6.7	6.1
Blue Collar Workers	41.5%	59.8%	36.0%	54.1%
Craft Workers	20.3	21.2	20.3	20.0
Operatives (including Transport)	15.6	27.3	11.0	24.0
Laborers (non farm)	5.7	11.3	4.6	10.0
Service Workers	8.4%	10.5%	8.4%	13.0%
Private Household	--*	--*	--*	--*
Protective Services	2.1	}10.5	2.4	1.2
Non-private Occupations	6.2		6.0	11.6
Farm and All Other Occupations	3.0%	8.7%	2.8%	10.7%

* Less than .01% reported working in this occupation.

Note: All figures have been converted to percentages and may not equal 100 percent due to rounding.

Source: 1970 data for white men: Composed from U.S. Bureau of the Census, *General Social and Economic Characteristics, Part 6: California,* Table 54, p.397 (April, 1973). 1970 data for Chicanos: U.S. Bureau of the Census, 1970, Census of Population, *Subject Reports,* "Persons of Spanish Origin," PC(2)-1C (June, 1973). 1980 data: Composed from 1980 Census/EEP Special File, "Summarized Occupational Categories by Race, Hispanic Origin and Sex: California."

This stability of Chicano employment patterns and the minimal progress of Chicana women contrasts starkly with the gains made by white women during this time. A survey of the occupational profile of white males in California reveals less overall participation in white collar and service employment than that experienced by white women. White males tend to be distributed within the high paying craft jobs, professional categories, and executive occupations. A comparison of white males and females in the white collar sector seems to indicate that they are approaching parity. For example, in 1980, 15.8 percent of white males and 10.5 percent of white females were administrators with white women slightly surpassing white males in professional job categories. This apparently progressive movement is contradicted by the persistent income differentials between white women and men in the same type of jobs.

A 1981 report by the U.S. Department of Labor, Bureau of Labor Statistics, demonstrated that wages for men and women in the same occupations were not the same. For example: the median weekly wage for female lawyers was $407; but male lawyers were paid $574. In addition, six of the top twenty occupations in terms of wages for women were in public service employment as opposed to only one (out of 20) for males.[11]

If we examine the income distribution (Table 3) for Spanish origin and white men and women in full-time, year-round employment in the U.S. in 1981, several startling differences emerge. First of all, the incomes of Spanish-origin and white women can be compared only in three categories: operative, clerical and service. Apparently the data base in the other categories was too small for the Census Bureau to delineate income.

Among clerical jobs, Chicanas earned 98 percent of the wages of both white women and Spanish origin men; however, they earned only 64 percent of white male income. A similar pattern existed among service jobs. Among operative workers, the wages of Chicanas were 83 percent of those of white women, but only 42 percent of those of white males. Overall, Spanish origin men and women were paid 69 percent and 49 percent respectively, of the earnings of white males. White women earned 55 percent of the wages of their male counterparts in full-time employment.

This income pattern is significant at several levels. First, the overall income statistics place Chicanos and women in similar situations relative to white males. Secondly, the income at each occupational level (that can be compared) demonstrates a closer relationship according to gender than by race—except at the clerical and sales worker levels.

The dual wage standard by race and gender is not a new discovery (Hartmann, 1976; Barrera, 1979; Morrissey, 1983;

Table 3. Median Earnings by Sex and Spanish Origin According to the Longest Job Held by Full Time Workers in the U.S. for 1981

	White		Spanish Origin	
	Male	Female	Male	Female
Total in non-agricultural industrial labor force (numbers in thousands)	27,386	14,971	1,717	907
Professional, Technical and Kindred Workers	$26,954	$16,681	$24,376	(B)
Managers & Administrators	27,290	14,998	20,981	(B)
Sales Workers	22,306	11,307	(B)	(B)
Clerical and Kindred Workers	17,794	11,687	11,962	11,471
Craft and Kindred Workers	20,812	13,133	17,066	(B)
Operatives (including Transport)	17,650	10,464	14,361	8,739
Laborers	15,415	10,470	11,422	(B)
Service Workers	11,687	8,101	9,762	7,561
Total Median Earnings	$21,241	$11,816	$14,704	$10,512

(B) Insufficient data base (less than 75,000).

Source: U.S. Bureau of the Census, *Current Population Reports*, Series P-60, No.137, "Money Income of Households, Families and Persons in the United States: 1981."

Rowbotham, 1973; Falk, 1975). Feminist and minority group scholars have pointed out that there is a long tradition in this country (and abroad) to pay white men higher wages than women and minorities for similar jobs. A related issue of contemporary relevance is the "comparable worth" debate which studies the wage differentials between female-dominated and male-dominated occupations that require similar levels of education and work experience yet pay dissimilar wages.

The few comparable worth debates that have attained national recognition have been organized largely by professional women (i.e., librarians and nurses) in the public service sector. Inasmuch as there are few Chicanas in this labor market, comparable worth does not have any immediate relevance to Chicanas.

Chicanas, like white women, continue to be concentrated in the "female-dominated" clerical occupations and comprise a major portion of the service sector as well. But there the comparison ends. Chicanas do not occupy positions or earn incomes similar to white women in the professional and managerial categories. In fact, their position in this regard is closer to that of Chicano males. In addition, both Chicano men and women have a disproportionate share of the unskilled and semi-skilled operative occupational categories. With respect to Chicana cannery workers, Zavella (1982) points out that they are fighting to obtain and keep jobs that pay "decent" wages as opposed to struggling for wages comparable to jobs held by men. Given the evidence, a need clearly exists for a reformulation of the concept of comparable worth that takes into account the different jobs of Chicanas who are found in distinct labor markets.

With respect to income and occupations, wage differentials between men and women demonstrate the stratification process by gender within the labor market. This gender stratification maintains women in an economically subordinate position relative to white males. The evidence for this conclusion is strengthened by the persistent income differentials unfavorable to women despite their progress in climbing the white collar professional and managerial ladders. Wage differences between white men and women and Chicanos illustrate stratification by race within the labor market. The result of the interplay between race and gender is the consistently lower income and status of Chicanas relative to Chicano males and to the majority white population.

Unemployment

To complete the demographic profile of Chicanas, an examination of the variations in unemployment rates by race and gender is crucial. Table 4 provides the unemployment rates of Chicanos and majority men and women in the United States.

It is readily observable that Chicanos, male and female, have significantly higher rates of unemployment than the majority white population. The levels of unemployment for white women are closer to those of white males than they are to Chicanas. Similarly, the high unemployment levels of Chicanas are closer to those of Chicanos. This suggests that Chicanas are affected by labor market processes to a greater degree than the other populations examined. California statistics reaffirm this relationship (see Appendix C). All of the information in this section indicates that race is a significant factor in limiting occupational choices, and distinguishes the Chicana experience from that of white women. Thus, the occupational stratification of Chicanas, including their weaker labor market position as demonstrated by high unemployment levels, illustrates the critical interplay between race and gender unique to this population.

**Table 4. Unemployment for
Selected Years in the United States**

	White		Chicano	
	Male	Female	Male	Female
1980	6.1%	6.5%	9.7%	10.7%
1976	5.9	8.7	11.1	14.9
1970	3.6	5.0	6.4	9.1
1960	4.7	4.7	8.1	9.5

Sources: For 1980: U.S. Department of Labor, Bureau of Labor Statistics, *Special Labor Force Report 244*,"Employment and Unemployment: A Report on 1980," Unemployment rates by race and Hispanic origin, Washington, D.C.: USGPO, April, 1981. For 1960, 1970 and 1976: U.S. Commission on Civil Rights, *Social Indicators of Equality for Minorities and Women,* Washington, D.C.: USGPO, August, 1978.

This profile necessarily begs the question of possible reasons for the lower incomes of Chicanas and their disproportionate placement in low-paying occupations. The following section will discuss cultural variables, education, labor market segmentation and the race/class segmentation approach to gain insight into the pervasive socio-economic inequality of Chicanas in the United States.

Chicana Labor: The Cultural Explanation

In their 1970 landmark study, *The Mexican American People*, Leo Grebler, Joan W. Moore and Ralph C. Guzman hypothesized that the limited labor force participation rate of Chicanas reflected an ethnic, or cultural tradition. The authors explained this traditional view as specifying:

> ...the woman's place is in the home, and the husband's or father's pride would be hurt if a wife or daughter were to hold a job.[12]

These authors represent the view that traditional, or cultural attributes among Chicanos hamper the entry of women into the paid labor force, and can inhibit their occupational mobility.

Within the cultural approach is the study of higher fertility levels of Mexican women and the effect on social integration. Based on a large Texas sample, Alvirez and Bean (1976), found that women's entry into the paid labor force is hampered by a "traditional" preference for staying home, as well as the large families for which they are responsible. [13]

The most recent study on Mexican American women, *La Chicana* (1979), by A. Mirandé and E. Enriquez, seeks to explain the origin and maintenance of traditional ethnic patterns. They assert that current cultural orientations among Chicanas have their roots in Aztec society.[14] Additionally, they point out that traditional Mexican culture "tends to be male oriented," where "a girl's educational and occupational goals are considered less important, because she will eventually have a man to take care of her."[15]

The culturally deterministic views of Chicanas have been criticized by several scholars (Baca Zinn, 1982; Tienda, 1981). In a review of *La Chicana*, Baca Zinn discusses the shortcomings of the cultural framework of the authors. She points out that the linkage of Chicana oppression to Mexican cultural antecedents (including Aztec society) obscures the role of social institutions, labor market structures and majority group ideologies in favor of a pejorative "blaming the victim" approach.

Marta Tienda (1981) also criticizes the cultural explanation for Chicana subordination within society. Tienda objects to the causal linkage between culture and low socio-economic status because of the lack of methodologically sound empirical evidence supporting this position. Tienda connects the persistence of Chicanos in the "lower echelons of the social structure" to the historical role of institutions that has limited their ability to become upwardly mobile.[16] Thus, an understanding of occupational mobility among the Chicano population involves an examination of the educational system as well as those labor market processes that limit initial entry into jobs by Chicanas.

Chicanas and Education

Education as a key to occupational mobility and socio-economic betterment is a theme that finds favor with many Americans. Increasingly, the educational institution has become responsible for providing the tools of acculturation to the diverse elements within society. Teaching United States History and Civics, English and Literature within a compulsory (and free) public school system ensures that "American values" will be spread and maintained throughout the country. Yet education has another role: it provides (or limits) entry into occupations in the private and public sectors.

The majority of professional and managerial jobs require a degree from an accredited four-year college or university in an appropriate field of study. Clerical jobs require a high school diploma or G.E.D. (General Education Diploma) along with "good English skills." Craft occupations that require apprenticeship training often limit their openings to those who pass the G.E.D. To be a Nurse's Aid, a low paying service job, requires a high school diploma and special training courses. Pre-school teachers, another low paying, often part-time job, must hold credentials from a college program in Early Childhood education. In those instances where education is not a major obstacle for obtaining better-paying jobs, ethnic and gender stereotypes are often barriers.

Clearly our society places great weight upon the acquisition of educational credentials for entry into a variety of occupations. Whether this emphasis is relevant to worker productivity on the job is a matter of debate and speculation (Berg, 1970; Jencks et al., 1972; Bowles and Gintis, 1976). The high correlation between education and better jobs is not debatable and as such is important to discuss with respect to Chicanas. It must be noted, however, that the explanation of the relationship between education and future occupational status should not be separated from the economic variable of family background given the linkage between them.

An examination of the educational attainment of Chicano males and females in society reveals several important patterns (see Table 5). Clearly Chicanos, male and female, possess significantly less education than the majority white population. Over twice as many Chicanos did not graduate from high school than white males and females.

**Table 5. Education of Chicano and
White Labor Force Participants by Sex for 1976**

	Chicano		White	
	Male	Female	Male	Female
Not a High School Graduate	60.2%	53.4%	26.2%	23.9%
High School Graduate	24.8	33.6	40.3	45.4
College	16.1	12.9	33.6	30.6
Percent	100.0%	100.0%	100.0%	100.0%
Total (number in thousands)	1,517	876	49,651	32,799

Source: U.S. Bureau of Labor Statistics, Bulletin 1970, *Workers of Spanish Origin: A Chartbook,* Table C-5, p.56. Washington D.C.: USGPO, 1978.

In addition to the 1976 statistics, a study of the youth workforce (ages 16-24) revealed that in 1978, 33 percent of Chicanos in this age group were "school dropouts." Thirteen percent of white youth were similarly classified.[17] A recent *Los Angeles Times* series on "Latinos in Southern California" (July/August 1983), reported that the dropout rate of Chicanos over the past twelve years has averaged 45 percent.[18]

Among Chicanos in the public schools, only 23 percent are performing "satisfactorily" at each grade level. Possessing lower educational levels, Chicanas are placed at a disadvantage in competing for jobs with majority-group males and females.

With respect to Chicanos who enter college, only seven percent of all advanced degrees are awarded to them.[19] The Stanford University study, "Chicanas in California Post Secondary Education," reported that in March 1979, only 2.8 percent of Chicanas over the age of 25 had completed four years or more of college.[20] Additionally this study found that the majority (85 percent) of Chicanas (and Chicanos) in higher education are enrolled in the two-year community college system with few transferring to four-year colleges.[21] The *Los Angeles Times* (1983) reported that of the 83,000 Ph.D.s conferred annually in the U.S., only 600 go to Chicanos, with 110 being earned by Chicanas.[22] This same report pointed out that only six percent of all teachers and public school administrators in California are Latino although Chicano enrollment is at least 25 percent.

The problem of realization of an equal educational experience for Chicanos has been the subject of much analysis (U.S. Commission on Civil Rights, 1971, 1972, 1974, 1978; Carter and Segura, 1975; Weinberg, 1977). These and other reports have focused their attention on two major outcomes of lower educational attainment for the Mexican origin population: (1) placement in lower-skilled, low-wage jobs; and (2) reinforcement of the image of Chicano culture as placing a low premium on education.

To begin to assess the relative merit of family background or educational variables with respect to job entry and mobility requires an examination of Chicana high achievers to provide a more balanced portrayal of the social and cultural factors that are involved in labor market selection.

Chicana High Achievers

The experiences of upwardly mobile Chicanas are critical to examine, given their small but slowly growing proportion in the labor market. The barriers these women face in terms of their similarity to other Chicanas and women is an issue in need of much analysis—a brief discussion will be presented here.

Patricia Gandara's study of 17 Chicanas who successfully completed advanced (Ph.D., J.D., M.D.) degrees describes a situation where inner turmoil is common inasmuch as their achievements contradict ethnic, gender and class traditions.[23] Emotional support from their families is critical to the success of these high achieving Chicanas. This support, coupled with the acquisition of a high degree of knowledge of the dominant culture, are integral components for success in higher education for this group of Chicanas.

This profile is distinct from the Chicano male who usually enjoys greater public and familial support when he is able to seek higher education. Gandara found that Chicano men credited themselves for their accomplishments, whereas Chicanas tended to connect their success to their families.[24] Additional reinforcement for Gandara's observations on gender differences among Chicano high achievers is given by the 1982 Stanford study. Also, a literature review on this subject by Melba Vasquez (1982) agreed with Gandara, but added that "mother encouragement to do well in school" is essential for the success of Chicanas in higher education.[25]

All of these studies, while acknowledging the unfavorable effects of sex role socialization on Chicanas, emphasize that a variety of structural barriers, such as "ability-grouping" in the public schools, standardized testing, and the low socio-economic status of Chicano parents, operate to preclude the participation of Mexican American women in higher education. Whether the participation of Chicanas in higher education would be improved by changing familial socialization patterns or schools is a matter of continuing debate. Nevertheless, these studies demonstrate that educational achievement can be positively affected when there is a consensus between the family and the school with respect to the future possibilities of individual Chicanas.

The relationship between aggregate low levels of education and low wages of Chicanas requires additional information to that provided by studies of educational achievement. It is for this purpose that I propose to examine economic theories that claim to shed light on this situation. With this in mind, neoclassical and radical traditions within labor economics that analyze wage differentials and discrimination in the labor market will be analyzed as they pertain to Chicanas.

Chicana Education and Human Capital Theory

A major spokesman for the neoclassical human capital theoretical perspective is Gary Becker (1971). Briefly stated, human capital theory analyzes current wages in terms of the productivity of the worker on the job (marginal product). Worker productivity depends on education, experience and specific human capital (skills related to a particular job). It is individual decision and initiative that determine the amount of human capital in which a person chooses to invest. Jobs requiring high levels of education tend to pay greater monetary rewards. Therefore if an individual wants to enter these high-wage occupations, it is necessary to invest in greater amounts of education, and in acquisition of job-specific skills (or human capital).

Lower wages of a minority group reflect their low levels of education as well as a "taste for discrimination" practiced by white employers. Becker asserts, however, that unrestricted competition will abolish employer discrimination against minorities as firms that hire minorities drive the more discriminatory firms out of business. It should be noted that this model evaluates Chicanas ad other women and men of color against the norm, or experiences of white male workers.

The human capital view is popular for several reasons: (1) it reaffirms the ideology of reward according to "individual merit"; (2) it does not question the manner in which institutional processes operate—particularly within the field of education; and (3) it implies social remedies that can be translated into policies (e.g. Compensatory Education programs, CETA (Comprehensive Education and Training Act of 1973) programs, etc.). Its major strength, however, lies within the positive relationship between amounts of human capital to high-level, white collar jobs that even critics find difficult to dispute.[26]

The implication of the human capital model for Chicanas is that improvement in occupational mobility will occur when individual Chicanas "choose" to acquire greater amounts of education. This argument implies that the quality of education can be equalized. Additionally it downplays the historical record that has documented discrimination based on race and gender which has often curtailed the ability of groups in society to acquire human capital. The factor of discrimination is problematic within human capital models because of the difficulties of assigning it a precise figure within a general equation of earnings differentials. Increasingly, Becker himself notes that the "average money rates on education are not the same for all groups."[27] Becker does not view these different "rates of return" (which vary by race and gender) as contradictory to his assumption that the acquisition of human capital—notably education, facilitates occupational mobility.

The explanatory power of this model is suspect given its primary assumption that all individuals freely select their place in the economic hierarchy. Another serious flaw within the human capital model is the assumption that acknowledging discrimination is the same as analyzing its persistence and complexity. For example, the human capital model does not adequately address the subjective processes within schooling (i.e. ability grouping) and employment; or the poverty that might inhibit the ability of Chicanas to choose an investment in higher amounts of human capital.

In spite of its limited applicability to women and minority populations, the human capital theory continues to exercise a strong influence on labor economists and policy makers. Its popularity, however, has been challenged by "radical" labor economists, notably David Gordon (1972), Michael Reich (1981) and Richard Edwards (1979).

Chicanas and Labor Market Segmentation Theory

Reich, Gordon and Edwards (1973) critique the weaknesses in neoclassical thought as stemming from the assumption:

> ...that profit maximizing employers evaluate workers in terms of their *individual* characteristics and predicts that labor market differences will decline over time because of competitive mechanisms.[28]

These critics suggest that workers are not evaluated as individuals, but as members of groups which are pitted against one another in competitive labor markets. Radical economics questions the assumption that competitive mechanisms will erode discrimination against subordinate groups such as women and minorities.

Integral to radical economic thought is the assumption that the current organization of the labor force is not accidental, but part of a larger dynamic that has operated to maximize the maintenance of a capitalist system of production (Gordon, Reich, and Edwards, 1973, 1982; Gordon, 1972; Edwards, 1979). The growth and reinforcement of capitalism has required the transformation of labor and work processes to erode the potential power base of workers to change the organization of production. Chicanas, as a class of workers located at the lower end of the occupational hierarchy, have been part of this transformation of the workplace.

Edwards (1979), and Gordon, *et al.*, (1982), trace the development of the organization of work and the role of technology in the curtailment of worker activism and solidarity. As workers compete among themselves for relatively greater access to better jobs and wages, they become divided according to race, class and gender. Classical Marxism holds such divisions as denoting false consciousness by obscuring the relationship between capitalist and proletariat. Radical economists, such as Gordon, Reich and Edwards, seek to reconcile these labor market divisions within a coherent explanation of the working class. They assert that capital seeks to divide workers to maximize profits. Gender and race are exploited to keep the working class divided. The most urgent concern for Gordon, Edwards and Reich (1982) is to seek an explanation of the failure of the working class to heal these divisions and remedy an exploitative situation by embracing socialism.

The theoretical model of Gordon, Reich and Edwards—labor market segmentation—draws on the concept of the dual labor market to describe a division in the industrial work force between primary and secondary segments. Primary jobs are characterized by good working conditions, stability of employment, relatively high wages, and promotional job ladders. Secondary jobs reflect high turnover of personnel, do not require stable working habits, pay low wages and provide few avenues for advancement (Reich, *et al.*, 1973:359). Secondary jobs according to this model are filled mainly by women, minorities and youth.

The historical analyses of the development of the dual labor market by Gordon, Edwards and Reich (1982), Edwards (1979) and Reich (1972) revealed "tripartite" rather than "dual" divisions among workers that blossomed after World War II. Jobs within the primary labor market have become separated into two broad categories: subordinate and independent.

Subordinate primary jobs are routinized and require dependable workers who accept the goals of the firm and are mindful of authority.[29] Both factory and office workers are represented in this segment. On the other hand, independent primary jobs require individuals who possess a high level of initiative and problem-solving abilities.[30] Independent primary jobs reward creativity as opposed to obedience. These working conditions coupled with relatively good wages make them desirable jobs. Gordon, et al., (1982), point out that the growth in independent primary jobs is due principally to expansion within the public service sector.[31] By 1970, each segment accounted for about one-third of the paid labor force.[32]

The divergence between primary and secondary jobs is analyzed within the context of a separation between core and periphery industries. Part of the labor market segmentation model places all of independent primary jobs, and the majority of subordinate primary jobs within core (or market-dominant) firms. It is the fact of market preeminence that enables these industries to pay higher wages and reinforce the occupational stratification process. Periphery, or competitive firms, on the other hand, tend to pay low wages within the secondary (and subordinate primary) segments of the labor market. Offering low wages, and unstable employment, periphery industries tend to employ large numbers of minority and female workers (e.g., cannery operatives and temporary clerical workers, etc.).

Divisions within the labor force according to gender and race are discussed by labor market segmentation theorists, but are not totally integrated into this model. The labor market segmentation theory is first and foremost an attempt to locate the rise of a system of segmentation according to occupational changes. Race and gender are viewed as prior forms of stratification that operate within a larger framework of occupational segmentation.

Women are viewed by these theorists as suffering from a labor market structure that reinforces their concentration in various sex-typed jobs.[33] Similar to other Marxist analyses, women are viewed as a reserve pool of labor that fluctuates according to the needs of the labor market (Sokoloff, 1981; Braverman, 1974).

In their examination of the proletarianization of labor tied to the emergence of capitalism, Gordon *et al.* (1982), briefly describe the early patriarchal control of women's labor by men in the following description of the Lowell textile industries:

> In these boarding mills, women provided the bulk of the labor....They were subject to supervision by the male foremen, surrogate fathers, as it were, who continued patriarchal authority.[34]

This acknowledgement of patriarchal authority in the labor force is not integrated, however, into the growth of capitalism. Neither is the historical base of this connection explained, including the development of sex-segregated labor markets within this framework. These shortcomings issue from the reluctance of Gordon, Reich and Edwards to recognize the autonomy of patriarchy. The development of gender-divided labor markets, then, must be analyzed with the same scrutiny as technology or the organization of production for us to understand the divisions within the labor force.

With respect to race, the labor market segmentation theorists observe that minority workers tend to be concentrated in race-typed jobs that reinforce negative stereotypes and inhibit occupational mobility. Their labor force participation within the different occupational segments tends to be at the lower levels within each sector. Within their analysis of labor market structures within "core" firms, Gordon *et al.* observe that reorganization within these firms often creates secondary labor markets, with minorities filling lower level positions (i.e., janitor, file clerk, machine operator, etc.).[35] These secondary jobs are separate from the internal labor market of primary jobs within core firms.

Analyses of occupational distributions of minorities and women reveal their over-representation in low-wage jobs within the secondary labor market. Gordon, Edwards and Reich note that 60 percent of blacks are employed in secondary jobs. Fifty percent of Hispanics are similarly located.[36] Distinct job placement and unequal rates of employment that vary by race and gender demonstrate the extent of labor market segmentation. These theorists conclude that the only hope for change in the lower socio-economic class positions of women and minorities is for all workers to realize the structural divisions among them and begin to devise effective means for overcoming their relatively weak class positions.[37]

Critiques of the Labor Market Segmentation Model

Critiques of the labor market segmentation theory have been diverse and numerous.[38] Rather than present all of them, I shall focus on three major points of contention that are directly related to the issue of Chicana and Chicano labor in the United States.

Marietta Morrissey (1983) questions the usefulness of the dual labor market theory. Her major question concerns whether the barrier between primary and secondary labor markets is impenetrable for minority workers.[39] She asserts that dual labor market theorists have not proved a causal linkage between monopoly firms with primary occupations and competitive firms with secondary jobs. Given the ambiguity in classification of jobs and their locations in carefully qualified market sectors, Morrissey views the model as having limited usefulness, especially since Chicanos occupy different occupations in different regions of the United States.

Heidi Hartmann (1976), in a Marxist-feminist critique of the dual labor market theory, analyzes the persistent occupational segregation of women as an extension of the sex-ordered division of labor. Hartmann maintains that the sex-segmented nature of the labor market relegates all women to lower-paying jobs thereby reinforcing their dependence on men. While appreciating the value of the dual labor market model, Hartmann asserts that to overcome their subordinate position, it will be necessary for women to wrest away privilege from men.[40] This process of struggle needs to occur within the family as well as in the labor force. Accordingly, the close connection between women's roles in the family and in the labor force must be extended to all classes and racial groups of women given the fact that all men gain by female subordination. Unlike Gordon, Reich and Edwards, Hartmann does not believe in the inevitability of a class struggle that will erase social stratification according to race, sex and class. Patriarchy preceded capitalism, and there is no reason to assume that a different mode of production will erase its organizing principle.

Mario Barrera (1979), questions the direct applicability of the labor market segmentation model to the Chicano/Chicana population given its emphasis on the structural arrangement of the various segments according to occupation as opposed to race or gender.[41] Barrera is unsatisfied with the subordination of race stratification in the labor market to the issue of worker stratification by occupation. This type of analysis according to Barrera serves to obscure the fact that white workers do benefit to a certain degree from the dual labor market by receiving higher wages on the average than Chicanos and by being spared the "worst" work.[42] Although employers gain more than white employees who compete within the working class, the benefits garnered by the white population at the expense of the nonwhite population should not be minimized. These criticisms of radical thought have been integrated by Barrera into a coherent theory of racial inequality. This race/class segmentation approach, with its focus on the development of a subordinated Chicano labor force, forms the next section of analysis in this paper.

The Race/Class Segmentation Approach

Utilizing an historical and interdisciplinary case study approach, Barrera (1979) describes the Chicano experience in the southwestern part of the United States from the U.S.-Mexican War to the present time. Within this general framework, Barrera reformulates the labor market segmentation model with race as a central focus. It is Barrera's contention that the class position of Chicano males and females is integrally linked to the status of their racial/ethnic identities. The manner in which race and ethnicity became synonymous with cheap labor and lower class status with respect to Chicanos forms the base for his race/class segmentation approach to labor.

Barrera examines the relationship between capitalist development in the Southwest and racism. He finds that in the decades immediately following 1848, Chicanos as a group increasingly became limited to a subordinate or "colonial labor force." The development of the colonial labor system was facilitated by conquest, land displacement and the loss or denial of access to political power.[43] Prevailing racial ideologies of the time reinforced the unequal treatment of Chicanos by providing justification at the cultural level for a dual wage standard and occupational segregation.

According to Barrera, a colonial labor force segmented by race and gender emerged by the end of the nineteenth century with Chicano and nonwhite workers occupationally segregated within the ranks of unskilled labor.[44] Chicanas suffered the effects of a labor market stratified by race and gender resulting in lower wages relative to Chicanos, white males and white females. The unfavorable structural position of Chicanas has remained to the present day, even though a greater degree of occupational variation exists. Nevertheless, it is Barrera's contention that the segmentation process will continue to work against the struggle of Chicanos to achieve equality in this society.

Chicana Labor: An Analysis

In the preceding section, various theoretical models were presented to provide a framework for an analysis of Chicana labor and occupational mobility. Demographically it was illustrated that Chicanas as a group have made little progress in terms of educational attainment, occupational status and income during the past decade. During this same time, white women made modest gains primarily within the white collar sector, at the managerial and professional levels. When compared to the occupational distribution of Chicanas vis-à-vis Chicanos, the occupational distribution of white females is comparable to white males. Nonetheless, the incomes of these white women remain significantly lower than those of white men. This suggests that gender continues to operate to the disadvantage of women.

In addition, the situation of income inequality and occupational segregation by gender serves to maintain the principle of male domination, or patriarchy in society as Hartmann observed earlier.

Hartmann points out that the principle of patriarchy does not operate exclusively in the market place. It operates within the family as women continue to bear the major responsibility for unpaid household labor—a category of socially necessary work that economists, neoclassical and radical, do not include in their discussions of labor.

The issue of the family as it relates to the labor force participation of Chicanas is problematic. The reason for the hesitation of some Chicano scholars to critically confront the relationship between the family and the labor market lies in the damaging analyses of some earlier researchers that depicted the Mexican family as backward and patriarchal to a pathological degree (Heller, 1966; Lewis, 1961; Hayden, 1966; Madsen, 1964).

As a response to these attacks on Chicano culture, Chicano scholars have channeled their energies into analyses of structural factors such as labor market processes, education and immigration. The maintenance and reproduction of a sex-based division of labor within the Chicano family is often obscured by Chicano and Chicana scholars studying the "rise of egalitarianism" within that unit (Ybarra, 1977, 1982; Cotera, 1976; Sotomayer, 1971). By analyzing the growth of equality between men and women in Chicano families, these scholars obscure the sex role dichotomization that affects future job preferences and expectations.

Critical to an understanding of Chicana labor force participation and occupational mobility is an analysis of the effects of family relationships upon employment options in addition to studies of the effects of employment upon familial structure. The brief presentation on "Chicana High Achievers" made clear that familial support (especially that of mothers) is an important factor in Chicana advancement. A central concern for future research should be to study the effects of the family upon Chicanas entering the labor force with respect to their points of entry and occupational advancement. This type of question, combined with an assessment of institutional constraints and labor market structural arrangements, can reveal a composite picture of the Chicana experience in the U.S.

The role of education, alone and within the human capital model that reduces Chicana mobility to one of individual choice, is important to scrutinize given its wide adherence. But this model lacks relevance to Chicanas in view of the limited choices they can exercise related to the low socio-economic status of Chicano families. Still, the human capital model does describe one aspect of the important relationship between education and occupations. Inasmuch as education operates to screen potential employees for employers, the variable of educational background is a critical reflector of socio-economic status. Chicanas can strive to improve their educational levels, but without supportive mechanisms (equal employment opportunities, reduction in discrimination, etc.), their mobility will remain minimal.

Racial discrimination by employers is a critical variable, and operates to isolate the Chicana experience from that of white women. Although both groups of women are concentrated in the clerical occupations, white men and women tend to supervise, whereas Chicanas tend to be supervised. An example of this hierarchical relationship is provided by employment figures for the civil employees of the State of California for 1978-1979 (State Personnel Board, 1979). During this year, 30 percent of white clerical workers were supervisors, as opposed to 14 percent of Chicanos occupying similar positions. The consistency of lower occupational and employment levels for Chicanas suggests that discrimination in the labor market, as well as in the acquisition of different educational levels, are critical to the race, class and gender stratification of this group.

As an alternative to the human capital approach, the labor market segmentation theory deserves a prominent place in this analysis. This model, by its critique of neoclassical and liberal paradigms, has shifted the locus of blame from the individual to societal mechanisms. Through an examination of the historical development of capitalism as predicated upon the division and control of the labor process by employers, the limitations on individuals by structural constraints are revealed. Although this model lacks historical specificity to the Chicana experience, other works (especially Barrera, 1979) have refined it to emphasize race.

In his analysis of Chicano incorporation into society since 1848, Barrera reformulates the dual labor market model within the context of the historical development of a "colonial labor force."[45] It is Barrera's contention that the class position of Chicano males and females is integrally linked to the status of their racial/ethnic identities. Due to their lack of integration into the industrial activities of the "integrated" sector of the economy, Chicanos have been confined to a colonial or reserve labor force status.

What is critical in Barrera's "class-differentiated" segmentation model is that race and gender are major tenets as opposed to descriptive elements. According to Barrera, race has operated to maintain Chicanos in the colonial, reserve labor force in marginal industries. Chicanas suffer from the colonial labor force status of all Mexicans in the U.S. and are located at the lower levels within the class hierarchy. In addition, Chicanas are affected adversely due to the lower status of all women relative to men. As labor force participants, Chicanas are located at the bottom of the occupational hierarchy via their Mexican origin and their gender which reproduces an unfavorable class position *vis-à-vis* the white population.

Barrera's reformulation of the dual labor market approach supplies us with a useful analytic tool to understand the Chicana experience. Inasmuch as his model is historically specific to Chicanos in the U.S., Barrera has accomplished the difficult first step in providing a conceptual model relevant to Chicanos—male and female. His model is not, however, without flaws. Of primary concern is its lack of a feminist perspective.

Although Barrera describes the sexism Chicanas endure, he does not analyze this oppression as integral to the operation of capitalism. Similar to other Marxist accounts, gender is subsumed under an analysis of race and class inequality in the labor market. Without a critical perspective on the pervasive power of patriarchy, he fails to address the gender oppression of Chicanas within the Chicano community and society at large. It is crucial for Barrera and other Chicano scholars not only to *acknowledge* but to *analyze* the reproduction of gender inequality as integral to the organization of material life.

The existing evidence illustrates that a triple oppression of race, class and gender operates to inhibit the quest of Chicanas for socio-economic equality in society. Ideologically, politically and economically, racial oppression has maintained Chicanas in a subordinate position to the white majority via discrimination and the growth of labor market segmentation. This interplay works against Chicanas within the process of acquiring skills and credentials to compete for jobs.

Prominent within the Chicana experience is the additional constraint placed on them by virtue of their gender. We have observed that Chicanas as women are concentrated in the lowest-paying jobs that have become historically prescribed by gender. Moreover, even when they are in the same jobs as men, they have been affected by a dual wage standard that makes them earn significantly less than white males.

Both race and gender are interrelated within the dynamic of class. Depending on class background, the means for social and economic opportunities are either proscribed or prescribed. As members of a racial/ethnic minority group predominantly located in the lower-income brackets, Chicanas begin the quest for socio-economic improvement at a fundamentally different position than the majority population—male and female. This difference must be recognized and critically evaluated if we are to devise and implement strategies for change.

With respect to future work on Chicana labor, this essay has suggested that the race/class segmentation approach be refined to incorporate the centrality of gender oppression. The relationship between capitalism and patriarchy is critical to an understanding of the

persistent social and economic subordination of Chicanas within the
labor force and society at large. Analyses of Chicanas and other
women of color need to be expanded to incorporate a four-way comparison between white and nonwhite, male and female, in all social
arenas to assess the interplay between race, class and gender. The
growth of the Chicana population makes this research of high priority
if we are to avoid the continuation of women of color as exploitable
and expendable laborers in this society.

Appendix A

Part I. Labor Force Participation
Rates for Selected Years in the U.S.

Year	White		Chicano	
	Male	Female	Male	Female
1970	77.4%	40.6%	78.3%	36.4%
1976	77.4	46.3	80.3	43.9
1980	78.3	51.3	87.1	49.1

Sources: For 1970: U.S. Bureau of the Census, *Subject Reports*, PC(2)-1C, "Persons of Spanish Origin;" PC(2)-1D, "Persons of Spanish Surname," (1973), cited in Almquist, E. and Juanita L. Wehrlie-Einhorn, "The Double Disadvantaged: Minority Women in the Labor Force," p.66. For 1976: U.S. Bureau of Labor Statistics, *Employment and Earnings,* Vol. 28, No. 1 (1981), p.197. For 1980: (Chicano) U.S. Bureau of Labor Statistics, *Employment and Earnings*, Vol. 28, No. 1, p.197; (White) U.S. Bureau of the Census, *Current Population Reports*, Series P-20, No. 363, "Population Profile of the United States: 1980," (1981).

Part II. Labor force Participation
Rates for Selected Years in California.

Year	White		Chicano	
	Male	Female	Male	Female
1970	78.0%	41.7%	79.0%	39.4%
1976	79.1	50.6	80.8	50.3
1980	76.4	51.7	81.1	51.3

Sources: 1970: Briggs, *et al., The Chicano Worker,* p.28. 1976: U.S. Department of Labor, Bureau of Labor Statistics, "Survey of Income and Education," Spring 1976, *Work Experience and Earnings in 1975, by State and Area*, Report 536. 1980: data composed from U.S. Bureau of the Census, *General Social and Economic Characteristics, Part 6: California*, p.154.

Appendix B

Part I. Occupation of Longest Job
in 1975 and 1981 for White and Spanish Origin
Civilian Female Workers 18 Years and Over in the U.S.

	1975 White	1975 Spanish Origin	1981 White	1981 Spanish Origin
Total number (in 1,000s)	35,071	1,617	43,104	2,426
White Collar Workers	65.1%	43.0%	66.9%	50.0%
Professional, Technical and Kindred Workers	16.2	7.5	17.4	8.9
Managers & Administrators (non-farm)	5.8	2.5	7.5	4.7
Sales Workers	7.6	4.9	7.6	5.0
Clerical and Kindred Workers	35.6	28.0	34.4	31.3
Blue Collar Workers	15.0%	30.7%	13.5%	26.5%
Craft and Kindred Workers	1.5	2.3	1.9	2.3
Operatives (including Transport)	12.4	27.0	10.3	22.9
Laborers	1.1	1.4	1.3	1.4
Service Workers	19.0%	21.7%	18.7%	20.7%
Private Household	1.8	4.0	1.7	3.5
Non-Private Occupations	17.2	17.7	17.0	17.2
Farm Workers	--*	4.4%	--*	2.8%

* Less than 1% reported working in this occupation.

Note: All figures have been converted to percentages and may not equal 100 percent due to rounding.

Sources: All 1975 data composed from U.S. Bureau of the Census, *Current Population Reports*, Series P-60, No. 105, "Money Income in 1975 of Families and Persons in the United States," p.234, USGPO: Washington, D.C. (1977). All 1981 data composed from U.S. Bureau of the Census, *Current Population Reports*, Series P-60, No. 137, "Money Income of Households, Families and Persons in the United States: 1981," USGPO: Washington, D.C. (1983).

Appendix B

Part II. Occupation of Longest Job
in 1975 and 1981 for White and Spanish Origin
Civilian Male Workers 18 Years and Over in the U.S.

	1975 White	1975 Spanish Origin	1981 White	1981 Spanish Origin
Total number (in 1,000s)	50,347	2,409	55,588	3,468
White Collar Workers	42.1%	22.9%	43.5%	24.5%
Professional, Technical and Kindred Workers	15.4	7.5	16.3	7.9
Managers & Administrators (non-farm)	14.5	6.0	14.8	6.7
Sales Workers	6.1	3.3	6.4	3.1
Clerical and Kindred Workers	6.0	6.1	6.0	6.7
Blue Collar Workers	45.7%	57.7%	44.7%	56.7%
Craft and Kindred Workers	21.8	19.4	21.9	20.7
Operatives (including Transport)	16.8	26.2	15.9	25.3
Laborers	7.1	12.1	6.9	10.6
Service Workers	7.8%	12.6%	8.2%	13.5%
Private Household	--*	--*	--*	--*
Non-Private Occupations	7.8	12.6	8.2	13.5
Farm Workers	4.4%	6.8%	3.6%	5.3%

* Less than 1% reported working in this occupation.

Note: All figures have been converted to percentages and may not equal 100 percent due to rounding.

Sources: All 1975 data composed from U.S. Bureau of the Census, *Current Population Reports*, Series P-60, No. 105, "Money Income in 1975 of Families and Persons in the United States," p.234, USGPO: Washington, D.C. (1977). All 1981 data composed from U.S. Bureau of the Census, *Current Population Reports*, Series P-60, No. 137, "Money Income of Households, Families and Persons in the United States: 1981," USGPO: Washington, D.C. (1983).

Appendix C

Unemployment Rates In California for Selected Years

	White		Chicano	
	Male	Female	Male	Female
1970	5.7%	6.8%	7.0%	9.6%
1976	7.9	9.7	12.7	16.7
1980	5.5	5.4	9.5	11.2

Sources: For 1970: U.S. Bureau of the Census, Census of Population, *General Social and Economic Characteristics, Part 6: California*, Table 53, p.395 (1973). For 1976: U.S. Bureau of Labor Statistics, Survey of Income and Education, *Work Experience and Earnings in 1975 by State and Area*, Report 536, Table 8, Spring 1976 (1978). For 1980: U.S. Bureau of the Census, *Census of Population, Part 6: California*, Table 101 (1983).

Footnotes

1.   In this paper, Chicano/Chicana refers to persons (male and female) of Mexican descent living in the United States. It is used interchangeably with the terms "Mexican-American" and "persons of Mexican origin." The terms "Spanish origin" and "Hispanic" are broader terms that refer to persons of Spanish and Latin American heritage. For additional information on the origins and use of the term Chicano (especially its political implications), see Marta Tienda, "The Mexican American Population," 1981, p. 6; Fernando Penalosa, "Toward an Operational Definition of the Mexican American," 1970, pp. 1-12; and Mario Barrera, *Race and Class in the Southwest*, 1979.

2.   Additionally, population statistics are significant because: 1) the totals are used to determine "rates of parity" in employment for women and minorities; and 2) they are guidelines for allocations of federal and state monies targeted for social and economic programs for various groups.

3.   U.S. Bureau of the Census, *Current Population Reports*, Series P-20, No. 363, "Population Profile of the United States: 1980," 1981. Also note that in 1980 7.9 million Mexicans were identified by the Census Bureau (4,076 male and 3,856 female—numbers in thousands); in U.S. Bureau of the Census, *Current Population Reports*, "Persons of Spanish Origin in the United States: March 1980 (Advance Report)," Series P-20, No. 361, p. 5, May 1981.

4.   U.S. Bureau of the Census, 1980 Census of Population, Vol. 1, Chapter B: General Population Characteristics, Part 6: California, PC80-1-136, Washington, D.C.: USGPO, July 1982. This report tabulated the total population for California as 23,667,902, of whom 15,763,992 were white; 4,544,330 were of Spanish origin, with 3.6 million identified as Mexican. In the California tables presented, the term "Chicana" was used in recognition of the fact that approximately 80 percent of Spanish origin people in this state are of Mexican origin.

5.   Vernon M. Briggs, Walter Fogel and Fred H. Schmidt, The Chicano Worker, p. 28.

6.   Ibid.

7.   Composed from: U.S. Bureau of the Census, General Social and Economic Characteristics, Part 6: California, p. 154, July 1983.

8.   For an explanation of the comparability between the 1970 and 1980 census, see U.S. Bureau of the Census, 1980 Census of Population and Housing, Supplementary Report, Part 6: California, PH C80-S2-6, January 1983, Appendix B, pp. B-3 through B-5.

9.   See Maria Patricia Fernandez-Kelly, "Feminization, Mexican Border Industrialization and Migration," Working Paper No. 3, Center for the Study, Education and Advancement of Women, University of California, Berkeley, 1982, on work in the garment industry; and Patricia J. Zavella, "Women, Work and the Chicano Family: Cannery Workers of the Santa Clara Valley," unpublished Ph.D. dissertation, University of California, Berkeley, August 1982.

10. Virginia Escalanté, Nancy Rivera and Victor Valle, "Inside the World of Latina," Los Angeles Times, (July/August 1983), Special Series on Latinos in Southern California.

11. U.S. Department of Labor, Bureau of Labor Statistics, 1981 Annual Summary, "Employment in Perspective: Working Women," Report 663, (1981).

12. Leo Grebler, Joan W. Moore and Ralph C. Guzman, The Mexican-American People, 1970, p. 206.

13. David Alvirez and Frank D. Bean, "The Mexican American Family," in Charles H. Mindel and Robert W. Habenstein (eds.), Ethnic Families in America: Patterns and Variations, 1976, pp. 271-292.

14. Alfredo Mirandé and Evangelina Enriquez, La Chicana, 1979, p. 98.

15. Ibid., p. 134.

16. Marta Tienda, "The Mexican American Minority," in Amos Hawley (ed.), The Future of Nonmetropolitan America, Chapel Hill: University of North Carolina Press, 1984, p. 510.

17. Anne McDougall-Young, "The Difference a Year Makes in the Nation's Youth Work Force," Monthly Labor Review, Vol. 102, No. 10, (October 1979), p. 35.

18. Robert Montemayor, "Latino Students Advance, Only to Fail," Los Angeles Times, Special Report Series, Latinos in Southern California, (July/August, 1983).

19. *Ibid.*

20. *Ibid.*

21. Maria Chacon, Elizabeth Cohen, Margaret Camarena, Judith Gonzalez and Sharon Stover, "Chicanas in California Postsecondary Education," A Special Report in *La Red/The Net*, Newsletter of the National Chicano Council on Higher Education," Winter 1983, p. 3.

22. *Ibid.*

23. Patricia Gandara, "Passing Through the Eye of the Needle: High Achieving Chicanas," *Hispanic Journal of Behavioral Sciences*, 4, No. 2 (1982), pp. 167-179.

24. *Ibid.*, p. 177.

25. Melba J.T. Vasquez, "Confronting Barriers to the Participation of Mexican American Women in Higher Education," *Hispanic Journal of Behavioral Sciences*, 4, No. 2, (1982), p. 160.

26. See Paul Osterman, "An Empirical Study of Labor Market Segmentation," *Industrial and Labor Relations Review*, 28, No. 4, (July 1975), p. 520.

27. Gary S. Becker, *Human Capital*, p. 7.

28. Michael Reich, David M. Gordon and Richard C. Edwards, "A Theory of Labor Market Segmentation," *The American Economic Review*, Vol. LXIII, No. 2, May 1973, p. 359.

29. *Ibid.*, p. 360.

30. *Ibid.*

31. David M. Gordon, Richard C. Edwards and Michael Reich, *Segmented Work, Divided Workers: The Historical Transformation of Labor in the United States*, 1982, p. 212.

32. *Ibid.*

33. *Ibid.*, p. 204.

34. *Ibid.*, p. 72.

35. *Ibid.*, p. 209.

36. *Ibid.*

37. *Ibid.*, p. 227.

38. See Michael Wachter, "Primary and Secondary Labor Markets: A Critique of the Dual Approach," in Arthur M. Okum and George L. Perry (eds.), *Brookings Papers on Economic Activity*, 3: 1974, pp. 637-693; Robert E. Klitgaard, "The Dual Labor Market and Manpower Policy," *Monthly Labor Review*, 94, No. 11, November 1971, pp. 45-48; and Natalie Sokoloff, *Between Money and Love*, Chapter 2.

39. Morrissey, "Ethnic Stratification and the Study of Chicanos," *The Journal of Ethnic Studies*, 10, 4, (Winter 1983), p. 79.

40. Heidi Hartmann, "Capitalism, Patriarchy and Job Segregation by Sex," in Martha Blaxall and Barbara Reagan (eds.), *Women and the Workplace*, p. 167.

41. M. Barrera, *Race and Class in the Southwest*, p. 210.
42. *Ibid.*, p. 213.
43. *Ibid.*, Chapter 3, pp. 34-60.
44. *Ibid.*, pp. 43-46.

References

Almquist, Elizabeth and Juanita L. Wehrlie-Einhorn. 1978. "The Double Disadvantaged: Minority Women in the Labor Force," in Anne H. Stromberg and Shirley Harkess (eds.), *Women Working: Theories and Facts in Perspective*, Palo Alto: Mayfield Publishing.

Alvirez, David and Frank D. Bean. 1976. "The Mexican American Family," in Charles H. Mindel and Robert W. Habenstein (eds.), *Ethnic Families in America: Patterns and Variations*, New York: Elsevier North Holland, pp. 271-292.

Arroyo, Laura E. 1973. "Industrial and Occupational Distribution of Chicana Workers," *Aztlan, Chicano Journal of the Social Sciences and the Arts*, 4,2 (Fall), Chicano Studies Center: University of CA, Los Angeles, pp. 343-398.

Baca, Reynaldo and Dester Bryan. 1980. *Citizenship Aspirations and Residency Rights Preference: The Mexican Undocumented Worker in the Binational Community*, Compton, CA: Sepa Option, Inc.

Baca Zinn, Maxine. 1982. "Mexican-American Women in the Social Sciences," *Signs*, 8,2: 259-272.

Barrera, Mario 1979. *Race and Class in the Southwest: A Theory of Racial Inequality*, Notre Dame, IN: University of Notre Dame Press.

Becker, Gary S. 1975. *Human Capital*, Chicago: University of Chicago Press; second edition, 1980.

Berg, Ivar. 1970. *Education and Jobs: The Great Training Robbery*, New York: Praeger.

Bowles, Samuel and Herbert Gintis. 1976. *Schooling in Capitalist America*, New York: Basic Books, Inc.

Briggs, Vernon M. Jr., Walter Fogel and Fred H. Schmidt. 1977. *The Chicano Worker*, Austin, TX: University of Texas Press.

California State Personnel Board. 1979. "Report to the Governor and the Legislature, July 1979," *Annual Census of State Employees, 1978-1979*, Sacramento, CA.

Carter, Thomas P. and Roberto D. Segura. 1979. *Mexican Americans in School: A Decade of Change*, New York: College Entrance Examination Board.

Chacon, Maria, Elizabeth Cohan, Margaret Camarena, Judith Gonzalez and Sharon Stover. 1983. "Chicanas in California Postsecondary Education," A Special Report in *La Red/The Net*, Newsletter of the National Chicano Council on Higher Education, Winter, Ann Arbor, Michigan, pp. 1-5.

Cornelius, Wayne A. 1981. "The Future of Mexican Immigrants in California: A New Perspective for Public Policy," *Working Papers in U.S. —Mexican Studies*, 6, La Jolla, CA: Center for U.S.-Mexican Studies, University of California, San Diego.

Cornelius, Wayne A., Leo R. Chavez and Jorgé Castro. 1982. "Mexican Immigrants and Southern California: A Summary of Current Knowledge," *Working Papers in U.S.-Mexican Studies*, 36, La Jolla, CA: Center for U.S.-Mexican Studies, University of California, San Diego.

Cotera, Marta. 1980. "Feminism: The Chicana and Anglo Versions," in Margarita B. Melville, (ed.), *Twice A Minority*, St. Louis, Missouri: The C.V. Mosby Co., pp. 217-234.

------. 1976. *Diosa Y Hembra*, Texas: Statehouse Printing.

Doeringer, Peter B. and Michael J. Piore. 1971. *Internal Labor Markets and Manpower Analysis*, Lexington, MA: Heath, Lexington Books.

Edwards, Richard C. 1979. *Contested Terrain*, New York: Basic Books, Inc.

------. 1972. "Systems of Control in the Labor Process," in Richard C. Edwards, Michael Reich and Thomas Weisskopf (eds.), *The Capitalist System*, New Jersey: Prentice-Hall, Inc., 1978, pp. 194-200.

Escalanté, Virginia, Nancy Rivera and Victor Valle. 1983. "Inside the World of Latinas," in *Los Angeles Times*, Special Report on Latinos in Southern California, July/August.

Falk, Gail. 1975. "Sex Discrimination in the Trade Unions: Legal Resources for Change," in Jo Freeman (ed.), *Women: A Feminist Perspective*, Palo Alto, California: Mayfield Publishing Co., pp. 254-276.

Fernandez-Kelly, Maria-Patricia. 1982. "Feminization, Mexican Border Industrialization and Migration," *Working Paper No. 3*, Berkeley, CA: Center for the Study, Education, and Advancement of Women, University of California, Berkeley.

Fogel, Walter. 1967. *Mexican Americans in Southwest Labor Markets*, Advance Report 10, University of California, Los Angeles.

------. 1968. "Job Gains of Mexican American Men," *Monthly Labor Review*, 91, pp. 25-28.

Gandara, Patricia. 1982. "Passing Through the Eye of the Needle: High Achieving Chicanas," *Hispanic Journal of Behavioral Sciences*, 4, No. 2, pp. 167-179.

Gordon, David M. 1972. *Theories of Poverty and Underemployment*, Massachusetts: D.C. Heath and Co.

Gordon, David M., Richard Edwards and Michael Reich. 1982. *Segmented Work, Divided Workers: The Historical Transformation of Labor in the United States*, Cambridge: Cambridge University Press.

Grebler, Leo, Joan W. Moore and Ralph C. Guzman. 1970. *The Mexican-American People*, New York: The Free Press.

Grosman, Allyson Sherman. 1982. "More than Half of All Children Have Working Mothers," Special Labor Force Reports—Summaries, *Monthly Labor Review*, February, pp. 41-43.

Hartmann, Heidi. 1979. "The Unhappy Marriage of Marxism and Feminism: Toward A More Progressive Union," *Capital and Class*, Summer, pp. 1-33.

-------. 1976. "Capitalism, Patriarchy and Job Segregation by Sex," in Martha Blaxall and Barbara Reagan (eds.), *Women and the Work Place*, Chicago: University of Chicago Press.

Hayden, Robert. 1966. "Spanish Americans of the Southwest: Life Style Patterns and Their Implications," *Welfare in Review*, 4, No. 10.

Heller, Celia. 1966. *Mexican-American Youth: Forgotten Youth at the Crossroads*, New York: Random House.

Jencks, Christopher, *et al.* 1972. *Inequality*, New York: Harper and Row Publishers.

Kane, Tim D. 1973. "Structural Change and Chicano Employment in the Southwest, 1950-1970," *Aztlan*, 4, No. 2, Fall, University of California, Los Angeles: Chicano Studies Center, pp. 383-398.

Klitgaard, Robert E. 1971. "The Dual Labor Market and Manpower Policy," *Monthly Labor Review*, 94, No. 11, November, pp. 45-48.

Lewis, Oscar. 1961. *The Children of Sanchez*, New York: Vintage Books.

Madsen, William. 1964. *The Mexican Americans of South Texas*, San Francisco, CA: Holt, Reinhart and Winston.

Maram, Sheldon L. 1980. "Hispanic Workers in the Garment and Restaurant Industries in Los Angeles County," *Working Papers in U.S.-Mexican Studies*, 12, La Jolla, CA: Center for U.S.-Mexican Studies, University of California, San Diego.

Melville, Margarita B. (ed.). 1980. *Twice a Minority*, St. Louis, Missouri: The C.V. Mosby Co.

Mirandé, Alfredo and Evangelina Enriquez. 1979. *La Chicana*, Chicago: University of Chicago Press.

Montemayor, Robert. 1983. "Latino Students Advance, Only to Fail," in *Los Angeles Times*, Special Report Series—Latinos in Southern California, (July/August).

Montoya, Alfredo C. 1981. "Hispanic Workforce: Growth and Inequality," *Perspectives*, (Summer/Fall), Washington, D.C.: U.S. Government Printing Office (USGPO), p. 37.

Morrissey, Marietta. 1983. "Ethnic Stratification and the Study of Chicanos," *Journal of Ethnic Studies*, 10,4, (Winter), pp. 71-99.

McDougall-Young, Anne. 1979. "The Difference A Year Makes in the Nation's Youth Work Force," *Monthly Labor Review*, Vol. 102, No. 10, October, p. 35.

Osterman, Paul. 1975. "An Empirical Study of Labor Market Segmentation," *Industrial and Labor Relations Review*, 28, No. 4, (July), pp. 503-523.

Penalosa, Fernando. 1970. "Toward an Operational Definition of the Mexican American," *Aztlan*, I, (Spring), pp. 1-12.

Quiroz, Victor Garcia. 1981. *Undocumented Mexicans in Two Los Angeles Communities: A Social and Economic Profile*, Monographs in U.S. Mexican

Studies, No. 4, La Jolla, CA: Center for U.S.-Mexican Studies, University of California, San Diego.

Reich, Michael. 1972. "The Development of the Wage-Labor Force," in Edwards *et al.*, *The Capitalist System*, New Jersey: Prentice-Hall, pp. 179-185.

-------. 1981. *Racial Inequality*, New Jersey: Princeton University Press.

Reich, Michael, David M. Gordon and Richard C. Edwards. 1973. "A Theory of Labor Market Segmentation," *The American Economic Review*, Vol. LXIII, No. 2, (May), pp. 359-365.

Romero, Fred E. 1979. *Chicano Workers: Their Utilization and Development*, Monograph No. 8, University of California, Los Angeles: Chicano Studies Center Publications.

Rowbotham, Sheila. 1973. *Woman's Consciousness, Man's World*, England: Penguin Books.

Sackrey, Charles. 1973. *The Political Economy of Urban Poverty*, New York: W.W. Norton and Company.

Sassen-Koob, Saskia. 1980. "Immigrant and Minority Workers in the Organization of the Labor Process," *Journal of Ethnic Studies*, 8, (Spring), pp. 1-34.

Sokoloff, Natalie J. 1980. *Between Money and Love*, New York: Praeger.

Sotomayer, Marta 1971. "Mexican American Interaction with Social Systems," in Margaret M. Mangold (ed.), *La Causa Chicana*, New York: Family Service Association of America.

Tienda, Marta. 1981. "The Mexican American Population," in Amos H. Hawley and Sara M. Mazie, (eds.), *Nonmetropolitan America in Transition*, Chapel Hill: The University of North Carolina Press, pp. 502-548.

United States Commission on Civil Rights. 1978. *Social Indicators of Equality for Minorities and Women*, (August).

-------. 1974. *Women and Poverty*, (June).

-------. 1974. *Toward Quality Education for Mexican Americans*, Report VI, (February).

-------. 1972. *The Excluded Student*, Report III, (May).

-------. 1971. *Civil Rights Digest*, Vol. 4, No. 4 (December).

United States Department of Labor, Bureau of Labor Statistics. 1981. "Employment in Perspective: Working Women," *1981 Summary*, Report 663, Washington D.C.: United States Government Printing Office (USGPO).

-------. 1978. *Workers of Spanish Origin: A Chartbook*, Washington, D.C.: USGPO.

United States Department of Commerce, Bureau of the Census. 1983. "Money Income of Households, Families, and Persons in the United States: 1981," *Current Population Reports*, Series P-60, No. 137.

-------. 1982. 1980 Census of Population, Vol. 1, Chapter B: *General Population Characteristics, Part 6: California*, PC80-1-136, (July).

-------. 1982. "Population Profile of the United States: 1981," *Current Population Reports*, Series P-20, No. 374.

-------. 1981. "Population Profile of the United States: 1980," *Current Population Reports*, Series P-20, No. 363.

-------. 1981. "Persons of Spanish Origin in the United States: March 1980 (Advance Report)," *Current Population Reports*, Series P-20, No. 361, (May).

-------. 1974. "Persons of Spanish Origin in the United States: March 1973," *Current Population Reports*, Series P-20, No. 250.

-------. 1973. 1970 Census of Population, Vol. 1, *Characteristics of the Population, Part 1, United States Summary*, Section 2, (June).

-------. 1973. *Subject Reports*, "Persons of Spanish Origin," PC(2)-1D, (June).

-------. 1973. 1970 Census of Population, *Characteristics of the Population, Part 6: California*, Section 2:1, (April); and Section 1:1, (April).

-------. 1971. "Persons of Spanish Origin in the United States: November 1969," *Current Population Reports*, Series P-20, No. 213, Washington, D.C.: United States Government Printing Office (USGPO).

Vasquez, Melba J.T. 1982. "Confronting Barriers to the Participation of Mexican American Women in Higher Education," *Hispanic Journal of Behavioral Sciences*, Vol. 4, No. 2.

Wachter, Michael J. 1974. "Primary and Secondary Labor Markets: A Critique of the Dual Approach," in Arthur M. Okum and George L. Perry (eds.), *Brookings Papers on Economic Activity*, 3, pp. 637-693.

Weinberg, Meyer. 1977. *A Chance to Learn: A History of Race and Education in the United States*, London: Cambridge University Press.

Whiteford, Linda. 1980. "Mexican American Women as Innovators," in Margarita M. Melville (ed.), *Twice A Minority*, St. Louis, Missouri: C.V. Mosby Co., pp. 109-126.

Wood, Charles H. and Frank D. Bean. 1977. "Offspring Gender and Family Size: Implications from a Comparison of Mexican Americans and Anglo Americans," *Journal of Marriage and the Family*, 39:1, (February), pp. 129-139.

Ybarra, Lea. 1982. "When Wives Work: The Impact on the Family," *Journal of Marriage and the Family*, (February), pp. 169-177.

-------. 1977. *Conjugal Role Relationships in the Chicano Family*, an unpublished Ph.D. dissertation, University of California, Berkeley.

Zavella, Patricia. 1982. *Women, Work and the Chicano Family: Cannery Workers of the Santa Clara Valley*, an unpublished Ph.D. dissertation, University of California, Berkeley (August).

CHAPTER 5

Day Work in the Suburbs: The Work Experience of Chicana Private Housekeepers*

MARY ROMERO

INTRODUCTION

Most research on domestic service begins with a set of assumptions based on the experience of European immigrant women. For these white, rural immigrant women, domestic service often represented a path to assimilation into the dominant American culture. As most foreign-born (and native-born) white domestics have historically been young and single, the occupation usually functioned as an interim activity between girlhood and marriage. Domestic service could also offer a first step toward employment in the formal sector and mobility into the middle class. Hence, domestic service became known as the "bridging occupation" (Broom and Smith 1963).

The experience of minority women differs radically. For women of color, domestic service has not resulted in social mobility but rather has trapped them in an occupational ghetto (Glenn 1981). Most minority women have not moved into other occupations as a result of their experience as domestics; instead, they have remained in domestic service throughout their lives. Minority women are usually married and work to support their families. Married black domestics have usually remained employed, whether they lived in or were day

*I am indebted to numerous persons who commented on the original version of this paper. Many of these people attended the conference on "Women and Work: Integrating Qualitative Research" (Racine, Wisconsin, 1985), where I presented the present version. In particular, I wish to thank Arlene Kaplan Daniels, Dee Ann Spencer, Judith Wittner, Evenly Glenn, and Sandra Porter. I also want to thank Frances Kleinman for her editorial comments.

workers, and they have not experienced intergenerational mobility (Lerner 1972; Katzman 1981; Rollins 1985); married Japanese-American (Glenn 1981) and Chicana domestics (Romero 1987) who were primarily day workers experienced some intergenerational mobility. Examination of the work histories of minority women domestics has led several researchers to abandon the traditional emphasis on assimilation and mobility and to focus instead on the actual work experience, particularly the employer/employee relationship.

Several researchers have documented the caste-like situation faced by generations of black women workers in the United States (Chaplin 1964; Katzman 1981). Their limited job opportunities in the South can be inferred from the fact that black servants were found even in lower middle class and working class white families. Better working conditions and higher wages attracted black women to Northern households. As factory and other job opportunities outside the home opened up for foreign-born white women, black women began to dominate the domestic occupation in the North. For a short period during the Depression, black women found themselves replaced by white domestics; but, in general, there were not enough white domestics to offer serious competition and the white women's positions as servants was short-lived. In 1930, 20 percent of household workers were native-born white and 41 percent, foreign-born white; by 1949, the proportion of foreign-born white had dropped to 11 percent. Moreover, while two-thirds of all black women were employed as domestics in 1930, this had only dropped to 50 percent by 1940. It was only after World War II that black women entered other fields in large numbers (Coley 1981).

The majority of Japanese-Amercian women working in the Bay Area prior to World War II were employed as domestics, a disproportionate concentration that persisted for more than one generation. Glenn's study (1986; 1981; 1980) of Japanese-American women in the San Francisco Bay Area identified several characteristics that made domestic service a port of entry into the labor market:

> The nonindustrial nature of the job, the low level of technology, and the absence of complex organization made it accessible; its menial status reduced competition from other groups who had better options; and the willingness of employers to train workers provided *issei* and *nisei* women with opportunities to acquire know-how and form connections outside the family and away from direct control of fathers and husbands (Glenn 1981: 381–82).

At the same time, successful generations of Japanese women became trapped by established pathways that provided access to the job in the beginning, but later separated them from other opportunities and resources. Consequently, Japanese women frequently continued to work as domestics even after marriage.

Because both domestic and mistress are women, their gender designates them as responsible for housework. In the case of white European domestics, the mistress frequently assumed a benevolent or even motherly role. However, this cannot be assumed with regard to minority women serving as domestics, as in this instance the mistress is in the position of delegating low-status work to women not only of a lower class but also of a different ethnic and racial group. In the case of black women, the domination/subordination pattern of the relationship grew out of attitudes developed during slavery that black servants were inferiors and nonpersons. Racism prevented white mistresses from assuming the surrogate mother role with their black domestics; instead, they adopted a benevolent role, treating the women as "childlike, lazy and irresponsible," hence requiring white governance (McKinley 1969).

In short, studies of black and Japanese-American women indicate that domestic service is not a "bridging occupation" offering transition into the formal sector. These studies have raised additional questions about minority women's experience as domestic workers. Rather than approaching domestic service in terms of acculturation and intergenerational mobility, researchers can approach the occupation from the worker's point of view. The following study explores domestic service as a serious enterprise with skills that have been either dismissed or ignored by previous researchers.

METHOD

This study is based on interviews with 25 Chicanas living in an urban western city. I conducted two- to three-hour open-ended interviews in the women's homes. I asked the women to discuss their work histories, particularly their experience as domestics. Detailed information on domestic work included strategies for finding employers, identification of appropriate and inappropriate tasks, the negotiation of working conditions, ways of doing housework efficiently, and the pros and cons of domestic work. The accounts included descriptions of the domestics' relationships to white middle class mistresses and revealed the Chicanas' attitudes toward their employers' lifestyles.

A snowball sampling method was used to identify Chicana domestic workers. Several current and former domestic workers I knew introduced me to other workers. Churches and social service agencies also helped to identify domestic workers in the community. In a few cases, community persons also assisted. The respondents ranged in age from 29 to 58. The sample included welfare recipients as well as working class women. All but one of the women had been married. Four were single heads of households; the other women were currently living with husbands employed in blue-collar occupations, such as construction and factory work. All of the women had children. The smallest family consisted of one child and the largest family had seven children. At the time of the interview, the women who were single heads of households were financially supporting no more than two children. Nine women had completed high school, and seven had no high school experience. One woman had never attended school at all. The remaining eight had at least a sixth-grade education.

RESEARCH FINDINGS

Work Histories

The majority of the women had been employed in a variety of jobs over their lifetimes. They had been farm workers, waitresses, factory workers, sales clerks, cooks, laundresses, fast-food workers, receptionists, school aides, babysitters, dishwashers, nurse's aides, and cashiers. Almost half of the women had worked as janitors in hospitals and office buildings or as hotel maids. About one-fourth of the women had held semiskilled and skilled positions as beauticians, typists, medical record clerks, and the like. Six of the women had worked only as domestics.

Only three women had worked as domestics prior to marriage; each of those three had worked in live-in situations in rural areas of the Southwest. Several years later after marriage and children, these women returned as day workers. Most of the women, however, had turned to nonresidential day work in response to a financial crisis; in the majority of cases, it was their first job after marriage and children. Some of the women remained domestics throughout their lives, but others moved in and out of domestic work. Women who returned to domestic service after employment elsewhere usually did so after a period of unemployment. Because of the flexible schedule, most of the women preferred housework to other employment during their children's preadolescent years. Many of the older women had returned to domestic service because the schedule could be arranged around their family responsibilities and health problems. For all of the women, the occupation was an open door: they could always find work as a domestic. Their experience as domestics had lasted from 5 months to 30 years. Women 50 years and over had worked in the field from 8 to 30 years, while 4 of the women between the ages of 33 and 39 had 12 years experience.

The women's opportunities in the labor market were apparently not significantly improved by working as domestics. No matter how intimate the relationship between employee and employer, the domestic was never included in a broader social network that might provide other job opportunities. As long as community resources were limited to low-paying; low-status positions, the women found it difficult to obtain employment that offered benefits and a higher salary. Still, it is important to keep in mind that horizontal mobility can make significant differences in the quality of one's life. As Becker noted:

> All positions at one level of work hierarchy, while theoretically identical, may not be equally easy or rewarding places in which to work. Given this fact, people tend to move in patterned ways among the possible positions, seeking that situation which affords the most desirable setting in which to meet and grapple with the basic problems of their work. (Becker 1952, 470).

While the women I interviewed preferred factory positions because of their pay and benefits, many found themselves hired during the peak season and subsequently laid off. Women unable to obtain regular factory positions usually remained in domestic service until they retired or health problems emerged. Most of their clerical experience was in community-based organizations. Only when jobs increased in the Chicano community — for instance, through CETA or bilingual education programs — did the women have an opportunity to develop skills useful in applying for jobs elsewhere. These programs usually freed the women from daywork as a domestic. Only after retirement or periods of unemployment did these women again return to daywork to supplement the family income.

FINDING DAY WORK

In acquiring most of these jobs, the women relied upon word of mouth. Their sources for information on job openings included husbands, sisters, cousins, friends, and neighbors. Thus, their networks were usually confined to the Chicano community. Women reported that family members usually assisted in obtaining employment as a domestic. For instance, one woman had been working in the fields with her family one day when her husband returned from the owner's home with a job offer to do housework. Sisters, cousins and in-laws frequently suggested housekeeping and willingly provided the contacts to obtain employers. Several women joined the ranks in response to a relative's need for a replacement during an illness, vacation, or family obligation. One woman started out with a cleaning agency. However, she quickly abandoned the agency, preferring to work independently. This pattern of using informal networks in job searches is consistent with other research findings on work (Reid 1972; Katz 1958).

Younger women's introduction to domestic service frequently began with an apprenticeship period in which they accompanied a relative or friend. Two women would work together for a certain period of time (several days or weeks) until the newcomer decided she was ready to take on her own employers on a regular basis. This training provided newcomers with an opportunity to acquire tips about cleaning methods, products, appliances, the going rate, advantages and disadvantages of charging by the house or the hour, and how to ask for a raise.

Most women found their first employers through the community network of other domestic workers. Later, new employers were added with the assistance of current employers who recommended their employees to friends and neighbors. Two women reported using ads and employment agencies along with relatives and friends. But most voiced a strong preference for the informal network. Recommendations and job leads from the informal network of family and friends provided women with a sense of security when entering a new employer's home.

In many ways these women demonstrated employment patterns similar to other working women in traditionally female occupations. Movement in and

out of the labor market coincided with stages of family life. Husbands' unemployment, underemployment, or financial crisis were the major reasons for reentry into the work force. And, like most other women, domestic workers found
employment in low-paying, low-status jobs. However, their ability to obtain
immediate employment may distinguish them from other women who seek
employment during times of financial crisis. These Chicana workers were
unique in that they could always find employment as domestics. The challenge
was to find a job *outside* domestic service.

Work Conditions of Day Work in the Suburbs

Most of the domestics interviewed for this study drove 20 to 60 minutes
every morning to work. In two cases, the employer provided transportation.
All of the women worked for non-Hispanic families. The usual arrangement
was to work for one household per day; however, with an increase in the number
of professional, middle class people living in smaller units, such as con-
dominiums, cleaning two apartments a day had become a more common pattern. Exceptions in the present sample included two women working solely
for parish priests and another woman working for one family five days a week.
The average work week ranged from three to five days a week. Almost half of
the women worked six- or seven-hour days, and the others worked half-days.
During the course of interviews, it became apparent that norms were
changing regarding the type of tasks associated with general housekeeping.
Older women with 20 or more years experience considered ironing, laundry,
window cleaning, cooking, and babysitting as part of the job; however, none
of the women currently employed as domestics identified such requests as the
norm. Several current domestic workers and younger informants distinguished
between "maid" work and "housekeeping" on the basis of these tasks. Glenn
(1986) found similar trends. Twenty years ago, domestics service usually meant
ten- to twelve-hour days and often included yard work and cleaning the cars
or the garage. Today the work usually consists of vacuuming all the rooms (frequently moving the furniture), washing and waxing the floor, dusting, and cleaning the bathrooms and kitchen. Each home typically requires four to seven
hours.
After the first two workdays in an employer's home, the women established a routine for housecleaning. For instance, the women would arrange a
schedule to work around members of the employer's family who were at home.
Domestics identified themselves as professional housekeepers with responsibility
for maintaining the employer's home. Maintenance involved bringing the
employer's house up to a standard that would then be maintained on a weekly
basis. Domestics established a routine for incorporating extra tasks on a rotating
schedule: for example, cleaning the refrigerator or oven once a month. The
employer's cooperation in establishing a routine played an important part in
the employee's decision to keep a particular job.
Most women earned between 30 and 65 dollars a day depending on the
number of hours worked. Most women averaged 8 dollars an hour. Employers

usually paid by cash or personal check each day the domestic came. A few paid by personal check once a month. Although none of the women received health care benefits, some employers offered other benefits. Four of the older women were paying into Social Security; this had been initiated by long-term employers who expressed concern over their employees' welfare. Paid vacations were another benefit obtained by women who had worked several years for the same employer. As with Social Security, a paid vacation was the exception rather than the norm. A few of the women received Christmas bonuses. None of the women received automatic annual raises. Because very few employers offered a raise, the women were forced to make the request. Since the only power the women had was to quit, the most common strategy was to pose an ultimatum to the employer — "Give me a raise or I'll quit." Sometimes a woman would announce to her employer that she had to quit because she faced a problem with transportation or childcare. In this instance, the hope was that the employer would offer a raise to keep the employee from quitting.

Most people clean house once or twice a week and assume the domestic's experience is comparable. However, the domestic's routine recurs everyday: carrying the vacuum up and down the stairs; vacuuming sofas and behind furniture; washing and waxing floors; scrubbing ovens, sinks, tubs, and toilets; dusting furniture; emptying wastebaskets; cleaning mirrors. Backaches from scrubbing and picking up toys, papers, and clothes are common. All of the work is completed while standing or kneeling. Beyond the physical demands of the job, many women faced the additional stress of having their work treated as non-work. Several domestics recalled occasions when employers' children or guests spilled drinks on the floor or messed up a room and expected the worker simply to redo her work. All of the women refused, pointing out that the work had already been completed. Although domestics are paid for housework, the job is treated no differently than housework done by housewives (Oakley 1974).

Maximizing Work Conditions

Housework itself offers few intrinsic rewards; therefore, women who choose domestic service over other low-paying, low-status jobs typically strive to maximize their working conditions. The women interviewed for this study put a great deal of thought into identifying ways to improve work conditions, and they had very clear goals in establishing conditions with employers.

Flexibility in their work time was the crucial factor for many of the women who wanted to be home with their children. As Mrs. Lopez[1] explains:

> I'd always try to be home when the children went to school and be home
> when they came home. . . . I would never leave my children alone. I always
> arranged with the ladies [employers] — always told them that I had children
> and that I had to come home early.

1. I have changed the subjects' names to protect their anonymity.

Domestic work allowed the women to arrange their own hours, adding or eliminating employers to lengthen or shorten the work week. Determining their own schedule allowed the women to get their children off to school in the morning and be back home when school was over. It also provided a solution for women with preschool age children:

> Most of the people I've worked for like kids, so I just take the kids with me. It's silly to have to work and pay a sitter; it won't work (Mrs. Montoya, age 33, 12 years' experience, mother of two).

> So that's mainly the reason I did it [domestic work], because I knew the kids were going to be all right and they were with me and they were fed and taken care of (Mrs. Cordova, age 30, 8 years' experience, mother of two).

Domestics were thus able to fulfill family obligations without major disruptions at home or work.

> You can change the dates if you can't go a certain day, and if you have an appointment, you can go later and work later, just as long as you get the work done. . . . I try to be there at the same time, but if I don't get there for some reason or another, I don't have to think I'm going to lose my job or something (Mrs. Sanchez, 54 years old, 18 years' experience, mother of six).

> That's one thing with doing daywork — if the children are sick or something, you just stayed home because that was my responsibility to get them to the doctor and all that (Mrs. Lopez, age 64).

Since the domestics worked alone and had a different employer each day, they could control the number of days and hours spent cleaning. Women who needed to attend to family responsibilities found employers for two or three days a week and arranged to clean the houses in five hours. In contrast, women whose major concern was money could work six days a week and clean two houses everyday. In order to control the number of days and hours worked, women established a verbal contract identifying what tasks constituted general housekeeping. This agreement was flexible and was adjusted to particular situations as they arose. As Mrs. Sanchez explained:

> Suppose one day they [the employers] may be out of town, and that day you go to work. You won't have much work to do, but you'll get paid the same. And then maybe some other time they're going to have company and you end up working a little more and you still get paid the same. So it averages about the same, you know, throughout the month (Age 54, 18 years' experience).

Maintaining a routine for accomplishing necessary tasks allowed domestics to control the work environment and eliminated the need for employers to dictate a work schedule. Once an agreement was made, the workers determined how quickly or slowly they would work. Contract work provided employees with considerable autonomy, as well as recognition of their skills by employers.

On the other hand, a few women found contracts inadequate in controlling the amount of work requested. Instead, they clearly stipulated the number of hours they would work. Then they would do as much work, at their own pace, as the time allowed. By establishing a set number of hours, the domestic forced the employer to choose particular tasks to be rotated each week.

Planning and organizing the work permitted the domestic to feel like her own boss. When the employer permitted, domestic work offered a variety of advantages not available in many other jobs. Key among these advantages was autonomy. Once the employee was no longer taking orders and receiving instructions about how to clean, she had the freedom to structure the day's work. Mrs. Portillo spoke about the importance of this job characteristic:

> Once the person learns that you're going to do the job, they just totally leave you to your own. It's like it's your own home. That's what I like. When you work like in a hospital or something, you're under somebody. They're telling you what to do or this is not right. But housecleaning is different. You're free. You're not under no pressure, especially if you find a person who really trusts you all the way. You have no problems (Age 68, 30 years' experience).

All of the informants preferred to work alone in the house. Women who achieved a degree of autonomy in their work environment were often able to substitute mental labor for physical labor. Planning and organization were essential for maintaining the house and arranging the work tasks in the most efficient manner. Several of the women were responsible for keeping an inventory of cleaning supplies as well as for maintenance of housekeeping equipment. It was not uncommon for the women to be called upon to rearrange furniture and fixtures. Therefore, autonomy in the work environment made it possible to unite the mental and manual labor involved in housework. Most of the women noted that this combination made the work more interesting and meaningful.

The Relationship between Mistress and Domestic

Class differences have always existed between mistresses and domestics; however, cultural differences are a relatively recent phenomenon in domestic service. Historically, mistresses have defined the employment of ethnic minority women as a benevolent gesture, offering to the less fortunate the opportunity to culturally and morally upgrade themselves. Mistresses frequently pry into or comment on domestics'personal lives without invitation. Sometimes they treat domestics like children. Racism is a reality of the job. Although many incidents are difficult to resond to, most women quit employers who make racist comments, such as "Chicanas have too many children" or "Chicanas lack ambition."

155

Several of the women in this study felt they were treated as cultural curiosities. Often mistresses would limit questions and discussion topics to Chicano culture and attempt to explain differences in their experiences as cultural. For instance, one woman recalled that an employer had decorated her house with Santos purchased on her annual trips to northern New Mexico. The employer was quite shocked to realize the domestic did not own a large wooden statue of her patron saint. Most of the mistresses' inquiries were about ethnic food. Several employers asked the domestic to make tortillas or chile, but the women were very hesitant about sharing food. All of the women felt the request for Mexican food was inappropriate, except when they considered the employer a friend. Even though the women engaged in conversations about Chicano culture, history, or social issues, inquiries frequently created tension. Consequently, such discussions were avoided as much as possible.

In past research, researchers assumed that employers transmitted cultural values and norms to the employee, providing a "bridge" to a middle class lifestyle. However, the women interviewed for this study strongly expressed the opposite view. They found that domestic skills did not transfer to any other setting, nor did they provide the legitimate "work experience" needed to move upwards in the formal sector. Often the domestics felt a sense of being trapped because they lacked suitable job experience, opportunities, and education. Mrs. Fernandez spoke of her limited alternatives in an assessment of her job skills:

> I'm not qualified to do much, you know. I've often thought about going back to school and getting some kind of training. I don't know what I would do if I would really have to quit housework because that wouldn't be a job to raise a family on if I had to. So I would have to go back and get some training in something (Age 35, 9 years' experience, mother of 4, eleventh grade education).

The two oldest women interveiwed (68 and 64 respectively) saw discrimination and racism limiting their job choices.

> There was a lot of discrimination, and Spanish people got just regular housework or laundry work. . . . There was so much discrimination that Spanish people couldn't get jobs outside of washing dishes — things like that (Mrs. Portillo, 30 years' experience, 68 years old, mother of two).

This study found the cultural exchange between domestic and employer to be much more diffuse than that described in research on domestics at the turn of the century (Katzman 1981) and in Third World countries (Smith 1971). However, I did find that material culture was frequently transmitted to the domestic who developed a need for particular appliances and products. Several women had acquired new appliances, such as microwave ovens, in the last few years. Some of the younger women had incorporated a "white middle class" decor and style of arranging furniture in their own homes. Many of the women acquired a taste for objects similar to those in the employer's home. However, it is difficult to attribute this interest solely to the work experience because of the substantial influence of the media. Younger women were more apt to incorporate new ways of doing things into their own homes. Although there was evidence of acculturation in the arrangement of furniture and wall decorations, certain traditional items remained, such as family pictures and religious art. I would argue that this readiness to incorporate material culture reflects class aspirations rather than assimilation to white American culture.

Cultural diffusion was not one way. Employers who turned over the control of the work process allowed workers to introduce new cleaning products and methods. A few of the older women became surrogate mothers to their employers and were called upon to discuss childrearing practices. The amount of cultural exchange was determined by the degree to which employers accepted domestics as experts in housekeeping.

Minimizing the Personal Cost of Being a Domestic

Many women found the stigma attached to domestic work painful. A few manifested embarassment and anger at being identified as a housecleaner. Other women were very defensive about their work and attempted to point out all the benefits associated with flexible work schedule and autonomy.

The women used several strategies for coping with the personal pain of being a domestic. They attempted to eliminate the stigma attached to the occupation by making a distinction between the positions of maid and housekeeper, defining the former as involving personal service. The younger women, in particular sought to redefine the job. Mrs. Fernandez noted the distinction between maid and housekeeper in the following story:

> They [the employer's children] started to introduce me to their friends as their maid. "This is our maid Angela." I would say, "I'm not your maid. I've come to clean your house, and a maid is someone who takes care of you and lives here or comes in everyday, and I come once a week and it is to take care of what you have messed up. I'm not your maid. I'm your housekeeper." (Age 35, 9 years' experience).

By identifyig themselves as professional housekeepers, the women emphasized their special skills and knowledge and situated their work among male-dominated jobs that are treated as semiskilled, such as carpet cleaning. This also served to define their relationships to their employers. Mrs. Montoya illustrated the relationship:

> I figure I'm not there to be their personal maid. I'm there to do their house-cleaning — their upkeep of the house. Most of the women I work for are professionals, and so they feel it's not my job to run around behind them. Just to keep their house maintenance clean, and that's all they ask. (Age 33, 12 years' experience).

157

The women redefined their employers as clients, vendors, and customers. Defining themselves as professionals, these domestics no longer saw themselves as acting in the subordinate role of employee to the dominant role of employer. Without recognition of their authority, however, the domestics had to rely on mistresses' cooperation. This is similar to women's lack of authority in other female-dominated occupations such as nursing and teaching. (See Ritzer 1977 and chapters by Spencer and Corley and Mauksch in this volume.)

Another strategy women used to lessen the stigma of doing domestic work was to focus on the benefits to their families. By praising aspects of domestic service compatible with traditional mother and wife roles, the woman's social identity was shifted to family rather than work roles. Since the status of motherhood is much higher than that of domestic worker, identifying with the tradidional family role served to minimize the stigma attached to the work role. Again, this strategy was found particularly among younger and more educated women. Mrs. Montoya, a high school graduate and mother of two, stressed that domestic work was preferable to other jobs because it did not interfere with her role as a mother:

> I make my own hours so I can go to [school] programs when I'm needed. I go to conferences when I'm needed. When the kids are ill, I'm there. . . .It's one of the best jobs that I could find in my situation where I am home with my family before and after school. I'm always around.

The women were usually available to participate in school functions, and many played an active role in the community. The fact that these women identified primarily with traditional family roles is consistent with other research findings suggesting that jobs are not the central interest of workers' lives (Dublin 1956).

Women tended to deny that they were actually employed, as did their families. Many of the women remarked that their families did not consider them to be working outside the home; their employment was dismissed as "shadow work," the peculiarly nonwork status commonly given to housework (Oakley 1974; Illich 1982). Therefore, the women's families saw no reason to give them credit or to help out at home. A few husbands did not want their wives working and retaliated by becoming more demanding about housework, laundry, and meals. This attitude was particularly common in families where mothers worked part time. The women received little help from their husbands or their children in doing cooking, laundry, and housekeeping. Children occasionally helped with the housework, and retired husbands were described as sporadically cooking a meal, removing the laundry from the dryer, vacuuming the living room, or "telling the children what to do." Consequently, women working six- to seven-hour days, five days a week as domestics experienced the common "double day" syndrome known to many working mothers regardless of their occupation.

The women described their wages as providing "extras" not afforded by their husbands' incomes. The items listed as "extras" were: food, children's clothes, remodeling the house, savings, children's tuition, and payment of bills. Clearly, their contributions enhanced their family's subsistence and went beyond the stereotypical 'pin money.' The notion that their employment provided extras rather than subsistence for the family was part of these women's strategy for coping with the stigma of being a domestic worker. In essence, they maintained a social identity based on the family rather than on the work role. Since the status attached to being a mother and wife is much higher than that assigned to the domestic, women defined their work as adding to the fulfillment of their traditional female role.

DISCUSSION

Chicana domestic workers share experiences similar to those of other minority women. Although a few of those interviewed worked on a live-in basis prior to marriage, they only worked on a nonresidential basis after marriage. This is quite similar to the pattern found among Japanese-American women (Glenn 1981). Chicana domestic workers also experience domestic service as an "occupational ghetto" as have so many Japanese-American and black women in the United States. Minority women have not moved into the formal work sector as a consequence of their experience as domestics, but have continued to have few options. The present investigation begins to explain why domestic service does not constitute a "bridging occupation" for minority women.

The use of informal networks to obtain daywork as described by Chicana domestics is also found in the Japanese-American community; while community resources provide Japanese-American women with immediate employment as a domestic, the residential and social segregation also "tend to insulate members from information about other occupations" (Glenn 1981, 380). This method of job searching has likewise been documented for various other workers, including professionals (Reid 1972; Katz 1958; Caplow and McGee 1958). It follows that potential for social mobility is related to expanding resources within the community rather than to simple assimilation into another community's norms and values. I would argue that domestic service serves as a bridging occupation only when employers make their informal networks available to domestics. Research on minority women in domestic service indicates that employers do not share these informal networks; that is, domestics do not become "just one of the family." As a result, domestics experience social segregation and do not gain access to other occupations.

Analysis of the work histories collected from Chicana domestic workers shows that they found their options limited in low-paying, low-status, dead-end jobs. The women's choice of domestic service over another job (such as waitressing or farmwork) was most often based on the flexible schedule and potential for autonomy on the job. Selecting employers who worked outside the home and establishing verbal contracts were attempts to increase autonomy. The women also tried to modernize their occupation by redefining themselves as professional housecleaners. These strategies are all essentially individualistic. However, as unionization among housekeepers increases, these women will be able to pursue collective approaches to the struggle for better working conditions.

REFERENCES

Becker, H.S. 1952. "The career of the Chicago public schoolteacher," *American Journal of Sociology* 57:470.

Broom, L., and J.H. Smith. 1963. "Bridging occupations," *British Journal of Sociology* 14:321–34.

Caplow, T., and R. McGee. 1958. *The Academic Marketplace.* New York: Basic Books.

Chaplin, D. 1964. "Domestic service and the Negro," In *Blue Collar World,* edited by A.B. Shoistak and Wl. Gomberg, Englewood Cliffs, N.J.: Prentice-Hall. pp. 527–536.

Coley, S.M. 1981. "And Still I Rise: An Exploratory Study of Contemporary Black Private Household Workers." Ph.D. diss., Bryn Mawr College, Bryn Mawr, PA.

Dublin, R. 1956. "Industrial workers' world: A study of the central life interests of industrial workers," *Social Problems* 3:131–42.

Glenn, E.N. 1980. "The dialectics of wage work: Japanese-American women and domestic service, 1905–1940," *Feminist Studies* 6:432–71.

———. 1981. "Occupational ghettoization: Japanese-American women and domestic service, 1905–1970," *Ethnicity* 8:352–86.

———. 1986. *Issei, Nisei, War Bride: Three Generations of Japanese-American Women in Domestic Service.* Philadelphia: Temple University Press. University Press.

Illich, I. 1982. *Gender.* New York: Pantheon Books.

Katz, F.E. 1958. "Occupational contract network," *Social Forces* 41:52–5.

Katzman, D.H. 1981. *Seven Days a Week: Women and Domestic Service in Industrializing America.* New York: Oxford University Press, 1978.

Lerner, G. 1972. *Black Women in White America: A Documentary History.* New York: Pantheon Books.

McKinley, G.E. 1969. "The stranger in the gates: Employer reactions toward domestic servants in America, 1825–1875." Ph.D. Diss., Michigan State University, East Lansing.

Oakley, A. 1974. *The Sociology of Housework*. New York: Pantheon Books.

Reid, G. 1972. "Job search and the effectiveness of job-finding methods," *Industrial and Labor Relations Review* 25:479–95.

Ritzer, G. 1977. *Working Conflict and Change*. Englewood Cliffs, NJ: Prentice-Hall.

Rollins, J. 1985. *Between Women: Domestics and Their Employers*. Philadelphia: Temple University Press.

Romero, M. 1987. "Domestic service in the transition from rural to urban life: The case of La Chicana," *Women's Studies*, forthcoming.

Smith, M.L. 1971. "Institutionalized servitude: The female domestic servant in Lima, Peru." Ph.D. Diss., Indiana University, Bloomington.

YOLANDA PRIETO

Cuban Women in the U.S. Labor Force: Perspectives on the Nature of Change

ABSTRACT

This article looks at the factors responsible for the high rate of labor force participation among Cuban women in the United States by studying a sample of 107 Cuban-born women in Hudson County, New Jersey. It is perplexing that so many Cuban women in the United States work, given the strong disapproval of female work outside the home in prerevolutionary Cuba. This study suggests that one of the strongest reasons behind the high labor force participation of Cuban women in the sample is the predominantly middle-class origin and/or ideology of Cuban immigrants. The upward mobility of the Cuban family in the United States seems to justify the massive entrance of women into the labor force.

RESUMEN

Este artículo examina los factores reponsables por la alta tasa de participación laboral de las mujeres cubanas en los EE.UU. mediante el estudio de una muestra de 107 mujeres nacidas en Cuba en el Condado de Hudson, New Jersey. Resulta sorprendente que tantas mujeres cubanas trabajen en los EE.UU. dada la fuerte desaprobación hacia el trabajo femenino fuera del hogar que existía en la Cuba pre-revolucionaria. Este estudio sugiere que una de las razones primordiales que explican la alta participación laboral de las mujeres cubanas en la muestra es el origen predominantemente de clase media y/o la ideología de los inmigrantes cubanos. La mobilidad ascendente de la familia cubana en los EE.UU. parece justificar la entrada masiva de mujeres en la fuerza laboral.

The challenge to the traditional place of women in Cuban society was one among the many changes brought about by the 1959 Revolution. The attempt to transform structures and deeply rooted attitudes that had kept women at the bottom of the social ladder generated enthusiasm but also a great deal of anxiety among males and females who had accepted "the woman's destiny" as something natural or inevitable.

One of the ways in which the new government began to promote the integration of women into society was to make their massive entrance into the labor force a goal. In prerevolutionary Cuba there was a strong disapproval of women working outside the home. The ideal place for women was "la casa" (the home), as opposed to "la calle" (the street). This distinction had moral connotations: good women would stay home, where they belonged, and avoid the street, where they would be exposed to the dangers of male sexuality. Thus, working outside the home was seen to be risky and done only if absolutely necessary. However, staying at home was possible only for those women, generally from the middle and upper classes, whose fathers or husbands could provide sufficiently for the family. The majority of working women were poor and needed their jobs for economic survival. Many were domestics, some worked in other service occupations, and a small percentage had industrial jobs. But in general, the total percentage of women in the labor force in 1956–57 (when the last prerevolutionary census was taken) was rather low (14.2 percent).[1]

The dramatic changes in the role of women as a result of the Revolution has been one of the numerous reasons that many families left Cuba after 1959. The "destruction of the family" was, according to Cuban men interviewed in a study conducted in Chicago in 1969, an outcome of the revolutionary government's policies concerning women (Fox, 1970: 279). These men pointed out that women not only worked outside the home, but also performed rough work in paid and unpaid agricultural labor and participated in the armed forces and in revolutionary committees. This confirmed their fears that socialism had a deleterious effect on women and the family.

In light of this historical experience, it is interesting that those who left Cuba after the Revolution, once believers that the natural place for women is the home, have significantly changed their behavior. While in 1970 the percentage of women in the labor force in Cuba was 18.3, the 1970 U.S. Census showed that the proportion of Cuban women in the U.S. labor force was almost three times as large as that of their counterparts in Cuba (55.1 percent) (Junta Central de Planificación, 1975; U.S. Bureau of the Census, 1973). In 1980, Cuban women exhibited the highest rate of labor force participation of all females in the three major Hispanic groups in the United States: 55.4 percent, compared with 49 percent Mexican-American and 40 percent Puerto Rican (U.S. Bureau of the Census, 1983).

What are the reasons behind this significant behavioral change on the part of Cubans in the U.S. concerning women and work? Is it economic need due to migration? Is it contact with an advanced, industrial society, where a great number of women have always worked? Is it the availability of jobs where Cubans have settled? Is economic mobility a valued family goal that justifies the massive entrance of women into the labor force?

This article will attempt to shed some light on these questions by examining the results of a study conducted in Hudson County, New Jersey, the second largest concentration of Cubans in the United States. The sample consisted of 107 Cuban-born women. Data on labor force participation and on attitudes about work outside the home were gathered primarily through structured and in-depth interviews with the respondents.

From Cuba to the United States: Economic Achievement and Middle-Class Ideology

The post-1959 Cuban migration to the United States, at least until the 1980 Mariel boatlift, was not representative of the Cuban population. As is well known, Cubans leaving the island were predominantly white, professional or semiprofessional, and mainly from urban areas. Consequently, the Cuban migration of the 1960s has been defined as a middle-class phenomenon by many authors, the media, and the general public. However, this is not quite accurate; even before Mariel, Cubans migrating to the United States represented a mixed population. Persons of working-class origin were also leaving the country, due in part to Cuba's difficult economic situation, especially in the late 1960s (Portes, 1969; Amaro and Portes, 1972; Prohias and Casal, 1974; Portes, Clark, and Bach, 1977).

The predominantly middle-class origin of the Cuban emigrés to the United States has been said to assist the group in becoming economically integrated into U.S. society. Moreover, Cubans' middle-class ideology, in particular their work ethic, is believed to be responsible for the economic success experienced by the group in a relatively short time.[2]

Studies about Cubans in the United States have interpreted their relatively successful economic integration into U.S. society precisely along the lines of Cuban "middle-classness." Even though studies vary in emphasizing different characteristics of the migrants and the communities they have established, their interpretations of Cubans' economic success are ultimately related to the predominant social class of origin of the group under scrutiny. Thus, many studies stress the importance of transferable abilities that Cubans brought with them when they came to the United States, such as occupational skills and education. Some focus on the development of strong enclave immigrant economies. Others call attention to specific characteristics of Cuban households, such as low fertility rates, the economic contribution of most family members, and a high level of female labor force participation (Portes, 1969; Amaro and Portes, 1972; Prohias and Casal, 1974; Portes, Clark and Bach, 1977; Portes and Wilson, 1980; Perez, 1986; Rogg, 1974; Rogg and Santana-Cooney, 1980).

The role of class ideology or belief systems has not been sufficiently examined in studies of Cubans' economic integration in the United States. This is understandable because "ideology" is much harder to define, operationalize, and ultimately "prove." However, to examine such belief systems becomes important if we want to understand more fully the dynamics that shape and differentiate the behavior of various groups in a complex society such as that of the United States.

At the theoretical level, there has always been an interest in the relationship between one's location in the social structure, belief system, and economic behavior. For example, classical sociological theory provides a starting point for this discussion. Karl Marx and Max Weber attributed an important role to ideas in influencing people's economic actions. Of course, neither implied a mechanical connection between ideas, individual or group action, and class location in society. Beliefs, according to Marx and Weber, are socially determined and differ from one group to another. Though working from very different perspectives, these thinkers concur remarkably when studying the motivation and the logic in the ideas and behavior of the middle strata of society. Thus, if we believe that some of their theoretical propositions can be applied to the here and now, we could refer to Marx's "class interest of the petite bourgeoisie" or to Weber's "work ethic as the ascetic trait of the middle class" as essentially describing the same phenomenon: individual or group action guided by a world view that emphasizes economic achievement.

It is precisely this relationship between socioeconomic or social class of origin, the ideology or belief system of that particular class or group, and economic behavior, that I am concerned with in this article. If we accept that middle-class individuals predominate among Cuban migrants, it would be logical to assume that their values correspond with the dominant achievement-oriented ideology of the U.S. middle class. Even when considering that not all Cubans in the United States come from the middle class (and most who did lost that status when migrating anyway), a generalized image develops about Cubans that the general public and the migrants themselves share, and which is to a great extent real. This image embodies middle-class characteristics (a respect for hard work, ambition, and abiding by the law) and persists regardless of former or present class position. Precisely because this middle-class image is maintained and reproduced in society even after one's original structural position has disappeared (that is, a middle-class position in Cuba), I believe that ideology plays an important role in influencing the behavior of these immigrants—especially economic behavior. The strong work ethic of Cubans, product of a previous middle-class position and ideology, generates a high degree of economic activity and, for many, economic success in the new country. The contribution of Cuban women to this economic success is vital. It is mainly in this context that the high incorporation of Cuban women into the labor force in the United States is analyzed in this essay.

Cuban Women in the United States: A Case Study

Cubans have settled primarily in Florida, but there are other areas of concentration in the United States. New Jersey contains a large Cuban settlement with about 10 percent of the total 806,223 Cubans listed in the 1980 U.S. census. In New Jersey, Cubans live mainly in Hudson County, a 46.4-square-mile area located within minutes of New York City. The county seat is Jersey City. Cubans reside primarily in Union City and West New York, where they constitute 32 percent and 39 percent of the population, respectively.

Since Cuban women have an even higher rate of labor force participation in New Jersey than they do nationally (59.4 percent, compared with 55.4 percent nationally), this site provides a particularly appropriate context in which to ask our initial research question.

The Labor Market in Hudson County

Traditionally, the largest single source of employment in Hudson County has been manufacturing, of which the apparel and textile industries are extremely important. These industries are labor-intensive, requiring many workers. Immigrants, especially minorities and women, have provided a steady supply of labor. But even though manufacturing continues to be the most important source of employment in this area, its decline since 1960 has been staggering. Between 1970 and 1980 Hudson County lost a total of 42,315 jobs in the manufacturing sector (Hudson County Planning Board, 1974; U.S. Department of Commerce, 1982). Yet the apparel industry has not been the hardest hit. In Hudson County, despite the employment decline in manufacturing over the past decade, small and competitive firms (some of them owned by Cubans and other immigrants) still provide jobs for women and minorities. For example, in 1980, 82 percent of the economically active population of Hudson County of Spanish origin was employed in manufacturing (U.S. Bureau of the Census, 1982). This fact may help explain the high rate of incorporation of Cuban women into the area's work force. These local, smaller firms are able to remain in business partly because of the mainly female pool of immigrant labor that has traditionally been available in Hudson County.

Methodology

In order to investigate why so many Cuban women work, I drew a sample of Cuban-born women in the Jersey City Standard Metropolitan Statistical Area (equivalent to Hudson County). Data collection took place between July 1979 and May 1981. Random and nonrandom techniques were used in the selection. The random and nonrandom components of the sample were drawn in two different stages. Because I lacked a sampling frame that included all Cuban women in Hudson County, my alternative was to approximate a multistage cluster sample, employing census tracts.

Using the 1970 census figures, I assigned a percentage of interviews per tract proportionate to the percentage of Cubans living in each tract. Once I determined the number of interviews per tract, I assigned the same number of blocks as designated interviews for the tract. Twenty-two tracts were included in the study out of a total of twenty-seven. The final number of cases selected was 107. Respondents had to be at least thirty years old so they would be able to compare their experiences in Cuba and in the United States.

During the data collection period, a new wave of refugees came to the United States from Cuba through the port of Mariel. Some of these new refugees came to the study area. This event gave me an opportunity to find out if the newcomers were significantly different from the earlier Cubans, and to evaluate the impact of their presence on the basic research questions. The randomized interviews represent 26 percent of the total sample; 74 percent had already been interviewed. There were still six census tracts, a total of twenty-eight blocks, to complete. I decided to randomize the rest of the sample to see whether the new wave was changing the general patterns of the Cuban community of the area. I drew a randomized multistage cluster sample by listing each household of the remaining twenty-eight blocks and randomly selecting the interviews assigned per block.[3] The final numbers of new immigrants from Mariel selected and interviewed was five, that is, 4.7 percent of the total (107). In general the new cases were not too different from the rest of the community. All of them except one were relatives of families in Union City and West New York; they had been expecting to leave Cuba for years and seized the first opportunity to do so.

An initial run using cross-tabulation analysis was performed on every variable by random and nonrandom sample. No significant statistical difference was found between the two on any of the variables. Thus, these two subsamples were collapsed and treated equally as one single random sample.

I collected data primarily through interviews using a structured questionnaire. In addition, I interviewed in depth a smaller subsample using recording tapes. These interviews were open-ended. Broad questions were asked and generally the women talked freely.

The structured interviews lasted about one and a half hours each. The taped interviews were much longer; some of them ran from three to four hours. The refusal rate was very low (4.7 percent), and with the exception of one woman, the excuse given was lack of time.

In the following pages I will describe some of the salient characteristics of the sample of Cuban women in Hudson County and explore how these characteristics relate to labor force participation. My conclusions suggest that the attitudes about women, work, and the family expressed by the respondents are related to their former class positions and/or ideology.

Selected Characteristics of the Hudson County Sample and Labor Force Participation

Women in the Hudson County sample had an even higher rate of participation in the labor force (68.2 percent) than other women in the

TABLE 1
Female Labor Force Participation Among Selected Hispanic Groups in the United States, 1980 (in percent)

	Total Female Population	Mexican-Americans	Puerto Ricans	Cubans	Total Spanish-Speaking
United States	49.9	49.0	40.1	55.4	49.3
New Jersey	50.6	52.1	43.1	59.4	50.6
Hudson County, N.J.	49.2	—	—	—	52.2
Hudson County sample[a]	—	—	—	68.2	—

Sources: U.S. Bureau of the Census, *U.S. Summary, 1980* (1983), and *New Jersey, 1980* (1983).

a. Drawn from the present study, conducted July 1979–May 1981.

area and higher than Cuban women in New Jersey and the nation (see table 1). Women interviewed in the Hudson County sample (median age, 49.7 years) were considerably older than Cuban and other Hispanic and non-Hispanic females nationally. This was partially due to the sample selection procedure, which established a minimum age of thirty.

A great majority, 73.8 percent, were married. Having a husband has traditionally meant having someone to depend on economically, but this was not the case here. As can be seen in table 2, 70 percent of the married women in the sample participated in the labor force. This is a higher percentage than women in the category that included divorced, separated, and widowed women. The explanation is that some of these women were beyond working age, while others were unmarried heads of households taking care of young children. In general, however, a significant proportion of the women in each category worked for pay.

Children, especially if they are young, have traditionally kept women from joining the work force. The mean number of children among women in the sample was 2.0, while the mean number of persons per household was 3.2. In 50.5 percent of the cases, the children were living with their parents. Thirty-one percent of the women interviewed reported that some of the children were living at home and some lived elsewhere. Generally, those living elsewhere were married. In fewer cases there were children away at school. Most college-attending children of the women in the sample commuted to a nearby campus.

TABLE 2
Marital Status and Labor Force Participation of 107 Cuban Women in Hudson County, N.J., 1979–81

	Single		Married		Divorced, Separated, Widowed		Total	
	%	N	%	N	%	N	%	N
Working women	83.3	5	70.1	56	54.5	12	68.2	73
Women who do only housework	0.0	0	21.5	17	36.4	8	23.4	25
Retired women	16.7	1	6.3	5	4.5	1	6.5	7
Women seeking, but unable to find work	0.0	0	1.3	1	4.5	1	1.9	2
Total	100.0	6	100.0	79	100.0	22	100.0	107

Sources: See table 1.
Note: Chi square = 6.18; significance = 0.4; degrees of freedom = 6. Sample drawn from the present study, conducted July 1979–May 1981.

The percentage of women with children under age six in the sample was low, 3.7 percent. (Remember that respondents had to be at least thirty years old). Even so, we found a difference between workers and nonworkers by number and age of children. Only 3.3 percent of the workers had children under six, while 6.3 percent of the nonworkers were in this category. Similarly, 21.3 percent of the workers have no children at all, while all of the nonworkers had children. Child care responsibilities, especially for young children, explained why some women did not participate in the work force.

Table 3 shows that almost half (48.1 percent) the women interviewed in this sample had worked for pay in Cuba before coming to the United States. The fact that so many women in the sample had worked in Cuba reflects at least two things. First, the assumption that few Cuban women did not work outside the home (or for pay) may have been more a myth than a reality, especially in the decade preceding the Revolution. It is quite possible that many salaried women were not counted by the census as part of the labor force. Some of the occupations that sample members reported (such as working as a seamstress) could have been carried out at home.

Second, the majority of women in the Hudson County sample came to the United States during the late 1960s and early 1970s. During those years one of the goals of the revolutionary government had been to incorporate more women into production. Opportunities for women, therefore, were opening up in Cuba that did not exist earlier. Work outside the home was becoming more acceptable. Many of the women in the sample who worked in Cuba did so because jobs were

TABLE 3
Labor Force Participation of 106 Cuban Women in Cuba and the United States

| | Cuba | | | | United States | |
| | Did Not Work | | Worked | | | |
	%	N	%	N	%	N
Working women	70.9	39	66.7	34	68.8	73
Women who do only housework	23.6	13	23.5	12	23.6	25
Retired women	5.5	3	5.9	3	5.7	6
Women seeking, but unable to find work	0.0	0	3.9	2	1.9	2
Total	51.9	55	48.1	51	100.0	106

Sources: See table 1.
Note: Totals differ slightly from table 2 because of one missing case. Sample drawn from the present study, conducted in Hudson County, N.J., July 1979–May 1981.

available and they could earn money without incurring disapproval. Their joining the work force was independent of their later decision to leave the country.

As seen in Table 3, having worked or not having worked in Cuba does not have an impact on labor force participation here. The distribution of women according to their economic activity in Cuba is almost identical among those who opted to work in the United States and those who did not.

As previous studies have indicated, the Cuban community of Hudson County, unlike the Cuban population nationally, contains a significant proportion of persons from rural and semirural areas and small towns in Cuba (Rogg, 1974). They have not achieved the educational levels of the rest of the country. For example, while 44 percent of Cubans in the United States are high school graduates, only 12.4 percent of the respondents in our sample had attained that level. There was little variation between the educational level of married women and that of their husbands.

The large majority of the working women in the sample were in blue-collar occupations in the apparel and textile industries. This fact is not surprising, given the lower educational level of the sample and the predominance of blue-collar, especially manufacturing, employment in this area. As shown in table 4, more women in the sample were concentrated in the blue-collar occupations (generally as operatives) than their husbands. The older age of Cuban women in the Hudson County sample and their poor knowledge of English may account for their high concentration in factory work. By contrast, 14.3 percent of men were in the service category, compared with only 4.1 percent of the women.

Also interesting was the difference in the professional, technical, and managerial category, where 8.1 percent of the women were concentrated, as opposed to only 1.4 percent of the men. Yet more men than women owned businesses. Since the difference in educational levels between males and females was not significant, the fact that there were more women professionals indicates that it was easier for some educated Cuban women to enter traditionally acceptable professions for women, such as teaching or social work. For example, of the women interviewed who had been lawyers in Cuba, most were working in social service agencies in Jersey City or New York. Educated men, on the other hand, may have concentrated their efforts in business.

Cubans suffered a significant loss of occupational status after coming to the United States (Moncarz 1969; Rogg 1974). But they appear to have adapted their old values and aspirations to their new circumstances even when their new social location was not the same. To

TABLE 4

Occupations of Employed Cuban Women in Hudson County, N.J., and Husbands, 1979–81 (in percent)

	Total Women[a]	Husbands
Owning a business	6.8[b]	12.9
Professional, technical, managerial work	8.1	1.4
White-collar work	10.8	11.4
Blue-collar work	67.6	51.4
Service work	4.1	14.3
Self-employment	1.4	1.5
Other	1.2	7.1

Sources: See table 1.
Note: Sample drawn from the present study, conducted July 1979–May 1981.
   a. Includes both married and unmarried women; 5 of the total working women were single; 12 were separated, divorced, or widowed (see table 2).
   b. Many women reported owning businesses with their husbands.

determine the degree of occupational mobility experienced by the sample, we compared occupational status in Cuba and the United States. Broad occupational categories were used: blue-collar and service work were considered low-status occupations; white-collar work and being self-employed, a middle status; and owning a business or practicing a profession, high status. Data for husbands as heads of households in Cuba and in the United States were used for this purpose, since not all women in the sample had occupations in Cuba. Table 5 compares the occupational status levels of husbands in Cuba and in the United States.

Although there is a significant association between occupational status in Cuba and in the United States (because a sufficient number of people maintained the same occupations), there is also a pattern of downward mobility. For example, 47.2 percent of white-collar and self-employed workers in Cuba became blue-collar or service workers in the United States, and 52.6 percent of those owning businesses or in the professions in Cuba moved down to the white-collar category in the United States. Conversely, a high percentage (68.2 percent) of those having blue-collar or service jobs in Cuba remained in the same category after emigration. Among those in the blue-collar and service categories in Cuba, 22 percent moved up to white-collar jobs in the United States, and 9.1 percent became business owners or professionals.

The majority of women who worked for pay in Cuba and also went to work in the United States experienced downward mobility. Fifty-six percent of those who worked in Cuba and held white-collar jobs in their country moved down to blue-collar occupations in the United

TABLE 5
Husbands' Occupations in Cuba and in the United States (in percent)

	Cuba							
	Blue-Collar Work and Service Work[a]		White-Collar Work and Self- Employment		Owning a Business and Professional Work		United	States
	%	N	%	N	%	N	%	N
Blue-collar and service work	68.2	15	47.2	17	10.5	2	44.2	34
White-collar work and self-employment	22.7	5	44.4	16	52.6	10	40.3	31
Owning a business	9.1	2	8.3	3	36.8	7	15.6	12
Total	28.6	22	46.8	36	24.6	19	100.0	77

Sources: See table 1.
Note: Sample drawn from the present study, conducted July 1979–May 1981. Chi square = 17.70; significance = .01; degrees of freedom = 4.
   a. Does not include professional services.

States. This movement obviously reflects the difficulties that most working women had in maintaining the same occupation after emigration. Language problems were the main impediment to staying in the same occupational field. Women in white-collar, professional, and business occupations in the United States had held similar positions in Cuba. This pattern indicates that those women in Cuba in the professions and with higher levels of education and knowledge of English could transfer their skills more easily to the United States.

Why Do so Many Cuban Women Work?

This discussion can only refer to Cuban women and work in the Hudson County sample. However, the answers of these respondents may suggest general patterns in the behavior of Cuban women in the United States. We asked the women in the sample their main reason for working. Eighty-three percent said to help the family financially; 5 percent said to pay for their children's education. Others gave more personal reasons, such as becoming economically independent (9.5 percent) and self-realization (2.7 percent).

The answers confirmed what many studies about immigrant women in the United States have found: working outside the home is a response to the economic needs of the family. Wage labor was viewed by Cuban women as an extension of their family obligations and as an important contribution to the family economy. In general, women's economic contribution represented about 40 percent of the total family income.[4]

The central importance of family in explaining why so many Cuban women work outside the home is reflected in the way they spend their salaries. When given a series of categories to indicate how they spent their money, 70.1 percent mentioned food first. Paying the rent or mortgage was another top priority for 53 percent. For 32.4 percent, utilities were among the three most important expenditures. Education of the children was one of the top priorities for 15 percent of the women.[5]

In the opinion of many of the respondents, having small children at home was the most powerful reason why a woman should not work: 57.5 percent said they should not work when children are young. On the other hand, 36.8 percent responded that having small children was no impediment to work, although some qualified this statement by saying that there was no reason a mother should not work if children are cared for by a trustworthy person, preferably a relative. Only 3.8 percent said women with children should never work, 0.9 percent responded that women with children should not work if their husbands objected, and the same proportion stated that women with children should never work unless there was a great need in the family.

Employment outside the home was seen as necessary to supplement the needs of the family. However, one central element here is that most Cuban women in the sample clearly expressed that they worked to help the family regain what it had lost in Cuba as a result of the Revolution, and for that end, any type of work became acceptable. Thus, female employment outside the home is seen as vital not only for survival, but also for the upward mobility of the family.

An elementary school teacher in the Hudson County sample illustrates the above points:

I always worked in Cuba because I enjoyed my career. Maybe it was because I always saw my mother work (she was a teacher) and it became so natural. Here, I do the same kind of work I used to do in Cuba and I like it. I am an elementary school teacher. Even though my husband has a business now I want to continue working. I think it would be inconsiderate on my part to stay home while he works. Life is very expensive and we Cubans are used to living comfortably. . . . No wonder most Cuban women have jobs here. Cuban women have been forced to help their families recuperate in only a few years the standard of living they had achieved in Cuba before communism took over.
—Married white woman, forty years old, middle-class
with university education in Cuba, from Las Villas.

The reasons for this strong emphasis on participating in the labor force are intimately connected to the specific characteristics of the Cuban migration.. Cubans have a strong work ethic. This is in part geared toward substituting for the social and economic rewards that the family lost in the homeland (even if this work ethic can satisfy only material wants at first). Therefore, factors pertaining to the specific nature of the Cuban migration to the United States and the reception offered the group in this country have to be taken into account. The high level of participation of Cuban women in the U.S. work force is one way in which the family can achieve faster economic success and substitute for the lost economic and social rewards enjoyed in Cuba.

Cuban "refugees" of the 1960s, like those from other socialist countries, were determined to succeed in U.S. society and brought skills that allowed success in many cases and reinforced their drives. Thus, the high incorporation of Cuban women into the U.S. labor force has to be seen in the context of a migrant group that wants to regain a middle-class life and its symbols: owning a home, sending the children to college, and saving for the future. These material achievements may not be the equivalent of obtaining a middle-class status in U.S. society—Cubans are a Hispanic minority in the United States—but it paves the way for the mobility of the family (especially of the children) to that status in the future. This goal justifies the massive entrance of women into the labor force and their acceptance of manual, blue-collar work.

These generalizations apply to the workers who left in the late 1960s and early 1970s as well as to former middle-class Cubans. Former working-class women in the sample were from families aspiring to middle-class status before the Revolution. In their view, coming to the United States was the only way in which their aspirations could be realized.

A formerly working-class woman talked about her family's reasons for leaving Cuba in the early seventies and about why she thinks Cubans work so hard in the United States:

Why did we leave Cuba? Well, because we didn't like that system ["no nos gustaba aquello"]. The reason was political. In Cuba there was no place to better yourself. The Revolution brought many people down instead of helping them to improve themselves. That is why Cubans work so hard here, because they are used to always struggling to have something and to secure a better future for their children. They did that in Cuba, too, no matter how poor they were.

> —Married white woman, forty-three years old, working-class with some secondary education in Cuba, from Havana.

Being a "burden" to the U.S. government, to relatives, or to society in general was a concern for many interviewees. A former secondary school teacher reflected on the reasons why Cubans work so hard and how this is seen by other groups:

Cuban women work out of necessity unless they have a profession they like. The husband's salary is not sufficient. In Cuba, it was enough if the man worked. You could even have servants. But here, life is different. If there are children in the family, both husband and wife have to work to provide these children with a good education. I think the main reason for working is economic need. Many people say that Cubans work hard because they want to have two cars and many other things. I think that is not totally true. Many other people are envious of us because we work hard. Even the Americans sometimes! For example, my daughter has the highest point average in her class, and many kids (especially American kids) resent the fact that she is Cuban and number one. But the reason why we are successful is because we work hard and are responsible. . . . When we came to this country we had a lot of debts. We went to Spain first, and our relatives here had to send the plane tickets for us to come here, plus money to live on during the months we had to wait in Spain. When we got here we wanted to work doing *anything* to pay our relatives back. So we didn't work to buy luxuries then but to support ourselves and pay our debts. Only when we finished paying them did we start thinking about buying things. It is not right to be a burden to this government or to people who have helped you, even if they are your relatives.

— Married white woman, forty-eight years old, middle-class with secondary education in Cuba, from Las Villas.

As the above quotes suggest, a strong factor behind the high level of labor force participation among Cuban women is their predominantly middle-class origins or aspirations and a middle-class ideology of upward mobility. Although these findings apply only to the sample studied here, similar reasons may explain the equally high level of labor force participation of Cuban women nationally and in the Cuban concentrations in the United States. (For data, see Wilber, Jaco, Hagan, and del Fierro, 1976, vol. 3; Ferree, 1978; Diaz, 1981).

Thus, we see that the characteristics of Cuban immigrants explain in part their heightened economic activity. But these characteristics would not mean much if there were no labor market for these human resources. The correspondence between the needs of industries for workers and the high motivation of Cubans to work explains the high levels of Cuban women in the work force in Hudson County, New Jersey.

177

Conclusion

This article attempts to explain the high level of labor force participation of Cuban women by analyzing a sample of Cuban-born women in Hudson County, New Jersey. Given the negative attitudes existing in prerevolutionary Cuba about women working outside the home, it becomes important to understand this paradoxical behavioral change among Cubans who left the island, among other things, to escape radical changes affecting the traditional role of women and the family.

Although unusual characteristics of the sample—such as there being fewer children, and children of older age than is the case with other Hispanic groups—account for higher female labor force activity, the strongest factor behind the intense economic activity of Cuban women (as for Cubans in general) is the combination of middle-class values or aspirations, a rejection of the socialist revolution taking place in their homeland, and positive attitudes about the U.S. economic and political system. These strong beliefs, common among refugees from socialist countries, are manifested in a powerful work ethic and aspirations for social mobility. Primarily to compensate for the lost rewards in their home country, this group justifies the massive entrance of women into paid production.

These conclusions raise other questions, however. Do Cuban women in the United States feel that they are more "liberated" now because they work outside the home? Moreover, is female labor force participation in general an indicator of female emancipation? This last question has been indeed posed by feminist scholars studying women and work. Like Cuban women, immigrant and other women in the United States and elsewhere have seen work outside the home as a way to help the family and not as a means to sexual liberation.

However, the process of participating in the labor force appears to confer an independent identity (perhaps only an economic one at first) on women, whether or not they are conscious of an identity change. For example, despite the fact that the overwhelming majority of women interviewed maintained that the principal reason for work was to help the family economically, 64.4 percent said that they would work even if their families did not need the money. A much lower percentage (35.6 percent) stated that they would prefer to stay home under those circumstances.

Many women workers in the sample admitted feeling more independent as a result of having a job. The process of participating in the labor force may make Cuban women more cautious of the significance of work in their lives, beyond that of meeting the needs of their families. It is to be hoped that incorporation of Cuban women into the U.S. labor force will pave the way for their increased participation in other public spheres in the Cuban community and in American society at large.

NOTES

This article, from my Ph.D. dissertation, is part of a larger research project supported by the Ford Foundation. It is adapted from two earlier articles: "Women, Work and Change: The Case of Cuban Women in the U.S.," Latin American Monograph Series 9, Northwestern Pennsylvania Institute for Latin American Studies, Mercyhurst College [Erie, Pa.], 1979; "Cuban Women and Work in the United States: A New Jersey Case Study," in *International Migration: The Female Experience,* ed. Rita J. Simon and Caroline Brettell (Totowa, N.J.: Rowman and Allanheld, 1986).

1. Consejo Nacional de Economía, 1958. In the late 1940s and early 1950s, increasing numbers of lower middle-class and upper-class women joined the labor force, the former group mainly because of changes in the Cuban economy (Kaufman-Purcell, 1970:260–61). Economic expansion, U.S. investments in utilities, communications, oil refining, and tourism generated white-collar work opportunities, particularly for educated lower middle-class women.

According to census figures, between 1943 and 1953, the number of female typists and stenographers increased from 1,253 to 5,420; the percentage of female elementary teachers increased from 77.5 to 84.3, and that of female professors increased from 53.6 to 67.8. Many women also became service workers (waitresses and janitors), undoubtedly because of the growth of tourism. More women also became domestics, as more families could afford their services.

2. "Middle-class" here denotes professional, semiprofessional, and entrepreneurial categories, in which a certain level of education is needed and aspirations to economic success are implied.

3. I could not use a random selection process because of the impossibility, given limited time, resources, and research assistants, of listing every household in every block in order to construct a sampling frame.

4. Median income in the sample was $6,336. Median total family income, out of six income categories, was between $13,000 and $15,999.

5. Even though most women interviewed stressed the importance of education to upward mobility, few cited their most important reason for working as to provide for their children's education. This discrepancy is explained by the fact that some women gave "education of the children" as a motive for working, while others included that motive in the response "helping the family financially." Indeed, financial self-sufficiency was encouraged in children. In most cases, because of the older age of the sample, children had already finished college; and many had received financial aid and/or had worked to pay for their education.

REFERENCES

Amaro, Nelson, and Alejandro Portes. 1972. "Situación de los grupos cubanos en Estados Unidos." *Aportes* 3.
Consejo Nacional de Economía. 1958. *El empleo, el subempleo y el desempleo en Cuba.* Havana: CNE.

90 : YOLANDA PRIETO

Diaz, Guarione, ed. 1981. *Evaluation and Identification of Policy Issues in the Cuban Community*. Miami: Cuban National Planning Council.
Domínguez, Virginia. 1977. "The Nature of Change: Cuban Women in the United States." Presented at the Conference on Women and Change, Boston University, May 6–7.
Ferree, Myra Marx. 1979. "Employment Without Liberation: Cuban Women in the United States." *Social Sciences Quarterly* 60 (June).
Fox, Geoffrey E. 1970. "Honor, Shame and Women's Liberation in Cuba." In *Female and Male in Latin America*, ed. Anne Pescatello. Pittsburgh, Pa.: University of Pittsburgh Press.
Hudson County [N.J.] Planning Board. 1972. "Distribution of Cuban Population. Map No. 8." *Hudson County Population Study*. Jersey City, N.J.: County of Hudson.
———. 1974. *Economic Base Study*. Jersey City, N.J.: County of Hudson.
Junta Central de Planificación. 1975. *Censo de población y viviendas, 1970*. Havana: Editorial Orbe.
Junta Nacional del Censo. 1945. *Censo de 1943*. Havana: P. Fernández y Cía., S. en C.
Kaufman-Purcell, Susan. 1970. "Modernizing Women for a Modern Society: The Cuban Case." In *Female and Male in Latin America*, ed. Anne Pescatello. Pittsburgh, Pa.: University of Pittsburgh Press.
Marx, Karl, and Frederick Engels. 1974. *The German Ideology*. New York: International Publishers.
Moncarz, Raul. 1969. *A Study of the Effect of Environmental Change on Human Capital Among Selected Skilled Cubans*. Washington, D.C.: Clearinghouse for Federal Scientific and Technical Information, U.S. Department of Commerce, National Bureau of Standards.
Oficina Nacional de los Censos Demográfico y Electoral. 1955. *Censos de población, viviendas y electoral. Informe General, 1953*. Havana: P. Fernández y Cía, S. en C.
Pérez, Lisandro. 1986. "Immigrant Economic Adjustment and Family Organization: The Cuban Success Story Reexamined." *International Migration Review* 20 (Spring).
Portes, Alejandro, Juan M. Clark, and Robert L. Bach. 1977. "The New Wave: A Statistical Profile of Recent Cuban Exiles to the United States." *Cuban Studies* 7 (January).
Prohías, Rafael, and Lourdes Casal. 1974. *The Cuban Minority in the United States: Preliminary Report on Need Identification and Program Evaluation*. Boca Raton: Florida Atlantic University.
Rogg, Eleanor M. 1974. *The Assimilation of Cuban Exiles: The Role of Community and Class*. New York: Aberdeen Press.
Rogg, Eleanor M., and Rosemary Sanatana Cooney. 1980. *Adaptation and Adjustment of Cubans: West New York, New Jersey*. Hispanic Research Center Monograph No. 5, Fordham University.
U.S. Bureau of the Census. 1973. *Final Report, 1970*. Washington, D.C.: GPO.
———. 1983. *Characteristics of the Population, General Social and Economic Characteristics, U.S. Summary, 1980*. Washington, D.C.: GPO.
———. 1983. *General Social and Economic Characteristics, New Jersey, 1980*. Washington, D.C.: GPO.
U.S. Department of Commerce. 1982. *County Business Patterns, 1980*. Washington, D.C.: GPO.
Weber, Max. 1958. *The Protestant Ethic and the Spirit of Capitalism*. New York: Charles Scribner's Sons.
Wilber, George, D. E. Jaco, R. J. Hagan, and Al del Fierro. 1976. *Minorities in the Labor Market*. Vol. 1: *Spanish Americans and Indians in the Labor Market*. Vol. 3:

Metropolitan and Regional Inequalities Among Minorities in the Labor Market. Lexington: University of Kentucky Press.

Wilson, Kenneth L., and Alejandro Portes. 1980. "Immigrant Enclaves: An analysis of the Labor Market Experience of Cubans in Miami." *American Journal of Sociology* 86, no. 2.

Yans-McLaughlin, Virginia. 1971. "Patterns of Work and Family Organization: Buffalo's Italians." *Journal of Social History* 2 (Autumn).

SE ME ACABÓ LA CANCIÓN: AN ETHNOGRAPHY OF NON-CONSENTING STERILIZATIONS AMONG MEXICAN WOMEN IN LOS ANGELES

Carlos G. Velez-I

INTRODUCTION

"Se me acabó la canción" is a phrase which was repeated quite frequently by one of ten Mexican women[1] who were sterilized without their consent between 1971 and 1974 in Los Angeles, California.[2] The phrase literally means, "my song is finished," but the connotations are far more important. From the point of view of the Mexican women "the song" is the melody of life which is inextricably linked to the ability to procreate children. This melody is the core of the social identity not only of the women, but interdependently it extends to Mexican males as well, in their ability to sire children.

The analysis of the social, cultural, and psychological effects of the forced termination of this melody is the focus of the ethnography of this work, but it is not the totality. For this is

also an ethnography of the attempts to redress what for most human beings is a basic right. In addition, this is an explanation of the theories and techniques that were utilized to structure legal actions on the women's behalf, as well as their methodological implementation, and their efficacy in a court of law. But beyond this, through the use of theoretical constructs we will understand the genesis of negative differential treatment of working and non-working class Mexican people in the United States in analogous behavioral environments.[*] Lastly, however, it is also an ethnography of naïve applied anthropology.

BASIC ASSUMPTIONS

There are two primary assumptions that guide the following analysis, and they should be clearly stated. First, in the general area of "applied anthropology," in which this work may be placed, a built-in assumption can be perceived. As Bastide (1971) points out, much applied work depends on stratification models

*See Note 3 for an explication of behavioral environments.

Carlos G. Velez-I is Assistant Professor of Anthropology at the University of California, Los Angeles. Versions of this paper were presented before the International Congress of Anthropological and Ethnological Sciences, New Delhi, India, December 10–18, 1978 and at the post-congress of Applied and Action Anthropology, Calcutta, India, December 19–20, 1978 © 1980 by Carlos G. Velez-I and focuses on the subordinate and super-ordinate relations between dominant and minority sectors. This work is not different from this traditional concern. However, opposed to Bastide's suggestion that in the intraethnic sphere most applied anthropologists yearn for the assimilation of minorities in plural socie-ties, I remain uncommitted to such a view. Sec-ond, much of the work in the United States con-cerning ethnic and racial relations has been, as Van den Berghe suggests: "the handmaiden(s) to the meliorative and reformists attempts of the well-intentioned liberal establishment . . ." (1970). It follows as a corollary that scholars should drop their pretenses of "objectivity," and state with as much precision as possible their position.

These two assumptions, then, must be con-sidered in order to understand clearly the his-torical conditions discussed, and the theoreti-cal constructs utilized. Certainly, the first bias is obvious in that I chose to serve in the capa-city of consulting cultural anthropologist in favor of the plaintiffs—the Mexican women who had been allegedly sterilized without their consent. I would not have served the defendants with equal conviction if I had been asked. There-fore, I certainly adhere to the applied anthropo-logical tradition in this manner. However, I drop the positivist credo of "objectivity" by stating that as a Mexican in the United States, I have experienced numerous behavioral environments in which I was the object of differential negative treatment because of my ethnic minority status, and I have witnessed the same treatment on other occasions. It follows, then, that this ex-perience filters and colors my selection of the theoretical constructs used in the analysis and conclusions derived in this study. Neverthe-less, I have attempted to keep within the bounds of the basic cannons of anthropological re-search. As will be shown, the course of events proved the theoretical constructs and hypothe-ses to be valid.

BASIC THEORETICAL AND METHODOLOGICAL CONCERNS

In order to appreciate the significance of the events analyzed here, it must be made clear that these occurred within a highly industrial-ized capitalist nation-state in which variance

and heterogeneity of culture, rather than com-monality and replication organize behavior and behavioral environments.[3] Since class, ethni-city, socially defined racial groups, and special interest sectors form subcultures of various sorts within the nation-state, most complex societies are culturally plural by definition. Yet this diversity of culture is organized in the nation-state by a prism of behavioral expecta-tions which reflect a subcultural ideal in which economic and social values are the valid indi-cators of citizenship and nationality. In the United States this "subcultural prism" holds true. Citizenship, nationality, and ethnic iden-tity reflect the dominant ethnic group of Anglo-Saxon Americans.[4] It is indeed a curious para-dox of all nation-states that while pretending universalistic criteria for its citizens, in reality it distributes rights and duties according to a preconceived specific subcultural ethnic group ideal. That ideal often reflects the dominant ethnic group holding political and economic power, regardless of which "ism" the nation adheres to. Enloe (1973) suggests:

If the group's ethnic identity is closely bound to the nation's identity it may not even appear to be an ethnic group. It will simply be the norm, the mainstream into which all minorities are submerged. Only when minorities [or oppressed majorities (numerical ones)] self-consciously assert the worth of their own cultures is the ethnicity of "invisible" ethnic communities exposed. Ukranian nationalism reveals the ethnic chauvinism of the Great Russians;[5] Turk-ish nomad's resistance to the Red Army reveals the ethnicity of the Han Chinese (1973, pp. 213–214).

In the United States it was not until the Chicano, Black and Indian power movements of the 1960s that the ethnicity of WASPs was re-vealed.[6] On the other hand, throughout Latin America there is little of the national subcul-tural prism that is invisible. The "mestizo" or "ladino" prism is the overt, explicit, national model and except for nations like Mexico that pay lip service to "indianism" (Indigenismo), most Latin American nations suffer a cultural ethnocentrism which seeks to assimilate or eradicate its indigenous populations. Brazil, Paraguay, and Venezuela have used particularly violent methods of implanting their national subcultural prism.

THE IDEOLOGY OF CULTURAL DIFFERENCES

For ethnic and racial minority groups revelation of the existence of such a prism leads to the understanding that an "ideology of cultural differences" has been used as the *raison d'etre* for the continued differential treatment of ethnic and racial minority groups. Kuper (1974) has suggested that the ideology of cultural differences is an elaborate rationalization. A dominant group, regardless of actual differences in culture, points to a subordinate group's inferior relationship with the dominant group as the aftermath of unresolvable differences in social organization, political systems, economic relations, religious and ideological beliefs and values, and certainly the expression of these differences in behavior. The thieving Mexican has been a rather traditional cultural characteristic associated with this ethnic group. As Paredes (1958) states in discussing the incessant conflicts between Mexicans and Anglos along the border frontier between Mexico and the United States:

> The picture of the Mexican as an inveterate thief, especially of horses and cattle, is of interest to the psychologist as well as the folklorist. The cattle industry of the Southwest had its origin in the Nueces-Río Grande area, with the stock and the ranches of the Rio Grande rancheros. The "cattle barons" (Texans) built up their fortunes at the expense of the Border Mexican by means which were far from ethical. One notes that the white southerner took his slave women as concubines and then created an image of the male Negro as a sex fiend. In the same way he appears to have taken the Mexican's property and then made him out a thief (p. 20).

This ideology of cultural differences is used then to screen out other groups as too different from the subcultural prism to allow for access to resources unless they become "mainstream Americans" by acculturation and assimilation. Regardless of historical conditions and structural relations, the onus of undifferentiated access to resources lies in the hands of the ethnic minority. It may also be the case, however, that the ideology of cultural differences defines the ethnic minority as so different that only complete physical separation, as in South Africa, can be articulated as the national policy.

Such rationalizations are a contrast to the cross-cultural record. For the most part there are efficient conditions which have defined the quality of the relations between dominant ethnic national groups and subordinate ethnic national groups. Certainly as a point of departure, the Mexican ethnic minority in the United States, as is the case for many minorities in the New World, can trace their subordination to a war of conquest and other acts of violence. While violence as Wagley and Harris (1964) have pointed out, is not a universal characteristic for the rise of minority groups, the presence of violence ". . . in the process of birth of minority groups frequently provides an important key to understanding intergroup hostilities" (p. 252). Furthermore, the economic relegation of workers to subservient positions as sources of cheap labor in times of economic expansion of the nation-state may also generate subordinate minority relations between ethnic groups. Also the appearance of minority groups is always associated with the emergence or expansion of the nation-state so that cultural groups become overwhelmed by others who represent the national prism.

In addition to these elements which foster intergroup hostilities and subservient domination of one group by another, there also lie efficient conditions for a virulent sort of domination; that is, social racism which arises when two populations who differ phenotypically and culturally intersect in the aforementioned circumstances: conquest, violent confrontation, economic subservience, and nation-state expansion. The end result for the dominated population is differential negative treatment in most behavioral environments. When such conditions are coupled with an "ideology of cultural differences" and the national subcultural prism becomes economically, educationally, politically, and socially institutionalized, then clearly those who were annexed, conquered, enslaved, economically colonized, and materially denied will be placed in a structurally asymmetrical and subordinate status.

MEXICANS AND THE UNITED STATES: A HISTORICAL STRUCTURAL PRÉCIS

Recently, a number of stratification indices were used to rank ethnic and racial groups in the United States.[7] Of the fourteen groups mentioned the lowest four consistently retained that position during the twenty-year period (1950–1970) in which the data was collected. Significantly, these four groups are all ethnic or racial minorities who historically emerged from conquest (Mexicans, Indians), enslavement (Blacks), economic colonization (Mexicans, Indians, Puerto Ricans and Blacks), and annexation (Mexicans and Puerto Ricans). In addition, all four groups were to different degrees culturally and phenotypically distinct from the national subcultural prism. The other ten groups mentioned do not in fact comprise populations who have been colonized economically or were subjected to conquest or enslavement. Although other ethnic groups may differ phenotypically and culturally, intergroup hostility such as that between Japanese and Anglo-Saxons has been limited to extremely short periods, as during World War II.

Of all the ethnic populations in the United States, Mexicans and Indians have passed from conquest, annexation, purchase, and into economic colonization. For Mexicans, their subject population status is the result of having provided land and labor for 130 years to a national dominant subcultural group of Anglo-Saxons. As the aftermath of the "Texas War of Independence (1836)," the Mexican War of 1846, and the so-called Gadsden Purchase of 1853, the United States gained roughly half of Mexico and a population of 75,000 Mexicans. Thus through annexation, conquest, and the forced purchase of mineral-rich southern Arizona and the Mesilla Valley of southwestern New Mexico, the United States managed to acquire territory greater in extent than Germany and France combined (McWilliams 1968).[8] In addition, Mexican labor has been used, drawn, discarded, and repatriated by United States mining, agriculture, railroad, and heavy industrial corporate interests. Most recently the garment industry has been a particularly intensive user. For 130 years, depending on the state of economic conditions in the United States, such labor has been both welcomed and expelled. It is clear from the Bracero programs[9] of the 1940s to the so-called twin-cities border projects,[10] that Mexicans have composed an extremely important segment of the cheap labor supply to various sorts of large corporate industrial interests.

Goldschmidt (1976, 1978) empirically shows that the correlation is extremely significant between the ownership of the means of production by large corporate industrial interests in agricultural contexts, and the ensuing size of lower-class populations. Thus ". . . as the proportion of product by the large (agribusiness) farm increases, the proportion of lower-class persons also increases" with a .76 statistical correlation. According to Goldschmidt the social structures of industrialized agricultural communities differ markedly from family farm communities, as his table illustrates.

It follows that use of the labor of an ethnic population by corporate modes of production has had very significant social structural implications for the communities in which they reside. For Mexicans who have always composed a large cheap labor force for corporately controlled industrial enterprises in either rural or urban contexts, community social structures largely reflect the agribusiness mode of production in which Mexicans are selected for the lowest sector of such a social structure.

When these various historical structural relations are combined with a largely chauvinistic national subcultural prism and "depigmented" phenotypic racist ideal, the probability of intergroup hostility and conflict remains very high.[11] Thus, basically a working-class and underclass ethnic minority population, Mexicans in the United States have received differential negative treatment in myriad behavioral environments.

THE DISTRIBUTION OF DIFFERENTIAL NEGATIVE TREATMENT IN BEHAVIORAL ENVIRONMENTS

A basic problem arises in the discussion of differential treatment of any minority population if only structural or historical arguments are articulated. Especially in a heterogeneous, complex, industrial state like the United States, differential negative treatment of its traditional

TABLE 1
Comparison Between a Family Farm and Agribusiness

Community in California

	Family Farm Town	Agri- business Town
Economic base is the same		
Total farm sales (millions)	$2.5	$2.4
Farm size is different		
Average farm size in acres	57	497
Farm size adjusted for productivity	87	285
Population characteristics differ		
Total population	7,400	6,200
Self-employed & white collars	970	240
Percent of labor force	51	19
Agricultural labor	550	800
Percent of labor force	51	65
Economic conditions differ		
Number of retail businesses	141	62
Total retail sales (millions)	$4.4	$2.4
Level of living (percent above combined mean)	70	30
Community affairs differ		
Number of civic organizations	21	7
Participation (members per 100 population)	42	29
Number of churches	15	9
Church attendance (percent)	72	59
Public parks	2	0
Civic affairs differ		
Participation in school activities (percent)	28	16
Newspapers (issues per week)	4	1
Local government (incorporation)	yes	no

SOURCE: W. Goldschmidt, *The Rural Foundation of the American Culture*. A Gregory Foundation Memorial Lecture. (Columbia, Missouri, 1976, p. 16.)

ethnic and racial minority groups is "distributed" according to the structure of the behavioral environments in which representatives of the dominant ethnic group intersect with subordinate populations. Thus it is simply just not valid that all Mexicans, in all circumstances, at all periods in history will receive negative treatment by Anglos and their representatives. Rather, there are specific behavioral environments that select for differential treatment where an "ideology of cultural differences" can be utilized as the *raison d'etre*, as the justification for the structurally asymmetrical relations that unfold in the course of social intercourse between Mexicans and Anglos.

The sort of behavioral environments that select for such treatment have their genesis in working-class or underclass environments, but not necessarily in the specific environments in which actual labor processes are carried out. Instead there is a higher probability that such differential treatment based on ethnicity will be expressed in behavioral environments that are characterized by high levels of paternalism and structural dependence. Thus the distribution of differential negative treatment can be predicted utilizing a probabilistic model in which various factors are identified as indicators of paternalism and dependence. Those behavioral environments, however which are characterized by competitive structural relations will not select for differential treatment of a population based on other than class factors. It may be the case, as it is with the Mexican population in which its male working force is made up of largely working-class and underclass sectors (82 percent),[12] that there is little respite from differential treatment since either competitive or paternalistic environments are the very basis of existence for the great majority of Mexicans.

Among those behavioral environments marked by paternalism and dependence are those in which groups and persons cannot make demands upon those who control services, resources, information or material goods. Such contexts require behavior patterns of extreme deference articulated through a routinized and elaborate etiquette. Thus, the use of titles of reference, indicating superior status will generate social distance and status differentials. In addition, expected responses within the environment will be "client"-like; that is, passivity rather than demands are the expected responses. Questioning of interaction or its quality will result in negative responses, sometimes in an argot available only to the "selected." The argot itself will be highly developed and in fact will mark the included from the excluded. Elaborate cultural rationalizations are in fact worked out as the only proper "institutionalized" method of communication. Furthermore, spatial separation ensures the relationship of dominance and subordination. There are spaces where only the "clients" are allowed to congregate, and others in which the paternal figures have access to the physical space of the client whenever they choose to move. Such physical segregation not only ensures boundaries but in fact accentuates the difference in roles between clients and paternal figures. Also there is a high probability that costumes and other attire will also mark the status difference between client and paternal figure so that there is little mistaking the two if a physically neutral space should happen to become availabe for social intercourse. In such contexts a "everybody knows their place" and despotism controls the quality of the social intercourse in such paternalistic behavioral environments.

Moreover, "clients" will be perceived as childish, immature, ignorant, and not informed of the specifics of the behavioral environment, a knowledge which is solely that of the paternal figures. The exclusive knowledge will be couched in a special argot available only to the specialist paternal figures who command the behavioral environments. Such artifacts are congruent with aristocratic, oligarchic, autocratic, or colonial political relations between clients and paternal figures which in turn will generate relations based on ascription and a priori definitions of statuses and roles. Such linguistic codes do ensure their maintenance. At no time during the life of the behavioral environment does the client become a paternal figure. Clients may "horizontally" change identity to other kinds of clients, but never vertically. However, paternal figures may acquire greater ascendancy within the boundaries of the behavioral environment. As a corollary, it follows that all paternalistic behavioral environments will be hierarchical and unequal. Social stratification of such behavioral environments is in fact castelike, and the behavior expected within each caste division will be homogeneous. The very institutional processes which allow entry into the upper-caste regions of the paternal systems are themselves so highly articulated that the homogeniety of the controlling paternal figures is almost assured.

Since the behavioral environment is hierarchical and oligarchic then it follows that value consensus is imposed and withdrawal of services, commodities, material goods, or information is the means by which value consensus is assured. Ideological conflict between social divisions is largely eliminated by the traditional etiquette and enforced value consensus. While conflict is endemic to this kind of structure because of the divergent social sectors which make up the paternalistic behavioral environments, there are few alternative choices for the subordinated clients since the information, resources, commodities, or material goods that are in the control of the paternal figures are valued and scarce to the subordinated clients. Thus scarcity makes value greater, a relationship which the paternal figure exploits in this type of context. The manipulation of value consensus is the fulcrum of control in a paternalistic behavioral environment.

These aspects of paternalistic behavioral environments will more than likely lead to differentiated negative treatment of a historically subordinated ethnic minority, especially those of working-class or underclass origin. Thus when Mexicans and Anglos have intersected in behavioral environments with paternalistic relations and characteristics, then Mexicans usually will suffer negative differential treatment and the liberal utilization of an "ideology of cultural differences" will form the *raison d'etre* for such differential treatment. The history of Mexicans in the United States is replete with countless examples.[13]

THE CASE IN POINT: STERILIZATION OF MEXICAN WOMEN IN LOS ANGELES

Twenty-four women have alleged that they did not or could not have given informed consent to sterilization procedures that were carried out during 1971 and 1974 at the "Medical Center," one of the major county hospitals in Los Angeles. Ten of the twenty-four women filed a civil action suit against the Medical Center in which the sterilizations were performed, and each has described the specific circumstances in which they occurred in affidavits and in Findings of Fact and Conclusions of Law.[14]

The evidence illustrates practices by the hospital staff (nurses and doctors) to pressure patients into signing consent forms during intensive labor stages by withholding medication, not soliciting consent for sterilization, or not informing the patients of the permanency of such procedures. In addition, some husbands were pressured to sign consent forms for their wives without their wives' knowledge. Even though there were no medical indications for such procedures to be performed, consent was obtained from the husbands after their wives had refused to sign the consent forms. There was even a recorded refusal by one woman to submit to sterilization, this appears on her medical chart at 5:00 a.m., and after having been given demoral, consent forms appear to have been signed by 6:28 a.m.—the time in which the surgical procedures were performed. One woman was falsely told that a tubal ligation was necessary because the State of California did not allow more than three Cesarian sections. Her third child was to be born in this manner as had her two previous children. According to her physician, conception of a fourth child had to be avoided since this one would also have to be delivered by C-section.

It is a remarkable fact that among the ten women, four did not learn of the sterilization procedures until after they had sought birth control devices. One woman did not become aware that such a procedure had been performed until four years later during a medical examination.

In each case the Medical Center reflects the basic characteristics of a paternalistic behavioral environment. In fact a stay in any hospital exposes an individual to a condition of passivity and impotence not often replicated easily in other environments, except perhaps in judicial contexts. Certainly, in each woman's case, the consent of sterilization was not informed due to the unusual pressures applied and the specific physical conditions in which most of the women were suffering. Furthermore, their lack of knowledge regarding the irreversibility of the procedures, the sedated condition of some of the women who did sign, and the total lack of written consent of three of the women, all point to unilateral, oligarchical, and paternalistic conditions within the behavioral environments in which they were a part.

THE HOSPITAL AS THE BEHAVIORAL ENVIRONMENT

Within the confines of the Medical Center relatively defenseless Mexican women were selected out for differential negative treatment and hostility exemplified by nonconsenting sterilizations. In part, such an abuse is greatest in public hospitals, such as the Medical Center in which the sterilizations of these women occurred, because these are institutions where the poor are regarded as practice cases for medical students. Interns gain status by the number of operations they perform, so it is unlikely that they would turn down the surgical opportunities which a dependently oppressed minority represents. According to one source, a doctor told a group of physicians training at a southern California county hospital as part of their entry into obstetrics:

> I want you to ask every one of the girls if she wants her tubes tied, regardless of how old she is. Remember, every one who says yes to getting her tubes tied means two tubes (practice) for some resident or intern and less work for some poor son-of-a-bitch next year (Kennard 1974).

In addition, there is a general neo-malthusian ideology that permeates the medical profession. Dr. H. Curtis Wood, Jr., a medical consultant and past president of the Association for Voluntary Sterilization indicated this point of view:

> People pollute, and too many people crowded too close together cause many of our social and economic problems. These in turn are aggravated by involuntary and irresponsible parenthood. As physicians, we have obligations to the society of which we are a part. The welfare mess, as it has been called, cries out for solutions, one of which is fertility control (1973).

At the Medical Center where the ten women were sterilized, Dr. Bernard Rosenfeld, coauthor of a Ralph Nader Health Research Group study on surgical sterilization and one-time OB/GYN resident at the Center stated:

> Surgical teaching programs are having increasing difficulty in finding patients because they·

have traditionally had to rely upon the availability of indigents. With the increase of third party payments (insurance), the number of indigents has decreased, causing the Medical Center to resort to "selling" and various forms of coercing patients into consenting to surgery.

I estimate that while I was at the Medical Center, between 20 to 30 percent of the doctors pushed sterilization on women who either did not understand what was happening to them or who had not been given the facts regarding their options (Interview quoted in Siggins 1977).

Another "insider" also commented on the coercive practices at the Medical Center at the point in time in which the sterilizations of the ten women were taking place:

I saw various forms of actual physical abuse used to force women in labor to consent to sterilization. There were incidences of slapping by doctors and nurses. A syringe of pain-reliever would be shown to a woman in labor and she would be told "we will give you this and stop the pain if you will sign" (Benker press conference 1975).

Such abuses then point to a "neutralization" of the minority person as a human being and the objectification of the practice as a necessary one due to population rationalizations, surgical practice procedures for the interns, or for the "social good" of the patient. Whatever the genesis, they all point to differentiated negative treatment and, in each case, to an "ideology of cultural difference," as the core rationalization for such practices. Through sterilization the subcultural prism of the dominant group has articulated its power in the behavioral environment. In fact, this is an extension of cultural sterilization into the physical sphere.

ENTER THE ANTHROPOLOGIST: QUALITATIVE INDICATORS OF SUBCULTURAL RURAL STRATEGIES OF THE WOMEN

From November 1, 1977 through May 30, 1978, the field studies of these women and their families were designed to accurately gather data which would "place" them in relation to a heterogeneous Mexican population. The studies sought to establish the "subcultural strategies" which these women shared within the cultural boundaries of the Mexican/Chicano population in the southwestern United States. Using participant observation, unstructured interviews and questionnaires, it was determined that in fact the women shared subcultural rural Mexican strategies that were adaptive in urban contexts. These findings even surprised the lawyers who themselves had not quite known what to make of the reactions that these women had expressed in regard to the sterilizations.

The data showed that nine of the ten women were born in small rural communities such as rancherias or ejidos and had been socialized in such environments through the age of fourteen.[15] In Mexico, these women had fulfilled agricultural chores from milking cows to planting and sowing corn. The one woman who had not been born in a rural Mexican setting was born in Dallas, Texas, but had adopted equivalent strategies in Mexican barrios. We can infer that their socialization experiences from early ages were strictly divided according to sex. Also among other adaptive patterns, they learned high values on child bearing and strict divisions of labor.

In such social environments, fictive kinship, extended familial networks, and dense friendship networks assist emotional survival. In urban Los Angeles such extensive and intensive networks were generated by all of the women and their spouses. Thus compadrazgo relations were shared by all the women. All ten women had extensive fictive kinship ties for the four traditional occasions in which such ties are generated: baptism, confirmation, communion, and marriage. For some of the women who had four children, compadres and comadres alone numbered eighteen persons. Five of the ten women maintained extended generational ties so that a three-generational tier was valued and experienced.

In addition, the mean number of children in the women's families of orientation was 7.5 and in their spouses families of orientation it was 9.5. Thus not only were they from large families, but these consanguineal relatives could be regarded as possible network supports. Visitations between consanguines was intensive and Sundays were generally the days in which the gathering of both fictive, consanguineal, and ascending generational relations would meet for commensal activities or for the celebration of birthdays or feast days. Another means of network expansion was that generated through amistad (friendship). Their functions were not only primarily affectionate, but also material. The males assisted each other and reciprocated repair and construction work, the women visited and exchanged information, and in all, they formed borrowing and lending networks for household goods. In addition, all of the women and/or their spouses had participated with their families in tandas or revolving credit associations.

Such consanguineal, fictive, and amistad relationships were identified as rewarding or not, based on sentido familiar (familial sentiment). That is, persons who did not generally reciprocate in exchange relations within these various networks were considered to be lacking in sentido familiar. This sentido familiar had as its basis, however, two core elements as organizing principles: first, marriage and children mark adulthood and responsibility; and second, as a social corollary of the first principle, is the internalization of the social identity of una mujer and un hombre. For the women in the case, although having had ritual markers through quinceñera (debut) to announce the passage from adolescence to adulthood, in fact adulthood was defined once marriage had taken place and children had been procreated. Without such circumstances and regardless of statuses gathered in other contexts such as professional standing or educational achievement, a female was not considered privy to the councils of discussion among women on such topics as sex, behavior of men, or topics of seriousness such as death, and other aspects of the life cycle. It is interesting to note that as long as one of the female lawyers in this case was not married she in fact had no access to the discussions these women shared regarding their marital difficulties experienced as the aftermath of the sterilization procedures. It was not until the lawyer married that she gained access to their discussions.

While marriage marks entrance into adulthood, as a ritual it also legitimizes sexual intercourse for the specific purpose of propagating children. While all of the women were Roman Catholics, it was not only specific Church doctrine to which they pointed as the rationalization of this central principle. Rather, they adhered to a traditional belief that sexual relations were the mechanisms for bearing children and

not for the distinct pleasure of the male and female. Thus, the potential for bearing children and concomitantly the potential for siring children were given expression in the belief that sexual relations were primarily for the propagation of progeny. This potentiality quotient is the main vehicle by which continuity of all relations can be assured through sentido familiar. As long as children were likely to be born, reciprocal relations were likely to be generated and the various social networks in which these women and their spouses participated could be assured of continuation.

The social corollary of the first organizing principle which defines adulthood through marriage and children is that the social identities of the women, and in part that of the males who were their spouses, were measured not just by the potential for bearing and siring children, but by their actual manifestation. The actual manifestation of childbearing for these women of this subcultural strategy was the means by which their adult status was reinforced and articulated within the domestic group. There these women received prestige and were recognized as valued adults because of the potential and ability to bear children, a potential and ability which was reinforced by the continued presence of small children in the household. To be una mujer was to have children. During the various network activities previously described the private domestic value of the women's social identity as una mujer was assured by the adult female members of those various networks. Constant references during social intercourse about the ages of the children of the women present, the short spacing between children in order to ensure maximal peer relations and caretaker roles available, and in fact the various household duties assigned to females during such network activities as cooking, serving, washing dishes, and feeding children contributed to a total domestic social identity.

For males, on the other hand, prestige among cohorts and within the network activities was indirectly associated with the potential for siring children. This potential took a slightly different political avenue for men because it was also used as the measure of political control over the female within the domestic household. Within the networks, a pregnant woman was the symbolic presentation of the male ability to control her social existence within the domestic household. Therefore, un hombre was able to control una mujer through impregnation. In addition, un hombre was assured continued existence through his progeny since they bore his name. They assured also the efficacy of the various social networks to which he belonged. As will be seen, for males this control of the female and of her continued social existence was one of the central social principles that was greatly compromised as the aftermath of sterilization.

For the most part, then, social identity of these women was closely associated to the domestic group, but more importantly to the potential for bearing children and the potential for their spouses to sire children as domestic group political leaders. Certainly, within the domestic group activities, such relations were expressed in the division of labor not only of the spouses but in the division of labor of their children. For the most part, male children had responsibilities distinct from that of female children with the latter primarily fulfilling caretaker household duties including feeding and caring of younger brothers and sisters. For the most part, male siblings were assigned protective roles regardless of age and tasks unassociated with the household. Gardening, collection of garbage, and permissive explorations were largely in the hands of male siblings. When asked at one point during the course of the work as to why none of the male children were observed participating in kitchen tasks, the general response from the women was that their husbands did not want them to be maricones (effeminates).

For the most part, then, such qualitative findings point to a subcultural rural Mexican strategy for both spouses since all husbands had been born in small towns in Mexico, except for one spouse who was born in rural Imperial Valley in California. Certainly the composition of their past networks had been very much in keeping with traditional means of support and help. They generated fictive kinship, amistad relations, maintained intragenerational solidarity, and planned for large numbers of children.

The socioeconomic characteristics do not point to such cultural systems and in fact the mean age of these women was 32.6 with a range of 24–39 at time of sterilization; a mean income of $9,500 per year which was the median family income for that of the total U.S. population; a mean education of 8.5 years which is only .6 years below that of the median of Mexican females in the United States, and stable housing and employment characteristics. In no way could a "culture of poverty" be suggested as the core of behavioral principles.

QUANTITATIVE INDICATORS OF SUBCULTURAL RURAL STRATEGIES

The qualitative data however, would remain inconclusive unless the notion of subcultural rural strategies could be operationalized and control groups could be provided with instruments by which comparisons could be made. One central hypothesis generated was that the women in the case would more significantly express such strategies in their beliefs and values than two control groups that were randomly selected from two networks of Mexican and Chicana females who had not been sterilized. First, however, an instrument was devised which would elicit for or against responses of a rural sort; twenty-eight scales were responded to by nine of the women in the case, nine randomly-selected urban and rural Mexican-born married unsterilized females from a fifty-two person network, and eight randomly-selected urban U.S.-married unsterilized females from a thirty-seven person network. The instrument was derived from questionnaires previously constructed for equivalent purposes by Grebler, Guzman and Moore (1969), ethnographic statements by Madsen (1964), and Farris and Glenn's (1976) scales on familism. From the total twenty-eight scales, 61 percent were randomly selected for analysis and the responses (seventeen) all weighed equally.[16] Table 2 illustrates the mean response on rural strategies. Significantly, all the sterilized, rural Mexican females scored high. A rank order of percentages of these women reveals that no women scored under 71 percent, while four scored 94 percent or better. Among the unsterilized rural Mexican-born women one scored 100 percent, and the rest of the rural and urban women scored below that. Although scoring 30 percent below the sterilized rural Mexican women, more than half (seven) of these women were from urban Mexico which would account for higher negative responses. Nevertheless, the score of 56.4 percent is sufficiently high to insist upon the relation between rural

TABLE 2
Response on Rural Strategies

	All Sterilized Women	All Unsteriled Rural & Urban Mexican	All Unsteriled Urban Chicanas
Mean Responses: Rural Strategies	+ 14.6 − 2.3	+ 9.6 − 7.4	+ 4.9 −12.1
Percent for Rural Strategies	86.4	56.4	28.9

subcultural experience and positive responses to the rural scales, even from unsterilized urban and rural Mexican women. The further verification of the hypothesis however occurred in the analysis of the unsterilized urban Chicana women. Their mean score of 28.9 percent is again 30 percent less than that scored by the unsterilized rural and urban Mexican women. That is, the percentages of positive responses are reduced 30 percent by each of the control groups; so the less important the rural strategies to the group, the greater the increase in lower positive percentages. Thus, the negative response of the unsterile urban-rural Mexican women slightly more than doubled over the responses of the women in the case, and the Chicanas slightly less than doubled the negative responses to that of the unsterilized Mexican women. In comparison to the sterilized Mexican women, the Chicanas negative responses were quadrupled. One can suggest, then, that there is a strong relation between the degree of importance of subcultural rural strategies and the negative responses. The less the importance of the rural strategy, the greater the increases in negative responses. The greater the importance of the rural strategy, the fewer the decreases in positive responses.

An analysis of variance (ANOVA) confirms the hypothesis of significant differences between each of the three groups at α (Alpha) 0.05 (95 percent level of significance). In addition, analysis of variance between all three groups at α (Alpha) 0.01 (99 percent level of significance) show significant differences between sterilized Mexican women and unsterilized urban Chicanas. Furthermore, there are significant differences between the sterilized women and both groups of unsterilized Mexican/Chi-

cana women at the α (Alpha) 0.005 level as evidenced by a t-test comparison.

From these quantitative data, then, and in addition to the qualitative data which was presented in the previous section, the study concluded that the women who were sterilized had in fact shared subcultural rural strategies which contrasted significantly with those of the control groups. Within urban contexts such rural cultural and social systems fulfilled equivalent functions of self-help, and cooperation. The extensive networks of kin, friends, and ascending generational members, as well as the values and beliefs concerning *sentido familiar,* marriage and children all served as the basis for social living even within the urban environment. These social and cultural aspects served equivalent affective and material functions to those which were fulfilled in rural contexts. It is only within these cultural and social patterns that the effects of sterilization can then begin to be understood.

QUALITATIVE CONCLUSIONS OF THE STATE AND STRESS OF THE SUBCULTURAL SYSTEMS OF THE STERILIZED WOMEN

From the knowledge gained of the manner in which the social and cultural systems had worked before sterilization, it was then necessary to ascertain the "state" of the sociocultural systems after sterilization. On a social level, it was discovered that most of the women had gone through a process of social disengagement, beginning with the husband-wife dyadic relationship. Two of the husbands remained highly supportive of their spouses and no appreciable damage seemed to have resulted in their relationship. One of the two husbands, however, compensated for the loss of his wife's ability to procreate by showering her with gifts at most inopportune times. The other remained a saddened, but not bitter, male who counseled his wife and was extremely supportive of her. The other eight relationships suffered irreparable damage to different degrees. Three couples filed for divorce prior to the completion of the judicial procedures on July 7, 1978. The other five relationships were marked largely by jealousy, suspicion, and in two cases—physical violence and abuse. Jealousy and suspicion arose in three of the husbands due to the change they perceived in their political control over their wives' sexuality. Basically they feared that their wives would avail themselves of the sterile state, or that other males would make overtures toward their wives once their sterile state was revealed. In this regard, their wives' social identity had changed from respectable woman to possible whore.

The relationships between mothers and children for eight of ten women shifted as well. Physical punishment of children had increased to the point that in at least five of the cases, children sought to remove themselves from their mother's presence at every opportunity. Children themselves had begun to express anger to their own siblings so that sibling conflict had also increased. Aggression between mothers and their children and between siblings shifted the qualitative relationship from affection and nurturance to that of fear and violent reaction.

In all cases fictive and *amistad* relations suffered and visitations which germinated such relations decreased dramatically. Saints days, parties, fiestas, and Sunday exchanges have been largely avoided by all the women through withdrawal from fictive and amistad relations. For the most part, the women agreed that it was less painful to withdraw from these relationships than to answer questions regarding either the sterilizations or the reason why more children have not been sired, since the last born were, by this time, at least four years old. To inquiries about future pregnancies the retort that they were "guarding against pregnancies" was short-ranged. Such questions were exceedingly painful since, of the ten women, five had already chosen names for their future progeny. For the most part these were names of paternal or maternal grandparents.

Consanguineal relations were also affected. Six of the women did not share the fact that they had been sterilized with immediate siblings, and in three of the cases with their own mothers. This denial, of course, could only take place if social relations were themselves withdrawn by the women in order to avoid the topic altogether. In addition, this also meant that their spouses' consanguineal relatives were also avoided so that this provided another source of conflict between husbands and wives.

Such conflict became so endemic that in three of the relationships, the husbands lost their employment, two became alcoholics, and one left the family and has not been seen for four years from the date of the sterilization.

The degree of cultural disruption has been immense. The basis of social identity and self-image has been largely eliminated for all of the women. In the place of the culturally constituted social definition of self, a substitution of what can be termed the "Mula (Mule) Syndrome" has been generated. The mula syndrome refers to the cultural redefinition of the women as "unnatural," "insufficient," or "incomplete women" for they are no longer of domestic value. One woman expressed her situation: "I can no longer be a companion to my husband." Cultural symbols of self-worth were negated and in their place symbols of self-deprecation and self-blame took hold. Of course, these led to feelings of guilt, shame, worthlessness and self-blame. They blame themselves for what has occurred and are blamed in part by some of the husbands for not resisting sterilization, they then turn in anger against themselves. This situation has been expressed in acutely vivid dream content. Thus, one woman dreamt she found herself traveling to Mexico without her children and upon arrival becoming embarrassed when asked by relatives where they are. Another has nightmares in which her children have been stolen, killed and eaten by unidentified figures. Others have dreamt of finding themselves alone with dead persons, or totally alone and lost without their children or husband, while others recall seeing their children drowning in lakes.

The sense of personality loss, and worthlessness, all part of the grief reaction to the sterilization procedures, led to acute depression. For each woman her sense of continuity with the past had been fractured, her sense of self-worth had been shattered, self-blame had been internalized, and a new social identity of impotence had been generated. Each woman in fact is now stigmatized. The sterilization procedures stand as visible and permanent marks of humiliation which they can never remove. The greater the effort at denial, the greater the anger and self-hate generated. The greater the anger and self-hate, the greater the necessity of expression upon themselves or upon others. The greater the expression, the greater the increase in conflict, social disengagement and cultural disruption.

RURAL STRATEGY, CULTURAL DISRUPTION, AND PREDICTIVE DEPRESSION

From the qualitative analysis presented of the effects of sterilization, a hypothesis was developed. The greater the importance of the rural strategy had been among the women's sociocultural systems, the higher the probability of deeper depression as the aftermath of cultural disruption. This hypothesis was based on the notion that although beliefs do not define actual behavior, they were nevertheless central to the personality of individuals and had been extremely important in assessing the moral worth of others and assessing themselves. This is not a causal argument. It suggests that if the subcultural systems which the women had shared, including their spouses, were such that few alternatives for social identity were available after their disruption, or if the spouses in their reaction upheld the core values of such social identity by denying alternative rewarding roles for their wives, then more than likely the depression for the women would be concomitantly high.

From observed contexts and knowledge of the environments of each woman, each was ranked according to what had been the degree of importance of such strategies to their entire sociocultural systems prior to sterilization. Thus each woman was ranked according to the following system and given a score (see tables 3 and 4).

TABLE 3

Degree of Importance of Rural Strategy

(VH)	Very High	—	16 - 17
(H)	High	—	14 - 15
(M)	Medium	—	12 - 13
(L)	Low	—	10 - 11
(VL)	Very Low	—	8 - 9

My qualitative judgment was the following:

TABLE 4

Woman	Degree of Importance of Rural Strategy	Score
Madrigal	VH	16 - 17
Bienavides	VH	16 - 17
Figueroa	H	14 - 15
Hurtado	H	14 - 15
Hernandez	H	14 - 15
Rivera	H	14 - 15
Hermosillo	H	14 - 15
Acosta	M	12 - 13
Orozco	M	12 - 13

A second set of scores was quantitatively derived from the rural strategies questionnaire. In turn these scores were compared to the qualitatively derived ranking. This comparison appears in table 5.

For each matched score a numerical value of two points was allowed, for each error of one interval a score of one point, and for errors of more than one interval zero points. In summing the numerical values of accurate versus inaccurate scores according to the process above, it was possible to predict a degree of importance of the rural strategies with a total score of thirteen out of eighteen possible points for an accuracy of 72 percent.

TABLE 5

Woman	Qualitative Judgment	Quantitative Score from Questionnaire
Madrigal	VH: 16–17	VH: 16
Bienavides	VH: 16–17	M: 12
Figueroa	H: 14–15	VH: 16
Hurtado	H: 14–15	VH: 17
Hernandez	H: 14–15	H: 15
Rivera	H: 14–15	H: 15
Hermosillo	H: 14–15	VH: 16
Acosta	M: 12–13	M: 13
Orozco	M: 12–13	M: 12

Then the qualitative judgments and the quantitative comparisons were combined for a new ranking by order of *depression* according to the degree of the importance of rural strategies exhibited in the sociocultural systems of which the women had been a part and their responses on the questionnaires. The following are the ranked estimates according to the degree of depression on a scale of one to ten with one the highest, ten the lowest (see table 6).

TABLE 6

Woman	Degree of Depression
Madrigal	1
Figueroa	2
Hernandez	3
Acosta	4
Hurtado	5
Bienavides	6
Rivera	7
Hermosillo	8
Orozco	9
no respondent	10

The next step for verification was to ask the consulting psychiatrist on the case, Dr. Terry Kuper, to provide his ranked estimates according to the degree of depression, as well as for the female attorney's judgment of the degree of depression according to her best knowledge. The psychiatrist had been working on the case for three years prior to my request and the lawyer for four years. His opinion would provide a professional perspective, her's a popular one. At no time had we spoken concerning the degree of depression suffered by each woman, but unfortunately at this time the psychiatrist was only able to provide me with the top and bottom two, since he had no immediate access to his records when this information was solicited. Therefore, his ranking is incomplete (see table 7).

From the ranked data appearing above, the major hypothesis of the relation between the rupture of traditional rural beliefs and their sociocultural systems and degrees of depression is verified by the independent ranking of the psychiatrist who has agreed with extreme accuracy with the anthropologist. The popular

TABLE 7

| Woman | Degree of Depression | | |
	Velez-I	Kuper	Lawyer
Madrigal	1	2	1
Figueroa	2	1	3
Hernandez	3	0	4
Acosta	4	0	2
Hurtado	5	0	6
Bienavides	6	0	7
Rivera	7	0	5
Hermosillo	8	8	9
Orozco	9	9	8

judgment of the lawyer was slightly off in ranking the second most depressed person but was in complete agreement with both psychiatrist and anthropologist concerning the bottom two. All of these steps were necessary to present to a court of law, as an empirically sound judgment, the effects of sterilization on the sociocultural systems of the women and the relationship between the disruptions of those systems and the generation of acute depression and its distribution. The greater the importance of rural strategies had been among the women, the higher the probability of deeper depression as the aftermath of cultural disruption and social fracturing of networks.

These findings and the verified hypotheses were then presented in a court of law as part of the evidence in behalf of a law suit which these women had filed in federal court. As will be seen, it is ironic that the very evidence used to illustrate the damages done to the social and cultural systems of these women, was in fact partially used by the court to rationalize a decision against them. The court processes and the final decision, however, do verify the theoretical position this work assumed: that in paternalistic behavioral environments, Mexicans would be treated negatively. The court is one such behavioral environment.

MADRIGAL V. QUILLIGAN: THE TRIAL AS A BEHAVIORAL ENVIRONMENT

On May 31, 1978, a civil suit for damages began in District Court for the Central District of California. The complaint was entitled

"*Dolores Madrigal et al.,* Plaintiff v. *E.J. Quilligan et al.*" The action was brought against Dr. E.J. Quilligan, chairman of Medical Center's Department of Obstetrics and Gynecology, and eleven other doctors on behalf of the ten women. In order to appreciate the final outcome of the suit, however, we should recall the central contention that "paternalistic behavioral environments" foster differential treatment of Mexicans when the efficient conditions are present. The trial will be treated as such a behavioral environment and the efficient conditions articulated.

The courtroom was very much like most in that spaces were defined in proper domains for the judge, the plaintiffs' attorneys and the defendants' attorneys. Since the trial was a nonjury type the focus of all the attention by the attorneys on both sides was on the judge. Neither the trial per se nor the judicial arguments will be detailed since both are much beyond the scope of this work. Instead, the contrasts within the confines of the trial will be addressed in order to understand the behavioral environment within the total context of the social question involved.

These contrasts were most immediately apparent in the attorneys. The plaintiffs' two Mexican lawyers were from a local poverty legal center. One of the lawyers was a thirty-five year old male who had graduated in the top of his class a few years previously. He was legally blind from a childhood disease so that the enormously thick glasses he wore accentuated and distorted his dark brown eyes. For the most part, this soft-spoken, medium-sized, and slightly pudgy man, shuffled as he moved between the plaintiffs' table and the podium that sat squarely in the middle of the room facing the judge's panelled bench. The other lawyer was a recently graduated Mexican woman, and like the other lawyer, had been working on the case for four years. Dark, thin, and well-dressed, the young female lawyer moved assertively between the plaintiffs' table and the podium. She spoke in a clear, clipped and slightly-accented diction. They differed little from the ten plaintiffs in court, except for variance in quality of dress.

In opposition, the defendants' lawyers were the best that money could buy. Both the male and female lawyer were from one of the more prestigious Beverly Hills law firms and both seemed quite relaxed in their roles in the courtroom. She moved assertively and quickly from the defendants' table even though she was about thirty pounds overweight. Well dressed, articulate, and quite polysyllabic, this unattractive Anglo woman did not in fact actually present any of the defendants nor did she cross-examine witnesses. Instead she largely was responsible for making legal motions, registering legal requests, and seemed to assist her partner. He was like his fair counterpart, fiftyish, well groomed, articulate and quite polysyllabic without the stuttering that seemed to mark the presentations of the plaintiffs' lawyers. Both in hue and in presentation of themselves, there were obvious contrasts which seemed to divide the courtroom into the Mexican side and the Anglo side. The judge seemed to sit in the middle, or so it seemed.

The judge, the Honorable Jesse W. Curtis, a white-haired seventy year old person, seemed like the stereotype of the paternalistic figure commanding the courtroom. Firm-jawed, angular faced, with piercing blue eyes set beneath profuse eyebrows that moved in unison in mostly frowns, this Nixon-appointee to the federal bench was known by reputation as a conservative judge who lived aboard his yacht in Newport Beach, one of the most prestigious areas in southern California. He and the defendants' lawyers were obvious analogues and stark contrasts to the plaintiffs and their lawyers. The judge did not in fact sit in the middle.

For two and a half weeks the plaintiffs' lawyers presented evidence that under duress, after hours of being in labor and under medication, the plaintiffs could not have given informed consent. Dr. Don Sloan, an internationally known gynecologist and obstetrician, testified that given the circumstances surrounding the sterilization procedures, none of the women could have provided informed consent. Each woman in turn provided their testimony in Spanish, in which they detailed the contexts of their sterilization. A handwriting expert examined the signatures of those women who had signed consent forms and concluded that in fact each woman had been suffering great distress and stress at the time. Dr. Terry Kuper presented his evidence of the sterilization procedures on each woman and concluded that to different degrees each woman had suffered irreparable psychological damage and that long periods of psychotherapy would have to be undertaken by each one. I offered the data discovered in this work in much the same manner and development, except initially the judge was not going to permit my testimony. When Judge Curtis was made aware of my impending testimony, he remarked from the bench that he did not see what an anthropologist was going to say that would have any bearing on damages and that if I was getting paid, that my testimony would not be worth a "plugged nickle." He concluded that after all "We all know that Mexicans love their families." Nevertheless, I was able to present the data contained and except for minor cross-examination, no opposing expert was presented to refute my testimony. Of interest to note, however, were the concluding questions that Judge Curtis addressed to me which would be of significance in the final opinion.

After having concluded my testimony, the Judge asked me how long I had spent on the case. I answered that I had spent 450 hours of time between field work, creation of the instrument, selecting the control groups, and ascertaining what the effects had been on the women's sociocultural systems. He then asked me if I would have undertaken the study in any other manner. I responded that I would not have since ". . . as an anthropologist to have done otherwise would not have been worth a hill of beans." He repeated the same question again, slightly rephrased, and I answered that professional ethics would have prevented me to come to the conclusions that I did unless I rigorously followed the methodology I had used. The Judge thanked me and I stepped down.

The defense presented no rebuttal of expert witnesses and did not cross-examine the plaintiffs. Instead they called each one of the doctors in question and from the plaintiffs' medical files commented on the medical procedures contained. At no time did any of the doctors recall any of the women but they all asserted that their "custom and practice" was not to perform a sterilization unless a woman had consented and understood what she was doing. When cross-examined as to whether they spoke Spanish well enough to detail the procedures, they responded generally that they knew enough "obstetrics Spanish" to get them by. When pressed for details about the individual women,

they all answered that they could not recall them as patients since there were so many.

The final decision was handed down June 30, before Judge Curtis left for a lengthy Scandinavian vacation. It stated rather succinctly that the judgment was entered for the defendants. The women lost, but the judge's rationalization is interesting and informative because it in fact verifies the theoretical position which underlies this exposition—that in paternalistic environments in which Mexicans are differentially treated in a negative manner, the "ideology of cultural differences" will be used as a rationalization for the structural and asymmetrical characteristics of the environments.

The Judge's remarks are as follows:

Communication Breakdown

This case is essentially the result of a breakdown in communications between the patients and the doctors. All plaintiffs are Spanish speaking women whose ability to understand and speak English is limited. This fact is generally understood by the staff at the Medical Center and most members have acquired enough familiarity with the language to get by. There is also an interpreter available whose services are used when thought to be necessary. But even with these precautions misunderstandings are bound to occur. Furthermore, the cultural background of these particular women has contributed to the problem in a subtle but significant way. According to the plaintiff's anthropological expert, they are members of a traditional Mexican rural subculture, a relatively narrow spectrum of Mexican people living in this country whose lifestyle and cultural background derives from the lifestyle and culture of small rural communities in Mexico. He further testified that a cultural trait which is very prominent with this group is an extreme dependence upon family. Most come from large families and wish to have large families for their own comfort and support. Furthermore, the status of a woman and her husband within that group depends largely upon the woman's ability to produce children. If for any reason she cannot, she is considered an incomplete woman and is apt to suffer a disruption of her relationship with her family and husband. When faced with a decision of whether or not to be sterilized, the decision process is a much more traumatic event with her than it would be with a typical patient and, consequently, she would require greater explanation, more patient advice, and greater care in interpreting her consent than persons not members of such a subculture would require.

But this need for such deliberate treatment is not readily apparent. The anthropological expert testified that he would not have known that these women possessed these traits had he not conducted tests and a study which required some 450 hours of time. He further stated that a determination by him based upon any less time would not have been worth "beans." It is not surprising therefore that the staff of a busy metropolitan hospital which has neither the time nor the staff to make such esoteric studies would be unaware of these atypical cultural traits.

It is against this backdrop therefore that we must analyze the conduct of the doctors who treated the plaintiffs in this case.

Doctors' Custom and Practice

Since these operations occurred between 1971 and 1974 and were performed by the doctors operating in a busy obstetrics ward, it is not surprising that none of the doctors have any independent recollection of the events leading up to the operations. They all testified, however, that it was their custom and practice not to suggest a sterilization unless a patient asked for it or there were medical complications which would require the doctor, in the exercise of prudent medical procedures, to make such suggestion. They further testified that it was their practice when a patient requested sterilization to explain its irreversible result and they stated that they would not perform the operation unless they were certain in their own mind that the patient understood the nature of the operation and was requesting the procedure. The weight to be given to such testimony and the inferences to be drawn therefrom will be determined in the light of all the testimony relating to each doctor's conduct.[17]

The Judge's final opinion also excluded the testimony by the handwriting expert, the psychiatrist on the case, and refuted the testimony by Dr. Sloan, the gynecologist and obstetrician, by saying that his statements ". . . completely defy common sense." Why they do so, he did not explain. His conclusion, however, is quite enlightening in that he admits that in fact all of the women had suffered. He states:

This case had not been an easy one to try for it has involved social, emotional and cultural considerations of great complexity. There is no doubt that these women have suffered severe emotional and physical stress because of these operations. One can sympathize with them for their inability to communicate clearly, but one can hardly blame the doctors for relying on these indicia of consent which appeared to be

unequivocal on their face and which are in constant use in the Medical Center.

Let judgment be entered for the defendants.

Jesse W. Curtis
Senior United States
District Judge (19)

CONCLUSIONS

First it must be obvious that within paternalistic institutionalized behavioral environments, Mexicans have a high probability of being negatively treated. Certainly the medical sterilizations and the legal judgments uphold this fact. Regardless of the overwhelming evidence to the contrary, the judge disregarded evidence and testimony presented and chose instead to consider the "custom and practice" of the doctors, rather than following rules of evidence.

Second, his misuse of the anthropological data in which he identified the women as belonging to a "relatively narrow spectrum of Mexican people" was not presented as empirical evidence. Instead this commentary was used to illustrate the "atypicality of their cultural traits." In other words, the women were so culturally different that the doctors could not have known that the sterilizations would have affected them in so adverse a manner. This belief removes the legal and moral responsibility for their actions. The "ideology of cultural differences" then is used as the very basis for an unjust and detrimental decision against a group of largely defenseless Mexican women. After all, how could the doctors have been aware that the sterilizations would have such an effect on Mexican women since the hospital in which these operations were carried out is in the middle of the largest Mexican barrio outside Mexico City. The judge legitimized the doctors' actions and his action against the women by noting that the doctors were too busy to note these cultural differences and even more importantly, they were so different that the doctors could not have known the effects of sterilizations unless they had carried out studies similar to the one I carried out in the case.

Third, all the work which went into the presentation of this material is still very much in the "meliorative and reformists attempts" of the well-intentioned liberal establishment. I too blundered and in fact was responsible for providing the judge with exactly the ammunition he needed to utilize the "ideology of cultural differences." Ironically, while fairly objective empirical findings of effect were presented which were too overwhelming to ignore on the record, the judge's only recourse was to utilize the data against the women since it could not be refuted.

Fourth, and last, all of the activities which make up this work occurred within the confines of an industrial capitalist state in which the diversity of culture is organized and controlled by a national prism which reflects a dominant ethnic group of Anglo-Saxon Americans. Both the sterilization of the physical ability of a group of ethnic minority women to procreate, and the resultant cultural sterilization of the same group of women were in fact provided legitimization by the court. The decision reinforces that national prism and ensures the superordinate ethnic group of Anglo-Saxon Americans continued domination by whatever means.

As one woman so astutely observed: Se me acabó la canción.

NOTES

1. On November 1, 1977, I met with two attorneys to discuss the effects of alleged unconsented sterilization procedures that had been conducted on ten Mexican women in Los Angeles, California. I had received a telephone call earlier from one of the lawyers who represented a civil suit against a major metropolitan hospital in Los Angeles for allegedly permitting sterilization procedures to be conducted on non-consenting Chicano women. Both lawyers presented the case from the perspective that ten "Chicanas" had been sterilized without their consent. They then asked for my assessment of the possible cultural and social ramifications of such practices on the ten women.

   I replied that I could not offer an informed judgment without analyzing the case and the women. However, I felt able to venture an opinion, an educated one at best. I suggested that quite variable responses could be expected dependent on the behavioral contexts in which these women had been a part, their cultural histories, and their present support networks. Furthermore, at that time, I postulated, and it must be emphasized that it was merely a postulate, the following. If the women had been born in Mexico in rural contexts or in the United States in equivalent circumstances, then sterilization could have severe psychocultural and social results even beyond those expected of other women in the United States. Also, I suggested that the degree of damage could vary with the background of the women. Thus, if the women were urban Chicanas and

part of lower-class sectors,then their reaction could also be severe, but perhaps their social beings may not be as importantly related to the potential for bearing children. In either context, the severity of a nonconsenting sterilization on the women would be dependent on a variety of exogenous and endogenous variables including class, ethnic maintenance, social networks, work experience, and the psychological well-being of each woman prior to the sterilization procedure.

   The lawyers then asked me if I would be willing to serve as a consultant on the case in order to test out the postulates that I had suggested. I explained that I could not entertain any a priori conclusions in regard to the women, but that I would be willing to undertake a basic field study of the individuals involved and the circumstances of their sterilization. From the data I would submit an informed opinion of the effects, if any, of the surgery. Consequently, I agreed to serve as a consulting cultural anthropologist for their clients, with the stipulation that whatever conclusions I reached would have to be validated by empirical findings.

2. I use the term "Chicana" to designate U.S.-born women of Mexican heritage who are socialized within industrially-structured population centers in either agricultural or urban contexts. Cultural specifics from language to belief systems are "distributed" according to class and occupational sectors. "Mexican" is the term I use to designate Mexican-born persons who are socialized within rural or urban contexts and in a possible variety of structural settings from industrial to small village "close corporate" communities. Cultural specifics from language to belief systems are "distributed" according to class and occupational sectors. The differences between populations will be both cultural and structural; however, similarities will also be reflective of cultural specifics arising from equivalent structural conditions. The term "working class" Mexican denotes little specifically and assumes a homogeniety of experiences that is ahistorical in content.

3. Theodore Schwartz (1971) states that the behavioral environment is the environment as conceived by the member of a society. It includes those physical features which are culturally relevant, as well as all culturally recognized beings and forces and their relation to man. One might term the study of cultural constructs of the behavioral environment "phenomenological ecology." If we take "environment" as the objective or real situation in which a people live, "ecology" would be the culturally mediated relation between man and environment.

   In addition, however, I characterize behavioral environments as temporal and spatial extensions of culturally constituted constructs. Thus, a "working area" is an extension of constructs upon the environment and "becomes" a working area when time, space, social relations, artifacts, goals, and values all intersect from the extensions provided by living beings who form and shape the specificity of the working area. I use the word "extensions" as projected information bits which carry the constructs containing the specifics of the working area(s). While the extensions carrying the cultural constructs may be partially "congealed," as physical artifacts these become active only within a socially stimulated context. A factory may contain all the congealed data within its machinery to function automatically, but only an extended cultural construct(s) and its social context provide it with temporal and spatial "life."

I utilize the concept of behavioral environment as an important construct which may be fruitful in designating those situations that promote negative differential treatment. Some environments can be considered "paternalistic" when the cultural constructs demand extreme deference articulated through a routinized and elaborate etiquette, titles of reference and superiority, a specialized argot or jargon, differentiated costumes and attire, allocated physical spaces, and segregated activities. Social relations are based on dependence asymmetry, social distance, and ascribed status differentials without vertical mobility for the client population. "Clients" are perceived as immature, childish, ignorant, and underdeveloped so that the controlling figures in the environment have political control over them and economic access which commands the allocation of valued resources, services, material goods, or information. Enforcement is based on the withdrawal or threatened withdrawal of such resources so that ultimately the roles fulfilled by "clients" vis-à-vis their "patrons" are based on coercive support. (For an elaboration of the differences between coercive and legitimate support see the discussion by Marc J. Swartz in his "Introduction" to *Local-Level Politics*, Chicago, Aldine, 1968.)

Yet, "competitive behavioral environments" in comparison to paternalistic ones are marked by factors of achievement, affective neutrality, mobility, rational legitimate support, and are legalistic, representative, and "earned." The relations between participants, although hierarchical are not passive-dependent but active-interdependent. These may be asymmetrical, but all concerned here expect change and development through participation. Competition is designated within boundaries and conflict is defined and agreed to within parameters that do not threaten the relations between members in the environments. There is a general value consensus without coercion, and resources are allocated to those who can best meet the goals of the behavioral environment. Both "paternalistic" and "competitive" models are polar types and operationalization is still to be developed.

The basic notions of paternalistic and competitive relations are owed to Pierre Van den Berghe's two fine basic works in ethnic and race relations: *Race and Racism*, (New York: John Wiley & Sons, 1967) and *Race and Ethnicity*, (New York: Basic Books, 1970). In these two works, the author uses the characteristics of paternalism and competition as independent and dependent societal variables which mark the nature of the relations between dominant and subordinate groups within a developmental polar model. I contend that, regardless of larger societal developments, paternalistic and competitive behavioral environments will coexist in even the most "competitive industrialized" social contexts. In the most rational of institutionalized bureaucratic contexts, paternalistic factors may very well mark most relations between participants.

4. See Charles Wagley and Marvin Harris, *Minorities in the New World*, (New York and London: Columbia University Press, 1964) and Richard M. Burkey, *Ethnic and Racial Groups*, (Menlo Park, Calif.: Cummings Press, 1978) for a discussion of the relation between nationality, ethnicity, and citizenship.

5. From the Soviet perspective, ethnic chauvinism of the Great Russians does not exist. Y. Bromley (1978) explains that Soviet culture, not Russian culture, is the prism of the Soviet Union and that the Soviet Union is not a nation-state but a state of collected nationalities and minorities integrated to develop a new historic entity—the Soviet people. The Russian language, for example, is the *lingua franca* necessary for socialist construction, the requirements of the national economy, and the growth of towns with multiethnic and multilingual populations (p. 24). For Bromley, the adherence to an internationalist socialist perspective has resulted in a cultural syncretism of all nationalities into a Soviet culture which has a single socialist content. "Thus, not merely a national but a whole Soviet culture takes shape in the course of the mutual influence and mutual enrichment of the intellectual cultures of the peoples of the USSR and the assimilation of the achievements of world culture" (p. 25). This ideological belief is most interesting in light of the agitation of ethnic minorities such as Soviet Jews in the Soviet Union.

6. Ibid.

7. See Burkey, *Ethnic and Racial Groups* for the fourteen groups which were stratified according to four indices, pp. 300–400.

8. See Rodolfo Acuña, *Occupied America: The Chicano's Struggle Toward Liberation*, (San Francisco: Canfield Press, 1972) in which Acuña states that as a matter of historical record the chief negotiator for the United States in fact threatened his Mexican counterparts with the ultimatum that if Mexico did not accept the terms offered, the United States would take the territory under negotiation.

9. The Bracero program for contract labor was initiated in 1942 in the United States to fill manpower shortages generated by World War II. The program was resumed in 1951 with the enactment of Public Law 78. Recent hysteria concerning the undocumented worker of Mexican descent in the United States has generated calls for the reinstitutionalization of such a program in order to stem what is seen as a "brown tide" of humanity spilling into the United States. Yet as David Weber pointed out in a recent article (*Los Angeles Times*, January 14, 1979), Mexican documented and undocumented workers have a long historical cultural tie to the Southwest and contribute immensely economically, socially, and developmentally to the United States. See also Mauricio Mazon "Illegal Alien Surrogates: A Psychohistorical Interpretation of Group Stereotypes in Time of Economic Stress," *Aztlán: International Journal of Chicano Studies Research*, 1975, Vol. 6, No. 2, pp. 305–324.

10. The twin-cities programs are joint capital intensive projects in which light industry is created in Mexico for the express purpose of using cheap Mexican labor in a border area and then shipping the assembled product to the United States for sale. The Nogales Sonora-Arizona and El Paso-Cd. Juarez cities are among the most notable examples.

11. See Wagley and Harris, *Minorities in the New World* for the efficient and necessary conditions for intergroup conflict and its maintenance.
12. See *A Study of Selected Socio-Economic Characteristics of Ethnic Minorities Based on the 1970 Census: Volume I: Americans of Spanish Origin.* Department of Health Education and Welfare (Office of Special Concerns: July, 1974).
13. See Tomás Almaguer "Toward the Study of Chicano Colonialism," *Aztlán,* 1971, Vol. 2, No. 1, Spring, pp. 7-21, and also his "Historical Notes on Chicano Oppression: The Dialectics of Racial and Class Domination in North America," *Aztlán,* 1974, Vol. 5, Nos. 1 and 2, pp. 27-56. Carey McWilliams' *North From Mexico,* (New York: Greenwood Press, 1968, originally 1949) is the seminal work on the differential treatment of Mexicans and the historical antecedents to continued intergroup conflict. David J. Weber's *Foreigners in Their Native Land* also details the historical events comprising intergroup conflicts. For union and labor struggles, the issue of *Aztlán* devoted to labor history (1975, Vol. 6, No. 2, pp. 137-324) is the best yet written on the topic.
14. See "Findings of Facts and Conclusions of Law," filed by Los Angeles Center for Law and Justice (May 31, 1978:1-78), and also "Affidavit" by Maria Figueroa (June 18, 1975), "Affidavit" by Georgina Hernandez (June 15, 1975), "Affidavit" by Consuelo Hermosillo (June 18, 1975), "Affidavit" by Estela Benavides (June 18, 1975), "Affidavit" by Rebecca Figueroa (June 18, 1975), and "Affidavit" by Guadalupe Acosta (June 18, 1975). Also see Antonia Hernandez "Chicanas and the Issue of Involuntary Sterilization: Reforms Needed to Protect Informed Consent," *Chicano Law Review* (1976, Vol. 3, pp. 3-37).
15. Rancherias are small agricultural settlements in which the population density of the residential area is equal to the area used for subsistence. Ejidos are communal lands assigned to a community by the Mexican federal government.
16. The selected scales solicited information of social identity, traditional beliefs of witchcraft and medicine, sex roles, acceptance of outside agency or control, and familism.
17. See Judge Jesse W. Curtis "Opinion," (No. CV 75-2057-JWC, United States Federal Court, June 30, 1978, pp. 1-19).

REFERENCES

1975   Acosta, G. Affidavit, June 18.
1974   Acuña, Rodolfo. *Occupied America: The Chicano's Struggle Toward Liberation.* San Francisco: Canfield Press.
1974   Almaguer, Tomás. "Historical Notes on Chicano Oppression: The Dialectics of Racial and Class Domination in North America." *Aztlán: Chicano Journal of the Social Sciences and the Arts* 5:27-56.
1971   _____. "Toward the Study of Chicano Colonialism." *Aztlán: Chicano Journal of the Social Sciences and the Arts* 2:7-21.

1975   *Aztlán: International Journal of Chicano Studies Research* 6:137-324.
1973   Bastide, Roger. *Applied Anthropology.* New York: Harper and Row. Originally published in French by Payot, 1971.
1975   Benavides, E. Affidavit, June 18.
1975   Benker, Karen. Statement made before a press conference at the Greater Los Angeles Press Club, December 6.
1977   Briggs Jr., Vernon M. et al. *The Chicano Worker.* Austin and London: The University of Texas Press.
1978   Bromley, Yulian. "Cultural Aspects of Ethnic Processes in the USSR." *Soviet Studies in Ethnography* 72:16-26.
1978   Burkey, Richard M. *Ethnic and Racial Groups.* Menlo Park, California: Cummings Press.
1978   Curtis, Jesse W. Opinion, June 30, No. CV 75-2057-JWC: 1-19.
1973   Enloe, Cynthia. *Ethnic Conflict and Political Development.* Boston: Little, Brown and Company.
1976   Farris, Buford E., and Norval D. Glenn. "Fatalism and Familism Among Anglos and Mexican Americans in San Antonio." *Sociology and Social Research* 60:395-402.
1975   Figueroa, R. Affidavit, June 18.
1973   Gaylin, Willard. "Editorial: The Patient's Bill of Rights." *Saturday Review of Science* Vol. 22.
1947   Goldschmidt, Walter. *As You Sow.* New York: Harcourt, Brace and Company.
1976   _____. *The Rural Foundation of the American Culture.* A Gregory Foundation Memorial Lecture. Columbia, Missouri.
1970   Grebler, Leo, Joan W. Moore, and Ralph C. Guzman. *The Mexican American People: The Nation's Second Largest Minority.* New York: The Free Press, A Division of the Macmillan Company.
1975   Hermosillo, G. Affidavit, June 18.
1976   Hernandez, Antonia. "Chicanas and the Issues of Involuntary Sterilization: Reforms Needed to Protect Informed Consent." *Chicano Law Review* 3: 3-37.
1978   Hernandez, Antonia, and Charles D. Nabarrete. Findings of Fact and Conclusions of Law, *Dolores Madrigal et al., Plaintiffs* v. *E.J. Quilligan et al.,* United States District Court, June 2: No. CV 75-2057-EC.
1975   Hernandez, G. Affidavit, June 15.
1974   Kennard, Gail. "Sterilization Abuse." *Essence,* October: 66 ff.
1974   Kuper, Leo. *Race, Class and Power: Ideology and Revolutionary Change in Plural Societies.* London: Gerald Duckworth & Company Limited.
1964   Madsen, William. *Mexican Americans of South Texas.* New York: Holt, Rinehart and Winston, Inc.
1975   Mazón, Mauricio. "Illegal Alien Surrogates: A Psychohistorical Interpretation of Group Stereotyping in Time of Economic Stress." *Aztlán: International Journal of Chicano Studies Research.* 6: 305-324.
1949/   McWilliams, Carey. *North From Mexico.* New
1968 rpt York: Greenwood Press.
1974   Office of Special Concerns. *A Study of Selected Socio-Economic Characteristics of Ethnic Minorities Based on the 1970 Census: Vol. 1: Americans*

1958 *of Spanish Origin.* Department of Health, Education and Welfare, July.

1958 Paredes, Américo. *With His Pistol in His hand: A Border Ballad and His Hero.* Austin and London: University of Texas Press.

1971 Schwartz, Theodore. "A Glossary of Terms for Culture and Personality." Mimeographed. University of California, San Diego.

1977 Siggins, Richard V. "Coerced Sterilization: A National Civil Conspiracy to Commit Genocide Upon the Poor?" Unpublished manuscript. Loyola University, School of Law, Los Angeles.

1968 Swartz, Marc J. "Introduction." In Marc J. Swartz (Ed.), *Local-Level Politics.* Chicago, Illinois: Aldine.

1970 Van den Berghe, Pierre, ed. *Race and Ethnicity.* New York: Basic Books.

1967 _____. *Race and Racism: A Comparative Perspective.* New York: John Wiley and Sons.

1958/ Wagley, Charles, and Marvin Harris. *Minorities in*
1964 rpt *the New World.* New York and London: Columbia University Press.

1973 Weber, David J., ed. *Foreigners in Their Native Land.* Albuquerque: University of New Mexico Press.

1979 _____. "Mexico, So Far From God, So Near the U.S. and Now So Rich." *Los Angeles Times,* Part 5, January 14: 2.

1973 Wood, Jr., H. Curtis. "Statement of Address." *Contemporary OB/GYN.* January. Quoted in Kennard "Sterilization Abuse," *Essence,* October: 86.

VIRGINIA MARTINEZ

Virginia is Associate Counsel and Director of the Mexican-American Legal Defense and Education Fund, Chicago, Illinois Office. She is also director of the national MALDEF Chicana Rights Project. Ms. Martinez earned a Juris Doctor from De Paul University and was admitted to the bar in Illinois.

134

CHICANAS AND THE LAW
by Virginia Martinez

The legal system is one useful tool for the Chicana's effort to achieve her rightful place in the American mainstream. Historically, this has not been the case. In the aftermath of the Mexican-American War, the experience of Chicanas in American justice was grim. In 1851, Josefa Segovia was the first person hanged in "occupied" California.[1] While in her third month of pregnancy, Josefa was lynched for stabbing a drunken Anglo who had attacked her (her husband was exiled). Not long after that, in a similarly cruel incident, Chipita Rodriguez became the only woman ever to be legally sentenced to death and executed in Texas. She earned this distinction in 1863 while in her sixties. This Chicana, a respected citizen, was hanged based on the evidence that the body of an Anglo horse-trader was found near her home.[2]

More recently, the Chicana experience with the legal system remains tragic, if less extreme. The Los Angeles Zoot Suit Riots of 1943 are said to have been provoked by Anglo sailors' advances towards Chicanas. Regardless of how the riots began, the resulting media coverage came down hard on Chicanas, "...during the rioting, one Los Angeles newspaper ...published a story to the effect that the Cholitas and Pachucas were cheap prostitutes, infected with venereal disease and addicted to the use of marijuana."[3] The Chicanas in Los Angeles had no recourse in 1943. They were at the mercy of Anglo sailors, the Anglo community, and they were open for attacks from the Anglo press.

The arrival of the fifties, McCarthyism, and the Immigration Act of 1952 afforded Chicanas no relief. The threat of deportation plagued all activists, especially many Chicano and Chicana leaders. Between 1952 and 1956 more than two million Chicanos and Mexicans were deported. One important Chicana leader, Luisa Moreno, was deported along with Frank Corona

135

and Antonia Salgado.[4] She was active in labor disputes and was a national organizer for the United Cannery, Agricultural and Packing Workers of America. She was primarily responsible for the first national, non-labor oriented Chicano conference in 1938. In a similar case, Rosaura Revueltas was arrested and deported in 1953 as a result of her work in the film, "Salt of the Earth".[5] Her film portrayal of the role of women in mining strike efforts was too controversial for paranoid America of 1953.

The sixties brought an end to the witch hunt era and the beginning of a new activism. From a nationwide cry for civil rights sprang "El Movimiento". Chicano activism became established. Within the context of the Chicano movement, the Chicana began to assert her own identity, confronting the movement with its shortcomings. This activism led to Chicana organization efforts and conferences. Chicanas began to express their desire and ability to lead. By the early seventies, Chicanas were organizing themselves at Movimiento conferences and at their own conferences throughout the Southwest.

While Chicanas were making great strides in terms of organization and their own consciousness, they had a very limited impact on the socio-economic status of the Chicano population generally. Huge disparities exist in this area today, barely affected by the years of struggle and sacrifices. The Farrah strike and boycott in Texas in 1972 is but one example of Chicanas utilizing their organizing skills and leadership abilities in an effort to establish control over their own lives. Their success in this effort reflects the strength of their determination to overcome injustice.

The legal system is another means of opposing some of the causes of the disparities that exist, and of eliminating injustice for Chicanas. The Mexican-American Legal Defense and Educational Fund (MALDEF) recognized this possibility as well as the need for an organized effort to defend the rights of Chicanas. In 1974, MALDEF established the Chicana Rights Project

136

(CRP) as an expression of their commitment to the protection of the civil rights of Chicanas. This project is unique in its interest in Chicana issues and has pursued litigation in the areas of prison reform, CETA programs, maternity benefits, banking, media, health issues, displaced homemakers' needs, battered women, and is interested in the "comparable worth" issue, and any issue that affects Chicanas and Hispanic women generally.

Chicanas continue to assert themselves, in and outside of their homes. In 1975, the case of Inez Garcia became a feminist cause. This Chicana was convicted of killing a man who had helped rape her. The case was controversial because the shooting occurred several hours after the rape. The case was appealed and Inez Garcia was acquitted in retrial.[6] A few years later, in 1978, Idalia Mejia was also acquitted of charges related to a fatal shooting. This battered wife had endured fourteen years of terror with her husband and shot him in self-defense.[7]

The Chicana is still not getting a fair shake in the justice system. However, recent efforts are beginning to have an impact on the Chicana's life. Agencies and programs like the Chicana Rights Project and many that are represented at this conference, are dedicating tremendous energy on behalf of Chicana issues. Conferences, like the Chicana Conference held in Sacramento on October 2-3, 1981 and the Illinois Hispanic Women's Conference held in Chicago in October, 1981, are significant illustrations of the fact that Chicanas are increasingly active in exercising their leadership strength. However, until Chicanas no longer represent the lower end of the socio-economic scale, and as long as discrimination exists in this country, there will also continue to be a need for guardians of the rights of Chicanas.

There is some question as to whether the women's movement is an element of the Chicana's struggle. The question of the relationship between the Chicana and the women's movement has been controversial since the inception

137

of Chicano activism. Any perspective must consider the fact that for Chicanas, the experience of sexism must be considered in light of the experience of racism. Since in the case of the Chicana the two cannot be separated, it becomes difficult to evaluate the Chicana's benefits from and responsibility to the women's movement. It must be recognized that the gains made by feminists stand to benefit Chicanas. However, until it is recognized that poverty and racism are also women's issues, the relationship between Chicanas and feminists will be strained.

From a legal standpoint the issues affecting Chicanas are clear: discrimination, immigration law, education, labor and health issues are a few. The laws affecting these issues are relevant to Chicanas in distinct ways. Chicanas are affected differently than women in general and differently than Chicanos. This is why it became necessary to establish the Chicana Rights Project, to ensure that Chicanas as a distinct group are defended and protected. The simple fact is that the issues that are most pressing among Chicanas are generally not among the priorities of the Anglo feminist. "For some women of the barrio, their hope is to achieve that measure of control over their own lives which many Anglo women already have."[8]

Another aspect of conflict between Chicanas and feminists is the question of the Chicana's minority status within the Anglo-dominated feminist movement. "While Chicanas do not want to sacrifice themselves as the instrument of compromise between Chicanos and the dominant society, they must ask themselves if they can become free from the Chicano's anger and frustration through the Anglo feminist movement, a segment of the very society which has been the source of so much of their oppression.[9]" This issue has more than one dimension. One part of the question is whether the Chicana should align herself with a segment of the society that oppresses her. Another part is the problem of the Chicana's second-class status within the women's movement. These issues profoundly disturb the relationship between Chicanas and feminists.

138

Other less emotional issues that hinder this relationship are legal questions like affirmative action. The issue of affirmative action concerns both women and minorities. However, contrary to popular attitudes, Chicanas do not generally benefit doubly from their status as female and minority. "Too often affirmative action for women has been interpreted to mean for Anglo women, while that for minorities has been interpreted to mean for minority males."[10] Thus, a concept that would seem to induce cooperation between Chicanas and feminists, in application produces a competitive relationship.

The institutionalization of sexism has made women, as a class, poor. It is minority women, particularly Hispanas, who bear this burden. Statistics show that Hispanic women had the lowest income of any racial/ethnic group in 1978. Hispanas earn about fifty-one cents for every dollar earned by a White male. The Anglo women's average income is not much better.[11] Thus, it is in the interest of the Chicana, as well as most women, to share in the efforts of the women's movements struggle for equality and an end to sexual discrimination. Just as important, it is in the interest of the women's movement to address the issues of poverty and racial discrimination in order to raise the living standard for all women.

This becomes increasingly clear upon examination of some of the legislative issues that are currently in question. The most pressing legislative issue for women and for the Chicana is the proposed EQUAL RIGHTS AMENDMENT. Until the ERA is passed, the rights of women are protected only by limited existing legislation (like Titles VII and IX) and precedent set by case law. This limited protection is slowly deteriorating with regulations and funding for enforcement agencies in jeopardy. Additionally, legislative budget cuts have adversely affected recent court decisions that have favored women's rights issues like maternity benefits and abortion funding for Medicaid patients.[12] While the specific issues are important, the

139

passage of the ERA would ultimately provide the only legal tool that could ensure the protection of the rights of women.

This issue is of particular relevance to Chicanas because it stands to benefit poor and working class women above all. Chicanas, being part of this population, are highly vulnerable to the attacks against labor and the poor that are becoming increasingly popular. Chicanas are severely affected by recent anti-abortion legislation and welfare cutbacks, and are highly vulnerable to discrimination on the job. In the current atmosphere that favors big business and militarism, it is doubtful that the rights of the poor and working people will be protected or guaranteed. The urgency of passing the ERA grows more pressing with each budget cut and with each government proposal to reduce safety regulations and laws.

President Reagan's recent proposal regarding immigration will have a devastating effect on Mexican families within the United States and Mexico. Aside from the strong moral, political and civil rights concerns about the proposal generally, there are several aspects of the plan that would prove very severe for the Chicana and her sisters in Mexico. The proposed "amnesty" program does not allow families separated by the border to be brought together in this country. As proposed, an individual who could prove residency prior to January 1, 1980 would be eligible for amnesty or "renewable term temporary residency". The spouse and family members of the individual, who remain in Mexico or who could not prove residency back to the aforementioned date, would not be legally permitted to join an individual under the amnesty program. The "guest worker" proposal has similar drawbacks.

Furthermore, an individual under the amnesty visa status would be required to work and pay taxes for ten years, yet they would be ineligible for benefits that other Americans enjoy, such as social security and unemployment compensation. The Reagan proposal would create a "sub-class" for

140

all undocumented workers who are eligible and choose to participate. It would place a burden on the ineligible relatives of these individuals. The proposal reflects a complete lack of concern for and understanding of this population by the Reagan Administration. The burden of the misunderstanding is borne by the spouses and children of the undocumented who are working in the fields, factories and restaurants of this nation.

Another recent legislative issue that will prove to be burdensome to the Chicana population is the Hyde Amendment. This legislation, which has been upheld by the Supreme Court, prohibits the federal government from funding abortions for Medicaid recipients.[13] The decision to continue funding abortions was left up to individual state governments. Approximately ten states have assumed that responsibility while several others have chosen not to. This issue is of crucial importance to all poor women, and Chicanas particularly. The government has decided that poor women must carry to term unwanted babies, placing a physical and financial burden on these women and their families, as well as reducing their choices and any control they have over their bodies.

Also in the medical field, the abuse of the sterilization procedure has been a problem for Chicanas in the past. The introduction of regulations regarding "informed consent" provided a guard for Medicaid patients, protecting them from mistaken or unwanted sterilization. However, a recent study found that despite any gains brought by regulations, the abuse of indigent women's health rights still occurs with some frequency.[14] Many states have been found to be in violation of certain aspects of the informed consent rules. Thus, it is becoming increasingly clear that the gains fought for since the sixties are in jeopardy today. Only diligent monitoring of the agencies that serve our communities will ensure that the treatment we receive is fair and just.

141

In the field of education, Title IX has been the first comprehensive legislation that ensured women an equal educational opportunity. Of course, education is a fundamental issue in our community and any law that guarantees the Chicana an equal opportunity in the educational system is invaluable. In 1973, the drop-out rate for Chicanas was 61.8%[15], and in a later study, the median years of school completed by adult Chicanas over 25 was 8.4 years.[16] These educational statistics are indicative of the sorry state in which Chicanas find themselves generally. The current attacks on Title IX, bilingual education, and other educational protections, are also attacks on Chicanas.

In the past, Chicanas have benefited from sympathetic legislation and a political atmosphere conducive to the promotion of civil rights. The 1980's bring new elements into question and consequently the outlook for the Chicana is changing. There are two very significant factors that influence the outlook of the Chicana; they are the 1980 Census and the recent change in administration.

The results of the 1970 Census confirmed for the general population what Chicanos were already aware of. The Hispanic population had become something to be reckoned with. Though still smaller than the Black population, Hispanics became recognized as increasingly visable and significant. The 1980 Census has served to further clarify this truth. It is said that the 1980's will be the "Decade of the Hispanic" and that soon we will outnumber Blacks and become the largest minority.

It is believed that there is power in numbers. However, our numbers will prove meaningless if we do not exercise our power, if we are not unified, if we do not carry on the efforts that won the gains brought by the sixties. If we are not careful, the only news brought by the census may be a warning that there will be more unemployed, more high school drop-outs, and more families living under the poverty level. It may warn us

142

that the problems faced by the Chicana will only become more prevalent and more serious.

This year has been the first time that many Latino populations have had the skills to respond to legislative redistricting. This is significant because our potential voting power would be meaningless without fair reapportionment. On another level, it reflects the fact that there are increasing numbers of Chicano professionals and technicians. While Chicanos make up less than two percent of the college student population[17], the number of educated Chicanos that are able to contribute to our community is growing.

Thus, while the problems of our growing population may become more evident, our ability to address these problems will also be increasing. One result of our growing visability will be an increased focus on the needs of Chicanas and hopefully an increased understanding by the mainstream society.

It is also true that the general political atmosphere is growing increasingly conservative. It has been mentioned that recent legislation has not been supportive of Chicana needs. Budget cuts that are being implemented are hard on poor women and therefore their effects are particularly felt by Chicanas.

The only certainty in the future of the Chicana is that the coming decade will be decisive as to where we are headed. It will take hard work and persistance to overcome the obstacles that confront us today.

The following issues are offered as goals which should be among our priorities as Chicanas:

1. Passage of the Equal Rights Amendment.

2. Participation in national coalitions and networks to salvage as much as possible from federal budget cuts.

3. Active, coordinated efforts to increase effectiveness of Chicana organizations.

143

4. Participation in lobbying efforts for legislation which secures for Chicanas equal participation in every aspect of American life.

5. Monitoring enforcement of protective laws.

6. Seeking research on the problems which Chicanas face and methods to correct them.

7. Encouraging and assisting young Chicanas to seek training and in the professions and non-traditional jobs.

144

NOTES

[1]Cotera, Martha, Profile on the Mexican American Woman, (Austin, TX: Educational Laboratory Publishers, Inc., 1976) p. 60

[2]Ibid, pp. 60-61

[3]McWilliams, Carey, North from Mexico, the Spanish Speaking People of the United States, (New York: Greenwood, 1968) p. 257

[4]Nuestro Magazine, Vol. 5, No. 5, June/July, 1981, p. 21

[5]Martha Cotera, p. 97

[6]Nuestro Magazine, Vol. 5, No. 5, June/July, 1981, p. 51

[7]Ibid, p. 59

[8]Nieto, Consuelo, The Chicana and the Women's Movement, a Perspective, p. 38

[9]Gonzalez, Sylvia, "The White Feminist Movement: The Chicana Perspective", The Social Science Journal, Vol. 14, No. 2, April, 1977, p. 71

[10]Nieto, p. 41

[11]National Commission on Working Women Publications: "An Overview of Women in the Workforce"

[12]Oliver, Myrna, "ACLU asks for Restoration of Abortion Funds", Los Angeles Times, July 17, 1981, pp. 3 and 26

[13]Supreme Court Decision: Harris v. McRae, (1980) 448 US 292

[14]"The Rowen Report", Carl T. Rowen, August 21, 1981

[15]Nieto, Consuelo, "The Working Chicana, Forging a New Identity", Affirmative Action in Progress, Vol. 3, No. 3, October, 1973

[16]Chicana Rights Project Monograph Series

[17]Nuestro Magazine, Vol. 5, No. 5, June/July, 1981, p. 59

LAW

Panelists

Virginia Martinez
Attorney, Moderator
National Director
MALDEF
Chicana Rights Project
Chicago, Illinois

Anna M. Caballero
Attorney
California Rural Legal Assistance

Carol Cantu
U.S. Probation Officer

Cristina Cruz
Nelles School
Los Angeles, California

Monica Herrera-Smith
Placentia, California

Recommendations

1. Work for the passage of the Equal Rights Amendment.

2. Participation in lobbying offices for legislation which secures equal participation of Chicanas.

3. Enforcement of protective laws should be motivated.

4. Participation in national coalitions to salvage as much as possible from federal budget cuts.

146

HISPANIC WOMEN BREAKING NEW GROUND THROUGH LEADERSHIP

Gloria Bonilla-Santiago[*]

Although the white women's movement in the United States has gained and accomplish strong professional links with Hispanic women leaders, exchangés between them have been largely unidirectional, with ideas and practice methodologies flowing from the dominant feminist culture to the Hispanic\Latina women culture. These activities have perpetuated the belief-so prevalent in the feminist Anglo culture-that Hispanic\Latina women will prosper only if they adopt the dominant feminist movement cultural tradition. Rejecting this view, the author argues in this descriptive analysis of Hispanic Women and Leadership, that the feminist movement to an extent has failed Hispanic\Latina women for several major reasons. First, because the way in which Hispanic women's experiences and their diversity has been brought into their movement, is one of token treatment and marginality. They bring one successful Hispanic women and ask her to be part of their board and expect her to be the representative of all Hispanic women. This is a result of the racial and class bias in the white women's movement as a whole. The second reason deals with the need to develop new ways of incorporating traditions and strategies which do not isolate Hispanic women from within the movement. The structure of the movement is exclusive of the needs of Hispanic women from a social structure point of view. And third, the failure of the feminist movement to create a positive environment in their organizations in which all women can participate. Approaches which keep Hispanic women and other women of color in the periphery of the movement have failed to address critical issues of racism, diversity, and classism. Isolating their participation and representation from the traditional feminist movement, the white women's feminist movement fosters ideas that contribute to the blaming of the victim. The author calls for Hispanic women leaders to unravel the dual conflicting system, one that is based on cultural consciousness and a knowledge of the demands and strategies of their immediate environment, and another that devalues and rejects their immediate environmental system. Hispanic women leaders need to pay attention to their strengths and resources as they move away from this conflict.

Historical Overview of Hispanic Women Leadership in the United States

The task of rethinking, revising, redefining, and enhancing the feminist white women's movement to incorporate the experiences of Hispanic women is one of the most significant challenges this presentation brings to feminist scholarship. Unlike Hispanic women and other racial ethnic groups that have been marginalized and isolated in the periphery of society, the feminist white women's movement has had a more positive reception. White women, to an extent, have benefited from the civil rights movement, from affirmative action

* All correspondence should be sent to: Professor Gloria Bonilla-Santiago Ph.D., Rutgers University, Graduate School of Social Work, 327 Cooper St., Camden, New Jersey, 080102

programs, and have been given the opportunity to compete with minorities from upper mobility opportunities to the point of "breaking through the glass ceiling." Their movement and leadership grew out of the re-awakening of a women's rights struggle centered around the demand for full integration of women into the mainstream and symbolized by the formation of commissions on the status of women and the founding of the National Organization for Women (NOW) during the middle '60s (Bunch, 1987). Unlike them, Hispanic women, minority men, and other women of color are beginning to break ground into the labor force.

In less than fifteen years, with the help of the women's and civil rights movements, Hispanic women have made a significant impact on American society. This paper is part of a monograph that I am preparing for publication with Praeger and is a ground breaking study, the first one to analyze how Hispanic women's educational and employment backgrounds, career goals, aspirations, cultural differences, obstacles and styles of leadership have contributed to or made a difference in the way that they have managed their lives as they developed into leaders.

The relationship of Hispanic women leadership to women leaders in the United States has been neglected and left out of the social sciences and feminist scholarship research. This is due to the limited research on Hispanic women and the lack of understanding on the part of social scientists on how to bridge and bring together Hispana or Latina women ("Hispana", "Latina" is the word of choice for many Hispanic women) contributions, diversity and the uniqueness about the way they organized their movements and leadership styles from that of the dominant society. The limited research conducted on Hispanic women reveals the need for a massive effort to enhance the leadership development of middle management, as well as young emerging Hispanic women leaders.

Recent research on Hispanic women indicates a need to aid this population in overcoming several societal-induced barriers, including sex and ethnic discrimination, lower levels of educational attainment, lower earning levels, and traditional sex-role socialization. Although there are some studies that illustrate programs developed to address these barriers, a larger number of studies simply indicate the continuing obstacles Hispanic women face in their economic and professional development. Although research is beginning to reach consensus on the hindrances to Hispanic women's development, (Ortiz and Cooney, 1984; Romero, 1986; and Carranza, 1988) such as lack of education and deeply-ingrained cultural norms, little work has been done to find out how to begin helping Hispanic women overcome these problems and to make personal and professional strides. The idea of enabling potential Hispanic women leaders to learn from the knowledge and experience of established Hispana leaders, while seemingly necessary, has not yet been the focus of research endeavors. However, a sampling of some diverse research findings indicates that such a study would be a significant component of any successful effort to provide potential Hispanic leaders with the opportunity and support needed to develop and enhance their skills to succeed better in society.

Several studies have looked at the status and /or demographic of Hispanic professionals and of Hispanic women in particular. Lopez (1984) found that the integration of Mexican- American women into higher education administration has been minimal, with most of the respondents holding mid-management level positions. While expressing satisfaction with current positions, respondents generally held low expectations for future promotions or advancement into institutional decision making levels. A study looking at the representation of minority groups in the news work force between 1976 and 1986 shows that blacks and Hispanics made little progress into management levels and remained underrepresented in both electronic and print media (Stone, 1987). Another study compared the careers of nontraditional engineering graduates (e.g. women, Hispanics, and blacks) with their traditional peers (Lebold et., al., 1983). While technical responsibilities increased with experience with no significant sex\ethnic differences, men reported higher supervisory responsibilities and salaries ten years after graduating than did women. Men were more likely to assess athletic and mechanical abilities higher than women's. Women rated their artistic, mathematical and interpersonal abilities higher than men.

As in the United States, Hispanic women in Latin America are finding obstacles to success. One study finds that while Latinas have been prominent in politics, they are only now obtaining business power in a geographic area that has long relegated them to a second class status in high administrative positions. It is difficult for them to advance to the top executive posts because most private firms belong to family groups which traditionally give management positions only to males.

Barriers, such as the male-only management practice in some U.S. Latin American firms, come in different forms and at different times in Hispanic women's lives. Some obstacles develop so early through the socialization process that the potential of many talented Hispanic girls and women is hidden for years or, tragically, for a lifetime. Although several educational projects have been developed for use in primary and secondary school classrooms to teach students about Hispanic women leaders not all schools use them in their curriculum (National Women History Project, 1985; Wood, 1974; Herrera and Lizcano, 1974). In addition, there are few Hispanic women in academic leadership positions to provide role models to young Hispanic girls in school (Crocker, 1982).

In the United States a 1982 (Project on Equal Education Rights) PEER report finds that Hispanic women earn less, own fewer businesses, and are less represented in politics than almost any other population segment. These realities can be explained, in part, by a history of low educational attainment. In 1981, while 69% of the total U.S. population completed four or more years of high school, only 42% of the Hispanic females reached the same level. With an average of 10.2 years of schooling, Hispanics lag behind black females at 11.9, and white females at 12.5 average years of schooling. Economic need, language barriers, family responsibility, and educator attitudes all contribute to a high Latina drop out rate which is twice as high as the 16% national rate (Crocker, 1982).

In addition to these problems, Hispanic high school females receive inadequate counseling, and vocational education enrollments clearly show that Hispanas are being steered into life cycles with little career or income potential. The pattern of disadvantage continues at the college level, with Hispanic women less likely than black or white women to complete four or more years (Crocker, 1982). At the graduate school level, a study shows that Hispanic women encounter problems in developing leadership or mentor relationships due to: conflicts within their culture, conflicts with the majority culture, and educational/financial barriers. Without an academic faculty mentor, the Latina student might find graduate study extremely difficult or impossible to complete (Quezada, 1984).

In addition to structural barriers, such as lack of positive role models, mentors and economic hardship, Hispanic girls and women face the constraining sex-role expectations ingrained in Hispanic culture. The typical sex-role stereotypes of the macho.male and submissive female still pervasive in society today seem even more powerful in Hispanic culture. The associated attitude can be so debilitating that it hinders or precludes Latina women from leaving the domestic domain of home and family, entering the labor force, gaining leadership roles, or acquiring a formal education. An analysis of 1979 interview data from the youth cohort of the National Longitudinal Surveys of Labor Market Experiences found that first generation Hispanic females held significantly more traditional sex-role attitudes than did second and third generation Hispanic females or non-Hispanic white females. Both first and second generation Hispanic females were significantly less likely to participate in the labor force than were non-Hispanic white females. This study found that the Hispanic-white difference in labor force participation was due more to differences in educational attainment than to sex-role attitudes (Ortiz and Cooney, 1984). One could argue that educational level was, in part, determined by sex-role attitudes. While studies reviewed so far, and many studies in general, focus on barriers to success for Latina women, others look at the characteristics and skills of successful Hispanic women leaders. Still other studies have investigated programs to help Hispanic women develop their potential for professional/personal development and leadership roles. In these studies, the term leadership has varied somewhat in definition and in the context in which it is applied (e.g. business, education administration, community work). Case studies have included such women as Dr. Maria Urquides, who has held numerous offices in local, state and national education organizations and worked to pass the Bilingual Education Act. Dr. Urquides had a strong mentorship system composed of elementary and high school teachers and her parents. She also maintained strong Hispanic cultural ties, she was a "truly bicultural person", developed strong coping skills and a positive life perspective, and gained leadership skills through her involvement and participation (Gonzales, 1986). Other studies have profiled women business executives, like Carmen Abril, who operated La Canasta Mexican Foods Products International , and Linda Vasquez, an executive of McDonald's Corporation (Arizona Business Gazette, 1986 and Lanier, 1984). One comparative study looked at the demographic, management skills, and personality characteristics of 468 females entrepreneurs in the United States and 30 in Puerto Rico. Ninety percent of American women and 73% of Puerto Rican women classified their businesses as service related. In Puerto Rico and the U.S., women rated themselves highest in people management and product innovation and entrepreneurs. Overall, a female entrepreneur in both geographic areas is married to a self-employed man, is approximately 35 years old, and holds an undergraduate degree (Hirsch, 1984).

Another study, which looked at business women in Latin America, included the Director of Braniff Airlines operations in Chile. She believed that performing the dual family life professional role has helped increase their awareness of human potential. Some Latin-American business women believe that they possess certain inherent advantages over their male peers, such as the ability to manage money better (Taylor, 1984).

In addition to looking at characteristics of already established leaders, some investigations have studied the effects of programs directed at developing leadership skills in Hispanic women. The federal Bureau of Occupational and Adult Education sponsored a program to develop and motivate minority women, especially those of Hispanic origin, in the Washington, D.C.

metropolitan area to undertake business ownership and management. This training program sought to equip potential managers with information about the management skills needed for functioning competently in a business ownership, corporate management, or personal life management situation. Trainees learned functional skills in motivation and personal development, communications, essentials of management process, and financial management. With an 87 percent retention rate, the 43 trainees completing the program indicated that their needs were addressed; the concept they learned were applied and the materials were practical and valuable. Individual participants experienced attitudinal and behavioral changes (Miranda, 1976).

While the cited studies have focused on women in business or education, one investigation emphasized women as grass-roots community leaders. The study's purpose was to see how people cope with the demands of their environment and to observe the relationship between learning competent coping behaviors and self-reported well being. The study sample was composed mostly of Mexican-American women in their middle-aged years who were both members and non-members of a citizen action organization in East Los Angeles. The citizen action group concentrated on developing community leaders by promoting spiritual beliefs and family values as shared community resources. Neighborhood leaders were encouraged to engage in risk-taking and confrontation tactics, taught problem-solving skills, and provided with social support. Slightly more members than non- members were willing to undertake confrontation. A substantial proportion of those who were confronters reported feeling well in comparison to their non-member counterparts. Ethnic pride was positively associated with participation in the organization and with self-reported well-being (Arzac, 1982).

In response to the lack of knowledge and understanding of the work done on Hispanic professional women, and their educational experiences, the National Network of Hispanic women completed a nationwide survey of 303 Latina respondents who were in management positions and/ or who owned small businesses in 1986. Both professional and entrepreneurial women were included. The survey helped identify the successes and strengths of Hispanic women who have overcome obstacles and are succeeding in the professional world. According to the survey the sociodemographic and family characteristics of the survey respondents depart from Hispanas in general. The sample seemed to represent a highly selected group of professional, upwardly- mobile women who were educated in the 1960's and 1970's when educational opportunities were available for racial/ethnic minorities. The average age of the respondents was 38 years with 18 years of schooling, including high school plus six years of graduate study. Some of the major findings suggested that the respondents marital status was comparable to other women: about 50 percent were married. An interesting deviation, however, appear in the divorce rate, which was twice as high for Hispanas. The study also showed a relatively high outmarriage rate, which was twice as high for Hispanas than non-Hispanas: over one third of the sample were married to Anglo-American men. This seemed to confirm findings from other studies correlating higher educational levels and social class standing with intermarriage rates. The majority of women were in middle or senior level positions in the workplace. In addition managers were also asked about progress in prior employment. Those who had progressed rapidly represented 57.4 percent of the sample. The remaining 42.6 percent felt they did not progress rapidly primarily because of the lack of mentors or sponsors in the organization (Carranza, 1988).

Zambrana (1988), suggest that although few definitive conclusions can be drawn from this survey, it helped identify the successes and strengths of Hispanas who have overcome obstacles and are succeeding in the professional world. Moreover, the data described Hispanic women entrepreneurs who earlier had been an invisible and neglected group.

In reviewing recent conference proceedings about Hispanic women, the information points to factors that influence career choices of Hispanic women. Hispanic women are not willing to relocate, not willing to separate from family, and feel insecure because they are the first in their family to pursue a professional career (Castillo, Sylvia, 1986). In terms of organizational experiences of Hispanic women managers, there are indications that often the value system of Hispanic women intersects with mobility in subtle ways. Hispanic women don't know how to react to discrimination because they can't determine if the source is gender-based or race related. Hispanic women suffer psychologically because they hold loyalties to two conflicting goals; success in the mainstream and attachment to the Hispanic culture. On the positive side, they have strong nurturing values. In addition, there are other conflicts; doing the right thing versus doing what is the politically responsible. Most Hispanic women are trained to believe in the notion that if you work hard you get ahead.

For many Hispanic women, cultural values suggest that power is unfeminine and is viewed as a negative quality. Therefore they have been socialized and trained to eliminate conflict instead of facing it; they learn early not to take risks, and they place a high value on security; they want to create stability and do not understand the necessity for change in the corporate world; they often do not understand the vision or mission of the organizations for which they work; they value loyalty, and expect loyalty from their subordinates; they do not value the power of bargaining, if something does not feel right they back out instead of negotiating (Romero, 1986).

HISPANIC WOMEN

25

For some Hispanic women leaders the most successful mentors are "white males" because they know how to survive in the mainstream culture (Romero, 1986) and minority mentors may not understand the mainstream culture and may see Hispanic women as competitors. Some Hispanic women may find this hard to accept because they feel that they are being disloyal to their culture and community. However some Hispanic women in general tend to feel that white male mentors offer both emotional and material support, but they need to accept this support without feeling that there are sexual overtones.

When examining the success and leadership stress factors in the CORO leadership programs (an experiential leadership program designed for Hispanic women highly educated from a variety of difference experiences), Miranda, (1986) highlights internal and external factors that their women reported while climbing up the ladder for private sector positions. Most internal stresses were derived from their own lack of self- confidence. The fear of attempting something new and proceed with a task that basically had no structure. She suggested that despite the experience and informal training, they failed to recognize the transferability of skills they already had. Hispanic women tended to freeze-up instead of taking charge when confronted with conflict and tended to be bashful at promoting themselves.

In observing some of the women's behaviors, the CORO leadership reported that Hispanic women in supervisory positions, feel that they must maintain an "in charge" posture for fear that they might be perceived as weak, regardless of how stressful a position is. By doing this, women close themselves off and have no one to discuss the difficulties they encounter. They pay the price of isolation due to their fear that they will be perceived as incapable of handling the job. Hispanic women are also afraid of delegating responsibility because they feel that they are ultimately responsible. In this program there were a significant number of women who were single or did not have children. In general, the women with children were more responsible, more task oriented, better at commitment, and more punctual. These women had a better sense of organizing their lives due to the demands of a family, unlike single women whose life after the job had little structure. Some major findings reflect the inner conflict over how Hispanic women should modify their behavior and values in order to conform to the mainstream culture. Many still tend to pursue the more feminine occupations as a way to enter the work setting because they do not understand the organizational cultures in their work settings (Miranda, 1986).

Hispanic women studied to a large extent had been first born and had assumed a large amount of responsibility in the family. They became accustomed to large amounts of responsibility which carried over to their work settings. These roles often operate on an unconscious level. Consequently, they tend to be overlay-formal especially in job interviews and towards powerful decision makers. This was partly due to cultural differences and partly to sexual differences. One reason is because Hispanic women tend to move up the ladder in isolation. They learned the game within one arena, but, when exposed to a different arena, they needed to keep a distance. Another reason for formality is their inability to "read" a situation correctly, since they enter a situation without a feeling of equality. The external factors perceived as stereotypes of Hispanic women have become external barriers. Contrary to those perceived stereotypes, Hispanic women to a large extent in the CORO program were found to be very intelligent and articulate.

For the most part, corporations have resisted hiring Hispanic women, and, when they have, they restrict them to public affairs and community affairs as opposed to policy making positions. Corporations usually stop after they have hired one or two Hispanic women, they feel they have done their job. These "token" women then have the burden of representing all Hispanic women as well as the burden of proving that they are qualified. Often there is a conflict with white women. Corporations believe that if they hire a woman then they have done their part for all minorities (Ybarra, 1986). This is one of the double standard barriers posed by Hispanic men in organizational settings. Hispanic men expect women to remain in traditional fields and tend to be more tolerant of white women than Hispanic women. Hispanic men are often more competitive and insecure with Hispanic women. Institutional and sexist barriers to promotions for Hispanic women are evident. There is a lack of experience and resources available to help train and prepare Hispanic women for a competitive market. There is a lack of interaction and supportive networking with leaders from numerous occupations (Miranda, 1986). Some recent research suggests that Hispanic women are in the workforce because they want to work. For white women the biggest barrier in the workforce is their husband's income and family considerations. The biggest barrier for Hispanic women in the workforce is education. Hispanic women have a high drop out rate due to family's economic status. Although Hispanic females are less likely to drop out of school than are Hispanic males, they are more likely than other groups of women to be high school dropouts. Census data from October 1986 showed that, among Hispanic females between 14-17 years of age, 18.4 percent had left high school without a diploma. In 1986, of Hispanic women aged 16-24, 27.2 percent were high school dropouts, compared to 32.8 percent of Hispanic males, 11.1 percent of White females, and 13.4 percent of Black females (U.S. Bureau of the Census, 1986). For example, Hispanic women occupy a marginal position in the labor market. Their labor force participation rates are the lowest of all women, and their median weekly earnings are the lowest of all workers in the labor market. Their low level of educational attainment has contributed to occupational segregation in low-skilled, low paid jobs, vulnerability to high rates of unemployment and a precarious economic position for them and their families (Escutia and Prieto, 1988).

Hispanic Women Relationship to Other Women's Movement

I argue that the feminist movement to an extend has failed women of color for several major reasons. First because of the way in which Hispanic women's experiences and their diversity has been brought into their movement. That is one of token treatment and marginality. They bring one successful Hispanic women and ask her to be part of their board and expect her to be the representative of all Hispanic women. That is a result of the racial and class bias in the white women's movement as a whole. The second reason deals with the need to develop new ways of incorporating traditions and strategies which do not isolate Hispanic women from within the movement. The structure of the movement is not inclusive of the needs of women of color from a social structure point of view. And third, the failure of the feminist movement to create a positive environment in their organizations in which all women can participate. Approaches that keep Hispanic women and other women of color in the periphery of the movement have failed to address critical issues of racism, diversity, and classism. Consequently, isolating their participation and representation from the traditional feminist movement. Out of this frustration the white women's feminist movement fosters ideas that contribute to the blaming of the victim. Hispanic women become isolated from the main stream society and are forced into an environment of survival which requires to create a new place for themselves and their families. They have learned to survive in a dual conflicting system, one that is based on cultural consciousness and a knowledge of the demands and strategies of their immediate environment, and another that devalues and rejects their immediate environmental system.

Although Hispanic women's involvement in the community has increased considerably in recent years, there are countless theories why Hispanic women and other Third World women have not identified with contemporary feminism in large numbers. Smith suggests "that racism of white women in the movement has certainly been a major factor. The powers that be are also aware that a movement of progressive Third World women in this country would alter life as we know it" (1979:47). Consequently, this has kept Hispanic women and other women of color from organizing autonomously and with other women around women's political issues.

Hispanic Women's Movement: Feminism and Organizing

According to some Hispanic researchers, the origins of the Anglo feminist movement stem from within a society that has transmitted, through its many institutions, oppressive attitudes toward minorities. Since the male traditionally bears the brunt of this offense to his personal pride and dignity because of greater opportunities for social interaction, his home has become the target for his misguided value as a human being or reactionary macho.

Hispanic women organizing in the United States of America began developing as early as 1968, when Dr. Hector Garcia, the founder of the G.I. Forum, met with Polly Baca Barragan, (the first Hispanic women Senator from Denver) and Dr. Sylvia Gonzales, (one of the first Hispanic women advocates for Latina rights) to discuss the formation of a national Chicana organization. Polly Baca was charged with meeting with Washington Chicanas to test the waters for such an organization. In 1971, the first attempt to form a national organization for Hispanic women was initiated by Lupe Anguiano, a Chicana employed with the Department of Health, Education, and Welfare. A group of Puerto Rican women from New York were invited (Lourdes Miranda King, Diana Lozano, Ana Maria Perera and others). Throughout these two attempts to organize there were many organizational and turf conflicts about who the organization was going to serve, who was going to be the leaders, headquarters and all kinds of ideological battles, all of which led the organizational efforts into a failure.

It was not until 1971, that the Chicanas group held a national conference in Houston, Texas. Resolutions generated by the conference called for legal abortions, birth control and child-care centers. At the same time Puerto Rican women on the East Coast founded the National Conference of Puerto Rican Women under the leadership of such women as Carmen Delgado Votaw and Paquita Vivo. Other communities around the country began to organize. In Los Angeles, the Commission Femenil Mejicana and The Chicana Service Action Center were founded to respond to the needs of California Chicanas. In Miami Florida, the Cuban Women's Club advanced the cause of Cuban women through the creative efforts of Maria Fernandez, Silvia Unzueta, Yvonned Santa Maria and many others (Gonzales, 1981).

During the 1980's Hispanic women entered a new phase of organizational development. This decade began with the National Hispanic Feminist Conference. Hispanic women leaders gather after a decade of attempts of organizational failures, ideological disputes, political and ideological battles between groups of women. In the process of looking for an organizational role model

HISPANIC WOMEN

29

that would aspire an united action, the group of women adapted a "Paulo Freire" approach of organizing for the conference. The National Hispanic Feminist Conference was held in San Jose, California. A group of Chicana leaders began to boycott the conference hotel because they were not included as keynote speakers. They sufficiently disrupted events and disoriented participants to handicap the unifying efforts of the meeting. Although the conference proceeded successfully, the several agendas and platforms about the inclusion of Gay rights, refugees issues, and antifeminist positions from the many long time Chicano activists sought to establish their historical position in the Chicana leadership hierarchy.

As always the conference prevailed and Hispanic women decided to be inclusive of gay rights, condemn right wing governments, while displaying a sensitivity to the boycott by moving conference workshops from the hotel. This conference was very particular in the history of Hispanic women because of the persistence and eventual resolution of leadership struggles which have caused so much conflict in the past and to some extent continues to cripple the present.

During the late 1960's the Chicano and other Latino groups bible or organizing principle was Paulo Freire's *Pedagogy of the Oppressed*. Freire's book became the handbook for the Hispanic oppressed. Dr. Sylvia Gonzales tells us that the reason this movement faltered was because although they read Frei

re's work and instinctively identified with its message, they were unable to internalize his methodology because of the strength of the social norms to which they were bound. It was very difficult for the movement to release the image of the "oppressor" and assume autonomy and responsibility for their condition. According to some of these women leaders "we put too much energy in anti feelings rather than in creating a new system or mode of operandi". The lessons learned from this movement for the leadership of the National Hispanic Feminist conference are indeed significant to the understanding and survival of any Hispanic women's movement. The contradiction was one of wanting a model or organizing that allow the women to become part of the system which for them was adopting the "oppressors model and in reality seeking the power of the "oppressor". The timing for the organization ideological formulation was one that provoked community and grass-roots competition, negative undermining and destructive disruptions. The view of "the piece of the pie", became the slogans for wanting to be with the "Oppressor". Wanting to be a leader became the "intermediary Oppressors" of the Latino communities. Dr. Sylvia Gonzales advices Hispanic women leaders to read Paulo Freire with the clear understanding that his methodology will not gain any one a "piece of the pie, but show us how to change the pie" (Nuestro 1981:45-47). She adheres to the fact that the reason why the feminist movement and Hispanic women have not gotten together is because they are trapped by this model. Some Hispanic women leaders refer to the white women benefiting from Affirmative Action more than minorities. Some say that they are chastising them for taking a "piece of the pie". Some analyst suggest that what started as a grass-roots consciousness-raising women's movement turned into labeling the model "the new girls network". That's the model that is used during the early 1980's for organizing Hispanic women.

During this same time of National-level struggles, the International Women Conference was held in Mexico City and Chicana women organized to speak about the differences and lack of inclusion of Chicana women issues in the feminist movement. They initiated a campaign to ensure their representation and their presence increased their awareness of the sorrowful position Chicanas occupy within the United States feminist movement. Anglo woman found themselves in the same ironic contradiction as the Chicanas as they approached the Mexico City conference, having to leave behind racial prejudices in pursuit of true international sisterhood. The disagreement with this notion had to do with the fact that Anglo women patronize the black members of her movement, while neglecting other ethnic minority women such as Chicanas, Puerto Ricans, Asians, and American Indians. This serious neglect, according to the Hispanic women's movement, stemmed from a group of white feminist from the East coast perspective, where black women were in the majority and did have greater visibility than other minority women. However, when minority women were included in feminist activities, commissions, clubs or organizations, it was always under the title of committee or subcommittee on minority women and never as president or chairwoman. Before and after the Mexico conference, numerous other conferences and workshops were held throughout the nation to discuss the issues. Planning committees and program announcements showed that panels on minority women were subtopics and were under lengthy list of major topics discussed by Anglo women organizers. The continuous failure to address the women of color, issues from a social structure position has led Hispanic women, in the marginality of society. Consequently, they have organized their own organizations.

Hispanic women generally faced both external and internal constraints to other organizational efforts due to their economic position. Most of the women have been and continue to be at the bottom of the ladder with regard to education, employment, income, adequate health care, political representation, and fair housing. Oppression occurs because of race, sex, low socioeconomic status, lack of facility with the English language and their weak entry-level

HISPANIC WOMEN

31

bargaining position in the labor force. There are numerous examples of Hispanic women organizing to help themselves and their communities. This is because of the way white feminist movements have treated Hispanic women. The first major Chicana women's conference was held in Houston (Women Conference, Por La Raza held May 28-30, 1971, Houston, Texas). Another is cited by Longeaux and Vazques on the Colorado conference where a representative said that "it was the consensus of the group of women not to want to be part of the white women's movement" (Conference in Colorado in Enriqueta Longeauz y Vazquez, 1972). Other Chicana women organizing examples are the Chicana Service Action, Los Angeles: MALDELF; Chicana Rights Project; San Antonio Welfare Rights groups; Chicana Foundation, and others. Historically very few Hispanic women obtained leadership positions in Hispanic organizations, labor, business, education, government and even in religious groups. In the Chicano community, for examples, a few women excel in taking leadership. These women and others (Adelitas, Lucia Gonzales, de Parsons, Mujeres del Primer Congreso Mexicanista, Erma Tenayuca, Graciela Olivares, Polly Baca Barragan, Gloria Molina, Dolores Huerta, Dr. Alicia Cuaron, Dr. Antonia Pantoja, Dr. Helen Rodriguez, and others), served as role models for Hispanas. Together they provided evidence for Hispanic women in positive self-assessment as a strong, capable, intelligent individuals who can and must play a viable role in defining and obtaining their liberation and that of their people.

Carmen Delgado Votaw, a Puerto Rican activist who attended the International Women's Year Conference in Mexico City representing the National Conference of Puerto Rican Women, 1976, pointed to the fact that the process of changes comes hard for Hispanic women. This is so because they come from a traditional society to which they want to conform, and they have few role models to emulate, ..."most Latinas are very traditionally minded", she explains. "They're reluctant to openly express women's movement views that to them seem outlandish. Their culture hasn't prepared them to discuss things like sexual freedom" (Agenda, 1976, p.16). Ada Peña, National Vice President of for the Midwest of the League of United Latin American Citizens (LULAC), agreed with Carmen Votaw in her evaluation of the role of Hispanic women within the mainstream feminist movement of this country — "we have both been able to identify with it, basically I think it's because we are concerned with other issues. We know that there's discrimination because of sex, but we still haven't gotten beyond discrimination in education, in housing, and in other vital areas".....

"they don't welcome you , they don't say 'you are part of us; when we talk about sex discrimination, we include Spanish-speaking, and blacks. What they say is 'When we talk about discrimination, we mean all women.' But it is not so" (Votaw, 1981:18). These two women represent the opinions of Hispanic women about the Women's movement of the sixties and seventies. In the 1980's, Hispanic women feminist activism, is for the most part invisible.

More recently, Vasquez (1988) claims that Anglo women primarily experience oppression through sexism, while class issues and racism are much more a reality for Hispanas. "We don't deny that sexism is a problem, but our needs are even more basic. We need jobs. We're not just a small percentage of lawyers, we're a minuscule percentage. Access to education and job training are much more important to us" (1988:10). She further argues that to empower and organize themselves, Hispanic women need to work with movements that address their immediate and real concerns. "In that way Hispanas can become more established within their own community. Then after a while, they will be a force to be reckoned with by other movements".... there is a need to raise the consciousness among both women and men in our communities about sexism, how it affects us, and where it intersects with class issues" (Vasquez, 1988:10).

The Hispanic women's movement, the African American Movement, the Women's movement overall has recently brought some positive changes for Hispanic women professionals. Carranza (1988) argues that although it is true that there is a large number of Hispanic women trapped in poverty, there is a growing number of Hispanic women entering managerial and professional jobs. She argues that some of these women are beginning to overcome obstacles of race, gender, culture and class to become highly successful in the professional world. Terie Flores Baca (1988) concurs with this argument, suggesting that "some Hispanic women as a rule are better educated, can compete for higher paying jobs and is slowly being recognized for their achievement"(Carranza, 1988:22). Sylvia Castillo also suggests that "in ten years we have seen more women earning college degrees and moving into the public and private sectors. We now see women in decision making positions and not just in entry level jobs in manufacturing industries. Unfortunately affirmative action gains have not been too significant. Affirmative Action has helped us increase our numbers at some decision making levels, but Hispanic women are competing against Hispanic men for those one or two affirmative action jobs. By and large, affirmative action has not affected the general pool of workers. In terms of a hopeful outlook, I think that with more Hispanic women working outside of the home are beginning to influence decision makers and leaders" (1988:22). Although this trend is evident in many Hispanic communities throughout the country, it does not change the reality for thousands of working class poor Hispanic women who are struggling to make it and are trapped in poverty.

Currently, national Hispanic women organizations have taken the leadership

HISPANIC WOMEN

33

in advocating for political, economic and social change. For example, (The Mexican American National Women Organization), MANA has been very active in voting and registration projects, has worked on reproductive rights, education reform, housing, labor organizing, antiracist organizing, immigration issues and welfare rights. (The National Puerto Rican Women Rights Organization) NACOPRO, has also advocated for Hispanic women and health issues such, as building campaigns against Aids, sterilization, welfare rights and educational reform. The National Network of Hispanic Women has held corporate and round table consultations to discuss and highlight Hispanic women issues and agendas that are inclusive of the needs of Hispanic professional women. Commission Femenil Mexicana Nacional (National Commission of Mexican Women) LA MUJER, they advocate for Latinas and Reproductive Rights, and other organizations such as the National Association of Working Women who advocate for grass-roots women issues including Hispanic women. But very few Hispanic women organizations have been successful in advocating for new policy changes in the structure of the economy at the national level. Some Hispanic women organizations have been successful at their local levels. One successful example is the New Jersey Hispanic Women's Task Force of New Jersey, a young vibrant Hispanic women's group has successfully advocated Hispanic women programs via the state legislature, and others.

Conclusion

As the Civil Rights Movement took root and grew during the fifties and antiwar sentiment dominated the sixties, the seventies signaled the growth of women's consciousness. By the eighties, women had entered corporate America in force and struggled to "break through the glass ceiling." No doubt, Hispanic women, children of their time, environment, and circumstances, felt the impact of the women's movement. All women did. But this analysis points to the specific differences in the response of Hispanic women to the issues raised by the white female majority.

Although the Hispanic women leaders understand the historical significance of the feminist movement, they continued to label it a white, middle-class movement. The daily struggle to survive in the social and political climate of their communities consumed all their energy and distracted them from linking and networking with white feminist groups. Many of these leaders had, and have, the ability to form a critical consciousness of their community's circumstances, yet the mainstream feminist issues – abortion, equal rights for women – have not engaged their involvement. Hispanic women felt isolated from white feminists. They continue to be held back from meaningful participation in women's movement activities. Consequently, these women have become victims of the mistaken notion that any improvements in the status of white women is a remarkable accomplishment for them, too. In essence, when one looks at the conditions of poverty in general, the condition of Hispanic women in poverty has vastly improved. For professional Hispanic women, there seems to be very little, if any, advancement in terms of gaining access and positions through the movement. Many of these leaders have succeeded only through their community struggles, and by advocating on behalf of their Hispanic community they have created a place for themselves.

Hispanic women in general have not profited from the movements the Hispanic men initiated nor from the feminist movement. They have began to move into their own organizations within a climate of declining resources, self righteous negativity, and antifeminist and minority agendas. In essence, Hispanic women leaders have paid their dues and that has kept them honest and focused. The leadership that they want to aspire is one of cooperation, community training and awareness, and changes for their future generations within the system.

References

Arzac, Adriana Maria. 1982. "The Development of Community Competence through a Neighborhood Organization." Ph.D. diss., University of Texas, Houston School.

Bunch, Charlotte. 1987. *Passionate Politics: Feminist Theory in Action.* (New York: St. Martin's Press).

"Carmen Cashes in on Her Tortilla Chips". *Arizona Business Gazette*, 13 January 1986, A-4.

Carranza, Ruth. 1988. "Leaders Reply: In What Ways are Hispanic Women Better Off/Worse Off Today than Ten Years Ago." *Intercambios Femeniles*, 3:10.

Carranza, Ruth. 1988. "Hispanas and the Women's Movement." (Interviews with Terrie Florez Baca and Sylvia Castillo). *Intercambios Femeniles*, 3:22.

Carranza, Ruth. 1988. "Research Findings on Marriage, Income and Stress of Professional Women." *Intercambios Femeniles*, (3):6-9.

Castillo, Sylvia. "The Economic Labor Force Participation of Hispanic Women". in *The Hispanic Professional Women Worklife and Leadership Experience, National Network of Hispanic Women Roundtable Reunion, Summary of Discussions and Recommendations.* San Francisco, California, 13 June 1974.

Cooney, Rosemary S. and A. Colon. 1980. "Work and Family: The Recent Struggle of Puerto Rican Families". In Clara Rodriguez, Virginia Sanchez-Korrol and Jose Alers, eds., *The Puerto Rican Struggle: Essays on Survival in the United States* (New Jersey: Waterfront Press).

HISPANIC WOMEN

35

Cooney, Rosemary S. 1975. "Changing Labor Force Participation of Mexican American Wives: A Comparison with Anglos and Blacks." *Social Science Quarterly*, 56:252-261.

Crocker, Elvira Valenzuela. 1982. "The Report Card on Educating Hispanic Women." Washington, D.C.: NOW Legal Defense and Education Fund.

Escutia, Marta and Margarita M. Prieto. 1988. "Hispanics in the Workforce, Part II: Hispanic Women." Report. Washington, D.C.: National Council of La Raza.

Gonzalez, Sylvia. 1981. "The Latina Feminist: Where We've Been, Where We're Going". *Nuestro*, 5:45-47.

Gonzalez, Sylvia. 1982. "La Chicana: An Overview". In Conference on the Educational and Occupational Needs of Women, The National Institute of Education. Washington, D.C.: U.S. Department of Health, Education and Welfare :186-212.

Gonzalez-Quiroz, Elizabeth. *The Education and Public Career of Maria L. Urquidez: A Case Study of a Mexican American Community Leader*. Ann Arbor, Mich.: University Microfilms, 1986.

Herrera, Gloria and Lizcano Jeanette. 1974. "La Mujer Chicana". (Crystal City, Texas: Office of Education (DHEW)

Lopez, Gloria Ann. 1984. "Job Satisfaction of the Mexican American Woman Administrator in Higher Education". Doctoral Dissertation. The University of Texas at Austin.

Miranda Towns, Luz. 1974. "Examination of Success and Leadership Stress Factors." Paper presented at The Hispanic Professional Women Worklife and Leadership Experience, National Network of Hispanic Women Roundtable Reunion, Summary of Discussions and Recommendations, 13 June, at San Francisco, California.

National Women's History Project. 1985. "Women as Members of Communities, Third Grade Social Studies." Abigail Adams, Sarah Winnemucca, Helen Keller, Shirley Chishlom, March Fong Eu, and Carmen Delgado Botaw. Women"s Educational Equity Act Program: Washington D.C.

Ortiz, Vilma and Rosemary Santana Cooney. 1984. "Sex Role Attitudes and Labor Force Participation among Young Hispanic Females and Non-Hispanic White Females." *Social Science Quarterly*, 65: 392-400.

Romero, Mary. 1986. "Twice Protected?: Assessing the Impact of Affirmative Action on Mexican-American Women." *Ethnicity and Women*, 5:135-156.

Smith, Barbara. 1986. "Some have truths on the Contemporary Black Feminist Movement." in Nan Van Den Bergh and Lynn B.Cooper, eds., *Feminist Visions Social Work* (National Association of Social Work, Silver Spring, Maryland: National Association of Social Work).

Stone, Vernon A. 1987. "Minority Employment in Broadcast News 1976-86." Paper presented at the Annual Meeting of the Association for Education in Journalism and Mass Communication, San Antonio, Texas, August 3.

Taylor, Frank. 1984. "Women Grab Management Power in Home Machismo." *International Management* (European Edition), (39) : 24-27.

U. S. Bureau of the Census. 1986. "Current Population Reports," ser.:20, no. 421. Washington, D.C.

U.S. Department of Labor. 1987. Bureau of Labor Statistics, "Dislocated Worker Survey." Washington, D.C.

LATINO STUDIES JOURNAL

36

Votaw, Carmen D. 1981. "Cultural Influences on Hispanic Feminism." *Agenda*, 11:44-49.

Zambrana, Ruth E. 1987-88. "Latinas in the United States." In Sara E. Rix (Ed.) *The American Woman, 1987-88: A Report In Depth* (New York: W.W. Norton and Company).

HISPANIC WOMEN

37

Political Familism: Toward Sex Role Equality in Chicano Families

Maxine Baca Zinn

The Chicano family has been described by social scientists against a backdrop of inflexible tradition. Recent studies, however, reveal changes in Chicano families. This paper analyzes family and sex role transformations. I refute the notion that changes in the family result simply from the modernization or acculturation of an ethnic group. Chicano family structure and sex role relationships are indeed undergoing some far-reaching changes. But I propose that many of these changes are generated because of conditions unique to the Chicano experience—conditions which necessitate responses to structural domination in U.S. society.

Participation of total family units in the Chicano movement has on one level an integrating function, and on another level a role equalizing function. On the one hand it pulls the family, the community, La Raza, together to fight racial discrimination. On the other hand it requires an alteration of traditional sex role relationships and the creation of new associations and linkages between men and women.

Acculturation and Family Structure

Social science has assumed that the process of acculturation changes traditional relationships in "ethnic" families. The assumption has been that there is a general movement in acculturating groups toward family

©Copyright 1975 by Maxine Baca Zinn

13

egalitarianism. Ethnic or subordinate group family transformations are seen in an evolutionary perspective of world-changing family patterns. Overall shifts occur from extended kinship units with rigid sex role divisions to nuclear, autonomous, egalitarian family units.[1] With industrialization, urbanization, and modernization, the family as an institution is expected to move gradually from an extended structure to a nuclear structure. This modernization is said to give rise to a new "modern" orientation among women and to bring about a trend toward greater equality between the sexes.

Concern with acculturation of the Chicano family is reflected in earlier studies of this institution.[2] Recent investigations of the Chicano family indicate that it is moving in the direction of the ideal typical nuclear family with its emphasis on sex role equality. A 1967 study by Manual Ramírez on the identification of Chicano family values revealed that Chicanos identified with traditional Mexican family values of conformity, strict child rearing, and authoritarian submission. However, he found that Chicanos exhibited signs of "Americanization" in the form of decreasing identification with traditional patterns of male authority and separation of the sexes.[3]

In examining changes in marriage roles which accompany the acculturation of Chicanas, Tharp et al. found that the more acculturated the wife, the greater the marriage role resembled an egalitarian-companionate pattern.[4]

In *The Mexican American People,* the family is presented as an institution which has undergone significant departure from the traditional pattern. Shifts in the structure of the family are explained in terms of movement of substantial sections of the population into the urban middle class. According to the study, familism and patriarchy, two characteristic features of traditional Chicano families, no longer define family structure.[5]

Ellwyn Stoddard in his book, *Mexican Americans,* gives considerable attention to changing family patterns. He concludes that the traditional family is giving way to a modern family life style characterized by greater rates of exogamy and increased geographical, social, and occupational mobility. This trend, he continues, is much like trends that have occurred in other immigrants who have been assimilated into the dominant society.[6]

Each of these works interprets changes in the structure of the Chicano family as inevitable changes which accompany modernization and acculturation of ethnic groups. They view changes in sex role relationships in developmental terms, as the results of Americanization and gradual assimilation to the dominant society. However, interpretations of Chicano social institutions which rely exclusively on assimilationist analytic frameworks, result in neglect of certain sociological realities. Thus they must be considered incomplete, erroneous, or both.

Racism, Resistance, and Family

An alternative framework must be adopted. It is necessary to steer analysis away from assimilation and toward a perspective which includes the concepts of oppression, opposition and change. The internal colonialism framework best incorporates these notions. This framework, based on similarities between classic colonialism and oppression of racial groups in the U.S. posits that the subordination of Chicanos is the result of oppression by a dominant Anglo minority.[7] It also posits inevitable opposition by those groups subject to racial subordination. In this resistance and opposition to colonial status we find conditions specifically relevant to changing familial patterns occurring among Chicanos.

Social and political activism of Chicanos must be seen in light of attempts by racially oppressed groups, both within and outside of the United States, to alter those conditions which render them powerless. Although nationalist liberation movements in the third world and El Movimiento have developed out of structurally different sociopolitical conditions, both are responses to common processes of social oppression. As diverse and expansive as the Chicano movement is, it is nevertheless a response to the pervasive structural control which Anglo society maintains over Chicanos. Broadly conceived, El Movimiento is a decolonization movement. Of course, questions arise concerning the revolutionary versus reformist orientations of organizations and activities which constitute El Movimiento. Obviously, it is impossible to characterize the entire Chicano movement as either reformist or revolutionary. However, insofar as Chicano movement activities seek to make fundamental changes in institutions of the dominant society which control the lives of Chicanos, the movement is revolutionary. Insofar as masses of Chicanos are politicized in an intensive manner and imbued with the idea of creating a new order of things, the movement is revolutionary.[8] What is more immediately relevant to this discussion is that regardless of how it is categorized, the Chicano movement aims to decolonize Anglo-Chicano relationships.

Decolonization struggles occur at many different levels and exhibit many ranges of activity. They involve conscious, continual development and modification of political strategies and traditional behavior patterns. The Chicano movement has had an impact not only on structures of the dominant society that have served to maintain racial subordination, but also on sociocultural traditions of Chicano people.

A guiding principle of the Chicano movement which cuts across specific organizational goals and tactics is the preservation and maintenance of family loyalty. Ideologically, this principle is expressed by two concepts: La familia de la Raza and carnalismo. La familia de la Raza unites Chicanos to struggle as a family tied together by carnalismo, the spirit of brotherhood. Organizationally, these concepts take the form of total family participation in ongoing struggles for racial justice.

This fusing of cultural and political resistance may be referred to as political familism. It is a process of cultural and political activism which involves the participation of total family units in the movement for liberation. Political familism is a phenomenon in which the continuity of family groups and the adherence to family ideology provide the basis for struggle. El Movimiento has gone into the Chicano home. It has become a family affair which demands total involvement from all family members.[9] While this phenomenon has not yet been empirically documented, there is evidence which points to the profound importance of the familia in the Chicano movement.

César Chávez' early successes in the farmworkers' movement may be partly attributed to the fact that he converted the Huelga into a strike of families by basing the union structure on the strong family structure.[10] The triumphant Chicano revolt against the Crystal City, Texas, School District in 1969 (an event which helped precipitate the formation of La Raza Unida Party in that state) drew its organizational support from the Chicano family.[11] José Angel Gutiérrez, the leading figure in the formation of La Raza Unida Party in Texas, expresses the political significance of total family participation:

> You know, civil rights are not just for those under 21. They're for everybody —for grandma, for daddy and mamma, and los chamaquitos and primos and sisters and so on. We've all got to work together. That means that all of us have to pitch in. . . . You see, La familia mexicana está organizada.[12]

At the first Chicano Youth Liberation Conference held in Denver in 1969, a position paper entitled "El Plan Espiritual de Aztlán" expressed commitment to a family-based movement of Chicanos:

> Our cultural values of home and family will serve as powerful weapons to defeat the gringo dollar system and encourage the process of love and brotherhood.[13]

The Denver-centered Crusade for Justice operates on a family principle: a system of family ties extending beyond the immediate family to a family of all Chicanos. At its weekly meetings, both young and old participate in what amounts to a family gathering, a strictly non-Anglo phenomenon.[14]

Family activism, a defining feature of the contemporary Chicano movement, is not restricted to the political arena. Cultural and schooling programs also utilize the familia as a basic organizing principle. Describing

Chicano pursuits at the University of California at Davis, Jesús Leyba explains:

> The easiest way to understand the organizational structure under MECHA (Movimiento Estudiantíl Chicano de Aztlán) is to compare it to the extended family. . . . If you think of MECHA as the core family unit, then the other activities would be carried out by members of the extended family units: this insures that everyone has a voice in and understands what every subunit is doing.[15]

Project Consejo at the University of New Mexico aims to secure college admission for the "high risk" students and to assist them to use their talents, skills, and cultural values to successfully complete a university education. Project Consejo's unique approach to counseling students is based on the familia concept:

> This stresses the close family ties in Chicano families starting with the children and working its way up the family ladder to the grandparents. It is based on a spirit of cooperation and unity.[16]

The key to unity for La Raza has been found in the various manifestations of Chicano nationalism. According to movement leader and philosopher, Rodolfo "Corky" González, Chicano nationalism arises from La Familia Chicana:

> What are the common denominators that unite the poeple? The key common denominator is nationalism. . . . nationalism becomes La familia. Nationalism comes first out of the family, then into tribalism and then into alliances that are necessary to lift the burden of all supressed humanity.[17]

Making the traditional family the basis of a decolonization movement is not unique to the Chicano movement. Tanzania, under the leadership of Julius Nyerere, assumed ideological unity with the concept "ujamaa" or family-hood. After Tanzania's independence from Britain, the process of decolonization was carried forth by adherence to family ties, symbolized by the traditional African family which was based on "practices and attitudes which together meant basic equality, freedom and unity."[18] This is not to suggest that African socialism and Chicano nationalism are altogether parallel. However, the use of the family, a basic traditional social institution, in these two anti-colonial movements may indicate something about resistance by racially oppressed groups.

In the process of becoming independent or maintaining separation from the dominant society, oppressed peoples take those cultural patterns which have fostered their survival in the face of oppression, and use them as political guides for resistance and revolution. Cultural revitalization phenomena become important in anti-colonial movements.[19] In many respects, El Movimiento's emphasis on family unity and family participation is an expression of cultural revitalization. It is important to ask why the familia has emerged as a basis for the collective movement. Very likely the familia's present cultural and political significance is not simply a return to, or a rejuvenation of Mexican cultural tradition. Rather, the present significance of the familia has strong roots in the historical function which the Chicano family has performed in protecting individuals from the hostilities of Anglo White society. Melford E. Spiro, writing about "ethnic" groups in the U.S. notes that family traditionalism serves to reduce the stress of culture contact by offering solidarity support.[20] Chicanos, unlike European ethnic groups, have remained subject to control by institutions of the dominant society. They have thus required the protection which the family affords long after the initial period of contact with the dominant society. Robert Staples' historical analysis of the Chicano family treats the institution as one which has undergone various adaptations in order to meet the changing requirements of society. The extended traditional family, being an essential cultural component, has functioned as a protective device against the larger society.[21] The Chicano kinship system, based on intensity and primacy of the familia, has functioned as a source of trust, refuge and protection in a society which systematically exploits and oppresses Mexicans.

The first and most characteristic cultural resistance to colonialism is the maintenance of values and ways of life in the face of modernization.[22] The Chicano family has operated as a mechanism of cultural resistance during periods when political resistance was not possible. Adherence to strong family ties and to a pattern of familial organization with distinct sex role differentiation has not indicated a mere passive acceptance of tradition. This adherence has afforded protection, security, and comfort in the face of the adversities of oppression: it has expressed Chicano cultural identity in a society that destroys cultural distinctions.

The political significance of the family has its roots in the history of Chicano political organization. Miguel Tirado's analysis of organizational behavior since 1910 points to involvement of families as a contributing factor to the longevity and vitality of political organizations.[23]

Contemporary political familism has significant consequences both in terms of its impact on the Chicano movement, and in terms of those changes which it has brought about in the Chicano family. Family involvement in political activities has made possible the retention of special bonds between family members at a time when the trends toward urbanization and atomization of family life move to eliminate extended family ties. Although the structure of family life among urban Chicanos may be described as nuclear, familism has not been abandoned. Rather, its focus has been shifted to another institutional setting—the social movement for racial justice. As the familia concept has taken on a new meaning, it has created new organizational and ideological bonds between Chicanos who are politically united as a familia in La Causa.

Political familism has wrought considerable changes in Chicano families. Organizational commitment to total family involvement in the Chicano movement results in new patterns of behavior as women take part in movement activities. Political activism places Chicanas in situations requiring modification of both male and female traditional roles. The dynamics of political familism are such that while it enables Chicano groups to maintain familial ties, it also provides conditions for the transformation of traditional sex roles.

Revolution, Family Structure, and Women's Roles

El Movimiento's demands for Chicano activism are not incongruent with men's traditional sex role expectations; however, they do place new role expectations on women. As Chicanas have become involved in movement activities which seek to change patterns of racial equality, many aspects of their subordination as women have come to the surface. By involving themselves in activities of El Movimiento, women have found that they have had to confront not only an externally imposed system of racial domination, but also a system of sexual domination within their own cultural setting.

The history of women's involvement in revolutionary struggles is one in which women have encountered opposition as they become involved in activities which challenge traditional male dominance. Sheila Rowbatham's book, *Women, Resistance and Revolution,* identifies a relationship between social revolution and feminism. She has found that while the specific conditions of revolution remain distinct, women's experience in revolutionary movements is repeated. Political activity challenges women's and men's traditional positions; it changes women's relationship to the family, and it generates conditions for the emergence of women's consciousness.[24]

Recognition of the common structural position of women in revolutionary movements should not obscure the unique historical conditions of Chicanas or their unique struggles in El Movimiento. Adaljiza Sosa Riddell provides an insightful historical analysis of the experiences of women in México. She discusses the conquest by Spaniards, and the subsequent experiences of women who became Chicanas either as a result of the conquest of México by the United States, or by migration to this country. Both these incidents of colonization imposed two forms of domination on Mexican women: racial and sexual. Reflecting the views of the Catholic church on women, the Spanish conquerors regarded the native women as heathens in need of redemption, and as loose women who could be exploited without fear of punishment. Chicanas experienced similar treatment in the United States. They entered the U.S. economic and political system at the lowest stratum. Again they were sexually and economically exploited, this time by Anglo White colonizers.[25]

The history of the revolutionary emergence of women in colonized societies accentuates women's unconventional modes of cooperation in political revolt. Departures from traditional sex role behaviors made necessary by revolution lead women in nationalist liberation movements to discover their own powers, strengths, and talents—to demand changes in the system of power relationships based on sex. Such departures also bring about efforts by men to defend their established positions of dominance. As far as the position of women is concerned, the Chicano movement echoes previous nationalist revolutionary movements. Conditions for a sex role revolution within a political revolution have been generated. Attempts to equalize the Chicano movement in sexual terms have resulted in unique activities and expressions of Chicana consciousness.

Social science literature abounds with descriptions of Chicano sex role relationships in which males are aggressive, tough, and dominating, while females are submissive, suffering, dependent, and passive. It is necessary to refute stereotypes which describe Chicanos as passive reactors to traditional values. Although most sex role descriptions are static, one-dimensional, and in need of refutation, the inescapable truth remains that sex role relationships in Chicano sociocultural systems are characterized by patterns of male dominance.

Political familism has provided the conditions for changes in patriarchal patterns of Chicano relationships. Participation of total Chicano family units in political and quasi-political activities has placed women in situations which require new forms of behavior, thus restructuring their relationships with Chicano men. By saying that assertiveness and independence are required of women as well as of men who are challenging the dominant system and demanding a better life for their people and their children, I do not mean that Chicanas have not been active, assertive, or strong women in the past. I believe that they have always possessed these traits, and that historical research will uncover the importance of women's activities in the Chicano experience. I am suggesting that the call for total family participation in the Chicano struggle has resulted in necessary changes in relationships between men and women. Women's involvement in El Movimiento has begun to transform patterns of male exclusiveness as women participate in meetings and strikes, as they seek and acquire meaningful schooling and employment, and as they forge new directions for achieving the collective goals of La Raza.

The Chicano movement calls for changes not only in conditions which are externally imposed by the dominant society, but also in Chicano behaviors. Movement rhetoric makes much of the creation of "La Raza Nueva." This emphasis undoubtedly provides opportunities for Chicanas to act autonomously as new expectations are placed on them. Nevertheless, Chicanas often find themselves in the ambiguous position of consciously striving to alter traditional subordinate roles while at the same time having to defend Chicano cultural conditions.

Chicanas are increasingly articulating the conviction that cultural integrity and the elimination of their traditional subordination are not incompatible. Elena García makes this point about Chicana consciousness:

> Chicana consciousness is an integral part of the new breed, the Chicano movement, Chicanismo. Chicana consciousness defined is not a white women's liberation movement being that we are working within a cultural context, a Chicana context. . . . Chicana consciousness can thus be defined as working within the cultural context, yet not upon limitations of the self, the new Chicana self. As Chicanas we respect our men. We respect the home, the familia. This is all dealing within the cultural context. Yet times are changing. You are coping with a new Chicana, a Chicana working within the college system. A Chicana who is seeing that her place need not only be in the home. She is sensing her ability beyond that, yet not excluding it.[26]

Enriqueta Longeaux y Vásquez' writings on the Chicana, which have appeared in many publications, also emphasize change within a cultural context. Consider the following passages from the essay, "Soy Chicana Primero:"

> The Chicana is needed by her people for part of the equality of Raza is cultural survival. . . . In working for her own people a Raza woman becomes more capable and gains confidence, pride and strength. This strength is both personal and as a people. She gains independence, security and more human strength because she is working in a familiar area, one in which she puts her corazón and love. . . . This is the kind of spirit and strength that builds and holds firm La Familia de La Raza.[27]

Chicanas are consciously creating for themselves new role models which differentiate them from other types. In a pamphlet written for Chicanas, Gloria Guardiola and Yolanda Garza Birdwell deal with the following concepts: Chicano culture, the traditional woman, the middle class woman, the professional woman and "the Chicana." The Chicana stands out as the ideal, the aim, the type of woman Chicanas should aspire to become because of her active political and social participation. The authors urge Chicanas to work toward a new social order which guarantees the equal involvement of the whole Chicano family.[28]

Political familism has jarred the Chicano family at one level because total family participation results in changes in the relative position of men and women. Such changes have hurled Chicanas out of their traditional subordinate roles. It would be inaccurate to conclude that male dominance has disappeared, but political activism of the women of La Raza has weakened the patriarchal patterns. Political familism has disrupted the sex role stability of Chicano families. Ideologically, Chicanos may support the virtues of total family involvement, but for individual men and women, this involvement may present difficulties as they attempt to adjust to the changes which political familism demands.

Machismo

The male-dominated Chicano family is frequently discussed in terms of the machismo cult. The importance which the notion of machismo has acquired in social science literature and in El Movimiento necessitates the following discussion.

In social science literature, machismo is most often associated with irresponsibility, inferiority, and ineptitude.[29] This culture trait as well as the adoption of a tough pose in family relationships, has been attributed to Mexican and Chicano males and is said to be a compensation for feelings of inadequacy and worthlessness. Both machismo and female submissiveness are said to reinforce one another to impede productive, instrumental achievement-oriented behavior.

Analysis of colonization often fosters misuse of the macho concept. This misuse takes the form of identifying a system of economic, political, and psychological colonization. Where objective conditions of oppression and subordination exist, inferiority is said to be internalized by members of the colonized group who develop psychological mechanisms to compensate for their subordination. Rowbatham, in his discussion of colonized women, notes the presence of psychological colonization:

> ... the man's reaction is partly the age-old response of the male oppressor, but it is also something else. The White imperialists not only colonize economically, but psychologically. They usurped the men from their "manhood;" they took over from the colonized men control of their women.[30]

The widely accepted interpretation of machismo is that it is an attempt by men to compensate for their inferiority. This interpretation (whether one locates the cause of oppression in the social structure or in psychological characteristics of the oppressed) attributes machismo and its corresponding pattern of female submissiveness to pathological characteristics of the oppressed. In effect this interpretation finds Chicanos themselves responsible for their own subordination due to their dysfunctional cultural reponses.

The validity of this prevailing social science interpretation of machismo is open to serious question.[31] This is not to say that the concept itself must be abandoned. However, if the concept is to be more than a cultural stereotype, it must be used in a discriminative manner. One viable approach is to examine the way in which machismo is perceived and defined by Chicanos themselves, rather than relying exclusively on social science categories for definition. Such an investigation would undoubtedly yield some indication of the positive dimensions of machismo. This approach may enable us to ask questions which would lead to an understanding of male dominance and aggression of the oppressed as a *calculated* response to hostility, exclusion, and racial domination in a colonized society. It is possible that aggressive behavior of Chicano males has been both an affirmation of Mexican cultural identity and an expression of their conscious rejection of the dominant society's definition of Mexicans as passive, lazy, and indifferent.[32]

The machismo issue has become central to questions concerning women's roles in the Chicano movement. Machismo is seen by many Chicanas as an obstacle to revolutionary struggle. Jennie Chávez' description of the dilemmas she faced as a woman in a university Chicano organization has a familiar ring to many Chicanas:

> As soon as I started expounding my own ideas the men who ran the organization would either ignore my statement, or make a wisecrack about it and continue their own discussion. This continued for two years until I finally broke away because of being unable to handle the situation.[33]

Lionela López Saenz denounces machismo, stating that the Machismo syndrome advocates absolute power and authority, thus subordinating Chicanos to submissiveness.[34] Mirta Vidal claims that the awakening of Chicano consciousness has been promoted by the machismo which women encounter in the movement. Furthermore this behavior, "typical of Chicano men," is a serious obstacle to women anxious to play a role in the struggle for Chicano liberation.[35] Such calls for an end to male domination have caused dissent within the Chicano movement, but they have not gone unheeded.

The Black Berets of Albuquerque have redefined machismo in terms of revolutionary struggle:

> We want equality for women. Machismo must be revolutionary . . . not oppressive. Under this system our women have been oppressed both by the system and our own men. The doctrine of machismo has been used by our men to take out their frustrations on their wives, sisters, mothers and children. We must support our women in their struggle for economic and social equality and recognize that our women are equals within our struggle for liberation. Forward hermanas in the struggle.[36]

Armando Rendón has attempted to move machismo beyond its negative sex role connotations and to link it with the Chicano movement in a political sense:

> The essence of machismo, of being macho, is as much a symbolic principle of the Chicano revolt as it is a guideline for the conduct of family life,

female relationships, and personal self-esteem. To be macho in fact is an underlying drive of the gathering identification of Mexican Americans which goes
beyond a recognition of common troubles. The Chicano revolt is a manifestation
of Mexican Americans exerting their manhood and womanhood against the
anglo society. Macho, in other words, can no longer relate merely to manhood,
but must relate to nationhood as well.[37]

Whether a redefinition of machismo as a political concept can be
reconciled with women's full and equal participation in revolutionary
struggle remains to be seen. Chicanas' censure of machismo is important in that such demands for sexual equality stem *not* from the adoption
of Anglo patterns of sex role relationships, but rather from Chicanas'
experiences, which have shown how patterns of traditional male dominance have inhibited the active participation of women in Chicano liberation struggles.

As social and political involvement of Chicanas flourishes, so does
their consciousness as women take shape. The question of the role of
women in society, of Chicanas in El Movimiento, is a much debated
issue. Because male dominance has been a major pillar of Chicano life,
the issue has become a highly emotional one. Never before have Chicanos, both men and women, discussed so openly and intensely questions relating to sex roles in the Chicano community. An ongoing dialogue
continues between men and women, between young Chicanas and their
mothers, between those who claim to be "brown" feminists, and those
who resist any affiliation with feminism. In spite of these differences, it
has become clear that a new mode of liberation is evolving out of Chicano liberation.

Conclusion

Changes in the structure of Chicano families cannot be attributed
solely to acculturation or modernization. While sex roles are moving in
the direction of equalization, this movement should not be taken to signal
the assimilation of Chicanos.

The Chicano movement has fostered a situation in which nationalism
and feminism are both important components. They are in some ways
contradictory, yet as political familism has taken on real meaning, men
and women have come to need and depend on each other in new ways.
Political familism itself does not transcend sex role subordination. But
within the varied expressions and manifestations of El Movimiento are
changes in sex role relationships and family structure, as well as the
seeds of new roles for the women and men of La Raza.

Notes

1. William J. Goode, *World Revolutions and Family Patterns* (London: The Free Press of Glencoe, 1963), pp. 1-26.

2. See for example Alice B. Culp, *A Case Study of 35 Mexican Families*. 1921. Reprinted by R and E Research Associates (1971); Ruth Tuck, *Not with the Fist* (New York: Harcourt Brace and Company, 1946), and Norman D. Humphrey, "The Changing Structure of the Detroit Mexican Family," *American Sociological Review*, Vol. 9 (December 1944), pp. 622-26.

3. Manuel Ramírez, "Identification with Mexican Family Values and Authoritarianism in Mexican Americans," *Journal of Social Psychology*, Vol. 73, (1967), pp. 3-11.

4. Roland G. Tharp, Arnold Meadow, Susan G. Lennhoff, and Donna Satterfield, "Changes in Marriage Roles Accompanying the Acculturation of the Mexican American Wife," *Journal of Marriage and the Family*, Vol. 30, (August 1968), pp. 404-412.

5. Leo Grebler, Joan Moore, and Ralph Guzmán, *The Mexican American People* (New York: The Free Press, 1970), pp. 350-370.

6. Ellwyn Stoddard, *Mexican Americans* (New York: Random House, Inc., 1973), pp. 103-104.

7. See Tomás Almaguer, "Toward the Study of Chicano Colonialism," *Aztlán*, Vol. 2, No. 1 (Spring 1971); Rodolfo Acuña, *Occupied America* (New York: Canfield Press, 1972); Joan W. Moore, "Colonialism: The Case of the Mexican American," *Social Problems*, Vol. 17, No. 4 (Spring 1970); Mario Barrera, Carlos Muñoz, and Charles Ornelas, "The Barrio as an Internal Colony," in *People and Politics in an Urban Society*, Harlan Hahn, ed., Vol. 6, *Urban Affairs Annual Reviews*, (Beverly Hills: Sage Publications, 1972).

8. Ron E. Roberts and Robert Marsh Kloss argue that the differentiating factor between revolution and reform lies in the degree of mobilization of the masses of people: "Many successful reforms have been effected without great commitment by the masses. The case is different with a successful revolution. In this case, the masses must be mobilized to overturn elites and to make basic institutional changes," *Social Movements: Between the Balcony and the Barricade* (St. Louis: The C. V. Mosby Company, 1974), pg. 38.

9. Abelardo Delgado, "The Chicano Movement; Some Not Too Objective Observations," (Denver: Totinem Publications, 1971), pg. 3.

10. Carey McWilliams, *North From Mexico* (New York: Greenwood Press, 1968), introduction.

11. Armando G. Gutiérrez, "Institutional Completeness and La Raza Unida Party," in *Chicanos and Native Americans,* Rudolph O. de la Garza, Z. Anthony Kruszewski, and Tomás A. Arciniega, eds., (Englewood Cliffs, New Jersey: Prentice Hall, 1973), pp. 113-123.

12. Excerpts from a speech by José Angel Gutiérrez in *Viva La Raza,* Julian Nava, ed. (New York: D. Van Nostrand Company, 1973), pg. 145.

13. "El Plan Espiritual de Aztlán." Paper presented at the Chicano Youth Liberation Conference, Denver, Colorado (March, 1969).

14. Armando B. Rendón, *Chicano Manifesto* (New York: Macmillan Company, 1971), pg. 169.

15. "A Sense of Togetherness," *La Luz,* Vol. 3, No. 3 (June 1974), pg. 40.

16. From the University of New Mexico *Lobo* (November 14, 1973).

17. From Rodolfo "Corky" González, "What Political Road for the Chicano Movement," *The Militant* (March 30, 1970); Reprinted in *A Documentary History of the Mexican Americans,* Wayne Moquin and Charles Van Doren, eds. (New York: Praeger Publishers, 1971), pg. 488.

18. Julius K. Nyerere, *Freedom and Unity* (London: Oxford University Press, 1967), pg. 10.

19. Robert Blauner, *Racial Oppression in America* (New York: Harper and Row, 1972), pg. 95.

20. Melford E. Spiro, "The Acculturation of American Ethnic Groups," *American Anthropologist,* Vol. 57 (1955), pg. 1247.

21. Robert Staples, "The Mexican American Family: Its Modification Over Time and Space," *Phylon,* Vol. 32, No. 2 (1971), pp. 179-192.

22. Blauner, op. cit., pg. 116.

23. Miguel David Tirado, "Mexican American Community Political Organization: The Key to Chicano Political Power," *Aztlán*, Vol. 1, No. 1 (Spring 1970), pp. 53-78.

24. Sheila Rowbatham, *Women, Resistance, and Revolution* (New York: Vintage Books, 1971).

25. Adaljiza Sosa Riddell, "Chicanas and El Movimiento," *Aztlán*, Vol. 5, No. 1 and 2 (Spring and Fall 1974), pp. 155-165.

26. Elena García, "Chicana Consciousness; A New Perspective, A New Hope," in *La Mujer en Pie de Lucha*, Dorinda Moreno, ed., Espina del Norte Publications, pg. 4.

27. Enriqueta Longeaux y Vásquez, "Soy Chicana Primero," *El Cuaderno*, Vol. 1, No. 1 (1970), pp. 17-22.

28. Gloria Guardiola and Yolanda Garza Birdwell, "The Woman: Destruction of Myths, Formation and Practice of Free Thinking." 1971, n.p.

29. Miguel Montiel, "The Chicano Family: A Review of Research," *Social Work*, Vol. 18, No. 2, pp. 22-31.

30. Rowbatham, op. cit., pg. 205.

31. For a critique of uncritical use of the machismo concept, see Miguel Montiel, "The Social Science Myth of the Mexican American Family," *El Grito*, Vol. 3, No. 4 (Summer 1970).

32. For a discussion of characterizations of the oppressed as a rejection of the oppressors stereotype, see Stephen R. Warner, David T. Wellman, and Leonore J. Weitzman, "The Hero, The Sambo, and The Operator: Three Characterizations of the Oppressed," *Urban Life and Culture*, Vol. 2, No. 1 (1973).

33. Jennie V. Chávez, "An Opinion: Women of the Mexican American Movement," *Mademoiselle*, Vol. 74 (April 1972), pg. 82.

34. Lionela López Saenz, "Machismo, No! Igualdad, Sí!" *La Luz*, Vol. 1, No. 2 (May 1972), pg. 19.

35. Mirta Vidal, "New Voices of La Raza: Chicanas Speak Out," *National Socialist Review*, (October 1971).

36. From "Venceremos I," (July 1971). Reprinted in Stoddard, *Mexican Americans*, pg. 105.

37. Rendón, op. cit., pg. 104.

Marital Decision-Making
and the Role of *Machismo*
in the Chicano Family

Lea Ybarra

Exactly who has the power and control in the Chicano family? Who decides what will or will not be done? According to much of the previous social science literature on Chicanos, the total power would seem to lie with the husband. The Chicano family has generally been viewed as forming a totally patriarchal situation characterized by the unquestioned and absolute supremacy of the husband and the absolute self-sacrifice of the wife, (Humphrey, 1944; Madsen, 1964; Rubel, 1966; Peñalosa, 1968). The male has been characterized as overly dominant, violent, and obsessed with sexual fantasies while the woman is characterized as being at the other extreme. Mexican and Chicana women are considered to be submissive, subordinate, mistreated women who are not only forced into this type of situation but who also accept, and sometimes even like their position (Aramoni, 1972; Madsen, 1964; Rubel, 1966; Stephens, 1973). Ideas such as these have been perpetuated largely through the unquestioning use of a domination/submission model commonly referred to as *machismo*.

Since very few systematic and empirical studies have been done on the Chicano family, many social scientists have merely relied on their own ethnocentric misconceptions of *machismo* and other aspects of Chicano culture and created a distorted view of the Chicano family. Distortions were bound to continue as long as there was a lack of empirical information to refute these previously established stereotypes about the family.

The present study was conducted to determine the type of roles that were in fact exhibited in Chicano marital relationships. The guiding hypothesis was that Chicano families would exhibit a wide range of variations in the structure of their marital relationships, ranging from patriarchal to egalitarian. Thus, they would not be totally patriarchal nor as obsessed with *machismo* as has been previously assumed.

METHOD

The present study was conducted in 1978, in Fresno, a central California city. Fresno then had a population of 170,000, with Chicanos constituting about 25% of the population. Census data were utilized to identify neighborhoods which had varying concentrations of Chicanos. Neighborhoods representing low socioeconomic working-class and middle-class families were selected for the sample. The actual addresses and respondents to be interviewed were then chosen at random. Since the wealthier upper-class Chicano families do not live in neighborhoods with a high concentration of Chicanos, a name list of upper income Chicanos was obtained by compiling lists from professional and community organizations and from individual referrals. Random selections were made from the listings obtained.

One of the objectives of the study was to see what effect, if any, factors of socioeconomic class, occupation, education, and outside employment of wives had on the structure of conjugal role relationships. Therefore, an effort was made to include every major sector of the Chicano community. These sectors were differentiated along the following dimensions: 1) economic class—interviews were conducted among low, middle, and upper income families; 2) occupation—although this is sometimes closely tied to income, farmworkers as well as lawyers, and blue collar workers as well as teachers, were represented; 3) age—a distribution among individuals was obtained ranging from twenty years old to sixty-seven years old; and 4) a nearly equal distribution of families with housewives and wives employed outside the home. The objective was to obtain as varied a number of individuals as possible with a sufficient number of respondents in specific categories so as to allow for comparative analysis between various subgroups.[1]

The data base for the present sample of Chicano families consists of one-hundred three-hour intensive interviews. All the interviews were with individuals who were married, and both spouses in each family were interviewed. The interviewers worked in pairs so that if both husband and wife were at home at the same time, they were always interviewed separately. The interviewers were Chicano, and the interviews were conducted in either English or Spanish, depending on the preference of the respondent. The majority of the individuals interviewed seemed very willing to cooperate. Of those approached for interviews, only 15% declined to participate. Thus, no major problems arose in obtaining access into the interviewees' homes, but the administration and coding of interviews proved difficult and time-consuming.

The interview instrument consisted of one-hundred questions, 60 of them open-ended. This allowed for flexibility of responses rather than forcing them into preconceived categories. The various sections considered husband-wife relationships relative to: a) decision-making, b) household tasks and child care, c) attitudes towards *machismo*, and d) male-female roles. These variables and the particular family relationships they engendered were then analyzed to determine if they were affected by a family's level of acculturation, level of education and income, and whether or not the wife was employed outside the home.

Since much of the original questionnaire dealt with open-ended responses, categories were created during the coding process. Thus, only after all the interviews were completed, were respondents' answers categorized. Since very little empirical research has been done on Chicano families, this method seemed to be the least prejudicial way of establishing categorized responses for coding, rather than simply coding artificial categories created beforehand.

RESULTS

Results indicated that the Chicano families interviewed exhibited a wide range of conjugal role patterns, ranging from a patriarchal structure, or segregated conjugal role relationships, to an egalitarian structure, or joint conjugal role relationships, with many combinations of these two polar opposites evident. For the purpose of this study, the terms "conjugal roles" and "conjugal role relationships," as defined by Bott (1957), will be used to refer to husband-wife roles and husband-wife relationships, respectively. Bott's typology of "segregated" and "joint" conjugal role relationships will also be used. Segregated role relationships, where there is a clear differentiation of tasks, will be seen as indicative of a patriarchal family structure, and "joint" role relationships, where husband and wife carry out many tasks together, will be seen as indicative of an egalitarian family structure. Following Harold Christensen's definition (1964), patriarchal family structure is defined as a father-dominated family where the father makes the decisions in all areas of family life. An egalitarian family is defined as more democratically structured with husband and wife sharing family responsibilities equally.

A great deal of data was generated by this study and specific data were tabulated in a variety of categories. For the purposes of this paper, only the following categories will be discussed: a) decision-making, b) household chores, and c) attitudes towards *machismo*.

Decision-making. One section of the questionnaire focused on decision-making. The intent was to measure not only who actually made *what* decisions, but also the attitudes regarding decision-making. Available social science literature on Chicano and Mexican families has consistently emphasized that husbands make all the decisions and wives merely submit to them (Madsen, 1964; Rubel, 1966; Peñalosa, 1968; Stephens, 1973). The present study, however, provides an empirical basis for questioning this assumption.

The study indicated that 80% of the respondents stated decisions in their households were always discussed between husband and wife, 11% stated they discussed decisions "in some cases," and only 9% stated that one spouse made all the decisions. The percentages varied as to who made the final decisions in areas such as large purchases, purchase of furniture, employment, matters affecting the children, and deciding the family budget.

TABLE 1

Participation by Husband and Wife in Household Decision-Making

"Who makes decisions in your household in the following areas?"

	Both	Husband	Wife	Entire Family	No Response or Not Applicable
Large Purchases	66%	24%	3%	6%	1%
Purchase of Furniture	59%	16%	18%	6%	1%
What Clubs to Join	55%	17%	5%	-	23%
On Who Works and Type of Job	71%	23%	3%	-	2%
Matters Affecting Children	57%	15%	13%	2%	13%
Division of Household Chores	39%	5%	54%	1%	1%
Family Budget	45%	20%	33%	1%	1%

As indicated in Table 1, women play a major role in joint decision-making with their husbands. Decisions on the family budget, for example, are made the majority of time by both husband and wife or by the wife. Thus, it appears that Chicana wives have a much larger role in decision-making than has been previously assumed.[2]

The majority of couples felt sharing decision-making was important. The most frequent comments were that "marriage is 50-50 and both should be involved," that it prevented arguments and thus helped "keep peace in the family." Of the 16% who did *not* share decision-making, 4% believed that the husband should have the last say-so because some of the women did not "want the pressure" or because the man himself felt that someone had to take the responsibility and "be accountable." Another 4% believed that it prevented arguments, while 8% stated that although their relationship was not equal, they thought it should be. However, what seemed to be emphasized most was that how the relationship "should be" really depended on a number of issues. These included: what a couple agreed upon; who was better at, or liked doing certain things such as keeping a budget; and what way worked out best for each particular couple.

An interesting discussion arose when respondents were asked if decision-making had changed since the beginning of their marriage. Thirty-nine percent stated they and their spouses had always discussed decisions, "that they had agreed on it from the beginning." Another one-third stated that their relationship had become more egalitarian and that decisions were shared more now than at the beginning of their marriage. A frequent comment regarding this change was that initially some of the women used to "leave it to the husbands," and some of the men themselves felt they should make all the decisions. As one woman stated, "At the beginning it was stormy because my husband was more hardnosed and both of us wanted to be right. But now we've learned to compromise—unless we get mad." The general feeling among the respondents was that now wives are taking a much stronger role in decision-making because both men and women have realized that "equal decision-making is a necessity." They also feel they have moved to a more egalitarian relationship because it leads to a better understanding between the spouses.

When respondents were asked if, in general, spouses get along better if they share decisions, 96% said "yes," only 3% said "no," and 1% did not know. The most frequent comment by respondents was that marriage is a partnership and "problems are created if decision-making isn't shared." Others felt that "sharing saves a lot of arguing and frustrations and creates a better understanding," and that "you need to get your partner's opinion on things because your decisions affect each other's lives." In addition, the majority of respondents mentioned that sharing decisions created a better family relationship, that to "create a good home life, both need to be a part of it."

"The wife has as much right" was the most frequently given answer to the question of whether or not a wife should voice her opinion as much as the husband. An overwhelming 94% said "yes" while only 6% said "no" or "sometimes." Besides having the right to do it, respondents felt the wife should express her opinions because "she has a mind of her own," "she's got brains too," and because "she has ideas and can provide a better perspective." Many of the women felt it was important to express their opinions rather than keeping them "bottled up inside" because this would lead to frustrations.

Some of the male respondents stated they felt threatened at first by their wives expressing their opinions but then realized it was beneficial. A few (2%) stated that the wife could give her opinion "if she was not too aggressive" or "if her ideas were sensible," but this type of answer was in the clear minority. The fact that most Chicana wives do give their opinions is probably best stated by one male respondent, "You might as well let them express their opinion, they do it anyway."

The views on husband-wife egalitarianism shifted a little downward when respondents were asked if, in general, a husband and wife should have equal power in the home. Seventy-five percent stated "yes" while 25% said "no" or that "it depended on the situation." Of those that said yes, the consensus seemed to be that sharing responsibilities and power "led to a more harmonious and productive relationship," that it was "only fair" to share authority. As one female respondent stated, "If one person dominates all the time, it makes you feel inferior." Another respondent stated that having equal power "encourages growth among both of them in terms of the relationship and respect for one another."

The reasons given among those who felt there should not be equal authority between husband and wife were that the husband should have the "final say-so," "sort of a 51%-49% relationship," as one male stated. Some women also felt that the man should have more authority, especially when it came to disciplining the children, either because she did not want the responsibility or because that was "just the way it should be." The majority of respondents felt that in one way or another women did exercise power in the home. As one woman stated, "It doesn't make any difference whether or not he has the last word, because he usually does what I want anyway."

From these data we can see that while Chicano families do not exhibit complete egalitarianism in decision-making, they certainly exhibit a great deal more than has been assumed. It is important to realize the relative positions of Chicano husbands and wives in the family decision-making structure since the supposed 'powerlessness' of the wife and the complete domination by the husband are at the base of the stereotypes on the Chicano family. Findings from this study indicate that the wife does have power in decision-making areas in the family and that in the majority of families she is an integral part of decision-making.

Household Chores. Another part of the study dealt with who actually performed household chores. The division of labor regarding household chores was considered to be another measure of the extent to which roles in a marital relationship were segregated or joint. The results indicate that the participation of the husband and wife in household chores varied depending on the task (see Table 2). For example, the wife was involved in washing dishes two-thirds of the time while the husband was involved in washing them one-third of the time. In yardwork, however, the husband was involved half of the time while the wife did yardwork 45% of the time.

While most chores appear to be done along traditional male-female roles, this pattern does not seem to differ too much from the dominant Anglo-American conjugal role relationship. The findings also indicate a much larger sharing of tasks in the Chicano family than has been previously assumed. This sharing is even more apparent when one considers that only when spouses were *equally* responsible for doing a particular chore, was it coded as "both." There were many other respondents who stated, for example, that while the wife may have the major responsibility of washing dishes or cooking, the husband helped her frequently in doing all these things.

TABLE 2

Participation by Husband and Wife in Household Chores

"Who does the following household chores?"

	Husband	Wife	Both	Entire Family	Wife and Children	Husbands and Sons	Others
Washes Dishes	2	47	19	12	18	-	2
Cooks	2	51	28	6	11	-	2
Washes Clothes	2	62	15	2	16	1	2
Groc. Shopping	8	39	50	-	3	-	-
Makes Beds	4	55	14	15	10	-	2
Vacs/Mops	5	55	14	10	14	-	2
Gen. Hskg.	3	53	21	10	10	1	2
Yard Work	42	10	22	12	3	9	2
Heavy Work	48	12	19	9	4	1	7
Car Repair	76	2	3	1	-	-	18
Home Repair	73	5	15	1	-	-	6

When respondents were asked why they did specific chores, the largest percentage (34%) stated they did them because it was their "obligation" or "responsibility." The next highest percentage (25%) stated that if they "didn't do them, they wouldn't get done." Other answers varied from doing certain chores because they liked to do them (20%), or because they were more capable of doing them. In addition, the answers of male respondents and female respondents were compiled separately. A greater number of women than men tended to feel that if they didn't do certain chores, they wouldn't get done. More men than women appeared to like what they did but this difference was not significant. About the same number of men and women, however, felt they were "obligated" to do certain chores. The majority also felt that their spouse did particular chores out of obligation.

The findings also suggest an increase in the tendency of husbands to help their wives over time. Thirty percent of the respondents stated that the husband helped more now than at the beginning of their marriage. Others stated there had been no change because the husband had always helped (22%), or the wife had always done everything (16%). Of those where the husband was helping more, the increase occurred especially after the wife had started working. Others stated that if the wife did start working, the decisions on who did the chores "would have to be re-evaluated." Whether or not the wife was employed, there was still a change towards the husband helping more. One male respondent stated, "I realized I had to consider her health, happiness . . . I had burdened her with all the house chores and I realized it had to change." Others stated that their duties have varied depending on the time each spouse has available.

One-fifth of the respondents also stated that the husband had helped more at the beginning of their marriage when the children were small, and now that the children were older, he expected them to assume the major responsibility of helping the wife although he still helped occasionally. This general attitude was exemplified by one respondent's comment, "My husband has always helped in housework and taking care of the kids. He feels the kids should help more now and that everyone should carry their load."

With respect to household chores then, it is evident that tasks within the Chicano family are shared in varying degrees, contrary to characterizations of it being completely patriarchal with a strict segregation of household roles and labor. An additional conclusion is that their family roles are not static; many had changed since the beginning of the marriage or were in the process of changing.

Machismo is a concept that has continually been used as a basis of explanation in studies of the Chicano family and it has also become a widely used word in this society. The concept of *machismo*, therefore, merits close scrutiny. How and in what ways does it play a part in the Chicano family? What do Chicanos themselves think of *machismo*?

Respondents were first asked to define what *machismo* was to them. Fifty-eight percent of those interviewed defined *machismo* as "male dominance" or as having negative characteristics. Thus, they saw *machismo* as "Doing what you want to do with no consideration for anybody else," or "being accustomed to the old ways when the man was boss and the woman didn't count," and in general, a man thinking he was superior to women. Others saw it as "a big mistake" or "a phony sense of superiority."

The remainder of the respondents (42%) stated *machismo* was just a neutral term meaning "male" with no positive or negative characteristics or that it had positive connotations. To them, being *macho* meant being "Brave, responsible, mature, level-headed and strong." Also, it meant a "man who respects his fellow man and shows culture and good upbringing." All of those who defined *machismo* in negative terms felt it was wrong and a frequent comment was that being a *macho* was not equivalent to being a man. As one male respondent stated, "I have heard some people say to be *macho* is to be more manly than someone else, but that's not being a man. That kind of *machismo* only causes problems. To be a man is to feed and take care of your wife and family." The same type of thought was echoed by a female respondent, "A man who drinks, goes out, doesn't take care of his family . . . I don't call that being a man, I call that being a coward!" Another stated, "A man has to realize that to feel and to love is being a real man." There was a higher tendency among men (22%) than women (6%) to attribute positive characteristics to *machismo*. That is, more men defined *machismo* as being a responsible man or a good father.

Another assumption in this area was that the Chicano family, like many other families, was going through a process of change with regard to male-female roles. Apparently respondents themselves also perceived such a change. When defining *machismo* in negative terms, respondents stated there had been a change towards less *machismo* among their male friends and relatives and males in the Chicano community in general. Eighty-three percent felt the change towards less *machismo* was "good" and 17 percent felt it was "bad."

The few who stated it was "bad" said that while in the long run it might be good, now it led to a confusion of roles. The majority who felt it was a "good" change stated it was especially good for the woman because she should have an equal say in everything. Women were now being given "more recognition and respect" and being recognized as "just as intelligent and capable as men." As one female respondent stated, "It makes the woman feel more independent . . . If the man does everything, the woman won't know how to do anything and she won't get a chance to develop." In addition to being good for the woman, others felt the change towards less *machismo* was important for the entire family and for the community as well. This sentiment is exemplified by the following comment: "The entire status of the Chicano community, social as well as economic, is improving by capitalizing on the talents and intelligence of the female sex."

There was a difference between male and female respondents in their response to how *machismo* could become lessened or enhanced. The most frequent answer given by women is that *machismo* is lessened when the wife asserts herself (32%). Men stated it lessened "with education," as the man became more educated and realized what "being a man is really about" (36%). The low level of response to this question is worth noting. Many respondents (45%) found it difficult to answer, either because they did not have a response or because they had previously given a neutral or positive definition of *machismo* and the question was not applicable.

Both male and female respondents felt that education played an important part in decreasing *machismo* and that it also decreased "when a family shares responsibility and authority." Twenty-six percent stated that people were getting away from *machismo* now, and times were changing. Others also stated that "many wives work and they are having more say in the family" and are therefore less dependent on men. A female respondent added, "With women's lib, the woman has become more involved and more her own boss regardless of color."

In terms of what would cause *machismo* to increase, the female respondents mainly stated it increased if the woman was "docile" and the males stated it increased if the man was "not aware or not responsible." Both felt that it really depended a lot on whether or not the wife "gives in." However, it is interesting that each sex mainly saw the root of the problem of *machismo*, or the answer to it, as based in their own sex. In other words, the man saw *machismo* as decreasing as men became more educated and the women saw it decreasing as women became more assertive. They tended not to blame each other.

Implications For Future Research.

One of the major implications of the present study is that the findings call into question the previously held assumptions of the Chicano family as being a completely patriarchal system. Since studies on Chicano families are sometimes based on what social scientists assume to be correct data on the Mexican family, we must begin to investigate and question these assumptions as well. Their studies on Mexican families have similarly begun to question many commonly held assumptions by providing data which suggest a strong trend toward egalitarian decision-making in Mexican conjugal pairs (DeLenero, 1969; Cromwell, et al., 1973).

Current empirical data on both Mexico and on Chicanos is thus being provided to enable social scientists to discard old stereotypes and to take into account factors which have been previously ignored. Two such factors, which are clear in this study and others, are that Mexican/Chicano family structures have been and are now undergoing change and that the Mexican/Chicana woman has not been given sufficient credit for the important decision-making role she has assumed in the family.

As the concept of *machismo* undergoes re-examination, assertions such as the following are being seriously challenged—"the ideal male role is defined by the concept of *machismo* and every Mexican-American male tries to make his life a living validation of the assumption that the man is stronger, more reliable, and more intelligent than the female" (Madsen, 1964, p. 20). While some individuals may engage in this type of behavior, it is evident, from the data, that such behavior does not always "elicit respectful admiration" as has been stated (Stephens, 1973, p. 60). The majority of respondents reacted negatively to this type of behavior. Therefore, the concept of *machismo*, as it has been defined in social science literature, should not be regarded as an integral part of Chicano culture. It should also not be seen as the basis for male-female roles in the family until it has been theoretically and empirically investigated. So far, terms such as *machismo* have been uncritically and loosely applied and no empirical verification has been made of its prevalence in Chicano and Mexican culture. This has led to distortions in both the definition and the usage of *machismo*.

To say that the use of *machismo* as a basis for the study of the family has distorted the results, is not to say that *machismo* does not exist, but only to emphasize that male domination exists in most societies. And, just as in all societies, so in Mexican and Chicano society, it exists in varying degrees in some family structures but not all, nor necessarily most, families. A problem in the study of Chicano families has been that *machismo* is seen as the basis for all familial relationships and has been utilized as a mono-causal explanation for all changes that occur within the family structure. For example, if family structure is traditional and patriarchal, then it is considered to be only because of *machismo*; if it exhibits shared authority, then it is considered to be because of acculturation. The family seems to be studied in a vacuum without taking into account all the varied factors which continually influence it. Familial roles should be analyzed in a variety of ways with many factors being taken into account.

One factor, for example, which has been shown to cause some change in conjugal role relationships, and which could be more effectively utilized in studying Chicano families, is the effect of women joining the paid labor force. The great majority of wives, in the present study, stated that working is what caused them to demand help in household chores and child care. If the wife was employed, there was a much greater likelihood that she would have a greater role in decision-making, that household chores and child care would be shared between spouses, and that, in general, they would have a more joint conjugal role structure than couples where the wife was not employed.

Changes, similar to these, seem to be affecting families in other cultures and other countries as well (Goode, 1963; Oppong, 1971; Babchuk and Balweg, 1972; Cromwell, et al., 1973; Magnarella, 1972; Pleck, Note 1). Magnarella (1972), conducted a study in a Turkish town and found that conjugal role relationships were becoming more joint in nature with husbands and wives carrying out more activities together. He believes this change is the result of several factors, including a more modern economic structure creating increased industrialization and new jobs for both men and women, in addition to an increasing secular education in the community's population. He further states that the Turkey experience is not unique but is an example of a universal process whereby these factors are altering conjugal role relationships so they become more joint in nature.

Chicanos are not immune to these processes. Our respondents demonstrated considerable awareness of factors such as these which were affecting their lives. This has important implications when attempting to understand changes that are occurring in some Chicano families. Previous studies of Chicano families have largely ignored factors such as the increased employment of Chicana women, level of education and income of spouses, and universal changes that are occurring to all families, as explanatory models for understanding Chicano family structure. Much of the previous literature stressed that Chicano families were "typically" patriarchal and that if they were changing toward more egalitarian relationships, it was principally because they were becoming more acculturated into Anglo-American society and thus adopting the values and ideals of the Anglo-American family (Madsen, 1964; Rubel, 1966; Tharp, Meadow, Lennhoff & Satterfield, 1968).

This idea is based on two false premises: first, that the Chicano family shows no variations from traditional role patterns until it achieves acculturation; and secondly, that the ideal of egalitarianism is unique to, and widely practiced in, Anglo-American culture. These assumptions should be questioned before they are so readily accepted, especially the assumption that acculturation fully explains why the Chicano family is undergoing change.

In order to better understand Chicano familial dynamics, it is important to go beyond the model of acculturation. To do this, it is necessary to realize that the almost exclusive reliance by social scientists on "acculturation" is too prevalent a pattern to be dismissed as a chance or random occurrence. There has been an underlying negative or pejorative attitude towards Chicanos and other ethnic cultures in general which has led social scientists to depict them negatively (Lieberman, 1973; Staples, 1971).

Social scientists may not have created the negative stereotypes of the Chicano family but they have certainly helped to perpetuate them. The model of acculturation, if not misused, can be a research tool. When studying a phenomenon, however, regardless of which model is employed, a people's interpretation of their own situation—of their own values, norms, and definitions—must be taken into account before an accurate portrayal of that phenomenon can be achieved. This has typically not been the case with past studies of Chicano families. As a result, narrowly focused definitions of Chicano familial processes have been instituted and alternative explanations to the acculturation model have not been sufficiently explored. This has, in turn, prevented a scholarly and accurate portrayal of family life.

In future research, Chicano family structure should not be seen as exhibiting certain patterns only because of adherence to a particular culture, but as a result of interaction with many different factors or as a reponse to certain conditions. The necessity to fulfill functional requirements may be one factor. For example, if the majority of Chicana and Mexican women stay at home, instead of analyzing this situation superficially by stating the Mexican male's *machismo* will not allow his wife to work, other variables should be considered. Oftentimes the wife must stay home and care for the house and children due to lack of educational and work skills and lack of child care facilities. It is both impossible and unprofitable for her to go to work. When education and employment opportunities are available to Chicanas, however, the necessity for different role functions arise. The same is true for Chicano men when they are provided with increasingly varied educational and employment opportunities.

Further research needs to be done on the socio-psychological implications of changes in male and female roles as husband/wife/parent and in children's roles within the family. Both the immediate and long-term effects these changes might have in overall family structure need to be studied. An analysis would also have to consider the changes Mexican family structure has undergone in the United States. It is, therefore, necessary to determine which values characterized the family at given periods. Economic, social, historical, and geographic factors should be studied. An analysis of the Chicano family must not be based on the idea that it has remained static and intact, over time and over varying geographic areas, whether this encompasses movement from Mexico to the U.S. or movement within the United States itself.

The fact that Chicanos as a group are undergoing many changes should not overshadow the fact that, as individuals, their responses to these changes also differ. The idea that Chicanos exhibit a "marked lack of internal differentiation" (Heller, 1968), is not a valid one. Chicanos must be seen as a mobile, changing people with as many patterns and variations in their familial structure as any other culture.

If it is to be assumed, as it has been, that the Chicano family is very important in shaping the attitudes and values of its members toward education, employment, and life in general, then the "negative" aspects attributed to the Chicano family should not be consistently and selectively pointed out while the positive aspects are either ignored or considered exceptions to the rule. This has resulted in the family being viewed as "pathological" and as a detriment to the growth and advancement of Chicanos. Most important, a class analysis should be utilized in explaining the structure of the Chicano family. In that way, factors of poverty, racism and oppression, which permeate every aspect of life, could be considered.

CONCLUSION

When taking into account factors such as decision-making, household chores, and *machismo*, the data indicated that Chicano families do exhibit a wide degree of variations in their conjugal role structure. These variations range from a patriarchal to an egalitarian structure, with only a small minority being strictly patriarchal. The majority of Chicano married couples shared decision-making. A large number of Chicano husbands helped their wives with household chores and child care. The majority of Chicana wives played an important or equal part in all facets of conjugal role relationships. This clearly contradicts the negative stereotyping of the Chicano family in previous social science literature, especially the distorted and overly used *machismo* model.

Many factors need to be analyzed in further research on the Chicano family and future studies must formulate different hypotheses to take these various factors into account. It is essential that these hypotheses be tested by a variety of empirical methods. Studies of the family must therefore move beyond any model of analysis which is based on mono-causal or one-dimensional modes of explanation. A new basis for further research can then be established and new theoretical and empirical models for study of the Chicano family can emerge. Otherwise, incomplete and distorted perspectives will be perpetuated.

In order to avoid an incomplete perspective on another level, the reader should be aware of the limited applicability of these and other data. While certain generalizations about Chicano families may be made from the data collected and reported here, it should be emphasized that variations in family structure and ideology would probably be evident if a similar study were conducted among Chicanos in another state or even in a more urbanized area in the same state. Therefore, data from studies in one area should not be automatically considered as representative of the attitudes or lifestyles of Chicanos in other areas. More than one model of analysis and more than one area of study will be necessary to accurately portray Chicano families with their multi-faceted and continually changing lifestyles.

NOTES

[1] As a result of random sampling, several categories, e.g., families with housewives or employed wives, had a good chance of having a fairly equal distribution in the final number of questionnaires obtained. Other categories tended to randomly select more in one area than another, such as more low income than high income respondents. In these cases, after obtaining representative sampling from each category, if in any category an area was highly over-represented, questionnaires were randomly selected out of the over-represented area. This sampling procedure produced a respondent pool with varied demographic characteristics. For example, the male-female ratio was exactly 50 percent. One-third of the respondents were between 20-30 years of age, one-third were between the ages of 31-44 years old, and the remaining one-third were between 45-70 years of age. Approximately 30% of the sample had less than eight years of formal schooling. Another 30% had attended high school. Fifteen percent had attended college for between one to two years. Nearly 25% had graduated from college. Regarding family income, some 20% of the respondents earned less than $5,000 per year. Approximately one-third of all respondents earned between $16,00-25,000 per year. The balance, nearly 15%, earned above $25,000 per year. Nearly 40% of the female respondents classified themselves as housewives. Approximately 35% were employed full-time and the balance, 25%, were employed on a part-time basis. The number of years respondents had been married was fairly evenly distributed. Some 15% of the sample had been married five years or less. One-quarter had been married between 6-10 years, one-quarter had been married 11-20 years, one-quarter had been married 21-30 years, and the remaining 10% had been married between 30-50 years. Only 10% of the couples interviewed were childless. Nearly 45% of those interviewed had between 1-3 children. Thirty percent had 4-6 children, and 15% of the sample had seven or more children.

[2] Because married couples were first interviewed separately and then together, it provided interviewers the opportunity to verify one spouse's answers with the other spouse, after the interviews were completed and were being coded. Only about 8% of the

spouses contradicted each other. That is, in the majority of cases, if the wife stated she had power in the home and participated in decision-making, he also stated that she did. If she stated that her husband made all the decisions, her husband stated that in his interview. The same occurred with household chores. Husbands seemed equally open in admitting they did help in household chores or that they did not. This was verified by the wife stating that the husband did or did not help. Although it is difficult to gauge complete honesty and to ascertain how one actually behaves, the data about respondents' behavior and attitudes was at least basically verified. This serves, therefore, to bring into question social science studies which assumed that not only do we not practice egalitarianism, but that we do not even understand the concept.

REFERENCES

Aramoni, A. "Machismo." *Psychology Today*, 1972, *5*, 69-72.

Babchuk, N. & Balweg, J.A. "Black family structure and primary relations," *Phylon*, 1972, *33*, 334-347.

Cromwell, R.E., Corrales, R., & Torseillo, P.M. "Normative patterns of marital decision-making power and influence in Mexico and the United States: A partial test of resource and ideology theory." *Journal of Comparative Family Studies*, 1973, *4*, 175-196.

De Lenero, D.C. *Hacia donde va la mujer Mexicana?* Mexico City: Insituto de Estudios Sociales, A.C., 1969.

Gordon, M.M. *Assimilation in American life*. New York: Oxford University Press, 1964.

Goode, W.J. *World revolution and family patterns*. New York: Free Press, 1963.

Heller, C.S. *Mexican American youth: Forgotten youth at the crossroads*. New York: Random House, 1968.

Humphrey, N.D. "The changing structure of the Detroit Mexican family: An index of acculturation." *American Sociological Review*, 1944, *9*, 622-626.

Lieberman, L. "The emerging model of the black family." *International Journal of Sociology of the Family*, 1973, *3*, 10-22.

Madsen, W. *Mexican Americans of South Texas*. New York: Holt, Rinehart and Winston, 1964.

Magnarella, P.J. "Conjugal role relationships in a modernizing Turkish town." *International Journal of Sociology of the Family*, 1972, *2*, 179-192.

Oppong, C. "Joint conjugal roles and extended families: A preliminary note on a mode of classifying conjugal family relationships." *Journal of Comparative Family Studies*, 1971, *2*, 178-187.

Peñalosa, F. "Mexican family roles." *Journal of Marriage and the Family*, 1968, *30*, 680-689.

Rubel, A.J. *Across the tracks: Mexican Americans in a Texas city*. Austin: University of Texas Press, 1966.

Staples, R. "Towards a sociology of the Black family: A theoretical and methodological assessment." *Journal of Marriage and the Family*, 1971, *33*, 119-138.

Stephens, E.P. "Machismo and Marianismo," *Society*, 1973, *10*, 57-63.

Tharp, R.G., Meadow, A., Lennhoff, S.G., & Satterfield, D. "Changes in marriage roles accompanying the acculturation of the Mexican American wife." *Journal of Marriage and the Family*, 1968, *30*, 404-412.

REFERENCE NOTE

1. Pleck, J.H. *Work and family roles: From sex-patterned segregation to integration.* Paper presented at the meeting of the American Sociological Association, San Francisco, August 1975.

CHICANAS AND THE ISSUE OF INVOLUNTARY STERILIZATION: REFORMS NEEDED TO PROTECT INFORMED CONSENT

Antonia Hernandez**

The purpose of this article is to inform the public and its government representatives about practices which have caused the involuntary sterilization of Chicanas. These unauthorized medical practices have occurred within the area presently governed by laws which sanction voluntary sterilization. The right to procure a voluntary sterilization is not challenged, but the duty to provide an opportunity to render informed consent is in need of more stringent guarantees. In too many instances women have been coerced into undergoing sterilization surgery without their informed consent.

Most of the areas to be reviewed involve women who are poor, usually on welfare, and of a racial minority. With respect to Chicanas an additional element, lack of English fluency, deserves considerable attention. Furthermore, any concrete form of analysis cannot ignore the fact that women eligible for welfare not only must contend with the doctor-patient relationship, but also with government participation. At present, the federal and state governments provide substantial assistance to hospitals and women unable to afford medical care on their own. Consequently, doctors and hospitals which receive government subsidies to perform sterilization surgery, but violate a patient's right to informed consent, not only violate existing government regulations but raise the issue of inadequate government enforcement.

A thorough examination of this topic would not be complete without some understanding of the attitudes which cause unwanted sterilizations. Special focus will be directed toward the ethical beliefs held by many medical practitioners, and the transference of these beliefs into nationwide practice. The interrelationship between government and the medical profession also requires some mention of the Supreme Court decision in *Buck v. Bell*.[1] A state

---

* Co-authored by Richard Avila.
** A.A. 1969, East Los Angeles College; B.A. 1971, U.C.L.A.; J.D. 1974, U.C.L.A. Staff attorney, Los Angeles Center for Law and Justice.
1. 274 U.S. 200 (1926). A Virginia statute which authorized the involuntary sterilization of an institutionally committed woman was upheld, because both the woman's mother and illegitimate child were mentally incompetent.

3

policy which required that a woman institutionalized in a mental facility be sterilized prior to her release was upheld. So long as the state's procedures satisfied due process standards, the inability of the woman to render an informed consent did not bar the involuntary condition.

Chief Justice Holmes sanctioned the government's right to exact this condition as the price for freedom in the following terms:

> It is better for all the world, if instead of waiting to execute degenerate offspring for crime, or to let them starve for their imbecility, society can prevent those who are manifestly unfit from continuing their kind. The principle that sustains compulsory vaccination is broad enough to cover cutting the Fallopian tubes.[2]

Such an unequivocal endorsement of the government's right to forcefully deprive an individual of the decision to procreate lessens personal freedom. The *Buck* decision's broad language provided a license for public officials to subject individuals considered "manifestly unfit from continuing their kind." By 1966, for example, twenty-six states had eugenic sterilization laws: twenty-three of these were compulsory.[3] These statutes applied to mentally retarded persons but a dozen extended to certain criminals as well.[4] When compared with similar attitudes held by many doctors, the social implications posed by the tangible existence of the Holmesian philosophy raises the real threat of a professional and governmental denial of a protected right.

To emphasize the gravity of coerced sterilization, the problems which confront Chicana hospital patients will be considered first.

I. PROBLEMS CONFRONTING CHICANA PATIENTS

A condensed clinical explanation of the tragic circumstances forced upon Chicanas must yield to a graphic narrative of personal harm. The personal experiences attested to by twelve Chicanas in a recent suit, *Madrigal v. Quilligan*,[5] brought against the U.S.C.-Los

---

2. *Id.* at 207.
3. Ferster, *Eliminating the Unfit: Is Sterilization the Answer?*, 27 OHIO ST. L.J. 591 (1966).
4. *Id.* California, for example, once authorized the sterilization of those adjudged guilty of carnal abuse of a female person under the age of ten years (1923). But by 1976, this could only be accomplished with the informed consent of the prisoner, and could not be made a term or condition of probation or parole. CAL. PENAL CODE § 645. As of 1974, CAL. PENAL CODE § 2670 was amended to prohibit the punitive sterilization of recidivist prisoners for the crimes of rape, assault with intent to commit rape, or seduction, or who exhibit evidence of moral or sexual depravity.
5. Brief for Plaintiffs, Madrigal v. Quilligan, No. 75-2057 (C.D. Cal., filed June 18, 1975) (hereinafter referred to as *Madrigal*). Joined as defendants were the Director of Obstetrics, U.S.C.-Los Angeles County Medical Center (hereinaf-

Angeles County Medical Center (hereinafter referred to as the Medical Center), relate the abuses perpetrated against them. All of them alleged that they were unduly pressured into accepting an operation to be sterilized.

Dolores Madrigal,[6] on or about October 12, 1973, was admitted to the Medical Center for the delivery of her second child. Even though she had dismissed the suggestions of a staff doctor and nurse that she submit to a sterilization, she was presented with sterilization consent forms while in labor and told to sign them. Under the severe pain of labor, and after being assured that the operation could be easily reversed, she signed these forms and was sterilized. The forms signed by Mrs. Madrigal were printed in English. Her primary language was Spanish, which made it impossible for her to determine the content of the forms. Only after the sterilization operation was completed was she informed that it was effectively irreversible.

Maria Hurtado[7] appeared at the Medical Center for a routine medical checkup on or about December 6, 1972. The doctors who examined her determined that her baby should be delivered by caesarean section. She was anesthetized with a spinal injection for the delivery of her child. After the delivery of the child, she was given general anesthesia. While under this unconscious state, she was surgically sterilized by a staff doctor without her consent. She was not informed about the sterilization until six weeks later when she appeared for a routine checkup. She spoke only Spanish and did not recall signing a form authorizing the operation.

On or about September 13, 1973, Jovita Rivera[8] went to the Medical Center for the delivery of her baby. She was given general anesthesia in preparation for a delivery by caesarean section. While groggy and incoherent she was approached by a staff doctor who told her that she should have her "tubes tied," because her children were a burden on the government. She was never made aware of the definition for "tying tubes," but signed the consent forms. She received no counseling or advice from her doctor or other staff members to inform her of the operation's consequences. She did not learn until some time later that the operation was effectively irreversible. Mrs. Rivera spoke and read

---

ter referred to as the Medical Center); Dr. John Doe, physician on the staff of the Medical Center; Jerry Bosworth, Executive Director of the Medical Center; Mario Obledo, Secretary of the Health and Welfare Agency of California; Jerome Lackner, Director of the Department of Health of California; and Caspar Weinberger, Secretary of the United States Department of Health, Education and Welfare.

6. *Id.* Affidavit by Dolores Madrigal, June 18, 1975.
7. *Id.* Affidavit by Maria Hurtado, June 18, 1975.
8. *Id.* Affidavit by Jovita Rivera, April 29, 1975.

only Spanish, and could not read or understand the consent form given to her to sign even if she had been lucid.

As an expectant mother at the Medical Center, and while in labor, Maria Figueroa[9] was approached by a staff doctor who prompted her to undergo a sterilization operation by tubal ligation.[10] He falsely told her that the operation involved "tying," not cutting, her "tubes." She refused the operation, but was solicited again by the same doctor during her stay in the delivery room, and after general anesthesia had been administered to her. As the moment of birth neared, she reluctantly agreed to a tubal ligation, but only if the baby to be delivered was a boy. A baby girl was born to her in June, 1971; nevertheless, she was sterilized. At no time did she consent to the surgery or sign any forms indicating consent.

During the month preceding the delivery of her son, Helena Orozco[11] was repeatedly solicited by Medical Center doctors and staff members to undergo sterilization surgery. She refused these invitations, and stated her preference for birth control pills as the means to achieve family planning. At no time during these solicitations was she ever counseled regarding the irreversibility of tubal ligation. On or about July 11, 1972, she was admitted to the Medical Center for the delivery of her baby. As she experienced regular contractions, which substantially weakened her, Mrs. Orozco was informed by a Medical Center staff member that her "tubes" were to be "tied," and that she sign a consent form. Under these circumstances, she signed the consent form and was sterilized.

In August, 1973, Guadalupe Acosta[12] was admitted to the Medical Center after having suffered labor pains throughout the day. The attending physician in the delivery room pushed violently upon her abdomen in order to induce delivery. Delirious with pain, she flailed at the doctor who responded by punching her in the stomach. Her child was later born dead. It was during the performance of the delivery that the attending physician unilaterally decided to sterilize Mrs. Acosta. She did not learn of her

9. *Id.* Affidavit by Maria Figueroa, June 18, 1975.
10. Tubal ligation is defined by three procedures: (1) *Postpartum* (within 24 hours after delivery). The Fallopian tubes are severed. (2) *Elective* (not with delivery). The Fallopian tubes are cut and tied by entering the abdominal cavity through the vaginal wall. (3) *Transabdominal Laparoscopy or Laparoscopic Tubal Ligation.* The surgeon makes a small hole into the abdomen and through this fills it with about three to four liters (about a gallon) of a gas (carbon dioxide). He then puts in a metal cylinder through which he can visualize the Fallopian tubes and the other abdominal organs. Through this metal cylinder he can first cauterize (burn) and then cut the tubes, one at a time. *Id.* Affadavit by Dr. Bernard Rosenfeld, June 18, 1975.
11. *Id.*
12. *Id.* Affidavit by Guadalupe Acosta, June 18, 1975.

sterilization until more than two months later when she returned to the Medical Center to request birth control pills. The sterilization surgery was never formally requested. She was later hospitalized in October, 1973, for a hemorrhage attributable to the tubal ligation.

Spanish was the primary language of Georgina Hernandez[13] when she was admitted to the Medical Center on April 6, 1972. She was prepared for childbirth and taken to the area of the maternity ward commonly referred to as the labor room. A doctor informed her that her child would be delivered by caesarean section because it would be too dangerous to deliver naturally. She signed a consent form which was written in English for what she believed to be her permission for the caesarean surgery. At 1:00 a.m., on April 7, as she painfully tried to rest in the labor room, two doctors asked her if she wanted to have her tubes tied. After being informed that the operation would result in permanent sterilization, she refused to consent. The doctors persisted in attempting to obtain her consent by emphasizing that her Mexican birth and poverty would make the proper care and education of any additional children unlikely. Four hours later she was anesthetized and taken to the delivery room where she gave birth to a son. When she returned to the Medical Center on April 26, she was informed for the first time that a tubal ligation had been performed on her.

Consuelo Hermosillo[14] was taken to the Medical Center's labor room during the evening of September 1, 1973. Her doctor determined that the baby would have to be delivered by caesarean section. He falsely advised her that a sterilization operation would be necessary, because her third caesarean section delivery made the eventuality of a fourth pregnancy hazardous to her life. Groggy and weak from medication, Mrs. Hermosillo signed the consent forms handed to her without comprehending their content. As a result, she was sterilized.

The fear of death from pregnancy, falsely instilled in Estela Benavides[15] by her attending physician, compelled her to consent to a sterilization by tubal ligation. She had gone to the Medical Center on March 7, 1974, for the scheduled birth of her baby by caesarean section.

Rebecca Figueroa[16] had carefully planned for the birth of her child. A devout Roman Catholic, she had already paid for pre-

13. *Id.* Affidavit by Georgina Hernandez, June 15, 1975.
14. *Id.* Affidavit by Consuelo Hermosillo, June 18, 1975.
15. *Id.* Affidavit by Estela Benavides, June 18, 1975.
16. *Id.* Affidavit by Rebecca Figueroa, June 18, 1975.

natal care and the delivery of her baby at Santa Marta Hospital. But on October 18, 1971, at about 2:00 a.m., she woke up and discovered that she was bleeding profusely. Her husband immediately took her to the Catholic hospital. Upon her arrival and examination, the Santa Marta staff decided that they did not have the necessary equipment to care for Mrs. Figueroa. She was taken by ambulance to the Medical Center, where she was again examined and injected with medication. A member of the staff had her call her husband, to inform him that she could not have any more babies and that her "tubes were going to be tied." A nurse intervened throughout the entire telephone conversation. When she finally asked her husband about what the nurse had said, he told her that the nurse had communicated the wife's decision to be sterilized. Mrs. Figueroa informed her husband that she did not want the surgery, but if the child was born healthy, then she would consent. The nurse again intervened in the conversation, informing Mr. Figueroa of his wife's agreement, and then told the patient to sign a form. The form was written in English, a language foreign to the patient. She signed the form at a time when she was under sedation. After the operation was completed her husband also signed the form. As a result, Mrs. Figueroa not only lost the opportunity to procreate, but suffers from severe nervous seizures.

On August 18, 1973, Laura Dominguez[17] was admitted to the Medical Center for the delivery of her third child. As she began her labor several nurses attempted to convince her to accept sterilization surgery. The nurses accused the patient of "burdening the taxpayers" with her children. She consented to the surgery under the physical pain induced by labor, and the psychological promptings of the nurses. A uterine infection spared Laura Dominguez from the irreversible damage. As she recuperated from the infection and pregnancy, the opportunity to resist the coerced sterilization was seized. The attending physician supported her decision, but he no longer practices at the Medical Center. Mrs. Dominguez has since remarried and has had one child by her new husband.

During her pre-natal care at the Medical Center in April, 1974, Blanca Duran,[18] a Medi-Cal recipient, was solicited by a nurse at the Family Planning Clinic for sterilization surgery. Not being able to read or speak English, she made a "good faith" verbal agreement with the nurse. She agreed to sign the sterilization consent form, but accept an actual sterilization only upon the condition that she give birth to a boy. On May 16, 1974, her

---

17. *Id.* Affidavit by Laura Dominguez, June 18, 1975.
18. *Id.* Affidavit by Blanca Duran, June 30, 1975.

attending physician made sure that she understood the consent form. At that point she informed the doctor about the verbal agreement with the nurse. When she gave birth to her fifth daughter no attempt was made to subject her to a tubal ligation.

In all of the cases just reviewed there existed a number of common conditions. All of the victims and near victims belonged to a racial minority, were poor, and.could not readily understand the English language. Most were approached for sterilization surgery while under the duress of labor, drugged, and confined. All of them entered the Medical Center without any intent of becoming sterilized, and all were persistently solicited for the operation. Many of the women encountered doctors and nurses who were openly hostile to them because of their ethnicity or poverty status. The solicitors did not satisfactorily inform the patients of the consequences attendant to such surgery. Because of their low-income status all of the Chicanas were eligible for public medical assistance, but none were on welfare.

What these allegations point out is the existence, at one of our major hospitals, of an unbridled discretion which permits medical personnel to coerce expectant Chicana mothers to accept sterilization. Furthermore, the Medical Center is the recipient of state and federal funds for use in providing sterilization surgery to low-income persons pursuant to federal statute.[19] It was under this professional-governmental relationship, therefore, that these unwanted operations took place.

Of special importance, then, is an analysis of the existing regulations which govern procedures for sterilization.

II.   REGULATIONS GOVERNING STERILIZATION PROCEDURES

A.   *Controlling Federal Regulations*

On May 18, 1971, the United States Department of Health, Education and Welfare (hereinafter referred to as HEW) began to include sterilization as part of its health program. HEW's family planning projects are funded by its Public Health Service[20] and its Social and Rehabilitation Service.[21] The Public Health Service manages the allocation of federal funds to state health agencies and to public and private programs for the provision of family planning services to the poor.[22] The Medicaid and Aid to Families with Dependent Children programs are funded through the Social and

---

19.   §§ 703(a)(3), 602(a)(19), 139(d)(a)(4)(c), 42 U.S.C. §§ 300 *et seq.*
20.   Public Health Service Act, §§ 310, 314(d,e), 42 U.S.C.A. §§ 242(h), 246 (d,e).
21.   39 Fed. Reg. 4730-34 (1974).
22.   § 708(a), 42 U.S.C. §§ 300 *et seq.*

Rehabilitation Service.[23]   To support the "full range of family planning services," except abortion, was the intent of Congress,[24] and regulations were to be issued by the Secretary of HEW.[25]

Prior to February 6, 1974, federal funds were directed to family planning facilities without the benefit of comprehensive regulations.   Interim regulations were then issued to guide the recipient agencies of federal family planning funds.[26]   The purpose of these interim guidelines was to safeguard the right of legally competent adults to "informed consent" in obtaining sterilization surgery.[27] This would be accomplished, according to the intent of HEW, by requiring a written and signed document indicating, *inter alia*, that any applicant for sterilization surgery be aware of the benefits and costs involved, and the guaranteed option to withdraw from the surgery without suffering any loss of federal benefits.[28]

The interim regulations included a provision to protect legally competent persons under the age of 18. To ensure the most careful review of these cases, a special *Review Committee of independent persons from the community* must certify that the requested operation is in the best interests of the minor.[29] The Committee must consider two general concerns: (1) the expected mental and physical effects of pregnancy and motherhood on the female applicant, or the anticipated psychological impact of fatherhood on the male applicant; and (2) the expected immediate and protracted mental and physical consequences of sterilization on the person.[30]

More specifically, the Committee was charged with (1) reviewing the minor's medical, social and psychological background, alternative family planning methods, and the adequacy of consent; and (2) interviewing the applicant, both parents of the minor (if available), and all other individuals which could shed light on the appropriateness of the surgery.[31] Parents were required to be consulted, *but parental consent was not required.*[32]

The exclusion of the parental consent requirement, however, was offset in respect to legally incompetent minors. Not only

---

23.   §§ 1396 *et seq.*, 42 U.S.C. §§ 601 *et seq.* Aid to Families with Dependent Children, 42 U.S.C. §§ 601-610; Medicare and Medicaid, 42 U.S.C. § 602(a)(14).
24.   H.R. Rep. No. 91-1472, 91st Cong., 2d Sess. 10 (1970), U.S. Code Cong. & Admin. News 1970, at 5068. 42 U.S.C. § 300(a)(6).
25.   42 U.S.C. § 216.
26.   38 Fed. Reg. 4730-34 (1974).
27.   42 C.F.R. § 50.202(f). 45 C.F.R. § 205.35(a)(2)(ii).
28.   42 C.F.R. § 50.202(f). 45 C.F.R. § 205.35(a)(e)(ii).
29.   42 C.F.R. § 50.206(a). 45 C.FR. § 205.35(a)(4)(i).
30.   42 C.F.R. § 50.206(a). 45 C.F.R. § 205.35(a)(4)(i).
31.   42 C.F.R. § 50.206(b)(1,2). 45 C.F.R. § 205.35(a)(4)(i)(A,B).
32.   42 C.F.R. § 50.203(c). 45 C.F.R. § 205.35(a)(5)(ii).

would they be provided with the aforementioned safeguards, but a state court of competent jurisdiction would have to rule on the propriety of sterilization in each case.[33]   However, *personal consent was not made mandatory*.[34]   A request for sterilization by the minor's "representative" was deemed as sufficient evidence of consent.[35]   HEW's interpretation of the term "representative," as including any person empowered under state law to consent to an incompetent minor's sterilization, finds no explicit support in the regulations.[36]   It is within the Committee's delegated authority, therefore, to arrange for the required court determination.[37]

Each Committee was also charged to maintain records[38] of its determinations, including a summary of the reasons therefor, and all relevant documentation.   This information would become part of the patient's permanent record.   All such files were made subject to inspection by the Secretary or his designated representative, to measure compliance with the regulations.

The crucial language focused on the "voluntariness" of each applicant:

> The acceptance by any individual of family planning services . . . provided, through financial assistance under this title (whether by grant or contract) *shall be voluntary* and shall not be a prerequisite to eligibility for a receipt of any other services or assistance from, or to participation in, any other program of the entity or individual that provided such service or information.[39]

In compliance with this requirement, and in response to various court suits, Frank Carlucci, Acting Secretary of HEW, announced that the Department's preexisting moratorium,[40] enjoining the allocation of federal money for any sterilization to be "performed on an individual who is under the age of 21, or who is himself legally incapable of consenting to the sterilization," would continue.[41] This federal moratorium was again extended on April 16, 1974.[42]

As of April 18, 1974, HEW required that all family planning programs under its revised Sterilization Restriction regulations had to document informed consent.   This would be effected by having each applicant sign a consent document, or acknowledge that oral

---

33. 42 C.F.R. § 50.203(c).   45 C.F.R. § 205.35(a)(1)(iv)(A,B).
34. 42 C.F.R. § 50.203(a).   45 C.F.R. § 205.235(a)(1).
35. 45 C.F.R. § 50.203(a).   45 C.F.R. § 205.235(a)(1).
36. 45 C.F.R. § 50 *et seq.*
37. 45 C.F.R. § 50.203(c).   45 C.F.R. § 205.35(a)(1)(iv)(A,B).
38. 45 C.F.R. § 50 *et seq.*
39. 42 U.S.C. § 300a-5.   42 U.S.C. §§ 602(a)(15), 708(a).
40. 38 Fed. Reg. 20930-20931 (Aug. 3, 1973).
41. 39 Fed. Reg. 10431-10432 (Mar. 20, 1974)
42. 39 Fed. Reg. 13873 (Apr. 18, 1974).

counseling was provided. Furthermore, each written consent document had to prominently display the following legend:

> Your decision at any time not to be sterilized will not result in the withdrawal or withholding of any benefits provided by programs or projects.[43]

Every applicant electing to be sterilized, therefore, was given the right to a fair explanation of the medical procedures, a description of the attendant discomforts, risks, and benefits to be expected, information covering the available alternative family planning methods, *and the affirmation that such surgery is irreversible.*[44] All applicants were also entitled to have any inquiry about the medical procedures answered, and withhold or withdraw voluntary consent at any time prior to the surgery without incurring any loss of future care or program benefits.[45]

The revised regulations mandated each federally assisted family planning program "not to perform nor arrange for the performance of a *nontherapeutic sterilization*[46] sooner than 72 hours following the giving of informed consent."[47]   To assure compliance with the revisions, HEW ordered each family planning program to supplement the existing reporting procedure:

> In addition to such other reports specifically required by the Secretary, the State agency shall report to the Secretary at least annually, the number and nature of the sterilizations subject to the procedures set forth in this section, and such other relevant information regarding such procedures as the Secretary may request.[48]

B.   *Applicable California Regulations*

California's applicable regulations are examined here in light of the harm suffered by Chicanas at the Medical Center, and also because its population of Chicanas is the highest in the nation. The jurisdictional basis for standing provided in the statutory scheme follows.

The Administrative Procedure Act provides that "any interested person may petition a state agency requesting the adoption

---

43.   39 Fed. Reg. 13873.
44.   *Id.*
45.   *Id.*
46.   22 Cal. Adm. Code § 1266.1(e) defines *Nontherapeutic sterilization* as any treatment, procedure, or operation, the primary purpose of which is to render an individual permanently incapable of producing offspring, and which is neither: (a) a necessary part of the treatment for an existing illness or injury, or (b) medically and surgically indicated as an accompaniment of a surgical procedure on the genito-urinary or reproducing organs.   (Mental or emotional incapacity is not considered an illness or injury).
47.   39 Fed. Reg. 13873, 13887.
48.   39 Fed. Reg. 13873, 13888.

. . . of a regulation as provided" in the Government Code.[49] Jurisdiction may also be invoked under the Health and Safety Code[50] and the Welfare and Institutions Code.[51]   Under these code sections, the Department of Health is obligated to carefully license and regulate all health care facilities in the state.   Specifically, Health and Safety Code, section 1276, provides that "regulations shall prescribe standards of . . . services based on the type of health facility and the needs of the persons served thereby."

On March 13, 1975, the Administrative Code was revised in respect to the regulations governing sterilization.[52]   The purpose of these revisions was to conform state procedures with those enacted by the federal government.   As a result, the requirements for nonemergency therapeutic[53] and nontherapeutic sterilizations were augmented.   The new regulations substantially emulated the federal regulations.   Each applicant must voluntarily request the surgery,[54] no person can be penalized for a refusal of the operation,[55] legally informed consent must be obtained from each applicant,[56] and no such surgery can be performed sooner than 72 hours after informed consent is given.[57]   California makes two exceptions to this 72 hour limit.   This occurs when the sterilization surgery is in response to an emergency medical condition,[58] or, to a life threatening disease.[59]

The regulations further provide that the attending physician

---

49.   CAL. GOV'T CODE §§ 11426 *et seq.*
50.   §§ 1250-1276, 429.50, 429.64, 429.66, 1100-1111, 1177, 1178, CAL. HEALTH AND SAFETY CODE §§ 1100 *et seq.*   Sections 1250 *et seq.*, require that the Department of Health approve an application and issue a license to those who wish to operate health care facilities.   Under the authority of section 1276, the Department must establish by regulation the requirements to be fulfilled by any licensed health facilities.
    Sections 1100 *et. seq.*, authorizes the Department of Health to provide financial aid to assist local public health agencies in providing "effective public health services to all the people of the state."   Section 1111 charges the Department of Health to adopt rules and regulations necessary to ensure that the aforementioned directive be complied with.
    The Director of the Department of Health, under section 1177, is empowered to make loans and provide technical assistance to Health Maintenance Organizations.   The services provided by such organizations must be delivered, according to standards set by the Department of Health, pursuant to section 1178.
51.   CAL. WELFARE AND INSTITUTIONS CODE §§ 14132, 14124.   Section 14132 provides for Medi-Cal coverage of family planning services.   Reasonable rules and regulations must be established by the Department, under section 14124.5, to protect any recipient of family planning services under the Medi-Cal program.
52.   22 Cal. Adm. § 1266.1(e).
53.   *Therapeutic sterilization*, as defined under 22 Cal. Adm. § 1266.1(e), is any treatment, procedure, or operation, the primary purpose of which is to correct or treat a medically recognized abnormal condition, or disease, but which also secondarily results in a permanent inability to reproduce offspring.
54.   22 Cal. Adm. § 1266.1(e)(1)(A).
55.   22 Cal. Adm. § 1266.1(e)(1)(B).
56.   22 Cal. Adm. § 1266.1(e)(1)(C).
57.   22 Cal. Adm. § 1266.1(e)(1)(D).
58.   22 Cal. Adm. § 1266.1(e)(1)(D)(1).
59.   22 Cal. Adm. § 1266.1(e)(1)(D)(2).

sign a form[60] attached to the surgical request document[61] for nonemergency therapeutic and nontherapeutic sterilization procedures. In addition, telephone authorization shall not be accepted.[62] It is with reference to "legally effective informed consent," however, where the state regulations differ most from the federal scheme.

One major difference applies to the age level of legal competence to give informed consent. Whereas federal law sets this limit at age 21, California permits 18 year olds to make a unilateral decision.[63] Federal law did provide the same opportunity for persons under the age of 18 prior to the moratorium, but only after a rigorous review procedure was applied.[64] Since April, 1974, the federal government has discontinued its funding of any sterilization performed on individuals under age 21.[65]

The state expands the required description of the medical procedure by requiring the following: (1) an explanation of the surgical techniques, (2) a description of the anesthesia to be used, (3) the approximate duration of hospitalization and expected recuperation, and (4) the consequences of the operation.[66] The latter description includes the disclosure of the anticipated and potential side effects, complications, and any important psychological or emotional effects.[67] A patient must also be informed about the surgical procedure's novelty or experimental nature when applicable.[68]

The regulations not only provide for a disclosure of alternative birth control methods, but also for an explanation of *alternative sterilization procedures* available in nontherapeutic situations.[69] The same requirement applies in the case of therapeutic surgery, including the disclosure of whether such alternative treatments result in sterility.[70] An explanation of the procedure must also include specific information relative to the applicant's medical history when material to the issue of consent.[71]

Moreover, all of this information must be contained in a Medical Information Statement, attached to the Consent Docu-

60.   22 Cal. Adm. § 1266.1(e)(1)(E). *See* Form MC 128: *Certification of Compliance with Requirements for Sterilization.*
61.   22 Cal. Adm. § 1266.1(e)(1)(E). *See* Form entitled: *Treatment Authorization Requests.*
62.   22 Cal. Adm. § 1266.1(e)(1)(F).
63.   22 Cal. Adm. § 1266.1(e)(2).
64.   42 C.F.R. § 50.206(a). 42 C.F.R. § 205.35(a)(4)(i).
65.   38 Fed. Reg. 20930-20931 (Aug. 3, 1973). 39 Fed. Reg. 10431-10432 (Mar. 20, 1974). 39 Fed. Reg. 13873 (Apr. 18, 1974).
66.   22 Cal. Adm. § 1266.1(e)(2)(A)(4).
67.   *Id.*
68.   22 Cal. Adm. § 1266.1(e)(2)(A)(5).
69.   22 Cal. Adm. § 1266.1(e)(2)(C).
70.   22 Cal. Adm. § 1266.1(e)(2)(E).
71.   22 Cal. Adm. § 1266.1(e)(2)(F).

ment.[72] Applicants for the surgery are required to be presented with these two documents.[73] However, any distribution of the documents to the applicants must be supplemented. Every applicant must be informed of the presiding physician's name.[74] It is required that this physician discuss with the applicant the nature of the operation relative to the patient's medical history and preoperative examination.[75] Any proposal of a surgical procedure not contained in the Medical Information Statement requires full notification to the applicant.[76]

A fundamental departure from the federal regulations in securing "legally informed consent" is the requirement that any Consent Document be co-signed by the applicant and an auditor-witness.[77] This auditor-witness cannot be affiliated with the physician or the medical facility, but must be independently selected by the person contemplating the surgery. It follows from this emphasis on an independent decision that any signature indicating consent, obtained during labor or delivery, or while the patient is under the influence of drugs, shall be invalid.[78] As a further precaution, the revised regulations provide that the entire process established to provide legally informed consent be presented "in easily understandable lay language."[79] Included in the language requirement is the provision that all instructions, both written and oral, be provided in English, Spanish, Cantonese or in the language of the applicant.[80]

California now authorizes its Department of Health to demand from any health agency a report disclosing the number of therapeutic and nontherapeutic sterilization operations conducted by the agency, evidence of compliance with the documented consent process, and demographic data of the sterilized individuals.[81]

As a result of these modifications to solidify the consent process, the broad discretion exercised by medical personnel to the detriment of Chicanas has been technically, but not effectively, narrowed. Regardless of these revisions, there remain areas which the federal and state regulations fail to properly supervise. The subsequent survey of ethical and empirical evidence which follows

---

72. 22 Cal. Adm. § 1266.1(e)(3)(A,B,C). The Medical Information Statement shall be framed by the State Department of Health, after the submission of recommendations by consumer and health organizations, and be updated by the Department not less than once every 12 months.
73. 22 Cal. Adm. § 1266.1(e)(4).
74. 22 Cal. Adm. § 1266.1(e)(4)(A).
75. 22 Cal. Adm. § 1266.1(e)(4)(B).
76. 22 Cal. Adm. § 1266.1(e)(4)(C).
77. 22 Cal. Adm. § 1266.1(e)(4)(D).
78. 22 Cal. Adm. § 1266.1(e)(4)(D)(1).
79. 22 Cal. Adm. § 1266.1(e)(5).
80. *Id.*
81. 22 Cal. Adm. § 1266.1(e)(6).

should illuminate the issue, and give impetus to a more comprehensive reform of the existing regulations.

III. THE CONFLICT BETWEEN REGULATORY INTENT AND MEDICAL PRACTICE

The intent of the regulations was to ensure that every applicant for sterilization surgery be afforded the protection of an explicit consent process. Several cases indicate that this has not transpired. Both raise doctrinal arguments considered basic to an understanding of the rights of patients and the duties of medical personnel.

A. *The Relf Case*

The Relf family resided in east-central Alabama where both parents worked as farmhands. Illiterate and unskilled, they lost their jobs when machines made manual labor expendable. They were compelled to move the family, which included three daughters, to Montgomery in search of employment. Unprepared to compete in an urban economy, Mr. and Mrs. Relf resigned themselves to a shack in the city garbage dump. Welfare authorities eventually provided the family with money for food and child support, an apartment in a housing project, free medical care, and family planning services.

The Montgomery Community Action Agency, a federally funded organization,[82] supervised the issuance of Depro-provera, an experimental birth control drug,[83] to Minnie, Mary Alice, and Katie Relf. Katie, the oldest daughter was also told to accept an intra-uterine device (I.U.D.). In June, 1973, nurses from the agency took the younger daughters to be sterilized. Mrs. Relf was informed that Minnie and Mary Alice were to receive additional birth control drugs, and based on this information she signed a consent form with her "X." The signed form provided the technical consent of the parent necessary for the resultant sterilization of the children. Katie, however, successfully dodged the attempts by

---

82. 42 U.S.C. §§ 2781-2837 (1964).
83. Investigational drugs, as defined by the Federal Drug Administration (hereinafter referred to as F.D.A.), are those which have not been approved for distribution. A drug may be approved for a certain use where its safety is verified, but unapproved for other uses.

Such drugs may be legally administered in two situations. (1) Local physicians may prescribe an approved drug for an unapproved purpose, because the F.D.A.'s jurisdiction does not extend to the local level. *See Hearings on S. 974 before the Subcomm. on Health of the Comm. on Labor and Public Welfare*, 93d Cong., 1st Sess., pt. 1, at 41 (testimony of F.D.A. Commissioner), 74 (testimony of Marcia Greenberger) (1973). (2) A license may be obtained from the F.D.A. to investigate the drug's effects, authorizing the interstate shipment and use of the drug, provided that strict recording and consent procedures are followed.

the nurses to sterilize her by locking herself in a bedroom. All of Mrs. Relf's daughters were under the age of 21.

The precise reason for the Agency's decision to sterilize the minors remains unascertainable. Mary Alice suffered from some form of educational disability and might have been partially mentally retarded.[84] Minnie, however, was a normal seventh grade student attending the public school system. Without evidence to the contrary, it can be fairly implied that the sole reason for the compelled operation was to prevent the girls from bearing children.

Joining the Relf sisters in their suit against HEW were Dorothy Waters and Mrs. Virgil Walker. Each received assistance under the federal categorical grant program known as Aid to Families with Dependent Children (hereinafter referred to as AFDC).[85] Their eligibility for AFDC also entitled them to services available under Medicare and Medicaid.[86] HEW program funds paid for the prenatal care of Ms. Waters when she became pregnant with her fifth child. Her physician was Dr. Clovis H. Pierce, who regularly cared for welfare mothers in Aiken County, South Carolina. He conditioned the rendering of his professional services upon Ms. Waters' submission to sterilization surgery. Threatened by possible lack of medical care, she agreed to be sterilized following the uncomplicated delivery of her child. Mrs. Walker also relented in her refusal to be sterilized when Dr. Pierce threatened to have her removed from the relief roles. She was then pregnant with her fourth child.

All of the plaintiffs were Black.

B. *The Brown Case*

Dr. Pierce was also involved in another suit brought by Mrs. Shirley Brown, and the aforementioned Mrs. Walker, for damages.[87] In September, 1973, Mrs. Brown was approached by Dr. Pierce, one day following the delivery of her child. He demanded that she be sterilized. Her refusal resulted in her dismissal as a patient at the Aiken County Hospital. This retaliation, alleged Mrs. Brown, placed the life of her infant in jeopardy. Both women were legally separated from their husbands and had long relied on public assistance.

---

84. Tests conducted by a separate public agency prior to the sterilization operation showed that Mary Alice was at least trainable and she had been selected to begin a special training center for handicapped children. Brief in Support for Motion for Preliminary Injunction, Relf v. Weinberger, 372 F. Supp. 1196 (D.D.C. 1974) (hereinafter referred to as *Relf Brief*). Joseph J. Levin, Jr., Southern Poverty Law Center, Inc., P.O. Box 548, Montgomery, Alabama 36106.
85. 42 U.S.C. §§ 601-610.
86. 42 U.S.C. § 602(a)(14).
87. Brown v. Pierce, (D.C. S.C., 1975), in the Los Angeles Times, July 27, 1975, at 7.

The federal court held that Mrs. Brown's civil rights had been violated, but assessed only nominal damages of five dollars because the jury concluded that she had not suffered serious harm.[88] Recovery was also denied to Mrs. Walker. This discouraging finding resulted, even though Dr. Pierce testified that his personal policy was to prevent welfare mothers from bearing children after their third or fourth pregnancy.[89]

As a matter of litigation strategy, the result in *Brown* should not discourage the use of damage claims as a way of countering medical malpractice in sterilization cases. Unlike the Chicanas in *Madrigal*, the women in *Brown* were welfare recipients and were unmarried or without the father's presence in the home. The human element probably played an important role in the jury's determination. Even though one half of the jury was composed of Blacks, the moral prejudice against women on welfare who bear children out of wedlock was very likely a crucial factor. The only note of guidance advanced by U.S. District Judge Solomon Blatt, Jr., was the muffled conclusion that the trial presented "novel legal questions." However, as a way to protect the right to procreate from an abuse of professional authority, the award of large damages for a denial of that right would seem to be one of the most effective methods.

C. *Constitutional Guidelines*

Federal law has a pervasive influence in determining the exercise of the sterilization option for family planning. The leading example is *King v. Smith*,[90] which stands for the proposition that in programs using both federal and state funds, the federal law prevails over nonconforming state rules. In relation with this decision, HEW is delegated with the duty of compelling the states to comply with federal law.[91] Should a state fail to comply, the Secretary is required to discontinue federal assistance to the delinquent program.[92] Under the AFDC statute, regulations issued by the Secretary are binding on the states.[93] When compliance is not enforced by the controlling federal agency, suit can be brought in a federal court for an order to compel enforcement.[94] Such orders are "to be obeyed until they expire . . . or [are] . . . set aside by

---

88. *Id.*
89. *Id.*
90. 392 U.S. 309, 316 (1968). *See also* Townsend v. Swank, 404 U.S. 282 (1971); Rosado v. Wyman, 397 U.S. 397 (1970).
91. *Id.*
92. 42 U.S.C. § 304. *See* LEVY & LEWIS, CASES AND MATERIALS ON SOCIAL WELFARE AND THE INDIVIDUAL 81-82 (1971).
93. Lewis v. Martin, 397 U.S. 552 (1970).
94. *See Relf Brief*, note 84, *supra.*

appropriate proceedings, appellate or otherwise."[95]   As a result of the availability of this equitable relief, the *Relf* sisters case succeeded in causing HEW to revise its regulations.[96]

Relf v. Weinberger, therefore, resulted in a court declaration of HEW's then existing regulations as unreasonable and arbitrary in application.[97]   Only the voluntary, knowing and uncoerced consent of individuals competent to give consent would satisfy the reasonableness test.   The case of *Madrigal v. Quilligan* raises the issue of individual competence to render consent, since the federal and state regulations defining consensual age are inconsistent.[98] This inconsistency necessarily exposes state licensed health facilities to a loss of federal funds for certain medical procedures.   The less strict California regulations are consequently vulnerable to attack based on *Smith*[99] under the supremacy clause, and subject to revision through the *Relf*[100] approach.   Such a relationship is highly significant since most states are heavily dependent upon federal funds to continue family planning services.

D.   *Constitutional Protections*

The issues raised by *Madrigal* focus on the right to procreate and to due process of law.

In *Hathaway v. Worcester City Hospital*,[101] a city hospital's prohibition of the use of its facilities for consensual sterilization violated the equal protection clause, since no other surgical procedures of equal risk, including nontherapeutic procedures, were barred.   A compelling state interest was required to justify a denial of the fundamental right to procreate or not to procreate.   Furthermore, a parity formula, based on a woman's age and number of children, would probably not withstand a *Stanley v. Illinois*[102] test. An irrebuttable presumption cannot be erected to deny an individual's qualification for sterilization.

Ever since *Meyer v. Nebraska*,[103] there has developed a substantial body of law tending to make certain family associated functions protected from government intrusion.   It is now considered a fundamental right to create a family unit through mar-

---

95.   U.S. v. United Mine Workers of America, 330 U.S. 258, 294 (1947).
96.   38 Fed. Reg. 4730-34 (1974). 39 Fed. Reg. 13873.
97.   Public Health Service Act, § 1007, 42 U.S.C.A. § 300a-5; Social Security Act, §§ 402(a)(15), 508(a), 1905(a)(4), 42 U.S.C.A. §§ 602(a)(15), 708(a), 1396(d)(a)(4).
98.   22 Cal. Adm. § 1266.1(e)(2).
99.   392 U.S. 309, 316 (1968).
100.   *See Relf Brief*, note 84, *supra.*
101.   475 F.2d 701 (1st Cir. 1973).
102.   405 U.S. 645 (1972).
103.   262 U.S. 390 (1923) (dictum).

riage,[104] to decide privately and personally when and whether to have children, [105] and to raise and educate the offspring of the union.[106] The right to procreate, therefore, is so intertwined with marriage, child bearing, and the quality of child rearing that it must also be considered fundamental.

A key element in this discussion focuses on the meaning of privacy. In *Eisenstadt v. Baird*, Justice Brennan made the distinction between private rights and public interests more definite:

> If the right of privacy means anything, it is the right of the individual, married or single, to be free from unwarranted government intrusion into matters so fundamentally affecting a person as the decision whether or not to beget a child.[107]

The right at issue, said the Supreme Court in *Roe v. Wade*,[108] encompassed the "[w]oman's decision whether or not to terminate her pregnancy." Reference was not only made to the doctrine of government exclusion from the decision not to bear children, but in *Griswold v. Connecticut*,[109] Justice Goldberg directly addressed the issue of the parental right to procreate.

> Surely the government . . . could not decree that all husbands and wives must be sterilized after two children have been born to them . . . [if] a law outlawing voluntary birth control by married persons is valid, then, by the same reasoning, a law requiring compulsory birth control also would seem to be valid. In my view, however, both types of law would unjustifiably intrude upon rights of marital privacy which are constitutionally protected.[110]

Privacy emanates from the concept of personal liberty embodied in the first, fifth, ninth, and fourteenth amendments. Each individual is guaranteed the autonomy necessary to make decisions of a personal nature. The decision to procreate or not centers on the people's basic freedom from the government's interference. When this freedom involves a fundamental right, such as the private decision to procreate, only a compelling state interest can justify its denial.

The Chicanas victimized in *Madrigal* suffered from a direct government relationship with the medical profession. Coupled with the unauthorized practices of medical personnel, the government's permeation of the entire sterilization process has served to deprive Chicanas of the right to procreate. If government author-

---

104. *See* Loving v. Virginia, 388 U.S. 1 (1967).
105. *See* Eisenstadt v. Baird, 405 U.S. 438 (1972).
106. *See* Pierce v. Society of Sisters, 268 U.S. 510 (1922).
107. 405 U.S. at 453. *See* note 103.
108. 410 U.S. 113 (1973).
109. 381 U.S. 479 (1965) (Goldberg, J., concurring).
110. *Id.* at 496-497.

izes certain practices which touch upon fundamental rights, its failure to properly supervise those practices negatively intrudes upon personal liberty. Even though the intent behind the intrusion be benign, the actual application has resulted in damaging effects. This same finding was alluded to in *Relf* when the court explained that "it is for Congress and not individual social workers and physicians to determine the manner in which federal funds should be used to support such a program."[111]

IV.   ETHICAL ATTITUDES EFFECTING THE QUESTION OF REGULATORY REFORM

An examination of current ethical premises among medical personnel is necessary, to fully appreciate the need to promulgate regulations which will satisfactorily protect Chicana patients.

After surveying the available medical literature, V. B. Marrow arrived at the conclusion that most physicians consider their own "vast experience and common sense" determinative in ethical decisions.[112] According to Dr. Samuel Vaisrub, doctors should be their own philosophers: "[the] ethical dilemmas of medicine often defy rational solutions [and are] more in need of the intuitive perceptions of Aeschylus rather than of the logical analysis of an Aristotle."[113] Writing in 1936, Dr. H. J. Stander indicated that medical practitioners exercised one standard of consultation with solvent patients, and another with poorer patients, when sterilization was considered attendant to a caesarean section.[114] The availability of proper medical care in the poorer communities was considered crucial in arriving at a decision to sterilize.[115] But poor women were generally categorized for sterilization without consultation, as the following quotation indicates:

> [I]f she is weak-minded or diseased and is liable to become a public charge, the operation is justifiable. In general, with pauper patients, it is our practice to effect sterilization at the third [caesarean] section.[116]

Modern medical practice assigns a high priority to surgical experience. This preoccupation with "cutting" encourages hospital personnel to solicit consent for sterilization operations for the purpose of training interns. Generally, the patients selected for this training are poor women. A good record of surgical participa-

---

111. 372 F. Supp. at 1204.
112. Marrow, *Medical Ethics: Should Healers Think?*, MEDICAL DIMENSIONS, at 31-32 (March, 1975).
113. *Id.*
114. DR. H.J. STANDER, WILLIAMS OBSTETRICS (7th ed. C.D. Appleton-Century, 1936).
115. *Id.*
116. *Id.*

tion usually results in residency certification and specialty board qualification.   This experience is ultimately converted into higher financial rewards.

Based upon a report by the acting director of obstetrics and gynecology at a New York City municipal hospital, an unwritten policy exists within most of the City's teaching hospitals to perform elective hysterectomies on poor Black and Puerto Rican women, with only minimal medical indications, in order to train residents.[117]   Dr. A. Shapiro asserts that such an attitude does not protect the interests of the patient: "We have got to stop people who are doing [sterilization] for their own profiteering motives or referring for that reason."[118]   Supporting this view is Dr. J. Knowles, former head of the Massachusetts General Hospital who stated:

> Human beings rationalize what they do without any conscious effort to be dishonest or greedy . . . . Doctors are human.   A significant number of them, 20 to 30 percent, are *de facto* fleecing the public while 'knowing they are doing good'.[119]

It would be unfair to condemn the entire medical profession for the unethical motives of a few, but the minority of doctors performing unjustified sterilizations warrants regulatory attention. Perhaps, as has been generally argued, society expects too much from the presently inadequate supply of doctors.   Dr. C. E. Lewis focused on the impact felt by overworked doctors when he said:

> "Because her husband is absent so much, the surgeon's wife may seek tangible compensations such as a better house or a fur coat.   And medicine is one of the few fields . . . where if a wife wants a new coat, all you have to do is a couple more hysterectomies, and she can buy it."[120]

Yet even the most coercive violations of individual rights are often ignored, sometimes even applauded, by medical associations. This raises a question pertinent to the efficacy of self-regulation in such cases.   For example, the South Carolina Medical Association responded to the *Brown* decision by unequivocally supporting the practices of Dr. Clovis Pierce.   The Association's resolution declared that "it is entirely ethical for a physician to inform a woman who desires to become his patient that he will require her to agree to sterilization as a condition to accepting her as a patient."[121]

---

117.   Newsday, Jan. 2, 1974, at 4A.
118.   Medical World News, Nov. 1972, at 19-20.
119.   Hospital Physician, Feb. 1973, at 35-40.
120.   *Id.*
121.   *S.C. Society Calls Sterilization Precondition in Taking Patient Ethical,* Obstetrician and Gynecology News, Aug. 1, 1974.

Entirely ignored was the unconscionable position of the patient which would compel her to yield under pressure.

Some doctors have relied on a pragmatic stance to justify the increased spread of sterilization surgery. Leaders of the Association for Voluntary Sterilization support this trend as the most effective means of avoiding the harm engendered by the radical growth of population. They particularly dismiss the studies purporting to cite the psychological ill effects associated with sterilization. A past president of the Association, Dr. Curtis Wood, summed up this philosophical position:

> People pollute, and too many people crowded too close together cause many of our social and economic problems. These, in turn, are aggravated by involuntary and irresponsible parenthood. As physicians we have obligations to our individual patients, but we also have obligations to the society of which we are a part. The welfare mess, as it has been called, cries out for solutions, one of which is fertility control.[122]

There is also evidence indicating that this attitude is not limited to medical practitioners. Proposals have been introduced in the legislatures of eight states, to punish by sterilization those welfare recipients who have given birth to a number of children in excess of a set limit.[123] This attitude could help to explain why, in an alarming number of recent cases, women have awakened from minor surgery to be informed of their sterilization.

The conclusion recently framed by several prominent members of the medical profession condemns the stated justifications for involuntary sterilization. Specifically criticized is the proliferation of abuse suffered by minority women. They characterize such tragic results in ironic terms:

> [W]hereas middle class women have had to go to court to obtain voluntary sterilization, poor women are in danger of the procedure being performed without their consent.[124]

It has also been recommended that the value of sterilization as a method of contraception may be lessened unless careful attention is paid to any potentially harmful psychological effects. Another major argument is that "a contraceptive method with harmful side

---

122. 1 CONTEMPORARY OBSTETRICS & GYNECOLOGY 31-40 (1973).
123. *Panel Recommends Caution in Federal Family Planning.* Obstetrician and Gynecology News, Dec. 15, 1974, at 2. Address by Dr. James E. Allen of the School of Public Health at the University of North Carolina, at the annual meeting of the American Public Health Association.
124. GYNECOLOGY AND OBSTETRICS: THE HEALTH CARE OF WOMEN (S. Romney ed. 1975), at 12, 48, 49, 577. The textbook was edited by Seymour L. Romney, M.D., Professor in the Department of Gynecology and Obstetrics at the Albert Einstein College of Medicine and by five other professors of obstetrics and gynecology from different universities.

effects released on large sections of the population will ultimately do more to retard than advance the cause of family planning."[125]

It is not enough, therefore, if the motives of medical practitioners are lofty when the techniques of duress they employ violate a patient's privacy and due process rights, and result in irreversible sterilization. No less an authority than Dr. Julius Paul has warned about this danger:

> Where the persons who are affected by these laws or administrative decisions are mentally incompetent (by some standard), poor, or in any fashion or form vulnerable to blandishments of various kinds, the problem of protecting personal rights is even more difficult, and the obligation of the administrator to protect personal rights should be even higher.[126]

The obligation to protect personal rights is even more significant when one considers the magnitude of current sterilization programs, the lack of compliance with existing regulations, and empirical data indicating a disturbing frequency of postoperative complications.

V. THE EMPIRICAL CASE FOR REGULATORY REFORM

A. The Expanded Use of Sterilization for Contraception

Federal support for family planning services has rapidly increased since 1967. By 1973, the amount of annual federal expenditures had grown from $11 million to $149 million.[127] Dr. Louis Hellman, Assistant Secretary of HEW for Population Services, estimated that $1 billion would be spent on the program by 1975. The federal government now pays 90 percent of the total contribution for birth control services offered to Medicaid recipients, and obliges every state to provide such services to every woman on welfare.[128] With the expansion of federal expenditures has come a comparable increase in sterilization surgery.

During the period 1970 to 1974, the number of yearly female sterilizations increased from 192,000 to 548,000.[129] At the Medical Center there was a 450 percent rise in the number of steriliza-

---

125. 4 BRIT. MED. J. 297-300 (Oct. 1970).
126. Paul, *Population "Quality" and "Fitness for Parenthood" in the light of State Eugenic and Sterilization Experience: 1907-1966*, 11 POPULATION STUDIES 3, at 295 (Nov. 1967). *See also* AMERICAN PHILOSOPHICAL SOCIETY, YEARBOOK, at 379, 380-381 (1967).
127. *D.H.E.W. 5-Year Plan Report: Program Served 3.2 Million in FY 1973,* 3 FAMILY PLANNING DIGEST (May 1974).
128. *Birth Curb Leaders Cite Future Needs,* AMERICAN MEDICAL NEWS, May 16, 1974, at 16.
129. 39 Fed. Reg. 237 (1974). *See also* E. KRAUSS, *Hospital Survey on Sterilization Policies,* March, 1975 (American Civil Liberties Union, 22 E. 40th St., New York, N.Y. 10016) (hereinafter referred to as KRAUSS).

tions performed just between 1968 and 1970.[130]   This included elective hysterectomy,[131] elective tubal ligation, and tubal ligation after delivery.   The largest expansion occurred in the performance of hysterectomies, almost 750 percent.[132]   This is not surprising since hysterectomies rank as the fourth common operation performed in the country.[133]   Such an augmentation reflects a relaxation of prior restrictions based on a patient's age, parity (number of children) and marital status.   Similar expansion has taken place in other parts of the country.[134]   For example, the number of sterilizations performed at the Mount Sinai Hospital in New York City increased 200 percent from 1970 to 1974,[135] and a large hospital in St. Paul, Minnesota, reported that the ratio of tubal ligations to births had increased from 1:9.2 in 1968-1969 to 1:4.3 in 1973.[136]

Women who are poor and of a racial minority experience a higher incidence of sterilization than do other women.   Among those women who undergo the surgery with less than a high school education, 14.5 percent were Caucasian but 31.6 percent were Black.[137]   Thirty-five percent of Puerto Rican women, aged 15 to 44, have been sterilized and two-thirds of these women are under age 30.[138]   The Minnesota report indicated that over half of the hospital's patients were Caucasian, but only 40 percent of those sterilized were Caucasian; one third of the patients were Black, but they constituted 43 percent of those sterilized.[139]   This information becomes even more relevant when postoperative complications are considered.

B. *Postoperative Complications*

According to Dr. Curtis Wood, as women become better informed about contraception, they will increasingly realize that "over all, sterilization is the safest of all methods."[140]   The evi-

130.   *Sterilization: Women Fit to be Tied*, HEALTH POLICY ADVISORY CENTER BULLETIN, Jan. Feb., 1975, at 2.
131.   DR. G. ROSENFELD & DR. S. WOLFE, *A Health Research Group Study On Surgical Sterilization: Present Abuses and Proposed Regulations*, October, 1973. (Health Research Group, funded by Public Citizens, Inc., 2000 P. Street, N.W., Washington, D.C. 20036) (hereinafter referred to as ROSENFELD).
132.   The surgical removal of all or part of the uterus.
133.   See ROSENFELD, note 129, *supra* at 1.
134.   Brief for Plaintiff at 5, California Coalition for the Medical Rights of Women v. California Dept. of Health, (unfiled). Prepared by B. Grubb, S. Wolinsky, Public Advocates, Inc., 433 Turk St., San Francisco, CA 94102. Tonsillectomy, hernia repair and gall bladder removal rank ahead of hysterectomy in frequency of performance.
135.   Newsday, Jan. 2, 1974, at 4A.
136.   L. Edwards & E. Hakanson, *Changing Status of Tubal Sterilization: An Evaluation of Fourteen Years' Experience*, 115 AMER. J. OB. & GYN. 347 (1973).
137.   See note 128, *supra* at 3.
138.   1 FAMILY PLANNING DIGEST 6 (May, 1972).
139.   See note 134, *supra* at 347.
140.   1 CONTEMPORARY OBSTETRICS & GYNECOLOGY 31-40 (1973).

dence seems to contradict this view. In terms of psychological impact, the existence of sterility in a marital relationship has been found significant. Extensive research suggests that the inability to procreate has a profound emotional effect on married couples, and hastens marital dissolution.[141]   Dr. M. H. Johnson has described the serious psychological repercussions derived from sterilization as long "a matter of common medical knowledge."[142]   One study found that 12 percent of the women sterilized suffered postopera- tive harm.[143]   More recent data suggests that this incidence of mental regret may be as high as 25 percent.[144]

The risk of physical harm is also very significant. A surgery for tubal ligation "sounds attractive to the uninformed, but a serious complication rate exists."[145]   A survey of obstetricians and gynecologists who had participated in 7000 tubal ligation opera- tions found that a major complication rate .6 percent or 6000 per million women, resulted.[146]   Data applying to the mortality rate dif- fer somewhat, but still tends to affirm the gravity of risk involved. For example, one study determined that the mortality rate was .15%, or 1500 per million women, with the failure rate at .3 per- cent, per million women.[147]   Another study indicated that the mor- tality rate was as low as 25 per 100,000 women;[148] but associated with a post-operative morbidity rate of from 2 to 4 percent, usually from bleeding or infection.[149]   In comparison with hysterectomy, tubal ligation produces less certain results but is also less expensive, requires a shorter period of convalescence, and causes less com- plications.[150]

Information gathered by Dr. Lester Hubbard, Professor of Obstetrics and Gynecology at the Medical Center, points out that the complication rate resulting from hysterectomy is 10 to 20 times greater than for tubal ligation.[151]   It costs 4 to 5 times more for the surgery, and the convalescent period is six weeks compared to the few days required after a tubal ligation.[152]   The high rate of complications, manifested as bladder trauma, excessive blood loss and pelvic hematomas, persuade many physicians to forego hyster- ectomy unless there are additional indications for the operation.[153]

141.   See ROSENFELD, note 129, supra at 16, 20.
142.   121 AM. J. PSYCH. 482-486 (July 1964-1965).
143.   4 AM. MED. J. 297-300 (Oct., 1970).
144.   Whitehouse, Sterilization of Young Wives, BRIT. MED. J. (June 19, 1973), at 707.
145.   See ROSENFELD, note 129, supra at 14.
146.   10 J. REPR. MED. 301 (1973).
147.   See ROSENFELD, note 129, supra at 13-14.
148.   Presser, Voluntary Sterilization: A World View, REPORTS ON POPULATION & FAMILY PLANNING 1970), at 1.
149.   Id.
150.   See ROSENFELD, note 129, supra at 14.
151.   112 AM. J. OB. & GYN. 1076 (1972).
152.   Id.
153.   114 AM. J. OB. & GYN. 670 (1972).

Not included as a valid interest is a history of previous caesarean sections, unless the object is to remove a cancerous growth or an intractable uterine hemorrhage.[154]   Death from this operation occurs 300 to 500 times for every 100,000 operations.[155]   The mortality rate is, in fact, greater than that for uterine cervical cancer.[156]

C.   *Impact on Minors and Incompetents*

Considered within this context the term "voluntary" requires "that the individual have at [her] disposal the information necessary to make   a   decision and the mental competence to appreciate the significance of that information."[157]   The case of *Relf v. Weinberger* presented uncontroverted evidence that minors and incompetents had been sterilized with federal funds, and had been improperly coerced into accepting the surgery.[158]   Dr. Louis Hellman, reported that only between 2,000 and 3,000 individuals under the age of 21, and fewer than 300 under age 18, had been sterilized.[159]   At the Baltimore City Hospital twelve women, most of whom were between the ages of 18 and 21, were coerced under duress to give consent to sterilization surgery just minutes before undergoing caesarean section.[160]   No authority for the federal funding of such procedures relative to minors and mental incompetents is discernable from the Social Security,[161] or Public Health Service Acts.[162]   The court's reaction in *Relf* was to enjoin the further allocation of federal funds for the sterilization of incompetent minors and adults.[163]   So even though the number of minors and incompetents sterilized may be comparatively small, the need to protect their personal rights is no less mandatory.

D.   *Summary of Compliance with the Requirement of Informed Consent*

After the federal court order of March, 1974, which required HEW's revision of its sterilization regulations to ensure informed consent, it was reported that 76 percent of 51 hospitals surveyed

---

154.   *See* ROSENFELD, note 129, *supra* at 10.
155.   C. Porter, Jr. & J. Hulka, *Female Sterilization in Current Clinical Practice,* 4 FAMILY PLANNING PERSPECTIVES 35 (Winter 1974).
156.   *See* note 132, *supra.*
157.   *See, e.g.,* Dusky v. United States, 362 U.S. 402 (1960); Elder v. Crawley Book Machinery Co., 441 F.2d 771, 773 (3d Cir. 1971), Pearson v. United States, 117 U.S. App. D.C. 52, 325 F.2d 625, 626-667 (1963).
158.   372 F. Supp. at 1199.
159.   *Id.* at 1198.
160.   *See* ROSENFELD, note 129, *supra* at 4.
161.   42 U.S.C. §§ 330 *et seq.*
162.   Public Health Service Act, §§ 310, 314(d,e), 42 U.S.C.A. §§ 242(h), 246(d,e).
163.   372 F. Supp. at 1201.

continued in complete noncompliance as of January, 1975.[164] Another 12 hospitals failed to comply with part of the revised regulations.[165]   For example, only 15 of the hospitals had a policy prohibiting staff members from discussing sterilization with patients in labor.[166]   Twenty-one hospitals completely failed to provide for an oral and written description of medical indications to patients requiring therapeutic sterilization.[167]   Only 15 hospitals gave the required protective notice to welfare recipients.[168]   Moreover, there was extensive noncompliance with the required 72 hour waiting period, the content of the consent form, the requirement that all pertinent information be communicated to each applicant in clearly understandable terms, and mention that the surgery is irreversible.[169]   Not surprisingly, though, each consent form found out of compliance due to an ambiguous explanation of surgical procedures contained a very concise statement absolving the medical personnel from liability.[170]

A recent study[171] of 17 hospitals in San Francisco yielded similar results.   Four out of the ten East Bay hospitals studied, including the hospital with the largest volume of obstetric and gynecology patients in the area, were completely uninformed about the regulation changes.[172]   Ten of the 17 total hospitals surveyed could not recall having received printed regulations from HEW, and 9 hospitals had no knowledge of the specific revisions.[173] Furthermore, some of the hospitals did not even provide consent forms to patients prior to performing sterilization operations.[174]

The extent of noncompliance may be the result of both a relaxation of precautionary measures once considered mandatory, and the widespread belief that sterilization is particularly effective in controlling population growth among the poor.   For example, in 1970, the American College of Obstetricians and Gynecologists withdrew its guideline recommending the signature of two or more doctors plus a psychiatric consultation as necessary prior to effecting a sterilization.[175]   Commensurate with this adoption of a less stringent standard was an attitudinal shift favoring the expanded

---

164. See KRAUSS, note 127, supra at 20.
165. Id.
166. Id. at 16.
167. Id. at 13. Therapeutic sterilization refers to any treatment, procedure, or operation, the primary purpose of which is to correct or treat a medically recognized abnormal condition, or disease, but which also secondarily results in a permanent inability to reproduce offspring.
168. Id. at 14.
169. Id. at 8, 10, 15.
170. Id. at 11.
171. See note 132, supra.
172. Id.
173. Id.
174. Id.
175. See note 128, supra at 3.

use of sterilization surgery. One study indicated that between 45 percent and 94 percent of the doctors surveyed "encourage" the compulsory sterilization of welfare mothers and "any woman who has more than two illegitimate children."[176] A different poll showed that only 6 percent of the doctors surveyed would recommend sterilization as a contraception method for *private* patients, but 14 percent considered sterilization as the primary contraceptive method for *public* patients.[177] This same poll also revealed the following attitudinal prevalence:

> The obstetrician-gynecologists were the most punitive of the doctors surveyed, 94 percent favoring compulsory sterilization or withholding of welfare support for unwed mothers with three children.[178]

The motive behind such a menacing posture may be the belief that poor women are less likely to use less drastic contraceptive methods. On the contrary, a number of studies have supported the opposite conclusion.[179]

VI. SPECIAL CONCERNS OF CHICANAS

The circumstances in *Madrigal* present additional shortcomings in the existing regulations. It was discovered that consent documents, informational materials and oral presentations were not given in the primary language of the patients.[180] No provision was made that consent forms be legible.[181] Guidelines were not established to protect patients with limited reading ability, or those unable to read.[182] Medical terms, such as therapeutic and non-therapeutic, were not defined in terms which could be readily understood by each patient.[183] When federal regulations were considered separately, the failure to specify against the practice of considering caesarean delivery as a valid medical indication for sterilization was found to be a harmful omission.[184] In addition, the federal regulations did not prohibit the practice of approaching patients to consider sterilization and to sign consent forms while

---

176. H. Werley, J. Ager, R. Rosen, F. Shea, *Medicine, Nursing, Social Work, Professionals and Birth Control: Student and Faculty Attitudes.* 5 FAMILY PLANNING PERSPECTIVES 42-49 (1973).

177. *Physician Attitudes: MDs Assume Poor Can't Remember to Take Pill*, 1 FAMILY PLANNING DIGEST 3 (Jan., 1972).

178. *Id.*

179. *Poor Women Good Pill Users, Study Finds*, 1 FAMILY PLANNING DIGEST 1-2 (1973); H. Davis, The I.U.D. (The Williams & Wilkens Co., Baltimore, 1971); M. Vessey & P. Wiggins, *Use-Effectiveness of the Diaphragm in a Selected Family Planning Clinic Population in the United Kingdom*, 9 CONTRACEPTION 15 (1974).

180. *Madrigal*, note 5, *supra.*

181. *Id.*

182. *Id.*

183. *Id.*

184. *Id.*

they were in labor and under anesthesia.[185] Regulatory concerns alone, however, cannot explain the depth of hurt felt by the victims.

Cultural values vary from individual to individual, but among Chicanas a pervasive set of beliefs are still given great weight. These beliefs are as important in weighing the extent of damage suffered as the physical impact itself. Sterility not only strikes at traditional religious values but also at the viability of the marital relationship

Catholicism, though not universally accepted among Chicanos and Chicanas, continues to be a powerful influence within the community. For centuries it has been established among the Mexican people as the source of moral authority. The faith has given definition to the spiritual essence of the human experience. This spiritual commitment varies and is subject to flux, but the longevity of the Church gives testimony to a continuous acceptance.

The Church operates one-fourth of the hospitals in the United States. A staunch position on sterilization and birth control reflects cherished principles of human conduct. The following directive was issued by the National Conference of Catholic Bishops:

> Sterilization, whether permanent or temporary, for men or for women, may not be used as a means of contraception. Similarly excluded is every action which, either in anticipation of the conjugal act, or in its accomplishment, or in the development of its natural consequences, proposes, whether as an end or as a means, to render procreation impossible.[186]

Allen v. Sisters of Saint Joseph,[187] provided an opportunity to test the Church's right to implement its anti-sterilization policy. A Catholic hospital which received federal and state funds was held not to be operating under the color of law when it refused to use its facilities to perform a requested sterilization operation. The court could not find a "compelling reason appearing to issue an injunction in order to prevent irreparable harm and injury to the life and health" of a patient.[188]

Even though the woman who requested the surgery would have been required to undergo separate operations for a caesarean section and sterilization, instead of combining both procedures, this was held not to be sufficient grounds for ordering the hospital to

---

185. *Id.*
186. CATHOLIC HOSPITAL ASS'N OF THE U.S. AND CANADA, ETHICAL AND RELIGIOUS DIRECTIVES FOR CATHOLIC HOSPITALS (3d ed. 1972).
187. 361 F. Supp. 1212 (N.D. Texas 1973).
188. *Id.* at 1214.

reverse its policy. The court explained its decision on First Amendment grounds:

> The interest that the public has in the establishment and operation of hospitals by religious organizations is paramount to any inconvenience that would result to the plaintiff in requiring her to either be moved or await a later date for her sterilization.[189]

This religious philosophy underlines related attitudes about the spousal relationship. Two examples from the *Madrigal* case suggest the importance of the family as an institution to Chicanas. Guadalupe Acosta was led to believe that her husband had authorized her sterilization, but he believed that his consent was limited to her caesarean section. The wife angrily blamed the husband for the tragic result, and the husband came to feel that his wife's inability to procreate made their eight year common law marriage severable.[190]

Maria Diaz was informed some weeks after the operation about being sterilized. She cried when she heard the news. The doctor responded by saying, "Don't cry. It's best for you that you not have any more children. In Mexico, the people are very, very poor and it's best that you not have more children."[191] Mrs. Diaz has revealed that her involuntary sterilization has caused great friction in her relationship with her husband. He has already warned her that they would part.[192]

Among Chicanos and Chicanas the purpose of marriage continues to be, for the most part, the bearing and rearing of children. Without children the prized continuation of the family, and all of the cultural values embodied therein, is lost. The reality of the situation burdens the sterile woman with decreased prospects for marriage, and the increased possibility of marital discord and dissolution. So when a Chicana is made sterile she not only loses the opportunity to procreate, but also the chance to live a precious cultural role.

Thus, the impact of a coerced sterilization strikes at the heart of the woman's existence within the culture. Guadalupe Acosta gave expression to this loss of identity when she related the following sentiment:

> Ever since the operation, I am very inattentive. Not forgetful, inattentive. People sometimes have to tell me things twice. It's not that I don't understand them, it's that I'm not there.[193]

---

189. *Id.*
190. C. Dreifus, *Sterilizing the Poor.* THE PROGRESSIVE (Dec., 1975), at 14.
191. *Id.*
192. *Id.*
193. *Id.*

When the evidence is considered, including the cultural reality of Chicanas, the necessity to make sure that low-income consumers receive complete and understandable information pertinent to sterilization is underscored.   Only a reform of the existing regulations can ensure voluntary and informed consent.   To accomplish this fundamental goal, the following solutions are recommended.

VII.   SOLUTIONS RECOMMENDED TO SECURE INFORMED CONSENT

The following provisions should become a mandatory part of the existing federal regulations and all state regulations where applicable.

A.   The right to be free from a physical intrusion into the body is as fundamental a part of the right to privacy as the decision whether or not to beget children.[194]   For this reason *any nonemergency sterilization must be initially requested by the patient or potential patient, and the medical record must indicate that the request for surgery originated with the patient.*   The necessity for this measure is substantiated by Drs. Barner and Zuspan: "Where the procedure is proposed by the attending physician, approximately 32 percent of the patients become unhappy, compared with only 9 percent if initiation of the idea is with the couple."[195]   As a prerequisite of this request provision, *only those persons who are 21 years of age or older shall* be eligible for the surgery.   Such a policy was recently supported through injunctive relief by federal Judge E. Avery Crary in the *Madrigal* case.[196]

B.   The following statement must be printed directly above the patient's signature line on the consent form in bold face type:

"I UNDERSTAND THAT THE PURPOSE OF THIS OPERATION OR SURGERY IS TO MAKE ME STERILE, AND THAT I WILL NEVER BE ABLE TO HAVE A CHILD IN THE FUTURE."

Furthermore, *a written consent form must be properly signed, witnessed, and made a part of the hospital record 30 days before the actual performance of the surgery, or, in expectation of a postpartum sterilization, 60 days before the expected date of con-*

---

194.   *See* Roe v. Wade, 410 U.S. 113 (1973) (Douglas, J., concurring); Mackey v. Procumier, No. 71-3062 (9th Cir., Apr. 16, 1973); Kaimowitz v. Dept. of Mental Health, No. 73-19434 (Mich. Cir. Ct. of Wayne County, Jul. 10, 1973) (three judges).
195.   89 AM. J. OBST. 395-400 (1964).
196.   *Madrigal*, note 5, *supra*.   The court enjoined state health officials from using federal funds for voluntary sterilizations of women between 18 and 21 years of age.   California presently allows the voluntary sterilization of anyone over 18 years of age, but federal law limits this procedure to persons 21 years of age or older.   *See also* Calderon, *Sterilization Suit by Chicanas*, 2 La Raza 21 (1975).

finement. Dr. T. W. Adams' study, conducted at a hospital where this rule was applied, showed that of those patients dissatisfied with the results of the operation, 36 percent had undergone a sterilization in disregard of the rule compared to a 16 percent dissatisfaction rate among those in compliance.[197]   Such an extended waiting period is necessary because studies have consistently indicated that women below age 30 are more likely to regret sterilization than women over 30.[198]   In addition, sterilization is not any safer physically than continued use of oral contraceptives, and is more dangerous than the I.U.D. or diaphragm.[199]

C.   *For persons who speak and understand only Spanish, or a language other than English, the prescribed "informed consent" can be obtained only after all pertinent information is provided in the patient's own language.*   This must include verbal counselling and all written forms; particularly in regards to the *alternative methods available to effect contraception and sterilization.   All consent forms must be written at a sixth grade education level of comprehension.*

There can be no informed consent to sterilization as mandated by the federal regulations when counseling is provided in a language which the patient does not understand, nor where the consent form is written in a language which the patient cannot read. Even though this provision may entail additional administrative costs, increased costs cannot justify the abrogation of the fundamental right to procreate.   This policy was clearly stated in *Castro v. California.*[200]

> Avoidance or recoupment of administrative costs, while a valid state concern, cannot justify the imposition of an otherwise improper classification, especially when, as here, it touches on 'matters close to the core of our constitutional system'.[201]

While there exists a strong societal interest in the uniformity of language, as the Court said in *Meyer v. Nebraska,*[202] basic consti-

---

197.   89 AM. J. OBST. & GYN. 395-401 (1964).
198.   *See* ROSENFELD, note 129, *supra.*   The mathematical likelihood of such things as divorce and remarriage or a child dying during a woman's reproductive years is much greater for younger women than older women.
199.   *See* ROSENFELD, note 129, *id.* at 18.
200.   2 C. 3d 223 (1970).
201.   *Id.* at 242.   In *Castro,* the California Supreme Court invalidated the state's constitutional provision conditioning the right to vote upon the ability to read the English language as applied to persons who are literate in Spanish but not in English.   The Court balanced the state's concern in avoiding the cost and administrative burden of providing a bilingual electoral system against the fundamental right to vote and found that the importance of the individual's right to vote outweighed the state's interest.
202.   262 U.S. 390 (1923).

tutional rights cannot be violated for the sake of linguistic homogeneity:

> The protection of the Constitution extends to all, . . . to those who speak other languages as well as to those born with English on the tongue. Perhaps it would be highly advantageous if all had ready understanding of our ordinary speech, but this cannot be coerced by methods which conflict with the Constitution, . . . a desirable end cannot be promoted by prohibited means.[203]

In addition, *every person who voices a desire to undergo nontherapeutic sterilization surgery must be provided with an illustrated booklet, written in the language of the applicant, which clearly describes the surgical procedures and effects of the operation.*

D. *Every hospital providing sterilization surgery must also present to every applicant a detailed audio-visual explanation, in the language of the applicant, which accurately describes the surgical procedures and effects of the operation.*

E. *The results of a preoperation examination must be made available to the applicant.*

F. *An auditor-witness, independent of the medical facility, and chosen by the applicant, must be present for the entire counseling and consent process. This provision may be waived by the applicant by a written statement on the consent form. Spousal consent is not necessary, but a spouse's participation in the process of securing informed consent should be encouraged. A spouse may act as an auditor-witness.*

G. *No person under the influence of any anesthetic, hypnotic, narcotic, tranquilizing or mood altering substance (unless the person is a chronic user of such substance, the withdrawal of which would be seriously detrimental to his or her health) shall be solicited for a nontherapeutic sterilization.*

H. *Consent for a nontherapeutic sterilization shall not be solicited from any person undergoing the labor of pregnancy. Nor shall consent be solicited for a period less than 30 days following delivery, an abortion, or any other postpartum surgery.*

I. *A copy of the consent document shall be provided to the patient who signs it.*

J. *To qualify for federal assistance, each state department of health must disseminate copies of the regulations, and prototype copies of the illustrated booklet and audio-visual material, to all licensed physicians within its jurisdiction.*

---

203.   262 U.S. at 401.   *See also* Note, *El Derecho de Aviso: Due Process and Bilingual Notice*, 83 YALE L.J. 385 (1973).   F. Terry v. Alabama, 21 Ala. App. 100, 105 So. 386 (1925) (deaf mute).

K.   *Copies of the regulations shall be posted in all health agencies performing sterilizations and shall be made available to all patients or potential patients upon request.   All of the facility's personnel, including medical and support staff, shall be made aware of the contents of the regulations.*

L.   *California's Department of Health shall commence and maintain all necessary actions and proceedings to enforce the regulations in accordance with Section 205 of the Health and Safety Code. Penalties for violations shall include, but not be limited to, those provided for in Sections 1290[204] and 1293,[205] and 1294[206] of the Health and Safety Code.   Similar sanctions must be established by all of the states.*

VIII.   CONCLUSION

For Chicanas, the crucial issue is the assurance that their right to procreate is respected and safeguarded.   The current extent of governmental funding and direction over family planning agencies, absent adequate safeguards, has enabled medical personnel to violate this basic right in too many cases.   Even in cases currently covered by regulations abuses have taken place because the doctor-patient relationship has not been closely monitored.   Enforcement of the regulations must be more strictly compelled.   Under the existing structural relationship between the medical profession and government, which permits doctors to enjoy a large amount of autonomy, the most prominent instrument to compel the enforcement of the existing regulations is legal action by patients aggrieved by practitioner abuses.   Respect for the right to procreate on the part of doctors and medical staffs is more adequately

---

204.   Section 1290 of the HEALTH AND SAFETY CODE reads as follows: Any person who violates any of the provisions of this chapter or who willfully or repeatedly violates any rule or regulation promulgated under this chapter is guilty of a misdemeanor and upon conviction thereof shall be punished by a fine not to exceed five hundred dollars($500) or by imprisonment in the county jail for a period not to exceed 180 days or by both such fine and imprisonment.

205.   Section 1293 of the HEALTH AND SAFETY CODE reads as follows: The district attorney of every county shall, upon application by the state department or its authorized representative, institute and conduct the prosecution of any action for violation within his county of any provisions of this chapter.

206.   Section 1294 of the HEALTH AND SAFETY CODE reads as follows: The state department may suspend or revoke any license or special permit issued under the provisions of this chapter upon any of the following grounds and in the manner provided in this chapter:

(a)   Violation by the licensee or holder of a special permit of any of the provisions of this chapter or of the rules and regulations promulgated under this chapter.

(b)   Aiding, abetting, or permitting the violation of any provision of this chapter or of the rules and regulations promulgated under this chapter.

(c)   Conduct inimical to the public health, morals, welfare, or safety of the people of the State of California in the maintenance and operation of the premises or services for which a license or special permit is issued.

ensured when they must pay substantial monetary damages for the harm they perpetrate.

The emphasis on enforcement, however, does not understate the necessity of regulatory reform. In order to correct the existing deficiencies, the regulations must be reformed to effectively provide stricter adherence to the standards of procedural due process. One major way to satisfy this constitutional requirement is to mandate that oral counseling and written consent forms be provided in Spanish. This would make it possible for medical personnel to meet the standards of *Canterbury v. Spence.*[207] In *Canterbury*, the right of the patient to expect, and the duty of the physician to impart, information concerning the details of the therapy was established.[208] The existing regulations were intended to accomplish this end, but they have not been efficiently enforced, and, in many instances, have proved inadequate. In response to similar situations, courts have long held that a right can be infringed not only by unconstitutional laws but also by the unconstitutional actions of public officials.[209] Such is the case under the current regulations governing sterilization surgery.

There is a difference between an inconvenience and a constructive denial of the right to undergo sterilization surgery. The harm experienced by Chicanas and other poor women require greater controls on the doctor-patient relationship within this context. The amount of time needed to make an informed decision is already available to the better educated middle class woman. Sterilization in her situation is usually the result of extensive consultation with a private physician, and an even longer period of discussion with the male spouse. It may inconvenience some women to read a consent form written at a sixth grade comprehension level, or view an audio-visual presentation, but when compared to the threat of involuntary sterilization, inconvenience must give way to considerations of health, safety, and the fundamental right to procreate. Middle class women who have striven to acquire greater control over their own bodies should not view the inconvenience of stricter regulations as an obstacle to this end, especially when such an inconvenience is necessary to safeguard the physical and psychological well being of their less fortunate sisters. Judge Gesell expressed the necessity for this position quite precisely in *Relf*: "Under these circumstances it is well established that one does not have to forfeit fundamental rights before he or she may com-

---

207.　464 F.2d 772 (D. Col. 1972).
208.　*Id.* at 782. This included the goals to be expected and the risks involved.
209.　*See* Goldberg v. Kelly, 397 U.S. 254 (1970) (due process), Yick Wo v. Hopkins, 188 U.S. 356 (1886) (equal protection).

plain, so long as the threat is real and immediate, as it is here."[210] To undermine this threat, and to protect the rights of Chicanas, the recommendations submitted herein need to be adopted and enforced.

---

210.   372 F. Supp. at 1201.

Privacy and the Regulation of the New Reproductive Technologies: A Decision-Making Approach*

ANTOINETTE SEDILLO LOPEZ†

I. Introduction

Today scientists are able to harvest eggs from women,[1] fertilize them *in vitro*[2] with sperm which has been separated so that it contains con-

*Copyright © 1988 Antoinette Sedillo Lopez. All rights reserved.

Author's Note: Footnotes that contain medical citations deviate from standard *Blue Book* form by including first initials of authors. This will facilitate research in this area.
†Ms. Sedillo Lopez, J.D. UCLA 1982, is an assistant professor of law at the University of New Mexico School of Law. She gratefully acknowledges the contributions of Professors Richard Delgado, Robert Schwartz and Lee Teitelbaum. She also thanks Dean Parnall for his support—personal, professional, and in the form of a summer research grant.

1. *See* L. Mettler, M. Seki, V. Baukloh & K. Seem, *Human Ovum Recovery via Operative Laparoscopy and In Vitro Fertilization*, 38 Fert. & Steril. 30 (1982) (describes use of laparoscopy, which involves cutting through abdominal muscles and examining the interior with a special scope to recover oocytes for use in *in vitro* fertilization (IVF)); S. Lenze & J. Lauritsen, *Ultrasonically-Guided Percutaneous Aspiration of Human Follicles under Local Anesthesia: A New Method of Collecting Oocytes for In Vitro Fertilization*, 38 Fert. & Steril. 673 (1982) (describes use of needle guided by ultrasound through abdomen to collect oocytes for *in vitro* fertilization. This method is less expensive and less traumatic than laparoscopy. It is usually called the "transvesical method"); M. Wikland, L. Nilsson, R. Hansson, L. Hamberger & P. Janson, *Collection of Human Oocytes by the Use of Sonography*, 39 Fert. & Steril. 603 (1983) (describes further developments in the transvesical method introduced by Lenz and Lauritsen); N. Gleicher, J. Friberg, N. Fullan, R. V. Giglia, K. Mayden, T. Kesky & I. Siegel, *Egg Retrieval for In Vitro Fertilization by Sonographically Controlled Vaginal Culdocentesis*, 2 Lancet 508 (July–Sept. 1983) (describes use of needle guided through vagina by ultrasound to collect oocytes for IVF; this is usually called the "transvaginal method"); M. Wikland, L. Enk & L. Hamberger, *Transvesical and Transvaginal Approaches for the Aspiration of Follicles by Use of Ultrasound in In Vitro Fertilization and Embryo*

centrations of male or female chromosomes,[3] and implant the embryo[4] in a surrogate (a woman who will carry the embryo to term).[5] Scientists can discover information about the sex, gene structure, and some diseases of the resulting conceptus. Based on this information, a decision to terminate the pregnancy can be made.[6] Future advances in technology[7]

Transfer, 442 ANNALS N.Y. ACAD. SCI. 182 (M. Seppala & R. G. Edwards eds. 1985) (discusses transvesical and transvaginal methods and compares them to other methods).

2. *See generally* HUMAN CONCEPTION IN VITRO (R. G. Edwards & J. M. Purdy eds. 1982); *In Vitro Fertilization and Embryo Transfer,* 442 ANNALS N.Y. ACAD. SCI. (M. Seppalla & R. G. Edwards eds. 1985); L. ANDREWS, NEW CONCEPTIONS: A CONSUMER'S GUIDE TO THE NEWEST INFERTILITY TREATMENTS INCLUDING IN VITRO FERTILIZATION, ARTIFICIAL INSEMINATION AND SURROGATE MOTHERHOOD (1984).

3. Sex is determined at the time of fertilization in humans. A man's sperm contains either an X chromosome or a Y chromosome. A woman's egg contains only X chromosomes. A sperm with a Y chromosome creates a male (XY) offspring. A female offspring is created when the sperm fertilizing the egg contains an X chromosome (XX). Researchers have separated X and Y chromosomes by chemical treatment and centrifugation. The X and Y chromosomes are of slightly different weights. When sperm is centrifuged in a density gradient, the heavier sperm settle to the thicker and lower layers of the density gradient. If such separated sperm are used to fertilize the egg, presumably the chances of conceiving a child of the desired sex is increased. A process which concentrates Y sperm to approximately 70 percent of the specimen was first used for cattle breeding. W. L. G. Quinlivan, K. Preciado, T. L. Long & H. Sullivan, *Separation of Human X and Y Spermatozoa by Albumin Gradients and Sephadex Chromotography,* 37 FERT. & STERIL. 104 (1982). The technique is now used in at least seven United States clinics and is advertised for sex selection and for male infertility. *See generally* A. CLASS & R. CRUCCAAN, GETTING PREGNANT IN THE 1980's: NEW ADVANCES IN INFERTILITY TREATMENT AND SEX SELECTION (1982).

4. Scientists can discover such things as sex, gene structure, disease, etc., about the potential offspring by analyzing the fertilized egg at the blastocyst stage of development. *See generally* BIOLOGY OF THE BLASTOCYST (R. J. Blandeau ed. 1971).

5. *E.g.,* J. D. Biggers, *In Vitro Fertilization and Embryo Transfer In Human Beings,* 304 NEW ENG. J. MED. 336 (1981).

6. *See* Note, *Sex Selection Abortion: A Constitutional Analysis of the Abortion Liberty and a Person's Right to Know,* 56 IND. L.J. 281 (1981).

7. Over the past twenty years procreation or biological reproduction has become subject to increasingly intrusive medical technological intervention. *See generally* Wertz, *What Birth Has Done for Doctors: A Historical View,* 8 WOMEN & HEALTH 7 (1983). For example, medical technology has made possible a wide range of alternative forms of conception, including artificial insemination. Wadlington, *Artificial Conception: The Challenge for Family Law,* 69 VA. L. REV. 465, 468 (1983); *in vitro* fertilization, *see* note 2 *supra;* surrogate gestation, *see* KEANE & BREO, THE SURROGATE MOTHER (1981); Handel, *Surrogate Parenting, In Vitro Insemination and Embryo Transplantation,* 6 WHITTIER L. REV. 783 (1984); and perhaps, in the future, cloning, *see* Watson, *Moving Toward the Clonal Man,* 227 ATL. MONTHLY 50 (1971).

Other types of techniques connected with the new reproductive technology include *in utero* fetal therapy. *See* Robertson, *The Right to Procreate and In Utero Fetal Therapy,* 3 J. LEGAL MED.—CHI. 333–66 (1982); fetal destruction, *see, e.g.,* Kerenyi & Chitkara, *Selective Birth in Twin Pregnancy with Discordancy for Down's Syndrome,* 304 NEW ENG. J. MED. 1525 (1981) (the doctors examined the twin fetuses and chose to abort the one with Down's Syndrome; the other remained in the womb to term); and fetal experimentation, *cf.* R. G. Edwards, *Fertilization of Human Eggs In Vitro: Morals, Ethics and the Law,* 49 Q. REV. BIOLOGY 11, 13–14 (1974). Another technique is embryo-freezing; *see* A. Trounson & L. Mohr, *Human Pregnancy following Cryopreservation, Thawing and Transfer of an Eight-cell Embryo,* 305 NATURE 707 (1983) (describes embryo freezing procedures). A review of the different techniques available by the development may bring the possibility of manipulating the egg,[8] sperm, embryo, or fetus to alter characteristics of potential offspring even more dramatically.[9]

A number of critical issues must be confronted in society's decision to enter the brave new world of the new reproductive technology.[10] The legal system, society's traditional mechanism for enforcing values and priorities,[11] will inevitably be called upon to grapple with the difficult issues which use of the new reproductive technology[12] will raise.[13] Policymakers and lawmakers presently have two alternatives. One is to wait and decide whether to regulate each potential use of the new

---

of the new reproductive technology reveals that they can be categorized as follows: (1) those which are used as therapy for infertility; (2) those which require the participation of third parties; and (3) those involving manipulation of potential offspring. Each of these uses raises different concerns.

8. Research in manipulating eggs has been conducted in mice. R. D. Palmiter, G. Norstedt, R. E. Gelinas, R. E. Hammer & R. L. Brinster, *Methaliothionein-Human GH-Fusion Genes Stimulate Growth of Mice*, 222 SCIENCE 809–14 (1983) (reported results of a study in which mouse genes and human genes were fused and then injected into fertilized mouse eggs. Mice which incorporated the genes (transgenic mice) grew larger than control mice). *See also* R. H. Lovell-Badge, *Transgenic Animals: New Advances in the Field*, 315 NATURE 628 (1985) (review of research on gene manipulation in animals); R. D. Palmiter & R. L. Brinster, *Transgenic Mice*, 41 CELL 343 (1985) (review of research involving gene manipulation in animals); R. L. Brinster & R. D. Palmiter, *Introduction of Genes into the Germ Line of Animals*, 80 HARVEY LECTURES 1 (1984–85); and W. F. Anderson, *Prospects for Human Gene Therapy*, 226 SCIENCE 401 (1984) (discusses applying research in gene manipulation to humans).

9. Gene manipulation in animals has already been used for commercial purposes. *See* J. J. Rutledge, G. E. Siedel, *Genetic Engineering and Animal Production*, 57 J. ANIMAL SCI. 265 (Supp. 2 1983). And the new reproductive technology has been applied to manipulative uses in the context of selective abortions and genetic screening. *See supra* note 7, *infra* notes 108–24, and accompanying text.

10. For a discussion of some of these issues, *see, e.g.*, ETHICS ADVISORY BOARD, U.S. DEPT. OF HEALTH, EDUCATION, & WELFARE, HEW SUPPORT OF RESEARCH INVOLVING HUMAN IN VITRO FERTILIZATION AND EMBRYO TRANSFER (1979); R. G. Edwards, *Fertilization of Human Eggs In Vitro: Morals, Ethics, and the Law*, 49 Q. REV. BIOLOGY 3 (1974).

11. *See* Teitelbaum, *Family History and Family Law*, 1985 WIS. L. REV. 1135 (1985). Professor Teitelbaum discusses the history of governmental intervention in the family and demonstrates that governments and courts assumed substantial roles in childrearing, education, regulation of marriage, child custody, and spousal support during the nineteenth and early twentieth centuries.

12. This article uses the term reproductive technology to refer to any medical procedures which are used in childbirth. The *new* reproductive technology refers to medical procedures developed after the late 1970s which manipulate the process of childbirth so that children who would otherwise not be born are born, or that characteristics of those children who would be born are altered.

13. There are proposed statutes concerning surrogate motherhood reprinted in 1982–85 HUM. REPRODUCTION & L. REP. (Legal Medical Studies) R71–109 (1984). This is an example of commentators preparing for the legal problems raised by this particular method of utilizing the reproductive technology. *See* Note, *Surrogate Motherhood: Contractual Issues and Remedies under Legislative Proposals*, 23 WASHBURN L.J. 601 (1984), for an overview of legal issues and proposed solutions to the problems raised by the practice of surrogate motherhood.

reproductive technology as it becomes available and as problems arise with its use. The other option is to anticipate potential developments and to formulate policies and laws that will guide researchers and medical professionals in their pursuits. For example, the government might prohibit procreative techniques that threaten the future gender and genetic composition of society.[14]

This article maps out the territory that must be explored in this very complex area and analyzes the implications of governmental regulation of the new reproductive technology.[15] It suggests that the central issue for analysis is the extent to which authority to make decisions concerning reproductive potential should be allocated to individuals rather than to the government. The article describes approaches to allocating decision-making authority with respect to procreative issues. The first is a rights-based approach which emphasizes individual autonomy; this approach will not permit governmental regulation which interferes with personal autonomy in decision making, at least without good reason. The second approach accepts regulation which impinges on individual decision making for the public good.

The traditional two-tier substantive due process analysis incorporates both models by categorizing and balancing.[16] This approach strengthens the perception that private and public spheres of human existence should be kept separate on the basis that the public sphere (i.e., work and politics) may be regulated, while the private sphere (i.e., home and family) is somehow beyond regulation. This idea has historically oppressed women by justifying their exclusion from the public sphere; its effect has been to perpetuate and legitimate a power imbalance in the private sphere. However, in the area of reproduction,

---

14. Presently the only use of reproductive technology which is regulated to some extent is the use of artificial insemination. *See* UNIF. PARENTAGE ACT § 5, 9 U.L.A. 593 (1980).

15. There is a tension in this article between advocating a new analysis and maintaining that the Court has already laid the groundwork for this analytical framework; the article thus predicts future analysis. In this article, I demonstrate that allocating decision-making authority and considering autonomy and societal benefit is something that the Court has already done in the area of substantive due process. However, the Court has not analyzed any questions concerning the new reproductive technology and has not set out a framework for considering procreational privacy questions in the way this article does. Professor Karst identified this tension as existing in most writing that addresses emerging legal doctrines. Karst, *The Freedom of Intimate Association*, 89 YALE L.J. 624, 626 (1980).

16. To illustrate, the first step in the traditional analysis is to consider whether regulation impinges on a fundamental right. This entails determining what rights are fundamental. The Court has held privacy to be such a right, but it has not yet decided whether it extends to decisions to use the various medical techniques available in aid of procreation. If the Court determines that a fundamental right is implicated, the Court looks to the state interests in the regulation to determine whether they are substantial. If so, the Court determines whether the regulation is the only practical means of furthering those interests.

the rights-based notion of individual autonomy has empowered women. The article concludes that the problems associated with separate spheres can be minimized if the analysis focuses precisely on the application of the new reproductive technology and on the impact of individual autonomy on women and society.

This article maintains that that which is implicit in privacy analysis must become explicit. We must look closely at individual decisions to use procreative technology to see whether they implicate autonomy so strongly as to be deemed fundamental. After examining the effect of the regulation on autonomy in decision making, courts should examine the potential effect of decisions to use technology on others. Whenever possible, the courts should seek a solution that maximizes autonomy and concurrently prevents harm to others.

Three applications of the new reproductive technology will be analyzed: (1) treatment for infertility, (2) multiple-parent procreation, and (3) reproductive manipulation. After describing the medical technology available in each category, arguments for and against regulation are evaluated in light of their implications for autonomy and society. The article concludes that individuals should be free to choose the new reproductive technology as treatment for infertility unhindered by state interference; oversight and recordkeeping regulation adequately addresses societal needs in this instance. States should have the power to regulate multiple-parent procreation in order to protect innocent children and potential surrogates. Finally, manipulation of the reproductive process should be regulated only to the extent necessary to protect autonomy, prevent private gender discrimination, prevent the skewing of the gender and genetic pool, and prevent any one person or entity from controlling and upsetting the genetic development of future generations.

II. Decision Making

A principle issue in cases involving reproductive decisions is the allocation of decisional authority. For example, the crucial question in abortion cases is not whether an abortion will be performed, but whether, under the circumstances, the power to make that decision resides in the state or in the individual.[17] The state may be regarded as a decision

_____

17. That is, for example, in the case involving the decision to obtain an abortion, the court is not necessarily deciding whether an abortion will be performed but is deciding whether the power to decide whether an abortion will be performed will reside in the state or the pregnant woman. *See* Tribe, *Forward: Toward a Model of Roles in the Due Process of Life and Law*, 87 HARV. L. REV. 1, 11 (1973). Sometimes the parental autonomy notion collides with the individual right to privacy, for example in those cases invalidating statutes requiring parental consent for minor child's abortion. *See* Belotti v. Baird, 443 U.S. 622 (1979). *See also* Planned Parenthood v. Danforth, 428 U.S. 52 (1976) (invalidating a statute requiring the husband's consent to an abortion).

maker to the extent that regulation of access to the new reproductive techniques, as well as the use thereof, effectively limits individual choice.

The range of governmental regulation can be placed on a continuum. At one extreme, regulation in the form of prohibition may completely preempt individual decision making; a law prohibiting surrogate mother contracts would be such a regulation. An absolute ban obviously removes the freedom of individuals to choose to hire a woman to bear a child. It would also affect the surrogate's freedom to choose to bear a child and to choose to terminate her parental rights.

At the other extreme, the state might resolve not to regulate, thereby leaving individuals free to make their own decisions. Between these two extremes on the continuum falls regulation which limits, but does not wholly curtail, individual decision making. An example of such regulation is regulation which requires some form of minimum protection for the surrogate (perhaps including a minimum wage) and psychological evaluations of all parties to the surrogacy contract. Thus, the courts must consider the question of how to allocate decision-making authority and the extent to which autonomy may be affected by such regulation.[18]

A. *Approaches to Allocating Decision-Making Authority*

One approach to allocating decision-making authority is a rights-based autonomy theory.[19] This view supports individual choice as the primary value which is protected by a zone of noninterference.[20] The rights

---

18. Although these concepts have been analyzed as a question of market alienability or inalienability in a market-based approach to the allocation of resources, the primary concern in the marketplace is whether buyers and sellers can make unimpeded decisions in the marketplace or whether their ability to make decisions in the market will be impeded by other factors—in this case regulation. *See* Radin, *Market Inalienability*, 100 HARV. L. REV. 1849 (1987). In this article, Professor Radin provides a theory which fills the gap between an economic view that views all things as freely exchangeable on an open market and a view that rejects markets entirely. She describes how the liberal view is pushed toward the economic view. She explores and finally rejects attempts based on economic analysis and liberal philosophical doctrines to justify particular distinctions between things that are and things that are not appropriately bought and sold in open markets. She proposes a pragmatic approach to market inalienability which relates to an ideal of human flourishing. She addresses the issue of full and partial commodification of sexuality and reproductive capacity and concludes that to the extent that we must not assimilate our conception of personhood to the market, prohibitions in trading certain aspects of personhood are justified.

19. Johnstone, *The Right to Privacy: The Ethical Perspective*, 29 AM. J. JURIS. 73, 81 (1984).

20. Professor Teitelbaum describes this idea: "Rights theory, however, usually supposes a 'space' around the individual." He goes on to state that this "space" has a special claim not well accounted for in utilitarian approaches and which seems reflected in cases and commentary that emphasize family autonomy and family privacy. Teitelbaum, *Moral Discourse and Family Law*, 84 MICH. L. REV. 430 (1985).

stem from traditional liberal concepts[21] which give priority to the individual and resist intrusions by the state.[22]

A contrasting view assigns priority to the common good, which requires determining the impact of particular rules or decisions on society in general.[23] Cases which subordinate individual interests in autonomous decision making to the good of society reflect this value.[24] Both individual and societal concerns are at stake in the controversy over reproductive technology.[25]

A problem with the rights-based approach is that it strengthens the conceptual distinction between the private and the public spheres of human existence. The private sphere of the home and family (the woman's domain) is considered to be somehow beyond regulation, whereas the public sphere of work and politics (the man's domain) is properly regulated.[26] This distinction is problematic on several grounds. First, it may not be defensible on closer examination.[27] Moreover, it has historically served in our legal system to justify barring women from participating in the world outside the private sphere.[28] At the same

---

21. *See. e.g.,* Kuflik, *The Inalienability of Autonomy,* 13 PHIL. & PUB. AFF. 271, 296–98 (1984).

22. This concept has also been described as "negative" liberty. *See* I. BERLIN, *Two Concepts of Liberty,* in ON LIBERTY 122 (1969). Using this analysis, decision-making authority should reside in the individual. This rights-based autonomy ideal presumes autonomous moral agency—it assumes that individuals are equal in having subjective will. *See, e.g.,* Kuflik, *The Inalienability of Autonomy,* 13 PHIL. & PUB. AFF. 271, 296–98 (1984).

23. I. BERLIN, ON LIBERTY (1969).

24. *See* notes 47–48 and accompanying text.

25. On the one hand, a rights-based approach might maintain that the government should not intrude and that individuals should make decisions concerning their reproductive potential without interference from the government. Johnstone, *The Right to Privacy: The Ethical Perspective,* 29 AM. J. JURIS. 73, 81 (1984). Autonomy would be the dominant value. Utilitarian notions would more readily accept state regulation if it appeared that society's goals would be furthered by such regulation. *See generally* I. BERLIN, ON LIBERTY (1969).

The rights-based autonomy approach to decision making poses problems for those who believe that as a society we should prohibit some decisions which could pose harm to self, others, and/or to society. Mill, *On Liberty,* in THE CASE AGAINST MILL 126 (1975); J. FEINBERG, HARM TO SELF 75–79 (1986); Taylor, *What's Wrong with Negative Liberty,* in THE IDEA OF FREEDOM 175 (A. Ryan ed. 1979); R. NOZICK, ANARCHY, STATE AND UTOPIA 331 (1974) (a free system would allow an individual to sell himself into slavery).

Conversely, utilitarianism is criticized as an infringement on freedom. Regan, *Paternalism, Freedom, Identity and Commitment,* in PATERNALISM 113–17 (R. Sartorius ed. 1983). The next section will demonstrate that traditional constitutional analysis incorporates elements of both autonomy and of utilitarianism.

26. This notion became popular when industry effectively took production outside of the home and into the factory. *See generally* A. OAKELY, WOMEN'S WORK (1974).

27. Olsen, *The Myth of State Intervention in the Family,* 18 U. MICH. J.L. REFORM 835 (1985); Teitelbaum, *Family History and Family Law,* 1985 WIS. L. REV. 1135.

28. Bradwell v. State, 83 U.S. 130 (1872).

time, it has fostered an unequal power balance within the family unit by deferring to the privacy of the family and declining to intervene.[29]

Yet, the treatment of birth control decisions and abortion decisions as beyond the scope of regulation has given women more control over their own reproduction, and thus has empowered them in this aspect of their lives. Although some have argued that privacy decisions primarily served men's needs and only incidentally served women's interests,[30] a central aspect of power is control. The ability to control their reproduction has given women the opportunity to achieve additional gains in the workplace and in the political realm. Despite the risk of strengthening a harmful distinction, advocacy for the protection of women's choices does not pose the problems the distinction raises.

This article focuses on a central aspect of empowerment, i.e., the ability to choose. The authority to make decisions normally gives the decision maker control. The elimination of decision-making authority from a woman disempowers her. Important concerns are raised when one permits individual autonomy and declines to intervene, which creates a potential negative effect on women.

B. *Reproductive Choice in the Liberal Tradition*

The privacy cases seem to demonstrate the U.S. Supreme Court's special concern with autonomy as opposed to the needs of the state. Throughout the last century, the Court has protected autonomy in private family decision making at the expense of state interests.[31] The Court has found that some types of reproductive decisions fall within the zone of privacy; these decisions should be protected by the U.S. Constitution as fundamental rights.[32] For example, the decision to use

---

29. McGuire v. McGuire, 157 Neb. 226, 59 N.W.2d 336 (1953) (the court refused to order spousal support in an ongoing marriage). This is peculiarly a problem with treating the "family" as an entity with its own autonomy claims.

30. *See* A. Dworkin, Right-Wing Women 104–105 (1982).

31. In *Pierce v. Society of Sisters*, 268 U.S. 510 (1925), the Court considered an action brought to challenge the constitutionality of an Oregon statute requiring children to attend public schools. The Supreme Court affirmed a lower court ruling that the statute deprived the private schools of property and the parents of liberty without due process. *Id.* at 534–35. The Court stated that "the Act of 1922 unreasonably interferes with the liberty of parents and guardians to direct the upbringing and education of children under their control." *Id.* at 534–35.

Meyer v. State, 262 U.S. 390 (1923), concerned the constitutionality of a statute which prohibited the teaching of foreign languages to a child who had not finished the eighth grade. The Supreme Court held that parents have the right to decide how the child will be reared and taught.

See also Moore v. City of East Cleveland, 431 U.S. 494 (1977). The court stated: "This Court has long recognized that freedom of personal choice in matters of marriage and family life is one of the liberties protected by the Due Process Clause of the Fourteenth Amendment." *Id.* at 499 (quoting Cleveland Board of Education v. LaFleur, 414 U.S. 632, 639–40 (1974)).

32. Roe v. Wade, 410 U.S. 113, 152 (1973) ("only personal rights that can be deemed fundamental . . . are included in this guarantee of personal privacy"); Skinner v. Oklahoma, 316 U.S. 535, 541 (1942) (procreation is a fundamental right).

contraceptives[33] and a woman's decision to obtain a first trimester
abortion[34] have been protected from state regulation.[35]

The traditional two-tier method of constitutional analysis[36] used to
decide privacy issues does not currently offer much guidance in addressing issues raised by the new reproductive technology. With respect

---

33. In *Griswold v. Connecticut*, 381 U.S. 479 (1965), the Supreme Court struck down
a Connecticut statute prohibiting the use of contraceptives and abetting of the use of
contraceptives. The Court distinguished this regulation from economic regulation and
found that this law "operates directly on an intimate relation of husband and wife and
their physician's role in one aspect of that relation." *Id.* at 482. Thus, the Court declined
to defer to the legislative wisdom in the *Lochner v. New York*, 198 U.S. 45 (1905),
tradition. Justice Douglas, writing the majority opinion, reviewed the Bill of Rights and
determined that they describe a protection against governmental invasions "of the sanc-
tity of a man's home and the privacies of life." *Griswold* at 484 (quoting Boyd v. United
States, 116 U.S. 616, 630 (1886)).

The Court said that regulating the use of contraceptives seeks to achieve the goals
(without stating what the goals of the legislation were) by means having a maximum
destructive impact upon a relationship lying within the zone of privacy created by several
fundamental guarantees found in the First, Third, Fourth, Fifth and Ninth Amendments.
Thus, for the first time, the Court viewed a group of amendments as fashioning a zone
of privacy upon which the state could not intrude. *Griswold* at 484.

In *Eisenstadt v. Baird*, 405 U.S. 438 (1972), the Court reaffirmed the right to privacy
and extended it to protect unmarried individuals. The Court considered the conviction
of Baird under a Massachusetts statute prohibiting the giving of contraceptives to unmarried persons. The Court overturned the conviction on equal protection grounds using
very broad language: "If the right of privacy means anything, it is the right of the
individual, married or single, to be free from unwarranted governmental intrusion into
matters so fundamentally affecting a person as the decision whether to bear or beget a
child." *Id.* at 453 (emphasis in original).

34. The landmark case, *Roe v. Wade*, 410 U.S. 113 (1973), seemed to extend the right
to privacy, holding that the right was "broad enough to encompass a woman's decision
whether or not to terminate her pregnancy." *Id.* at 153. The Court assumed that a woman
has a fundamental right of privacy and balanced this privacy right with the state interests
in protecting potential human life and in protecting the mother's health. *Id.* at 150. The
Court struck the balance by concluding that the woman's privacy interests were para-
mount in the first trimester, and the decision whether to abort could not be interfered
with by the state. However, the state's interests became more compelling as the pregnancy progressed. Thus, reasonable regulation to protect the mother's health was permissible in the second trimester and regulation to protect the fetus would be permissible
after viability. *Id.* at 63. Later in the opinion, however, the Court stated: "it is not clear
to us that the claim asserted by some amici that one has an unlimited right to do with
one's body as one pleases bears a close relationship to the right of privacy previously
articulated in the Court's decisions." *Id.* at 154. The Court may have been presaging
issues concerning homosexuality. See Bowers v. Hardwick, 478 U.S. 186, 106 S. Ct.
2841 (1986).

35. Even before the landmark cases of *Griswold* and *Roe*, Justice Douglas had found
procreation to be a fundamental right. In *Skinner v. Oklahoma*, 316 U.S. 535 (1942), he
wrote for the majority: "We are dealing here with legislation which involves one of the
basic civil rights of man. Marriage and procreation are fundamental to the very existence
and survival of the race. The power to sterilize, if exercised, may have subtle, far-
reaching and devastating effects. . . ." *Id.* at 541. *See infra* note 36 for a discussion of
Skinner.

36. Using the current constitutional analytical framework, it is important to determine
whether the decision to use the new reproductive techniques is encompassed by the
right to privacy and, thus, is a fundamental right. The Court has considered procreation
as a right only twice.

In 1927, the Court in *Buck v. Bell*, 274 U.S. 200 (1927), considered a case involving
Carrie Buck, a woman committed to a mental institution. The Court considered the

to whether the use of the new reproductive technology can be characterized as fundamental, the Court's categorization of activities as fundamental does not have a coherent conceptual framework; consequently, the nature of the right to privacy is unclear in important aspects.[37]

The usual argument made in favor of protecting an individual's right to use the new reproductive technology can be stated simply: a state's attempt to curtail an individual's quest for a child violates that individual's right to procreative autonomy.[38] If the Constitution protects

---

interests of society and compared sterilization to compulsory vaccination and decided that the interests of society should prevail. The Court thus denied her due process and equal protection challenges. The Supreme Court stated: "it is better for all the world, if instead of waiting to execute degenerate offspring for crime, or to let them starve for their imbecility, society can prevent those who are manifestly unfit from continuing their kind. The principle that sustains compulsory vaccination is broad enough to cover cutting the Fallopian tubes." *Id.* at 207.

Without overturning *Buck v. Bell,* the Court reached a different result in *Skinner v. Oklahoma,* 316 U.S. 535 (1942). Mr. Skinner was convicted of three felonies, and the state instituted proceedings under statutory authority to have him sterilized. The statute provided for sterilization of habitual criminals, who were convicted two or more times of certain felonies. The Court struck down the statute on equal protection grounds because the statute did not treat all felons equally. Although the Court looked to the disparate treatment in deciding the case on equal protection grounds, it stated: "We are dealing here with legislation which involves one of the basic civil rights of man. Marriage and procreation are fundamental to the very existence and survival of the race." *Id.* at 541. Thus, while not basing its decision on a right to procreate, the Court alluded to such a right.

The Court's traditional two-tier substantive due process analysis first requires courts to consider whether the prohibition burdens a fundamental right. Roe v. Wade, 410 U.S. 113, 153 (1973). If not burdening a fundamental right, the state action justifying the regulation will not be rigorously reviewed but will be upheld if it is reasonably related to some legitimate state interest; *see, e.g.,* San Antonio Indep. School Dist. v. Rodriguez, 411 U.S. 1 (1973) (education is not a fundamental right, thus traditional standard of review, which requires only that the state's system be shown to bear some rational relationship to legitimate state purposes, will be applied to a state's funding scheme). If the right implicated is found to be fundamental, the challenged state action will only be upheld if, upon a balancing of the various interests, the regulation is necessary to further a compelling state interest. Zablocki v. Redhail, 434 U.S. 374 (1978). *See also* Kramer v. Union Free School Dist., 395 U.S. 621, 627 (1969). Because the burden of justification is so high, most challenged legislation fails when it infringes on the exercise of a fundamental right. Thus, the Court's traditional analysis makes a broad distinction between fundamental rights and other rights; it generally permits individuals to exercise fundamental rights without government interference, unless the government has some compelling interest to further and tailors its legislation narrowly. Using the Court's analysis, the matter is set up as a conflict between the rights and interests of the individual in decision making and the needs and interests of the state in interfering with those decisions.

37. For example, the right to choose to abort a pregnancy is within the right to privacy; *see* Roe v. Wade, 410 U.S. 113 (1973). The right to choose sexual practice is not; *see* Bowers v. Hardwick, 478 U.S. 186 (1986). For a proposal that would explain the concept of privacy as a right to intimate association, *see* Karst, *The Freedom of Intimate Association,* 89 Yale L.J. 624 (1980).

38. Doe v. Kelley, 106 Mich. App. 169, 307 N.W.2d 438 (1981), *cert. denied,* 459 U.S. 1183 (1983) (Doe contended that baby broker statutes prohibiting the exchange of money or other valuable consideration infringes the constitutional right of privacy). *See also,*

the decision not to procreate, it must protect the decision to procreate even if the means for such procreation are unusual.[39] Although the argument is plausible, the Court has yet to determine the argument's validity. Does the privacy right shield all forms of procreation,[40] including those requiring extraordinary medical technology?

A lower court, in striking down a Florida statute requiring parental and spousal consent to abortion, found that the concept of privacy protects the potential to procreate but not the opportunity to do so.[41] In this case, the husband argued that a spousal consent requirement protected the spouse's privacy right to procreation (as established in *Skinner*), since the fetus being aborted was his. The court responded to this argument:

> Although *Skinner* protected the individual's procreative rights, in practical terms these rights cannot be exercised alone. Hence, even without state interference, the right becomes meaningless in the absence of a willing partner. *Skinner*, therefore, did not guarantee the individual a procreative opportunity; it merely safeguarded his procreative potential from state infringement.[42]

This court's interpretation weakens the claim that the right to procreation protects decisions to use artificial forms of conception and gestation, since the potential to procreate and not the opportunity to procreate is protected. On the other hand, in the case of an individual who can have children only through artificial means, denial of those means affects his or her potential to procreate.

One justification for treating reproductive decisions as within the zone of privacy is that it would be almost impossible to enforce laws which interfere with these decisions because they are made in the privacy of the home.[43] But the Supreme Court's recent decision up-

---

e.g., Handel, *Surrogate Parenting, In Vitro Insemination and Embryo Transplantation*, 6 WHITTIER L. REV. 783, 788 (1984); Robertson, *Procreative Liberty and the Control of Conception, Pregnancy and Childbirth*, 69 VA. L. REV. 405, 414–20 (1983).

39. *See* sources cited *supra* note 38.

40. In Carey v. Population Services Int'l, 431 U.S. 678 (1977), the Court considered a challenge to the constitutionality of a New York statute which prohibited the sale of contraceptives to minors. *Id.* at 681. The Court struck down the statute, noting that the outer limits of the privacy right had not been marked, but that it included personal decisions concerning marriage, procreation, contraception, family relationships and childrearing and education. *Id.* at 684–85. The Court stated: "The decision whether or not to beget or bear a child is at the very heart of this cluster of constitutionally protected choices." Thus, the Court appeared to extend the right of privacy to include procreation. *See also* Paris Adult Theatre I v. Slaton, 413 U.S. 49, 65 (1973) ("privacy right encompasses and protects . . . family, marriage, motherhood, *procreation* and childrearing" (emphasis added)).

41. Poe v. Gerstein, 517 F.2d 787 (5th Cir. 1975).

42. *Id.* at 789.

43. Schneider, *Moral Discourse and the Transformation of American Family Law*, 83 MICH. L. REV. 1803, 1837–38 (1985). Professor Schneider states that the inefficacy of enforcing family law is not surprising in that the very nature of family law suggests it

holding state laws which punish sodomy casts doubt on this claim.[44]
And, in any case, the decision to use complex medical procedures or
medical procedures requiring third-party participation is rarely made
in the privacy of the home or even in the privacy of the confidential
physician/patient relationship. For example, persons seeking to use
surrogates must advertise for a surrogate and must use lawyers and
other individuals to help with the arrangements.[45] Moreover, it is possible to enforce regulations affecting collaborative conception and extraordinary medical procedures in connection with the state's power
to regulate the medical profession.

Finally, even in the liberal tradition of protecting individual autonomy,[46] the Court has found in exceptional circumstances that the needs
of the state take precedence over individual privacy in decision making.
Some cases stress the subordination of family privacy to the public
interest. They have upheld laws requiring parents to have their children
vaccinated so that the state could protect public health[47] and upheld a
state's conviction of parents for violating the child labor laws.[48] With

---

should be inherently difficult to enforce. First, much of what family law seeks to enforce
occurs in private. Second, the person against whom the law is enforced is often specially
able to injure the person the law intervened to protect. Finally, in many family law
situations, those whose conduct the law attempts to regulate are under psychological
and emotional pressure which make them hard to coerce into compliance with the law's
structure.

44. Bowers v. Hardwick, 478 U.S. 186 (1986).

45. Typically, persons seeking to use surrogates must advertise for a surrogate and
must use lawyers and other individuals to help with the arrangements. Ince, *Inside the
Surrogate Industry*, in TEST TUBE WOMEN 99–116 (R. Arditti, R. D. Klein & S. Minden
eds. 1984); M. KEANE & D. BREO, THE SURROGATE MOTHER (1981) (attorney Noel
Keane describes processing the paperwork for the surrogate mother's termination of
parental rights and subsequent adoption in at least six cases).

46. There is probably no more right to use the new reproductive technology than there
is a right to a heart transplant. *See* Annas, *Allocating Artificial Hearts in the Year 2002:
Minerva v. National Health Service*, 3 AM. J.L. & MED. 59 (1977). Nor does there appear
to be a right to choose among medical procedures without state interference. *See* United
States v. Rutherford, 442 U.S. 544 (1979). *Cf.* Maher v. Roe, 432 U.S. 464 (1977) (state
may fund childbirth but not abortions); Beal v. Doe, 432 U.S. 438 (1977) (Court upheld
state exclusion of welfare funding for nontherapeutic abortions). No Supreme Court
case has determined whether the right to privacy extends to decisions to use the new
reproductive technology. Justice Brennan was the only Justice who would have granted
certiorari in Doe v. Kelley, 106 Mich. App. 169, 307 N.W.2d 438 (1981), *cert. denied*,
459 U.S. 1183 (1983) (fundamental interest to bear and beget children does not extend
to protect contracts and compensation of surrogate mothers).

47. Jacobson v. Massachusetts, 197 U.S. 11 (1905). In *Jacobson*, the Supreme Court
upheld a compulsory vaccination statute by saying: "the liberty secured by the Constitution of the United States does not import an absolute right in each person to be at
all times, and in all circumstances, wholly freed from restraint. . . . There are manifold
restraints to which every person is necessarily subject for the *common good*." *Id.* at 26
(emphasis added).

48. Prince v. Massachusetts, 321 U.S. 158 (1944). Prince concerned the conviction of
a child's guardian for permitting the child to sell religious magazines in violation of the
Massachusetts child labor law. *Id.* at 159–60. Prince appealed her conviction on First

respect to reproductive decisions, courts have upheld the state's power to sterilize individuals in those cases where the state's interests were believed to outweigh the individual's right to procreate.[49]

Similar state interests weigh against uses of the new reproductive technology. Decisions to acquire a child by using the new reproductive technology implicate the government's interests in regulating the medical profession and protecting the welfare of its citizens. For example, the state may claim an interest in seeing that potential surrogates and egg donors are protected physically and psychologically.[50] Moreover, the state has an interest in protecting the children who might be separated from biological parents and ensuring that the children's best interests are protected.[51] Finally, the state may assert an interest in the health of the gene pool.[52]

Current fundamental rights analysis would require the Court to consider whether these interests are compelling or substantial. The Court's two-tier substantive due process analysis incorporates both a rights-based and a utilitarian approach to allocating decision-making authority: the individual's fundamental rights will be protected, unless the state's interests or the potential harm to others indicates that some interference with a fundamental right is warranted. Although the current approach focuses on the relevant considerations, the analysis should focus precisely on the different issues raised by the different uses to which the new reproductive technology may be put.

III. Proposed Analysis

Because the Supreme Court, in its early decisions, used grand, expansive language about the choice to "bear and beget a child" and procreation lying at the heart of protected liberties, some commenta-

---

Amendment religious freedom grounds and a claim of parental autonomy. *Id.* at 164. The Supreme Court upheld the conviction, stating that "[c]ustody, care and nurture of a child reside first in the parents, whose primary function and freedom include preparation for obligations the state can neither supply nor hinder. But the family itself is not beyond regulation in the *public interest.*" *Id.* at 166 (emphasis added).

49. *See* Buck v. Bell, 274 U.S. 200 (1927); *In re* Cavitt, 182 Neb. 712, 157 N.W.2d 171 (1968).

50. For a psychiatrist's study of the psychological makeup of surrogates, see Parker, *Surrogate Motherhood: The Interaction of Litigation, Legislation and Psychiatry,* 5 INT'L J.L. & PSYCHIATRY 341 (1982); Parker, *Making Better Babies in Surrogate Motherhood— The Adult Psychological Ingredient,* in CHANGING CONCEPTIONS: CHILDREN AND PARENTS IN THE NEW REPRODUCTIVE AGE (in press).

51. The prevailing standard for courts deciding cases affecting children is the child's best interest. *See, e.g., In re* Seiferth, 309 N.Y. 80, 127 N.E.2d 820 (1955) (a fourteen-year-old's father refused treatment for his son's harelip; the court found it was in the best interests of the boy to refuse to order treatment).

52. *See* C. GROBSTEIN, FROM CHANCE TO PURPOSE (1981) (advocates a state-mandated program of genetic selection).

tors focused on the nature of the right at stake, i.e., procreation, to conclude that government should have a very limited role in regulating the new reproductive technology.[53] Others maintained that the protection extends only as far as the Court has taken it (if there) and should not be extended.[54] In any event, it appears that most decisions to employ the new reproductive technology will raise a colorable constitutional claim.

Attention should now shift to the next set of issues: which applications of these technologies will be highly protected and which state interests will be permitted to override individual choice? The remainder of this article addresses these considerations. The next section reviews each type of technology by first describing it and then evaluating the extent to which regulation would be appropriate. In applying the proposed analysis, arguments will be evaluated in light of the effect of regulation on individual autonomy and on society.

A. *Treatment for Infertility*

One of the major uses of the new reproductive technology is the treatment for infertility. For example, *in vitro* fertilization is used to help a woman with blocked oviducts to conceive a child by fertilizing her egg outside the body with sperm. The conceptus is then implanted in her womb where it is brought to term.[55]

A law prohibiting infertility treatment would take away an individual's ability to choose whether to undergo medical procedures to bear a child. Some commentators have supported legislation prohibiting *in vitro* fertilization even in the "simple case" of a married infertile couple.

The most common objections to *in vitro* fertilization are (1) that this type of technology is "unnatural";[56] (2) that it separates the procreative

---

53. *See, e.g.,* Note, *In Defense of Surrogate Parenting: A Critical Analysis of the Recent Kentucky Experience,* 69 Ky. L.J. 877, 887 (1980–81).

54. *See, e.g.,* Smith & Iraola, *Sexuality, Privacy, and the New Biology* 67 Marq. L. Rev. 263 (1984).

55. An example of these procedures is the use of external fertilization and reimplantation which permits the possibility of giving women who are infertile because of nonfunctional, destroyed, or absent oviduct the opportunity to have a child. *See, e.g.,* P. Steptoe & R. Edwards, *Implantation of the Human Embryo,* Lancet 366 (Aug. 12, 1978). The authors are the doctors who helped Mrs. Brown give birth to Louise Brown in the much publicized case of the first "test tube baby" in 1978. *See* N.Y. Times, July 26, 1978, at 1, col. 5.; The Times (London) July 26, 1978, at 1.

56. *See, e.g.,* Kass, *Making Babies—The New Biology and the "Old" Morality,* 26 Pub. Interest 318, 349 (1972). Kass writes:

> Is there possibly some wisdom in that mystery of nature which joins the pleasure of sex, the communication of love, and the desire for children in the very activity by which we continue the chain of existence?
> My point is simply this: There are more or less human ways of bringing a child into the world. I am arguing that the laboratory production of human beings is no longer *human* procreation, that making babies in laboratories—even perfect babies—means a degradation of parenthood (author's emphasis).

and the conjugal aspects of marriage, thus damaging the marital relationship;[57] (3) that it brings us closer to a horrifying "brave new world"[58] scenario; (4) that it is risky for the offspring; (5) that it is expensive and the resources allocated to it would be better spent elsewhere; and, finally, (6) that adoption is a better solution to the problem of childlessness.

The first two objections limit individual choice with little benefit to society. If we were to object to modern medicine as "unnatural," we would object to many of the advances medicine has brought which have increased our life cycles and made many lives more pleasant. The implication of courts identifying and upholding only "natural" reproductive decisions is troubling, in part because there is little evidence that "unnatural" reproduction harms others. The courts would be seriously affecting individual autonomy without justification.

The objection to separating the procreative and conjugal aspects of marriage has been voiced by the Catholic Church[59] and other religious groups. The objection is based on a concern about the effect on the family. It is true that the legal system often attempts to reinforce the family unit with its family law principles; however, there is no evidence that allowing infertile couples to conceive by use of the new reproductive technology will injure their marriage or family. And, absent evidence, it seems plausible that use of the new reproductive technology as treatment for infertility could strengthen the family unit by allowing more couples to have children. Indeed, the desire for a child must be strong for an infertile couple to undergo the expense and inconvenience of the procedures.[60] Moreover, governmental enforcement of religious values is troublesome in its own right.[61] There is, therefore, no real evidence supporting this objection and the problem of church/state entanglement with it.

---

57. *Id.;* P. RAMSEY, FABRICATED MAN 38–39 (1970). ("We procreate new beings like ourselves in the midst of our love for one another, and in this there is a trace of the original mystery by which God created the world because of His love.")

58. A. HUXLEY, BRAVE NEW WORLD (1932). In this tale, the family was abolished and reproduction was handled by the state in state hatcheries in which embryos were produced, monitored, and modified in an artificial environment. The modifications were deemed necessary for the production of a stable society.

59. *Instruction on Respect for Human Life in Its Origin and on the Dignity of Procreation: Replies to Certain Questions of the Day.* Pope John Paul II Vatican Doctrinal Statement on Human Reproduction, reproduced in N.Y. Times, March 11, 1987, at A14, col. 1. The Vatican believes that the sacrament of marriage does not give couples a right to a child but the right to perform the acts necessary to create a child. Separating the marital conjugal act from procreation is morally illicit and cannot be approved. Every child who comes into the world, no matter how conceived, however, is to be accepted as a living gift of God and must be brought up with love.

60. *See, e.g.,* E. POHLMAN, PSYCHOLOGY OF BIRTH PLANNING 35–81 (1969) (discusses extent and sources of parents' desire for children); Kleiman, *Anguished Search to Cure Infertility,* Jan. 17, 1983 § 8 (N.Y. Times Magazine).

61. Abington School Dist. v. Schempp, 374 U.S. 203 (1963).

The third objection, i.e., that the new reproductive technology brings us closer to a scenario where children are manipulated and manufactured rather than born into families, impacts on techniques like genetic engineering[62] or ectogenesis.[63] However, this concern has little direct application to treatment for infertility. Children born through the use of the new reproductive technology as a treatment for infertility are born into families; other than the extraordinary medical procedures required to produce them, they are like children born into any other family.

The concern that the use of the new reproductive technology may alter the genetic pool of the human species is likewise misdirected in connection with the treatment for infertility. The argument presented is that permitting the infertile to conceive children will alter the natural genetic development of the human species, in that the infertiles' genes would otherwise disappear from the gene pool without the technology. However, infertility is normally not caused genetically but is more often caused by environmental factors,[64] contraceptives, venereal diseases, and other medical processes.[65] Thus, in the absence of external factors causing infertility, the infertiles' genes would naturally continue to appear in the gene pool.

The remaining three objections listed above have serious implications for individuals and society. Should the techniques fail, the risk of harm to potential offspring is a very serious consideration. Nonetheless, medical risks can be minimized by the supervision of peer review boards and agencies created by states and Congress.[66] Oversight regulation and record-keeping requirements, rather than prohibition, would address the concern more directly.

As for the objection to the use of scarce resources, it does seem incongruous in an overpopulated world with widespread hunger to use

---

62. *See infra* text and notes at 108–24.

63. Ectogenesis is the theoretical possibility of nurturing an embryo through term completely outside a woman's womb. R. FRANCOER, UTOPIAN MOTHERHOOD (1970). Some feminists are concerned about the consequences of such a possibility. G. COREA, THE MOTHER MACHINE 250–59 (1985). A. DWORKIN, RIGHT-WING WOMEN 187–88 (1983).

64. S. BARLOW, S. & F. SULLIVAN, REPRODUCTIVE HAZARDS OF INDUSTRIAL CHEMICALS (1982).

65. G. COREA, THE MOTHER MACHINE 144–65 (1985). Ms. Corea cites many medical sources pointing to the IUD, birth control pills, depo provera, DES, and venereal disease as causes of infertility.

66. A review of reported research reveals two abnormalities reported in *in vitro* fertilization: (1) a spontaneous abortion of a triploid fetus (a fetus with 69 chromosomes instead of the normal 46)—P. C. Steptoe, R. G. Edwards, & J. M. Purdy, *Clinical Aspects of Pregnancies Established with Cleaving Embryos*, 87 BRIT. J. OBSTET. & GYNECOL. 757 (1980); and (2) a child born with transposition of the major vessels of the heart—C. Wood, A. Trounson, J. S. Leeton, P. M. Renore, W. A. W. Watlers, B. W. Buttery, J. C. Grimwade, J. C. Spensley & V. Y. H. Yu, *Clinical Features of Eight Pregnancies Resulting from In Vitro Fertilization and Embryo Transfer*, 38 FERT. & STERIL. 105 (1982).

modern technology to create even more children.[67] Adoption would certainly be a more efficient way to alleviate the problem of childlessness and world hunger. This important concern must be weighed against autonomy values. In our liberal tradition, in which procreation is a fundamental right closely protected by the Constitution, fertile couples are not required to forego having large families or adopting unwanted children. Poor women are not required to undergo sterilization or abortion to reduce the welfare rolls.[68] These types of decisions are so firmly a part of our traditional notions of individual autonomy and freedom that only in a compelling situation should they be usurped by the government.[69]

Decisions to use reproductive technology in the simple case seem to be at the heart of the right to bear or beget children and, thus, would probably be protected as within the right to privacy. None of the state's interests described above are likely to be compelling enough to justify regulation prohibiting the decision to use the new reproductive technology. Oversight and record-keeping regulation would address the government's interests.

B. *Multiple-Parent Procreation*

In vitro fertilization and embryo transfer allow several individuals to participate in the creation of a family.[70] The participants can include a sperm donor, an egg donor, and a woman who carries and nourishes an embryo or fetus to term.[71] There are two typical versions of the multiple-parent procreation process. In the first, a couple contracts with a woman to be inseminated with the husband's sperm. She carries a child who is genetically related to her and to the sperm donor. Upon the child's birth, she terminates her parental rights.[72] The husband

---

67. An article in a Mexican feminist magazine questioned the wisdom of spending vast sums on creating children with so many uncared for children in the world. Lamas, *Las Feministas ante la Tecnologia Reproductiva,* FEM. 31 (Marzo 1987). The author also questioned whether third world women and other poor women would be used as breeders for the wealthy.

68. Justice Stevens (concurring) in a recent abortion decision discussed some implications of allocating decision-making authority to the state. Thornburgh v. American College of Obstetricians and Gynecologists, 54 U.S.L.W. 4618, n.6 (U.S. June 10, 1986) ("[I]f federal judges must allow the State to make the abortion decision, presumably the State is free to decide that a woman may never abort, may sometimes abort, or, as in the People's Republic of China, must always abort if her family is too large.")

69. *See supra* notes 31–35 and accompanying text.

70. *See infra* note 2.

71. *See* Comment, *New Reproductive Technologies: The Legal Problem and a Solution,* 49 TENN. L. REV. 303, 305 (1982) (reviews the legal status of children born through alternative means of reproduction and proposes modifications to the Uniform Parentage Act to provide for alternative statutory parentage for children born through these procedures).

72. Syrkowski v. Appleyard, 420 Mich. 367, 362 N.W.2d 211 (1985), is a case involving a surrogate mother contract and paternity issues. The court held that the state paternity act allows the court to determine paternity of the child born through the surrogate arrangement even though the mother was married.

190 *amily Law Quarterly, Volume XXII, Number 2, Summer 1988*

establishes paternity and his wife adopts the child.[73] In the second typical situation, a woman is paid to be implanted with an already fertilized egg.[74] She carries a child that, although not genetically related to her, develops in her womb and is nourished by her. Although some have questioned whether she is to be considered the "mother" of a child, at the time of birth she terminates her parental rights. The individuals who contracted with her take custody of the child and, if necessary, adopt it.[75]

Because a woman outside of the family unit is required,[76] arrangements to use this type of technology are usually made contractually.[77] At issue is whether a state's attempt to regulate such a contract between a couple[78] and a woman violates the constitutional right to privacy. The usual argument is that since procreation is implicated, the state should not interfere.[79]

The argument in favor of permitting surrogate contracts without regulation rests on the motion of moral agency or "freedom to contract."[80] This theory, which emphasizes individual autonomy, supposes that the participants, including the women who would be surrogates, should

---

73. *In re* Adoption of Baby Girl L.J., 505 N.Y.S.2d 813 (Sup. Ct. 1986). The surrogate parent contract was given legal effect where all parties agreed that the child should go to the couple who contracted for her birth. *But see In re* Baby Girl, 9 Fam. L. Rep. 2348 (BNA) (Ky. Cir. Ct. 1983) (surrogate mother does not have right to relinquish parental rights).

74. J. D. Biggers, *In Vitro Fertilization and Embryo Transfer in Human Beings*, 304 New Eng. J. Med. 336 (1981).

75. Note, *Redefining Mother: A Legal Matrix for New Reproductive Technologies*, 96 Yale L.J. 187 (1986) (proposes legal framework for delineating rights and duties of parties in surrogate arrangements).

76. Participation in the process is what distinguishes sperm donors and surrogate mothers. Sperm donors do not actively participate in the process, rather they simply supply genetic material and have no further connection in the creation of a child. *See supra* note 59. Also, artificial insemination is a well-established technique which was developed long before the techniques included in this article's definition of the new reproductive technology.

77. *See* N. Keane & D. Breo, The Surrogate Mother (1981). Attorney Keane describes his role as a go-between for surrogates and couples desiring to contract with them for a child.

78. Although this article uses a couple in the example, there are, of course, other possibilities. A single man or woman may want to hire a surrogate to bear a child. This raises public policy implications beyond the scope of this article.

79. See the father's argument in *In re* Baby M, 13 Fam. L. Rep. 2001, 2009 (BNA) (N.J. Sup. Ct. 1987). This case involved a surrogate's repudiation of a contract to bear a child. The court's analysis of the constitutional question was remarkably superficial.

80. *See* Comment, *Baby-Sitting Consideration: Surrogate Mother's Right to "Rent Her Womb" for a Fee*, 18 Gonz. L. Rev. 539 (1982–83). *See also, e.g.*, Muller v. Oregon, 208 U.S. 412, 421 (1908). ("It is undoubtedly true, as more than once declared by this court, that the general right to contract in relation to one's business is part of the liberty of the individual, protected by the Fourteenth Amendment to the Federal Constitution.").

have the right to enter into binding contracts.[81] Refusal to enforce surrogate contracts is paternalistic and is just as offensive as a regime which would not enforce a married woman's contracts.[82] Multiple-parent conception also avoids sterotypes about the role of women as mothers. Rather, it places an economic value on childbirth as if it were a service and permits women to make choices about their role as childbearers.[83]

However, despite notions of "freedom of contract," there are some types of contracts we decline to enforce. For example, to protect children, we do not endorse and, indeed, often prohibit agreements to sell children;[84] to protect potential slaves we do not enforce contracts to sell oneself into slavery;[85] and, to protect others, we do not enforce contracts to commit crimes. Although one can argue that refusing to

---

81. *See* Comment, *supra* note 80 at 556, 559. Havighurst, *Limitations Upon Freedom of Contract*, 1979 ARIZ. ST. L.J. 167, 183 (1979). The author states: "Every contract is not to be proscribed whenever judges, legislators, or administrators believe that its terms are unfair or unjust or in any degree opposed to the public interest. Just as there must be 'freedom for the thought we hate,' so there must also be, in a measure, freedom for the contract we hate."

82. Muller v. Oregon, 208 U.S. 412 (1908) (women are competent to enter into binding contracts and cannot be arbitrarily restricted by exertion of the police power of the state. It must be clear that there are issues of health, safety, and welfare at stake).

83. Landes & Posner, *The Economics of the Baby Shortage*, 7 J. LEGAL STUD. 323, 337 (1978). In discussing adoption, the authors state that medical and legal services are only part of the costs of "producing and selling" a baby. The major other costs are: (1) opportunity costs of the natural mother's time; (2) any pain or other disability of the pregnancy and delivery; (3) any value that attaches to keeping the child rather than giving it up; and (4) the costs of search of the middleman in locating "supplier and demander." *Id.* at 337. The authors advocate taking interim steps, which can be reversed, to a legal full-fledged "baby" market. *Id.* at 337. Posner has recently stated that he "did not advocate a free market in babies." Posner, *Mischaracterized Views*, 69 JUDICATURE 321 (1986).

84. Twenty-four states have enacted baby-selling statutes which prohibit the payment of money in exchange for a child. Katz, *Surrogate Motherhood and the Baby Selling Laws*, 20 COLUM. J.L. & SOC. PROBS. 3, 8 (1986). *See also, e.g., In re* Willey v. Lawton, 9 Ill. App. 2d 344, 132 N.E.2d 34 (1956) (a natural mother with custody and her second husband agreed to adopt her children by her first husband and thereby relieve the defendant father of his support obligation provided $5,000 was paid for the release. The court held that the contract was void as against public policy).

However, in Surrogate Parenting Assoc.'s. v. Commonwealth, 704 S.W.2d 209 (Ky. 1986), and *In Re* the Adoption of Baby Girl L.J., No. 358 (N.Y. Surr. Ct. 1986), the courts distinguished adoption under the baby-selling laws and surrogate contracts because the decision to sell the child is made before conception and the sperm donor is biologically related to the child. Why these factors make the practice *not* baby–selling is unclear from the case. *When* the decision is made is irrelevant as to whether a sale occurs. Also, the fact that one of the purchasers is related to the child does not obviate the fact that the surrogate mother is receiving money in exchange for relinquishing parental rights to her child. Childbirth should not be analogized to a "service" because a "product," the child, is transferred.

85. The Thirteenth Amendment assures that: "Neither slavery nor involuntary servitude . . . shall exist within the United States . . ." U.S. CONST. AMEND. XIII. A slave society degrades human life and thus injures us all.

permit surrogate contracts is paternalistic, an underlying basis for this type of prohibition is justifiable protection of the child,[86] an unquestioned concern of the state. Of course, it would have to be shown that children born of surrogacy arrangements were, in fact, harmed in some fashion.

An argument against multiple-parent procreation is that permitting surrogate contracts demeans motherhood by reducing it to a type of farming;[87] it relegates women who make these types of contracts to their biological function as reproducers, thus degrading and objectifying them as "mother machines."[88] Additionally, a surrogate contract is arguably an adhesion contract because there will generally be a disparity in incomes between those paying for the baby and the surrogate who carries the baby. Concern has been expressed as to the possible exploitation of third world women and other poor women, in that their economic situation will likely lead them to become breeders for the wealthy.[89]

Another argument for prohibiting surrogate mother contracts by regulation is that there is a critical bonding process that takes place between an infant and its mother. Enforcing surrogate mother contracts, thereby requiring surrogates to terminate their parental rights and relinquish all contact with their children, may damage both the surrogate and the child psychologically. The long-term consequences are unpredictable at this point in time because surrogacy is a relatively recent development. In addition to the possible harm to individuals affected by enforcement of the contract, society may be harmed in a much broader sense—the psychological harm to individuals is likely to have society-wide implications. Children and women damaged by the experience do not live in a vacuum. They interact with others; their psychological problems will affect those with whom they interact.

However, if there is potential for damage when the surrogate reneges on her contract, what if she does not want to renege on the contract but insists that the contract be enforced? Perhaps the psychological

---

86. "The sovereign has an interest in a minor child superior even to that of a parent; hence, there is a public policy against the custody of such a child become the subject of barter." S. WILLISTON, A TREATISE ON THE LAW OF CONTRACTS § 1744A (3d ed. 1961).

87. DWORKIN, The Coming Genocide, in RIGHT-WING WOMEN 174 (1983). The author argues that the farming model, like the brothel model of how women are socially controlled, exploits women. The author describes how the value and respect now granted to women in the farming model will be lost when reproductive capacity becomes an item of commerce.

88. See G. COREA, THE MOTHER MACHINE 213-49 (1985); see also A. DALLY, INVENTING MOTHERHOOD: THE CONSEQUENCES OF AN IDEAL (1982); A. RICH, OF WOMEN BORN: MOTHERHOOD AS EXPERIENCE AND INSTITUTION (1976).

89. Lamas, Feministas ante la Tecnologia Reproductiva, 11 FEM. 31 (Marzo 1987).

damage to the unwanted child and the corresponding damage to society will militate in favor of enforcement. Yet, the recent phenomenon of surrogates who regret the experience indicates that there may be psychological and emotional damage even if the surrogate does not renege on the contract.[90]

Apart from the concerns expressed above is the practical consideration that surrogacy may be unavoidable because of the infertiles' strong desire to have children. Since it is potentially impossible to curtail, the consideration of the interests of the children who are created looms large. One argument is that enforcing the contracts assures that the children born by use of these contracts will be cared for. This is illusory. If the person who pays for the child did not want the child for some reason, it would be impossible to force him to love and care for the child, just as it is impossible to make abusive and neglectful parents properly care for their children. Similarly, it is impossible to force the surrogate to care for a child she does not want if those who contracted with her change their minds.

All of the above considerations[91] should be examined in considering the implications of regulating multiple-parent procreation. In evaluating the arguments and the effect on the individual and society, two considerations emerge. The first is protecting the interests of the children. Children cannot speak for themselves or represent their own interests. We, thus, have an obligation to protect them.[92] The question should not be whether the contracting parties have a fundamental right to decide to enter into these types of agreements, but the extent to which legislatures can legislate to protect the children.[93] Second, the legislature should be able to protect potential surrogates who might be harmed or exploited. Therefore, the focus of regulation must be on the extent to which the state can regulate in order to protect children and surrogates.

---

90. *Mothers Urge Ban on Surrogacy as Form of Slavery,* N.Y. Times, Sept. 1, 1987, § A at 13, col. 1.

91. Do children have the right to know who their biological parents are? Many adopted persons now insist that they have the right to information about their biological parents. Arguably, children born through the use of the new reproductive technology should have similar rights. *See generally* J. TRISELIOTIS, IN SEARCH OF ORIGINS: THE EXPERIENCES OF ADOPTED PEOPLE (1973); Klibanoff, *Genealogical Information in Adoption: The Adoptee's Quest and the Law,* 11 FAM. L.Q. 185 (1977) (the rights to privacy of the adopted child and the natural parents must be balanced).

92. Annas & Elias, *In Vitro Fertilization and Embryo Transfer: Medicolegal Aspects of a New Technique to Create a Family,* 17 FAM. L.Q. 199, 219 (1983).

93. *See, e.g.,* Krause, *Artificial Conception: Legislative Approaches,* 19 FAM. L.Q. 185 (1985) (proposes that commercial surrogate motherhood should be made illegal with criminal sanctions on intermediaries. The primary concern of any legislation should be to protect the children resulting from surrogate activities).

C. *x. ,/roductive Manipulation*

The new reproductive technology can also be used to manipulate or change the characteristics of potential children and future generations. For example, genetic screening can influence the decision to have children by giving parents information about the characteristics their children are likely to have.[94] Amniocentesis provides information about the unborn and, coupled with selective abortions, permits the termination of pregnancies based on the information obtained about the fetus.[95] Finally, the fetus can be altered during pregnancy using *in utero* fetal therapy.[96] The future may bring chromosome or gene substitution and modification,[97] parthenogenesis,[98] and perhaps cloning.[99] These possibilities raise the same question noted earlier: who should make the decisions required when the new reproductive technology is used to manipulate the reproductive process and affect potential children and future generations?[100]

Many states passed compulsory, extensive sterilization laws between 1911 and 1930.[101] However, those laws have come into question.[102] Today individuals, in consultation with their physicians, decide whether to employ the technology that is presently available and whether they

---

94. Genetic screening may be defined as a search in a population for persons possessing certain genotypes that: (1) are already associated with disease or predisposed to disease; (2) may lead to disease in their descendants; or (3) produce other variations not known to be associated with disease. Committee for the Study of Inborn Errors of Metabolism, Genetic Screening, National Academy of Sciences 9 (1975).

95. Delgado & Keyes, *Parental Preferences and Selective Abortion: A Commentary on Roe v. Wade, Doe v. Bolton, and the Shape of Things to Come,* 1974 WASH. U.L.Q. 203; Note, *Sex Selection Abortion: A Constitutional Analysis of the Abortion Liberty and a Person's Right to Know,* 56 IND. L.J. 281 (1981).

96. *See, e.g.,* Harrison, Golbus & Filly, *Management of the Fetus with a Correctable Congenital Defect,* 246 J.A.M.A. 774, 775 (1981). In this case a defect was corrected.

97. *See, e.g.,* Cohen, *Gene Manipulation,* 294 NEW ENG. J. MED. 883–88 (1976); C. GROBSTEIN, FROM CHANCE TO PURPOSE: AN APPRAISAL OF EXTERNAL HUMAN FERTILIZATION 54–58, 123–25 (1981); Anderson, *Gene Therapy,* 246 J.A.M.A. 2737, 2739 (1981).

98. Daniloff, *Life Without Fathers?* Wash. Post, Feb. 3, 1980, at C1, col. 2. (scientists claim to have produced rats from unfertilized ovae); L. KARP, GENETIC ENGINEERING: THREAT OR PROMISE? 186–88 (1976) (explains parthenogenesis as the development of an unfertilized egg into an embryo-fetus-individual).

99. G. COREA, THE MOTHER MACHINE (1985). For a bibliographic index of the development of genetic engineering as followed by the media, see Smith, *The Genetic Engineering Revolution: A New Century Reality* (published by How. L.J. (1986)).

100. The conflict in decision-making authority raised when parents or guardians seek to make these decisions is beyond the scope of this article. *See* Note, *In re Guardianship of Eberhardy: The Sterilization of the Mentally Retarded,* 1982 WIS. L. REV. 1199 (1982).

101. *See* K. LUDMERER, GENETICS AND AMERICAN SOCIETY: A HISTORICAL APPRAISAL (1972); Beckwith, *Social and Political Uses of Genetics in the United States: Past and Present,* 265 ANNALS N.Y. ACAD. SCI. 46–58 (1976) (study of the early eugenics movement in the United States).

102. Skinner v. Oklahoma, 316 U.S. 535 (1942); Relf v. Weinberger, 372 F. Supp. 1196 (D.D.C. 1974).

wish to do anything about the results.[103] However, as the reproductive technology becomes more sophisticated, states may become interested in the potential for affecting its future citizens. States may be interested in having mandatory genetic screening programs, mandatory amniocentesis, or compulsory abortions to prevent the birth of babies with severe abnormalities (thereby reducing health care costs).[104] The state might want to improve the gene pool,[105] or perhaps the state may be interested in eliminating ''undesirables'' from society.[106] Of course, there are the even more chilling possibilities that the state might want to encourage social stability and eliminate potential dissenters from its midst.

Obviously, techniques to manipulate the reproductive process entail an intrusive invasion of the mother's body and expose the mother and her unborn child to possible risk. If the techniques fail, the mother and her child are the parties who will suffer the most. Thus, the effect on the individual is great; the weight is in favor of individual decision-making authority.

Permitting individuals to make choices concerning the characteristics of their potential offspring will further a pluralistic society in that individuals will probably choose to have offspring that resemble themselves. On the other hand, permitting individuals to make choices involving gender and genetic composition might result in skewing the population. For example, many couples prefer first-born boys.[107] Permitting individuals to make these types of decisions might, indeed, have a negative effect on society.[108] Thus, the state might want to

---

103. Currently pregnant couples can use amniocentesis to discover whether the child the woman is carrying has certain types of defects. If so, the parents can decide whether to abort it. *See generally* Carlton, *Perfectibility and the Neonate: Providers,* in THE CUSTOM-MADE CHILD (H. Holmes, B. Hoskins, & B. Gross eds.). *See also* Virshup, *The Promise and the Peril of Genetic Testing: Perfect People?* N.Y. MAGAZINE, July 27, 1987, at 26.

104. Virshup, *The Promise and the Peril of Genetic Testing: Perfect People?* N.Y. MAGAZINE, July 27, 1987, at 26.

105. *See* G. SMITH, GENETICS, ETHICS AND THE LAW (1981) (the author advocates a state mandated program of active eugenics on the grounds that it is in the interests of society to improve the gene pool; generally, the author sees no drawback to prohibiting the passing of ''bad'' genes).

106. In Buck v. Bell, 274 U.S. 200 (1927), the Supreme Court upheld the constitutionality of a Virginia statute providing for the sexual sterilization of inmates of institutions supported by the state who are found to be afflicted with a hereditary form of insanity or imbecility. The case has never been overruled; *see* STRICKBERGER, GENETICS 151–52 (2d ed. 1976), for an overview of eugenic sterilization of this country.

107. *E.g.,* C. RICE, BEYOND ABORTION 98 (1979) (women were more likely to abort if they were told that the sex of their child was female); Cutright, Belt & Scangoni, *Gender Preferences, Sex Predetermination, and Family Size in the United States,* 21 Soc. BIOLOGY 243 (1974). *But see* L. KARP, GENETIC ENGINEERING: THREAT OR PROMISE? 158 (1976) (suggests that any imbalance in the sex ratio would be short lived).

108. Scientists predict some of the following consequences of a society with a higher ratio of males in the population: a decrease in population growth, increased crime and wars, increased male homosexuality, increased polyandry, and finally, possible increased

prevent individuals from making decisions that could harm society. The state might want to prohibit potentially harmful decisions, such as the decision to abort a child solely because of its sex or because of some other benign characteristic, such as eye color, skin pigmentation,[109] etc. The state, for example, may want to prohibit sex-selection abortions on the grounds that this is an inappropriate, private gender-based discrimination which would result in an unnatural balance of the sexes in our society.[110]

However, if the state interferes with individual decision making by regulation prohibiting, for example, sex selection abortion, the concern is raised that it could also usurp these kinds of decisions and actually make decisions about the characteristics of potential children.[111] Yet, the fact that the state is permitted to prohibit some kinds of decisions which might have a harmful effect on society does not automatically give it the power to make decisions about the characteristics of our children. Our important interests in autonomy and pluralism indicate that the state should not have that power.

Respect for privacy and autonomy protects individuals from many forms of governmental intrusion when they make procreative choices about the characteristics of their future children. The state, thus, should only regulate to prevent private gender-based discrimination, to prevent genetic or gender skewing of the population, and to prevent any one person or entity, including the government, from being able to control the natural genetic development of the human species.

IV. Conclusion

Whether state control of decisions to use reproductive technology will be construed as within the zone of privacy, and, thus, a matter of individual autonomy, or a matter of grave social concern will depend

---

occurrence of first-child personality traits in males and later-child personality traits in females. Largey, *Reproductive Technologies: Sex Selection*, in 4 ENCYCLOPEDIA OF BIOETHICS 1439, 1443, cited in Note, *Sex Selection Abortion: A Constitutional Analysis of the Abortion Liberty and a Person's Right to Know*, 56 IND. L.J. 281, 287 n.23 (1981).

109. Skin cells indicative of pigmentation (melanocytes in the epidermis) begin to appear at about the fourteenth week of gestation. *See* Sagebiel & Odland, *Ultrastructural Identification of Melancytes in Early Human Embryos*, in PIGMENTATION: ITS GENESIS AND BIOLOGIC CONTROL 43, 44 (V. Riley ed. 1972), cited in Delgado & Keyes. *Parental Preferences and Selective Abortion: A Commentary on Roe v. Wade, Doe v. Bolton, and the Shape of Things to Come*, 1974 WASH. U.L.Q. 203 n.58.

110. One way for the state to achieve this goal would be to prohibit the use of medical testing for the sole purpose of identifying fetal sex. Another way would be to require doctors to determine the reason for the abortion and to prohibit the abortion if the sole reason for the abortion is the sex of the fetus. The easiest way might be to withhold information about the sex of the fetus on the grounds that it is irrelevant. Sex-linked diseases may be an exception.

111. *See generally* A. HUXLEY, BRAVE NEW WORLD (1932); G. ORWELL, 1984 (1946).

on the purpose or use to which technology is to be put. This article began by asking which applications of the new reproductive technology will be highly protected by the doctrine of privacy and which will be less so. It also asked which state interests justify overriding individual choice. It determined that the privacy doctrine treats the question as a conflict between individual autonomy and government interests in regulation. It found that treating these cases as conflicts between the autonomy of the individual and the needs of government strengthens the notion that the private and public spheres should be kept separate.

The notion of separate spheres has historically oppressed women. However, in the area of reproduction, the rights-based notion of individual autonomy has empowered women by permitting them to control their reproductive capacities. The article concluded that the problems associated with separate spheres can be minimized if the analysis focuses precisely on the application of the new reproductive technology and is sensitive to the effect of individual choices on women and society.

Applying the analysis proposed, the article found that the autonomy value outweighs concerns raised by the use of technology as treatment for infertility so that only minimal oversight and record-keeping regulation is warranted. With respect to the use of the new reproductive technology in multiple-parent procreation, it found that the possible exploitation of women and the potential harm to children are interests which can outweigh the interests of autonomy; regulation is thus justified in order to prevent exploitation and to protect children. Finally, in considering the regulation of the use of the new reproductive technology to manipulate characteristics of potential children, the article determined that the interests of preventing private gender discrimination and skewing of the gender and genetic composition of humanity permit regulation to further those interests but do not permit regulation which attempts to usurp decision-making authority so that the government would make substantive decisions about the gender and genetic composition of humanity.

Commentary: The Implications of Being a Society of One

By RACHEL F. MORAN

Professor of Law, Boalt Hall School of
Law, University of California, Berkeley;
A.B., Stanford University (1978); J.D.,
Yale Law School (1981).

—"America's first democratically distributed privilege was the
right to dream . . . ."[1]
—"What happens to a dream deferred?"[2]

Introduction

TODAY'S TALKS POIGNANTLY capture the strain induced by
a dream long-envisioned but only partially realized, a vision of
equal participation for minorities and women in the American legal
educational system. Professor Wright's reference to W.E.B. DuBois
illustrates the persistent difficulties generated by deferring the
hopes and aspirations of an entire people.[3] The stress created for
minorities attempting to attain prominence in the legal academy is
by no means a novel phenomenon. For example, Charles H. Houston, the grandson of slaves, entered Amherst College at age sixteen
and graduated in 1915 as class valedictorian and a member of Phi
Beta Kappa.[4] In 1922, he graduated from Harvard Law School in
the top five percent of his class and was the first black elected to
the editorial board of the *Harvard Law Review*. Subsequently,
Houston became the first black to earn a doctor of judicial science
degree from Harvard. He also received a doctor of civil law from
the University of Madrid. Houston later became dean of Howard
Law School and in two years converted it from an undistinguished

---

1. R. WIEBE, THE SEGMENTED SOCIETY 3 (1975).
2. L. HUGHES, SELECTED POEMS OF LANGSTON HUGHES 268 (paperback ed. 1974).
3. Wright, *The Color Line Still Exists*, 20 U.S.F. L. REV. *infra*.
4. G. SEGAL, BLACKS IN THE LAW 210 (1983).

503

night school into a full-time, fully accredited day school. Houston's students, including Thurgood Marshall, nicknamed him "Iron Shoes" because of his stringent standards and heavy demands. Houston eventually left the deanship at Howard to direct the NAACP's legal campaign and to work with Marshall on a lawsuit to desegregate the University of Maryland Law School. Houston worked himself to death, succumbing to a heart attack in 1950 at the age of fifty-four. In his last message to his six-year-old son, Houston wrote: "Tell Bo I did not run out on him, but went down fighting that he might have better and broader opportunities than I had, without prejudices or bias operating against him. In any fight some fall."[5]

The number of minority faculty present at this Conference demonstrates that Houston succeeded in opening up more opportunities, not only for blacks but also for Asian-Americans, Latinos, Native Americans, and women. Yet, as the perceptive remarks of our panelists make clear, he was unable to eliminate entirely the subtle prejudices, biases, and attendant stress that hinder the advancement of minorities and women in academe. In this commentary, I will first examine the debate surrounding the numbers of minorities and women appointed to law faculties. I will then examine two competing models of how the legal academy functions: assimilationism and pluralism. After describing the two models, I will discuss the implications for each of small numbers of minority and women faculty.[6]

I. THE LAW OF SMALL NUMBERS

In 1981, Professor David L. Chambers of Michigan Law School conducted a survey for the Society of American Law Teachers ("SALT") to learn how many minorities and women were in tenured or tenure-track positions at accredited American law schools.[7] According to Chambers' research, thirty percent of the re-

---

5. *Id.* at 210-11.

6. The scope of this comment does not permit extensive analysis of the differences between the experiences of minority and women faculty members. By treating these groups similarly, however, I do not mean to discount the possible significance of these differences.

7. Chambers, *SALT Survey: Women in Law School Teaching,* SALT NEWSLETTER 1 (July 1983) [hereinafter cited as *1983 Newsletter*]; Chambers, *SALT Survey: Minority Group Persons in Law School Teaching,* SALT NEWSLETTER 5 (Nov. 1982) [hereinafter cited as *1982 Newsletter*]; D. Chambers, SALT Report on Women in Teaching 1 (Mar. 14,

sponding schools had no minority faculty, thirty-four percent had only one, and twenty-one percent had two. Only fifteen percent of those schools responding had more than two minority faculty members.[8] Chambers also found that nearly one-tenth of the responding schools had five percent or fewer women on the faculty, approximately one-third had six to ten percent women, and another one-third had eleven to fifteen percent women. Only about one-fourth of the responding schools had more than fifteen percent women on the faculty.[9]

These findings indicate that the number of minority and women law professors remains discouragingly small despite faculty affirmative action. These statistics alone might explain Professor Banks' observation that "[f]or reasons which are understandable, most of the dialogue about equity and faculty affirmative action in higher education has focused on the numbers."[10] Nevertheless, I believe that additional factors have militated in favor of a narrow focus on numbers. Numbers are easy, numbers are specific, and they are not very threatening, as long as they are small.[11] More importantly, numbers never force us to look beyond the initial hiring decision to examine the quality of the academic experience for minority and women faculty members. It is, after all, much easier to assess how many minorities and women are on the faculty than

---

1983) (unpublished manuscript on file with the *University of San Francisco Law Review*).

Professor Chambers mailed questionnaires to a SALT member or to the dean at 172 law schools and received 97 responses. Because of tardy responses, only 94 schools were included in calculating minority law faculty representation; all 97 schools were included in a later statistical analysis of women law faculty. *1983 Newsletter, supra,* at 1; *1982 Newsletter, supra,* at 6 n.3; D. Chambers, *supra,* at 1. As Chambers points out, the sample of responding schools may not be representative because of differences between the responding and nonresponding schools. *1982 Newsletter, supra,* at 5; D. Chambers, *supra,* at 1-2.

8. *1982 Newsletter, supra* note 7, at 5.

9. *1983 Newsletter, supra* note 7, at 6; D. Chambers, *supra* note 7, at Table 2. For a good discussion of the pitfalls in statistical analysis of the number of women law faculty, see Zenoff & Lorio, *What We Know, What We Think We Know, and What We Don't Know About Women Law Professors,* 25 ARIZ. L. REV. 869, 871-73 (1983). For an earlier analysis of the representation of women on law faculties, see Weisberg, *Women in Law School Teaching: Problems and Progress,* 30 J. LEGAL EDUC. 226 (1979) (in-depth statistical discussion of women law professors based on 1975-76 ABA Review).

10. Address on behalf of Professor Banks, Black Scholars in the University: Roles and Conflicts, Minority Law Conference (Oct. 27, 1985) (on file with the *University of San Francisco Law Review*).

11. *See* W. NEWMAN, AMERICAN PLURALISM 218 (1973) (single racially identifiable family in otherwise racially homogeneous community is less likely to provoke extreme prejudice).

to determine how satisfied they are with their careers, how successful they are in the academic world, and how important they are in
the operation of the law school.

Quality is an intangible characteristic, and if independent ob-
servers were to try to measure it carefully, I think many academics
would feel threatened by this invasion of their decision-making
prerogatives. Their fears derive not only from a belief that such an
evaluation would infringe on their academic freedom, but also from
a suspicion that introspection could prove incredibly painful for
individuals who pride themselves on being at the forefront of reform. Reece McGee once went so far as to formulate McGee's Law
of Faculty Conservatism:

> Any faculty, given the choice between the admission of an un-
> pleasant truth about themselves or the institution with which
> they are affiliated, the recognition of which will make possible
> a universally desired progressive change, or the [maintenance]
> of a self-congratulatory myth the adherence to which will make
> the desired change impossible, will invariably elect to maintain
> the myth.[12]

The reluctance to engage in self-examination is especially pernicious because colleagues are apt to dismiss complaints by minority
and women law faculty as idiosyncratic reactions rather than treat
these grievances as predictable responses to institutional deficiencies. The structural limits on meaningful participation in the academic community are systematically ignored, thereby perpetuating
the isolation of minorities and women.

II. THE COMPETING MODELS OF ASSIMILA-
TIONISM AND PLURALISM: WHAT DOES MEM-
BERSHIP IN THE ACADEMY MEAN?

To analyze the experiences of minority and women law professors, it is necessary to understand how newly hired faculty members become integral parts of the law school. I will advance two
possible models of participation: assimilationism and pluralism.
These models are, of course, archetypal, and any law school proba-

---

12. Blassingame, *Comment*, in THE ROCKEFELLER FOUNDATION WORKING PAPERS ON
BAKKE, WEBER AND AFFIRMATIVE ACTION 211-13 (1979) (citing R. McGEE, ACADEMIC JANUS
(1971)).

bly embodies elements of both. Nevertheless, they constitute useful tools for evaluating the problems that small numbers of minority and women law faculty face in becoming full members of the academy.

A. *Assimilationism in the Academy*

The concept of assimilationism has not been uniformly defined. One author has defined assimilationism as a model of social organization that "stresses the importance of integration and absorption of various cultural traditions into a relatively homogeneous society. Assimilation envisions a unified society permeated by a single culture, a society in which conflict among groups is reduced by eliminating their differences."[13] Another author has distinguished between an exclusivist melting pot in which "assimilation is considered desirable only if the Anglo-Saxon cultural pattern is adopted as the ideal" and a permissive melting pot in which all cultures contribute to "a totally new blend, culturally and biologically, in which stocks and folkways of Europe were, figuratively speaking, indiscriminately (permissively) mixed in the political pot of the emerging nation."[14] Milton Gordon's classic treatment of assimilation demonstrates that the term encompasses a number of subprocesses and stages.[15] He contends that although immigrants have frequently become acculturated by changing their cultural patterns to resemble more closely those of the host society, other stages of assimilation have not followed acculturation in the United States.[16] In particular, structural assimilation, the large-scale entrance into cliques, clubs, and institutions of the host society, has not taken place. Consequently, ethnic and racial communal organizations persist.[17]

Gordon's distinction between acculturation and assimilation raises a critical problem for the minority or woman professor relying on assimilation to achieve acceptance in the law school community: Attempts to adopt academic values, attitudes, and behaviors will not necessarily lead to meaningful participation in scholarly

---

13. Comment, *Cultural Pluralism*, 13 HARV. C.R.-C.L. L. REV. 133, 136-37 (1978).
14. Castaneda, *Persisting Ideological Issues of Assimilation in America*, in CULTURAL PLURALISM 57-59 (E. EPPS ed. 1974).
15. M. GORDON, ASSIMILATION IN AMERICAN LIFE 68-71 (1964).
16. *Id.* at 104-10.
17. *Id.* at 110-14.

circles. In law schools, this problem is aggravated by the highly politicized nature of faculty affirmative action. As Professors Banks and Wright have indicated, minority and women law professors are less likely to find mentors who will facilitate the process of acculturation.[18] As Professor Banks has further remarked, minority faculty are frequently burdened with disproportionately heavy administrative duties. In addition to their teaching responsibilities, they may be asked to assist in minority recruitment, act as advisors to minority student organizations, and direct formal or informal tutoring programs for minority students.[19] These tasks divert minority and women law professors from legal scholarship, an important element of the traditional legal academic role. These added duties thereby impede acculturation, especially when colleagues are prompted to dismiss the minority or woman professor. as a political, rather than an academic, appointment.

In addition to having doubts about the relationship between acculturation and assimilation, the newcomer may be quite unclear as to the proper tradition to adopt in order to assimilate. Studies of assimilation frequently assume a dominant, homogeneous culture exists.[20] In fact, however, there may be a high degree of internal differentiation within a dominant population.[21] Under these circumstances, the process of assimilation raises difficult questions about how newcomers select among a variety of subcultural practices. Certainly, difficulties in ferreting out a single tradition confront the minority or woman professor seeking to assimilate into the academic community. Typically, the academy has prided intself on fostering a wide variety of substantive schools of thought. Nevertheless, legal academics do share a core tradition of professionalism that relies heavily on peer review.

This core tradition of professionalism focuses primarily on scholarship, although teaching and community service are also considered. Traditional peer review can seriously disadvantage minor-

---

18. Banks, *supra* note 10; Wright, *supra* note 3.

19. Banks, *supra* note 10; Hamlar, *Minority Tokenism in American Law Schools*, 26 How. L.J. 443, 564 (1983).

20. R. Rosaldo, Assimilation Revisited, Working Paper Series No. 9, at 12 (July 1985) (questioning theories of assimilation that treat dominant culture as monolithic) (unpublished manuscript on file with the *University of San Francisco Law Review*).

21. *See* W. NEWMAN, *supra* note 11, at 24-31 (describing internal differentiation in economic, political, and social-institutional structures of society).

ity and women law professors who pursue work on the problems of race, ethnicity, and gender if definitions of high-quality scholarship systematically exclude these challenging new perspectives.[22] Moreover, the peer review process may discount the importance of the disproportionate contribution of community service by minorities and women, especially if colleagues characterize this investment of time as a voluntary decision to devote less attention to scholarship. In addition to concerns about scholarship, teaching, and community service, faculty members are concerned about their long term relationships with minority and women faculty professors. As Derrick Bell explains:

> [M]ost faculty are looking—often more carefully—for good colleagues, that is, people with whom they will feel comfortable and who will 'fit' into the existing faculty group. This seldom-expressed qualification, until recently, virtually eliminated all women, blacks and Spanish-surnames from teaching, and even today can present an obstacle to the woman unable to act like a man, to the black unwilling to act as though he were white and to the Puerto Rican or Chicano unwilling to act as though he were pure Anglo-Saxon.[23]

In sum, peer review and commitment to professionalism based largely on traditional models of the legal academic role frequently disadvantage minorities and women who were historically unrepresented in the law school community. The unusual, and often highly politicized, status of the few minority and women professors on law faculties will frequently thwart assimilation, even if these individuals attempt to acculturate themselves to traditional roles.

Small increments in the number of minority and women law professors may significantly alter the chances for acceptance under a model that embodies elements of assimilationism.[24] The sole minority or woman law professor is more apt to be viewed as a novel

22. In making this observation, I am not suggesting that minority and women law faculty should invariably devote themselves to problems of race, ethnicity, and gender. However, many do, and their efforts should not automatically be devalued in the peer review process. See, e.g., Zenoff & Lorio, supra note 9, at 880-81 (83% of professors teaching "Women and the Law" courses are women; women are overrepresented in subjects considered nonprestigious).

23. C. CLARK, MINORITY OPPORTUNITIES IN LAW FOR BLACKS, PUERTO RICANS AND CHICANOS 72 (1974).

24. See C. EPSTEIN, WOMEN IN LAW 193 (1981) (describing experiences of women partners in Wall Street firms).

curiosity or a constant irritant. Although there is a possibility that the dominant academic community will close ranks to protect itself from larger numbers of minorities and women, this seems unlikely because any increase will probably be extremely gradual. However, there is no reason to believe that hiring practices will change drastically in the near future, as Professor Wright's description of the dismantlement of minority programs makes clear.[25]

B. *Pluralism: A Limited Alternative*

Because of the problems with a model of assimilationism for women and minority law faculty, an attractive possibility is reliance on a model of pluralism. As with assimilationism, the concept of pluralism defies simple definition. Pluralism is often vaguely described as respect for diversity or tolerance of different groups. In fact, theories of pluralism have sometimes been formulated out of distaste for the implications of assimilationism. In the early 1900's, for example, Horace Kallen, a Harvard-educated philosopher of Jewish immigrant stock, published a collection of essays on cultural pluralism largely in response to the excesses of pure Americanism.[26] Kallen's analysis was based on three central propositions: (1) assimilationism was an unrealistic doctrine because conscious identification with some distinctive group trait persisted despite acculturation; (2) each minority culture could make valuable contributions to American society; and (3) pluralism was inherent in an American ideology committed to equality despite ostensible differences between individuals and groups.[27]

Just as Kallen reacted to nativism, advocates of pluralism in American legal education frequently are responding to the rigidity and intolerance associated with assimilationism.[28] For reasons already mentioned, pluralists argue that assimilationism has not led to successful integration of minorities and women into law faculties. Instead, minorities and women remain identifiably different

---

25. See Wright, *supra* note 3; Lauter, *Gender Gap Gets Wider on Law Faculties*, Nat. L.J., Jan. 9, 1984, at 1, col. 4 (gap between proportion of women in the legal profession and the proportion on law school faculties has steadily widened since the late 1970's).

26. W. NEWMAN, *supra* note 11, at 67-68.

27. *Id.* at 68-69.

28. See Hamlar, *supra* note 19, at 558-59 (describing narrow academic outlook due to traditional hiring practices of law schools).

members of the legal community.[29] Pluralists further contend minorities and women have unique contributions to make to legal scholarship because of their special experiences, thus rendering assimilation inappropriate. As Christopher Edley has remarked, "*We teach what we have lived*, and this may be particularly true in a field like law, which is, after all, about life and how it is or ought to be ordered."[30] Because the experiences of many Americans were not considered in establishing the traditional model of the legal academy, pluralists reject simpleminded assimilationism that fails to rectify these long-standing omissions.[31]

Pluralists claim that the legal academy has already committed itself to promoting diversity in several different ways.[32] Legal academics have relied on academic freedom as a device for encouraging innovation and promoting multiple schools of thought. Moreover, law schools have at least acquiesced in legislative, administrative, and judicial determinations that the student body and faculty must contain a fairer representation of minorities and women. Moreover, the law school community has prided itself on its use of decentralized decision-making processes that discourage conformity and stimulate individual autonomy, freedom, spontaneity, creativity, dignity, and independence.[33]

Yet, to succeed as an alternative, pluralism must establish more than the inadequacy of an assimilationist model. It must create a viable method of promoting meaningful participation in the legal academic community. Pluralists must not overstate the current possibilities for diversity in law schools. As noted, legal academics share certain values and assumptions that shape a core tradition of professionalism. These values and assumptions may be so

---

29. *Id.* at 554-55, 562-63 (discussing unspoken quotas on minority hiring and negative faculty attitudes toward minority colleagues).

30. *Id.* at 68-69.

31. *Id.* at 566-73 (arguing for greater diversity in faculty and curriculum).

32. *See, e.g.,* AMERICAN BAR ASSOCIATION, STANDARDS FOR APPROVAL OF LAW SCHOOLS AND INTERPRETATIONS S211, I211, S212 (1984) (endorsing equality of opportunity in legal education and law school employment without discrimination or segregation on the ground of race, color, religion, national origin, or sex); AMERICAN BAR ASSOCIATION, APPROVAL OF LAW SCHOOLS 5-6 (as amended 1983) (same). *See also* American Bar Association, *The American Bar Association's Role in the Law School Accreditation Process,* 32 J. LEGAL EDUC. 195, 198 (1982) (law schools must demonstrate through concrete action their commitment to providing full opportunities for qualified members of historically disadvantaged groups, especially racial and ethnic minorities).

33. *See* C. PERROW, COMPLEX ORGANIZATIONS 32-33 (1972).

deeply rooted that they are treated as unassailable truths; disagreement with them may be classified as deviance, rather than diversity.[34] In addition, as Professor Banks' presentation makes clear, a formal appearance of decentralized decision-making may conceal more highly centralized, informal networks of communication.[35] A noted sociologist has described as a "myth" the claim that "the university is a collegial body having a minimum of hierarchy and status difference."[36] Informal hierarchical networks are likely to reduce the possibilities for pluralism. In fact, the inevitable disparity between the results of private collegial exchanges and those expected under a formally decentralized system will generate complaints from outsiders about opaque and impenetrable decision-making processes.

Moreover, because of the small number of minority and women faculty members, those who opt for pluralism will often constitute a "Society of One." A recent SALT position paper on minority hiring indicates most minority law professors are "isolated token presences on their campuses."[37] The psychological and social consequences of membership in a Society of One are pervasive and severe. The lone minority or woman professor is likely to encounter two extreme reactions. Some students and faculty will expect the minority or woman professor to serve as a representative of all minorities and women. These expectations will manifest themselves in demands for compliance with an impossible standard of performance. Another group will stigmatize the isolated minority or woman professor by assuming that he or she is inherently less capable than white male colleagues and was only appointed because of affirmative action.[38] These dehumanizing views ignore the unique individual characteristics of minority and women law professors by either elevating them to superhuman symbol or reducing them to substandard political appointment. Both reactions have devastating consequences. An impossible standard of

---

34. *See* C. EPSTEIN, *supra* note 24, at 61.

35. Banks, *supra* note 10.

36. C. PERROW, *supra* note 33, at 35.

37. SOCIETY OF AMERICAN LAW TEACHERS, STATEMENT ON MINORITY HIRING IN AALS LAW SCHOOLS: A POSITION PAPER ON THE NEED FOR VOLUNTARY QUOTAS 1 (1985).

38. C. EPSTEIN, *supra* note 24, at 233 (noting that a lone woman on the faculty was frequently perceived as representative of all women); *see* Hamlar, *supra* note 19, at 561-63 (citing negative attitudes toward isolated minority faculty in law schools).

performance is a surefire formula for disappointment and failure. A negative expectation about academic promise may become a self-fulfilling prophecy.[39] Neither characterization is consistent with a pluralist ideology predicated on the equality of alternative academic roles.

Ironically, the problems associated with the politicization of faculty affirmative action hinder reliance on both assimilationism and pluralism. A lone minority or woman law professor can not discount the salience of race, ethnicity, and gender in the legal academy. Yet, in standing apart as a Society of One, these professors cannot assume the limited diversity on law faculties implies equality or even a grudging respect.

Conclusion

Until minorities and women achieve more balanced representation in the academic community, neither assimilationism nor pluralism will be viable methods of ensuring full participation in law schools. Faced with a "no-win" situation, those minorities and women who presently serve on law faculties will inevitably find their experience a lonely and frustrating one. As Charles H. Houston noted, "In any fight some fall."[40] Hopefully, through panel discussions such as the one today, fewer will fall and more will endure successfully as Societies of One, until larger numbers of minorities and women make it possible to create Societies of Two, Three, and more. It takes courage and principle to stand as a Society of One and to preserve the dream deferred until it becomes a community dream. The skeptical will believe in our dream when they see it. We, as Societies of One, must nurture the dream of equality and meaningful participation, knowing that we will see it when we all believe it.[41]

---

39. *See* Hamlar, *supra* note 19, at 579-82 (discussing effects of negative expectations on minority student performance and arguing that the belief that minority students will do little more than meet minimum standards of performance becomes a self-fulfilling prophecy).

40. G. SEGAL, *supra* note 4, at 211.

41. For the imagery in this last paragraph, I am indebted to the haunting poetry of Langston Hughes, L. HUGHES, *supra* note 2, at 291, and the thought-provoking prose of Saul Alinsky, S. ALINSKY, REVEILLE FOR RADICALS 235 (1969).

TWO LEGAL CONSTRUCTS OF MOTHERHOOD: "PROTECTIVE" LEGISLATION IN MEXICO AND THE UNITED STATES*

ANTOINETTE SEDILLO LOPEZ**

I. INTRODUCTION

The United Nations Economic and Social Council recently adopted a wide range of recommendations promoting women's rights throughout the world, including a call for increased dissemination of information about women's legal and de facto social status.[1] In light of the proposed free trade agreements, which will increase interaction between the United States and Mexico,[2] developing an understanding of women's rights in both countries will become increasingly important.[3] A comparative analysis of women's legal issues can help us place a feminist agenda in a broader context.[4]

© 1991 by Antoinette Sedillo Lopez.

** Associate Professor of Law, University of New Mexico School of Law. Bachelor of University Studies 1979, University of New Mexico; J.D. 1982, University of California, Los Angeles. I would like to thank Anne Waters for research assistance and Robyn Smith for editing. This article is dedicated to Victor and Graciela.

1. 27 U.N. MONTHLY CHRON. no. 3, at 38 (1990).

2. Brenda Dalglish, *Rapidly Modernizing Mexico Wants to Create a Free Trade Zone with the United States and Canada*, MACLEANS, Dec. 3, 1990, at 48.

3. The United States and Mexico have an uneasy relationship. They are neighboring countries with vastly uneven economic resources. They share a violent and bitter history of hostilities toward each other. The peoples of each country also have very different cultures, education, and social development. Moreover, the countries' relationship with each other is challenged by their different legal systems. Mexico has furthered its tradition in the civil law since it was imposed by Spain. The United States has advanced its common law tradition after adopting the English common law. *See generally*, ALAN RIDING, DISTANT NEIGHBORS: A PORTRAIT OF THE MEXICANS 316-39 (1985) (discussing the power relationship between Mexico and the United States); PHILLIP RUSSELL, MEXICO IN TRANSITION 89-94, 121-27 (1977) (discussing the social structure and social services of Mexico).

4. For notable comparative work on women's legal issues, see MARY ANN GLENDON, ABORTION AND DIVORCE IN WESTERN LAW: AMERICAN FAILURES, EUROPEAN CHALLENGES (1987); MARGARET E. LEAHY, DEVELOPMENT STRATEGIES AND THE STATUS OF WOMEN: A COMPARATIVE STUDY OF THE UNITED STATES, MEXICO, THE SOVIET UNION, AND CUBA (1986); Marsha

239

The theme of this symposium, "Reconstructing Motherhood," requires an examination of laws designed to further traditional motherhood roles. Societal constructs of motherhood—women as child bearers and nurturers—have profoundly affected women's involvement in paid employment. Conversely, women's participation in paid employment affects how women experience motherhood. For example, a woman who does not work outside the home has a dramatically different mothering experience than a woman who works outside the home and leaves her children with a day-care provider. The legal system can affect the relationship between motherhood and employment opportunities for women by means of employment laws and policies. Sometimes protective legislation[5] is enacted in view of women's unique role as potential and actual mothers. Studying forms of protective legislation in different countries can help us to think about ways of reconstructing motherhood.[6]

In both Mexico and the United States, protective legislation has been enacted in ways that control women's experiences as mothers by attempting to further or maintain their traditional role in the family. One justification for the legislation is to protect women's health or the health of an unborn or potential fetus.[7]

This article briefly describes Mexico's unique equal rights amendment and examples of protective employment legislation under Mexican labor law.[8] For example, Mexico's federal labor laws include regulations designed specifically to protect women's health and to guard against potential harm to fetuses.[9] The article then outlines the United States' experience with protective legislation. Although the Equal Rights

---

Freeman, *Measuring Equality: A Comparative Perspective on Women's Legal Capacity and Constitutional Rights in Five Commonwealth Countries*, 5 BERKELEY WOMEN'S L.J. 110 (1990). *See also*, Heather Dashner, *Unionists Propose Women's Issues for NAFTA Negotiations*, NOTIMEX MEXICAN NEWS SERVICE, Feb. 10, 1992 (discussing the demands of a trilateral women worker's conference involving women from Mexico, Canada, and the United States).

    5. The term "protective legislation" will be used in this article to refer to laws affecting only women—ostensibly to protect their health and the safety or the health of an unborn or even yet-to-be-conceived fetus.

    6. Professor Catharine Wells asked me to comment on employment legislation and policy in Mexico and the United States, particularly in light of the recently decided case of International Union, United Automobile Aerospace and Agricultural Implement Workers of America v. Johnson Controls, 111 S. Ct. 1196 (1991). This article is a small piece of a larger body of work analyzing women's issues in Mexico and the United States, planned for publication by the University of New Mexico Press in 1992.

    7. *See infra* text accompanying notes 53-56, 72-73.

    8. *See infra* text accompanying notes 18-69.

    9. *See infra* text accompanying notes 42-58.

Amendment to the United States Constitution failed to pass, anti-discrimination laws have been used to strike down protective legislation under the theory that men and women must be treated equally.[10] Today, however, we see a resurgence of the notion of protective legislation in the laws enacted and policies pursued in purported attempts to protect fetuses.[11] But this new protective legislation does not protect fetuses as much as it controls women's reproductive role.[12] The *Johnson Controls*[13] case is a recent example of anti-discrimination law precluding such attempts to control women's reproductive role in society.[14] Evaluating both countries' experiences with protective legislation reveals a paradox.[15] Legislation designed to accommodate the unique needs of women as child-bearers and nurturers may limit their employment opportunities.[16] And, legislation that mandates absolute equality for women may reduce employment opportunities for women in light of their traditional role as child-bearers and nurturers.[17] Understanding the nature of the paradox can help us to think about alternative approaches to preserving equality while supporting women who choose the role of mother.

II. MEXICO'S EQUAL RIGHTS AMENDMENT AND PROTECTIVE LEGISLATION

Although Mexico declared itself independent from Spain in 1810, because of constant internal strife and political upheaval the country did not attain its current democratic government until the late 1850's.[18] Until then, according to Margaret Leahy, "the political rights of all Mexicans were limited, and the legal rights of women further circumscribed by Spanish law and, for a short time, the Napoleonic codes."[19] For example, "under both Spanish law and the Napoleonic codes, the concept of community property in marriage prevailed."[20] Although both parties had a theoretical right to share in the community property, the husband had the sole right to manage and control that property. Under

---

10. *See infra* text accompanying notes 74-79.
11. *See infra* text accompanying notes 88-93.
12. *See infra* text accompanying note 94.
13. 111 S. Ct. 1196 (1991).
14. *See infra* text accompanying notes 95-104.
15. *See infra* text accompanying notes 109-10.
16. *See infra* text accompanying notes 59-63.
17. *See infra* text accompanying notes 101-03.
18. *See generally* AGUSTIN CUÉ CANOVAS, HISTORIA SOCIAL Y ECONOMICA DE MEXICO: LA REVOLUCION DE INDEPENDENCIA Y MEXICO INDEPENDIENTE HASTA 1854 (1947) (discussing the turbulent history of Mexico from independence to the current democratic government).
19. M. LEAHY, *supra* note 4, at 47.
20. *Id.* at 134-35, n. 1.

both legal systems, marriage was a religious as well as a civil state and divorce was forbidden.[21] The Napoleonic codes forbade "a wife's employment without the express consent of her husband."[22] Finally, in any dispute or separation the father had custody and control of his legitimate children.[23]

The 1857 Constitution defined the rights and duties of citizens in the democratic Mexican Republic.[24] Although "[t]he 1857 Constitution did not explicitly exclude women from voting and holding office . . . the election laws restricted the suffrage to males . . . ."[25]

Mexican women's struggle for the franchise was long and bitter.[26] In 1953, women were finally given the vote, in large part because the ruling party, Partido Revolucionario Institucional (PRI), co-opted women's organizations and ensured that a female voting bloc would not affect the status quo.[27] In fact, winning the franchise splintered women's groups because they had a difficult time organizing around common issues.[28]

---

21. *Id.* at 135, n.1.
22. *Id.*
23. *Id.*
24. *Id.* at 47.
25. WARD M. MORTON, WOMAN SUFFRAGE IN MEXICO 1 (1962). *See also* MARIA ELENA MANZANERA DEL CAMPO, LA IGUALADAD DE DERECHOS POLITICOS 143 (1953) (discussing the meaning of the concept of equality as a political right).
26. The twin goals of the 1910 revolution were economic justice and political democracy (La Tierra y La Libertad). These goals were variously interpreted by the assorted groups, including many women's groups, who actively supported the revolution. During the revolution, many women were significant participants. Some were officers and rose to leadership positions, some exercised influence in their role as private secretaries to male leaders. Others participated in combat, especially in the Red Battalions of Workers. Many women expected that the revolution would result in suffrage for women. However, the struggle for women's suffrage may have been overshadowed by the new republic's fear of the power of the Catholic church, in that women were perceived as much more firmly entrenched in the Catholic church. They were seen as a potential voting bloc controlled by the church. So, in addition to laws forbidding parochial instruction and attempting to loosen church control over land, the specific right of women to vote was left unclear in the 1917 Constitution. M. LEAHY, *supra* note 4, at 47-48.
   President Carranzo's decree of September 19, 1910, set the first election date and "authorized . . . persons to vote who 'are considered residents of the states qualified to vote for Deputies to the Congress.'" W. MORTON, *supra* note 25, at 5 (quoting DIARIO OFICIAL, ÓGANO DEL GOBIERNO PROVISIONAL DE LA RÉPUBLICA MEXICANA, Sept. 22, 1916). However, only males were qualified to vote for deputies. Between that election law and the formal grant of suffrage in 1953, Mexican women were told they must be prepared for the grant of suffrage. Apparently it took over 40 years for them to prepare. *Id.* at 14-15.
27. *See* W. MORTON, *supra* note 25, at 61-84.
28. *Id.* at 88.

In 1975 Mexico City hosted the United Nations World Conference of the International Women's Year.[29] In that same year, Mexico passed a rather interesting equal rights amendment.[30] Article 4 of the Mexican constitution declares that men and women will be treated equally by law.[31] However, the very next sentence of article 4 states that laws shall protect the organization and the development of the family.[32] Because the family is not regarded as an egalitarian institution in Mexico[33] this

29. NATALIE KAUFMAN HEVENER, INTERNATIONAL LAW AND THE STATUS OF WOMEN 201 (1983).

30. In the civil law tradition, the primary emphasis is on the text of the code rather than on judicial interpretation. For example, a Mexican district court is not bound by a previous Supreme Court interpretation of a statute unless the Supreme Court has created binding precedent by ruling the same way in five consecutive cases. Mexican lawyers rarely cite cases in their legal briefs. If they cite anything other than the code, they will cite a treatise or other writing by a legal scholar. In addition, the power of the judiciary is limited. Judges do not have the power to declare statutes unconstitutional and thus void. If a litigant has a claim based on a deprivation of a right guaranteed by the constitution, he or she may use the *amparo* process. *Amparo* is a legal process roughly similar to a writ of habeas corpus in which the constitutionality of the government action is challenged. However, this proceeding is primarily used in criminal cases and is binding only on the involved litigants. The statute, even if found by the judge to be inconsistent with the constitution, stays on the books until the legislature changes it. Paul Bernstein, *El Derecho y El Hecho: Law and Reality in the Mexican Criminal Justice System*, 8 CHICANO L. REV. 40, 45-46 (1985) (citing J. MERRYMAN, THE CIVIL LAW TRADITION (1969)). Broad rulings such as *Roe v. Wade*, 410 U.S. 113 (1973), declaring restrictions on a woman's right to abortion unconstitutional and invalidating all statutes imposing such restrictions are not possible under the Mexican legal system.

31. CONSTITUCIÓN POLÍTICA DE LOS ESTADOS UNIDOS MEXICANOS title I, art. 4 (Mex.) (reprinted in English in CONSTITUTION OF MEXICO 1917 (General Secretariat of the Organization of American States 1977)).

32. *Id.*

33. According to Octavio Paz, a leading Mexican philosopher, the creation of the Mexican race of mixed Spanish and Indian blood caused a deep psychic pain in the Mexican people. On the one hand, the Mexican male feels anger at the Spaniard who raped his mother and, on the other hand, feels anger at his mother for betraying her Indian blood because of the rape. Paz calls this the Malinche syndrome, after Cortez's Indian mistress who served as an interpreter for the Spaniards and bore a son (the first *mestizo*, or mixed blood) who was fathered by Cortez. Some have claimed that this is the source of "machismo"—the exaggerated notion of male superiority and dominance thought to be a part of Mexican culture. Machismo has also created a mythical image of women in Mexican society. A woman is expected to be a pure, long-suffering wife and mother. It is much worse for her to betray her husband than it is for him to be unfaithful to her. *See* OCTAVIO PAZ, LABYRINTH OF SOLITUDE: LIFE AND THOUGHT IN MEXICO 35-40, 66-88 (1961).

In this society of machismo, the father is the undisputed head of the stereotypical Mexican family. He has a domineering relationship with his wife and children. He expects to be pampered at home, but spends much time with friends or a mistress. He neglects his wife and children. The wife, neglected by her husband, accepts his faults and often lives for and through her children. This pattern is repeated for generations in that sons adore and venerate their mother but emulate their father with respect to their wives. Daughters are supposed to repeat the role of their mothers. Alaide Foppa, *Para Que Sirve la Familia?*, 2 FEM. no. 7, at 41 (1978). *See* ALAN RIDING, DISTANT NEIGHBORS: A PORTRAIT OF THE MEXICANS (1985). *See also* FRANCISCO ZARAMA, CONSUELO ZARAMA, & ROBERT ZARAMA URDANATA, LA FAMILIA HOY, EN AMERICA LATINA (1980) (discussing common traits and structure of the family in Mexico).

244 REVIEW OF LAW AND WOMEN'S STUDIES [Vol. 1:239

article creates an inherent tension (if not contradiction) between the goals of guaranteeing equality and furthering women's roles within the family. The second sentence of article 4 justifies protective legislation such as mandatory maternity leave, mandatory *descansos* (breaks for nursing women), laws prohibiting night work and limiting hours, as well as other regulation of working conditions for women—pregnant women, nursing women, and mothers—all in the interests of furthering the family. Such legislation, while accommodating women's roles as mothers, without corollary laws prohibiting discrimination in hiring practices, tends to limit employment opportunities for women.

Recent estimates place the participation of women in the work force in Mexico at approximately 17.6% of females over the age of eight.[34] Women tend to be concentrated in domestic service and clerical positions.[35] Young women between the ages of sixteen and twenty-four are disproportionately represented in assembly line jobs in the border industries (the *maquiladoras*).[36]

In general, Mexico's constitution and labor laws appear committed to preserving workers' rights. Indeed, the Mexican revolution succeeded, in part, because of the alliance of peasants and workers in the revolutionary cause.[37] Revolutionary rhetoric about workers' rights was outlined in the 1917 Constitution.[38] Women's rights and labor reforms, advocated by General Salvador Alvarado, a member of the Constitutional

---

34. JORGE LEOPOLDO RENDÓN, LA PARTICIPACION DE LA MUJER EN LA FUERZA DE TRABAJO: SIGNIFICADO E IMPLICACIONES: EL CASO ESPECÍFICO DEL ESTADO DE MÉXICO 23 (1977). *See also* CÉSAR ZAZUETA, LA MUJER Y EL MERCADO DE TRABAJO EN MEXICO 65-70 (1981). Obviously, a greater percentage of men than women are employed in the work force. However, when the economy grows, the number of women participating in gainful employment increases. Women in urban areas are more likely to work outside the home than women in rural areas. Women in the age group between 15 and 24 are more likely to participate in the work force. Divorced, separated, or widowed women are more likely to work than women who have never married, married women, or women living with someone in an union *libre*. Generally, better educated women tend to work outside the home more often than women with minimal education. If other members of the family work, such as husbands, sons, daughters, cousins, or uncles, the mother of the family is less likely to work outside the home. In rural homes, with many young children in the home, the likelihood of a woman working outside the home is high. Thus, the biggest factor affecting whether women work outside the home is economic need. *Id.*

35. *Id.* at 55.

36. Susanna Peters, *Labor Law for the Maquiladoras: Choosing Between Workers' Rights and Foreign Investment*, 11 COMP. LAB. L.J. 226, 243 n. 91 (1990).

37. JOHN WOMACK, JR., ZAPATA AND THE MEXICAN REVOLUTION (1968); Mary K. Vaughan, *Women, Class and Education in Mexico 1880-1928*, in WOMEN IN LATIN AMERICA: AN ANTHOLOGY FROM LATIN AMERICAN PERSPECTIVES 69-70 (1979).

38. Vaughan, *supra* note 37, at 70-71.

Army, were incorporated into the Mexican Constitution of 1917.[39] General Alvarado believed in individual freedoms and competition, and he championed the liberation of women from religious discrimination, male domination, and economic servitude.[40] Specifically, General Alvarado advocated women's rights to divorce, political participation, education, increased vocational training, and admission to the professions.[41] His labor reforms, which were also incorporated into the Mexican Constitution of 1917, encouraged traditional family life by giving workers the right to organize and bargain, by setting minimum wages and maximum hours, by setting limits on and establishing protection of child labor, and by establishing maternity leaves and rest periods for nursing mothers.[42] Most of these reforms are presently reflected in article 123 of Mexico's current constitution and in the Federal Labor Act of 1970.[43]

The Mexican constitution requires equal wages for equal work regardless of sex or nationality.[44] Both the federal Mexican labor law and the Mexican constitution[45] require state and federal governments to provide pregnant women with a six-week paid maternity leave prior to

---

39. *Id.*
40. *Id.*
41. *Id.*
42. *Id.*
43. *See* CONSTITUCIÓN POLITICA DE LOS ESTADOS UNIDOS MEXICANOS title VI, art. 123 (Mex.); LEY FEDERAL DE TRABAJO [L.F.T.] (Spanish and English text of current Mexican federal labor law reprinted in MEXICAN LABOR LAW (Commerce Clearing House, Inc. 1978)).
44. CONSTITUCIÓN POLITICA DE LOS ESTADOS UNIDOS MEXICANOS title VI, art. 123, para. A-VII (Mex.).
45. *See* U.S. DEP'T OF STATE, 102D CONG., 1ST SESS., COUNTRY REPORTS ON HUMAN RIGHTS PRACTICES FOR 1990 696-700 (1991). This report states:

> The Constitution also provides for a minimum wage for workers, with variations for geographic zones and professional specializations. . . . The U.S. Labor Department study noted that the Government, in controlling the minimum wage (which serves as a benchmark) has not always been able to help workers keep up with inflation and the devaluations of the peso. It finds itself, according to the study, in the difficult position of trying to balance its desire to improve the social lot of workers with its desire to retain employers who might otherwise go elsewhere.
>
> The maximum legal work week is 48 hours. In recent years, the average workweek has declined considerably, to a level of approximately 42 to 43 hours. . . . The Constitution provides for required rest periods, stipulating that workers who do, in fact, put in more than 3 hours of overtime per day or work overtime more than 3 consecutive days must be paid triple his regular wage rate. Anecdotal evidence suggests that workers frequently exceed these work hours.
>
> With respect to occupational health and safety, legislation is relatively advanced and provides substantial protection. Health and safety standards are better observed in large firms. There appears to be a higher incidence of industrial accidents in smaller firms and on construction sites. This does not reflect inadequate legislation, but rather too few inspection personnel to monitor adequately health and safety regulations. Mexican labor law requires the formation of mixed commissions of government, labor, and workers to oversee security and hygiene; it also sets conditions for compensation due to work-related illness or injury.

Id. at 699-700.

birth and a six-week paid maternity leave after birth.[46] Further, under the federal labor law, non-government employers are also required to provide a six-week pre-birth paid maternity leave and a six-week after-birth paid maternity leave.[47] After the child's birth, the law allows for two additional breaks a day in order to allow a nursing mother to continue nursing when she is at work.[48] The employer must provide an adequate and sanitary place for this lactation period.[49]

During maternity leave, women are to receive full salary for the mandatory period; if they take an extension of the mandatory period, they are also entitled to fifty percent of their salary for up to sixty days.[50] They are entitled to return to their jobs if they return within a year after their child's birth.[51] Their maternity leave periods are included in computations of seniority.[52] Employers are directed to adopt measures to "ensure the greatest possible guarantee for the health and safety of workers" and, in the case of pregnant workers, for their unborn children.[53] Pregnant women are prohibited from working in jobs which would endanger the health of the woman or of her fetus and from working after ten in the evening.[54] In addition, a woman may not work over-time when her health or the health of her fetus is in danger.[55] The labor law also requires that sufficient chairs or seats be provided for pregnant

---

46. L.F.T. title fifth, art. 170, para. II; CONSTITUCIÓN POLITICA DE LOS ESTADOS UNIDOS MEXICANOS title VII, art. 123, para. V (Mex.).

47. CONSTITUCIÓN POLITICA DE LOS ESTADOS UNIDOS MEXICANOS title VII, art. 123, para. V (Mex.) ("They [women] shall necessarily be entitled to six weeks leave prior to the approximate date of child birth and to six weeks leave thereafter.").

48. L.F.T. title fifth, art. 170, para. IV; CONSTITUCIÓN POLITICA DE LOS ESTADOS UNIDOS MEXICANOS title VII, art. 123, para. V (Mex.).

49. L.F.T. title fifth, art. 170, para. IV.

50. *Id.* at title fifth, art. 170, paras. III, V.

51. *Id.* at title fifth, art. 170, para. VI.

52. *Id.* at title fifth, art. 170, para. VII.

53. CONSTITUCIÓN POLITICA DE LOS ESTADOS UNIDOS MEXICANOS title VI, art. 123, para. A-XV (Mex.).

54. L.F.T. title fifth, art. 166.

55. *Id.* Given the weak economy in Mexico, most people cannot support their family based on the 48 hour work week. Overtime is an economic necessity. Instead of receiving higher overtime pay from employers reluctant to pay it, Mexicans often take second jobs to survive. 1990 HUMAN RIGHTS REPORT, *supra* note 45, at 699.

working women to use.[56] Additionally, child care services are to be provided by the Mexican Institute of Social Security.[57] Mexicans are quite proud of these special protections for women.[58]

When employers comply with their legal obligations,[59] pregnant women may use these protections to tend to their traditional family role as child-bearer and nurturer. However, some problems exist. First, not all women want or need these provisions.[60] Many working women do not have children.[61] Even among women who have children, not all of them would choose to use the protections afforded them.[62] Second, Mexico does not have legislation prohibiting employment discrimination in hiring based on sex, pregnancy, or potential for pregnancy. Accordingly, some employers concerned with the potentially high cost of employing women who might need these mandatory benefits discriminate against women. In addition, some companies require women to state that they are infertile on job applications.[63] If a woman becomes pregnant after stating she is infertile, she may be fired for lying on the job application.[64] Thus, protective legislation has a negative effect on women's employment opportunities.

In Mexico, protective legislation furthers a concept of the family in which the husband is the head of the household and their wives are their dependents and the bearers and nurturers of their children.[65] Protective legislation is viewed by many Mexicans as progress in improving most women's lives.[66] The fact that protective legislation may reduce employment opportunities for women is viewed by some as positive support for

---

56. L.F.T. title fifth, art. 172.

57. *Id.* at title fifth, art. 171. Unfortunately, child care is not always adequate. Interview with Licenciada Patricia Begne, Professor, Universidad de Guanajuato, author of MANUAL DE LOS DERECHOS DE LA MUJER (1987) (Nov. 5, 1991).

58. Interview with Licenciado Juan Renee Segura, Mexican labor lawyer and Professor, Universidad de Guanajuato, Facultad de Derecho (Fall 1990) ("Mexico still believes that the most important unit in its society is the family. The United States believes that the most important unit in society is the almighty dollar.").

59. Most employers fail to comply with these provisions. *Id.*

60. Interview with Lic. Patricia Begne (June, 1990).

61. J. RENDÓN, *supra* note 35, at 77.

62. Pregnancy leaves may detrimentally affect the careers of some women. Interview with Lic. Begne, *supra* note 57.

63. *See, e.g.*, Marlise Simons, *Brazil Women Find Fertility May Cost Jobs*, N.Y. Times, Dec. 7, 1988, at A11, col. 1 (describing the identical problem in Brazil).

64. *Id.*

65. *See supra* note 33.

66. JOSÉ ANTONIO ALONSO, SEXO, TRABAJO Y MARGINALIDAD URBANA 96-97 (1981) (study of women's participation in the work force in Nezahualcoyotl. Only 24% of the women worked outside the home for a salary, and 46% worked in their own home. 38% of the women who worked

the traditional family.[67] Further, some feminists in Mexico advocate for enforcement of protective legislation such as day care and pregnancy leaves.[68] Others are aware of its negative impact on women's employment opportunities.[69]

III. PROTECTIVE LEGISLATION IN THE UNITED STATES

In the early 1900's feminists in the United States also supported protective legislation as a means to improve women's lives.[70] For example, in the United States Supreme Court case of *Muller v. Oregon*,[71] Louis Brandeis, representing several women's organizations, argued that Oregon laws limiting a factory woman's labor to ten hours a day should be upheld because, as potential mothers, women needed special legislation to protect them from jobs or occupational situations that could negatively affect their health.[72] However, the court in *Muller* did not focus on protecting women's health or improving women's lives. Rather, the Court focused on the health of potential *offspring*. In upholding the ten hour-a-day limit for female factory workers, the court stated: "[H]ealthy mothers are essential to vigorous offspring, the physical well-being of women becomes an object of public interest and care in order to preserve the strength and vigor of the race."[73] Thus, in 1906, protective legislation protected *women's* health as a corollary to protecting (and controlling) women's reproductive role in society.

When the Supreme Court in *Adkins v. Children's Hospital*[74] later declared a law setting minimum wage for women unconstitutional, the National Women's Party found this to be a victory for women's rights; however, many women's groups and labor organizations denounced it as

---

outside the home worked as domestics, 16% had small businesses, 9% were manual laborers, 1% were professionals, and 10% were factory workers).

67. Interview with Lic. Segura, *supra* note 58.

68. PATRICK OSTER, THE MEXICANS: A PERSONAL PORTRAIT OF A PEOPLE 270 (1989) (portrait of "la femenista": "[feminists] discuss whether Mexican women will ever get adequate day care or paid maternity leaves.").

69. Interview with Lic. Begne, *supra* note 57.

70. *See* ELEANOR FLEXNER, CENTURY OF STRUGGLE: THE WOMAN'S RIGHTS MOVEMENT IN THE UNITED STATES chaps. 9, 14, 18 (rev. ed. 1975); WILLIAM L. O'NEILL, EVERYONE WAS BRAVE: THE RISE AND FALL OF FEMINISM IN AMERICA 152-53 (1969).

71. 208 U.S. 412 (1908) (upholding Oregon's minimum hour legislation as applied only to women).

72. Mary Ann Mason, *Motherhood v. Equal Treatment*, 29 J. FAM. L. 1, 3-4 (1990-91). *See also* CARL N. DEGLER, AT ODDS: WOMEN AND THE FAMILY IN AMERICA FROM THE REVOLUTION TO THE PRESENT (1980) (discussing women's early support for protective legislation).

73. 208 U.S. at 421.

74. 261 U.S. 525 (1923), *overruled* by West Coast Hotel Co. v. Parrish, 300 U.S. 379 (1937).

a retreat from *Muller v. Oregon*.[75] Interestingly, the Court in *Adkins* did not retreat dramatically from the idea that protecting women's health was a constitutionally permissible objective.[76] Rather, the Court found a relationship between numbers of hours worked and women's health,[77] but little relationship between minimum wages for women and women's health.[78] Thus, the doctrinal basis for treating men and women equally was not developed in *Adkins*, despite the National Women's Party support for the opinion.[79]

More recently, after a long struggle, the proposed Equal Rights Amendment to the U.S. Constitution failed to pass.[80] However, antidiscrimination legislation such as the Civil Rights Act of 1964[81] and several executive orders,[82] together with the subsequent judicial interpretation of these laws, have served to dismantle protective legislation. The judicial effort has invalidated mandatory maternity leave,[83] laws restricting women's work hours and how much weight they could lift,[84] and other protections[85] that had been enacted during the first forty years of the twentieth century.

---

75. *See* C. DEGLER, *supra* note 72, at 403.

76. 261 U.S. at 554.

77. *Id.*

78. *Id.* at 555.

79. C. DEGLER, *supra* note 72, at 403. This conflict between protective legislation and equal treatment bedeviled feminists in this country for many years. *See, e.g.*, SUSAN D. BECKER, THE ORIGINS OF THE EQUAL RIGHTS AMENDMENT: AMERICAN FEMINISM BETWEEN THE WARS (1981). Further, this conflict is still an issue in the feminist debate between equal treatment and special treatment. *See, e.g.*, Alison M. Jaggar, *Sexual Difference and Sexual Equality*, in THEORETICAL PERSPECTIVES ON SEXUAL DIFFERENCES (Deborah L. Rhode ed. 1990); Christine A. Littleton, *Reconstructing Sexual Equality*, 75 CALIF. L. REV. 1279 (1987).

80. MARY FRANCES BERRY, WHY ERA FAILED: POLITICS, WOMEN'S RIGHTS, AND THE AMENDING PROCESS OF THE CONSTITUTION (1986); WILLIAM HENRY CHAFE, THE AMERICAN WOMAN: HER CHANGING SOCIAL, ECONOMIC, AND POLITICAL ROLES, 1920-1970, 112-32 (1972). *See generally* JANET K. BOLES, THE POLITICS OF THE EQUAL RIGHTS AMENDMENT: CONFLICT AND THE DECISION PROCESS (1979) (discussing the various pressures that came to bear in the attempted passage of the equal rights amendment).

81. 42 U.S.C. §§ 2000e to 2000e-17 (1988).

82. Exec. Order No. 11246, 3 C.F.R. 339 (1964-1965), *reprinted in* 3 U.S.C. § 2000e app. at 398-401; Exec. Order No. 11375, 3 C.F.R. 684 (1966-1970); Exec. Order No. 11478, 3 C.F.R. 803 (1966-1970), *reprinted in* 3 U.S.C. § 2000e app. at 402.

83. *E.g.*, Schattman v. Texas Employment Comm'n, 459 F.2d 32 (5th Cir. 1972) (upholding mandatory maternity leave after seven months of pregnancy), *cert. denied*, 409 U.S. 1107 (1973).

84. *E.g.*, Rosenfeld v. Southern Pacific Co., 444 F.2d. 1219 (9th Cir. 1971) (laws regulating women's work hours and weights they could lift violate Title VII of the Civil Rights Act of 1964).

85. *See, e.g.*, Krause v. Sacramento, 479 F.2d. 988 (9th Cir. 1973) (invalidating law prohibiting women from working as bartenders). *See also* WOMEN'S BUREAU, U.S. DEP'T OF LABOR, STATUS OF STATE HOUR LAWS FOR WOMEN SINCE PASSAGE OF TITLE VII OF THE CIVIL RIGHTS ACT OF 1964 (July 1, 1972) (discussing changes in state laws restricting hours women could work since passage of civil rights legislation).

Recently, more women have been entering the work force.[86] Unfortunately, despite the passage of the Equal Pay Act, women have consistently earned less than men.[87] Interestingly, there appears to be another "protective" movement gathering strength in the United States. After years of chipping away at abortion rights, massive attempts to finally reverse *Roe v. Wade*[88] have been launched.[89] The Supreme Court has permitted the government to deny federal funds to family planning clinics that counsel about abortion as a method of family planning.[90] Commentators urge states to use resources to punish or jail pregnant addicts rather than to treat them.[91] Court orders have been issued forcing women to have cesareans against their will in order to protect the fetus.[92] Employers have enacted fetal protection policies in the workplace to protect fertile women from working in jobs thought to be dangerous to the potential fetus.[93]

These laws and policies may appear to be an attempt to protect fetuses but, in fact, they control women's reproductive roles and only indirectly affect fetuses. If the government really wanted to ensure healthy fetuses, it would channel money to adequate prenatal care, daycare, birth control, treatment and education programs, and safe workplaces for all workers. This new wave of legislation and policies controls women's reproductive role in society by limiting women's ability to choose when to give birth and how to manage their pregnancies. This

---

86. In 1986, 55.3% of women over age 16 participated in the work force, up from 37.7% participating in 1960. BUREAU OF THE CENSUS, U.S. DEP'T OF COMMERCE, STATISTICAL ABSTRACT OF THE UNITED STATES 365, no. 607 (1988).

87. *See generally* WOMEN, WORK AND WAGES: EQUAL PAY FOR JOBS OF EQUAL VALUE (Donald J. Treiman & Heidi I. Hartmann eds. 1981) (report on the validity of compensation systems and methods for determining the relative worth of jobs, including the question of whether and to what extent existing pay differences between jobs are the result of discrimination).

88. 410 U.S. 113 (1973) (a state may not prohibit a woman's decision to terminate her pregnancy prior to viability of the fetus).

89. *See* ROBERT D. GOLDSTEIN, MOTHER LOVE AND ABORTION: A LEGAL INTERPRETATION 1-37 (1988) (a comprehensive description of the positions of "regulators" and "deregulators" in the current abortion debate).

90. Rust v. Sullivan, 111 S. Ct. 1759 (1991).

91. *See, e.g.*, Kathryn Schierl, *A Proposal to Illinois Legislators: Revise the Illinois Criminal Code to Include Criminal Sanctions Against Prenatal Substance Abusers*, 23 J. MARSHALL L. REV. 393, 402-07 (1990).

92. *See, e.g.*, Nancy K. Rhoden, *The Judge in the Delivery Room: The Emergence of Court-Ordered Cesareans*, 74 CALIF. L. REV. 1951 (1986).

93. *See, e.g.*, Wendy W. Williams, *Firing the Woman to Protect the Fetus: The Reconciliation of Fetal Protection with Employment Opportunity Goals Under Title VII*, 69 GEO. L.J. 641 (1981).

protective "movement" elevates the perceived interests of fetuses over the interests of women.[94]

However, antidiscrimination laws may provide a means to curb attempts to control women's reproductive role. For example, on March 20, 1991, in *International Union v. Johnson Controls*,[95] the Supreme Court unanimously struck down a "fetal protection policy" instituted by Johnson Controls, Inc. which excluded women who could not medically document their infertility from working in a battery manufacturing plant.

Justice Blackmun, writing the majority opinion, framed the issue as whether an employer may exclude a fertile female employee from certain jobs because of the employer's concern for the health of a fetus the woman might conceive. Despite evidence about the effect of lead exposure on the male reproductive system, Johnson Controls chose only to apply exclusionary policies to fertile females.[96] Thus, all women were treated as potentially pregnant, and no men were treated as at risk. The Court determined that such an exclusion violates the Pregnancy Discrimination Act and constitutes sex discrimination under Title VII,[97] and therefore found that the Johnson Controls fetal protection policy facially discriminated against women on the basis of sex and potential for childbearing.[98]

After finding that the policy constituted discrimination on the basis of sex under Title VII,[99] the Court went on to find that Johnson Controls could not show infertility as a bona fide occupational qualification because the protection of unborn potential fetuses did not relate to the "essence" of the business of manufacturing lead batteries.[100] The Court cited *Muller*[101] as a case where concern for a woman's potential offspring historically served as an excuse for denying women equal employment opportunities. The Court in *Johnson Controls* concluded: "It is no more

---

94. "Fetus-mania" is a term coined in seminar classes I have taught entitled "Reproductive Technology and the Law." Fetus-mania is defined as elevating the interests of fetuses over pregnant (or even non-pregnant) women. I am grateful to all the students who have taken the class for the many insights they have shared with me.

95. 111 S. Ct. 1196 (1991). This case and its relation to reproductive rights are also discussed in Laura C. Fry, *Is It Enough that* Johnson Controls?, 1 S. CAL. REV. L. & WOMEN'S STUD. 255 (1992).

96. 111 S. Ct. at 1199-1200.

97. 42 U.S.C. § 2000e(k) (1988).

98. Johnson Controls, 111 S. Ct. 1196.

99. *Id.* at 1203.

100. *Id.* at 1205-06.

101. *Id.* at 1210, *citing* Muller v. Oregon, 208 U.S. 412 (1908).

appropriate for the courts than it is for individual employers to decide whether a woman's reproductive role is more important to herself and her family than her economic role. Congress has left this choice to the woman as hers to make."[102] This is an example of the Court finding that antidiscrimination law prohibits an employer from controlling a woman's individual choices about her reproductive role. The District Court[103] and the Seventh Circuit[104] had both viewed all fertile women as pregnancies waiting to happen. All fertile women were potentially pregnant women. The lower courts then elevated potential fetuses' interests above the interests of the potentially pregnant women workers, thus treating women as vessels without autonomy to make choices relating to their reproductive roles. The Supreme Court's reversal is a message that women as individuals should be afforded choices by employers about their reproductive roles to the same extent as men. In short, antidiscrimination law in this case precluded an attempt to control women's reproductive role.

Despite the invalidation of protective legislation and the corresponding enhancement of employment opportunities, women are still concentrated in "pink collar" and service jobs and earn substantially less than their male counterparts.[105] Additionally, many middle class women who enter the work force find it difficult to balance their family roles with their employment responsibilities (a problem that many minority, working class, and poor women have experienced for generations).[106] Much has been written about the dilemma women face because of the double burden of family responsibilities and employment responsibilities.[107] Because men do not assume responsibility for children to the extent women do,[108] the burden of balancing family and work has not

---

102.   111 S. Ct. at 1210.

103.   680 F. Supp. 309 (1988).

104.   886 F.2d 871 (1989).

105.   *E.g.*, THE AMERICAN WOMAN 1988-89, A STATUS REPORT 387 (Sarah E. Rix ed. 1988).

106.   *See, e.g.*, Project, *Law Firms and Lawyers with Children: An Empirical Analysis of Family/ Work Conflict*, 34 STAN. L. REV. 1263, 1274 (1982); Mary Joe Frug, *Securing Job Equality for Women: Labor Market Hostility to Working Mothers*, 59 B.U.L. REV. 55 (1979).

107.   *See, e.g.*, Heidi Hartmann, *The Family as the Locus of Gender, Class and Political Struggle: The Example of Housework*, 6 SIGNS 366 (1981); Barbara Wolfe and Robert Haveman, *Time Allocation, Market Work and Changes in Female Health*, 73 AMERICAN ECONOMIC REVIEW 12, 134-39 (1983); Lee Teitelbaum, Antoinette Sedillo Lopez, Jeffrey Jenkins, *Gender, Legal Education and Careers*, 41 J. LEG. EDUC. (1991) (manuscript on file with author).

108.   Martha S. Hill, *Patterns of Time Use*, in TIME, GOODS, AND WELL-BEING 133 (F. Thomas Juster & Frank P. Stafford eds. 1985); Elizabeth Maret & Barbara Finlay, *The Distribution of Household Labor Among Women in Dual-Earner Families*, 46 J. MARRIAGE & FAM. 357, 360 (1984).

proven to be as problematic for men. Thus, equal treatment in employment opportunities does not address the real problems women face because of their traditional family role.

IV. CONCLUSION

The traditional structure of the family tends to define motherhood. Mexico, because of its cultural preference for *la familia*, has chosen to further its version of the traditional structure of the family with protective legislation because women's biological differences in childbearing and nurturing justify protective legislation. This has enabled some employed women in Mexico to attend to their role in the traditional family structure more easily after having children. However, protective legislation has also limited many Mexican women's employment opportunities.

In the United States, antidiscrimination laws have served to strike down legislative and employer attempts to control women's reproductive role in the family. Permitting women to make those choices has theoretically enhanced their employment opportunities. Thus, women are treated as autonomous, independent moral agents with the same choices afforded to men in balancing employment and family. Unfortunately, because of the traditional family structure, balancing employment with family responsibilities is more difficult for many women than it has been for men.

In comparing the two countries' approaches to women and employment, the paradox between protective legislation and equality becomes apparent. Protective legislation designed to accommodate women's pregnancy and childbearing, in the absence of antidiscrimination law, tends to limit women's employment opportunities. However, women in Mexico who choose to have children can more easily attend to their families. In contrast, in the United States, women's employment opportunities are not limited by protective legislation. However, because of women's traditional role in the family structure, pursuing employment opportunities and having families poses arduous difficulties which may de facto limit women's opportunities.

Perhaps what is needed is a combination of approaches which accommodate women's unique biological needs while ensuring that such accommodations do not attempt to control women's reproductive role. In reconstructing motherhood we should consider advocating for optional maternity leaves, paid for by the government,[109] and optional flexible work schedules.[110] We should support affordable quality day care. We should continue to support equal pay and antidiscrimination laws. These types of reforms would support women who choose the role of mother while serving the principle of treating men and women equally.

---

109. Of course, universal child care and health care would also solve many problems for working women as well as children in this country.

110. And we must think about creative ways of providing employers with incentives to provide flexible work schedules.

THE DEVELOPMENT OF CHICANA FEMINIST DISCOURSE, 1970-1980

ALMA M. GARCIA
Santa Clara University

The years between 1970 and 1980 represented a formative period in the development of Chicana feminist thought in the United States. During this period, Chicana feminists addressed the specific issues affecting Chicanas as women of color in the United States. As a result of their collective efforts in struggling against racial, class, and gender oppression, Chicana feminists developed an ideological discourse that addressed three major issues. These were the relationship between Chicana feminism and the ideology of cultural nationalism, feminist baiting within the Chicano movement, and the relationship between the Chicana feminist movement and the white feminist movement. This article describes the development of Chicana feminism and compares it with Asian American and Black feminism, which faced similar problems.

Between 1970 and 1980, a Chicana feminist movement developed in the United States that addressed the specific issues that affected Chicanas as women of color. The growth of the Chicana feminist movement can be traced in the speeches, essays, letters, and articles published in Chicano and Chicana newspapers, journals, newsletters, and other printed materials.[1]

AUTHOR'S NOTE: *Research for this article was supported by Rev. Thomas Terry, S.J., university research grant awarded by Santa Clara University. Two substantively different versions of this article were presented at the 1985 Annual Conference of the National Association of Chicano Studies, Sacramento, CA, and the 1986 International Congress of the Latin American Studies Association, Boston, MA. I would like to thank Maxine Baca Zinn, Ada Sosa Riddell, Vicki L. Ruiz, Janet Flammang, Judith Lorber, and the referees for their constructive criticism. I am grateful to Francisco Jimenez for his thoughtful editorial suggestions and for his moral support and encouragement during this entire project.*

REPRINT REQUESTS: *Alma M. Garcia, Sociology Department, Santa Clara University, Santa Clara, CA 95053.*

GENDER & SOCIETY, Vol. 3 No. 2, June 1989 217-238
© 1989 Sociologists for Women in Society

217

During the sixties, American society witnessed the development of the Chicano movement, a social movement characterized by a politics of protest (Barrera 1974; Muñoz 1974; Navarro 1974). The Chicano movement focused on a wide range of issues: social justice, equality, educational reforms, and political and economic self-determination for Chicano communities in the United States. Various struggles evolved within this movement: the United Farmworkers unionization efforts (Dunne 1967; Kushner 1975; Matthiesen 1969; Nelson 1966); the New Mexico Land Grant movement (Nabokov 1969); the Colorado-based Crusade for Justice (Castro 1974; Meier and Rivera 1972); the Chicano student movement (Garcia and de la Garza 1977); and the Raza Unida Party (Shockley 1974).

Chicanas participated actively in each of these struggles. By the end of the sixties, Chicanas began to assess the rewards and limits of their participation. The 1970s witnessed the development of Chicana feminists whose activities, organizations, and writings can be analyzed in terms of a feminist movement by women of color in American society. Chicana feminists outlined a cluster of ideas that crystallized into an emergent Chicana feminist debate. In the same way that Chicano males were reinterpreting the historical and contemporary experience of Chicanos in the United States, Chicanas began to investigate the forces shaping their own experiences as women of color.

The Chicana feminist movement emerged primarily as a result of the dynamics within the Chicano movement. In the 1960s and 1970s, the American political scene witnessed far-reaching social protest movements whose political courses often paralleled and at times exerted influence over each other (Freeman 1983; Piven and Cloward 1979). The development of feminist movements have been explained by the participation of women in larger social movements. Macias (1982), for example, links the early development of the Mexican feminist movement to the participation of women in the Mexican Revolution. Similarly, Freeman's (1984) analysis of the white feminist movement points out that many white feminists who were active in the early years of its development had previously been involved in the new left and civil rights movements. It was in these movements that white feminists experienced the constraints of male domination. Black feminists have similarly traced the development of a Black feminist movement during the 1960s and 1970s to their experiences with sexism in the larger Black movement (Davis 1983; Dill 1983;

Hooks 1981, 1984; Joseph and Lewis 1981; White 1984). In this way, then, the origins of Chicana feminism parallel those of other feminist movements.

ORIGINS OF CHICANA FEMINISM

Rowbotham (1974) argues that women may develop a feminist consciousness as a result of their experiences with sexism in revolutionary struggles or mass social movements. To the extent that such movements are male dominated, women are likely to develop a feminist consciousness. Chicana feminists began the search for a "room of their own" by assessing their participation within the Chicano movement. Their feminist consciousness emerged from a struggle for equality with Chicano men and from a reassessment of the role of the family as a means of resistance to oppressive societal conditions.

Historically, as well as during the 1960s and 1970s, the Chicano family represented a source of cultural and political resistance to the various types of discrimination experienced in American society (Zinn 1975a). At the cultural level, the Chicano movement emphasized the need to safeguard the value of family loyalty. At the political level, the Chicano movement used the family as a strategic organizational tool for protest activities.

Dramatic changes in the structure of Chicano families occurred as they participated in the Chicano movement. Specifically, women began to question their traditional female roles (Zinn 1975a). Thus, a Chicana feminist movement originated from the nationalist Chicano struggle. Rowbotham (1974, p. 206) refers to such a feminist movement as "a colony within a colony." But as the Chicano movement developed during the 1970s, Chicana feminists began to draw their own political agenda and raised a series of questions to assess their role within the Chicano movement. They entered into a dialogue with each other that explicitly reflected their struggles to secure a room of their own within the Chicano movement.

DEFINING FEMINISM FOR WOMEN OF COLOR

A central question of feminist discourse is the definition of feminism. The lack of consensus reflects different political ideologies and divergent social-class bases. In the United States, Chicana feminists shared the task of defining their ideology and movement with white, Black, and Asian American feminists. Like Black and Asian American feminists, Chicana feminists struggled to gain social equality and end sexist and racist oppression. Like them, Chicana feminists recognized that the nature of social inequality for women of color was multidimensional (Cheng 1984; Chow 1987; Hooks 1981). Like Black and Asian American feminists, Chicana feminists struggled to gain equal status in the male-dominated nationalist movements and also in American society. To them, feminism represented a movement to end sexist oppression within a broader social protest movement. Again, like Black and Asian American feminists, Chicana feminists fought for social equality in the 1970s. They understood that their movement needed to go beyond women's rights and include the men of their group, who also faced racial subordination (Hooks 1981). Chicanas believed that feminism involved more than an analysis of gender because, as women of color, they were affected by both race and class in their everyday lives. Thus, Chicana feminism, as a social movement to improve the position of Chicanas in American society, represented a struggle that was both nationalist and feminist.

Chicana, Black, and Asian American feminists were all confronted with the issue of engaging in a feminist struggle to end sexist oppression within a broader nationalist struggle to end racist oppression. All experienced male domination in their own communities as well as in the larger society. Ngan-Ling Chow (1987) identifies gender stereotypes of Asian American women and the patriarchal family structure as major sources of women's oppression. Cultural, political, and economic constraints have, according to Ngan-Ling Chow (1987), limited the full development of a feminist consciousness and movement among Asian American women. The cross-pressures resulting from the demands of a nationalist and a feminist struggle led some Asian American women to organize feminist organizations that, however, continued to address broader issues affecting the Asian American community.

Black women were also faced with addressing feminist issues within a nationalist movement. According to Thornton Dill (1983), Black women played a major historical role in Black resistance movements and, in addition, brought a feminist component to these movements (Davis 1983; Dill 1983). Black women have struggled with Black men in nationalist movements but have also recognized and fought against the sexism in such political movements in the

Black community (Hooks 1984). Although they wrote and spoke as Black feminists, they did not organize separately from Black men.

Among the major ideological questions facing all three groups of feminists were the relationship between feminism and the ideology of cultural nationalism or racial pride, feminism and feminist baiting within the larger movements, and the relationship between their feminist movements and the white feminist movement.

CHICANA FEMINISM AND
CULTURAL NATIONALISM

Throughout the seventies and now, in the eighties, Chicana feminists have been forced to respond to the criticism that cultural nationalism and feminism are irreconcilable. In the first issue of the newspaper, *Hijas de Cuauhtemoc*, Anna Nieto Gomez (1971) stated that a major issue facing Chicanas active in the Chicano movement was the need to organize to improve their status as women within the larger social movement. Francisca Flores (1971b, p. i), another leading Chicana feminist, stated:

> [Chicanas] can no longer remain in a subservient role or as auxiliary forces in the [Chicano] movement. They must be included in the front line of communication, leadership and organizational responsibility. . . . The issue of equality, freedom and self-determination of the Chicana—like the right of self-determination, equality, and liberation of the Mexican [Chicano] community—is not negotiable. Anyone opposing the right of women to organize into their own form of organization has no place in the leadership of the movement.

Supporting this position, Bernice Rincon (1971) argued that a Chicana feminist movement that sought equality and justice for Chicanas would strengthen the Chicano movement. Yet in the process, Chicana feminists challenged traditional gender roles because they limited their participation and acceptance within the Chicano movement.

Throughout the seventies, Chicana feminists viewed the struggle against sexism within the Chicano movement and the struggle against racism in the larger society as integral parts of Chicana feminism. As Nieto Gomez (1976, p. 10) said:

> Chicana feminism is in various stages of development. However, in general, Chicana feminism is the recognition that women are oppressed as a group and are exploited as part of *la Raza* people. It is a direction to be responsible to identify and act upon the issues and needs of Chicana

women. Chicana feminists are involved in understanding the nature of women's oppression.

Cultural nationalism represented a major ideological component of the Chicano movement. Its emphasis on Chicano cultural pride and cultural survival within an Anglo-dominated society gave significant political direction to the Chicano movement. One source of ideological disagreement between Chicana feminism and this cultural nationalist ideology was cultural survival. Many Chicana feminists believed that a focus on cultural survival did not acknowledge the need to alter male-female relations within Chicano communities. For example, Chicana feminists criticized the notion of the "ideal Chicana" that glorified Chicanas as strong, long-suffering women who had endured and kept Chicano culture and the family intact. To Chicana feminists, this concept represented an obstacle to the redefinition of gender roles. Nieto (1975, p. 4) stated:

> Some Chicanas are praised as they emulate the sanctified example set by [the Virgin] Mary. The woman *par excellence* is mother and wife. She is to love and support her husband and to nurture and teach her children. Thus, may she gain fulfillment as a woman. For a Chicana bent upon fulfillment of her personhood, this restricted perspective of her role as a woman is not only inadequate but crippling.

Chicana feminists were also skeptical about the cultural nationalist interpretation of machismo. Such an interpretation viewed machismo as an ideological tool used by the dominant Anglo society to justify the inequalities experienced by Chicanos. According to this interpretation, the relationship between Chicanos and the larger society was that of an internal colony dominated and exploited by the capitalist economy (Almaguer 1974; Barrera 1979). Machismo, like other cultural traits, was blamed by Anglos for blocking Chicanos from succeeding in American society. In reality, the economic structure and colony-like exploitation were to blame.

Some Chicana feminists agreed with this analysis of machismo, claiming that a mutually reinforcing relationship existed between internal colonialism and the development of the myth of machismo. According to Sosa Riddell (1974, p. 21), machismo was a myth "propagated by subjugators and colonizers, which created damaging stereotypes of Mexican/Chicano males." As a type of social control imposed by the dominant society on Chicanos, the myth of machismo distorted gender relations within Chicano communities, creating stereotypes of Chicanas as passive and docile women. At this level in

the feminist discourse, machismo was seen as an Anglo myth that
kept both Chicano and Chicanas in a subordinate status. As Nieto
(1975, p. 4) concluded:

> Although the term "machismo" is correctly denounced by all because
> it stereotypes the Latin man . . . it does a great disservice to both men
> and women. Chicano and Chicana alike must be free to seek their own
> individual fulfillment.

While some Chicana feminists criticized the myth of machismo used
by the dominant society to legitimate racial inequality, others moved
beyond this level of analysis to distinguish between the machismo
that oppressed both men and women and the sexism in Chicano
communities in general, and the Chicano movement in particular,
that oppressed Chicana women (Chavez 1971; Cotera 1977; Del
Castillo 1974; Marquez and Ramirez 1977; Riddell 1974; Zinn 1975b).
According to Vidal (1971, p. 8), the origins of a Chicana feminist
consciousness were prompted by the sexist attitudes and behavior of
Chicano males, which constituted a "serious obstacle to women
anxious to play a role in the struggle for Chicana liberation."

Furthermore, many Chicana feminists disagreed with the cultural
nationalist view that machismo could be a positive value within a
Chicano cultural value system. They challenged the view that
machismo was a source of masculine pride for Chicanos and
therefore a defense mechanism against the dominant society's racism.
Although Chicana feminists recognized that Chicanos faced discrimination from the dominant society, they adamantly disagreed
with those who believed that machismo was a form of cultural
resistance to such discrimination. Chicana feminists called for
changes in the ideologies responsible for distorting relations between
women and men. One such change was to modify the cultural
nationalist position that viewed machismo as a source of cultural
pride.

Chicana feminists called for a focus on the universal aspects of
sexism that shape gender relations in both Anglo and Chicano
culture. While they acknowledged the economic exploitation of all
Chicanos, Chicana feminists outlined the double exploitation experienced by Chicanas. Sosa Riddell (1974, p. 159) concluded: "It was
when Chicanas began to seek work outside of the family groups that
sexism became a key factor of oppression along with racism."
Francisca Flores (1971a, p. 4) summarized some of the consequences
of sexism:

It is not surprising that more and more Chicanas are forced to go to work in order to supplement the family income. The children are farmed out to a relative to baby-sit with them, and since these women are employed in the lower income jobs, the extra pressure placed on them can become unbearable.

Thus, while the Chicano movement was addressing the issue of racial oppression facing all Chicanos, Chicana feminists argued that it lacked an analysis of sexism. Similarly, Black and Asian American women stressed the interconnectedness of race and gender oppression. Hooks (1984, p. 52) analyzes racism and sexism in terms of their "intersecting, complementary nature." She also emphasizes that one struggle should not take priority over the other. White (1984) criticizes Black men whose nationalism limited discussions of Black women's experiences with sexist oppression. The writings of other Black feminists criticized a Black cultural nationalist ideology that overlooked the consequences of sexist oppression (Beale 1975; Cade 1970; Davis 1971; Joseph and Lewis 1981). Many Asian American women were also critical of the Asian American movement whose focus on racism ignored the impact of sexism on the daily lives of women. The participation of Asian American women in various community struggles increased their encounters with sexism (Chow 1987). As a result, some Asian American women developed a feminist consciousness and organized as women around feminist issues.

CHICANA FEMINISM AND FEMINIST BAITING

The systematic analysis by Chicana feminists of the impact of racism and sexism on Chicanas in American society and, above all, within the Chicano movement was often misunderstood as a threat to the political unity of the Chicano movement. As Marta Cotera (1977, p. 9), a leading voice of Chicana feminism pointed out:

The aggregate cultural values we [Chicanas] share can also work to our benefit if we choose to scrutinize our cultural traditions, isolate the positive attributes and interpret them for the benefit of women. It's unreal that *Hispanas* have been browbeaten for so long about our so-called conservative (meaning reactionary) culture. It's also unreal that we have let men interpret culture only as those practices and attitudes that determine who does the dishes around the house. We as women also have the right to interpret and define the philosophical and religious traditions beneficial to us within our culture, and which we have inherited as our tradition. To do this, we must become both conversant with our history and philosophical evolution, and analytical about the institutional and behavioral manifestations of the same.

Such Chicana feminists were attacked for developing a "divisive ideology"—a feminist ideology that was frequently viewed as a threat to the Chicano movement as a whole. As Chicana feminists examined their roles as women activists within the Chicano movement, an ideological split developed. One group active in the Chicano movement saw themselves as "loyalists" who believed that the Chicano movement did not have to deal with sexual inequities since Chicano men as well as Chicano women experienced racial oppression. According to Nieto Gomez (1973, p. 35), who was not a loyalist, their view was that if men oppress women, it is not the men's fault but rather that of the system.

Even if such a problem existed, and they did not believe that it did, the loyalists maintained that such a matter would best be resolved internally within the Chicano movement. They denounced the formation of a separate Chicana feminist movement on the grounds that it was a politically dangerous strategy, perhaps Anglo inspired. Such a movement would undermine the unity of the Chicano movement by raising an issue that was not seen as a central one. Loyalists viewed racism as the most important issue within the Chicano movement. Nieto Gomez (1973, p. 35) quotes one such loyalist:

> I am concerned with the direction that the Chicanas are taking in the movement. The words such as liberation, sexism, male chauvinism, etc., were prevalent. The terms mentioned above plus the theme of individualism is a concept of the Anglo society; terms prevalent in the Anglo women's movement. The *familia* has always been our strength in our culture. But it seems evident... that you [Chicana feminists] are not concerned with the *familia*, but are influenced by the Anglo woman's movement.

Chicana feminists were also accused of undermining the values associated with Chicano culture. Loyalists saw the Chicana feminist movement as an "anti-family, anti-cultural, anti-man and therefore an anti-Chicano movement" (Gomez 1973, p. 35). Feminism was, above all, believed to be an individualistic search for identity that detracted from the Chicano movement's "real" issues, such as racism. Nieto Gomez (1973, p. 35) quotes a loyalist as stating:

> And since when does a Chicana need identity? If you are a real Chicana then no one regardless of the degrees needs to tell you about it. The

only ones who need identity are the *vendidas*, the *falsas*, and the opportunists.

The ideological conflicts between Chicana feminists and loyalists persisted throughout the seventies. Disagreements between these two groups became exacerbated during various Chicana conferences. At times, such confrontations served to increase Chicana feminist activity that challenged the loyalists' attacks, yet these attacks also served to suppress feminist activities.

Chicana feminist lesbians experienced even stronger attacks from those who viewed feminism as a divisive ideology. In a political climate that already viewed feminist ideology with suspicion, lesbianism as a sexual lifestyle and political ideology came under even more attack. Clearly, a cultural nationalist ideology that perpetuated such stereotypical images of Chicanas as "good wives and good mothers" found it difficult to accept a Chicana feminist lesbian movement.

Cherríe Moraga's writings during the 1970s reflect the struggles of Chicana feminist lesbians who, together with other Chicana feminists, were finding the sexism evident within the Chicano movement intolerable. Just as Chicana feminists analyzed their life circumstances as members of an ethnic minority and as women, Chicana feminist lesbians addressed themselves to the oppression they experienced as lesbians. As Moraga (1981, p. 28) stated:

> My lesbianism is the avenue through which I have learned the most about silence and oppression. . . . In this country, lesbianism is a poverty—as is being brown, as is being a woman, as is being just plain poor. The danger lies in ranking the oppressions. The danger lies in failing to acknowledge the specificity of the oppression.

Chicana, Black, and Asian American feminists experienced similar cross-pressures of feminist-baiting and lesbian-baiting attacks. As they organized around feminist struggles, these women of color encountered criticism from both male and female cultural nationalists who often viewed feminism as little more than an "anti-male" ideology. Lesbianism was identified as an extreme derivation of feminism. A direct connection was frequently made that viewed feminism and lesbianism as synonymous. Feminists were labeled lesbians, and lesbians as feminists. Attacks against feminists—Chicanas, Blacks, and Asian Americans—derived from the existence of homophobia within each of these communities. As lesbian women of color published their writings, attacks against them increased (Moraga 1983).

Responses to such attacks varied within and between the feminist movements of women of color. Some groups tried one strategy and later adopted another. Some lesbians pursued a separatist strategy within their own racial and ethnic communities (Moraga and Anzaldua 1981; White 1984). Others attempted to form lesbian coalitions across racial and ethnic lines. Both strategies represented a response to the marginalization of lesbians produced by recurrent waves of homophobic sentiments in Chicano, Black, and Asian American communities (Moraga and Anzaldua 1981). A third response consisted of working within the broader nationalist movements in these communities and the feminist movements within them in order to challenge their heterosexual biases and resultant homophobia. As early as 1974, the "Black Feminist Statement" written by a Boston-based feminist group—the Combahee River Collective—stated (1981, p. 213): "We struggle together with Black men against racism, while we also struggle with Black men against sexism." Similarly, Moraga (1981) challenged the white feminist movement to examine its racist tendencies; the Chicano movement, its sexist tendencies; and both, their homophobic tendencies. In this way, Moraga (1981) argued that such movements to end oppression would begin to respect diversity within their own ranks.

Chicana feminists as well as Chicana feminist lesbians continued to be labeled *vendidas* or "sellouts." Chicana loyalists continued to view Chicana feminism as associated, not only with melting into white society, but more seriously, with dividing the Chicano movement. Similarly, many Chicano males were convinced that Chicana feminism was a divisive ideology incompatible with Chicano cultural nationalism. Nieto Gomez (1976, p. 10) said that "[with] respect to [the] Chicana feminist, their credibility is reduced when they are associated with [feminism] and white women." She added that, as a result, Chicana feminists often faced harassment and ostracism within the Chicano movement. Similarly, Cotera (1973, p. 30) stated that Chicanas "are suspected of assimilating into the feminist ideology of an alien [white] culture that actively seeks our cultural domination."

Chicana feminists responded quickly and often vehemently to such charges. Flores (1971a, p. 1) answered these antifeminist attacks in an editorial in which she argued that birth control, abortion, and sex education were not merely "white issues." In response to the accusation that feminists were responsible for the "betrayal of [Chicano] culture and heritage," Flores said, "Our culture hell"—a phrase that became a dramatic slogan of the Chicana feminist movement.

Chicana feminists' defense throughout the 1970s against those claiming that a feminist movement was divisive for the Chicano movement was to reassess their roles within the Chicano movement and to call for an end to male domination. Their challenges of traditional gender roles represented a means to achieve equality (Longeaux y Vasquez 1969a, 1969b). In order to increase the participation of and opportunities for women in the Chicano movement, feminists agreed that both Chicanos and Chicanas had to address the issue of gender inequality (Chapa 1973; Chavez 1971; Del Castillo 1974; Cotera 1977; Moreno 1979). Furthermore, Chicana feminists argued that the resistance that they encountered reflected the existence of sexism on the part of Chicano males and the antifeminist attitudes of the Chicana loyalists. Nieto Gomez (1973, p. 31), reviewing the experiences of Chicana feminists in the Chicano movement, concluded that Chicanas "involved in discussing and applying the women's question have been ostracized, isolated and ignored." She argued that "in organizations where cultural nationalism is extremely strong, Chicana feminists experience intense harassment and ostracism" (1973, p. 38).

Black and Asian American women also faced severe criticism as they pursued feminist issues in their own communities. Indeed, as their participation in collective efforts to end racial oppression increased, so did their confrontations with sexism (Chow 1987; Hooks 1984; White 1984). Ngan-Ling Chow (1987, p. 288) describes the various sources of such criticism directed at Asian American women:

> Asian American women are criticized for the possible consequences of their protests: weakening the male ego, dilution of effort and resources in Asian American communities, destruction of working relationships between Asian men and women, setbacks for the Asian American cause, co-optation into the larger society, and eventual loss of ethnic identity for Asian Americans as a whole. In short, affiliation with the feminist movement is perceived as a threat to solidarity within their own community.

Similar criticism was experienced by Black feminists (Hooks 1984; White 1984).

CHICANA FEMINISTS AND WHITE FEMINISTS

It is difficult to determine the extent to which Chicana feminists sympathized with the white feminist movement. A 1976 study at the University of San Diego that examined the attitudes of Chicanas regarding the white feminist movement found that the majority of Chicanas surveyed believed that the movement had affected their lives. In addition, they identified with such key issues as the right to legal abortions on demand and access to low-cost birth control. Nevertheless, the survey found that "even though the majority of Chicanas... could relate to certain issues of the women's movement, for the most part they saw it as being an elitist movement comprised of white middle-class women who [saw] the oppressor as the males of this country" (Orozco 1976, p. 12).

Nevertheless, some Chicana feminists considered the possibility of forming coalitions with white feminists as their attempts to work within the Chicano movement were suppressed. Since white feminists were themselves struggling against sexism, building coalitions with them was seen as an alternative strategy for Chicana feminists (Rincon 1971). Almost immediately, however, Chicana feminists recognized the problems involved in adopting this political strategy. As Longeaux y Vasquez (1971, p. 11) acknowledged, "Some of our own Chicanas may be attracted to the white woman's liberation movement, but we really don't feel comfortable there. We want to be a Chicana *primero* [first]." For other Chicanas, the demands of white women were "irrelevant to the Chicana movement" (Hernandez 1971, p. 9).

Several issues made such coalition building difficult. First, Chicana feminists criticized what they considered to be a cornerstone of white feminist thought, an emphasis on gender oppression to explain the life circumstances of women. Chicana feminists believed that the white feminist movement overlooked the effects of racial oppression experienced by Chicanas and other women of color. Thus, Del Castillo (1974, p. 8) maintained that the Chicana feminist movement was "different primarily because we are [racially] oppressed people." In addition, Chicana feminists criticized white feminists who believed that a general women's movement would be able to overcome racial differences among women. Chicanas interpreted this as a failure by the white feminist movement to deal with the issue of racism. Without the incorporation of an analysis of racial oppression to explain the experiences of Chicanas as well as of other women of color, Chicana feminists believed that a coalition with white feminists would be highly unlikely (Chapa 1973; Cotera 1977; Gomez 1973; Longeaux y Vasquez 1971). As Longeaux y Vasquez (1971, p. 11) concluded: "We must have a clearer vision of our plight and certainly we cannot blame our men for the oppression of the women."

In the 1970s, Chicana feminists reconciled their demands for an end to sexism within the Chicano movement and their rejection of the saliency of gender oppression by separating the two issues. They clearly identified the struggle against sexism in the Chicano movement as a major issue, arguing that sexism prevented their full participation (Fallis 1974; Gomez 1976). They also argued that sexist behavior and ideology on the part of both Chicano males and Anglos represented the key to understanding women's oppression. However, they remained critical of an analysis of women's experiences that focused exclusively on gender oppression.

Chicana feminists adopted an analysis that began with race as a critical variable in interpreting the experiences of Chicano communities in the United States. They expanded this analysis by identifying gender as a variable interconnected with race in analyzing the specific daily life circumstances of Chicanas as women in Chicano communities. Chicana feminists did not view women's struggles as secondary to the nationalist movement but argued instead for an analysis of race and gender as multiple sources of oppression (Cotera 1977). Thus, Chicana feminism went beyond the limits of an exclusively racial theory of oppression that tended to overlook gender and also went beyond the limits of a theory of oppression based exclusively on gender that tended to overlook race.

A second factor preventing an alliance between Chicana feminists and white feminists was the middle-class orientation of white feminists. While some Chicana feminists recognized the legitimacy of the demands made by white feminists and even admitted sharing some of these demands, they argued that "it is not our business as Chicanas to identify with the white women's liberation movement as a home base for working for our people" (Longeaux y Vasquez 1971, p. 11).

Throughout the 1970s, Chicana feminists viewed the white feminist movement as a middle-class movement (Chapa 1973; Cotera 1980; Longeaux y Vasquez 1970; Martinez 1972; Nieto 1974; Orozco 1976). In contrast, Chicana feminists analyzed the Chicano movement in general as a working-class movement. They repeatedly made reference to such differences, and many Chicana feminists began their writings with a section that disassociated themselves from the "women's liberation movement." Chicana feminists as activists in the broader Chicano movement identified as major struggles the farmworkers movement, welfare rights, undocumented workers, and prison rights. Such issues were seen as far removed from the demands of the white feminist movement, and Chicana feminists could not get white feminist organizations to deal with them (Cotera 1980).

Similar concerns regarding the white feminist movement were raised by Black and Asian American feminists. Black feminists have documented the historical and contemporary schisms between Black feminists and white feminists, emphasizing the socioeconomic and political differences (Davis 1971, 1983; Dill 1983; LaRue 1970). More specifically, Black feminists have been critical of the white feminists who advocate a female solidarity that cuts across racial, ethnic, and social class lines. As Thornton Dill (1983, p. 131) states:

> The cry "Sisterhood is powerful!" has engaged only a few segments of the female population in the United States. Black, Hispanic, Native American, and Asian American women of all classes, as well as many working-class women, have not readily identified themselves as sisters of the white middle-class women who have been in the forefront of the movement.

Like Black feminists, Asian American feminists have also had strong reservations regarding the white feminist movement. For many Asian Americans, white feminism has primarily focused on gender as an analytical category and has thus lacked a systematic analysis of race and class (Chow 1987; Fong 1978; Wong 1980; Woo 1971).

White feminist organizations were also accused of being exclusionary, patronizing, or racist in their dealings with Chicanas and other women of color. Cotera (1980, p. 227) states:

> Minority women could fill volumes with examples of put-down, put-ons, and out-and-out racism shown to them by the leadership in the [white feminist] movement. There are three major problem areas in the minority-majority relationship in the movement: (1) paternalism or materialism, (2) extremely limited opportunities for minority women . . . , (3) outright discrimination against minority women in the movement.

Although Chicana feminists continued to be critical of building coalitions with white feminists toward the end of the seventies, they acknowledged the diversity of ideologies within the white feminist movement. Chicana feminists sympathetic to radical socialist feminism because of its anticapitalist framework wrote of working-class oppression that cut across racial and ethnic lines. Their later writings discussed the possibility of joining with white working-class women, but strategies for forming such political coalitions were not made explicit (Cotera 1977; Marquez and Ramirez 1977).

Instead, Del Castillo and other Chicana feminists favored coalitions between Chicanas and other women of color while keeping their respective autonomous organizations. Such coalitions would recognize the inherent racial oppression of capitalism rather than universal gender oppression. When Longeaux y Vasquez (1971) stated that she was "Chicana *primero*," she was stressing the saliency of race over gender in explaining the oppression experienced by Chicanas. The word *Chicana* however, simultaneously expresses a woman's race and gender. Not until later—in the 1980s—would Chicana feminist ideology call for an analysis that stressed the interrelationship of race, class, and gender in explaining the conditions of Chicanas in American society (Cordova et al. 1986; Zinn 1982), just as Black and Asian American feminists have done.

Chicana feminists continued to stress the importance of developing autonomous feminist organizations that would address the struggles of Chicanas as members of an ethnic minority and as women. Rather than attempt to overcome the obstacles to coalition building between Chicana feminists and white feminists, Chicanas called for autonomous feminist organizations for all women of color (Cotera 1977; Gonzalez 1980; Nieto 1975). Chicana feminists believed that sisterhood was indeed powerful but only to the extent that racial and class differences were understood and, above all, respected. As Nieto (1974, p. 4) concludes:

> The Chicana must demand that dignity and respect within the women's rights movement which allows her to practice feminism within the context of her own culture. . . . Her approaches to feminism must be drawn from her own world.

CHICANA FEMINISM:
AN EVOLVING FUTURE

Chicana feminists, like Black, Asian American, and Native American feminists, experience specific life conditions that are distinct from those of white feminists. Such socioeconomic and cultural differences in Chicano communities directly shaped the development of Chicana feminism and the relationship between Chicana feminists and feminists of other racial and ethnic groups,' including white feminists. Future dialogue among all feminists will require a mutual understanding of the existing differences as well as the similarities. Like other women of color, Chicana feminists must address issues that specifically affect them as women of color. In addition, Chicana feminists must address those issues that have particular impact on Chicano communities, such as poverty, limited opportunities for higher education, high school dropouts, health care, bilingual education, immigration reform, prison reform, welfare, and most recently, United States policies in Central America.

At the academic level, an increasing number of Chicana feminists continue to join in a collective effort to carry on the feminist legacy inherited from the 1970s. In June 1982, a group of Chicana academics organized a national feminist organization called Mujeres Activas en Letras y Cambio Social (MALCS) in order to build a support network for Chicana professors, undergraduates, and graduate students. The organization's major goal is to fight against race, class, and gender oppression facing Chicanas in institutions of higher education. In addition, MALCS aims to bridge the gap between academic work and the Chicano community. MALCS has organized three Chicana/ Latina summer research institutes at the University of California at Davis and publishes a working paper series.

During the 1982 conference of the National Association for Chicano Studies, a panel organized by Mujeres en Marcha, a feminist group from the University of California at Berkeley, discussed three major issues facing Chicana feminists in higher education in particular and the Chicano movement in general. Panelists outlined the issues as follows (Mujeres en Marcha 1983, pp. 1-2):

1. For a number of years, Chicanas have heard claims that a concern with issues specifically affecting Chicanas is merely a distraction/diversion from the liberation of Chicano people as a whole. What are the issues that arise when women are asked to separate their exploitation as women from the other forms of oppression that we experience?

2. Chicanas are confronted daily by the limitations of being a woman in this patriarchal society; the attempts to assert these issues around sexism are often met with resistance and scorn. What are some of the major difficulties in relations amongst ourselves? How are the relationships between women and men affected? How are the relationships of women to women and men to men affected? How do we overcome the constraints of sexism?

3. It is not uncommon that our interests as feminists are challenged on the basis that we are simply falling prey to the interests of white middle-class women. We challenge the notion that there is no room for a Chicana movement within our own community. We, as women of color, have a unique set of concerns that are separate from white women and from men of color.

While these issues could not be resolved at the conference, the panel succeeded in generating an ongoing discussion within the National Association for Chicano Studies (NACS). Two years later, in 1984, the national conference of NACS, held in Austin, Texas, adopted the theme "Voces de la Mujer" in response to demands from the Chicana Caucus. As a result, for the first time since its founding in 1972, the NACS national conference addressed the issue of women. Compared with past conferences, a large number of Chicanas participated by presenting their research and chairing and moderating panels. A plenary session addressed the problems of gender inequality in higher education and within NACS. At the national business meeting, the issue of sexism within NACS was again seriously debated as it continues to be one of the "unsettled issues" of concern to Chicana feminists. A significant outcome of this conference was the publication of the NACS 1984 conference proceedings, which marked the first time that the association's anthology was devoted completely to Chicanas and Mexicanas (Cordova et al. 1986).

The decade of the 1980s has witnessed a rephrasing of the critical question concerning the nature of the oppression experienced by Chicanas and other women of color. Chicana feminists, like Black feminists, are asking what are the consequences of the intersection of race, class, and gender in the daily lives of women in American society, emphasizing the simultaneity of these critical variables for women of color (Garcia 1986; Hooks 1984). In their labor-force participation, wages, education, and poverty levels, Chicanas have made few gains in comparison to white men and women and Chicano men (Segura 1986). To analyze these problems, Chicana feminists have investigated the structures of racism, capitalism, and patriarchy, especially as they are experienced by the majority of Chicanas (Ruiz 1987; Segura 1986; Zavella 1987). Clearly, such issues will need to be explicitly addressed by an evolving Chicana feminist movement, analytically and politically.

NOTE

1. For bibliographies on Chicanas see Balderama (1981); Candelaria (1980); Loeb (1980); Portillo, Rios, and Rodriguez (1976); and Baca Zinn (1982, 1984).

REFERENCES

Almaguer, Tomas. 1974. "Historical Notes on Chicano Oppression." *Aztlan* 5:27-56.

Balderama, Sylvia. 1981. "A Comprehensive Bibliography on La Chicana." Unpublished paper, University of California, Berkeley.

Barrera, Mario. 1974. "The Study of Politics and the Chicano." *Aztlan* 5:9-26.

———. 1979. *Race and Class in the Southwest*. Notre Dame, IN: University of Notre Dame Press.

Beale, Frances. 1975. "Slave of a Slave No More: Black Women in Struggle." *Black Scholar* 6:2-10.

Cade, Toni. 1970. *The Black Woman*. New York: Signet.

Candelaria, Cordelia. 1980. "Six Reference Works on Mexican American Women: A Review Essay." *Frontiers* 5:75-80.

Castro, Tony. 1974. *Chicano Power*. New York: Saturday Review Press.

Chapa, Evey. 1973. "Report from the National Women's Political Caucus." *Magazin* 1:37-39.

Chavez, Henri. 1971. "The Chicanas." *Regeneracion* 1:14.

Cheng, Lucie. 1984. "Asian American Women and Feminism." *Sojourner* 10:11-12.

Chow, Esther Ngan-Ling. 1987. "The Development of Feminist Consciousness Among Asian American Women." *Gender & Society* 1:284-99.

Combahee River Collective. 1981. "A Black Feminist Statement." Pp. 210-18 in *This Bridge Called My Back: Writings by Radical Women of Color*, edited by Cherrie Moraga and Gloria Anzaldua. Watertown, MA: Persephone.

Cordova, Teresa et al. 1986. *Chicana Voices: Intersections of Class, Race, and Gender*. Austin, TX: Center for Mexican American Studies.

Cotera, Marta. 1973. "La Mujer Mexicana: Mexicano Feminism." *Magazin* 1:30-32.

———. 1977. *The Chicana Feminist*. Austin, TX: Austin Information Systems Development.

———. 1980. "Feminism: The Chicana and Anglo Versions: An Historical Analysis." Pp. 217-34 in *Twice a Minority: Mexican American Women*, edited by Margarita Melville. St. Louis, MO: C. V. Mosby.

Davis, Angela. 1971. "Reflections on Black Women's Role in the Community of Slaves." *Black Scholar* 3:3-13.

———. 1983. *Women, Race and Class*. New York: Random House.

Del Castillo, Adelaida. 1974. "La Vision Chicana." *La Gente:* 8.

Dill, Bonnie Thornton. 1983. "Race, Class, and Gender: Prospects for an All-Inclusive Sisterhood." *Feminist Studies* 9:131-50.

Dunne, John. 1967. *Delano: The Story of the California Grape Strike*. New York: Strauss.

Fallis, Guadalupe Valdes. 1974. "The Liberated Chicana—A Struggle Against Tradition." *Women: A Journal of Liberation* 3:20.

Flores, Francisca. 1971a. "Conference of Mexican Women: Un Remolino. *Regeneracion* 1(1):1-4.

———. 1971b. "El Mundo Femenil Mexicana." *Regeneracion* 1(10):i.

Fong, Katheryn M. 1978. "Feminism Is Fine, But What's It Done for Asia America?" *Bridge* 6:21-22.

Freeman, Jo. 1983. "On the Origins of Social Movements." Pp. 8-30 in *Social Movements of the Sixties and Seventies*, edited by Jo Freeman. New York: Longman.

———. 1984. "The Women's Liberation Movement: Its Origins, Structure, Activities, and Ideas." Pp. 543-56 in *Women: A Feminist Perspective*, edited by Jo Freeman. Palo Alto, CA: Mayfield.

Garcia, Alma M. 1986 "Studying Chicanas: Bringing Women into the Frame of Chicano Studies." Pp. 19-29 in *Chicana Voices: Intersections of Class, Race, and Gender*, edited by Teresa Cordova et al. Austin, TX: Center for Mexican American Studies.

Garcia, F. Chris and Rudolph O. de la Garza. 1977. *The Chicano Political Experience*. North Scituate, MA: Duxbury.

Gomez, Anna Nieto. 1971. "Chicanas Identify." *Hijas de Cuauhtemoc* (April):9.

———. 1973. "La Femenista." *Encuentro Femenil* 1:34-47.

———. 1976. "Sexism in the Movement." *La Gente* 6(4):10.

Gonzalez, Sylvia. 1980. "Toward a Feminist Pedagogy for Chicana Self-Actualization." *Frontiers* 5:48-51.

Hernandez, Carmen. 1971. "Carmen Speaks Out." *Papel Chicano* 1(June 12):8-9.

Hooks, Bell. 1981. *Ain't I a Woman: Black Women and Feminism*. Boston: South End Press.

———. 1984. *Feminist Theory: From Margin to Center*. Boston: South End Press.

Joseph, Gloria and Jill Lewis. 1981. *Common Differences: Conflicts in Black and White Feminist Perspectives*. Garden City, NY: Doubleday.

Kushner, Sam. 1975. *Long Road to Delano*. New York: International.

LaRue, Linda. 1970. "The Black Movement and Women's Liberation." *Black Scholar* 1:36-42.

Loeb, Catherine. 1980. "La Chicana: A Bibliographic Survey." *Frontiers* 5:59-74.

Longeaux y Vasquez, Enriqueta. 1969a. "The Woman of La Raza." *El Grito del Norte* 2(July):8-9.

———. 1969b. "La Chicana: Let's Build a New Life." *El Grito del Norte* 2(November):11.

———. 1970. "The Mexican-American Woman." Pp. 379-84 in *Sisterhood Is Powerful*, edited by Robin Morgan. New York: Vintage.

———. 1971. "Soy Chicana Primero." *El Grito del Norte* 4(April 26):11.

Macias, Anna. 1982. *Against All Odds*. Westport, CT: Greenwood.

Marquez, Evelina and Margarita Ramirez. 1977. "Women's Task Is to Gain Liberation." Pp. 188-94 in *Essays on La Mujer*, edited by Rosaura Sanchez and Rosa Martinez Cruz. Los Angeles: UCLA Chicano Studies Center.

Martinez, Elizabeth. 1972. "The Chicana." *Ideal* 44:1-3.

Matthiesen, Peter. 1969. *Sal Si Puedes: Cesar Chavez and the New American Revolution*. New York: Random House.

Meier, Matt and Feliciano Rivera. 1972. *The Chicanos*. New York: Hill & Wang.

Moraga, Cherrie. 1981. "La Guera." Pp. 27-34 in *This Bridge Called My Back: Writings by Radical Women of Color*, edited by Cherrie Moraga and Gloria Anzaldua. Watertown, MA: Persephone.

———. 1983. *Loving in the War Years*. Boston: South End Press.

Moraga, Cherrie and Gloria Anzaldua. 1981. *This Bridge Called My Back: Writings by Radical Women of Color*. Watertown, MA: Persephone.

Moreno, Dorinda. 1979. "The Image of the Chicana and the La Raza Woman." *Caracol* 2:14-15.

Mujeres en Marcha. 1983. *Chicanas in the 80s: Unsettled Issues*. Berkeley, CA: Chicano Studies Publication Unit.

Muñoz, Carlos, Jr. 1974. "The Politics of Protest and Liberation: A Case Study of Repression and Cooptation." *Aztlan* 5:119-41.

Nabokov, Peter. 1969. *Tijerina and the Courthouse Raid*. Albuquerque, NM: University of New Mexico Press.

Navarro, Armando. 1974. "The Evolution of Chicano Politics." *Aztlan* 5:57-84.

Nelson, Eugene. 1966. *Huelga: The First 100 Days*. Delano, CA: Farm Workers Press.

Nieto, Consuelo. 1974. "The Chicana and the Women's Rights Movement." *La Luz* 3(September):10-11, 32.

———. 1975. "Consuelo Nieto on the Women's Movement." *Interracial Books for Children Bulletin* 5:4.

Orozco, Yolanda. 1976. "La Chicana and 'Women's Liberation.'" *Voz Fronteriza* (January 5):6, 12.

Piven, Frances Fox and Richard A. Cloward. 1979. *Poor People's Movements: Why They Succeed, How They Fail*. New York: Vintage.

Portillo, Cristina, Graciela Rios, and Martha Rodriguez. 1976. *Bibliography on Writings on La Mujer*. Berkeley, CA: University of California Chicano Studies Library.

Riddell, Adaljiza Sosa. 1974. "Chicanas en el Movimiento." *Aztlan* 5:155-65.

Rincon, Bernice. 1971. "La Chicana: Her Role in the Past and Her Search for a New Role in the Future." *Regeneracion* 1(10):15-17.

Rowbotham, Sheila. 1974. *Women, Resistance and Revolution: A History of Women and Revolution in the Modern World*. New York: Vintage.

Ruiz, Vicki L. 1987. *Cannery Women, Cannery Lives: Mexican Women, Unionization, and the California Food Processing Industry, 1930-1950*. Albuquerque: University of New Mexico Press.

Segura, Denise. 1986. "Chicanas and Triple Oppression in the Labor Force." Pp. 47-65 in *Chicana Voices: Intersections of Class, Race and Gender*, edited by Teresa Cordova et al. Austin, TX: Center for Mexican American Studies.

Shockley, John. 1974. *Chicano Revolt in a Texas Town*. South Bend, IN: University of Notre Dame Press.

Vidal, Mirta. 1971. "New Voice of La Raza: Chicanas Speak Out." *International Socialist Review* 32:31-33.

White, Frances. 1984. "Listening to the Voices of Black Feminism." *Radical America* 18:7-25.

Wong, Germaine Q. 1980. "Impediments to Asian-Pacific-American Women Organizing." Pp. 89-103 in *The Conference on the Educational and Occupational Needs of Asian Pacific Women*. Washington, DC: National Institute of Education.

Woo, Margaret. 1971. "Women + Man = Political Unity." Pp. 115-16 in *Asian Women*, edited by Editorial Staff. Berkeley, CA: University of California Press.

Zavella, Patricia. 1987. *Women's Work and Chicano Families: Cannery Workers of the Santa Clara Valley*. Ithaca, NY: Cornell University Press.

Zinn, Maxine Baca. 1975a. "Political Familism: Toward Sex Role Equality in Chicano Families." *Aztlan* 6:13-27.

———. 1975b. "Chicanas: Power and Control in the Domestic Sphere." *De Colores* 2/3:19-31.

———. 1982. "Mexican-American Women in the Social Sciences." *Signs: Journal of Women in Culture and Society* 8:259-72.

———. 1984. "Mexican Heritage Women: A Bibliographic Essay." *Sage Race Relations Abstracts* 9:1-12.

Alma M. Garcia is Associate Professor of Sociology and Ethnic Studies at Santa Clara University. Her article, "Studying Chicanas: Bringing Women into the Frame of Chicano Studies," was published in Chicana Voices *(Austin: Center For Mexican American Studies, 1986). Her current research focuses on Chicana entrepreneurs. She has been the national president of the National Association for Chicano Studies and Mujeres Activas en Letras Y Cambio Social.*

CHICANA STUDIES: IS THERE A FUTURE FOR US IN WOMEN STUDIES?

by Tey Diana Rebolledo
University of New Mexico

DISCOURSE ON METHOD
Demetria Martínez

JULY 10TH, MY MONTH'S BLOOD IS
BRIGHT
CANDLE AT THE TUB, KNEES AND BREASTS
IN A BUBBLE REEF, READING BLAKE
BY THREADBARE LIGHT.
A CHILD I DREAMED I WAS A KILLER
WHALE,
BLACK CRESCENT BELLYING THROUGH
SEAS,
EATING SHARK, BEARING YOUNG, FAR
FROM THESE ALTITUDES, THESE
NEON YEARS ONE MUST BEAR
UNTIL THE WORK IS DONE.

NIGHTLY MY EYES RETURN TO THEIR

32

WATERS,
PLUNGING LEAGUES WHEN I CLOSE MY
LIDS,
BACK AT DAWN WITH ACCOUNTS OF
WRECKS,
WITH FINS, COINS, REMAINS OF MEN.

.THOSE WHO LEARN TO SEE IN THE DARK
NEVER GO BLIND.
IT IS A GOOD YEAR TO BE WOMAN
AND WHALE AT THE SAME TIME.[1]

The topic of this essay is the connection and interrelationship between Chicana Studies and Women's Studies. It has been an extremely difficult paper to write because over the more than ten years I have been involved with Women Studies on a national level, I have increasingly, instead of decreasingly, found it difficult to work with Anglo women involved in Women Studies. Therefore I fear that what I have to say is fairly pessimistic vis a vis Women's Studies. I also hope that once the tensions, problems and difficulties between the two areas are delineated, we may be able to transcend them and arrive at a new understanding.

In 1984 I was hired at the University of New Mexico as Director of the Women Studies Program there, the first minority woman to be the Director of the Program and at the time, I believe, I was the only Chicana to be the Director of such a Program in the United States. It may be that I am still the only Chicana to be a Director. In any event the number of us must be very, very small. The Program in New Mexico is one of the oldest women studies programs in the United States, having been started in 1970 by a group of graduate students and women professors. Because New Mexico is such an intercultural crossroads, from the beginning the program had participation from minority women, particularly Chicanas, who taught the first courses on Chicana relations, history and literature and began courses on race, class, sexual preference and gender issues. Their voices were loud and clear and insistent. Through the years there were often conflicts between the minority women and the liberal Anglo feminists who ran the program: sometimes on the basis of course offerings, sometimes of race issues, sometimes (and most often) on hiring issues.

The year before I was hired tensions were high, the program was in disarray and the minority women coalesced in force. With their support (and their pressure) I was hired as the director. I can tell you that when I arrived on campus expectations of me were high. I was to represent minority women, especially Chicanas. I was to be a visible presence for the university on minority issues as well as women's issues. I was to stabilize the program. I was to focus on minority hiring within the program. I was to be diplomatic and normalize relations between program participants.

Because I am a Chicana some faculty members felt I would focus exclusively on Chicanas (I tried to do as much of that as I could). I was expected to generate grant proposals and to work with SIROW (the Southwest Institute for Research on Women) to bring research to UNM. In addition to this I was half-time in my Department (Modern and Classical Languages) where I was expected to gain tenure in one year and teach graduate students (I also taught in the Women Studies Program). Since I am trained as a Latin Americanist and as a Chicana scholar there were pulls on my time and my interests from the Latin American Institute and the Southwest Hispanic Research Institute. I believe that, to begin with, many of us who are selected to administer such programs are pulled in a great many different directions which at times even conflict with each other.

I do not mean this discussion to be one of my travails, because the years I spent working on the Women Studies Program were happy ones for me, years in which I learned a great deal and had many enriching experiences. Nevertheless in the last years I began to have grave doubts about what I was accomplishing, trying to combine my interests in Chicana literature and scholarship, and working with the Women Studies Program. More and more I found myself being pushed in directions away from

my own interests in minority women, more and more I was dealing with mainstream activities and administrative activities having little or nothing to do with Chicana Studies.

After four years I decided that I would have more impact on Chicana Studies if I were to go back full time into my department, focus on our Chicana/o students, integrating women's and Chicana literature into the modern and classical language curriculum, and finish my books. In fact, I am often more effective as a critic on the outside than I was as a participant on the inside. I am sure that the high visibility I had as Director of the Women Studies program insures some of this effectiveness. I am sure that some of the tactics I learned as an administrator also helps, but, for the most part, I have come to feel that we are most effective working full time on our own agendas, rather than trying to work our agendas into mainstream agendas. I would like to outline for you here some of the problems I see in the interface between Chicana Studies and Women Studies, and hope that in workshops and discussion we may begin to find a solution.

Most Women Studies Programs are directed and led by White Anglo Feminists who range in perspectives from traditional to liberal to radical. At times they remember that they need to include minority women in their courses and on their faculties. Certainly in recent years, with curriculum integration projects and with loud voices and commentary from minority women, many programs have made significant inroads in inclusion. Many have not, and I truly believe even in women who regard themselves as "liberals" there is still insensitivity, tokenism, and the necessity for us to constantly be educating. This attitude reminds me of a poem written in the early seventies by Marcela Aguilar called "No More Cookies, Please" where she explains that she is tired of attending coffees with white liberal feminists, constantly having to be nice and to explain herself, educating them. In the intervening years it often seems to me as if not

33

much has changed.

If any group of minority women have been able to cross boundaries, I believe it is Black women. More often that not they are included in curriculum, their works are read. The curriculum integration and clearing house project run by at Memphis State is doing very well. Chicanas are not half so well represented. Asian-American and Native American women are still almost invisible. We are still having trouble breaking into the mainstream, although some of you/us are doing quite well. We continue to be asked the question, is the work any good? are the writers any good? are you any good? or are you good enough? (And since we ourselves ask these questions of ourselves often enough, it doesn't take much to discourage us.)

I want to outline several areas which for me continue to be problematic.

1) Integrating our research into mainstream books, journals, etc. For a long time I have firmly believed in working on projects that would integrate our work into the larger canon. To this end I have published chapters in such works as The Desert is No Lady, Yale University Press and For Alma Mater, University of Illinois Press. And I have continued to publish extensively in Chicana/Chicano publications. Several years ago I received a letter, however, which has made me question the value of such integration. I would like to read you excerpt from it which will aptly illustrate what I am talking about...it may strike a familiar cord in some of you.

"Dear Professor Rebolledo;

My co-editor and I have just signed an advance contract with a University Press for a collection of essays on the fiction and/or autobiographies of twentieth-century British and American women writers. For some time now we have been searching for someone to write an essay on mothering on the fiction of a Chicana or Latina Woman writer."

(At this point and throughout I am going to be a Chicana

deconstructionist analysis of this letter. To begin, I must mention that I did not know these women at all. I read that the volume is already put together since they have an advance contract. The editor of the press told them that they needed to find a Chicana or Latina, it doesn't matter which, so that their volume will not appear to be racist. They have already pre-selected the topic, mothering, but they don't know any Chicana or Latina critics, or really anyone who knows any, since they have been searching for some time. In addition they don't know any universities where such knowledge might be found.)

"Your name was given to me by the Women's Studies Director at the University of...She also suggested a possible novel -- The Ultraviolet Sky (Bilingual Press, Tempe, AZ) but we are certainly open to suggestion about this."

(Here they have chosen the novel for me, but if I complain loud enough they would be willing to change. After all, they have read the novel so it doesn't make much difference.)

"We are limiting each essay to 8250 words* (23 pages, excluding bibliography), and our deadline is October 15, 1989. In fact it would be preferable if we could have an initial draft in September so that we can make editorial comments. Given the short notice, we do realize that this may be difficult to achieve."

(Ah yes, deadlines. The letter to me was dated July 14, with the 14th crossed out and 18th written in. I received it on July 28th. This gave me exactly a month and a half to write a paper on a subject chosen for me. Because what I write might not be any good, they ask for it a little early so they can edit it, it might be really radical...or, the more likely possibility is that it will be badly written in English, so changes will have to be made. It also assumes that I have nothing to do, but to write this paper. I was only involved in trying to finish 2 books, write this paper for MALCS, finish a promised chapter for a book on Chicano colonial literature, get my

34

classes organized and coordinate the National Associate for Chicano Studies Conference for 1990.)

The final paragraph. *"Please let me know as soon as possible. You may phone me at home or at State University. But I am rarely in my office during the summer. You may, of course, also write to me at the above address. I do hope to hear that you will contribute an essay to this book."*

(Deconstruction: Even though I have nothing to do with this project, she not only patronizes me but she places the burden of responsibility on me. I may phone her and moreover, I should track her down. Baring not finding her, I can write to her, soon, immediately with my excitement about having been invited to participate in this project.)

Now perhaps some of you will think I am overreacting to this letter. When you have received enough of them you will see how serious this is. Question: what to do? I took the easy way out, I didn't answer. Advice from colleagues ranged from writing them an angry letter telling them "que se chinguen", to a letter educating them by refusing to participate but explaining why I am offended, to doing a Chicana deconstruction of it. This letter is serious because the project has never been from the start an integrated project with input from minority writers about how best to combine these various papers and perspectives, it is tokenism at its worst because it is so genuinely insensitive and it makes so many assumptions about our work.

2) It is very important to generate public programs, workshops, etc. on issues that minority women feel strongly about. But minority women have to be at the center of the planning for such programs. When they are, you can have great results. Erlinda Gonzales-Berry and I planned a program on Redesigning the Traditional Literary Canon, invited female and male speakers, collaborated between Departments and it was a great success. But they have been other programs where this precisely has not been the case, and

they have resulted in memorable disasters.

One case in point is the Dark Madonna Conference held at UCLA several years ago and sponsored by the UCLA Center for the Study of Women and co-sponsored by many minority groups such as the African Studies Center, Chicano Studies, Hispanic Women's Council, etc. It seems like a well planned conference. On the night of the opening plenary session with over 500 women in the audience it quickly became apparent that all was not well. Of six speakers on the podium there were no minority women. (We had all been relegated to sessions the next day.) The evening dragged endlessly on with discussions about women and uses of convention, and garden clubs etc.

When time was allowed for questions, a woman stood up and I recognized her, Roberta Fernández. She said, and I paraphrase: "As you look at the audience you can see that we are of all races, the program was advertised as the Dark Madonna with an obviously Black virgin and child on its cover, why are there no minority women on the plenary session?"

As you can imagine, this left the persons on the stage in total confusion with all sorts of embarrassing statements to be said, such as well, there are minority women on the program tomorrow, we tried to include minority women (and they had invited quite a few of us), we didn't think, and, it's not my fault I am not the organizer.

My point is that this happens again and again. When there are no minority women on the planning committees, they forget about us.

As another example, last year I was invited to participate in a New Mexico Humanities Grant on women's rituals for a program sponsored by a Women Studies Program which was to be held in New Mexico. The program director used my part of the program as an example of cultural integration for the program. After the grant request went in, I didn't hear from the program sponsors again except for a short note in January saying that

35

they had received the grant and that they would be in touch. Several months later I had a call from the secretary of the department asking me if I had made my hotel reservations yet. For when, asked I? For tomorrow night, said she, adding that my presentation was scheduled for 4 p.m. the following afternoon.

When I explained that I had not been notified even when the program was to take place, much less at which hotel I was to make my reservation, she was surprised, though not more so than I. Of course, feeling obligated, I called the program director to ask what happened, and the answer was, oh, they must have forgotten to notify me about it. Strange to say that they would have forgotten to tell the cultural diversity person about the program. Of course I was unable to go on one day's notice.

3) I think that perhaps the greatest impact that we have been able to make vis a vis Women Studies has been in curriculum integration. At least at the University of New Mexico all the Women Studies courses taught have to have a strong racial and ethnic component in them. Truly integrating Chicanas on projects, however, has been a different story, even on the project of curriculum integration. I have often worked with SIROW on different projects, inviting minority women to participate in small numbers. Several years ago they received a grant from the Ford Foundation to participate in a curriculum integration project of a different sort. To integrate the work of minority women into the Women Studies Curriculum. I was asked if our program wanted to participate. I asked what minority women were on the planning committee: well, none. I asked who the project director was: well, a gringa. I asked who the coordinators were: well, a gringa and a Chicano. I said no, no thank you, that we didn't want to participate because we had no input. In their January 1989 newsletter I read that on 13 campus coordinators for the project only one was a Chicana, although Gary Keller and Estevan Flores were also included. Now, if you think Chicanas have no input into the matter...Later I heard that it was being circulated that I was a difficult person to work with.

When one takes into consideration how these different projects are being put together and presented, it becomes clear that we Chicanas are not only not represented, but that others are speaking for us...others who may be sympathetic, but who cannot presume to speak for us, not from our perspective. Once again others are shaping our world view and presenting it as ours. Is this better than not being represented at all? I will leave this for you to cogitate.

What can Chicanas do about this besides complain and whine? For one thing we need to concentrate on our own research, our own classes, our own agendas. We need to finish our dissertations, our articles, our books. We need to be clear on our perspective and to look to other Chicanas as a source of support. When we are invited to be speakers, present papers, collaborate on books, we must ask who the organizers are, who the planners are. Have they had input from minority women, are they asking for ours? Are we invited at the beginning of the project so that we may take a role in shaping it? If the answers to our questions are not satisfactory, we might perhaps refuse to participate, particularly if we are being used as tokens and are matronized. If we are feeling generous we might explain why we are refusing. We must express our concerns. If they hear this enough from enough of us, perhaps the message will sink in, and I won't be the only one who is difficult to work with.

4) In hiring program participants (faculty, secretaries, students) etc. in Women Studies Program it is very important that there be more than a few token minority women. The more minority women we had in the office and in the halls at UNM in whatever capacity, more minority students were also there. In the years since I left, there has been a noticeable drop in minority students and faculty and student who have been physically present in the program. We need to keep the pressure on Women Studies Programs.

36

There might be some home of connections between Chicana Studies Programs and Women Studies Programs. My feeling is that they need us more than we need them. Our work is breaking new grounds, is vital and exciting. In reality they know this. It takes time, but the time is now.

I would like to end this discussion, which is just a beginning, with a poem by a Nuevo Mexicana writer, Gloria Gonzales:

THERE IS NOTHING
SO LONESOME
OR SAD
THAT
PAPAS FRITAS
WON'T CURE.[2]

[1] In Las Mujeres Hablan: An Anthology of Nuevo Mexicana Writers. Eds: Tey Diana Rebolledo, Erlinda Gonzales-Berry, Teresa Márquez. Albuquerque : El Norte Publications, 1988. 194

[2] Las Mujeres Hablan, 184

37

Ain't I a Feminist?

Celina Romany[†]

I want to recover my faith in feminism during the 1990's. The feminism that gave me the strength to understand the story of a woman born and raised in a colony who migrates to the metropolis, feminism as a liberation project. The feminism which launches a multi-faceted attack on legal institutions that perpetuate substantial inequities.

The current state of feminist legal theory makes me wonder if I am still a feminist. The feminism I see myself associated with has a capital F. That which aims at eradicating the various forms of oppression that affect all women, a project overlooked by "small-town" feminism. I am willing to risk being outside current postmodern theoretical trends by supporting capital letters. My capital letters connote expansion, breadth and inclusion. Far from claiming privileged access to truth with a capital T, feminism with a capital F thrives in a room with a great view of narratives about intersections.

Feminist legal theorists belong to a norm-forming group involved in what Robert Cover has described as the creation of new legal meanings.[1] As he suggested, we need to examine the juris-generative operation of such a group and how the process of creating new legal meanings depends on sustaining narratives. Narratives that define both the vision of the juris-generative group and its location in making its work a viable alternative.

Today, I'd like to critique the feminist narratives that sustain the creation of feminist legal theory as new legal meaning. My principal claims are: 1) that the feminist narrative deployed as a foundation with its monocausal emphasis on gender falls short of the liberation project feminism should be about: the emancipation of all women, 2) that feminism so defined cannot adequately address the shortcomings of liberal legalism and 3) that postmodernism, although helpful in counteracting feminist essentialism by giving space and voice to a multiplicity of accounts, nevertheless lacks a material analysis of macrostructures of inequality and thus lacks translation potential for social change.

Feminist legal theory needs to allow room for the destabilization of gender as both a conceptual and practical tool of analysis. Feminist legal theory moves

---

† Celina Romany is Associate Professor of Law at City University of New York (CUNY) Law School. This piece is a close adaptation of the speech she gave on the panel *Broadening the Definition of Feminism* at the *Conference Feminism in the 90s: Bridging the Gap Between Theory and Practice*. I dedicate this article to those Puerto Rican Feminists who struggle against all forms of colonialism.

1. Robert Cover, *Foreword: Nomos and Narrative*, 97 HARV L. REV. 4 (1983).

Copyright © 1991 by the Yale Journal of Law and Feminism

in the right direction when it pursues the humanist project of agency and subjectivity and attempts to redefine subjectivity to redress gross gender-related exclusions. Yet, it needs to move beyond. The feminism with a capital F which I want to recover in the context of legal theory is that which redefines subjectivity in light of the key variables of subject formation: race, ethnicity, class and gender. A feminist theory of subjectivity can adequately elaborate an alternative vision to the liberal self by showing the centrality of the political and cultural history in which the subject is born; a context of personal and social de-legitimation. Through this route, the elaboration of feminist subjectivity can plausibly seize the deep meanings of difference, subordination and oppression. By not filling this gap, we only catch a glimpse of meaning and experience exclusion. Universalist assumptions deny intersubjectivity any opportunity to liberate us from the appropriation and objectification of *others*, to pave the way for a real recognition of differences and commonalities and to serve as a reminder that "the *other* is just as entitled as I am to her/his humanity expressed in her/his cultural reality."[2]

What is the special claim of feminism in challenging core assumptions of liberalism? The emergence of what is currently characterized as many feminisms or postfeminism makes the project of identifying its unique contribution to the challenge of liberalism much more difficult. The liberal system which is so fond of binary oppositions contained in the separate public/private arenas is endorsed by the allegedly neutral, objective and procedurally fair rule of law. In spite of the different twists and turns of feminism, we can recognize that both methodologically and substantively it has put on the table the subordination, oppression, and second-class citizenship brought about by the devaluation of the personal and the so-called domestic sphere. It gave personal experience epistemological standing, offering counternarratives which have served as critiques of the values and assumptions lying beneath our social and political organization, social contract included. It challenged male norms. As Teresa de Lauretis correctly points out, feminism defined subjectivity as the very site of the material inscription of the ideological.[3]

However, such material inscription of the ideological has insisted on the preeminence of gender subordination at the expense of other forms of oppression, missing a basic point. If feminism was to be about freedom for all women, it had to consequently address multiple experiences—not an easy task both for theoretical generalizations and for political strategy. There are historical and sociological explanations for the essentialism of the woman standpoint. First, there is the interplay of practice and theory: the cross-

---

2. *See* Marnia Larzreg, *Feminism and Difference: The Perils of Writing as a Woman on Women in Algeria*, 14 FEM. STUD. 81, 98 (1988).
3. Teresa de Lauretis, *Feminist Studies/Critical Studies: Issues, Terms and Contexts*, in FEMINIST STUD./CRITICAL STUD. 1 (Teresa de Lauretis ed., 1986).

fertilization between the political practice generated by the feminist movement and its theoretical conceptualizations. bell hooks and other women of color have done excellent work in documenting the schism existing between women of color and white women in the context of the feminist movement, and the influence of color and class composition on these conceptualizations.[4] Second, there is a history of frustration brought about by the political left's inability to grasp the centrality of gender subordination, as shown by the many indictments against feminists' alleged misunderstanding of a class analysis.

Although solidarity, empathy, altruism, and collective attachments are dimensions increasingly explored through the acquisition of a feminist consciousness, the power dynamics generated by institutions creating and perpetuating the cultural and psychological manifestations of racism and classism are left intact. The elaboration of theoretical arguments exclusively resting upon gender sustains the narratives emerging from such feminist consciousness. Race, ethnicity, and class are viewed as diluting the thrust of gender oppression. The biggest irony is that just as gender is dismissed by reductionist Marxist critiques, race, ethnicity, and class are assigned by essentialist feminism to maximum security and isolated confinement. They are allowed to join the general prison population only for good behavior: when the race, ethnicity and class categories learn to stay where they belong, when their subsidiary explanatory power is understood, when basic rules of grammar are comprehended and the auxiliary nature of the conjunction "and" is fully grasped. Bear in mind the by now familiar descriptions: gender *and* race, gender *and* class, gender *and* ethnicity.

I have critiqued elsewhere the essentialist and universalist character of feminist theorists,[5] with their substitution of the view from nowhere with the view from womanland. I have specifically targeted the work of Carol Gilligan and her reliance on Nancy Chodorow's essentialist account of reproduction and motherhood. My critique has focused on those feminist legal theorists who have uncritically and enthusiastically adopted some of her limited findings as the basis of their work. Likewise I have critiqued radical feminists' reductionist accounts of sexual oppression. Four examples follow.

1) Robin West, in trying to reconcile or at least understand the "fundamental contradiction" between cultural feminists largely defined by Gilligan and radical feminists largely defined by MacKinnon, asserts that women want to mother in spite of the compulsory nature of institutional motherhood and that women strive for intimacy even though they are oppressed

---

4. *See generally* BELL HOOKS, FEMINIST THEORY: FROM MARGIN TO CENTER (1984); TALKING BACK: THINKING FEMINIST, THINKING BLACK (1989); YEARNING: RACE, GENDER AND CULTURAL POLITICS (1990); AIN'T I A WOMAN (1981, 1984).

5. Celina Romany, The Intersection of Race, Gender and Class in the Critique of the Liberal Self, presentation at the Critical Legal Studies Conference (1988) (unpublished manuscript on file with the *Yale Journal of Law and Feminism*).

by it.[6] She uses Gilligan in a structuring way although Gilligan's work is more of a descriptive mechanism than a theoretical model. Thus, West ends up using a Gilliganesque model without rigorously examining the assumptions behind her positing of gender-specific characteristics.[7]

2) Martha Minow provides a sensitive discussion of the dilemma of difference, yet she also implicitly integrates Gilligan into her analysis when she concludes that by acknowledging and struggling against one's own partiality and by making an effort to understand the reality of others we will all move towards comprehending reciprocal realities.[8] In proffering such advice, Minow risks falling into a Gilliganesque model of problem solving, i.e. an examination of competing values and views. But where does her acknowledgement of differences take us? Were she to develop the power imbalances underlying "reciprocal realities," she could perhaps escape the criticism that simply talking to each other does not necessarily mean that we can hear one other.[9]

---

6. *See* Robin West, *Jurisprudence and Gender*, 55 U. CHI. L. REV. 1 (1988).

7. Other feminist jurisprudence scholars also make gender-based assumptions without sufficient analysis of the complex factors shaping gender. *See* Christine Littleton, *Restructuring Sexual Equality*, 75 CAL. L. REV. 1279, 1296-97 (1987). Even Elizabeth Schneider, who acknowledges the critique of Gilligan's work for "its insensitivity to race and class differences, and its disregard of historical context," believes that it is possible to set aside the problematic elements of Gilligan's analysis and assumptions. She concludes that "for my purposes, however, the significant aspect of her work is her insight into the way in which rights claims can be an aspect of psychological and social transformation—a moment in a dialectical process of change—and the way in which rights claims asserted as part of that process might be different." Elizabeth Schneider, *The Dialectic of Rights and Politics: Perspectives from the Women's Movement*, 61 N.Y.U. L. REV. 589, 617 (1987).

8. Martha Minow, *The Supreme Court 1986 Term-Foreword: Justice Engendered*, 101 HARV. L. REV. 10, 76 (1987).

9. Catharine MacKinnon has critiqued Carol Gilligan in this regard for not taking into account powerlessness in her work. In an informative conversation between several prominent figures in feminist jurisprudence, the following exchange between Catharine MacKinnon and Carol Gilligan illustrates this problem in a discussion of Menkel-Meadow's hypothetical mediation session between Jake and Amy:

CM: Power is socially constructed such that if Jake simply chooses not to listen to Amy, he wins; but if Amy simply chooses not to listen to Jake, she loses. In other words, Jake still wins because that is the system. And I am trying to work out how to change that system, not just how to make people more fully human within it.

CG: Your definition of power is his definition.

CM: That *is* because the society is that way, it operates on his definition, and I am trying to change it.

CG: To have her definition come in?

CM: That would be part of it, but more to have a definition that she would articulate that she cannot now, because his foot is on her throat.

CG: She's saying it.

CM: I know, but she is articulating the feminine. And you are calling it hers. That's what I find infuriating.

CG: No, instead I am saying she is articulating a set of values which are very positive.

3) Catharine MacKinnon's critique of Gilligan also adopts the essentialist standpoint of the silenced woman, without elaborating the multi-layers of oppression vividly represented by women of color. For MacKinnon, there is no female subjectivity, as women are defined by men. In effect collapsing all forms of oppression, she views sexuality as a "pervasive dimension of social life, one that permeates the whole, . . . a dimension along which other social divisions, like race and class, partly play themselves out."[10] Her totalizing theory of social reality based on sexual oppression does not admit to a concept of identity, and therefore, cannot account for the multilayered experience of women of color.[11] Symptomatically, even in her acknowledgment of the contribution of writings of women of color, in her most recent book, MacKinnon implies that these works lack a theoretical framework and, as such, others will have to build upon those writings in the coming years.[12] The experience of women of color seems to be viewed as the anecdotes that will unfold, with the passage of time, grand theoretical discoveries in sync with MacKinnon's overarching theory of sexual oppression.

4) Carrie Menkel-Meadow has explicitly used Gilligan as a starting point for her discussion of women's lawyering process. Despite the limitations of Gilligan's description of women's experience, Menkel-Meadow uses Gilligan's description to structure her analysis of the way in which women's values can inform their lawyering process. She assumes that if parties speak "directly to each other, they are more likely to appreciate the importance of each other's needs."[13] However, Menkel-Meadow's observations fail to explore the effect of power imbalances on mediated solutions. She has also discussed the

---

CM: Right, and I am saying they are feminine. And calling them hers is infuriating to me because we have never had the power to develop what ours really would be.

Ellen C. DuBois, et al., *Feminist Discourse, Moral Values and the Law: A Conversation*, 34 BUFF. L. REV. 11, 74-75 (1985). *See also* Ann C. Scales, *The Emergence of Feminist Jurisprudence: An Essay*, 95 YALE L.J. 1373, 1381 (1986) (arguing against lawyers' simplistic use of Gilligan's work to graft women's different voices onto rights-based system).

10. CATHARINE MACKINNON, TOWARD A FEMINIST THEORY OF THE STATE 130 (1989).

11. Marlee Kline's excellent critique of MacKinnon points out the tension in MacKinnon's work between her recognition of the multiplicity of race and class differences that exist among women and her emphasis on women's gender commonality. As Kline states "[e]ven where MacKinnon provides an in-depth analysis of the particular experiences of women of color, she does not allow those experiences to challenge the premise of her theory. . . . Thus, it is not surprising that about half of MacKinnon's examples of the particular experiences of women of color in *Feminism Unmodified* refer to racism only in the context of pornography or rape. The other examples of the particular experiences of Black women and First Nations women are confined to brief comments or footnotes." (citations ommitted). Marlee Kline, *Race, Racism and Feminist Legal Theory*, 12 HARV. WOMEN'S L.J. 115, 138-39 (1989). Kline further argues that MacKinnon's "construction of the feminist project [is] limited in its capacity to capture the complex impact of racism in the lives of women of color" and "neither the differences in interest and priority that exist between white women and women of color nor the unequal power relationship between the groups are confronted or dealt with in her work." *Id.* at 140-41.

12. MACKINNON, *supra* note 10.

13. Carrie Menkel-Meadow, *Portia in a Different Voice: Speculations on a Women's Lawyering Process*, 1 BERKELEY WOMEN'S L.J. 39, 51 (1985). *See also* Carrie Menkel-Meadow, *For and Against Settlement*, 33 U.C.L.A. L. REV. 485 (1985); Janet Rifkin, *Mediation from a Feminist Perspective: Promise and Problems*, 2 LAW & INEQ. J. 21 (1984).

"epistemology of exclusion." She remarks: "It has become too easy, I think, for those who have been excluded by the 'white male club' to be lumped together in exclusions. One bit of knowledge we have gained from feminist knowledge is the contextual particularity of our experiences."[14]

In support of this principle, however, she cites Gilligan, who has notably failed to particularize realities in terms of race. She later states: "Thus the knowing that comes from exclusion is based not on intrinsic characteristics, but rather on perverse oppositional knowledge that may be necessary for survival and adaptation to exclusion. The parallels to exclusion based on race and class should therefore be obvious."[15] Menkel-Meadow fails to spell out what she calls the "obvious" implications of this model for a subject considered to have a race and class as well as a gender. Furthermore, she concludes that although exclusion may create certain characteristics, we needn't reject those characteristics.[16] This position has dangerous implications for a truly feminist lawyering process in that a socially-constructed definition of women's skills and values becomes the norm for all women.[17]

* * * * *

Do feminist legal theory's sustaining narratives have the breadth required to challenge different strands of oppression within liberal legalism, as experienced by all women? Can this work, as Robert Cover suggested, offer a viable alternative? Think about the critique of rights, their affirmative and negative character, ascription of rights, the instrumental value of rights, the nature of adjudication, core principles such as property, the exchange of commodities (personal included), demarcations of the public and private, boundaries for state intervention and non-intervention, the discrimination principle, conflicts among different sources of discrimination, and reflect on the limited potential a gender-essentialist analysis has for a thorough analysis of these core institutions.

I am skeptical of the ability of a feminist legal theory based on exclusive gender narratives to deal with the overall challenge. Essentialist narratives overload feminism as a key tool in the critique of the liberal project and utterly fail to offer a comprehensive critical framework for liberal legal institutions. The paradigm selection process (the architectural design, selection of building materials, objectives, aesthetics) is informed by that limited experience. At

---

14. Carrie Menkel-Meadow, *Excluded Voices: New Voices in the Legal Profession Making New Voices in the Law,* 42 U. MIAMI L. REV. 29, 31 (1987) (footnote omitted).

15. *Id.* at 43.

16. *See also* Littleton, *supra* note 7, at 1296-97 (1987) (advocating "acceptance" model to grapple with difference which is attentive to "consequences of gendered difference, and not its sources").

17. *See, e.g.,* EEOC v. Sears Roebuck & Co., 628 F. Supp. 1264 (N.D. Ill. 1986), *aff'd,* 839 F. 2d 302 (7th Cir. 1988).

their best these narratives offer partial critiques with partial and insular results: small-town feminism generating small-town feminist theory and politics.

To the extent that a racial/ethnic/class "minority perspective" gets incorporated into the feminist redefinition of subjectivity, the latter's critique of rights and fairness also undergoes revision. The normative intuitions that are to guide such an analysis are "different." As the "minority" critique of critical legal studies scholarship points out, the evaluation of rights stems neither from what a critical legal scholar would describe as an alienating experience originating from the fear of connection, nor from what a feminist legal scholar would characterize as a gender experience of connection that spells solidarity and responsibility to others in lieu of atomized individualism. The intersection of race and gender in the redefinition of subjectivity and intersubjectivity points to a different legal consciousness. Rights that "separate" individuals also trace boundaries of mutual respect in such separation and (no matter what amount of false consciousness is involved) can strengthen identities.

If feminism, and feminist legal theory in particular, is to remain a liberation project, it needs to come to grips with its cognitive distortions and self-idealized universal discoveries. Feminism needs to put forth sustaining narratives that capture the centrality of intersections in the intersubjective formation of identities. In the meantime, we could use a heavy dose of modesty, giving pretentiousness a deserved vacation and publicly announcing the incorporation of the project as "Feminism, Limited."

Postmodernism has been recruited in an effort to counter the essentialist dimension of the woman standpoint. Although I am sympathetic to the efforts of those (in particular the work of Nancy Fraser and Linda Nicholson)[18] who are are trying to match feminism and postmodernism through the magic of supplementation (a match not necessarily made in heaven), I am highly skeptical of satisfactorily concrete outcomes. The postmodern fallibilistic and decentering approach moves away from a unitary concept of the woman standpoint and opens up the door for alternative accounts of difference. However, this new entrance leads us into a meeting of discourses rather than to an encounter of those differences at the very concrete level of power differentials and unequal distribution of privileges.

Discourse, the understudy for representation, supplants representation once it is discarded as an obsolete and decadent way of apprehending reality.[19] I

---

18. Nancy Fraser & Linda Nicholson, *Social Criticism Without Philosophy: An Encounter Between Feminism and Postmodernism, in* UNIVERSAL ABANDON? THE POLITICS OF POST MODERNISM 83 (Andrew Ross ed., 1988).

19. Although postmodern feminists have attempted to move away from some of postmodernism's main tenets, the social critique of power differentials remains inadequate and the primacy of discourse remains significantly unaltered. *See* FEMINISM/POSTMODERNISM (Linda J. Nicholson ed., 1990); JEAN-FRANCOIS LYOTARD, THE POSTMODERN CONDITION (1984); STEPHEN A. TYLER, THE UNSPEAKABLE: DISCOURSE, DIALOGUE AND RHETORIC IN THE POSTMODERN WORLD (1988); F. Jameson, *Postmodernism or the Cultural Logic of Late Capitalism,* 146 NEW LEFT REV. 53 (1984).

am highly suspicious of discourse accounts, especially when I run into the postmodernist discussion of colonialism, a paradigm for marginality with which I am quite familiar. There is nothing outside the text in the realm of discourse, there is no point from which opposition forms. As Benita Parry accurately points out in her critique of Gayatri Spivak's work, the move is one to place "incendiary devices within the dominant structures of representation and not to confront these with another knowledge;"[20] the subaltern voice is deemed irretrievable; counternarratives of resistance are labeled as reverse discourse.

Linda Nicholson and Nancy Fraser talk about adopting a fallibilistic approach which "would tailor its methods and categories to the specific task at hand, using multiple categories when appropriate and foreswearing the metaphysical comfort of a single 'feminist method' or 'feminist epistemology.'"[21] Their approach "would be more like a tapestry composed of threads of many different hues rather than one woven in a single color."[22] Not much is said, however, as to the relinquishment of privileges necessary for the multi-colored, multi-class composition of the weavers' labor force. I have levelled the same critique against those who, like Roberto Unger, in the elaboration of "context-smashers narratives" guided by empathy and solidarity, need to resort to the trinity of love, faith, and hope.[23]

When I attempt to figure out if there is life after postmodernism, the recurrent image I have is one where I stand in the middle of a ballroom, paralyzed, surrounded by dancers experiencing the *jouissance* generated by dances of heterogeneous and fragmented accounts. Paralysis skyrockets my anxiety because I love to dance and thought I knew a lot about dancing . . .

* * * * *

Ain't I a Feminist? I am a feminist with a broad and expansive liberation project. I advocate a broadening of horizons to show that the humanist project of subjectivity and agency need not be trashed but rather redefined. We have to expose those legal institutions which delay and obstruct the creation of conditions for strengthening identities, thereby enabling them to engage in dialogues which further refine our subjective perceptions and which serve as spaces for the creation of new narratives that are able to sustain the paradigm choices guiding the formation of new legal meanings.[24]

Autonomy and subjectivity have a lot of appeal to Third World women. Feminist scholars and feminist legal theories should pay more attention to the

---

20. Benita Parry, *Problems in Current Theories of Colonial Discourse*, 9 OXFORD LITERARY REV. 27, 43 (1987).

21. Fraser & Nicholson, *supra* note 18, at 101.

22. *Id.* at 101-02.

23. Celina Romany, Book Review, 54 U.P.R. L. REV. 587 (1985) (reviewing ROBERTO UNGER, PASSION: AN ESSAY ON PERSONALITY (1984)).

24. Cover, *supra* note 1.

work of Third World cultural theorists, who expose the intimate connections between political and national history and the constitution of the subject, stress the importance of revealing marginality conditions which bring about non-identity,[25] and grasp the meaning of the "border [which] houses the power of the outrageous, the imagination needed to turn the historical and cultural tables."[26] As the writings of Guillermo Gomez-Pena, George Yudice, and Juan Flores describe, "the view from the border enables us to apprehend the ultimate arbitrariness of the border itself, of forced separations and inferiorizations."[27]

Juan Felipe Herrera's poem *"What if suddenly the continent turned upside down?"* says it best:

> *What if the U.S was Mexico?*
> *What if 200,000 Anglosaxicans*
> *were to cross the border each month*
> *to work as gardeners, waiters,*
> *3rd chair musicians, movie extras,*
> *bouncers, babysitters, chauffers,*
> *syndicated cartoons, feather-weight*
> *boxers, fruit-pickers & anonymous poets?*
> *What if they were called waspanos,*
> *waspitos, wasperos, or wasbacks?*
> *What if we were the top dogs?*
> *What if literature was life, eh?*[28]

---

25. Abdul R. JanMohamed & David Lloyd, *Introduction: Minority Discourse—What is to be Done?*, 7 CULTURAL CRITIQUE 5, 16 (1987).

26. Juan Flores & George Yudice, *Living Borders/Buscando America: Languages of Latino Self-Formation*, 24 SOC. TEXT 57, 80 (1990).

27. *Id.*

28. *Id.* at 79.

Postscript

Some time ago I read a paper in which I attempted to describe what it meant to be the concrete embodiment of the abstract conversation of feminists at a feminist conference: my invisibility. I said:

I looked around and saw that notwithstanding my unique location, the only Latina in the room, eye contact was avoided so as to reinforce my social invisibility. The experience is not exactly new. Yet, as at other times, I somehow nurtured hopes and expectations that my presence, or for that matter the presence of any other woman of color, could stir some interest in addressing the multi-facetedness of oppression. While following and observing the dynamics in that room, I asked myself how many of those participants actually had a person of color as a good friend or lover. I knew that a high percentage of those who had children have at least had close contact with that woman of color which allowed them to pursue their professional careers and personal realization: the domestic servant. At a more distant level many had come into contact with them in the lower ladders of service. In fact, at that same conference we were served food by one of them.

Therefore my presence in that room served the dual purpose of reminding them of their previous limited contacts with women of color, evoking feelings of distance and separation, and generating a good deal of curiosity as to my presence in that group. By talking of the need to find commonalities while asserting differences, I became the concrete embodiment of their abstract conversation. At one point an assertive student—why is it that students usually have the ability to generate honest confrontations?—directly gazed at me and asked the facilitators to discuss how those alluded differences were integrated into their feminist works. Loving and hating that student for her directness which was an open invitation for my intervention, I realized that the secure, yet uncomfortable, position of *observadora* was coming to an end.

That student had spoiled my otherwise successful "observer approach" in American feminist conferences. Since the rage and indignation were, as usual, very much inside myself, it was easier than I thought to accept her invitation. My accent, my color, the Caribbean rhythm in my words felt "different." The established feminist authorities assented with their heads to my thoughts. Yet in their faces you could see their inability to grasp, apprehend my feelings and emotions. They were too distant, I was too "other." Their otherness as women allowed them to walk with me half-way. But only half-way.

Marisa, one of my students at CUNY, after having read that paper, wrote:

Dear Celina:

What was it like becoming the concrete embodiment of their abstract conversation? What was it like to become the personification of theory? Why were they too distant? Why were you too other? You wrote that "their otherness as women allowed them to walk with me half-way, but only half-way." Is there just one path? Many paths? A straight line, a direction? Is that direction involved with purpose? Or is it a continuum, reflecting each of our lives? I think you hedge on page 8 when you refer to your rage and indignation. Is it that this "genre" of writing does not allow for visceral truthfulness/primitive truthfulness? Level with me and talk about that rage and indignation.

What is it like being invisible? Being made invisible by the discourse, by deconstruction, by academia? Being invisible in a world you've chosen to be in; in a world you thrive in? Don't you see the paradox, the dichotomy, the schism? You passed the professional rituals—but still you are invisible. You seek to become truly visible in evaluating social structures based upon experiencing oppression as a way of being.

So why is this core forced into hiding? It is forced externally (I realize you talk about internalization and complicity yet I want to dwell in the external). The externality of tentacles and arms which have the ability to enter human flesh—which have the ability to penetrate and wound—the tension at the moment of penetration . . . once inside, the tentacles divide and turn themselves into open hands which reach out for and search for living essences, the heart, the brain-they reach and squeeze hard. The essences aren't destroyed, they merely escape and hide, hide behind the heart and mind and continue to exist within the grip of those tentacles, because the essences of life have gone into hiding so that the whole organism can survive. These essences live themselves in a shallow pool of water—crystal clear, walled in by purple flowers that are always in bloom, which grow to enormous heights as the grip becomes stronger.

What does your space look like? You see my space, I don't know if it is a space for feminist legal scholars, but it is mine. Where is yours?

I realized I was truly visible to Marisa.

Chicanas and El Movimiento

Adaljiza Sosa Riddell

The Chicano* movement is the all-encompassing effort to, on the one hand, articulate and intensify the Chicano existence, and on the other hand, to articulate and alleviate the suffering which has accrued to Chicanos precisely because of that existence. Of the important issues it faces that of Las Chicanas is perhaps the most problematic. Ordinarily, when the issue of Chicanas is raised, whether it be by Chicanos, Chicanas, or by those outside of the Chicano context, the concern is with the status and role of Chicanas within the Movimiento in general, within specific activist organizations, and within Chicano society. This is particularly unfortunate because expression of interest in Chicanas thus inspires a defensive attitude on the part of Chicanos included within any of those categories. These defensive Chicanos are not too different from the Mexican-Americans who, in the early days of the newly articulated Movimiento defended the status quo situation either because they had invested so much time and energy into attaining a certain status within it, or because they had reasoned, along with the Anglo social scientists, that there was something innately wrong with

---

*The term Chicano will be used throughout this paper in the generic sense, inclusive of male and female, unless otherwise specified or used in companionship with Chicana.

©Copyright 1974 by Adaljiza Sosa Riddell

155

the Mexican culture which resulted in the conditions within which the Chicano existed in the United States.

The tragedy of this situation is simply an extension of the all-too-familiar syndrome under which Chicanos have suffered. Chicanos are induced to define and describe their very being and existence in terms of external constraints and conditions imposed upon them by their colonizers or neocolonizers. Thus, what we have is the acceptance of certain externally-imposed stereotypes about Chicanas acting as a restraint upon actions or suggestions for changes among Chicanas; actions and changes which would not conform to the stereotypes or act to destroy the stereotypes.

Many of the stereotypes have been equated with aspects of Mexican-Chicano culture. Social scientists describe la Chicana as, "ideally submissive, unworldly, and chaste," or, "at the command of the husband, who (keeps) her as he would a coveted thing, free from the contacts of the world, subject to his passions, ignorant of life."[1] Social scientists also describe "machismo," as a masculinity syndrome particularly attributable to the Latin male, and, thus, by extension, to the Chicano male. These attitudes are echoed by Chicanos themselves in such contexts as in the song "The Female of Aztlán," by la familia Domínguez: "your responsibility is to love, work, pray, and help . . . the male is the leader, he is iron, not mush," and by statements such as those made at the Denver Chicano Youth Liberation Conference in 1969 emphasizing the role of la Chicana in the movimiento was to "stand behind her man."[2] More problematic, however, are the large numbers of Chicanas and Chicanos who have come to accept these descriptions and syndromes as part of their daily lives.

Obviously these stereotypes have little meaning to those who have lived the reality of the Chicano existence. Within each of our memories there is the image of a father who worked long hours, suffered to keep his family alive, united, and who struggled to maintain his dignity. Such a man had little time for concern over his "masculinity." Certainly he did not have ten children because of his machismo, but because he was a human being, poor, and without "access" to birth control. We certainly remember mothers and sisters who worked in the fields or at menial labor in addition to doing the work required at home to survive. Submissiveness, chastity, and unworldliness are luxuries of the rich and/or nearly rich. Machismo is a myth propagated by subjugators and colonizers who take pleasure in watching their subjects strike out vainly against them in order to prove themselves still capable of action. The following billboard sign in Los Angeles was certainly not written by any Chicano:

MACHO
Join the LAPD

The term macho is not applied to the Anglo-society itself.[3] Chicanos are faced with stereotypes of themselves which are standards they are goaded into emulating, and expected to achieve in order to be accepted by the dominant society, the colonizers. Strenuous efforts to achieve these externally imposed goals may thus result in excesses which can then be blamed, by outsiders, on cultural traits. Conversely, failure to achieve them can result in the same syndrome, that is, a view of a culture as somehow inferior and inflexible. Thus, to talk about change becomes a very real threat to Chicanos who wish to retain what they have defined as their culture. The stereotypes, the acceptance of stereotypes, and the defensive postures adopted by "culturalists" become the problems for Chicanos striving to bring about some changes, rather than the problems being defined as they more adequately could be, in terms of external forces.[4] Chicano activists, in turn, tend to define the changes they wish to see in internal terms rather than external terms so that we see articles written by Chicanas with such titles as: "Machismo No! Igualdad, Si![5] The clashes thus continue unabated over Chicana roles, and the Chicana continues to feel guilty about what she is, or is not, doing for her people, to and for, her man. The important point is that Chicanos have had and continue to have, very little control over their self images, cultural awareness, and self definition.

In order to comprehend adequately the pervasiveness of the external restraints which operate upon the quality of the Chicana existence it is necessary to evaluate the earliest descriptions of women in the societies of the valley of México. These early descriptions were provided by either Spanish conquerors or Spanish male settlers.[6] In either case, the Spanish role was one of imposition upon first, the native local cultures, and second, the individuals within that local group. What these early chroniclers described was the world as they saw it, through Spanish eyes, much as Anglo social scientists "see" Chicano barrios today. The Spanish chroniclers were not wholly concerned with describing local customs prior to the conquest itself. In most cases, what was described was a situation already changed under the impact of a brutal and thorough conquest. The women of México had never been exploited in the same manner and to the same degree that they were during the Conquest. Exploitation of contemporary Chicanas begins in a very real sense with the Spanish conquest, regardless of what conditions were among the native peoples prior to the Conquest.

Two other conditions render the descriptions of native customs provided by the conquering peoples unreliable. There was not *one* native group with its unique customs, but a multitude of native groups.[7] Thus, descriptions which consider all native groups as one entity should be immediately suspect. The Spanish conquerors, whether soldiers, settlers, or priests, were all themselves products of the Judaeo-Christian tradition. This tradition has been often and well described in terms of its racist and sexist attitudes. The effect of this combination of attitudes is that in word and in deed, the Spaniards relegated the native woman, and later the mestiza, to the lowest position in the structured society which came to dominate México.

The social structure for females in the conquered nation of México paralleled that of the overall population based upon race. The Spanish born residents of México were at the top of the socio-economic ladder, followed by the Mexican born criollos, with the Mestizos and the natives lumped together at the bottom. However, when individuals from the "bottom" group were able to act like the other two classes, by being light-skinned and adopting their way of life, that is, by assimilating, they were allowed to form a third class. This class was between the Criollos and the Indians and Mestizos who looked like and lived like their Indian ancestors.

The Catholic Church is as responsible for the Conquest of México as the Spanish soldiers, and is part and parcel of the Judaeo-Christian tradition. It not only dealt with the natives as subjects, but with the women as subjects of the subjects *and* the subjugators. The Spanish Catholic Church, an institution of Conquest, thus stands as a guardian and perpetrator of an ancient tradition whereby women were unequal to, and in need of the constant surveillance of, men, preferably white Catholic men. The social structure of Mexican society, and that of all the other lands conquered by the Spaniards, reflected the views of the Catholic Church on women and on native peoples. The Spanish woman, being white and Catholic, was often considered as religious, sacrosanct, pure, somehow like the Virgin Mary, untouched and untouchable, the ideal woman, wife, and mother. The Mestizas and the native women were regarded as heathens, women in need of redemption, loose women, thus women who could be exploited without fear of punishment.

The Indian and mestizo men saw quickly the need to protect their women. The women responded to this blatant abuse by the Conquerors by staying out of public view, because public meant being exploited, being raped. Women were, current female chauvinism not withstanding, most vulnerable because of their unique childbearing ability. In this situation the women were given no choice. The men themselves could not be effectively protective of the women when they themselves were subject to enslavement, torture, and death. Thus the new race was born, and this is a reality with which Chicanas and Chicanos must live.

The sexism and racism were translated in México, as they were in the U.S. into mechanisms of domination by those in control over the political system. The Spanish also dealt with the Indian and mestizo males separately and distinctly from the Indian females and Mestizas. Whether or not Indian females and Mestizas were the subjects of the Indian males and Mestizos is not primarily relevant to the Chicana condition because Chicanas are the direct heirs of the subjugation of the women of the valley of México to the Spanish conquerors. What is important is that the Indian male and Mestizo were unable to act as intermediaries for the women with the Spanish power structure, even when they attempted to do so. The peoples of México and the Mestizos became economic and political objects of the Spaniards and the Indian females and Mestizas became the sexual objects of the conquerors. Changes in the power structure throughout the years between the Conquest and the Mexican Revolution of 1910 did not substantially alter the situation.

The migration of Mexicans in large numbers to the areas north of the Rio Bravo did not mark an end to this colonization experience. It simply meant that Mexicano-Chicanos, having internalized a past colonial experience, added a second one to their existence. Since they were largely from the working classes of Mexican society and were Mexican they came into the U.S. economic and political system at the lowest stratum. The females were dealt with only through the males until they attempted to compete for jobs. It was when Chicanas began to seek work outside of the family groups that sexism became a key factor of oppression along with racism. Chicanas were more readily hired for farmwork when they were with their husbands and children, thus forming, or being required to form, a working unit. When Chicanas operated outside of this context, they were relegated to other positions of menial labor. Chicanas have suffered through both experiences and now suffer from two apparently contradictory stereotypes. This contradiction was described by Gracia Molina de Pick:

> Las mujeres somos tradicionalmente presentadas en una doblez, que por una parte nos hace gozar con el sufrimiento diciendo además que somos víctimas de nuestra cultura, mártires de nuestros hombres, excesivamente supersticiosas, fanáticas, sucias, perezosas, tontas, aparatos de reproducción, y sonrientemente resignadas, sin ninguna vida interior, emocional o intelectual. Pero también somos las mujeres seductoras, voluptuosas, sensuales, pasionales, immorales, en suma, la representación de la aventura sexual más provocadora.[8]

This contradiction of roles serves a dual purpose. First, it removes all blame for the social problems of Chicanos from the dominant society placing it upon Chicanas themselves. Second, it serves to keep Chicanas pre-occupied with their apparent "shortcomings," so as to keep them from looking outward. Chicanas, then, can be blamed by the Anglo society and its institutions for not being good mothers, for not keeping their family together, for working instead of staying home, or, conversely, for being too oriented to their family, for having too many children, for not working, for staying home.

Statistics compiled on California by the United States Equal Employment Opportunities Commission indicate the following situations.[9] (See Table 1). First, of the total Spanish surnamed employees, 68% are male and 32% are female. This percentage breakdown is not un-like that of the state's general population. Spanish surnamed females do not stay at home any more nor less than women in the general population. It would seem ethnicity is the most important factor working against Chicanas as against Chicanos in general. The ratio of women to men appears to be 1 to 1 (see table 1).

Graph 1

Spanish Surname White Collar Workers by Category and Sex

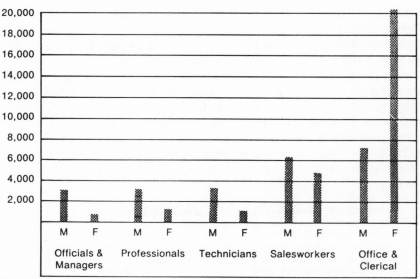

Source: United States Equal Employment Opportunity Commission, *California Section*, 1967, Table 5.

Table 1

California Spanish Surname Employment by Sex and Job Category

Sex	Total Population Employment — 1970*		Total Spanish-Surname employment 1967**		White Collar Spanish Surname Employment — 1967**		Blue Collar Spanish Surname Employment — 1967**	
	Number	%	Number	%	Number	%	Number	%
Male	5,285,220	63.4	167,721	68.6	25,519	47.4	123,682	75.8
Female	3,053,273	36.6	74,469	31.4	28,278	52.5	39,533	24.2
Total	8,338,493	100.0	237,190	100.0	53,797	100.0	163,215	100.0

*United States Bureau of Census, United States Department of Commerce, *Detailed Characteristics, California,* Table 164.

**United States Equal Employment Opportunity Commission, *California Section, 1967,* Table 5.

407

However, if we look at a detailed breakdown of white collar employment, we see in addition to ethnicity, sex mitigates against Spanish-surname females achieving certain positions within the category (see Graph 1). The highest proportion of females in the white collar category is in office and clerical work. Since Chicanos are not doing the majority of hiring, it is the dominant Anglo society which is responsible for such ratios in the hiring of Spanish-surname males and females.

Nonetheless some Chicanas perceive that it is the Chicano (male) who keeps them from attaining professional status. Linda Aguilar writes: "I have found that a Chicana has a better chance of being employed by an Anglo if she seeks any type of administrative position than by a Chicano."[10] This may very well be the case in the experience of Ms. Aguilar, but how often do Chicanas encounter Chicanos (males) in positions of administrative responsibility who are called upon to review them for hiring or promotion? This position can lead one to ignore important facets of our oppression. Chicanas may come to believe the external realities as equatable to the internal conditions. This is a dimension of being colonized, that is, coming to believe in one's own reference group as inferior to the dominant group. For the Chicana, racism is added to sexism and the result is the same manipulation, exploitation, and control by the superordinate group.[11] Chicanos, being part of the situation, can also be expected to express themselves in similar ways. Therefore, there is the very real possibility that, were there more Chicanos (males) in positions of administrative responsibility, they would be biased against Chicanas to a greater extent than Anglo males, for whatever reasons. It is this double oppression that we may ignore if we blame Chicanos for the problems of Chicanos.[12]

Chicanos and Chicanas and the Movimiento must now address themselves to these realities. If Chicanos act in such a way as to ignore the condition of double-oppression under which Chicanas suffer we must face the fact that they are not only perpetuating the stereotypes and the conditions which those stereotypes support, but they are also guilty of intensifying those conditions and their negative results. We should articulate specific proposals and goals which relate to the Chicana and should direct ourselves to relieving some of the unique burdens which the dominant society places upon Chicanas, thus separating her from her male counterparts.

Many Chicanas find the Women's Liberation movement largely irrelevant because more often than not it is a move for strictly women's rights. While women's rights advocates are asking for a parity share of the "American" pie, Chicanas (and Chicanos) are asking for something other than parity. The end which is desired by Chicanas is the restoration of control over a way of life, a culture, an existence. For a Chicana to break with this goal is to break with her past, her present, and her people. For this reason, the concerns expressed by Chicanas for their own needs within the Movimiento cannot be considered a threat to the unity of the Movimiento itself.

One of the questions to which Chicanos should be addressing themselves is what goals within the Movimiento can be constructed to relate to Chicanas in particular. If we recognize the external imposition of much of what defines and delineates the conditions for Chicanas, then it is obvious there must be a special effort to remove some of these unique burdens. La Malinche's situation symbolizes the problems which face Chicanas as they attempt to deal with the dominant Anglo society. She was, after all, as much a victim of the Conquest and of Cortéz as she was one of the keys to the Conquest. La Chicana is not only placed in a status below the Chicano (male), but in a category apart vis-à-vis the dominant society. That division is manipulated and exploited to further control Chicanos. To end the division by including Chicanas as an integral, not subordinate, part of the group we call Chicanos, is to also diminish the ability of outside groups to manipulate and exploit us. This should be one of the goals of the Chicano Movimiento.

Notes

1. The first example is from Arthur Rubel, "The Family", in John H. Burma, ed., *Mexican Americans in the United States*, p. 214. The second example is from Alfred White, *The Apperceptive Mass of Foreigners as Applied to Americanization, The Mexican Group*, Thesis, University of California, 1923, pg. 31.

2. The Denver Chicano Youth Liberation Conference was held in 1969 and one workshop which dealt with the question of Chicanas issued the statement that Chicanas do not want to be liberated. This is akin to saying that Black slaves loved their masters, and worse, saying this with pride.

3. Various authors have come to realize that machismo operates as much, if not more, in the dominant society. I.F. Stone in *The New York Reviews of Books* (May 18, 1972) entitles his article: "Machismo in Washington."

4. Culturalists in this paper are defined as those who wish to preserve certain aspects of the Chicano existence. Sometimes the concern with preservation of cultural characteristics becomes simply a status quo position as if cultures never change. At other times, culturalists border on traditionalists, that is, those who wish to go back to an earlier era, as if in that era "culture" was somehow pure and unadulterated by contact with Anglo society. The reality for the Chicano is that the contact has already occurred, and much of what was his past was no better than his present. The Chicano, then, exists in that diversity of truths which poses a problem for analysts who would like to define once and for all what Chicano culture consists of.

5. Lionila López Saenz, "¡Machismo, No! ¡Igualdad, Si!" *La Luz* (May 1972).

6. The two most famous chroniclers of the native societies included Bernal Díaz del Castillo, a soldier, and Fray Bernardino de Sahagún. Fray Sahagún's interest was in preserving knowledge of the history of the Conquest and of the civilizations which existed before the Conquest. Yet, by the time he began his chronicles, the Conquest was well established.

7. The word group, here is used instead of tribe because of the connotation, which appears to this writer as a negative one, accruing to the concept of tribe. A tribe is somehow inferior in the level of social development compared to contemporary groupings. This distinction is, to me, unacceptable, and certainly inapplicable to the type of social structures extant in the valley of México on the eve of Cortéz's arrival in México.

8. Gracia Molina de Pick, "Reflexiones Sobre el Feminismo y la Raza", *La Luz* (August 1972), pg. 58.

9. All statistics utilized are available from the United States Equal Employment Opportunities Commission. The data is on California for 1968.

10. Linda Aguilar, "Unequal Opportunity and the Chicana", *La Luz* (September 1972), pg. 52.

11. Robert Blanner in describing internal colonialism includes this aspect of being colonized in his definition of racism. See Robert Blanner, (ed), *On Racial Oppression in America*.

12. The term, double oppression, herein used refers to how this dominant Anglo society places Chicanas in categories and positions which denies them a modicum of dignity both because they are Chicanas and because they are females. Secondly, Chicanos, echoing the values of the dominant majority, often seek to confine Chicanas further.

Bibliography

Aguilar, Linda, "Unequal Opportunity and the Chicana," *La Luz*, (September, 1972), Vol. 1, No. 4, p. 52.

Blauner, Robert, (ed), *On Racial Oppression in America*. New York: Harper and Row, 1972.

Molina de Pick, Gracia, "Reflexiones Sobre el Feminismo y la Raza", *La Luz*, Vol. 1, No. 4, (August, 1972), p. 58.

Montiel, Miguel, "The Social Science Myth of the Mexican-American Family", from Romano, V., Octavio, (ed), *Voices*. Berkeley: Quinto Sol Publications, 1971.

Rubel, Arthur, "The Family", in John H. Burma, (ed), *Mexican-Americans in the United States*, pp. 211-234, New York, Shenkman Publishing Company, Inc., 1970.

Saenz, Lionila López, "Machismo, No! Igualdad, Sí!, *La Luz*, Vol. 1, No. 2, (May, 1972), pp. 19-24.

Shedd, Margaret, *Malinche and Cortez*, New York: Doubleday and Company, Inc., 1971.

Stone, I.F., "Machismo in Washington", *New York Review of Books*, (May 18, 1972), pp. 13-14.

United States Equal Opportunities Employment Commission, U.S. Government Printing Office, Washington D.C.

Vaillant, George C., *La Civilización Azteca*, México: Fondo de Cultura Económica, 1960.

White, Alfred, *The Apperceptive Mass of Foreigners as Applied to Americanization, The Mexican Group*, Thesis, University of California, Davis, 1923.

411

"ABNORMAL INTIMACY": THE VARYING WORK NETWORKS OF CHICANA CANNERY WORKERS

PATRICIA ZAVELLA

INTRODUCTION

Recent feminist research has greatly enhanced our understanding of women's networks in the past and present. We now examine the conditions that create variation in the structure and functioning of women's kin and social networks, conditions which allow women to cooperate with one another even in extreme instability, or which create conflict among women.[1] Further, the meaning provided by support networks of kin and friends varies by race and class. Middle-class white women of the nineteenth century found meaning, love, and support for community moral reform,[2] while working-class and impoverished black women also relied on network members for basic survival or to adapt to the new country after emigration.[3] And we have seen how women's networks have provided crucial means of support to political activists.[4]

At the same time, feminist labor historians have shown how women workers in a variety of occupational contexts create "work cultures" — shared understandings and practices — just as male workers do. Again, feminists emphasize that different conditions of work create variation in women's work culture. In the context of relative autonomy, sales clerks can create a "sisterhood" that inculcates new workers with lore and floor practices, and the occupational segregation of women sometimes creates great solidarity among female workers.[5]

We still know little about how these worlds of home and work intersect, however, and how networks affect women's consciousness. And because of still prevalent stereotypes, we have a limited view of the lives of some groups of women.

A constellation of stereotypes surrounds Chicanas — Mexican

Feminist Studies 11, no. 3 (Fall 1985). © by Feminist Studies, Inc.

American women. The literature on Chicano support networks[6] emphasizes the importance of kin ties above all others: more so than Anglos or blacks, Chicanos are thought to maintain cohesive ties with their extensive kin through frequent visiting and the exchange of goods and labor. Chicanos are said to regard support for emotional problems from relatives – especially close kin – as superior to other sources. Further, Chicanos tend to migrate to areas where relatives reside in order to utilize kin resources.[7] An implication of this research is that friendship is not considered to play an important part in Chicano support networks; at least most writers ignore this aspect of networks. In fact, some go as far as to claim that relatives are the primary source of support "*because* of the relatively low reliance of Mexican Americans on other informal resources such as fictive kin, friends, neighbors and coworkers."[8]

This view of Chicanos as solely reliant on kin parallels one that perceives Chicanas as solely kinswomen – as living outside the world of paid labor.[9] Yet along with other women, Chicanas have been rapidly entering the labor force. In the decade between 1960 and 1970, relatively more married Chicanas entered the labor force nationally than their white and black counterparts.[10] By 1980, the proportion of Chicanas who worked was similar to that of all women.[11] Yet there are very few discussions of Chicanas' work cultures.[12]

In this article, I address the following interrelated questions concerning the networks of Chicana cannery workers: How are work networks structured and operated, and why are work friendships important to Chicana workers? I show how women's work culture – of which coworker networks are an important manifestation – evolved within the context of canning production. My approach, however, goes beyond the factories and examines how women's work networks operate within women's private lives. I suggest that in order to understand the significance of and variation in women's work networks we must link the changing conditions of women's work with family changes. Further, working women develop a consciousness of their situation, or recognition of their collective circumstances as workers, by contrasting their work situations with their family situations. In this way, women's consciousness is "negotiated" – actively modified in response to their actual experiences on the job and within families.[13]

The research is based on fieldwork I did in 1977-78 in the Santa Clara Valley, the southeastern tip of the San Francisco Bay. The bulk of my data is in-depth, open-ended interviews with cannery workers conducted in their homes, some in Spanish. Informants were selected by "snowball sampling" – through contacts I established with cannery workers and labor activists. I interviewed a total of thirty-one workers, of whom fifteen were Chicanas. The mean age of my female informants is forty-six years, and the women had on the average sixteen years of plant seniority. Many of the women, however, had worked for as long as thirty years in the industry. Informants' names are fictitious. I also did participant observation in mainly public settings – informal social gatherings such as parties and barbecues. I was also a participant in a local union election campaign, which involved attending numerous meetings and support activities such as fundraisers. I was unable to secure a job in the canneries, so I made no on-the-job observations.[14]

CANNING PRODUCTION

Recruitment practices of canning firms are largely informal.[15] There is no hiring hall, and workers wait around outside company gates to be hired. When I was doing fieldwork, the overwhelming majority of job applicants were Chicanos and Mexicans. Women informants often went job hunting accompanied by female kin, particularly sisters, or were able to secure jobs with the help of relatives who were already employed in the cannery. These informal recruiting mechanisms have resulted in a predominantly Mexican American labor force in Santa Clara Valley canneries. Chicanos as a whole make up approximately 64 percent of the cannery work force; while Chicanas alone make up about 36 percent of the workers. In particular canneries, however, Chicanos comprise as much as 90 percent of the production work force.[16]

The cannery labor force is segregated by race and sex, and more recently even by age. The majority of the seasonal workers (who mainly work during summer months) are women, especially Chicanas. Various mechanisms such as a relatively closed internal labor market, women's lack of information about promotions, and sexual harassment by supervisors keep women in the lowest paying jobs. In addition, there are ethnic cleavages in the work force.

Italian Americans and Portuguese Americans entered canneries in earlier periods and have now risen to supervisory positions. Thus Chicanas are concentrated in the lowest paying jobs (such as sorting) and are usually supervised by white ethnic women. As one moves up the job hierarchy, men – especially white ethnics – predominate.

Increasingly, canneries are relocating to rural areas closer to where the produce is grown. Therefore, the number of cannery jobs in the Santa Clara Valley is diminishing. As a result, cannery workers – especially seasonal ones – are becoming a middle-aged labor force as only those with high seniority are able to keep their jobs.

Canning production is geared to a continuous conveyor belt that moves raw produce through various stages as it is processed, canned, cooked, and cased for storage or shipment to market. Production is highly mechanized except for sorting operations which require the largest number of workers. The actual process of sorting is fast paced and tedious, and women workers are immobilized. Sorters examine the produce and place it in various chutes, depending on the size and condition. My informants repeatedly noted that "it doesn't take much brains to work in a cannery." But the constant motion of so much produce on the conveyor belt, the humidity from water baths, the din of crashing cans and cooking machinery, as well as the nauseating odors of rotten produce and chemicals (such as chlorine) used in processing, make the job both distasteful and demanding. Supervisors (or "floor ladies" as they are called) constantly walk around inspecting the work and pressure women to work rapidly and carefully. Sorters have little room to control the pace or techniques of work and are forced to make instantaneous decisions regarding the quality of produce.[17]

WORK-BASED NETWORKS

When women first obtain jobs in canneries they are not formally trained. They are immediately placed on the job and learn from watching coworkers, with on-the-job instruction from the supervisor. Talking with coworkers is prohibited, and mandatory earplugs make it difficult to converse anyway. Supervisors must shout their instructions in order to be heard above the racket. New workers are often overwhelmed and feel dizzy or nauseated, and coworkers advise new women to adjust their equilibrium to the movement of the conveyor belt by concentrating on individual pieces of produce. Coworkers teach new employees how to perform their jobs so that the work is easier. They also point out that keeping up with the fast pace is not possible, nor even necessary. Training and advice by coworkers are given surreptitiously or during breaks, because if women do not concentrate on their work they will be fired.

Other jobs such as check weigher allow more flexibility. A check weigher, for example, grabs a handful of spinach, places it in a can, and weighs it for the proper amount. Women who are experienced learn to gauge the proper weight with their hands and bypass the weighing operation. Because they are paid by the piece rate, this shortcut is critical in enabling women to make more money. Here, coworkers teach new workers how to perform the job more effectively, or even how to rig the counting devices.

Coworkers also initiate women into the formal authority structure. Lisa Hernandez noted: "It's a big soap opera at the cannery. You know who hangs around the bosses and who 'makes the cans.'" Gossip provides important information about who belongs to different cliques. Euleria Torrez laughed: "You always know something about everybody." It helps to know supervisors in particular because work assignments are granted informally.

Line work provides conditions in which women are able to cooperate with one another, and this makes the work itself more pleasant. Connie Garcia recalled that "we all got along, you have to when you work that kind of work. We used to sing, make jokes." Further, women could anticipate staying on the line with many coworkers for years to come. Lupe Collosi observed: "Usually people in the cannery are good-natured; people have no problems. They're all so used to working hard that they don't complain." Workers try to keep their differences in check because of the constant menace of supervisors and the fear of losing their jobs. Vicki Gutierrez noted: "I got along pretty good with everybody. I wanted a job so I made it a point." Luz Betancourt said: "If you want to be working, you can't be fighting." These statements are in stark contrast with the competition and antagonisms among women workers when they were paid by the piece rate.[18] The hourly pay coupled with pressured working conditions allows women to establish camaraderie. But women's cooperation also helped managers by providing a trained work force.

Coworkers become an informal group—similar to the "sister-hood" of sales clerks that Susan Porter Benson discusses—which socializes women into the work culture. Yet these are not self-conscious groups. Most women claimed with disgust: "I trained myself," even though they had help, and did not view coworkers as constituting a group. The term "work-based networks" better characterizes these informal relationships with coworkers.

There are any number of work-based networks within a particular factory, and they tend to be composed of workers of the same gender and ethnic background. Seasonal workers tend to make friends with other temporary workers, while full-time workers (usually men) have their own networks. Women with relatives in the same plant have a ready-made training team that also includes them in socializing during breaks.

Lisa is a third-generation cannery worker. She described her first season on the job: "It's hard work, but I can't say I didn't enjoy it. Everywhere I looked I knew somebody, I had relatives to talk to. They baby me, give me cans. . . ." She also described her parents' participation in the work-based network: "My mom and my step-father live in the same world, the cannery world, with all the *chismes* [gossip]. In the cannery you can see them sitting together talking with all my aunts and their friends." Other women initiated friendships with coworkers through the informal training process. Connie observed: "You get to know all these people. You have this intimacy because you work with them at least eight hours a day." Vicki believes that work friendships detract from the monotony of the job: "You get to know everybody's little problems. It's interesting." Another woman characterized work friendships in a more cynical manner: "You have this *abnormal* intimacy. You make friends with people who are totally different than you, just because you work together." Nevertheless, many women believed they would not have stayed on the job without the help of coworkers.

The ethnic cohesiveness of networks replicated and perpetuated the segregation of the work force. A Chicana informant characterized Mexican-white friendships: "It's weird as I see it." One hapless Portuguese American woman described her social isolation until she made friends with other Portuguese women: "I used to sit with some Mexican women but they would only speak in Spanish. I felt so left out! I think it's only courteous to speak English." When she started working on the line she received little help from her coworkers because she could not communicate with them. "I don't know a lot of people; in three month's time you don't get close. This Spanish lady who works across from me doesn't speak English. So all we do is say hello or goodbye and smile." Yet after only twelve years of work, this woman was promoted to swing shift floorlady, while her Spanish-speaking compatriots with greater seniority remained behind. Participation in work-based networks provided information about promotions, and the exclusion of Spanish-speaking women was one way in which Chicanas became victims of discrimination.

Women also sanctioned those who left line work and no longer socialized with network members. Connie eventually took on a "man's job": she became a full-time checking clerk supervising the loading of box cars. She missed the friendship of her former coworkers. "It just seems like everytime that someone gets an advancement, there's a lot of things said. Petty things, like 'she thinks she's too good because she does all this stuff.' A lot of it is just jealousy."

By working on the line, women were able to establish friendships with one another. Yet because of working conditions, relationships at work were difficult to sustain. During the peak of the season, workers are on the job six or seven days a week. With half-hour lunches and only two twelve-minute breaks, there was little time to socialize. Besides, women occasionally preferred a silent retreat from the commotion inside the factory: "Sometimes I need to be by myself for that half-hour" (Vicki).

With work that has little intrinsic value and short occasions to socialize with coworkers, one could expect that union involvement would add meaning to the job.[19] It was difficult for Chicano workers, however, to find meaningful participation in their union local. Northern California cannery workers are affiliated with the International Brotherhood of Teamsters. Generally, cannery workers are dissatisfied with the Teamsters union,[20] and my informants were no exception. Some of them had almost a decade of rank-and-file activism within the local and established alliances with other dissident caucuses in northern California. The dissatisfaction stemmed from what workers perceived as a general lack of representation and union democracy. In addition, there was ethnic antagonism between the Italian American Teamster officials and Chicano caucus members, with mutual name-calling and red-baiting on the part of some union leaders. Chicano activists wanted the union contract translated into Spanish and for the local to hold bilingual meetings (among other things), but the union leadership refused. There was even a short-lived "Teamsters for [Cesar] Chavez" movement by Chicano cannery workers in the early seventies when the United Farm Workers and the Teamsters were having a jurisdictional battle in the fields. The Teamsters union was not a source of organizational support for most Chicano cannery workers.

In sum, the general work context included oppressive working conditions and an uninterested or even antagonistic union. Women's work culture was not conducive to the development of meaningful relationships at work. Work-based networks enabled women to bear the difficult conditions of their jobs and added the dimension of solidarity with other workers. Yet women had to develop these relationships outside the job.

WORK-RELATED NETWORKS

Work-related networks are expanded work-based networks that function outside the factories and whose members engage in social exchange. For the most part, work-related friendships began with only social motivations. Members frequently socialized with one another during the off-season (roughly from October through May). The women visited each other's homes, telephoned several times during the week, went shopping or out to lunch, or went out for drinks, all without their husbands. Connie elaborated on the difference between work-based and work-related networks. "I don't know how many times I remember telling a coworker that I became particularly fond of, 'Hey, I'll be sure to come and see you after the season.' I never made it because I have kids to raise, things to do, and I just never got around to it. And then there are others, like Elena, that you become so involved with and become very dear friends." But although women initiated activities with coworkers, once established, the networks also included husbands. Cannery workers occasionally got together as couples for parties, barbecues, short weekend trips, or even went on extended vacations together. Some of my informants organized large-scale activities in which a number of cannery worker couples and their kin and friends participated.

The structure of work-related networks varied between two poles. On one end were friendship networks composed entirely of coworkers. Regardless of whether they were recent immigrants from Mexico or third-generation Chicanas, women who had no kin residing in the area developed work friendship networks separately from kin networks. The opposite extreme was kin-dominant networks. These were composed almost entirely of cannery workers who were relatives. Often married couples met one another at the cannery. It was also common for women's children to work at least one season at the cannery before moving on to better jobs. Women in these situations usually had work-related networks in which kin predominated, and networks included members of their own nuclear families.

The presence of kin residing in the area who were also cannery workers, however, did not mean that kin and friendship networks coincided. Some women had numerous relatives working in canneries, and they developed extensive friendship networks that were integrated into kin networks. Other women developed friendship networks separately from kin networks that were largely made up of cannery workers. Women who did not consider their cannery worker relatives as being part of their friendship networks usually had different political values, other interests, and considered themselves to be marginal to cannery work culture. Other women had networks somewhere in the middle of the kin-dominant and friend-dominant types. Both their friends and kin were part of the work-related networks, but they differed in terms of whether the relatives and coworkers were largely separate or integrated. Of course, not every woman had large intense work friendship networks. One woman does not want to be "bugged" to socialize with coworkers: "We are friends while at work."

Although the networks varied in terms of the number of members, several were "close knit." This was because some of the women's friends were also *comadres* with one another; that is, they were ritual comothers who became fictive kin through Catholic baptismal rites.[21] Usually a woman chooses a friend and her spouse to sponsor a child at baptism with the intension of honoring them and solidifying the friendship. By selecting friends rather than kin to be *comadres,* Chicanas express their great affection and

respect.[22] The presence of fictive kin who are coworkers blurs the
distinction between friendship and kin networks, but adds to their
cohesiveness. The women were key in maintaining communication, organizing activities, and keeping the networks active. A few
women were core members, and they either organized get-
togethers such as birthday parties, or were honored at special occasions such as wedding anniversaries.

Work-related networks also operated like kin networks and
served as sources of exchange among members. In particular, network members were good sources of information regarding problems that arose from their work situation. Women found babysitters through their networks or learned from coworkers how to
qualify for unemployment benefits or how to claim disability pay.
Work friends were also sources of advice and emotional support.
Women discussed work and personal problems, especially those
concerning their children. Marital problems were important
topics, and work friends provided a crucial source of support in
women's struggles with their husbands. The standards of
housekeeping and how much labor their husbands should contribute was one problem; another was whether the woman should
return to work each season. About one-third of my informants'
husbands did not want them to work at all. Informants frequently
sought out a work friend when they just needed to talk, and greatly appreciated the support. Connie observed: "If I needed her she
was there. When I get real down, she is my moral support.
Everyone needs someone like that."

The context of work had other consequences for how work-
related networks operated. The lack of job mobility and unwilling-
ness of the union to meet the special needs of the Chicano work
force spurred some informants into labor organizing.

Although only a handful of the informants were politically active, these women's friends and kin were often also involved in
organizing. In some instances, work-related networks became
politicized after they were well established as social networks.
Connie and about twelve of her friends met frequently, and the
conversation inevitably turned to the work situation. They began
to devise ways to change working conditions. After the calloused
rebuffs from male union officials, the women decided to organize
women cannery workers themselves. They founded a women's
caucus (which included black and white women) and filed a com-

plaint with the Fair Employment Practices Commission. The women later became plaintiffs in a race and sex discrimination suit against California Processors Inc., which they eventually won. In addition, the women wrote articles for a cannery workers' newsletter, and one woman ran for president of the union. Her friends served as campaign manager and volunteers in a bitter election that was narrowly lost. The friendship network evolved into a militant organization.

Political activists' work friends became important in personal ways as well. Many of the women activists had conflicts with their husbands over their political involvement. Husbands complained that organizing took up too much time and that the women were neglecting their families. Indeed, one woman claimed that reluctant husbands were the biggest obstacles to organizing women workers. Some of these husbands either demanded that their wives stop organizing or that they restrict their activities to times that were convenient for their families. Several of the activists eventually divorced their spouses, partly because of their husbands' opposition to their political activism. Most of these women had attained better-paying jobs and were in a position to leave poor marriages. Work friendships served as a crucial means of support to those women who went through the painful process of divorce. One of these women claimed: "I don't know how I would have *survived* without my friends."

Other women intensified their relationships not only with network members, but also with spouses through their political activism. These women got involved with a dissident caucus whose membership was predominantly male. This caucus sponsored numerous activities: the members twice ran a slate of largely Chicano workers for union office and organized rallies, meetings, dances, and fundraisers. Through these activities, work networks became larger and more intense. Coworkers and *compadres*[23] were not only friends from work, but also political allies who shared all the frustrations and camaraderie of labor organizing.

Work-related networks also functioned in a politically conservative manner. Lisa, for example, avoided visiting her mother during the work season because the job harassment her mother received became increasingly difficult for Lisa to bear. She had advised her mother to talk with a lawyer and explore the possibility of legal action to stop the harassment, but Lisa's mother refused.

Lisa believed that her mother would not seek legal redress because
of the advice of an older sister married to a supervisor at the same
plant where Lisa's mother worked. The aunt actively discouraged
her sister from taking any action that might jeopardize her husband's position. None of the other relatives working at the plant
opposed the aunt's advice, so Mrs. Hernandez continued working
under stressful conditions. Lisa shrugged: "The cannery is a way of
life. You live in it and thrive on it." Thus, work-related networks
can serve to pressure women into acquiescence to unfair working
conditions.

Even if they were not politically involved, work friendships
were meaningful to my informants. Especially as they reach middle age and their children have either left home or no longer require so much attention, women have more time and desire to
socialize.[24] Because home responsibilities have lessened and financial obligations for their children are not as pressing, the meaning
of a job has changed for these women. They feel isolated at home
and long for social contact. They do not see housework as meaningful in its own right. Of course most women value a clean house,
but staying home full-time and cleaning house produces little intrinsic reward. Rather, homemaking is described as "doing
nothing" or "being lazy." If the children are gone, not only is there
little housework to do, but also "housework will always be
there"—it can be put off.

The women's need to socialize differed from their situations
when they started working and their children were young.[25] Vicki
explained: "I don't have to work anymore; we don't need the
money. But if I stay home, all I'll do is watch TV and get fat. I don't
have anything to do. There's not really much housework. No way!
No way am I going to stay home! I'm going to go work. Plus the extra money is always helpful." Celia said: "You look forward to
another season." Luz gave the rationale for continuing to work:
"Why not? The kids are gone, there's nothing for me to do at home,
and I like my job." Connie observed of her coworkers: "Most of the
women my age [forty-four] who work in the industry, their kids
are all grown. They've got grandkids already. So their life is just
cannery. The people they associate with are cannery workers;
they can't see beyond anything else that has to do with the cannery." The cannery provided women like these with an escape
from the solitary nature of homemaking, and work-related net-

works became the focus of their social lives.

Women's longevity on the job allowed friendships to flourish and provided expectations that they would endure. Especially if they were *comadres,* women were fictive kin and could feel free to develop *confianza* (trust or familiarity, usually reserved for kin) with coworkers. Women whose networks only included friends often characterized the relationships in kinship terms: "I don't know what I'd do without her, she's been like a sister to me." Another woman said of her work-related network: "It's like a little happy family. You look forward to seeing one another." Clearly, friendship networks were serving needs that kin networks typically provide, and in many ways work-related networks became surrogate kin networks.

CONCLUSION

Clearly, work friendships provided a crucial means of support for Chicana cannery workers. Work-related friendships were a second source of advice and personal support, especially for those women past the active childrearing phase. This information suggests that future studies of Chicano support networks must closely examine the various contexts in which people establish networks, in particular the situations in which women are confined to dead-end jobs. Although kin networks can continue to provide important material exchange and social support, long-term employment provides a context in which women factory workers can expand their social networks.

Further, women's work-based networks reflect contradictory and simultaneous processes occurring in the factories. On the one hand, women's work is considered unskilled, and little formal training is provided. Yet there are many skills, especially social ones that are necessary to work effectively, so women socialize with each other regarding shop floor practices. Although Chicana cannery workers do not have the autonomy of nurses or sales clerks, their work-based networks function in a manner similar to the "sisterhoods" described by Susan Porter Benson and Barbara Melosh. At the same time, although all women were in the same position as line workers, ethnic cleavages among the work force were reflected in exclusive work-based networks. In contrast to Louise Lamphere's factory worker informants (see this issue),

Chicana cannery workers formed their own networks and usually did not include their white ethnic compatriots. Within the context of working on the line, Chicanas established solidarity with their Chicana coworkers and maintained conflictive relations with other non-Chicana women.

Women's consciousness reflects these contradictory processes. Friendships initiated on-the-job function to "humanize" the workplace, and the camaraderie women develop in this process becomes an important positive feature of the job. Ironically, women's solidarity sometimes encourages women to bear the negative aspects of their jobs. Women's criticisms of work conditions are blunted, for they see work friendships as a way to create a "family" at work and thus the whole situation seems better.

For those women who were actively trying to change working conditions, work-related networks are a potent organizing means. Work-related networks not only bring meaning to the workplace, but they also become a focal point of their private lives. In a sense, these women bring work home as work relationships infuse their home and social activities, and at times women's political involvement even takes precedence over relations with their own families.

The conditions under which women's networks evolve contain contradictory processes, and this creates variation in women's consciousness and in the construction of meaning about work.

NOTES

I want to thank Felipe Gonzales, Louise Lamphere, Micaela di Leonardo, Rayna Rapp, Judith Stacey, and an anonymous *Feminist Studies* reviewer for their helpful comments on earlier versions of this paper. An expanded discussion of the issues raised in this article will appear in *Women's Work and Chicano Families: Cannery Workers of the Santa Clara Valley* (Ithaca: Cornell University Press, forthcoming).

1. Louise Lamphere, "Strategies, Cooperation, and Conflict among Women in Domestic Groups," in *Woman, Culture, and Society,* ed. Michelle Zimbalist Rosaldo and Louise Lamphere (Stanford: Stanford University Press, 1974); Suad Joseph, "Working-Class Women's Networks in a Sectarian State: A Political Paradox," *American Ethnologist* 10, no. 1 (1983): 1-22.
2. Carroll Smith-Rosenberg, "The Female World of Love and Ritual: Relations between Women in Nineteenth-Century America," *Signs* 1 (Autumn 1975): 1-29, reprinted in *A Heritage of Her Own: Toward a New Social History of American Women,* ed. Nancy F. Cott and Elizabeth H. Pleck (New York: Simon & Schuster, 1979); Nancy Cott, *The Bonds of Womanhood: "Woman's Sphere" in New England, 1780-1835* (New Haven: Yale University

Press, 1977); Mary P. Ryan, "The Power of Women's Networks: A Case Study of Female Moral Reform in Antebellum America," *Feminist Studies* 5 (Spring 1979): 66-86; Jessie Bernard, *The Female World* (New York: Free Press, 1981).

3. Elizabeth Bott, *Family and Social Network* (London: Tavistock Publications, 1957); Louise Lamphere, Filomena M. Silva, and John P. Sousa, "Kin Networks and Family Strategies: Working-Class Portuguese Families in New England," in *The Versatility of Kinship*, ed. Linda S. Cordell and Stephen Beckerman (New York: Academic Press, 1980), 219-50; Carol Stack, *All Our Kin* (New York: Harper/Colophon Books, 1974); Carol Stack, "The Kindred of Viola Jackson," in *A Heritage of Her Own*.

4. Blanche Wiesen Cook, "Female Support Networks and Political Activism: Lillian Wald, Crystal Eastman, Emma Goldman," *Chrysalis*, no. 3 (1977): 43-61, reprinted in *A Heritage of Her Own*, 415-44; Temma Kaplan, "Female Consciousness and Collective Action: The Case of Barcelona, 1910-1918," in *Feminist Theory, A Critique of Ideology*, ed. Nannerl O. Keohane, Michelle Z. Rosaldo, and Barbara O. Gelpi (Chicago: University of Chicago Press, 1981), 55-76.

5. Susan Porter Benson, "'The Clerking Sisterhood': Rationalization and the Work Culture of Saleswomen in American Department Stores, 1890-1960," *Radical America* 12 (March-April 1978): 41-55; Susan Porter Benson, "'The Customers Ain't God': The Work Culture of Department Store Saleswomen, 1890-1940," in *Working-Class America: Essays on Labor, Community, and American Society*, ed. Michael H. Frisch and Daniel J. Walkowitz (Urbana: University of Illinois Press, 1983), 155-211; Barbara Melosh, *The "Physician's Hand": Work Culture and Conflict in American Nursing* (Philadelphia: Temple University Press, 1982).

6. Most of the literature on Chicano support networks does not explicitly focus on women's networks. The exceptions are Brett Williams, "The Trip Takes Us: Chicano Migrants on the Prairie" (Ph.D. diss., University of Illinois at Urbana-Champaign, 1975); and Roland M. Wagner and Diane M. Schaffer, "Social Networks and Survival Strategies: An Exploratory Study of Mexican American, Black, and Anglo Female Family Heads in San Jose, California," in *Twice a Minority: Mexican American Women*, ed. Margarita B. Melville (St. Louis: C.V. Mosby Co., 1980), 173-90. I suggest that such a focus would yield interesting results and would change our conceptions of how Chicano kin networks function. For example, interviews with young married Chicana electronics and apparel factory workers show that women not only valued their work friendships highly, but at times *preferred* discussing sensitive matters with friends rather than kin because friends were socially distant and would not get involved in the problems. See my paper "Support Networks of Young Chicana Workers" (presented at the Western Social Science Association Meetings, Albuquerque, New Mexico, April 1983).

7. Jean M. Gilbert, "Extended Family Integration among Second-Generation Mexican Americans," in *Family and Mental Health in the Mexican American Community*, ed. J. Manuel Carlos and Susan B. Keefe, Monograph no. 7 (Los Angeles: Spanish Speaking Mental Health Research Center, UCLA, 1978); Susan B. Keefe, Amado M. Padilla, and Manuel L. Carlos, "The Mexican American Extended Family as an Emotional Support System," in *Family and Mental Health in the Mexican American Community*, Monograph no. 7 (Los Angeles: Spanish Speaking Mental Health Research Center, UCLA, 1978); Susan B. Keefe, "Urbanization, Acculturation, and Extended Family Ties: Mexican Americans in Cities," *American Ethnologist* (Spring 1979): 349-65; Carolyn J. Matthiasson, "Coping in a New Environment: Mexican Americans in Milwaukee, Wisconsin," *Urban Anthropology* 3 (1974): 262-77; Wagner and Schaffer; Maxine Baca Zinn, "Urban Kinship and Midwest Chicano Families: Evidence in Support of Revision," Special Issue on *La Familia, De Colores, Journal of Chicano Expression and Thought* 6, nos. 1-2 (1982): 85-98.

8. Keefe, Padilla, and Carlos, 148 (emphasis added).

9. Historically Chicanas have had lower labor force participation rates than Anglo or

black women. Unfortunately, some writers have placed the cause of this phenomenon with women themselves–the lack of work commitment by Chicanas, which stems from traditional cultural values, is said to prevent Chicanas from becoming wage earners. For this view, see Elizabeth M. Almquist and Juanita L. Wehrle-Einhorn, "The Doubly Disadvantaged: Minority Women in the Labor Force," in *Women Working: Theories and Facts in Perspective*, ed. Ann. H. Stromberg and Shirley Harkess (Palo Alto, Calif.: Mayfield Publishing Co., 1978), 63-88; Walter Fogel, *Mexican Americans in Southwest Labor Markets*, Advance Report no. 10 (Los Angeles: Mexican American Study Project, UCLA, 1965); Vernon M. Briggs, Jr., Walter Fogel, and Fred H. Schmidt, *The Chicano Worker* (Austin: University of Texas Press, 1977). For analyses that point to lower educational levels of Chicanas, a decline in traditional family values, or changes in labor markets as causes of Chicanas' recent *rise* in labor force participation rates, see, respectively: Denise Segura, "Labor Market Stratification: The Chicana Experience," *Berkeley Journal of Sociology* 29 (1984); Rosemary Santana Cooney, "Changing Labor Force Participation of Mexican American Wives: A Comparison with Anglos and Blacks," *Social Science Quarterly* 56, no. 2 (1975); and Patricia Zavella, "The Impact of 'Sun Belt Industrialization' on Chicanas," *Frontiers* 8 (Winter 1984): 21-27.

10. See Cooney.

11. The labor force participation rate for women over twenty years increased steadily. In 1971, 43 percent of all women worked; that figure grew to 52 percent in 1981. See U.S. Department of Labor, *Employment and Training Report of the President* (Washington, D.C.: GPO, 1982), 4. Chicanas (women of Mexican origin) had a labor force participation rate of 36 percent nationally in 1970. By 1980, 49 percent of all women of Spanish origin were in the labor force (statistics on Spanish-origin women were all that were available at the time of this writing). See U.S. Department of Commerce, Bureau of the Census, *United States Census of the Population, 1970: Persons of Spanish Origin*, PO (2)-10 (Washington, D.C.: GPO, 1973) and *Census of the Population, 1980: Provisional Estimates of Social, Economic, and Housing Characteristics*, PHO801S1-1 (Washington, D.C.: GPO, 1982).

12. Although they do not explicitly use the term "work cultures," the following historical pieces provide rich descriptions of the work contexts of Chicana food processing and garment workers and mention the relationships women established with each other. See Vicki L. Ruiz, "UCAPAWA, Chicanas, and the California Food Processing Industry" (Ph.D. diss., Stanford University, 1982); Laurie Coyle, Gayle Hershatter, and Emily Honig, "Women at Farah: An Unfinished Story," in *Mexican Women in the United States, Struggles Past and Present*, ed. Magdalena Mora and Adelaida R. Del Castillo (Los Angeles: Chicano Studies Research Center Publications, UCLA, 1980), 117-44; Magdalena Mora, "The Tolteca Strike: Mexican Women and the Struggle for Union Representation," in *Mexican Immigrant Workers in the U.S.*, ed. Antonio Rios-Bustamante (Los Angeles: Chicano Studies Research Center Publications, UCLA, 1981), 111-18.

13. Sarah Eisenstein, *Give Us Bread but Give Us Roses: Working Women's Consciousness in the United States, 1890 to the First World War* (London: Routledge & Kegan Paul, 1983). Eisenstein's formulation also examines how women's consciousness develops in response to contrasting ideologies of women's "proper place" and the radical critiques from social movements, a discussion beyond the scope of this article. Also see Micaela di Leonardo, *The Varieties of Ethnic Experience: Kinship, Class, and Gender among California Italian-Americans* (Ithaca: Cornell University Press, 1984); Jane Collier, Michelle Z. Rosaldo, and Sylvia Yanagisako, "Is There a Family? New Anthropological Views," in *Rethinking the Family: Some Feminist Questions*, ed. Barrie Thorne and Marilyn Yalom (New York: Longman, 1982), 25-39; Rayna Rapp, "Family and Class in Contemporary America: Notes toward an Understanding of Ideology" *Science and Society* 42, no. 3 (1978): 278-300.

14. Because the sample is small and not randomly selected, the data should be seen as illustrating only some of the processes that occur in the lives of Chicana cannery workers.

15. For a full discussion of the canning industry, the structure of the workplace, and women's attitudes toward their jobs, see *Women's Work and Chicano Families,* esp. chaps. 3 and 5; also see Martin L. Brown, "A Historical Economic Analysis of the Wage Structure of the California Fruit and Vegetable Canning Industry" (Ph.D. diss., University of California, Berkeley, 1981); Peter W. Philips, "Towards a New Theory of Wage Structures: The Evolution of Wages in the California Canneries – 1870 to the Present" (Ph.D. diss., Stanford University , 1979).

16. See *Women's Work and Chicano Families.*

17. For an amusing description of the work process by a former employee, see Steve Turner, *Night Shift in a Pickle Factory* (San Pedro: Singlejack Books, 1980).

18. Under the piece rate system, competition among women workers centered on the position they had on the line. Women who stood at the front of the line were able to choose the best produce and make more money. Supervisors gave out line positions, and the fair ones rotated the workers. See Ruiz.

19. Robert Blauner, *Alienation and Freedom: The Factory Worker and His Industry* (Chicago: University of Chicago Press, 1964).

20. Brown.

21. Women can also become *comadres* when their children marry one another, or when they sponsor children at other Catholic rites such as First Holy Communion or Confirmation.

22. Manuel Carlos, "Traditional and Modern Forms of Compadrazgo among Mexicans and Mexican-Americans: A Survey of Continuities and Change" (Atti Del XL Congresso Internazionale Degli Americanis, Roma-Genova: Tilgher, 3-10 Settembre 1972).

23. *Compadres* can refer to cofathers only or can mean coparents.

24. Lillian B. Rubin's analysis criticizes the literature that portrays the "empty nest syndrome" in which middle-aged women are said to experience crisis after their children leave home. Rubin's informants found a new meaning in life after their children left home and took on careers, sought education, and enjoyed social relationships more. See *Women of a Certain Age: The Midlife Search for Self* (New York: Harper & Row, 1979).

25. For a full discussion of women's obligations during the earlier years in their marriages, see *Women, Work, and Chicano Families,* chaps. 4, 6.

ACKNOWLEDGMENTS

I would like to thank Susan Halci, Sheryl Jimenez, Jonlyn Martinez, Roberta Marquez and Debbie Garcia for their research assistance. Debbie Garcia was funded by the Center for Regional Studies. I appreciate the Center's support for this project.

Del Castillo, Adelaida R. "Malintzin Tenépal: A Preliminary Look into a New Perspective." In Rosaura Sánchez, ed., *Essays on La Mujer* (Anthology No. 1 Chicano Studies Center Publication, UCLA, 1977): 124–49. Reprinted with the permission of the Chicano Studies Research Center, University of California, Los Angeles. Courtesy of Yale University Cross Campus Library.

González, Deena J. "The Widowed Women of Santa Fe: Assessments on the Lives of an Unmarried Population, 1850–80." In Arlene Scadron, ed., *On Their Own.: Widows and Widowhood in the American Southwest, 1848–1939* (Illinois: University of Illinois Press, 1988): 65–90. Courtesy of Yale University Cross Campus Library.

Ruíz, Vicki. "Dead Ends or Gold Mines?: Using Missionary Records in Mexican-American Women's History." *Frontiers* 12 (1991): 33–56. Reprinted with the permission of *Frontiers*, University of New Mexico. Courtesy of *Frontiers*.

García, Mario T. "The Chicana in American History: The Mexican Women of El Paso, 1880–1920—A Case Study." *Pacific Historical Review* 49 (1980): 315–37. Reprinted with the permission of the University of California Press. Courtesy of Yale University Sterling Memorial Library.

King, Lourdes Miranda. "Puertorriquenas in the United States: The Impact of Double Discrimination." *Civil Rights Digest* 6 (1974): 20–7. Reprinted with the permission of the *Civil Rights Digest*. Courtesy of *Civil Rights Digest*.

Segura, Denise. "Labor Market Stratification: The Chicana Experience." *Berkeley Journal of Sociology* 29 (1984): 57–91. Reprinted with the permission of the University of California Berkeley. Courtesy of *Berkeley Journal of Sociology*.

Romero, Mary. "Day Work in the Suburbs: The Work Experience of Chicana Private Housekeepers." In Anne Statham, Eleanor M. Miller, and Hans O. Mauksch, eds., *The Worth of Women's Work: A Qualitative Synthesis* (New York: State Univerity of New York Press, 1988): 77–91. Reprinted with the permission of the State University of New York Press. Courtesy of Yale University Law Library.

Prieto, Yolanda. "Cuban Women in the U.S. Labor Force: Perspectives on the Nature of Change." *Cuban Studies* 17 (1987): 73–91. Reprinted with the permission of the University of Pittsburgh Press. Copyright 1987 by the University of Pittsburgh Press. Courtesy of *Cuban Studies*.

Velez-I, Carlos G. "Se me acabó la canción: An Ethnography of Non-consenting Sterilizations among Mexican Women in Los Angeles." In Magdalena Mora and Adelaida R. Del Castillo, eds., *Mexican Women in The United States: Struggles Past and Present* (1980):71–91. Reprinted with the permission of the Chicano Studies Research Center. Courtesy of Yale University Cross Campus Library.

Martinez, Virginia. "Chicanas and the Law." In *La Chicana: Building for the Future* (National Hispanic University, 1981): 134–46. Reprinted with the permission of the National Hispanic Center for Advanced Studies and Policy Analysis. Courtesy of Antoinette Sedillo López.

Bonilla-Santiago, Gloria. "Hispanic Women Breaking New Ground through Leadership." *Latino Studies Journal* 2 (1991): 19–37. Reprinted with the permission of *Latino Studies Journal*. Courtesy of Gloria Bonilla-Santiago.

Zinn, Maxine Baca. "Political Familism: Toward Sex Role Equality in Chicano Families." *Aztlan* 6 (1975): 13–26. Reprinted with the permission of *Aztlan*. Courtesy of Maxine Baca Zinn.

Ybarra, Lea. "Marital Decision-Making and the Role of *Machismo* in the Chicano Family." *De Colores Journal* 6 (1982): 32–47. Reprinted with the permission of Pajarito Publications. Courtesy of Yale University Sterling Memorial Library.

Hernandez, Antonia. "Chicanas and the Issue of Involuntary Sterilization: Reforms Needed to Protect Informed Consent." *Chicano Law Review* 3 (1976): 3–37. Reprinted with the permission of the *Chicano Law Review*. Courtesy of Yale University Law Library.

López, Antoinette Sedillo. "Privacy and the Regulation of the New Reproductive Technologies: A Decision-Making Approach." *Family Law Quarterly* 22 (1988): 173–97. Reprinted with the permission of *Family Law Quarterly*. Courtesy of Antoinette Sedillo López.

Moran, Rachel F. "The Implications of Being a Society of One." *University of San Francisco Law Review* 20 (1986): 503–13. Reprinted with the permission of the University of San Francisco, School of Law. Courtesy of Antoinette Sedillo López.

López, Antoinette Sedillo. "Two Legal Constructs of Motherhood: 'Protective' Legislation in Mexico and the United States." *Southern California Review of Law and Women's Studies* 1 (1992): 239–54. Reprinted with the permission of the *Southern California Review of Law and Women's Studies*. Courtesy of Yale University Law Library.

Garcia, Alma M. "The Development of Chicana Feminist Discourse, 1970–1980." *Gender and Society* 3 (1989): 217–38. Reprinted with the permission of Sage Publications. Courtesy of Yale University Social Science Library.

Rebolledo, Tey Diana. "Chicana Studies: Is There a Future for Us in Women Studies?" In *Chicano Studies: Critical Connections Between Research and Community* (National Association of Chicano Studies, March 1992): 32–7. Reprinted with the permission of the National Association of Chicano Studies. Courtesy of Antoinette Sedillo López.

Romany, Celina. "Ain't I a Feminist?" *Yale Journal of Law and Feminism* 4 (1991): 23–33. Reprinted with the permission of the *Yale Journal of Law and Feminism*. Courtesy of *Yale Journal of Law and Feminism*.

Riddell, Adaljiza Sosa. "Chicanas and El Movimiento." *Aztlan* 5 (1974): 155–65. Reprinted with the permission of *Aztlan*. Courtesy of Yale University Sterling Memorial Library.

Zavella, Patricia. "'Abnormal Intimacy': The Varying Work Networks of Chicana Cannery Workers." *Feminist Studies* 11 (1985): 541–57. Reprinted with the permission of the publisher, Feminist Studies, Inc., c/o Women's Studies Program, University of Maryland, College Park, MD 20742. Courtesy of Yale University Sterling Memorial Library.